AMERICAN FOREIGN POLICY IN MEXICAN RELATIONS

THE MACMILLAN COMPANY
NEW YORK · BOSTON · CHICAGO · DALLAS
ATLANTA · SAN FRANCISCO

MACMILLAN & CO., Limited
LONDON · BOMBAY · CALCUTTA
MELBOURNE

THE MACMILLAN COMPANY
OF CANADA, Limited
TORONTO

AMERICAN FOREIGN POLICY IN MEXICAN RELATIONS

By

JAMES MORTON CALLAHAN

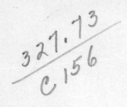

NEW YORK
THE MACMILLAN COMPANY
1932

Printed in the United States of America by
J. J. LITTLE AND IVES COMPANY, NEW YORK

PREFACE

THE recent pacification of Mexico by adjustments resulting from the mission of Dwight W. Morrow, following two decades of unsatisfactory Mexican relations, has stimulated an increased interest in American Mexican policy which suggests that the occasion is a fitting one for the appearance of a historical review of American foreign policy in Mexican relations. In the formulation and practice of policies the American government, representing a rapidly expanding people, has doubtless learned lessons which may prove useful in later experience in seeking adjustments with Latin American peoples.

American relations with Mexico, largely a result of its direct proximity and the problems of American peaceful economic penetration, but also influenced by frequent Mexican periods of disorderliness and instability of government arising from Mexican internal conditions, have often been disturbed by suspicion and irritating controversy. The American diplomatic mission at Mexico has been the most important and the most difficult on the American continent.

American policy in Mexican relations has been determined chiefly by self-interest, directly or indirectly, but, also, by neighborhood and larger community interests, especially in relation to problems of the Caribbean and isthmian area. It has been associated chiefly with American expansion on the Gulf and the consequent desire for a logical permanent boundary, American Cuban and Central American policy, diplomatic presentation of claims, antagonism to European designs or intervention in America, problems resulting from American economic enterprise and investments in Mexico and the questions arising from conflicts of Mexican revolutions and social reforms with American interests in Mexico.

Unfortunately, American policy, although always accompanied by an attitude of good will and frequently by unusual patience, has too often, possibly through lack of sympathetic insight, assumed an attitude of superiority and of impatience with Mexican arguments and delays which have characterized an independent people groping toward nationality and political stability through long struggle marked by repeated effort. In its earlier beginnings its success was restricted by various causes, including especially the political indiscretions of the American minister which, together with the hasty demands or discourteous farewells of later ministers, contributed to the misunderstandings, discords and distrust of the generation before 1860, and to the renewed irritations of the decade after 1867.

In this volume, based upon researches in American Caribbean policy begun many years ago in connection with a course of graduate lectures delivered at Johns Hopkins University, the author has attempted the first general historical view of American Mexican policy in the consideration and solution of continuous problems arising between the two countries. In his laborious researches for the period before 1907 he has chiefly relied upon the manuscript archives at the Department of State at Washington—especially upon the volumes of "Instructions" and "Despatches." For the first decade after 1907 he has relied chiefly upon published volumes of "Foreign Relations" and other government documents, and for the decade since 1920 (especially for the last half) he has largely supplemented the government documents by newspaper files and other periodical literature. Although incidentally he has treated diplomatic relations, he has constantly emphasized the problems and factors of American foreign policy, including interpretations of questions of international law. He has been aided by the studies of Manning, Rives, Reeves and Garber, covering limited periods of diplomatic relations before 1853, and also by the general survey of relations by Rippy, whose most valuable contributions were for the half decade before 1853 and the first decade after 1867. He has previously published monographic studies covering limited periods—especially from 1853 to 1861 and from 1861 to 1867. Parts of the earlier incomplete draft of chapters he has used as lectures at Johns Hopkins University and at other universities—Colorado, California, Washington and West Virginia.

In the preparation of this volume for publication the author gratefully acknowledges his obligations to West Virginia University and the Social Science Research Council for their cooperative encouragement in facilitating the collection of materials used as a basis for the completion of the study.

JAMES MORTON CALLAHAN.

CONTENTS

MAPS

AMERICAN FOREIGN POLICY IN
MEXICAN RELATIONS

CHAPTER I

HISTORICAL BACKGROUND: EARLY
AMERICAN INTERESTS AND
RECOGNITION

AMERICANS were early interested in the possibilities of trade with the chief Gulf ports of Mexico and after 1783 looked forward to Spanish American independence. In 1787 Jefferson, who foresaw the possible independence of all the Americas, feared that the Spanish American possessions would separate from Spain before the United States was ready for them. A more immediate and significant practical interest appeared in regard to Texas, whose western border first felt the influence of a Spanish settlement of 1598 on the upper Rio Grande and whose territory was first occupied in 1716 but ceased to attract Spanish interest after 1762.

As early as 1791 Americans were attracted to the Texas-Louisiana frontier by prospective profits from horse-trading.[1] Philip Nolan, whom Jefferson in 1798 asked for information concerning the herds of wild horses west of the Mississippi, possibly may have been engaged as a horse-trader between Natchez and San Antonio as early as 1785. In the winter of 1797, four years before he was killed in Spanish territory, his information concerning his observations or discoveries was submitted to Jefferson by General James Wilkinson. In October, 1800, with a passport from the governor of Louisiana he led an expedition of fourteen or more men from Natchez to the Brazos where after gathering about 300 horses he was attacked by a Spanish force of 100 men which had been sent from Nacogdoches to assist him. In the engagement which resulted, he was killed and the members of his party were arrested. Unfortunately, the

1

Mexican authorities erroneously suspected that the expedition had been secretly promoted by the American government. Such suspicion was a natural result of the schemes of Miranda for Latin American independence which attracted the attention of Hamilton and other prominent Americans in 1798-99. Hamilton, in planning war against France in 1799, and while proposing that the American executive should be given power to meet any attempt of France to execute her long-suspected project of taking Louisiana and Florida whose acquisition he regarded as essential to the permanency of the American Union, wrote Secretary McHenry that for eventual security against invasion by France or Spain "we ought . . . to squint at South America." Jefferson as early as November, 1801, contemplated the possibility of American expansion to the Isthmus. In writing to Monroe on the subject of establishing a penal negro colony in America, he said: "However our present interests may restrain us within our limits it is impossible not to look forward to distant times, when our rapid multiplication will expand itself beyond those limits and cover the whole northern, if not the southern continent." [2] About the same time and for several years thereafter, Dr. William Thornton, who doubtless exerted considerable influence on both Madison and Monroe, advocated the idea of extending the republican system over all North and South America and the adjacent islands, under thirteen distinct sections but united by one central government on the Isthmus. On the "healthy" hills near Panama was to be erected the great city called *America,* connected with both the Atlantic and the Pacific by a canal, and a center from which all longitudes were to be calculated. [3]

With the cession of Louisiana to the United States emerged a new problem of the destiny of Texas—a territory which was claimed as a part of Louisiana and which under the changed conditions became liable to foreign encroachments by the advance of American backwoodsmen who had not felt the restraint of the distant American government at Washington and had little respect for imaginary boundary lines. For a time the danger of frontier encroachment was increased by disagree-

ments which brought Spain and the United States to the verge
of war, but the storm passed and Spanish plans for defense and
settlement of Texas were abandoned. Jefferson, in 1803, claiming that the newly acquired territory of Louisiana extended
from the Perdido to the Rio Grande, saw no necessity for undertaking to exchange the western part of it for the remainder of
Florida which he expected rightfully to become a part of the
United States at the first favorable opportunity.[4] On July 29,
1803, and again in April and July 8, 1804, Monroe was instructed to obtain the views of Talleyrand and to join Pinckney
at Madrid in an effort to adjust the eastern and western boundaries of Louisiana, but the time was not propitious. Talleyrand
was opposed to any further extensions of American territory.
In the instructions of July, 1804, Morris and Pinckney were
informed that the President was averse to any perpetual re-
linquishment of territory eastward of the Rio Bravo, but were
authorized to regulate their demands according to the temper
and policy of Spain. Monroe reached Madrid on January 2,
1805, and left on May 26 without any progress in the proposed negotiations. Cevallos, on the basis of long possession of
coast and hinterland, refused to follow the American argument
and even declined to agree to a proposed compromise boundary
at the Colorado. Here the diplomatic discussions rested for
thirteen years. War seemed imminent and some arrangement to
prevent frontier conflict was needed. In September, 1805,
Jefferson wrote Madison: "Supposing, then, a previous alliance
with England to guard us in the worst event, I should suppose
this Congress should pass acts . . . to dislodge the new establishment of Spain between the Mississippi and the Bravo." [5]

Early in February, 1806, a small American military force
from Natchitoches drove a body of Spaniards westward across
the Sabine and soon thereafter the Jefferson government
ordered the reinforcement of Natchitoches. In September, 1806,
General Wilkinson, who was suspected of having a secret understanding to cooperate with Burr in an expedition against the
Spanish province of Mexico, wrote to John Smith that he
planned to push troops over the Sabine and stated that 5,000

mounted infantry would be necessary to reach "Mountel Ray" and an additional 20,000 or 30,000 to carry the conquest to California and the Isthmus of Darien.[6] Arriving at Natchitoches in September, he entered into negotiations with Spanish officers to arrange an agreement for a neutral ground between the Arroyo Hondo and the Sabine by which Spanish troops were restricted to territory west of the Sabine and American troops to territory east of the Arroyo Hondo.[7] In November, 1806, he and Herrera entered into a tacit agreement to establish a temporarily neutral ground in the disputed region (between the Sabine and the Arroyo Hondo) which thereby became a "No man's land"—a convenient asylum for refugees and marauders until 1819 (or 1821) and a contributory cause of subsequent troubles which increased Mexican distrust of the Americans and hostility toward them.

At the same time (in November, 1806), to obtain information concerning the topography and defenses of the route to Mexico City, he sent an agent who, on his return to New Orleans in March, 1807, reported that European conditions had encouraged plans for revolt in Mexico and recommended the route via the Rio Grande and "Monte del Ray" as the most favorable, either to conquer or to rescue the Mexicans.[8] Lieut. Z. M. Pike, eagerly accepting a proposition of Gen. Wilkinson, undertook a tour to the Southwest under authority of President Jefferson to observe or explore the Louisiana country west of the Big Bend of the Missouri and drained by the Arkansas and Red rivers. With this expedition went Dr. John H. Robinson as a volunteer to collect a claim of a Kaskaskia trader who had sent a trading expedition to Santa Fé in 1804. Penetrating Spanish territory west of the Rio Grande, Pike (on February 7, 1807) sent Robinson to Santa Fé on the pretext of collecting the trader's debt. A few days later he was arrested and escorted to Santa Fé by a Spanish cavalry force of 100 men and later he was sent to Chihuahua from which he was expelled and deported by Salcedo via Texas to Natchitoches under close guard. He reported that the Mexicans expected the Americans to aid them to secure independence and suggested that the

American government should adopt a policy which would prevent Napoleon from obtaining a foothold in that quarter.[9] In April, 1807, Jefferson, stating that the United States had kept her hands off perfidious Spain wholly out of respect to France who should either compel her to do justice "or abandon her to us," declared: "We ask but one month to be in possession of the City of Mexico." [10] Later in the year, considering the possibility of war between England and Spain, he said: "Our southern defensive force can take the Floridas, volunteers from the Mexican army will flock to our standard . . . and probably Cuba will add herself to our confederation."

After the news of the accession of Joseph Napoleon to the throne of Spain in 1808 Mexico showed a strong sentiment of resistance which however was at first divided on the question whether a Spanish junta or a Mexican junta should act for the deposed Ferdinand—a dispute quickly settled in favor of the *junta central* in September, 1808, by royalist seizure and deportation of the viceroy who had planned to summon a Mexican congress.

Soon thereafter, the American government began to consider the question of sending agents to Spanish American centers of revolt. In a letter to Jefferson written at Carlisle on October 1, 1808, and sent to Dearborn for delivery at his discretion, Wilkinson, enclosing a copy of a memorandum which he had sent to Herrera (governor of a Mexican province) and claiming (through an experience of twenty years) to know more of Spanish America than any other American and desiring an appointment in order to silence his slanderers, urged the prompt appointment of informed agents to Mexico to lead public opinion, to demonstrate sympathy and especially "to warn against the insidious encroachment of Great Britain." [11] Jefferson's cabinet on October 22, 1808, unanimously agreed to instruct special American agents to Cuba and Mexico to say that the United States government was content to see them under Spanish rule, but that, in case of danger from England and France, if they should declare their independence, it would act according to circumstances but with a "firm belief that our interests are intimately connected." Jefferson in 1809, just after his retirement from the presidency, wrote Madison, his successor, that Napoleon would be compelled to permit American seizure of the Floridas (if desired) and would doubtless "consent to our receiving Cuba into our Union to prevent our aid to Mexico and the other provinces."

The first attempt at armed insurrection for independence in Mexico was begun in September, 1810, under the leadership of Miguel Hidalgo, a parish priest, who (with his principal associates) was captured by a government force under Calleja in March, 1811, and shot. The republican insurrection was revived and continued thereafter under the leadership of another priest, José Maria Morelos, and others, but by 1816 its forces had been almost destroyed by Calleja (who was promoted to the office of viceroy) and by 1819 all organized resistance in Mexico was ended.

At the beginning of the Mexican revolution, Texas became the scene of considerable fighting in which adventurers from the Louisiana border participated. The first conspicuous movement was in the summer of 1812.

On June 16, 1810, immediately before the beginning of the first stage of the revolt of Mexico against Spanish rule and when it was feared that the Mexican authorities would refuse to recognize a regular consul, Secretary Robert Smith appointed William Shaler "Agent for seamen and commerce in the port of Vera Cruz and all other ports in the said province" to attend to regular consular affairs, but apparently Shaler did not serve at the post indicated.[12] On June 28, apprehending an approaching "crisis which must produce great changes in Spanish America," Secretary Smith began the regular policy of sending informal agents for promotion of good will and commercial intercourse [13]—a policy continued by Secretary Monroe. In November, 1810, stating that the United States was not an unconcerned spectator of the recent transactions in Spain which had produced in the Spanish American colonies a sensation tending to a change in the old-established polity, he announced that West Florida, in which the security of American rights had been placed in jeopardy, had been occupied by President Jefferson to the Perdido, leaving the question of sovereignty still open.[14] Significant in this connection was the encouragement given to John Jacob Astor who had secured a charter for the American Fur Company in 1808 and had organized the Pacific Fur Company in 1810, and established Astoria in June, 1812, on the Columbia River in territory still claimed by Spain as a part of Mexico.

Early in 1811, after De Onis in confidential letters to the Spanish commandant at Caracas had complained of the refusal of the American government to receive him as a representative of Spain, Secretary Monroe in an explanation said that the United States had received no minister from either party contending for the government of Spain and desired only to observe a policy of neutrality and friendly commercial intercourse with every part of the Spanish dominions under whatever authority.[15]

Secretary Monroe, under President Madison, largely determined the early American policy toward Mexico in conferences with a group of men who approached him in the guise of Mexican revolutionary agents. Preliminary diplomatic relations of Mexico and the United States through a self-constituted agent began the latter part of 1811. José Bernardo Gutierrez, who had aided in the revolt begun by Don Miguel Hidalgo, and had become a lieutenant colonel in the insurgent forces of northern Mexico, arrived at the "neutral zone" between Louisiana and Texas accompanied by José Menchaca and at Natchitoches was kindly treated by American officials who encouraged an appeal to Secretary Monroe.[16] Leaving his companion to organize the refugees of that region to undertake an invasion of Texas and to establish a provisional government there, he journeyed to Washington via Tennessee and Kentucky to seek from Secretary Monroe recognition and material aid (men, money and arms) for his embryo government. At Washington, although he arrived without either credentials or funds to insure proper respect for his mission, he presented letters of introduction which secured for him a cordial reception at the State and War departments and provision for entertainment and travel. The intermediary through whom official courtesy was extended was the chief clerk of the State Department, John Graham, who was fitted for the part by previous experience in Spain and Louisiana.

Monroe, although sympathetic and interested in the effort of mutually advantageous commercial treaties, and possibly hopeful of a Mexican constitution similar to that of the United States and of a pan-American confederation under American domination, was not ready to compromise with Spain or with the latter's ally (Great Britain), nor to compromise the American claim to the Rio Grande as a boundary. Aided by good fortune, he escaped any entanglements, but wishing to hasten the formation of a provisional government which might justify recognition, he paid the return expenses of Gutierrez to New Orleans, and apparently (through Graham) encouraged him to expect American aid in efforts to secure self-government.

The mission of Gutierrez had an interesting connection with that of other early revolutionary agents. It was closely associated with the mission of José A. de Toledo, a native Cuban who (with the aid of the American consul, Meade) visited Philadelphia in September, 1811, and, following a letter of November 16, and with the financial aid of A. J. Dallas, the United States district attorney,[17] visited Washington in the last week of December, became acquainted with Gutierrez whom he dominated in later plans, and obtained from Monroe expense funds for a return trip to Havana and a letter of introduction to William Shaler there. For a time he delayed his departure from Philadelphia, probably with expectation or hope of news of a revolutionary success in Mexico, and apparently claiming authority to act for leaders of the revolutionary movement in northern Mexico.[18] His correspondence with Monroe and Graham ceased in March, 1812. Later in 1812 he was joined at Philadelphia by Juan M. Picornell, a refugee from Caracas.

Gutierrez arrived at New Orleans by sea late in March, 1812, with Graham's letter of introduction to Governor Claiborne who provided for the remainder of his journey to Natchitoches and introduced him to William Shaler who had an appointment as American commercial agent to Mexico and was en route to the Texas frontier. With Shaler he journeyed to the frontier, causing both American and Spanish officials to infer that the Washington government approved the plans for the Mexican revolution. In May he severed relations with Shaler, and later he thoroughly discredited himself and his cause by recklessly organizing a filibustering raid (The Gutierrez-Magee raid of August, 1812) which drove the force from eastern Texas and compromised both the immediate leaders and the Philadelphia junta, and was a flagrant violation of American neutrality.*

Before learning of the filibustering project of Gutierrez in Texas, Monroe on recommendation of Col. Z. M. Pike on June 19, 1812,[19] employed Dr. John H. Robinson (Pike's friend) on a special mission to Salcedo, the general commandant of the internal provinces of New Spain,—the authority whom Gutierrez and Toledo were seeking to overthrow. His purpose in the mission was probably in part to prevent Spanish American colonials from aiding Great Britain in the war against the United States and possibly to suggest alliance against the European powers. In his instructions of July 1, he requested him to arrange with Salcedo some method to break up the lawless bands of the neutral ground between the Sabine and the Arroyo Hondo—marauders whom Col. Pike had unsuccessfully attempted to expel early in 1812 by troops under his command at Natchitoches. He also instructed Robinson to assure Salcedo that boundary disputes would be the "subject of amicable negotiation hereafter," to present documents to justify the American occupation of West Florida and to state that any

* Lieut. Augustus W. Magee, a graduate of West Point, had caught the spirit of the Wilkinson school of soldiers of the frontier, and was easily persuaded to join in an attempt to conquer Texas. The small army of 150 under Gutierrez began the march in June, 1812, captured Nacogdoches, and the fort at Spanish Bluffs on the Trinity River, crossed the Colorado, met a resisting force of Governor Salcedo at La Bahia (Goliad) and drove it to San Antonio, then captured the town (March 29, 1813), and treacherously put to death Salcedo and Governor Simon de Herrera and many Spanish officers. Soon thereafter the Republicans, increased to about 3000, deposed Gutierrez, and chose Toledo as their commander but were soon defeated (July, 1813) near Bexar by a royalist force of 2000 men and dispersed, many being butchered.

occupation of East Florida [20] which might be found necessary in the war against Great Britain should not be regarded as an act of hostility to Spanish possessions in North America.

These instructions may have been influenced by a letter of March, 1812, from Wilkinson to William Eustis, Secretary of War, stating that the obvious British policy was to acquire influence or control over Spanish America, recommending efforts to counteract the British in Mexico and at the same time to secure the friendship of the Mexicans.[21] Possibly the chief purpose of the mission to the Spanish colonial governor, like the missions of other agents to other parts of Spanish America, was to establish friendly commercial relations with the Mexican provinces. Already a contraband trade was increasing along the Texas border and a company of merchants had proposed to open trade between St. Louis and Santa Fé.[22]

Robinson was not successful in his mission. At San Antonio and Monclovova he was cordially received by Spanish officials, but at Chihuahua he was regarded with suspicion by General Salcedo, who, irritated by his bombastic speeches and seizing upon the irregularity of his credentials as a convenient pretext, refused to treat, and, after some delay, reported that his propositions would be referred to the viceroy or to Spain for reply through the regular diplomatic channels and courteously intimated that he should return at once from Spanish territory by the same route by which he had arrived. On his journey he enthusiastically encouraged the spirit of revolution. To those republicans who appealed for sympathy and aid he replied that the President felt a warm interest in their cause. With Shaler and Toledo, whom he encountered on the frontier, he had some kind of understanding, and when Monroe failed to respond to his report he entered into filibustering activities.

De Onis in January, 1813, complained that Robinson's mission ignored the regular diplomatic channels of communication. Some of the Spanish authorities suspected that Monroe's purpose was to tempt Governor Salcedo to act independently of his superiors in the territory over which he exercised practically independent jurisdiction, and thereby to encourage revolution.

Whatever was Monroe's purpose in these earlier missions, he aroused the hopes of those who were planning for independence, and excited among Spanish authorities bitter recriminations which complicated frontier problems and influenced the adoption of a more cautious policy by the Department of State. More effective American aid to the revolutionists of Mexico was doubtless prevented by the War of 1812. It was sought by authorized agents in 1814 and 1815 with even smaller measure of success, although American sentiment was probably expressed by Jefferson in his note of April 28, 1814, to De Onis suggesting that Spain, acting in self interest, might make firm allies and friends of her colonies by voluntary anticipation of their independence "which otherwise necessity will force."

Meantime, the republican movement in Mexico had been revived by Morelos who, after several victorious battles, called a congress which elected him generalissimo with power of chief executive. After publishing a declaration of independence (in November, 1813) Morelos sent Don José Manuel Herrera to represent the Mexican republic in the United States. After the degradation and execution of Morelos in December, 1815, closing the second period of the revolution for Mexican independence, the control was theoretically in the hands of the wandering congress but practically conducted by various regional republican leaders, with poorly equipped forces and without proper cooperation or definite plan of campaign. The chief leader, after a period of fruitless effort, occupied Galveston Bay in 1816 (with a band under Luis de Aury), raised the flag of the republic, established a government and opened a prosperous slave trade with New Orleans and by the spring of 1817 he had a body of about 600 soldiers under three commanders, but after various ill-fortunes Galveston was left in the hands of pirates under Lafitte. Aury, one of the commanders at Galveston, sailed to join McGregor at Amelia Island from whence he was driven out by the United States. Early in 1821 the piratical or privateering establishment at Galveston was broken up by the appearance of the United States brig *Enterprise* under Capt. Kearney.

In the second period of the revolution the leaders sought American recognition and on March 18, 1815, Juan Pablo y Anaya, Mexican agent, wrote from New Orleans to President Madison explaining the delay in establishing diplomatic communications with the United States at Washington and requesting protection in efforts to establish relations which he indicated should be on a basis of "absolute severance of America from Europe." [23] On July 14 a letter of President Morelos to President Madison, after briefly mentioning the improvements in the Mexican government which afforded an opportunity to open long-sought relations with the United States, and a prospect of treaties of alliance and commerce, announced the appointment of Don José Manuel Herrera as minister plenipotentiary and requested steps to recognize the independence of Mexican America. Herrera started on his mission to the American government on July 16 and on October 1, after detention on the Vera Cruz coast, finally reached New Orleans, where his departure for Washington was delayed for four months by various obstacles which finally induced him to return to Mexico in March, 1816, for assistance necessary to the success of his negotiations.[24]

American policy relating to Spanish America was criticized by Spain with whom official relations were restored after the dethronement of Napoleon. Luis de Onis, who had come to the United States in 1809 to represent the Spanish Junta but had not been accorded official recognition, was received late in 1815 as a special favor to Spain, although the President had preferred to receive some one else. Appointed to resume direct and official relations which had been broken since 1808, he reopened negotiations with the American government by presenting claims for losses from alleged depredations by expeditions fitted out at New Orleans to assist the insurgents of Texas and Mexico.[25] In December, 1815, referring to the insurgent bands which had conducted operations from New Orleans and Natchitoches with support from the authorities there he requested Secretary Monroe to obtain from the President orders for the prosecution of principal persons who he complained were then enlisting in

New Orleans men for new expeditions both by land and water, to invade the Spanish dominions. He named as the ringleaders José Alvarez de Toledo, José Manuel de Herrera, Dr. Robinson and others. He stated that Herrera had just arrived at New Orleans "with the appointment (as he says) of minister to the United States from the self-styled Mexican Congress, who has delivered to Toledo fifteen hundred commissions in blank from that body of insurgents, that he may confer them on a like number of officers which he is recruiting in the territory of the Union." In a letter of February 22, 1816, he complained that Toledo, Bernardo Gutierrez, Dr. Robinson and others whom he had named as the perpetrators of the horrible deeds at St. Antonio de Bexar were still in Louisiana where they were endeavoring to raise new forces to repeat the same excesses. He was especially severe in his denunciation of Robinson, accusing him of seducing the inhabitants of the interior provinces, of procuring the information which aided Gutierrez's cruel projects, and of inviting adventurers from the United States to form an army against Spanish territory.[26]

In reply to De Onis' letter demanding the apprehension of Toledo and other Spanish patriots and restitution of the Floridas, Monroe wrote a note reviewing the conduct of Spain for many years.

By January, 1816, the American government was urged by an increasing popular sentiment to take a more active stand in favor of the Spanish American revolutionists. General Scott and certain members of Congress proposed to join in the war against Spain at once. T. L. Halsey, writing to Monroe from Buenos Aires on July 3, 1816, urging prompt assistance to the revolutionists, suggested that since Spain by proximity of her most important colonies must sooner or later be at war against the United States, why should the United States not seize the opportunity to extend assistance in a righteous cause? [27]

The government had better advice from Jefferson who, on February 4, in a letter to Madison, after expressing his disapproval of the proposition of General Scott and others, stated that "although the colonies had a right to be free, and we had a right to aid them, we should defer alliance with Spanish America until open rupture with Spain could no longer be avoided."

On March 4, 1817, President Monroe, contemplating dangers from abroad, seemed to fear that war might cause the disintegration of the Union. In his message of December 2, 1817, although he admitted that the United States had watched the Spanish American contest with high interest, due in part to the natural sympathy of American citizens in the events which affected their neighbors, he asserted that the American government through every stage of the conflict had maintained an impartial neutrality, opening its ports to both contestants in the civil war (between parties nearly equal) and that it sought in commerce, or otherwise, no advantage not equally open to other nations. In later messages he continued his policy of neutrality, determined to defer recognition until the fact of independence was convincingly established. Secretary Adams had several times stated to Bagot that the United States should act in concert with Great Britain in regard to the Spanish American provinces.[28] After the Congress of Aix la Chapelle declined to interfere between Spain and her provinces, he informed Bagot that independence, which the United States had forborne to acknowledge in order to learn the course of Europe, must soon be recognized.

The question of American recognition was connected with other questions of policy—especially with the Florida negotiations, and questions concerning the interests of other powers in America. In March, 1818, Monroe received from Joseph Codina, a letter written at Philadelphia, enclosing a general plan for separating Spanish American dominions from Spain and for making them free under the protection of the United States, advising the negotiation of treaties of amity and commerce with South American countries and the formation of a coalition for mutual defense, and the occupation of the whole of the Floridas which were destined by nature to form a part of the United States (for safety and convenience). In this letter he was also advised, with cooperation of the Mexican patriots, to plan military occupation of the City of Mexico, Vera Cruz and other places as far as the Isthmus of Panama—"the point which . . . the judgment of every sensible man, is destined by God and nature to be the limits of the United States." He was especially urged to occupy Mexico which was regarded as desirable, to secure safe frontiers and as a policy calculated to discourage the royalists of Cuba and Porto Rico which thereafter would "with very trifling aid agree to form a union with the United States." [29]

When De Onis finally announced that he was authorized to propose arbitration or mediation of friendly European powers for the settlement of Spanish differences with the United States, Secretary Adams, on March 12, 1818, after reviewing relations with Spain and referring to the former boundless ambitions and assertions from which Spain had been compelled to recede reluctantly by ungracious gradations of three centuries, and to the recent pretensions to which the United States could never accede—informed Onis that the United States with a policy of peace had waited patiently for thirteen years with the hope of a satisfactory adjustment of the questions of boundaries and still preferred to await the favorable operation of time rather than to refer the questions to arbitration or mediation by European powers. Stating that the European states were connected by a multitude of important interests and relations with which the American government had no concern and with which it had always manifested the determination not to interfere, he respectfully declared that the United States "in justice to that fundamental system of policy which forbids them from entering the labyrinth of European politics must decline . . . the interference of any other government of Europe, for the settlement of their differences with Spain." [30]

On May 1, 1818, when Correa de Serra, the Portuguese minister, hinted that the European alliance had determined to participate against the Spanish Americans and that Russia would probably obtain a large foothold of the Mexican territory of Spain, Adams replied that "if they thought of settling affairs of such importance, and in which we have so deep an interest, without consulting us, they must not complain if we pursue our course concerning it without consulting them." [31] On May 20, in his instructions to Rush at London, in connection with questions of title on the Northwest coast, he said: "If the United States leave her (England) in undisturbed possession of her holds in Europe, Asia and Africa, with all her actual possessions in this hemisphere, we may very fairly expect that she will not think it consistent either with wise or friendly policy to watch with eyes of jealousy and alarm every possibility of extension of our natural dominion in North America which she can have no solid interests to prevent until all possibility of her preventing it shall have vanished." [32]

The final negotiations with Spain concerning the Louisiana boundary controversy were resumed and conducted by Adams under the personal supervision of Monroe who had conducted the negotiations of 1803 with France and of 1805 with Spain. Adams contended that Louisiana extended westward to the Rio Grande. This De Onis denied, claiming that Texas extended to the Mississippi. Adams then agreed to accept the line of the Colorado from its mouth to its source and thence to the northern bounds of Louisiana. De Onis then proposed to cede the Floridas and to establish the eastern boundary of Texas on one of the mouths of the Mississippi.[33] Finding no hope of success in his claims to Texas, Adams gradually retired from his extreme demand, compromised on the Sabine, and sought compensation in the establishment of the southern boundary of the Oregon country, first proposing the 41st parallel, but finally compromising on the 42d parallel, as the definite line of boundary between Oregon and Spanish territory to the South Sea. After the long discussions, he finally adopted the views of the President and the majority of the cabinet, refrained from pressing his demands for trans-Sabine territory which was not yet needed, and agreed that the United States ceded to Spain and renounced forever all its "rights, claims and pretensions" to Texas—in which Spain had first undertaken to establish a settlement at Matagorda Bay in 1720-21 and had reestablished missions in the interior west of the Sabine soon thereafter.

Monroe, who probably saw that the American title was much

weaker than the American argument in the case, had decided upon the expediency of accepting the Sabine for the western boundary. This decision, on which he was generally sustained by final approval of every member of his cabinet and by the sober judgment of the country, was in accord with his earlier instructions from Secretary Madison in 1804. The treaty which was immediately advantageous both to America and to Spain was finally signed on February 22, 1819.

The cession was criticized by those who believed that the Monroe administration had recklessly given away a good title to a vast and valuable territory. De Onis, however, after his return to Spain, published a memoir in which he said that the United States seemed to be "insatiable in the acquisition of territory," without reflecting whether by wide expansion it was "sowing the seed of its political dissolution." [34] Spanish ratification of the treaty was delayed for two years, during which Spain sought to prevent American recognition of her revolted colonies and unsuccessfully renewed efforts to secure from the United States a stipulation to this effect. During the period of delay the treaty was attacked by Clay in Congress (on April 3, 1820) on the ground that alienation of territory, to which America's unquestioned right had long been maintained by the executive department of the government, was unconstitutional without consent of Congress. In May, 1820, after the arrival of General Vives to extort new pledges before ratification of the treaty, Jefferson, who had not favored the abandonment of territory west of the Sabine, wrote Monroe that in case of non-ratification of the treaty by Spain the United States would expand into Mexico. Adams, while laboring to secure ratification, professed indifference to grumbling members of Congress. For a time both Monroe and Adams seemed ready to abandon the treaty. Monroe, foreseeing the expulsion of Spain from the continent, wrote Jefferson that the American government could arrange with Mexico a boundary which would give the United States more territory than would be safe for its internal peace. Notwithstanding his doubts in considering the international side of the question, he expressed his fears that the "acquisition of territory to the West and South involves difficulties of an internal nature which menace the Union itself." Although he concurred with Jefferson that in case Spain should fail to ratify the treaty "we might take Florida as an indemnity and Texas for some trifle as an equivalent . . . and with any new government which might be formed in Mexico . . . arrange the boundaries in the wilderness so as to include as much territory on our side as we might desire," he was reflecting upon the danger of exciting New England opposition by too rapid expansion. In a letter of May 22 (1819), referring to Eastern feeling, he said: "I have been decidedly of the opinion that we ought to be content with Florida for the present, and until the public opinion in that quarter shall be reconciled to any further change." [35]

An interesting American protest against the Sabine boundary provision of the Spanish treaty was the filibustering expedition into Texas led by James Long who had been a surgeon in the United States army and was related to General Wilkinson by marriage to his niece. Claiming that the United States had no right to abandon to Spain the territory of Texas without consent of the people, he left Natchez with 75 men in June, 1819, undertook to transform Texas into an independent republic by erecting a supreme council of 21 members at Nacogdoches and by issuing a proclamation.[36] Among the members of the expedition was Bernardo Gutierrez who had led the Magee expedition. During Long's absence from Nacogdoches for an unsuccessful conference with the pirate chief, Lafitte, his forces were scattered by Spanish troops. He escaped via Galveston to New Orleans, and after the revolutionary outbreak of 1821, formed a connection with the liberal leaders of Mexico and aided in the capture of La Bahia (October, 1821) but was later compelled to surrender with some of his followers who were thereafter detained in Mexico City until he was killed there. His followers were later released through the influence of the American minister, Poinsett. By 1821, Texas east of San Antonio was in a state of desolation. Nacogdoches was almost completely destroyed in 1821. The end of the era of the filibuster marked the beginning of a new era in which the permanent American settler was an important factor.

The Spanish ratification (in October, 1820) of the Florida treaty which was proclaimed in February, 1821, cleared the way for American recognition of the Spanish American republics which could meet the legal requirements. The independence of Mexico was finally consummated, February 24, 1821, two days after the exchange of ratifications of the Florida treaty, by an agreement between opposing military commanders—between Col. Augustin de Iturbide (acting under Apodeca, the viceroy of Mexico) and Vincent Guerrero, the only remaining prominent revolutionary leader of Mexico. This agreement, the unique plan of Igula, including both a proclamation of independence from Spain and a new constitution for the separate Mexican state, was proclaimed by Iturbide and soon won the adherence of both revolutionists and loyalists. The final revolt in Mexico was determined by the liberal spirit of the new rulers of Spain of 1820 which alarmed the Mexican clergy, resulting in the formation of a conspiracy and Iturbide's proclamation.

By July, 1821, the insurgents controlled practically all parts of the province except Mexico City, Acapulco and Vera Cruz. The new viceroy, General O'Donoju (successor of the deposed Apodeca), who arrived at Vera Cruz on July 30, finding a critical condition which first caused him to consider reembarkation, promptly opened negotiations with insurgent leaders, resulting in a meeting with the victorious Iturbide at Cordova. There on August 24, he and Iturbide signed the treaty of Cordova which provided for the surrender of the Spanish army and the independence of Mexico and ended the conflict, although it was later repudiated by Spain. On September 27, Iturbide led his victorious army into Mexico City. On May 29, 1822, by a *coup d'état,* following the news that Spain refused to sanction the treaty of Cordova, he managed, through the intimidated Mexican Congress, to have himself proclaimed constitutional Emperor of Mexico, under the title of Augustin I. Soon thereafter he was also declared Emperor in Central America to which he had sent a Mexican military force. After a short and stormy career of ten months in wielding the scepter which he said he "did not seek," and in discord with his congress which he finally dissolved (in October, 1822), he abdicated (in March, 1823) following a revolt begun by Santa Anna in favor of a republic.

Independent Mexico, left in a state of confusion by Iturbide's abdication in March, 1823, and Spain's refusal to recognize the validity of the treaty of Cordova, in November, 1823, through its authorities called a constituent congress to prepare a constitution which was adopted in October, 1824, and which was doubtless influenced in part by a project based on the principles of the United States Constitution submitted on March 29, 1823, by Stephen F. Austin who while at Mexico City became interested in the political reorganization of the country. Under the new constitution, Victoria was elected president by vote of the state legislatures. He assumed his duties on October 10, 1824, under somewhat hopeful conditions, but with a poorly organized and inexperienced government, a people largely indifferent and unfit for self-government and a vast northern frontier region almost unpopulated and unknown. This frontier extended from the mere missionary jurisdictions along the Pacific coast to the western borders of the United States, whose steady, unconscious expansion westward was due to individual initiative neither aided nor restricted by the American government, nor likely to respect an imaginary boundary line.

To the Americans who had aided the movement for Mexican independence, the Mexicans showed their gratitude by valuable colonization land grants which legalized and facilitated American emigration to Texas and proved a source of later troubles, producing increased suspicions and distrust and culminating in the Texan revolution of 1836.

Closely contemporary with the later part of the Mexican struggle for independence were the efforts of the Austins to establish a colony in Texas. In November, 1820, Moses Austin, a Connecticut Yankee—who had successively migrated to Philadelphia, and then to Richmond and later to Wyeth County, Virginia, and in 1798 to the Missouri region of the Louisiana territory—arrived at Bexar, after a long ride across the de-

serted wilderness of eastern Texas, and applied to Governor
Martinez for a tract of Texas land for a colony of 300 American families under a plan formed with his son Stephen in the
spring of 1819. From the indignant governor he received a peremptory order to leave Texas at once; but through the aid of an
old Louisiana acquaintance he managed to obtain a favorable
hearing and a recommendation of the grant which was later duly
authorized by the viceroy of Spain and certified by a letter of
Martinez of February 8, 1821, about three months before
Austin's death. The son, Stephen F. Austin, who had been a
member of the Missouri territorial legislature in 1814, and had
located the town of Little Rock, Arkansas, in 1819, and had
served as a newspaper editor at New Orleans in the winter of
1820-21, left Nacogdoches with a surveying party in July,
1821, after his father's death, and arrived at Bexar on August
12 to select the site for the colony. In the following December
he arrived on the Brazos with the first settlers of the colony. On
April 29, 1822, he arrived in Mexico City to obtain from the
Mexican Congress a confirmation of his grant, and there he
waited during the period of Iturbide's rise and fall. On April
28, 1823, he rode away carrying with him the evidence of the
official confirmation of the concession. Thereafter his colony
increased rapidly. In January, 1824, he established a code of
laws for it—seven months before the meeting of the first Coa-
huila-Texas legislature and three years before the adoption of
a state constitution.[37] Under the Mexican colonization act of
August, 1824, and the local state law of March, 1825, several
similar foreign colonial enterprises were authorized in Texas.
Among those of April, 1825, were the DeWitt colony and the
Robertson colony adjoining the Austin settlement and the
Hayden Edwards colony near Nacogdoches. Each emigration
from the United States to Texas was stimulated only by individual initiative and enterprise in seeking for better opportunities or new adventure, and without any encouragement or
stimulation from the American government. Each migration
proved useful in redeeming the deserts. In September, 1825,
the British minister, Ward, less than five months after his arrival

in Mexico, advised Canning that he expected serious difficulties to arise from the presence of the American backwoods settlers who by their dislike of all restraints might prove bad subjects and inconvenient neighbors.[38]

The question of American recognition of Mexico and the establishment of diplomatic relations became a pressing one in 1821-22. The provisional government of Mexico which was installed on September 28, 1821, immediately following the entrance of Iturbide's army into Mexico City, promptly sought to establish a legation at Washington. In the midst of the discord and struggle between Congress and the provisional executive (dominated by Iturbide) the latter urged Congress to take steps to open diplomatic relations.[39] On November 20, José Manuel de Herrera, the Mexican Secretary of Foreign Affairs, sent (by James Smith Wilcocks) his first diplomatic communication to Secretary John Quincy Adams announcing the triumph of the revolution which for eleven years had "kept the politicians of the whole world in suspense" [40]—a communication which reached Washington March 13, 1822, five days after Monroe had recommended that Congress take steps to enable him to appoint diplomatic representatives to the new Spanish American states. On September 24, 1822, Herrera announced the appointment of an envoy-minister, Don Manuel Zozaya, who sailed from Alvarado on October 27, reached Baltimore (via Hampton Roads) on November 20, and on December 3 sent his secretary to Washington to prepare for his reception while he made a short visit to Philadelphia. Zozaya arrived in Washington by December 10, was formally received on December 12 and was honored by a banquet given by the President on December 24.[41] In the midst of other honors which followed, he evidently had suspicious fears of future American policy in relation to Mexico—fears which arose in part from the published Memoirs of Onis, and which were probably strengthened by debates in Congress (including debates on the Oregon country). On December 26, in reporting to his government that he had discovered ambitious American views in regard to Texas, he added, "In time they will be our sworn enemies, and foreseeing this we ought to treat them as such from the present day." [42]

The real beginning of the Mexican legation was in November, 1824,—the date of the arrival of Parlo Obregon, envoy extraordinary and minister plenipotentiary, who was instructed to strengthen friendly relations and to learn what aid Mexico might expect from the United States in case of attack by European powers, and who remained at Washington until his death (by suicide) in September, 1828. His secret instructions of August 30, 1824, informing him of the report of Torrens, the Mexican chargé at Washington (or in Philadelphia), indicating American intentions as to Mexican territories in Texas, New Mexico and the Californias, stated that the negotiation of a treaty of limits was the chief object of the mission and urged him to secure acknowledgment of the Spanish treaty of 1819, which the imperial Mexican government (in preparing its secret instructions of October, 1822, to Zozaya) had regarded as valid.

Meantime on March 8, 1822, in reply to a request of January 30, Monroe sent to the House correspondence and several comments showing the political status of the new Latin American governments. He stated that five provinces were "in full enjoyment of their independence," that Spain was unable to restore authority over them and should become reconciled with them on the basis of unqualified independence. He suggested that Congress should make necessary appropriations to recognize the provinces which enjoyed independence. The time selected by Monroe for recognition of the new states was approved by Jefferson as neither premature nor disadvantageously delayed. In the House the vote on recognition was 167 to 1. To R. S. Garnett, who cast the negative vote, Monroe promptly suggested that he should change his vote in order to impress Spain with an unanimous vote in favor of the welfare of the Spanish provinces. [43]

In the following year Monroe announced his famous American non-intervention doctrine, whose fundamental idea had begun to develop from the earliest years of American national existence and which had begun to assume a more definite shape after Jefferson's administration—when Monroe, as Secretary of State, had carefully studied the many volumes of closely written despatches from American special diplomatic and commercial agents in Spanish America, beginning with those of General Thomas Sumter who was sent to Brazil in 1809 when the court of Portugal was moved to Rio Janeiro, and those of Joel R. Poinsett who was sent to South America in 1810 when events seemed to indicate that the European colonial system in America was about to end and who soon in 1812 actively participated in the extension of republican government along the Pacific side of the Andes.

The American government, after the adoption of a decisive policy toward Latin America, persistently urged Spain to acknowledge the independence of the new Spanish American nations, and to the latter it promptly reported the attitude of Spain toward these overtures. This policy was continued until it finally culminated in a treaty of peace and amity between Mexico and Spain in December, 1836.

Unfortunately the period from 1822 to 1825, in which America might have established friendly relations with Mexico, was wasted by delays in the appointment of a suitable American diplomatic representative. The position of minister to Mexico became a football of American politicians or a political pawn at Washington while the astute Canning was busy in establishing powerful British influence* which overshadowed the importance and influence of the earlier American recognition of Mexican independence and the declarations of Monroe. On

---

* Canning sent on a confidential mission Dr. Mackie who practically "began diplomatic relations" in July, 1823. Later he sent a special commission of three with instructions (of October 10, 1823) to renounce any selfish interests and to pledge protection against interference in Mexico by any power (in case of final separation of Mexico from Spain). Finally, on January 3, 1825, he announced his determination to recognize Mexico and sent Morier and Ward with instructions to guide them in negotiating a treaty which was signed on April 6, 1825 (but was rejected by Canning in the following July because of certain objectionable clauses which were omitted in a later treaty concluded near the end of 1826). One strong motive of Canning in recognition was to impose a barrier to the ambition and ascendency of the United States which he apprehended had designs to become the head of a trans-Atlantic league or confederacy.

May 4, 1822, Monroe signed an act of Congress appropriating $100,000 for expenses of "such missions to the independent nations in the American continent" as the President might consider proper. Although this act authorized the appointment of ministers to the new republics, he delayed action for almost a year. The chief cause of this delay he probably expressed in a discouraging letter of November 25, 1822, to Jefferson concerning the critical situation in Mexico. Later, he was probably influenced by the views of Jefferson who on December 1, in returning Mr. Taylor's lecture on Mexico, wrote him a letter rejoicing to learn that Iturbide was a mere usurper and slenderly supported and suggesting that it was "lawful to wish to see no emperors nor kings in our hemisphere and that Brazil as well as Mexico shall homologize with us," although he claimed no right to intermeddle with the form of government of other nations. Possibly, too, he may have been influenced by the news from St. Salvador ("one of the constituent states of Guatemala") which, fearing the menaces of Mexico, by decree of its congress on December 5, 1822, proposed its annexation to the United States—a proposal which was withdrawn after the overthrow of Iturbide.[44] Earlier in 1822, in Mexico, the United States was suspected of designs to acquire Texas to the Rio Bravo del Norte.[45] From General Wilkinson, who went to Mexico City in the spring of 1822,* Monroe received a letter stating that Mexicans desired annexation to the United States, and offered his services to further American negotiations looking toward that end.

To secure additional and more recent data concerning the probable durability of the imperial government, from which to determine a course of action as to diplomatic relations, Mon-

---

* Wilkinson evidently disliked both President Monroe and his predecessor Madison. Seeking a land concession from Mexico, he sailed from New Orleans to Vera Cruz in March, 1822, and by April 26 was at Puebla, evidently en route to Mexico City where he introduced Stephen F. Austin on May 15 and evidently remained from May, 1822, to June, 1824, or later, for the purpose of collecting accounts of persons for claims for advances to Mexican revolutionists years before. On March 6, 1823, he wrote from Mexico to Austin applying for a tract of land. He obtained a concession for Texas land but was unable to fulfill the conditions before his death in Mexico, December 28, 1825.

roe sent to Mexico City, in August, 1822, on a secret mission, Joel Roberts Poinsett (earlier special agent to South America) who early in 1823 (probably late January or in February) advised against recognition of Iturbide. Poinsett stated that Iturbide had neither talents nor scruples, that although he complimented American institutions he regarded them as unsuitable for his country and that his recognition would discourage the Republican party in Mexico.[46]

According to a later statement of Azcarate, one of Iturbide's officials, Poinsett, who was at first supposed to be an official envoy to Mexico (and was so presented to Iturbide), held with Azcarate an interview in which he traced on a map a line showing his desire that the United States should absorb all Texas, New Mexico and Upper California, and parts of Lower California, Sonora, Coahuila and Nuevo Leon—to which the angered Azcarate (who later predicted that the establishment of limits would be the American-Mexican apple of discord) responded that the Mexican government would always respect the Onis treaty and would never cede any territory.[47]

Already, on April 23, 1822, Adams, in reply to Herrera's note of November 30, 1821, had said that the President would appoint a minister to Mexico, but he suggested to the cabinet that action should be delayed until the arrival of an agent from Mexico. Early in January, after the arrival of Zozaya in December, the President decided to send a minister at once, and at his request Adams, on January 10, offered the post to the wealthy and able and polished Senator Brown of Mississippi, who declined on the ground that he did not regard the social conditions of Mexico suitable for his wife.[48] Coincident with the appointment of a minister to Colombia, on January 27, 1823, before the return of Poinsett from Mexico and before the arbitration of Iturbide, Monroe through Adams, and at Adams' suggestion,[49] offered the Mexican post to General Andrew Jackson, the hero of the battle of New Orleans and the first American governor of Florida (March-July, 1821). Jackson promptly and coldly declined (on March 15) as had been expected when the offer was made. His reasons for declining

appear in the following significant and diverting letter written
at the Hermitage on March 15 to Secretary Adams:

"I have received your letter of the 19th ulto and with it the
commission as Envoy Extraordinary and Minister Plenipotentiary to
Mexico—
"While I recognise in this act of my Government a further proof
of its approbation of my official conduct heretofore; and of a continuation of that confidence in me; still for various reasons, which have
been communicated in a letter to Mr. Monroe, I can not in justice to
myself or country consent to act on this mission—
"The present unhappy revolutionary state of Mexico, with an oppressed people struggling for their liberties against an Emperor; whom
they have branded with the epithets of usurper, and tyrant, convinces
me no minister from the U. States could at this period effect any
beneficial treaty for this country; and of the impolicy of a Republican
Representative at a court which might be construed as countenancing
the Empire in opposition to a Republic— The People of Mexico in their
honest efforts for freedom, command my warmest sympathies; and
their success is intimately the ultimate and general triumph of those
liberal principles for which our Revolutionary worthies bled; and
which now form the pride and boast of United America— With these
feelings and wishes, and which I believe to be in unison with my fellow
citizens generally; you may readily conceive that my situation at
Mexico would be embarrassing to me, independent of the conviction
that I was rendering no service to my country. To render service could
alone constitute any motive for again acting in a public capacity—
"The President has been kind enough to say, that not having consulted me before he made the nomination it is not obligatory on me
to accept; but that I will act as meets my convenience and approbation— The reasons stated above will shew that in consulting my own
feelings, I have not been uninfluenced by considerations connected with
the best interests of my country—" [50]

Writing Jefferson concerning international events, on April
14, 1823, Monroe said: "The situation of Mexico is peculiar
in our hemisphere. When a nomination of ministers to the new
governments was made Iturbide alone had sent a minister here.
To have nominated to the other governments and not to Mexico would have been so marked a proceeding that it would have
been felt by the holy alliance, as well as our neighbor. By the
nomination of General Jackson, that compliment was paid and

by his declining to accept the appointment, as was anticipated, the object, in not sending one there is attained, as no other will be made for the present." [51]

On December 12, 1822, Secretary Adams, nearly six months after recognition of Colombia by presentation of Manuel Torres, the Colombian chargé, completed the recognition of Mexican independence by presenting to President Monroe as minister plenipotentiary from the Mexican Empire, Jose Manuel Zozaya, whose appointment by the Iturbide government (in March, 1822), had been announced by Herrera (the Mexican Secretary of Relations) by letter of September 24. On January 28, 1823, James Smith Wilcocks, of Pennsylvania, who before October, 1821, had traveled on horseback from Guaymas on the Gulf of California to almost every part of Sonora and through other chief provinces of northern Mexico, was appointed the first American consul at Mexico City.[52] Trade intercourse with the United States, which was illegal before Mexican independence, was gradually begun in the period of revolt and about 1821 a regular commerce was established between St. Louis and Santa Fé, and with Vera Cruz.

On March 4, 1824, nearly a year after the nomination of Jackson, President Monroe * on the recommendation of Adams commissioned as minister to Mexico Senator Ninian Edwards of Illinois, who was confirmed by the Senate on March 4 and resigned before leaving for his post, but on April 22 was directed not to proceed but to await the orders of a congressional committee which was investigating a charge made by him against W. H. Crawford.[53] Under pressure from Monroe, Edwards resigned the Mexican post on June 22 and later refunded two-thirds of the $9,000 which had been advanced for the purchase of an outfit for the mission.[54] After considering several others who had been recommended for the place, among whom were Henry Wheaton, Thomas H. Benton and William Henry Harrison, he finally offered the place, in July,

* Monroe had favored G. M. Dallas, who was opposed by Adams on the ground that "he was not yet of the age and political standing suitable for that appointment." Both Edwards and Dallas were partisans of Calhoun, who had recently accepted the candidacy for vice president. (Adams, *Memoirs*, VI, pp. 227, 233, 234, 241 and 243.)

1824, to Joel R. Poinsett, of South Carolina, a pro-Jackson man, whose actual appointment was delayed by his unwillingness to resign his seat in Congress before the definite result of the presidential election could be determined, and whose credentials and instructions were finally issued in March, 1825, by the new administration in which the Calhoun partisans had hoped to secure his appointment as Secretary of State to prevent the appointment of Clay.

REFERENCES

1. I. J. Cox on "The Louisiana Frontier" (*Texas State Hist. Quarterly*, July, 1916).
2. *Jefferson's Works*, Vol. 4, p. 420 (Ford ed., Vol. 8, p. 104), Letter to Monroe, Nov. 24, 1801.
3. [WM. THORNTON], *Outlines of a Constitution for North and South Colombia*.
4. *Jefferson's Works*, Vol. 4; *Jefferson Papers*, 2nd series, Vol. 78; *Gallatin's Writings*, Vol. 1, p. 142.
5. *Jefferson Papers*, 1°, Vol. 11, No. 36; *Ford's Jefferson*, Vol. 8, p. 379.
6. *Jefferson Papers* (W), 2°, Vol. 85, No. 95a.
7. *Jefferson's Message* of December 2, 1806.
8. WILKINSON's *Memoirs*.
9. I. J. Cox, *Early Explorations of Louisiana*.
10. *Jefferson Papers*, 1°, Vol. 12, No. 130.
11. *Jefferson Papers* (W), 2°, Vol. 85.
12. *Mississippi Valley Historical Review*, Vol. II, p. 566.
13. *1 Despatches Consuls, 1800-17*, pp. 400-03.
14. *1 Despatches Consuls*, pp. 352-53.
15. *Ib.*, pp. 365-66.
16. *1 Consular Letters*, Mexico (1811-25).
17. *16 Domestic Letters; 35 Miscellaneous Letters*.
18. *36 Miscellaneous Letters*, January 4 and 7, 1812.
19. *Letters to Monroe, 1812-14*, Ford Collection, New York Public Library.
20. *Am. Hist. Review*, XVII, pp. 290-311.
21. WILKINSON's *Memoirs*, Vol. 1, p. 476.
22. *15 Domestic Letters; 53 Miscellaneous Letters*.
23. *1 Consular Letters*, Mexico.
24. *1 Notes from Mexican Legation*.

25. *2 Notes from Spanish Legation*, Oct. 20, 1809; *Jefferson Papers*, 2°; Vol. 58, No. 86, Monroe to Jefferson, Jan., 1816; *American State Papers*, Foreign Relations, II, p. 626.

26. *American State Papers*, For. Rels., IV, pp. 422 and 426.

27. 14 Jefferson Papers, 1°; 1 Consular Letters, Buenos Aires, No. 18.

28. *Lord Castlereagh's Letters and Despatches*, Vol. 12, p. 98, Bagot to Castlereagh, Jan. 4, 1819.

29. *Monroe Papers*, XVII, p. 2137.

30. *2 Notes to Foreign Legations*, pp. 282-355.

31. J. Q. ADAMS, *Memoirs*, Vol. 4, pp. 85-86.

32. *8 Instructions U. S. Ministers*, p. 190, No. 4, Adams to Rush, May 20, 1818.

33. J. Q. ADAMS, *Memoirs*, Vol. 4, p. 7; *American State Papers*, Foreign Relations, IV, pp. 450-60.

34. LUIS DE ONIS, *Memoria sobre las negociationes entre Espano y las Estados-Unidos que dieron motivo al trata de 1819*.

35. *Jefferson Papers*, 2°, Vol. 58, Nos. 138 and 139; *Writings of Monroe* (edited by S. M. Hamilton), VI, 119-23.

36. *Congressional Globe*, 29-2, Appendix, pp. 288 and 803.

37. *Austin Papers* (Report, Am. Hist. Ass'n, 1919).

38. *Texas Historical Quarterly*, IX, 140; G. L. Rives, *U. S. and Mexico*, I, 153-54.

39. *American State Papers*, For. Rels., IV, p. 841, Wilcocks to Adams, Oct. 25, 1821.

40. *1 Notes from Mexican Legation*.

41. W. R. MANNING, *Early Diplomatic Relations Between the U. S. and Mexico*, pp. 284-85.

42. *1 Diplomacia Mexicana*, p. 103.

43. *Jefferson Papers*, 2°, Vol. 58, No. 113; *7 Benton's Abridgment of Debates*, Mar. 28, 1822; *6 Monroe Papers*, p. 709, March 29, 1822.

44. *Jefferson Papers*, 2°, Vol. 58, Nos. 147 and 147a; *11 Instructions U. S. Ministers*, Guatemala, No. 1.

45. WARD's *Mexico*, II, 556.

46. J. R. POINSETT, *Notes on Mexico*.

47. W. R. MANNING, *Early Diplomatic Relations Between the U. S. and Mexico*, pp. 189-90.

48. J. Q. ADAMS, *Memoirs*, VI, 121-23.

49. *Ib.*, VI, 128; *9 U. S. Ministers' Instructions*, p. 169, Feb. 19, 1823.

50. *1 Mexico, Despatches*, March 15, 1823.

51. *Jefferson Papers*, 2°, Vol. 58, Nos. 148 and 149.

52. *American State Papers*, IV, 836.

53. *10 Instructions U. S. Ministers*, Apr. 22, 1824, p. 171.

54. *1 Mexico, Despatches*, June 22, 1824.

CHAPTER II

THE FIRST AMERICAN MISSION TO MEXICO: POINSETT'S NEGOTIATIONS

HENRY CLAY, whom President John Quincy Adams chose as his successor in the office of Secretary of State, was prepared for his new duties by two brief periods of service in the United States Senate (1806-07 and 1810-11) and almost continuous service as speaker of the House thereafter (1811-14, 1815-20 and 1823-25), and especially by his experience as American peace commissioner at Ghent in 1814. After his experience at Ghent, which stimulated a hope to succeed Monroe as Secretary of State, he had been offered the Russian post by President Madison and the English post by President Monroe, but had declined each offer. He had been a leading critic of the Monroe administration in which Adams directed foreign policy. In 1818 he had begun his campaign for recognition of the revolutionary governments of Spanish America. In 1819 he had left the speaker's chair to attack General Andrew Jackson for invasion of Florida and later had attacked the Florida treaty of Secretary Adams for its failure to include Texas as American territory. Toward Latin America he had a very friendly attitude, but he hoped that territory lost in the treaty with Spain could be recovered by treaty with Mexico. In Mexican relations, early influenced by Mexican distrust of American motives, Secretary Clay contended against serious obstacles.

Joel Roberts Poinsett, who at the age of 46 was sent to Mexico by the Adams administration with the expectation of establishing close and friendly relations, was a South Carolinian of Huguenot stock and with plenty of means. He had learned much from travel but was always proud of his American citizenship. After a brief period in a Connecticut school under Dr. Dwight, he had attended school in England and had studied medicine at Edinburgh. From 1801 to 1809 he had traveled extensively in Europe. At Paris in the winter of 1801-02 he had witnessed the beginning of the mighty task of Napoleon and formed some idea of the violent struggle between the old and the new as Napoleon fused them. After a visit to Italy he had stopped for awhile in Switzerland where, on the shore of Lake Geneva, he had met Madam de Staël and her father M. Necker who told him of the stormy scenes of the French Revolution. After a trip to Vienna and a short trip home, he returned to Europe in 1806 to visit Sweden and Russia. At St. Petersburg in the winter of 1806-07, two years before the United States had a minister there, he conversed and dined with the Emperor at the Palace. Then, after a visit to southeast Russia (the Caucasus provinces, Georgia and Armenia) and to Prussia, he had returned to Paris and in 1808 was present at the celebrated interview between Napoleon and Count Metternich at the Tuileries. Expecting a war between the United States and Great Britain to result from the *Chesapeake* affair, he hurried home. Invited by President Madison in 1809 (or 1810) to go on an official mission to South America (Buenos Aires and Chile) in 1812, he joined the insurgent forces as commander of a corps of troops and induced Chile to make war against Peru. Returning home in 1816, he declined Monroe's offer to send him as a commissioner to South America. From 1821 to 1825 he served as a member of Congress. In the latter part of 1822 he was sent on a secret mission to Mexico, where he made a favorable impression by his social manners and his easy command of the Spanish language. In connection with the collection of information upon which he based his prophetic report to the Department of State, he made extensive notes which were published in 1824. He was especially well qualified for the mission which Secretary Clay, considering the nearness of Mexico to the United States, regarded as a very important one—its purpose being "to lay for the first time the foundation of an intercourse of amity, commerce, navigation, and neighborhood which may exert a powerful influence for a long period upon the prosperity of both states."

As a general guide for his conduct he was furnished a copy of Secretary Adams' instructions of May 27, 1823, to Anderson, the American minister to Colombia—instructions which unfolded a system of relations expedient to establish with all the Spanish American governments. Specifically he was carefully instructed as follows by Secretary Clay,[1] who had been a leader in urging recognition of the Spanish American republics during the presidency of Monroe:

(1) To impress upon the Mexican government the friendly attitude of the American government—its sympathy in observing its long struggle for freedom, its haste to recognize Mexican independence at the earliest practicable moment (slightly more than a year after the proclamation of independence), and its protection against European interference through the warning declaration of Monroe—and to say that the American government, in return for its priority of recognition and other favors, asked no special favors or concessions or privileges to commerce and navigation not extended to European powers, but expected whatever was granted to others.

(2) To explain the purpose and scope and effect of the two "principles of intercontinental law in relations of Europe and America" asserted in President Monroe's message of December 2, 1823, and to "urge upon the Mexican government the utility and expediency of asserting the same principles on all proper occasions."

(3) To obtain (cautiously) agreement as to the limits, either by demarcation of the line on the basis of the Spanish treaty of 1819 (to which the addition of an article for mutual restraint of the Indians was desired) or by establishing a more logical and advantageous boundary beyond the Sabine and south of the Red and Arkansas—"if the Mexican government be not disinclined to fix a new line" which might relieve Mexico of territory too remote from its capital, and leave to American jurisdiction the troublesome Comanche Indians, and prevent future diffi-

culties and collisions which might result after extension of settlements.

(4) To ascertain and report the purpose and plans of Mexico in regard to Cuba following the recent victory of Bolivar against Spain in Peru, and frankly to reveal (whenever necessary) the American policy not to interfere with the existing condition of the island but to view with apprehension any change which might be attempted either by European powers or by concerted action of Colombia and Mexico, and to say that the position of the island "proclaims that it should be attached to the United States" in preference to any other American state.

(5) To assure Mexico that the project for construction of a road from the western frontier of Missouri to the boundary in the direction of Santa Fé had originated in a spirit of friendship for Mexico, to open a beneficial commerce and intercourse between the two countries in that direction, and with the supposition that Mexico would be willing to bear the expense of construction within Mexican territory; and to receive from the Mexican government any proposition which it might offer for regulating intercourse on the road.

(6) To express appreciation of Mexico's compliment in copying so largely the American Constitution and "to show on all occasions an unobtrusive readiness to explain the practical operation and the very great advantages which appertain to our system."

In Clay's concluding instruction, to show an unobtrusive readiness to explain to the Mexican government the working of the American Constitution which had been so largely copied by Mexico, Poinsett, overenthusiastic in maintaining the federal form of government against centralizing tendencies, found his only excuse for his later political activities (through the York rite Masons) which gave rise to Mexican charges against him.

Poinsett arrived at Mexico City May 25, and presented his credentials and was received by President Victoria on June 1, 1825. Delivering to a crowded room an address on the object of his mission, he took occasion to say (in the presence of the

British chargé Ward who had been received a day earlier, and
evidently with the purpose of counteracting English influence)
that the United States had taken the lead in recognition and
in the Monroe declaration of policy and had since been followed
by the freest government of Europe.[2] In this he probably reflected some regret at the time gained by Great Britain in opening negotiations—which was the beginning of his troubles. On
May 5 he had reported to his government from Vera Cruz
that the British agents, taking advantage of American dilatori-
ness, had anticipated him in making a treaty (on April 6)—a
treaty, however, which was rejected by Canning who later, in
1826, negotiated at London a more satisfactory one which was
ratified in 1827. Although he did not yet know how the British
had begun to gain a dominant influence by a pledge of October,
1823, not to take Spanish colonies nor to consent to their
seizure by others—a confidential pledge more positive than the
Monroe Doctrine and more clearly disinterested—he felt that
the influence was there and that it was unfriendly to the United
States. He believed that the British government was trying to
exert an influence hostile to the American system which had
been declared by Monroe and accepted by Poinsett as the guide
to relations between American states, but which was regarded
by Canning as a policy by which the United States planned "to
connect itself with all the powers of America in a trans-atlantic
league of which it would have the sole direction." He "scented
the conflict and prepared for the fray." To counteract undue
British influence, and to perpetuate the federal form of government and American institutions which he conscientiously
thought best for Mexico, he sought means to influence a change
in Mexican policy by the formation of an American party. Re-
capitulating in 1829 the events of the period of his mission and
emphasizing his purpose to encourage change through some
political organization, he said:

"We had not been long in the Country, before we became aware
of the determination of the democratic party to effect a revolution by
force. On this occasion, this Legation felt it their duty to interfere,
and to advise a milder course. A Revolution such as was contemplated

would have plunged the Country into a civil war, the result of which could not be foreseen, would have paralised commerce and have brought still greater discredit upon the Republican Institution of the new States of America. The history of diplomacy is full of instances of the interference of foreign ministers to sustain or to save the Institutions of the Country to which they are accredited, and few cases could be cited more important or more urgent than this. These people were told, that they had only to unite, to organise their party, to establish a press of their own, and to bring the whole weight of their numbers to bear upon the dictions in order to effect a great moral change, which would assist their views much more effectually, than could be done by force; especially as they were disposed to sustain the federal constitution." [3]

The details of his part in the struggle to form an American party may be studied in the official correspondence at Washington and in the fourteen folio volumes of Poinsett papers at the library of the Historical Society of Pennsylvania. To recover for his government the prestige lost by its delay, and with a desire to preserve republican institutions in Mexico and prevent encroachment of European powers, he used means which subjected him to charges of interference in internal affairs and produced increasing distrust and suspicions which postponed the satisfactory conclusion of pending negotiations, endangered peaceful relations, and finally led to public Mexican attacks which finally resulted in his recall. By aiding in the establishment of new (York rite) Masonic lodges as centers of republican principles, he certainly made an imprudent and unauthorized excursion into local politics which seriously interfered with the success of his mission. [4] At the same time he corrected the implication of Alaman (the Mexican Minister of Relations) that the declaration of Monroe gave Mexico the right to demand that the United States interfere in behalf of the new American states.

In a long dispatch of October 12, 1825, in cipher to Clay, Poinsett explained how Great Britain had secured an overwhelming influence since the overthrow of Iturbide—first through the unofficial British agent, Dr. Mackie, who had suggested that Mexico should offer certain commercial privileges for recognition, and later through the activities of the British commissioners and Mr. Ward—and stated that he had found it necessary to form a popular American party to resist centralizing tendencies in the government which the British had favored. This party, which he had advised to use moderate measures of organization instead of revolution by force, he later said had taken his advice and had been successful (by effecting a change in the ministry in September, 1825). He reported a reorganization of the cabinet in favor of the American party but apparently the change had little effect on his later negotiations.[5] Later, in explaining to Clay the part which he had taken in the organization of the York Masons, he expressed regret that Masonry had been made an instrument of political intrigue and said he had withdrawn from the meetings of the Yorkinos after they were publicly accused of perverting the organization to political purposes against the Mexican government; but after their success in the state elections of 1826 he knew their plans to capture the presidency two years later, and in October, 1826, he predicted the candidacy of Guerrero, whom he later persuaded in the interest of his candidacy and at the solicitation of his friends to abandon announced designs against expulsion of remaining European Spaniards from Mexico.[6] However, by his action in organizing the new lodges, which evidently increased the influence of the American or liberal party, he excited the violent hostility of such Mexican leaders as Alaman and others of their faction, who disliked him and properly characterized his conduct as unbecoming for a diplomat.

W. S. Parrott, who evidently had begun the formation of lodges in Mexico before the arrival of Poinsett and who later planned the extension of lodges into Texas, in a letter of November 7, 1827, to Stephen F. Austin said: "Every true American flocked to our standard, and we were soon able to outweigh the anti-republicans or Scotch party and they soon began to charge Mr. Poinsett with the crime of introducing a system or machine by which he intended to carry on all his intrigues. . . . Fear not but that the Yorkinos will gain the day. The poor

Scotch are making their last struggle. . . . I have just had an interview with the President. He assures me all will go well. He is a true patriot but slack of energy." [7]

By the middle of 1827 Poinsett was attacked by several Mexican legislatures in resolutions demanding the Mexican government to expel him for his political activity in establishing York lodges of Masons, to which most members of the government belonged—including President Victoria who, however, refused to take any definite action. On June 19, 1827, he was violently arraigned by the Vera Cruz legislature as a "hypocritical foreign minister" unfriendly to the prosperity of Mexico. To this attack he replied by a pamphlet in Spanish, reviewing the friendly policy of the United States and denying any interference in the internal affairs of Mexico unless his advocacy and explanation of republican institutions be so regarded; but, viewing with indulgence the errors of Mexico, he abstained from demanding satisfaction from the Mexican federal government which, although lamenting the attack, hesitated to take action against Vera Cruz. In July he received from the Mexican government an intimation that his recall would be demanded.[8]

The Adams administration early in August seemed inclined to disapprove part of Poinsett's conduct, and possibly contemplated his recall but, after reading Poinsett's explanatory letter of July 8 which arrived on August 31, it suspended judgment. Finally, on November 19, 1827, Clay politely reported that the President, having no complaint from the Mexican government, approved his conduct but suggested that he might return voluntarily in case his position had become unpleasant. Two months later he authorized Poinsett to remonstrate to the Mexican government against the attack of the Vera Cruz legislature and to terminate his mission at his discretion and inclination if his residence had become unpleasant.[9]

While Poinsett was seeking means to displace English influence in Mexico, the American policy in relation to Mexico was continuously affected by the serious international question of the destiny of Cuba and Porto Rico in connection with Spanish plans to continue the war against the revolted colonies. In Cuba, the "Key to the Gulf," the American government asserted a special interest which had its origin in incidents of 1803 and 1808, and was further developed after acquisition of the Floridas. American annexation of the island seemed logical in 1822 and was especially desired by Calhoun, although opposed by J. Q. Adams. Later, in March, 1823, Monroe, impressed with the serious situation, proposed to Great Britain a mutual pledge not to take the island from Spain. In 1825, Cuba was described by a London newspaper as the "Turkey of trans-Atlantic politics, tottering to her fall, and kept from falling by those who contend for the right of catching her in her descent." In this problem, resulting from mutual suspicions of nations concerning territory upon which Spain had only a feeble hold—a hold which had become more uncertain by her obstinate, threatening attitude toward Mexico and Colombia—the American government did not hesitate to assert a live interest, although, while opposing acquisition by any European power or by Mexico or Colombia, it declined to be drawn into a self-denying pledge against future acquisition by the United States. In the negotiations (and the forensics) in which seven nations were involved, it took an active and leading part.

Mexican interest in the problem first appeared in connection with a bill introduced in Congress at Washington for suppression of piracy in the West Indies. This bill awakened the suspicions of Obregon who in a letter to Michelena, the Mexican envoy at London, stated his fear that the proposed suppression of piracy might lead to American war with Spain and American seizure of Cuba, and in a dispatch to the Mexican government referred to an earlier proposal introduced in Congress by Poinsett to promote the independence of Cuba as an aid to the extermination of piracy there. In March, 1825, Michelena, in a conference at the British Foreign Office, stated that Mexico, on whom Cuba had always been dependent, had the best right to the island in case of its separation from Spain and asked whether Great Britain would be willing to see it attached to some power on the continent. For this communication he was rebuked by the Mexican government on the ground that he had announced pretensions and hopes which, until the formulation of a more definite plan, should have been concealed.[10]

Meantime, Clay, who, in his instructions (of March 26, 1825) to Poinsett, had requested him to ascertain the purpose of Mexico as to Cuba in which the United States had a larger interest than any other American state, and had clearly and frankly authorized him to state the American policy not to interfere with Spanish control of the island but to view with alarm any attempt of any other power to seize or acquire it. He also authorized the statement that he had directly urged Spain, in order to save Cuba and Porto Rico for herself, to terminate the hopeless struggle and recognize the new Spanish American states, and that with the same purpose he sought to induce Russia, France and England to use their influence in bringing pressure upon the court of Madrid.[11] "By a concerted system of action, direct and collateral," on Spain, he had hoped to impress the necessity of peace.

Soon after his efforts at combined mediation, he received the alarming information of certain mysterious movements of French vessels in the West Indies. These movements, which France later explained satisfactorily, the Mexican government, through Alaman (in August), brought to the attention of Poinsett and Ward declaring that they were hostile to the independent states of America and should be made the subject of a demand for explanations. In this connection, while giving information of efforts to prevent such movements, Poinsett corrected the implication that under the Monroe Doctrine Mexico had a right to ask for American interference, and also vigorously protested against the implication of a Mexican newspaper article suggesting that the French purpose was to protect Cuba "from the designs of the United States and from those attributed to Colombia and Mexico." [12] In October, Clay instructed Brown at Paris to inform the French government that its purpose in any such movement of its fleet hereafter in time of peace should be communicated to the American government which

20763

under no contingency could consent to the occupation of Cuba
and Porto Rico by any European power except Spain. Early in
1826, he received a reply admitting the right of the United
States to be informed concerning such a movement and agreeing in future to state the object of every such squadron sent
to that vicinity.[13]

To Canning's later proposal that Great Britain, France and
the United States should prepare Spain for peace proposals by
uniting in a disclaimer (of designs on her islands) to calm her
fears, Clay replied (through King) that such a policy relieving
Spain of the fear of seizure by the three powers might defeat
its avowed purpose and encourage the Spanish continuance of
the war.[14]

In August, following the report of the French fleet in the
West Indies, and again in September, Clay informed Mexico
of his efforts to secure concerted action in pressing upon
Spain a policy of recognition of her former colonies. On December 20, he requested the suspension of any project against
Cuba until Russia could have time to act upon Spain. A few
days later, in December (through Middleton), he informed
Russia of his efforts to secure a suspension of the anticipated
operations of Mexico and Colombia against Cuba while awaiting the results of the mediation, and, referring again to American policy, he significantly added that if Spain should obstinately
resolve to continue the war the President could see no justifiable
ground on which he could forcibly interfere against the plans
of Mexico and Colombia unless the latter should conduct war
against the islands in a desolating manner dangerous to American quiet and safety (and therefore justifying American seizure
of the islands). On April 13, 1826, Clay, in reply to Everett's
Madrid dispatch of January 1 suggesting that Spain might
welcome an offer to guarantee her possession of Cuba in return
for her recognition of the Spanish American states, declared
against any treaty stipulations of guaranty.[15]

Meantime Poinsett found some difficulty in interpreting
Mexican policy through the changing plans of the Mexican
government, which, after cashiering Santa Anna for prepara-

tions to invade Cuba from Yucatan, had, by the end of May, decided to aid the liberation of Cuba by military force. In June he wrote that Mexico, ambitious to act alone, had decided against joint action with Colombia. In September, 1825, he reported that distinguished officers of the Mexican army and members of Congress had united with the Cuban junta in favor of an expedition to Cuba. In October he wrote confidentially that the plan of the Mexican cabinet for the projected expedition had met opposition in Congress and might fail, and on December 2 added that it had been rejected by the lower house in secret session after the Spanish surrender of the Castle of Ulua at Vera Cruz. On February 1, 1826, after presenting to Mexico the Russian reply to Clay's proposition to influence Madrid, he reported that President Victoria was satisfied with the American attitude as to Cuba and had denied any intention to conquer the island but admitted the contemplation of a joint expedition to aid the Cuban revolutionists to expel the Spaniards and to achieve their independence. On March 8, he reported that the Mexican government feared neither Spain nor a European alliance but was apprehensive that the powers, in order to compel Spain to make peace, might guarantee to her Cuba and Porto Rico.[16]

Clay's efforts with Mexico in relation to Cuba proved more fruitful than his direct and concerted efforts with Spain. On May 31, Poinsett reported that President Victoria in his message to Congress had indicated that the projected Cuban expedition had been abandoned (or postponed for discussion at the Panama Congress).[17] To enable the American government to keep in touch with its interests relating to its Cuban policy, and especially with a view to influence in restraining Mexico and Colombia from any plans of attack upon Cuba and Porto Rico, President Adams urged American representation at the Panama Congress, which was expected to determine a definite American policy concerning the destiny of the Spanish islands of the Caribbean, and which was probably influenced by American expression of policy against any plans of attack. The Mexican government, which failed to ratify the conventions of

Panama, later concluded with Colombia a treaty of defensive alliance which, however, was confined to a pledge of mutual assistance in case of a Spanish invasion of the territory of either of the parties to the treaty. After the Panama Congress it was suspicious of rumored plans for a Colombian expedition against the islands; but however much it may have been tempted by aggressive arguments, such as those of its minister, Obregon, at Washington, in favor of the seizure of Cuba to end the war and to provide for the future safety of Mexico by balancing European influence in the Antilles, it was restricted by 1828 by factional strife which made foreign enterprise impracticable and greatly relieved the anxiety and watchfulness of the American government under Adams whose policy was continued under his successor.[18] Commodore David Porter, who was engaged in 1826 to command the small Mexican navy, destroyed considerable Spanish commerce off the Cuban coasts soon thereafter, but after a series of controversies with the Mexican government, he finally resigned in 1829.[19]

In July, 1828, and again a year later, the Mexican government became alarmed by reports that Spanish refugees from Mexico were in New Orleans planning, under José Lara, to cooperate with the Spanish authorities in Cuba in an expedition to the Texan coast. To Bocanegra's request of July 29, 1829, that such violation of neutrality should be prevented, Poinsett replied on July 31 that the reports had no foundation and suggested that they probably originated in the removal of exiled Mexicans from New Orleans to Cuba; and he added that the American government, although neutral, would be friendly and sympathetic in case of a Spanish attack on Mexico.[20]

In October, 1829, Poinsett sent to Secretary Van Buren the following dispatch indicating Mexico's designs which he suggested "should be promptly and effectually counteracted" in the interests of the United States:

"This Government has resolved to send a secret mission to Haiti, in order to concert measures with Boyer to excite the slaves in the Island of Cuba to revolt; and I have some reason to believe that Basandre has been charged with this commission, and that the mission to France is a mere pretext to cover the real object of his voyage. I have communicated my suspicions to the French Consul, and it is proper that the British Government should be informed of the attempt to excite a servile war in Cuba, but the conduct of the Legation of that Government at this Court, has prevented me from holding any confidential intercourse with it on this or on any other subject.

"I mentioned to the Secretary of State that I was aware of the intentions of this Government in relation to Cuba, and could not but disapprove of them. He did not attempt to deny them, and I then stated that I was well convinced my Government would not only highly disapprove of any such attempts, but would oppose them. I am convinced that the state of the Island of Haiti will not permit Boyer to take any active part in aid of the designs of this Government, and that even if he possessed the power and were so disposed, one word from France would restrain him from doing so. But these designs would command the active cooperation of Bolivar, and of a host of emigrants from Cuba who are scattered over these continents and the adjacent Islands." [21]

On November 30 Secretary Van Buren instructed Poinsett's successor in Mexico to remonstrate against the alleged plans of Mexico to excite a slave revolt in Cuba, but later learned that Mexico gave assurance that no such measure would be undertaken.[22]

Fear of Mexican territorial ambitions were not confined to Cuba. At the close of 1828, Clay received from Poinsett a dispatch indicating that he was alarmed by reports indicating that Mexico had designs on Central America. In a dispatch suggesting that Clay should send to Guatemala an intelligent accredited agent who might be able to calm the disturbances which were distracting that country, he said:

"I have been always aware of the existence of a party in Guatemala which prefers dependence upon Mexico to the dominion of the democracy of their own Country, and of the ambitious designs of Mexico to extend their territories by the acquisition of those provinces. The Mexican Minister who was in London at the time that a British Consul General was appointed to Guatemala went so far as to remonstrate with Mr. Canning, against a measure which he regarded as opposed to the Interests of his own Government; but without openly avowing what the intentions of Mexico were with regard to Central America.

"I am aware too that for the last two months active negotiations have been carried on between this Government and the chiefs of the Servile party in Guatemala thro their agent Don José Maria del Barrio the present Minister. Without having been able to ascertain their exact nature I have no doubt that they tend to affect the Independence of Central America. Mexico does not appear to be aware to what she exposes herself by attempting to establish the principle that a part of one federation is at liberty to depart from the original contract and to unite itself to another whenever it may think proper. I have expressed my disapprobation both of the principle and of the conduct pursued by this Government with regard to Guatemala, and as far as it has been in my power, without committing my own Government had opposed their views; but it is time the subject should be considered by the President, and instructions sent to this Legation, as to the course to be pursued in the event of Mexico interfering in the affairs of Guatemala, and resolving to admit the offers of the Servile party in that Republic. Central America cannot be appropriated by either of the great Powers which border upon it, nor partitioned between them, without materially affecting the balance of power in the Western Hemisphere." [23]

Poinsett's negotiations concerning the Sante Fé Trail were the result of the growing intercourse on the far northern frontier after 1821, the substitution of wagon trains for pack animals in 1824, the Benton law of March, 1825, which provided for a survey of a road from the Missouri River to the international boundary on the Arkansas River, and the necessity of measures to establish and protect the trade. On June 17, 1825, he opened the negotiations by emphasizing that the enterprise had originated in a friendly spirit, stating to Alaman that American commissioners had been appointed to begin the survey on the American side of the boundary and that he was authorized to receive Mexican proposals for construction of the road and regulation of intercourse thereon.[24] Efforts to secure the cooperation of Mexico in constructing the road were opposed by the Mexican government on the ground that the road should be postponed until the question of boundary line could be settled, but also probably because some of the officials, inheriting old Spanish views, did not welcome the news of the growing commerce. On July 20, Alaman stated that the separation of the negotiations concerning the road from those concerning limits and general commerce was not easy and that President Victoria proposed first to undertake the negotiations of the treaties of commerce and limits. This determination was strengthened early in August by a report received from the governor of Chihuahua stating that the purpose of the American plan to open commerce was to encourage American settlement in territory which should be colonized by Mexico, and intimating American designs of territorial acquisition which Clay promptly denied. Poinsett, who late in July still hoped that Victoria might change his decision and authorize Alaman to open negotiations concerning the road which furnished a cheaper commerce for Santa Fé, reported on August 17 that further propositions on the subject seemed useless, although in the following January he reported that Victoria had decided to submit the question to Congress which had a reputation for interminable deliberations.[25]

Meantime the American part of the survey was begun at Fort Osage on the Missouri on June 17 and completed to the Arkansas by September 11 under George C. Sibley, who immediately thereafter went to Santa Fé for cooperation with Mexico as to the completion of the survey and the removal of a few obstructions along the route, and for protection of trade on the route. On April 17, 1826, Poinsett informed the Secretary of Relations that Sibley, after waiting at Santa Fé with the American surveyors for several months, was now planning to return; and he induced the Mexican government to authorize the political chief of New Mexico to permit Sibley to *survey* the Mexican portion of the road as he returned, but could not get Mexican consent to erect markers nor to send an agent to cooperate in the survey. This restricted permission Clay did not consider satisfactory; but apparently the trade along the route favored by local authorities of New Mexico continued to grow without proper protection, and in 1829 it was finally favored by an American military force to protect the traders in transit, although Mexico at that time furnished no similar force to meet the caravans on the frontier. The road and the trade remained unregulated by internal agreement until the ratification of the commercial treaty of April, 1831, which accepted the practices in operation and provided for future regulation by mutual agreement between the executives of the two countries.

For over four years the negotiations for a commercial treaty were fruitless, and in this period Mexico twice allowed the time for exchange of treaty ratification to pass without action. Negotiations were begun by a conference of Poinsett with Alaman and Esteva (Secretary of the Treasury) on August 22, 1825, resulting in the selection of Poinsett to prepare a project of a treaty as a basis of discussion at a later conference. On September 13, Poinsett submitted the project which in various conferences met with objections from the Mexican plenipotentiaries. After the third conference, negotiations were disturbed by a ministerial change in which Poinsett probably exercised some influence and which he reported as a replacement of the British party by the American party—resulting especially in the resignation of Secretary Alaman whose temporary successor was Pedraza (who had been Secretary of War).[26] The chief initial obstacles to negotiation after the agreement to separate the question of commerce from that of boundaries were the attempt of the United States to modify the most favored nation clause by a new principle of "perfect reciprocity" (of tonnage dues) which was opposed by Mexico, and the demand of Mexico for an exception in favor of the new Spanish American states on the ground that they were engaged in a common contest against Spain in which the United States was not participating. In reply to the latter, Clay and Poinsett urged that the United States by maintaining neutrality had prevented the precipitation of a detrimental union of European powers against Americans and thus had been enabled to render assistance more valuable than military cooperation—assistance which entitled the American government to expect privileges such as were granted to the Spanish American countries.

Clay, on November 9, approving Poinsett's stand in the negotiations, and referring to the Mexican inconsistency in treating the United States as an American nation when it desired aid against a menacing attack from Europe but as a non-American nation in negotiations for trade relations, firmly declared in the conclusion of his instructions: "It is better to have no treaty than to subscribe to a principle wholly inadmissible, and which, being assented to in the case of Mexico, might form a precedent to be extended to others of the new states." [27]

Negotiations, after a postponement for seven months, were resumed by a sixth conference on May 6, 1826, and a seventh on May 7, and were continued by six additional conferences in June. Poinsett successfully made the omission of the proposed exception a *sine qua non,* but at the same time yielded on the proposed "perfect reciprocity" of tonnage dues and also withdrew an anti-British exception which he had proposed to the principle of "free ships make free goods"—an exception limiting the advantages of the principle to the property of enemies whose governments acknowledged the principle. In order to avoid breaking off negotiations a second time he allowed the insertion of an additional article, excepting from certain privileges all European Spaniards who had been naturalized in the United States since 1820.[28]

The treaty was signed on July 10, 1826, and on its arrival at Washington, still not ratified by Mexico, was promptly ratified (February 26, 1827) by the Senate after the insertion of Poinsett's proposed exception and the omission of an article excluding from Mexico all European Spaniards who had been naturalized in the United States since 1820—an article which was declared to be repugnant to the United States Constitution. Mexico still delayed to act, first objecting to the clause on the rendition of fugitive slaves, and later demanding an article settling the boundary dispute. Finally, after the hasty conclusion of a boundary treaty on January 12, 1828, followed by the quick settlement of disputed points, Poinsett obtained a new treaty (on February 14) which secured both the principle of "perfect reciprocity" and the exception to the principle of "free ships make free goods," and also provided for the return of fugitive slaves. This treaty ratified by the American Senate on May 1, 1828, failed in the Mexican Congress, both in the regular session in May, 1828, and in the special or extra session which Guerrero had called late in July, 1829, to consider and ratify what he had approved at the risk of weakening his hold on the government. Failure in the Mexican Senate was largely the result of objections to clauses relating to the return of fugitive slaves and the control of border Indians, but probably in part to prejudice against the United States and its republican institutions. In vain Poinsett applied his efforts to the lower house by supplying a friendly member of it with arguments to rebut those used by the Senate. A year later, in October, 1829, after the failure of the treaty in the special session, Van Buren severely blamed Mexico for refusing to sanction the obligation which its authorized agent had contracted in its name.[29] Finally, after firm but pacific American protests against her past unfriendliness, Mexico partly *redressed* the wrongs of the past by the ratification of the desired treaty. Over a year after the growing opposition to Poinsett had burst into a demand which had resulted in his removal, Anthony Butler (on April 5, 1831) secured a new treaty which was ratified and properly exchanged by both powers, and which contained practically all the articles of the Poinsett treaty except the clause providing for return of fugitive slaves, and also contained a new article providing for the regulation and protection of the Santa Fé trade from Missouri. With it the American government, according to promise, submitted to the United States Senate the pending treaty of limits which was thus revived after its obligatory character had been lost by the remissness of Mexico. Ratifications were exchanged on April 5, 1832, on the last day allowed under the treaty provision.

For a large part of his time, Poinsett was occupied in vain attempts to adjust the commercial controversies which, in the absence of a treaty regulation, continually arose over the rights and privileges of American merchants and merchandise—controversies relating to requirements of consular certificates, invoices of goods, unfair tariff charges, seizure of American vessels and cargoes on various pretexts, and the conduct of

Mexican naval vessels and Mexican privateers against commerce of Spain and their use of American ports, and losses to merchants and travelers at the hands of robbers and bandits.

In the negotiations relating to boundaries, Poinsett encountered cautious delays which may have resulted in part from the expression of his unofficial views of 1822 to Azcarate, the Iturbide official, who on June 3, 1825, reported (from memory) the incident to President Victoria and predicted that the establishment of limits would be the American-Mexican apple of discord. On July 12, at his first conference with Alaman on the subject, he made the suggestion that, although the American government held itself bound by the treaty of 1819, the two governments might prefer to attempt to establish a boundary more easily defined and more advantageous than the line already designated but not yet marked. This suggestion pleased Alaman who, suspicious and seeking delay, immediately proposed a joint reconnaissance by a joint commission to secure information as a basis for later negotiations. Poinsett objected to the proposed commission, which he said would delay the negotiations for two years, and he was supported by his government which urged the usual procedure of agreement upon the line before the appointment of the joint commission to mark it, but had no objection to a Mexican commission for examination if it involved no unnecessary loss of time.

On July 22, he reported that the Mexican government was jealously suspicious of all American movements toward Texas and New Mexico and that the Mexican people were apprehensive that the American government contemplated a renewal of the claim to the territory north of the Rio Bravo del Norte. On July 27, in reporting to Clay, he suggested the importance of extending American territory "toward the Rio del Norte either to the Colorado or at least to the Brazos" in order to secure a frontier with climate more suitable to a hardy race of white settlers; but, desiring to avoid any immediate proposition which might increase the apprehensions, sensibilities and jealous fears of Mexico, he felt that time might be gained by awaiting the effects of American immigration of grantees and squatters (into Texas) which by producing difficult problems of government might make Mexico less averse to cession of the territory.[30]

His suspicions that Mexico might seek to push the boundary farther east than the Sabine were verified, by September 20, by Alaman's suggestion that the ancient boundary of 1795 should be specified in the commercial treaty which was concluded before the treaty of limits. In reply to the latter, he declared that the treaty of 1819 with Spain was binding on Mexico and had been acknowledged by the accredited agent of Mexico, and that its execution had been delayed only by American motives of delicacy toward Mexico and by the proposal of a substitute treaty to secure a more advantageous line west of the Sabine (which was regarded as too near New Orleans) and suggested that the American claim to the Rio Bravo del Norte should be renewed in the commercial treaty. After the radical change in the Mexican ministry in October, 1825, although the Mexican government seemed favorable to federalism and to the United States, he found no favorable change in the Mexican attitude toward the treaty of limits. He soon discovered that the Florida treaty might be declared null and void on the basis of the ancient laws of the Indias, or ignored on the ground that it had not received the consent of the Mexican delegation in the Spanish Cortes.[31]

For more than a year, while American settlement was increasing in Texas, the question of a new treaty of limits rested. In March, 1826, Poinsett protested against a reported prospective Texan border grant to Indians from the United States, stating that such grant would be invalid if made while negotiations for the Texan territory were pending.[32]

Although American settlers in Texas usually maintained good order, a significant disorderly incident occurred near the close of 1826. Hayden Edwards, irritated by the governor's action in cancelling his contract and in banishing him because of a controversy in regard to confused titles in the Nacogdoches neighborhood, prepared for armed resistance to authority and attempted to create an independent state under the name of Fredonia. This attempted rebellion, which was promptly terminated by Mexican soldiers from Bexar aided by a body of militia from Austin's colony, awakened new Mexican suspicions of the conduct of the American colonists and the American government—although Secretary Clay, on February 19, 1827, in a formal note to Obregon expressed regret at the news of the disturbance, disavowed any sympathy with it, and notified him of the steps taken by the President to prevent any encouragement or aid to the participants by American frontier forces.[33] At least, it should have warned them of the possibility that even orderly and industrious American settlers in Texas would some time refuse to submit to the domination of a race which they regarded as inferior, or to obey legal authority of the distant government of Mexico City, distracted by factions and periodic revolutions.

Taking advantage of the apparently threatening situation, Clay, in accord with President Adams, decided to test Poinsett's earlier suggestion or prediction that American settlements in Texas would reduce Mexican objections to cession of the territory. On March 15, 1827, he again opened the question of boundaries through instructions introduced by the suggestion that the Mexican government, by numerous and extensive grants of land in Texas to American citizens, "authorized the belief that but little value is placed upon the possession of that province," and that, considering the recent collisions and anticipating future collisions which might be expected to result from these settlements,* the time seemed auspicious for negotiations to obtain a more logical boundary which would remove the dangers and motives of attack in case of the remote contingency

* Of interest in this connection was the plan of Robert Owen in 1828. After beginning a socialistic experiment at New Harmony on the Wabash (in Indiana) he sought a larger field for his philanthropic work and with this purpose in view, together with the desire to guard against a future American-Mexican war which might result from border jealousies and irritations, he presented to Mexico, through the Mexican representative at London, a request for a cession of the frontier provinces of Coahuila and Texas which he proposed should be formed into an independent state under a guaranty of Mexico, the United States and Great Britain. [Manning, *Early Diplomatic Relations between the United States and Mexico,* p. 323.]

of change of friendly relations. He authorized an offer of a million dollars for substitution of the Rio Grande (and its tributary, Rio Puerco) for the Sabine, or a half million for substitution of the Colorado—payable simultaneously with the delivery of the territory. Poinsett considered the offer too small, and evidently did not submit it, fearing it would provoke further unfriendliness; but on May 19, he sounded the Mexican government by a cautious approach through a note suggesting that the fortunate adjustment of the recent Texan difficulties indicated the importance of an early and permanent agreement on the boundaries for which he had full powers to treat. Early in January, 1828, he reported that he had abandoned any attempt at the proposed negotiations which he was convinced would fail. In reply to his private hint at a money consideration, he was assured that neither the Mexican government nor the Mexican Congress would consent to a sale or dismemberment of Mexican territory which was prohibited by the Constitution.[34]

Early in January, 1828, the boundary treaty was hastily negotiated. Poinsett reported that the Mexican Chamber of Deputies, while considering the treaty of commerce which had been concluded in July, 1826, had been influenced by the absurd attempt of one Hunter to start a revolution in Texas, and had declined to consider it further without the insertion of an article recognizing the validity of the Spanish treaty of 1819, and that the Mexican negotiators, without waiting for boundary information from the belated and useless Mexican commission, had prepared to renew negotiations by presenting the ultimatum of the deputies—possibly influenced by the rapidity of American migrations toward the southwest and by rumors of American plans to secure a mortgage on Texas for a large loan (of $12,000,000). Seeing no hope of any attempt to change the boundary, Poinsett accepted the proposal but suggested the more logical method of a separate treaty of limits to which the Mexican negotiators consented. The new treaty, accepting the limits of the treaty of 1819, was practically completed on January 10, and was signed on January 12 before the

Mexican reconnaissance commission had reached the border and about a month before the signing of the treaty of commerce. Its ratification was required to be exchanged within four months. The treaty was forwarded from Mexico City on February 22, reached Washington on April 21, and was ratified by the Senate on April 28 by a vote of 38 to 3. In Mexico, after considerable delay, it was ratified by both houses of Congress by April 26—too late for exchange of ratifications at Washington within the time limit required. When Obregon reported to Clay, on August 2, that he had just received instructions to effect the exchange, he was told that it would be necessary to re-submit the treaty to the Senate at the next session. In April, 1829, when Montoya (the Mexican chargé at Washington) asked Secretary Van Buren of the new administration whether he was ready to proceed with the exchange of ratifications, the latter promised to submit the treaty to the Senate at the next session and expressed the hope that the Mexican ratification of the treaty of commerce would arrive in time to submit at the same time.[35] Further delay resulted from the determination of the new administration of Jackson in August, 1829, to attempt the negotiations for a new treaty of limits in order to obtain Texas—negotiations which Poinsett had considered hopeless and useless, but which his successor used to beguile and delude the Jackson administration for over five years. The treaty of limits of January, 1828, renewed on April 5, 1831, finally became effective under the Jackson administration by exchange of ratifications on April 5, 1832, the last day of the time limit of one year and long after the close of Poinsett's mission.[36] Ratifications of an additional article of April 3, 1835, providing for commissioners to mark the boundary, were not exchanged until April 20, 1836, after the boundary situation had been changed by the independence of Texas.

The administration of Adams (and Clay) closed with its hopes of Mexican relations disappointed, and with Mexican suspicions increased. Poinsett was convinced that the United States could never expect to extend the boundary beyond the

Sabine without a quarrel which might drive Mexico to seek a European alliance. In August, 1829, when irritated by Bocanegra's complaints of rumored (or imaginary) American military movements on the frontier to which he thought the agents of the Mexican government gave too much credence, he suggested that the basis for such movements would be removed by ratification of the treaty of commerce, and reported to his government that General Teran, who had been placed at the head of the Mexican commission for reconnaissance of the boundary, had never ceased to arouse fears in regard to American designs on Texas. On August 22, referring to the violent majority faction in the Senate, which was opposed to the establishment of friendly relations between Mexico and the United States, he said: "These misguided men would delight to plunge the country into a war with the United States . . . which would overthrow the existing state of things, and trust to chance for the reestablishment of the power of the oligarchy which formerly governed the country." [37]

Until the end of his mission Poinsett remained an object of attack by a strong Mexican opposition which regarded him as an advocate and adviser of the Yorkino party. That he had a special interest in the success of the Yorkinos there was no doubt. On January 9, 1828, he reported that the Escoseses or anti-Yorkino party, led by the Vice President, General Bravo, despairing of regaining its influence by peaceable means, had appealed to arms—under the Plan of Montano, especially aimed against Poinsett whose immediate dismissal was demanded. A month later, after Bravo had been defeated and jailed by Victoria's able Secretary of War, Pedraza, and his party had been defeated by government troops under General Guerrero, Poinsett reported that he had not withheld his opinion when asked by the government or by those connected with it. Apparently he desired to escape from the attacks of the anti-government party, but decided to await the ratification of the treaties which he had negotiated. On September 25, 1828, he reported that Guerrero, the uneducated but popular nominee, had been defeated for the presidency by the educated Pedraza (by ten of the nineteen legislatures), resulting in a revolt of Vera Cruz Yorkinos under Santa Anna and military annulment of the election. In December, he reported the flight of Pedraza and the appointment of Guerrero as his successor (as Secretary of War) under President Victoria. On April 3, 1829, he reported the inauguration (on April 1) of Guerrero whose election as President was declared by Congress after Pedraza's claims had been renounced—resulting in a complete Yorkino victory, but establishing a dangerous precedent. In connection with threatened disturbance at the inauguration, he displayed the American flag from his balcony in order to disperse the insurgent mob which threatened his house, which stood in the street and in which the wife of the Spanish viceroy had sought refuge. Thereafter, he found that the opposition against him increased, blaming him for the victory of Guerrero and all the country's evils and demanding his withdrawal or dismissal. This opposition he attributed entirely to his efforts to prevent European encroachments or undue European influence and his uncompromising republican principles. At the end of July his dismissal was requested by the legislature of the state of Mexico, in a long memorial which recognized his ability and social qualities, but condemned him as a cause of discord; and this action was soon followed by requests from legislatures of other states—requests which he said were regretted and condemned by President Guerrero, who regarded them as attacks against his administration. The charges against him he denied in a published statement of August 2, expressing good will and appealing to Mexicans to imitate American institutions and characteristics. In his dispatch of August 7 to Van Buren, denying any interference in internal affairs, he admitted friendly intercourse with the popular party.[38]

The Jackson administration had been in power for six months before it fully realized the crisis in relations which prevented the satisfactory completion of pending negotiations. It finally decided to recall Poinsett, who had declared on August 22, 1829, that his residence in Mexico had become almost insupportable. Secretary Van Buren, on October 16, 1829, informed him that the President, although he could not apprehend that the embarrassing situation in relations with Mexico was due to the indiscretion of the American representative by inter-meddling in internal affairs of the country against the estab-lished policy of the United States, recognized that his stay in Mexico had become very unpleasant and that proper relations were seriously disturbed by the Mexican prejudices and sus-picions whatever their cause, and, in accord with the permis-sion granted by the Adams administration, assented to his resignation unless a change of Mexican sentiment should render his continuance agreeable there and useful to the American government. On the following day he added a postscript revok-ing the option of remaining and making the recall unconditional, although officially exonerating him on the basis of his assur-ances. This postscript was the result of a conference with the Mexican chargé, Montoya, who presented a letter of July 1 from President Guerrero stating that the general distrust and public clamor against Poinsett compelled and justified a request for his recall and might necessitate dismissal before the arrival of an answer from Washington.[39]

Meantime (in August) Poinsett reported a critical condition in Mexico—the danger of invasion from Spain, dissensions be-tween the Mexican states, state opposition to the federal system, and suspected plans of establishing a changed government under a foreign premier. He asked the attitude of the administration at Washington. On November 20, reporting that military officers from Jalapa had sent a committee to request General Guerrero to dismiss all members of the cabinet and to appoint others whom they designated "all violent members of the Scotch party and opposed both to federal and republican insti-tutions," he said: "Guerrero told me yesterday that he would resist this attempt at military usurpation to the death, and was decided never to admit any into his councils other than those whom he knew would aid him to support the existing form of Government. He considers this proposition of the Generals Bustamante and Santa Anna to be made, in order to further the wishes of a majority of the army to establish a central

Government. In my opinion any attempt to destroy this federation, and to establish upon its ruins a general Government, will fail; but it is to be feared that such an attempt may produce a dissolution of the Union, and call into existence new States and smaller confederacies, between which we should see acted over again, the scenes of bloodshed and civil wars, that distinguished the history of the Italian Republics in the middle ages, a period from which this people are not far removed." [40]

Late in 1829, following the defeat of the long threatened Spanish invading expedition by Santa Anna (on September 11) and the promulgation of several unpopular decrees, the incapable administration of President Guerrero was overthrown by Congress through the influence of the Vice President, Bustamante, who then became President and (by January, 1830) attempted to establish a military despotism. One of the newspaper charges against Guerrero was that he had criminally designed to sell Texas to the United States.

Poinsett, who on November 4 forwarded to Washington a request to leave Mexico, received Van Buren's letter of recall on December 9. At a conference with the provisional executive under Bustamante he took formal leave on December 25, two days after the arrival of Colonel Butler, his successor, and three days after Bustamante's forces had driven President Guerrero from the palace. On delivery of his letter of recall he expressed the friendly feelings of the American government and people, independent of persons, parties, or forms of government. On December 31 Bustamante, in a note to President Jackson, expressed his appreciation of the recall which he regarded as an expression of friendship. [41]

At home Poinsett rendered service more useful than he could have performed in Mexico. He aided Jackson in the maintenance of the Union; and in 1833, by request, he accompanied the President on a trip from New York to Boston. After nullification was over, he married and became a planter. Under Van Buren, acting as Secretary of War, he took an active interest in the Wilkes expedition and the founding of the Smithsonian Institution.

In the quibblings and misunderstandings of the period of Poinsett's Mexican mission, from 1825 to 1830 (largely a period of orderly government in Mexico), says Manning, may be found the origin and largely the explanation of the growing and apparently irreconcilable differences of the next two decades and the discord of half a century—which influenced in part the distrust of another half century.

REFERENCES

1. *10 U. S. Ministers Instructions*, pp. 225-238, No. 1, March 26, 1825; *American State Papers*, Foreign Relations, VI, 578; *House Report 701*, 45-2, April 25, 1878.
2. *1 Mexico, Despatches*, June 4, 1825.
3. *4 Mexico, Despatches*, No. 166, March 10, 1829.
4. *2 Mexico, Despatches*, April 26, 1827.
5. *1 Mexico, Despatches*, No. 24, Oct. 12, 1825.
6. *3 Mexico, Despatches*, Nov. 10, 1827.
7. *The Austin Papers*, Part 2, Report, Am. Hist. Ass'n, 1919, Vol. II, p. 1707.
8. *3 Mexico, Despatches*, (No. 94) July 8, 1827, and (No. 97) Aug. 10, 1827; J. Q. ADAMS, *Memoirs*, VII, 312.
9. *12 U. S. Ministers Instructions*, pp. 36-38, No. 25, Jan. 12, 1828.
10. W. R. MANNING, *Early Diplomatic Relations Between the United States and Mexico*, p. 103.
11. J. M. CALLAHAN, *Cuba and International Relations*, Chap. V; *10 U. S. Ministers Instructions*, p. 300, Clay to Everett, Apr. 27, 1825; p. 331, Clay to Middleton, May 10, 1825; p. 356, Clay to James Brown, May 13, 1825; p. 345, Clay to King, May 11, 1825.
12. *2 Mexico, Despatches*, Aug. 17, 1825; *1 Mexico, Despatches*, No. 43, May 6, 1825.
13. *10 U. S. Ministers Instructions*, p. 104, Oct. 25, 1825; *American State Papers*, V, p. 881, Jan. 10, 1826.
14. *10 U. S. Ministers Instructions*, p. 394, Oct. 17, 1825; p. 405, Oct. 26, 1825.
15. *10 U. S. Ministers Instructions*, pp. 385-391, No. 5, Sept. 24, 1825; *Ib.*, p. 424, Dec. 26, 1825; *11 U. S. Ministers Instructions*, p. 21, Apr. 23, 1826.
16. *1 Mexico, Despatches*, (No. 4) June 15, (No. 18) Sept. 13, (No. 25) Oct. 29, and (No. 30) Dec. 2, 1825, (No. 35) Feb. 1, (No. 37) Feb. 25, and (No. 38) March 8, 1826.

17. *1 Mexico, Despatches*, No. 46, May 31, 1826.
18. *2 Mexico, Despatches*, (No. 58) Sept. 23, 1826, and (No. 89) May 12, 1827; *4 Mexico, Despatches*, (No. 161) Dec. 30, 1828; *11 U. S. Ministers Instructions*, p. 139, (No. 13) June 23, 1826.
19. DAVID G. PORTER, *Memoir of Commodore David Porter of the U. S. Navy*, pp. 347-391; *2 Mexico, Despatches*, No. 49, July 8, 1826.
20. *4 Mexico, Despatches*, No. 175, Aug. 2, 1829.
21. *Ib.*, No. 184, Oct. 14, 1829.
22. *14 American States Instructions*, p. 148, Nov. 30, 1829.
23. *4 Mexico, Despatches*, No. 161, Dec. 30, 1828.
24. *1 Mexico, Despatches*, (No. 7) June 18, (No. 8) June 22, (No. 9) July 27, 1825.
25. *Ib.*, Jan. 18, 1826; *2 Mexico, Despatches*, No. 14, Aug. 17, 1825.
26. *1 Mexico, Despatches*, (No. 18) Sept. 13, and (No. 22) Sept. 28, 1825.
27. *10 U. S. Ministers Instructions*, pp. 407-414, No. 7, Nov. 9, 1825.
28. *2 Mexico, Despatches*, No. 50, July 12, 1826.
29. *4 Mexico, Despatches*, (No. 127) May 21, (No. 128) June 4, (No. 152) Sept. 25, Oct. 4, (No. 153) Oct. 22, (No. 156) Nov. 15, 1828; *14 American States Instructions*, p. 149, (No. 2) Oct. 16, 1829.
30. *1 Mexico, Despatches*, (No. 7) July 18, (No. 9) July 27, 1825; *House Executive Document 42*, 25-1; *10 U. S. Ministers Instructions*, p. 835, (No. 5) Sept. 24, 1825.
31. *1 Mexico, Despatches*, (No. 19) Sept. 20, 1825, and (No. 32) Jan. 4, 1826.
32. *Ib.*, (No. 39) March 18, and (No. 42) Apr. 30, 1826.
33. *2 Mexico, Despatches*, Feb. 26 and Apr. 26, 1827.
34. *11 U. S. Ministers Instructions*, p. 270, No. 21, March 15, 1827; J. Q. ADAMS, *Memoirs*, VII, 239-240; *3 Mexico, Despatches*, May, 1827, Jan. 8, 1828.
35. *2 Mexico, Despatches*, (No. 82) Apr. 10, 1827; *3 Mexico, Despatches*, (No. 113) Jan. 8, and (No. 115) Feb. 7, 1828; *4 Mexico, Despatches*, (No. 124) Apr. 24, and (No. 125) Apr. 26, 1828.
36. *House Executive Document 42*, 25-1, pp. 46-50; *House Document 351*, 25-2.
37. *4 Mexico, Despatches*, (No. 174) July 22, (No. 175) Aug. 2, and (No. 179) Aug. 22, 1829.
38. *3 Mexico, Despatches*, Jan. 9 and Feb. 9, 1828; *4 Mexico, Despatches*, No. 138, July 15 and Aug. 7, 1829.
39. *14 American States Instructions*, Oct. 16 and 17, 1829; *1 Notes from Mexico Legation*, Oct. 17, 1829.

40. *4 Mexico, Despatches,* (No. 176) Aug. 7, and (No. 191) Nov.
    20, 1829.
41. *Ib.,* (No. 187) Nov. 4, Dec. 9, (No. 197) Dec. 26, 1829, and
    Feb. 3, 1830.

CHAPTER III

QUESTIONS OF TEXAS AND CLAIMS UNDER JACKSON AND VAN BUREN, 1829-41

AMERICAN policy relating to the problem of Texas and American claims against Mexico in the twelve years from 1829 to 1841 was successively under the immediate direction of four secretaries of state: Martin Van Buren of New York, from March 6, 1829, to April 7, 1831; Edward Livingston of Louisiana, from May 24, 1831, to May 29, 1833, when he was appointed American envoy and minister to France; Louis McLane of Delaware, from May 29, 1833, to June 30, 1834; John Forsyth of Georgia from June 27, 1834, under Jackson, to the end of the administration of Van Buren on March 4, 1841. All were prominent men of public experience. Van Buren had served in the United States Senate from 1821 to 1828, when he resigned to become governor of New York. In 1831 he was appointed minister to Great Britain but his nomination was rejected by the Senate. He was elected vice president in 1832 and President in 1836. Livingston had served in Congress as a member of the House from New York (1795 to 1801) and as a member from Louisiana (1823 to 1829), and as a member of the Senate from Louisiana (1829 to May, 1831). McLane had served in Congress as a member of the House (1817 to 1827) and as a member of the Senate (March, 1827 to April, 1829). He had served as minister to Great Britain (1829 to 1831) and as Secretary of the Treasury (1831-33). Later (in 1837 to 1847), he was president of the Baltimore and Ohio Railroad and (in 1845-46) again served as minister to Great Britain. Forsyth had served in Congress as a member of the House (1813-18 and 1823-27), and as a member of the Senate (1818-19

62

and 1829-34). He had been American minister to Spain in 1819-23.

The American ministers to Mexico for this period, after the recall of Poinsett, were Anthony Butler, of Mississippi, who was commissioned as chargé on October 12, 1829, and his successor, Powhatan Ellis, who was commissioned chargé January 5, 1836, presented his credentials on May 11, demanded passports and withdrew the legation from Mexico on December 28, 1836, and was later commissioned as envoy and minister, February 15, 1839, and took final leave April 21, 1842 (over a year after the close of Van Buren's administration). Butler, an old comrade of Jackson and a speculator in Texan lands, had moral obliquities which unfitted him for a diplomatic position. He was known as a gambler and a drunkard, and Jackson later called him a liar. Ellis, who had moved from Virginia to Natchez, Mississippi, in 1816, had served as a United States senator from September, 1825, to July, 1832, and as a federal judge from 1832 to 1836.

American-Mexican relations in regard to Texas entered upon a new period following the Mexican attempts of September, 1829, and April, 1830, to stop American immigration into Texas—which, by 1830, had a population of about 20,000, chiefly from the United States, and a small slave population (possibly about 1,000). In September, 1829, through the influence of Tornel, President Guerrero issued a decree abolishing slavery, but, on receipt of a protest submitted through the local governor, on December 2 he excepted Texas from the decree. Other Mexican restrictive legislation, influenced in part by persistent American policy of acquisition, produced in Texas responsive protest and later responsive revolt which seriously threatened to disturb American-Mexican relations, even after the recognition of Texas as an independent state.[1]

The Jackson administration evidently became interested in the acquisition of Texas, or in a more natural western boundary, through Colonel Anthony Butler, a native of South Carolina, who had served under Jackson in the War of 1812, who had early migrated to Kentucky and then to Mississippi, and who had later become a Texas land speculator and, in the summer of

1829, had submitted a statement that the boundary really intended by the treaty of 1819 was not the Sabine but the more western river Nueces, which flowed into Sabine Lake.[2] Possibly Jackson was also impressed by the views of Senator Benton that the southwest had been injured by the provision of the treaty of 1819, giving to Spain large parts of the valleys of the Arkansas and Red rivers—clearly parts of the Mississippi basin which Spain had never claimed—and, also, by the desire to remove possible future sources of border collision by moving the boundary farther from New Orleans, and, at the same time, by the compensation to aid Mexico in repelling Spanish attempts at reconquest. President Jackson on August 13, 1829, influenced by the arguments of Colonel Butler, decided to renew the proposal for a change in the western boundary as fixed by treaty of 1819, and, in a memorandum, directed Secretary Van Buren to authorize Poinsett to offer a maximum of $5,000,000 for a convenient "desert" line following the watershed between the Nueces and the Rio Grande and thence northward along the watershed east of the Rio Grande to 42°, a line "forming a natural separation of the resources of the two nations" and leaving to the United States the Texan territory whose people under Mexican jurisdiction might become turbulent and, "taking advantage of their distance from Mexican authority, might endeavor to establish one independent of it." On August 15 he urged prompt action. On August 25 Van Buren, following orders, instructed Poinsett to reopen negotiations and entrusted a copy of the instructions and certain verbal messages to Butler who, traveling by way of Louisiana and Texas, reached Mexico City on December 19. Meantime, after receiving a despondent dispatch from Poinsett, and additional news from Commodore Porter (who returned from Mexico in disgust early in October), and a communication from the Mexican government requesting the recall of Poinsett, he had on October 16 authorized the return of Poinsett, and on October 17 had instructed Butler to assume the duties of chargé d'affaires and to continue the negotiations for the purchase of Texas and had especially cautioned him to avoid any interference in the domestic affairs of Mexico.

With these instructions, he had complained of the indifferent, unfriendly, ungrateful, suspicious and unjust attitude of the Mexican government toward the United States (and toward Poinsett). President Jackson, representing that Texas was useless to Mexico and predicting that it might become very troublesome, in a private letter expressed his confidence that the purchase which he regarded so important to future peace would be effected.

Poinsett, who received the October instructions on December 15, before the arrival of Butler, immediately asked for a final audience, which he was unable to obtain until December 25, after the Guerrero government had been driven from power by Bustamante. Butler, absolutely unfit for diplomatic service, had already spoiled his immediate prospects of successful negotiations by indiscreet leaks of information en route.[3]

Van Buren, after hearing Poinsett's gloomy views in a personal conversation at Washington in March, wrote Butler on April 1, 1830, that the President did not consider the time auspicious for the proposed purchase negotiations. That he was correct in his view of the situation was shown by the confidential report of Secretary Alaman to the Mexican Congress on February 8 presenting the supposed American policy to acquire Texas and proposing a Mexican policy of regulation and repression as a means to assert Mexican authority in Texas, and to prevent the success of the American designs on the coveted territory. In the preparation of this report, Alaman, the Mexican Minister of Foreign Affairs in the new Bustamante cabinet, was stimulated by the expectation of an early American proposal of five million dollars for the purchase of Texas. He especially emphasized the significance of the successive steps of American expansion policy, from colonial settlements to diplomatic intrigue, as illustrated in the American-Texan policy. He proposed to assert Mexican authority more effectually by location of troops, repeal of the colonization law of 1824, governmental encouragement of Mexican immigration into Texas, and the encouragement of the coastwise trade between Texas and other parts of Mexico. His recommendations were promptly adopted in legislative acts of Congress (in April, 1830) but the provisions for encouraging Mexican immigration failed. The attempt to prevent immigration and free importation of supplies from the United States led to smuggling and a series of irritating controversies between the "untamable" colonists and the Mexican officials under General Teran, culminating in an open conflict in May, 1832, when seven colonists were arrested without legal warrant near Anahuac on Galveston Bay, resulting in the Mexican evacuation of that post.[4]

Soon thereafter the Bustamante government, while embarrassed by the vigorous revolt of Santa Anna, found that its policy had stimulated Texan plans of separation which were favored (in September, 1832) by the withdrawal of the government military forces and customs collectors from Texas for the next three years, but which were doubtless delayed by the lack of any assurance of support from the American government. In December, 1832, Bustamante abdicated. By military agreement Pedraza was installed as President until the following March when the shrewd and ambitious Santa Anna, a man without political principles, was elected President with Farias as Vice President. The Texans approved the change, expecting the downfall of General Teran who had supported the policy of the Bustamante administration and who soon thereafter committed suicide.[5]

Meantime (June, 1831), Butler, in referring to the delicacy of the negotiations for Texas, suggested to his government the expediency of increasing the maximum offer to $7,000,000—a suggestion which the cabinet unanimously declined to approve. In October, 1831, at the end of nearly two years, during which he frequently reported to Washington promising prospects and excuses for delays or requested further instructions, he finally approached Secretary Alaman with caution on the subject of the proposed purchase; but, learning that the Mexican government could not constitutionally alienate its territory, he reported his decision not to press the matter. As previously indicated, he was finally more successful in obtaining Mexican ratification of the boundary and commercial treaties negotiated by Poinsett—the commercial treaty after a threat to close the legation, and the other with a hope that the American Senate would not ratify it. Ratifications were exchanged at Washington on April 5, 1832.[6]

In February, 1832, when the enforcement of Alaman's Texan policy was producing considerable discontent among the American colonists in Texas, Secretary Livingston instructed Butler to be active in efforts to remove any Mexican suspicions that the American government was fomenting or conniving at any such discontent. When Butler received this, following his return from a northern trip late in June, he had several communications with Alaman, who was no longer in office, but with whom he had expressed confidence of his ability to negotiate successfully. He especially urged the cession of Texas on the prophetic ground that it would probably soon be involved in a serious revolt which the Mexican government would never be able to suppress. Alaman simply asked him for a statement of American territorial desires.[7] Of his first conversation, of July 2, he furnished the following "minute" of the reasons which he presented for the establishment of a boundary farther west and Mr. Alaman's reply:

"That on our part it would leave entirely disembarrassed a portion of Territory now in the occupation of our Citizens, which in the opinion of some affecting accurate knowledge of the geography of the Country would be included in the province of Texas as the line would in all probability now go. That in such an event a novel, important and doubtful question would be presented—viz. Whether the General Government of the U. S. possessed the power of transferring any portion of the Citizens of the U. S. to a foreign Government without their consent? That I felt assured the assent would not be given and equally certain that the inhabitants of the Territory referred to would not relinquish their property unless the Mexican Government consented to make ample compensation, for the improvements made and money expended by the settlers on the Land they had purchased and occupied. . . . That these Lands covered two counties in the Territory of Arkansas including several thousand of inhabitants and many hundred thousand acres of Land. That my knowledge of the exhausted state of the Mexican Treasury forbid the expectation of the Government being able to command the means for making compensation either at the present moment, or within any defined period, and that I should suppose

Mexico would herself be desirous of avoiding so heavy a pecuniary responsibility. That an extension of the boundary West would obviate every difficulty. . . . That besides all this, he (Mr. Al.) was no stranger to the unsettled political conditions of Texas itself from the very frequent reports we receive of commotion amongst the people of that country . . . and although hitherto no serious convulsion had occurred, yet the danger of such an event at no very remote period was fully indicated by the rumors and alarms from Week to Week that a Revolution had already commenced. The Revolt once commenced must be successful, and Texas is lost to Mexico forever; upon this subject my Government feels the greatest anxiety. . . . We know the jealousy and suspicion hitherto entertained against our Government and people on this very subject, and how very readily that suspicion may be revived in the event of Texas declaring itself Independent as being a result of our secret encouragement and support, and we know how difficult it will be to remove such impression notwithstanding our good faith and fair dealing, and the effect which the indulgence of such suspicions may ultimately produce upon the Harmony of the two Nations. . . . It is to escape from a state of things so pregnant of discord betwixt the Governments and people of Mexico and the U. States that the President feels such an interest in concluding some arrangement that will forever remove the probability of such an event as I have imagined. . . .

"The Secretary replied that he concurred with me in many of the suggestions I had thrown out—but that the question presented many difficulties of embarrassing character, besides the one of How far we desired to extend the Cession West in establishing a new boundary? That he felt inclined to lend himself to any measure that would have a tendency to destroy all jealousies and suspicions between the two Nations and the two Governments. . . . He requested me to suspend any further remarks at the present time, but to meet him on the ensuing Tuesday Week with my Maps, on which we might trace the probable line by the Treaty as it now stands . . . and see to what limit it might prudently be extended West." [8]

On his second conversation, of July 10, he prepared the following record:

"We traced on the Map the supposed boundary between the two Nations, according to the provision of the Treaty of 1819 between Spain and the U. States. The Secretary followed the right branch of the River from the Sabine Lake (as I was convinced he would do) whilst I contended for the left branch. . . . This he strongly opposed, and rested his opposition upon the fact, that the left branch from the

Sabine Lake bore a different name—was never known as the River Sabine, whilst the right branch was always so designated.—To this I replied that as we were not the Commissioners appointed to adjust that question and establish the boundary under the treaty lately ratified, it would save the time that might be unprofitably spent, by leaving the question if it ever should arise, to those whose duty it would be to decide it. . . . That I hoped however we might be able to agree to some arrangement which would supersede the necessity of discussing that question altogether. That the very fact of this difference of opinion as to where the true line would be located, and the difficulties it might involve, would be a strong inducement as I must believe for establishing a new and different boundary. . . . That I would add one other remark, as he did not seem to be aware of all the difficulties with which this subject was pregnant . . . and hence the great advantage to both Governments as he must perceive in establishing a new boundary. I then proceeded to state that whatever names the two branches of the River which emptied into the Sabine Lake might have borne hitherto, and whatever names they may bear at present, he yet did not seem to be apprised of the fact of there being at this time two Rivers in the province of Texas bearing the name of the Sabine. . . . The one most Eastwardly emptied into the Sabine Lake and from thence was discharged into the Gulph of Mexico. . . . That another River now known, and always heretofore known to all Mexicans and others as the Sabine River, had its rise West of the Nueces, and discharged itself above Loredo on the Rio Grande, and which if it were established as the true boundary would give us more than we ask by the new line . . . and the question may perhaps be fairly made hereafter by the Commissioners . . . Which is the Sabine River meant as the boundary under the Treaty of 1819? . . . That I threw this out to apprise him of the many difficulties involved in the question as it now stood; and which I indulged hopes that with his cooperation we might be able to remove.

"We then proceeded to examine the Map and to determine on a proper location for the new boundary West. . . . I at once pointed to the desert or grand Prairie as the spot that seemed designed by nature as the boundary between the two nations. . . . Its great width and uninhabitable character whilst it rendered the Territory useless as a part of the National domain to either party; pointed it out as peculiarly fitted to be the dividing line between the adjoining nations. The Secretary thought it was going too far West and included a portion of the population of Texas purely Mexican, which it might be proper to retain in the event of deciding on a New boundary— but added:—this will be an after question; I now understand you and we may not differ greatly eventually. . . . So if you will be pleased to address an Official Communication to the department proposing a Review of this question of boundary between the two Nations, that Communication will be laid before the Vice President, and replied to with all convenient dispatch.

"The Communication was prepared and delivered on the 15 July." [9]

On July 18, 1832, Butler wrote President Jackson that he was very hopeful of the prospects for acquisition of Texas; but by August 12 his hopes were temporarily shaken. Later, in February, 1833, with nothing done and hope waning, in a note to Jackson he reverted to a proposal to get a mortgage on Texas. Jackson, who had heard (from the newspapers or from Houston) of the Texan plans for an April convention, which he supposed would result in a separation of Texas from Mexico rendering useless any further negotiations for a treaty of boundary with Mexico, gave orders to instruct Butler to bring the negotiations to a speedy conclusion—orders which Livingston promptly obeyed on March 20.[10]

Butler still wrote hopefully and looked forward to the arrival of Santa Anna at the capital, and, early in August, he claimed fresh hope from the discussions of the Texas problem in Farias' cabinet—whether to reduce the Texans to order or to cede the territory to the United States. Nearly two months later, on September 26 and again on October 2, seeing no hope of successful negotiations, and regarding Santa Anna as an unprincipled hypocrite (!), he advised Jackson to occupy Texas as he had occupied East Florida in 1818. On October 28 he hinted that the boundary might be arranged by bribery, an unprincipled policy which Jackson rejected. Soon thereafter, on January 13, 1834, the President, through McLane, instructed Butler to return home as soon as he could secure the Mexican signature and ratification of an article to make effective the treaty provision for marking the boundary. McLane asked him to explain that the President had been induced by imperative considerations connected with the public service to require his presence and that he intended as soon as possible to renew diplomatic relations—a request to return which was duplicated on June 18, but to which Butler, because of delay in securing the ratification of the desired article, neglected to act until the middle of 1835. Meantime, on March 7, 1834, Butler urged forcible occupation of the territory west of the Sabine to the Neches, and in July, 1834, he suggested that he be allowed to return for an interview with the President. In February, 1835, he confidentially wrote the President that his administration would get its wish. On March 31, 1835, he explained to Secretary Forsyth that his departure had been postponed by a new prospect of concluding a treaty since his audience of leave—an interview at which he had spoken to the President and the secretary very frankly and "energetically" upon the questions pending and had expressed regret that he could not report to his government a more favorable condition of affairs in Mexico.[11]

"At the close of the interview," wrote Butler, "The acting President (General Barragan) enquired whether it would be convenient for me to postpone for a short time my departure, in the event of the Government being disposed to entertain my proposition relative to the boundary question, and was answered that notwithstanding the delay in my departure would occasion some inconvenience to myself, still I would not hesitate to remain for a length of time sufficient for the accomplishment of that object, provided the President gave me assurances that no unnecessary delay would be suffered. When about to leave the Audience Chamber, the President observed that a Communication would be made to me before my departure, and as early as practicable. On the 29th a note from the Secretary of Foreign Affairs informed me that the Treaty should be immediately entered upon and concluded, announcing himself and the Secretary of the Treasury as the Plenipotentiaries on the part of Mexico.

"We met on the 30th inst., compared and exchanged our powers, and I was requested to prepare the project; this was done on the Evening of the same day and sent to the Plentipotentiaries, who appointed 2 o'clock today for the Conference, and where signing and sealing would have followed: At Eleven o'Clock the enclosed note was received from the Chief Clerk for the Department of Foreign Affairs postponing the meeting until tomorrow, and having other business to transact I attended at the Foreign Office at about 2 o'Clock and ascertained that the Cabinet had been in conclave the whole day, and the enclosed handbill published last night affords the clue to their deliberations.

"The fact is that a political storm is gathering and it will require all General Santa Anna's tact and popularity to weather it. I think he will do so, but unless he has address enough to quiet General Alvarez the struggle will be a serious and very probably a protracted one."

The situation encouraged him to expect within a few days a completion of the renewal of the treaty of limits, which he hoped to take to Washington on his return. "The Mexican Congress are now in Session," said he, "and the ratification on the part of Mexico will be obtained at once, and the Treaty be delivered to you in conformity with instructions sent me in January, 1834. The mere renewal of the Treaty is in itself a matter of importance to us, because I am convinced that we shall gain by it, jurisdiction over a very valuable Tract of Country, now either in an unsettled state or under the dominion of the Mexican Government. But this is not all we shall gain, for by the establishment of the true line a door will be opened to us through which we may enter for the satisfactory arrangement of a question of much deeper interest to us, than the mere marking of a boundary line. All this will be fully and, unless I am greatly mistaken, satisfactorily explained to you by documents and other information in my possession, that can be best communicated at a personal conference." [12]

Arriving at Washington on June 9, 1835, with the signed article extending the time for selection of commissioners to mark the boundary as agreed under the treaty of limits negotiated in 1828 and ratified in 1832, Butler proposed to Jackson and Forsyth a new plan of negotiation with Santa Anna, through bribery of Santa Anna's confessor, Hernandez, a treaty acquiring Texas—"the first of a series" which would finally result in the cession of New Mexico and all the Californias to the United States. After several interviews he was required to state in writing the status of the boundary negotiations and to explain the causes of delay. In his written explanation of June 17 to Forsyth, after referring to his "favorable" negotiations with Alaman which, he said, promised to result in a cession of all Texas east of the Colorado but were suspended by the unexpected successes of Santa Anna resulting in the dismissal of Alaman, he continued as follows:

"Upon General Santa Anna's accession to the Presidency, the Undersigned was invited by him in the most frank and cordial manner to an intimate intercourse, an intercourse, to use his own Language where we were to meet each other *as friends*, and not as public functionaries. I did not reject the overture, but endeavoured, discreetly to avail myself of all the advantages such an invitation might present; and at as early a period as seemed proper after the commencement of intercourse, the Undersigned addressed a private Note to the President, referring to what had passed under the previous Administration in relation to the boundary question, inviting his Attention to the Subject, as one of the highest interest to both Governments, and the final adjustment of which was alike demanded by a just regard to Treaty stipulations, and the maintenance of that harmony so happily subsisting between the two Nations. This Note Genl. Santa Anna never replied to, nor was any notice ever taken of it, in the many interviews between the Undersigned and himself, although great cordiality continued to prevail, and strong proofs of personal regard for the Undersigned were frequently indicated: It was difficult to comprehend at the time the reasons for a silence so studiously maintained on a subject of much interest, whilst the President permitted himself to converse with great freedom on all the prevailing topics of the day, manifesting always the most friendly feeling towards the United States and especially his regard for the President, declaring the strong desire by which he was animated to do at all times what would be agreeable to Genl. Jackson. The motive for this silence is no longer an enigma, it has been satisfactorily explained by the Author of the enclosed letter, and will be explained to yourself." [13]

With this explanation to Forsyth he submitted a letter of Hernandez (of March 21, 1835) indicating that the success of the negotiations was simply awaiting the delivery of the $500,000 for "judicious" application—a proposed bribery fund which Jackson still refused to approve, declining to countenance any payment or action (such as Butler's proposed modification of the disbursement of the money) which might bring against his government imputations of bribery.

Why Butler was returned to Mexico by the Jackson administration to renew negotiations is not clear. For some unexplained motive or reason, Forsyth, deciding to give him "another opportunity" to benefit his country (evidently through influence of the too patient President), on July 2 directed him to return to

Mexico, but without change of instructions and without any confidence of success and with the President's special command to conclude the negotiations at once (and return by December 1) so that the results could reach Congress promptly at the beginning of the session—a command which Butler later said he did not read at the time and which he claimed was contrary to the oral expressions of the President and Forsyth (!). A month later, the President for some unknown reason decided to offer to purchase Mexican territory reaching to the Pacific— possibly to please the whaling interests of New England. On August 6, Forsyth authorized Butler to offer to Mexico an additional $500,000 for a line which would include besides Texas the Bay of San Francisco, which was especially desirable as a resort for whaling vessels, and asked him to try first to secure the line of 37° from the Rio del Norte to the Pacific, but, in case of objection that this line was too near the Mexican settlement of Monterey, to explain that the American government had no desire to interfere with actual settlements of Mexico on the Pacific coast, and to agree to any provision which would secure the Bay of San Francisco and exclude Monterey and its immediate neighborhood.[14]

As Butler had left Washington promptly and returned to Mexico by way of Texas, which he visited just before the beginning of the Texan revolt, the Mexican government on October 31 requested his recall to avoid the necessity of his dismissal for "intrigues unbecoming a diplomatic agent"—including the stimulation of revolt in Texas. This official request Forsyth received promptly through Castillo, the Mexican representative at Washington, but postponed action while waiting to hear from Butler, from whom no dispatch had been received since his departure in July. Finally, on December 16, still without news from Butler, he notified him that Mexico had asked for his recall, that the time for his return had expired, that his mission would terminate December 1, and that his successor would be nominated to the Senate on the following day. Eleven days later, before the arrival of Forsyth's note, Butler, who had received a previous instruction (No. 94 and No. 100) to close his mission and return to the United States on December 1, wrote Forsyth that the doubt as to the situation which he occupied had paralyzed his exertions in attaining the object for which he had been laboring. Hoping that the restrictions as to the date of his return had been relaxed, he said: "For my satisfaction and for my guide also, it is proper that I should be informed whether I am here as the Minister of the United States or not—it is a matter of perfect indifference to me in what way the Government decides the question. If I were to consult my individual interest alone, it would be preferable to know that I was no longer the Agent of the United States." [15]

Powhatan Ellis, of Mississippi, whose apointment as chargé to succeed Butler was confirmed on January 8, 1836, received his personal and general instructions on January 29, and reached Mexico City by May 11.

Later Forsyth was embarrassed by Butler's continued residence in Mexico for several months after the arrival of his successor, and especially by his quarrels with the Mexican Minister of Relations and with the Mexican Secretary of War whom he personally insulted, necessitating an expression of regret by Forsyth, who was doubtless glad of his final retirement to Texas —by a journey which he inconsiderately undertook without the usual passports and with inconsiderate intimations that a conspiracy had been formed to assassinate him *en route*. In sending the correspondence between Butler and the Mexican government in relation to his privileges as a returning diplomatic agent, his successor, Ellis, on November 5, 1836, said:

"On the invitation of His Excellency the Minister for Foreign Affairs, in the early part of October, I had an interview with His Excellency the President ad Interim and his Cabinet, the object of which was to express the surprize and regret of this Government that my predecessor should persist in his determination to return to the United States through Texas—a rebellious province then at open war with Mexico. His Excellency the President remarked, that under such circumstances he had a right to interdict all communication with Texas, and more especially to one who, he had every reason to believe, was attached to the cause of those in open resistance to the authorities of the Country. He professed a strong desire to cherish those friendly

relations which had always existed between the two Countries—That
he was prepared to give Colonel Butler his passports and a guard to
protect him to any point of the Republic, except Texas—And that
he was willing to refer the whole matter to my discretion, reserving
the interdicted point as a principle that could not be conceded." [16]

The regret of the American government was expressed in the
following instructions of Forsyth to Ellis on November 16:

"The President has read with surprize and displeasure the two letters
which Mr. Butler, the late Chargé d'Affaires of the United States,
addressed to General Tornel, Minister of War of the Mexican Republic
on the 2nd of June, last, and subsequently, copies of which have been
transmitted to this Department, the former by Mr. Butler, the latter
by you. Nothing could be further from the sentiments which Mr.
Butler was instructed to manifest towards the Mexican Government,
than the language of insult and menace used in those letters towards
one of its high functionaries, and the President deeply regrets that
Mr. Butler, while claiming and enjoying the immunities of a diplomatic agent of the United States, should have so far disregarded the
obligations imposed on him by that character, both towards the
Mexican Republic and his own country.
"The President directs that you will make known to the Mexican
Government that Mr. Butler's conduct in writing those letters is
altogether disapproved by him, and express his hope that it will not
be permitted to disturb the friendly disposition which he has always
endeavored to preserve between the two countries." [17]

Unfortunately Butler's disgraceful mission of seven years,
reflecting discredit upon the Jackson administration, probably
increased Mexican distrust and suspicions against the United
States and contributed to the unsatisfactory course of diplomatic relations for the next decade.

Meantime, the movement which resulted in the independence
of Texas was passing from the earlier stage of struggle for
Mexican constitutional government to the final stage—the
struggle for independence. The chief events in the development
of the movement may be briefly summarized here. In October,
1832, the Texans, probably with no plans for independence,
met in a general convention at San Felipe to petition for separation from Coahuila, free importation of certain necessities and

repeal of the restrictive immigration law of 1830 which was aimed against American settlers. In April, 1833, another convention of delegates adopted a constitution for the proposed new Mexican state. Among the members of this convention was the later famous Sam Houston, who near the close of 1832 after a trip to Washington, D. C., rode from Indian Territory to Texas, probably to get information concerning the situation there, and immediately after February, 1833, moved from Indian Territory to Nacogdoches. Unfortunately both conventions were disapproved by Mexican officials who considered such assemblages as contrary to law and suspected that they were held in accord with secret American intrigues (under the lead of South Carolina!) to annex Texas to the United States. In March, 1833, the Mexican Minister of Relations wrote Butler that the "colonists of the department of Bexar" evidently planned to secede from Coahuila and to unite with the United States, whose western inhabitants had encouraged their plans. To prevent such plans, Mexico sent to the region of Coahuila and Texas, under General Filisola, a force which became mutinous and by the close of 1834 practically disappeared.[18]

In July, 1833, when the Mexican reformer, Vice President Farias, was temporarily serving as President in the place of Santa Anna who had overthrown Bustamante, Austin, on his arrival in Mexico City to submit the plea of the convention for Texan statehood, was arrested, but, before his departure in December, was finally able to influence Congress to repeal the provisions of 1830 against American immigration. At Saltillo he was rearrested by federal orders and imprisoned at Mexico City for eight months—probably for advising the formation of state government without waiting for the decision of the Mexican Congress. Curiously, Anthony Butler, the American chargé, whom the Mexicans had suspected of encouraging or stimulating the revolutionary movements in Texas in June, 1832, seemed pleased with the imprisonment, and in a dispatch to his government stated that Austin had prevented Mexico from consenting to the sale of Texas and that he was unfriendly to the United States. Austin, although he was released from prison by Santa

Anna, who reassumed the duties of President in April, 1834, was detained * on various pretexts until July, 1835, while Santa Anna, posing as the friend of the colonists, was considering a Texan policy. Returning to the Brazos River by schooner from New Orleans in September, 1835, carrying friendly messages from Santa Anna and others, and hopeful of the settlement of all differences, he found Mexican armed vessels making captures and also other evidences of threatened hostilities—finally causing him to join with those who advocated war for protection of their interests.[19]

Meantime, in October, 1834, the spirit of the Texas rebellion grew into that of separation, and the more radical inhabitants of Texas desired a new convention to declare independence. To secure concerted action in considering the situation, a third conference was proposed at San Felipe in July, and finally a convention of delegates was called to meet at Washington, Texas, in October, 1835, but it really met at San Felipe on November 5, 1835. This convention, although many of its members favored immediate independence from Mexico, expediently decided to declare in favor of the Mexican Constitution of 1824 and local self-government for Texas, but it denied the right of the existing Mexican federal authorities to govern within the limits of Texas and asserted the right of Texas to withdraw from the Mexican union if necessary to secure its rights. In November it adopted a provisional government with Henry Smith of Kentucky at the head and provisions for military defense under command of the picturesque Sam Houston who thereafter lived in the public eye and reformed his habits. Coincident with the organization of the provisional government, Texan volunteers were slowly planning to drive the Mexican force from Bexar on the western bank of the San Antonio River. Finally, in December, at the Alamo, the Mexican commander capitulated, and the Mexican troops retreated over the

* On May 26, 1834, Secretary McLane instructed Butler to interpose personal good offices in favor of Colonel Austin who had been arrested. On September 30, he sent to Butler a letter for Austin with instructions to forward to him with all possible safety and dispatch "whether he be in Mexico or returned to Texas, or wherever he may be." (15 *Mexican Instructions* No. 70 and September 30.)

150 miles to Laredo. Meantime Governor Smith, who favored independence and mistrusted Mexicans, was quarreling with his council who encouraged an expedition to Mexico under Mexican leadership. Finally the governor and the council, extending the quarrels, each refused to recognize the other. The break was irreparable. The new convention, which met on March 1, 1836, acted promptly, severing all political connection with Mexico, providing measures for safety and adopting a pro-slavery constitution and a new provisional government which took prompt steps to meet the new Mexican invasion planned by Santa Anna since the preceding June and which by February, 1836, was advancing by land by way of Matamoros and northward from Saltillo into Texas with considerable force to relieve Bexar.

Houston, appointed commander-in-chief on March 4, started westward for Gonzales on March 7, a day after the final assault of Santa Anna upon the defenders of the Alamo at Bexar, which prepared the way for the general Mexican advance eastward. On March 14, he began in a panic a precipitous retreat eastward from Gonzales to the Colorado, where he remained for a week opposite the site of Columbus; but, followed too closely by the Mexican advance and learning of the defeat of the Texan forces at Goliad, he continued eastward to the Brazos, reaching San Felipe on March 28 and Groce's Ferry (fifteen miles above) on the following day. There, having secured all boats in the vicinity, he rested securely while Santa Anna (arriving at San Felipe on April 7) moved down the river to Thompson's Ferry (April 11) and thence northeast to Harrisburg (April 15) from which he found that the Texan government had fled to Galveston. Finally, on April 11, coincident with Santa Anna's arrival at Thompson's Ferry he hesitatingly and slowly began to cross the Brazos and on April 16 began to move southeastward toward New Washington on the shores of Galveston Bay with plans to strike the final blow against a demoralized enemy. Adopting a policy of hasty pursuit, after an all-night march he halted near the San Jacinto River, and there on the following day (April 21) he directed a noisy, slaughterous rush on the unguarded Mexican line, resulting in a swift and complete victory which included the capture of Santa Anna. Houston declined Santa Anna's offer to recognize Texan independence conditional upon his own liberation, referring this question to the Texan government, but he made a preliminary demand that Santa Anna should issue an order for complete Mexican evacuation of Texas, to which Santa Anna promptly responded.

On May 14 at Velasco, selected as a safer place than Galveston for the Mexican prisoners, President Burnet obtained the signature of Santa Anna to two "treaties": one for cessation of all hostilities, Mexican evacuation, restoration of private property captured by the Mexicans, exchange of prisoners, and return of Santa Anna to Vera Cruz; the other (secret) securing Santa Anna's promise to arrange with the Mexican cabinet for reception of a Texan mission, the acknowledgment of Texan independence and the establishment of boundaries ("to go beyond the Rio Bravo del Norte"). Whether these promises, made by Santa Anna when his life was in serious danger, would be kept by Mexico was doubtful. On May 20, the Mexican Congress pronounced as null and void any stipulations of the imprisoned President in negotiations with the enemy; and, on July 9, Gorostiza,* who early in 1836 had been appointed Mexican minister at Washington, expressing the views of the Mexican government, officially notified Secretary Forsyth that no agreements of Santa Anna after his imprisonment in Texas would be regarded as binding.[20]

President Jackson, whom Santa Anna (at the suggestion of Austin) on July 4, 1836, wrote a letter requesting him to use his influence or mediation in securing the execution of the treaties and the independence of Texas, on September 4 declined

---

* Since June, 1831, when General Tornel left Washington, Mexico had been represented at the American capital by a succession of chargés d'affaires. Early in 1836 Mexico recognized the necessity or importance of a stronger representative at Washington to consider critical international questions and appointed as envoy extraordinary and minister plenipotentiary Manuel Eduardo de Gorostiza, who was educated in Spain from which he was banished in 1823, was experienced as a diplomatic representative of Mexico (1827-33) successively at Brussels, London and Paris, and was credited with some literary ability. Gorostiza devoted considerable time to complaints of "emigrations" and contraband exportations to aid the Texan insurgents, usually basing his assertions on newspaper clippings without satisfactory legal evidence.

to take any action which would have been regarded as interference with the policy of other powers, unless Mexico should request good offices for the purpose mentioned. He sent copies of the correspondence to Gorostiza. At the same time, on September 4, after considering Austin's request that he guarantee the execution of the treaties of Velasco, he notified Gaines that Mexico refused to recognize the legality of any act of Santa Anna after his capture, but he informed Gaines that he could properly pursue hostile depredating Indians across the boundary after he had clear evidence that Mexico was unwilling or unable to perform her international duty (or if she had instigated Indian warfare against the United States).[21]

Later, after various inconvenient experiences as a prisoner, Santa Anna, through the intercession of Austin, Houston and other influential Texans, was released, and with his faithful friend Almonte went by sea to New Orleans and thence up the Mississippi and the Ohio to Wheeling, and by the National Road to Washington, where, in January, 1837, he had a confidential conversation with President Jackson, apparently proposing to cede Texas for "fair consideration." To this proposal of cession, Jackson, although he was in accord with the idea that a voluntary cession of Texas and northern California to the United States might facilitate permanent tranquillity, stated that the United States could not act without an official Mexican proposition through the regular diplomatic channels and without some knowledge of the disposition of Texas with which the United States could not officially correspond until its independence had been recognized by the American Congress. On February 1, he mentioned to the Texan agents at Washington the substance of his interview with Santa Anna who a month later reached Vera Cruz by an American vessel on which the American government had offered him passage.[22]

American interest and public sympathy for Texas began to form by July, 1835, evidently originating in public meetings at New Orleans in July and October, 1835, and in the organization of a military company in Kentucky in November. Although the American government in November, 1835, published a warning of its intention to prevent interference in the domestic disputes of Mexico, recruiting of "emigrants" continued with various methods of evasions of the law. Interest was increased by the arrival of Austin and other Texans at New Orleans in January, 1836, and by the extension of their trip to Nashville, Louisville, Washington and New York, and was shown in February by enlistments of men, by loans and by shipments of contraband from New Orleans. It was further increased by the sad news of the fall of the Alamo and was expressed by the later joyous reception of the news of Houston's victory against Santa Anna in the battle of San Jacinto.[23]

President Jackson, although sympathetic toward the Texan revolt, apparently was sincere and faithful in efforts to observe the obligations of neutrality. He refused Austin's request to espouse the Texan cause by open aid with men and money. On November 9, 1835, through the Secretary of State, he instructed Butler to inform Mexico that he regretted the unhappy state of Texas and that the American government would continue to be neutral—permitting neither party to encroach on the territorial limits of the United States or to make American soil a battle ground for settling Mexican-Texan political differences. On January 29, 1836, Forsyth instructed Ellis to say that Mexican suspicions were unfounded and that the President had been actuated by the most scrupulous regard for justice and good faith. Late in January, 1836, following the news of Santa Anna's advance into Texas, he issued (through the War Department) to General E. P. Gaines, the experienced American commander at the south, an order to use troops at Fort Jessup (near Natchitoches) and along the Mexican frontier for enforcement of neutrality—to prevent either of the belligerents from crossing the boundary into the United States and to prevent any hostile Indian invasions from the United States into Texas. Unfortunately the execution of the delicate duties involved under this order led to serious diplomatic controversy. Gaines, advancing from his previous station of duty in Florida Territory, by way of Baton Rouge, reached Natchitoches on April 4 (a fortnight before San Jacinto), with the idea that he might anticipate lawless movements of the Mexicans and "their red allies" (if menacing American settlements)—that he might prevent anticipated attack of menacing forces by crossing the boundary to punish them within their own limits (as he had been ordered to do in Florida in 1817). For this idea he found new reasons for justification in the alarming current rumors of the violence of the approaching Mexican army and of expected Indian accessions at the Trinity River. He promptly decided to compel the Indians to return to their reservations and, also, on April 8, apparently influenced by Texan land speculators, he sent an unauthorized call upon governors of neighboring states for volunteers—a call which he rescinded following the news of the defeat of Santa Anna at San Jacinto. Meantime, on May 4, 1836, a few days before the news of San Jacinto, the President, contemplating the possible necessity of reinforcements to defend the southwestern frontier, approved the request of the Secretary of War for a congressional appropriation to pay expenses of a call for volunteers—a request granted only after considerable House debate concerning the propriety of the instructions of April 25 to Gaines which, although they did not materially aid Texas, seemed calculated to involve the United States in war with Mexico. Later in July, incorrectly informed that the Indians in Texas were planning trouble, Gaines sent to Nacogdoches a small force (of over 300 men) which was soon withdrawn after he was superseded. He also issued a new requisition for militia which the President promptly disapproved.[24]

The Jackson administration, by approving Gaines' proposal, found itself involved in a controversy with Gorostiza. Cass doubted whether the executive alone could authorize an invasion of foreign territory, except possibly in case of extreme danger; but the President, recalling Butler's suggestion that the Neches, west of the Sabine, should be regarded as the boundary intended as the Sabine in 1819, requested Cass to authorize Gaines to cross the Sabine, provided his advance did not go beyond Nacogdoches, which was in territory east of the Neches. On April 20 information of the purpose to send these instructions authorizing Gaines to take a position which would "enable him to preserve the territory of Mexico and the United States from Indian outrage," and to protect surveyors under the treaty of limits, was orally communicated to Gorostiza with the explanation that any advance or occupation beyond what Mexico might suppose was the American boundary should not be regarded as hostile or as a desire to establish a possession not justified by the treaty of limits. To this communication, the substance of which was submitted by Forsyth in a memorandum, Gorostiza, feeling the importance under existing conditions that former possession should be the only rule for mutual determination of limits, responded with an extended and angry answer indicating that he did not comprehend clearly the notice. On April 26, Forsyth, stating that the American government had no purpose to interfere in the disturbances of its neighbors or to decide whether the territory beyond the United States belonged to the Mexican government or to the newly declared Texan state, explained that the notice was not intended to express the intention to occupy a post within the acknowledged limits of Mexico, but to retire from any such post as soon as ascertained, unless continued possession should be indispensable to the safety of the United States and under circumstances which would justify the occupation. "The troops of General Gaines," he said, "will be used only in protecting the interests of the United States and those of Mexican territory according to the obligations of the treaty between the United States and Mexico. Whether the territory beyond the United States belongs to the Mexican government or the newly declared Texan state is a question into which the United States do not propose to go." Gorostiza, agreeing with Forsyth's main point and considering improper any hypothetical discussion of "what might be suitable for both countries, after the line shall have been marked," informally asked to be assured that Gaines' troops would not take a position on ground previously possessed by Mexico "within its known limits." Forsyth replied on May 3, stating in substance what he had previously said: *"Except in case of necessity, General Gaines will not occupy ground not indisputably in the limits of the United States. In case of neces-*

sity, whether the ground he may occupy is now or has heretofore been claimed by Mexico can not be made a question by that officer. He will take it to perform his duties to the United States and to fulfill the obligations of the United States to Mexico." Again, on May 10, in reply to Gorostiza, after seeking to impress the "important" distinction that "General Gaines is not authorized to advance to Nacogdoches but is ordered not to go beyond that point," he declared that American troops "might justly be sent into the heart of Mexico" to keep a friendly treaty agreement in regard to the Indians, and he declined to discuss with him any American claim to disputed territory of which Mexico was not then in possession but concerning which the United States was ready to execute the treaty provision in good faith. On August 1, 1836, replying to Gorostiza's request for a recall of the instructions to Gaines, Asbury Dickens, acting secretary, in a note briefly regretting that the statements of the American government as to Gaines had failed to reconcile the Mexican government, ventured to hope that Gaines might find the contemplated advance unnecessary. On August 31, Forsyth added that the United States was neutral in the civil war between Mexico and Texas, as it had been in the earlier war between Spain and Spanish America. On October 13, Dickens, in reply to Gorostiza's anxious complaint (of October 10) that the department had not kept its promise to answer his notes of July 28 and August 4 immediately upon the return of the President, stated that the President, after full consideration and basing his decision on the theoretical principle and duty of self-preservation (from a possible Indian invasion into American territory), had declined to comply with the request. The correspondence continued until October 20. On October 15, Gorostiza, failing to obtain an apology for what seemed to him an unwarranted action, courteously terminated his mission and asked for his passports after a lengthy note (of fifteen pages) to Dickens reviewing and summarizing his previous arguments concerning the order to General Gaines and expressing the feeling that the United States was unfriendly to Mexico by threatening its sovereignty and independence. Unfortunately, before leaving,* he discourteously published a pamphlet which the American government regarded as a violation of diplomatic usage, and asked the Mexican government to disavow, but which the Mexican government at that time approved, although a year later it satisfied the American demand for explicit disavowal.[25]

On December 10, 1836, Forsyth, referring to Gorostiza's prejudices and hasty action, undertook to explain to Mexico through Ellis the authorized advance of General Gaines, and closed by complaining of Gorostiza's unexampled publication. In the instructions to Ellis he said:

"Mr. Gorostiza has upon his own responsibility terminated his extraordinary mission to the United States. The President will not believe that the Mexican Government is under the influence of the obvious prejudices which have distorted and discolored every object seen here in the view of their functionary. The full and frank explanations of his motives and purposes, in the precautionary measures taken on the frontiers, should have satisfied that Government that nothing could have been further from the President's intentions than to injure Mexico in her interests or in her honor. Under this conviction, he trusts that the departure of the extraordinary mission will in no respect interrupt the friendly relations between the two Governments, and he instructs me to say that whatever feelings such a step was calculated to produce, it shall not be permitted to diminish his confidence in the amicable disposition of the Mexican Government, nor to operate in his mind prejudicially to its interests. Although the President supposes that the Mexican Government will have found, in the communications heretofore made by the Department to its Envoy Extraordinary, satisfactory grounds to justify the measure viewed so unfavorably by Mr. Gorostiza, yet his sincere and strong desire to prevent any misunderstanding on the subject induced him to determine, on the departure of that minister, to make such explanations as might prevent the Mexican Government from being misled into the adoption of the errors of their minister. Since my return to the seat of Government, the great pressure of other public business and the condition of the President's health, have delayed, until now, the execution of that purpose.

"So soon as the contest in Texas was found to be inevitable, it

* Gorostiza reached Mexico City by December 9, according to Ellis, who at that time was in the midst of a discussion of American claims against Mexico, and who, four days later, demanded his passports, although he did not leave Mexico until December 27 or 28.

became the President's duty to consider its probable consequences to the United States, with a view to guard against the injuries it might produce to our citizens and to the performance of the obligations of the Government to a friendly and neighbouring power. . . . You will perceive that Mr. Gorostiza in his conference with me, distinctly admitted our right in the event of hostility to the United States by Mexican Indians, to invade the territory of Mexico, either to prevent intended injury or to punish actual depredation. In a note written subsequently, he seeks to avoid the force of that admission, by confounding the principle upon which it obviously rests, with the right of making war for a violation of treaty engagement. You will find no difficulty in showing to the Mexican Government that it rests upon principles of the law of nations entirely distinct from those on which war is justified—upon the immutable principles of self-defence—upon the principles which justify decisive measures of precaution to prevent irreparable evil to our own or to a neighbouring people. . . . The President desires that you should give such explanations to the Mexican Government as these instructions will enable you to make, which if received in the proper and friendly spirit in which they are offered, will, he trusts, remove all ground for doubts and anxieties, if any have been entertained on the subject." [26]

Before the arrival of Forsyth's instructions, Monasterio informed Ellis that the Mexican government, after having heard Gorostiza and having examined impartially all his correspondence with the American government, could not but "coincide in every respect with what that Envoy has done in resisting so uncalled for an offence, and therefore approved his withdrawal from Washington with his Legation because of having been convinced that he could not obtain that just satisfaction which he demanded, notwithstanding he was supported by every argument and observation which reason and right could suggest."

"The Mexican Government," said he, "had desired, before acting in a definite manner upon the conduct observed by its Envoy in Washington, that Mr. Ellis should have previously given those explanations which were promised in the note of Mr. Dickens to Mr. Gorostiza of the 20″ of October last—the only object of which on the part of the United States should have been to prevent from the beginning all possible misunderstanding in so grave a matter. The Mexican Government has therefore awaited in silence and for the space of many days the corresponding communication from Mr. Ellis, flattering itself that in it would be found at last new and positive assurances that the United States have never desired nor do they now desire to offend voluntarily nor really to injure a neighbouring nation who has been wanting in nothing to them. Unfortunately Mr. Ellis has not thought proper thus to act up to this time; and the Government of the Undersigned cannot longer delay awarding to Mr. Gorostiza that act of justice which it owes to him in relieving him from the weight of responsibility which he has taken upon his own shoulders." [27]

The responsibility of the recognition of Texas Jackson cautiously threw upon Congress, which took no action until December, 1836. Following the news of San Jacinto, which reached Washington coincident with the arrival of Texan commissioners (G. C. Childress and Robert Hamilton), the question of recognition of Texan independence which had already been suggested prematurely was presented in both houses—especially through memorials and petitions—and, on May 23, the expressions in the Senate favored recognition in case the Committee on Foreign Relations could report reasonable proof on which to base such action. When Gorostiza (on May 24) complained of a Senate motion to refer to the Committee on Foreign Relations certain petitions for recognition of Texas, Forsyth replied (on May 27) that it was unnecessary to detain the Mexican minister by assignment of any reasons for occurrences in either house of Congress, but stated that the American government would make no decision not founded on the principles by which it was governed in the earlier disputes between Spain and the Spanish American states. The Senate report favoring recognition was presented on June 18, considered on July 1, and unanimously adopted. In the House the Senate resolutions were adopted by a large majority on July 4. Six weeks later the administration was vigilant in watching for any Mexican movement to secure aid for the subjugation of Texas.[28]

Meantime, late in June, President Jackson, through Secretary Forsyth, had sent H. M. Morfit to Texas to obtain information of the situation and by September he had received inpartial and cautious reports concerning the Texan government, and its policies and hopes—including an earlier ambitious plan to extend to the Pacific on the basis of rights claimed by conquest, and to construct a railway to the Gulf of California (!), and its well settled opinions in favor of annexation to the United States. He was informed that without foreign aid the ability of Texas to maintain its independence depended mainly upon the weakness of Mexico. Later, on December 20, he received unofficially William F. Wharton, whom the newly elected President Houston had appointed as minister to Washington, and who was disappointed to learn that the cautious American government, embarrassed by the Texan vote for annexation, preferred to act on recognition only after recognition by Great Britain or some other power. In accord with previous American foreign policy, he finally informed Wharton that he found it expedient to leave the question of recognition to Congress and cautiously to await further proof of the final outcome of the Texan contest with Mexico which threatened a new invasion. In a later interview, following his message of December 21 to Congress, he told Wharton that he would immediately concur in case the majority in Congress should recommend recognition. By February, 1837, he probably felt certain that Mexico would not be able to trouble Texas with another invasion, but possibly influenced in part by the unfriendly attitude of the Mexican chargé toward Santa Anna, and unwilling to act without certainty of the support of Congress which seemed more interested in other subjects, he left the problem of recognition to the administration of Van Buren. Finally, on March 3, the last day of his administration, he approved an act of Congress providing for the salary of a diplomatic agent to Texas whenever the President should decide that the evidence would justify recognition of independence.* Claiming that Congress had thereby decided the question, he promptly submitted for chargé d'affaires to Texas

* On January 11, 1837, Senator Walker offered a resolution for recognition which, by Northern influence, was postponed until March 1, when, partly through the influence of Calhoun and against the wish of Clay and Buchanan, it was approved by a vote of 23 to 19. Through the influence of Waddy Thompson, the House obtained a report from the Committee of Foreign Affairs on February 18, and finally on February 28 adopted the amended bill as indicated above and as adopted by the Senate on March 2.

the nomination of Alcée La Branche, and before midnight he notified the Texan agents at Washington. The nomination which he submitted was postponed by motion of Webster and was not confirmed until March 6—within the administration of Van Buren, which delayed the preparation of La Branche's commission until July 21, and the official reception of the Texan minister (Hunt) until July 6.* On March 17, Secretary Forsyth explained to the protesting Mexican authorities that the action of the American government was in accord with the settled policy followed in earlier cases, and was adopted with no unfriendly spirit or purpose against Mexico.[29]

Meantime, Forsyth had continued to discourage the Texan proposals for annexation, which had been submitted by Wharton at Washington in December, 1836. He explained that such action should await the conciliation of sectional interests in Congress. Later, in August, 1837, after receiving a new proposition in a long note (of August 4) from Hunt, he expressed the cautious waiting policy of the Van Buren administration by declining to enter into negotiations for annexation of the foreign independent state of Texas—a question which he said was very different (practically and constitutionally) from that involved in the earlier negotiations for acquisition of Louisiana and Florida, and might involve a war with Mexico with whom the United States was bound by the obligations of a treaty of amity and commerce. To Hunt's uncivil response which threatened to retaliate by unfriendly commercial arrangements, he made no reply. Poinsett, the new Secretary of War, however, encouraged hopes of a later change of policy, notwithstanding the strong Northern opposition to annexation at that time resulting in part from the rising anti-slavery movement. The Texan government, after withdrawing its proposal of annexation, soon dreamed of Texan expansion to the Pacific.[30]

The American government also declined at that time to press the question of recognition upon Mexico. In May, 1839, it con-

* The full recognition of Texan independence was delayed by France until September, 1839, and by Great Britain until November, 1840.

tinued the same cautious policy, as indicated by the following instructions of Forsyth to Ellis:

"Indications have very recently been given of a disposition on the part of the Republic of Texas to make a renewed application for the interposition of the United States in obtaining from Mexico an acknowledgment of its independence. It is not, however, the President's intention, under existing circumstances, to countenance or encourage such an application. He thinks that there is no occasion to deviate from the policy in relation to that subject marked out in the letter of his predecessor to General Santa Anna of the 4th of September, 1836. When, however, the event shall take place which by that letter is made the condition of our interference, all proper efforts will be cheerfully made by the President to bring about a peace between those two countries and to induce a recognition by Mexico of the independent sovereignty of her former province.

"Being in possession of these views, you will know what use to make of them should the minister lately sent by Texas to Mexico, or the Mexican government itself, sound you as to the present sentiments of this government with regard to the ostensible object of that mission, or should either open direct official communication with you on that subject." [31]

On the question of the treaty of limits, which had been affected by the independence of Texas, the American government decided to wait for an application from the Mexican government.[32]

The question of claims, which during the decade of negotiations for Texas and commerce had been somewhat neglected by the American government and ignored or evaded by the Mexican government—due in part to disturbed Mexican conditions—became prominent in the latter part of Jackson's administration and the chief diplomatic problem in the Mexican policy of the Van Buren administration.

Jackson, following his success in collecting the French spoliation claims and coincident with the Mexican attempt to suppress the Texan revolt, and possibly with the hope that the Mexican government, by its recent change in form, might be able to enforce on local authorities respect for the rights of foreigners, decided to press the long-standing American claims against Mexico. Before the close of 1833, Butler had presented many of these claims—for monies and munitions and services advanced to aid the Mexican revolutionary contest, for irregular and illegal exactions by Mexican customs officials, and for seizure and wrongful application of the property of American citizens. He was assured by the Mexican government that it was ready to proceed immediately with adjustment of claims, but preferred for convenience that the individual claimants should present themselves in person with documents and proofs—a plan which evidently was proposed with a view to evasion and delay, and to which was later added the refusal to investigate or decide any of the claims until after all claims had been submitted. On October 25, 1833, Butler, informing Secretary McLane of the unsatisfactory situation, also complained of the rude and almost insulting character of the language with which the Secretary of Relations had closed a note of October 24 to him. In June, 1834, Secretary McLane, stating that the President was dissatisfied with continued delays, instructed Butler to try to obtain a definite answer upon all the points at issue. He declared that the American government held the Mexican federal government alone accountable for any injuries to American citizens which merited national interposition and objected to the unreasonableness of the requirements that claimants present their demands in person at the Mexican treasury. "If you fail to get prompt response on this and other points at issue," he added, "you will present my letter to the Minister of Foreign Affairs and return home, but state that it is not the purpose of the President to disturb the existing amicable relations between the two countries." [33]

In order to press claims more effectually, Jackson appointed, as the successor of the unsuccessful Butler, the more experienced public man, Powhatan Ellis, a native of Virginia and a resident of Mississippi. Forsyth in his instructions of January 29, 1836, especially complained of the Mexican refusal to examine claims, and directed pressure for immediate payment of claims which the American government had too long treated with a policy of indulgence and forbearance—a policy which probably encouraged Mexicans to inflict additional injuries upon American citizens and their property. Later (on July 20), three months after the battle of San Jacinto, following Ellis' advice to use forcible means to impress Mexico, he authorized Ellis to make a strong but respectful presentation of the various unredressed complaints of accumulated injuries with a demand for reparation, and instructed him after three weeks to warn the Mexican government that his further residence would be useless unless redress was granted without unnecessary delay, and finally to give notice that he would request his passports unless he received a satisfactory answer at the end of two weeks, and after obtaining his passports to return to the United States, "bringing the archives of the Legation." [34]

Ellis, in a private note to the President, on August 26, 1836, and again on November 27, reported that he saw no present prospect of a just arrangement concerning claims, and apparently he saw little hope thereafter. Beginning in September and closing in December, he followed his instructions, strictly and uncompromisingly. On September 26, he presented to Secretary Monasterio a statement of specific claims, referred to others upon which action had been delayed by Mexico, and demanded prompt and proper examination of each claim and full reparation in each case. On October 20, with little hope of satisfactory reply, he gave notice that his longer residence would be useless unless redress could be had without unnecessary delay. Receiving a prompt reply (of October 21) which attempted to justify further delay by a plea of the necessity of time to collect and examine the documents (which should have been collected long before), and again promised to investigate without naming a time for report, on November 4 he gave notice of his instructions to demand his passports unless he received a satisfactory reply within two weeks. Monasterio's argumentative and oratorical reply of November 15—denying information or the propriety of diplomatic intervention in the cases presented, requesting specification of details in some cases, and agreeing to satisfy all claims properly proven—Ellis did not consider satisfactory. On December 7, further irritated by the seizure of the

American merchant brig *Fourth of July* and the United States sloop of war *Natchez* in the port of Vera Cruz, and by the recent promotion of objectionable General Gomez (who had executed prisoners at Tampico in December, 1835), he wrote a note beginning with an assertion that the method of redress for American citizens is not limited to that provided in Article 14 of the treaty with Mexico, and closing with a request for his passports and an escort to Vera Cruz.[35]

"With all these facts before him," he said, "the undersigned entertains no hope of a satisfactory adjustment of the questions in controversy between the United States of America and Mexico. He has patiently waited three weeks for some evidence of a more favorable disposition to render justice to his injured country—but he has waited in vain—and, whatever may be the consequences, he now feels it to be his duty, in compliance with instructions, to request that His Excellency the President *ad interim* will be pleased to furnish him with the necessary passports to leave the Mexican Republic, and that suitable orders may be given for a guard to protect him on the road to Vera Cruz."

This note, because of delay in copying and the intervention of three successive feast days which prevented the transaction of public business, he did not deliver to the Mexican Foreign Office until December 13. On the following day he wrote Forsyth in cipher: "I have the honor to inform you that I demanded my passports of this Government on the 13th instant [by note dated December 7] and shall repair to Washington City without delay. To the note embracing this demand, I have yet received no reply. The correspondence which led to this state of things I shall not be able to present to you previously to my return to the United States." On December 21 he again wrote Forsyth: "I have not received an answer to my note of the 7" Instant, demanding my passports of this Government, with a view to return to the United States. To-morrow I shall address a second note to the Acting Minister of Foreign Affairs demanding them within a given time, and if they are not sent to me, I shall leave this Capital without them."

On December 22, he forwarded to Forsyth additional correspondence relating to reclamations, which had led to his demand for his passports. On December 27, he left Mexico City and, traveling by way of Vera Cruz and New Orleans, reached Washington by February 1, the date on which he delivered Monasterio's note of December 27. With the latter he also delivered the unanswered notes of December 21 as to the withdrawal of Gorostiza from Washington, and of December 24 requesting the causes of Ellis' proposed departure—both of which were regarded as "discourteous."

The note of December 27 as to passports was as follows: "The Undersigned, Acting Minister of Foreign Affairs, has received an order from His Excellency the President to do himself the honor of addressing the Hon. Mr. P. Ellis, Chargé d'Affaires of the United States of America, and to say: That the very natural desire of His Excellency to investigate the true motives which have influenced Your Excellency in determining to return to your country, leaving unsettled the grave questions which are now pending between that and this nation, was that which prompted the note addressed to Mr. Ellis, by the Undersigned, under date of the 21″ Instant.

"The silence which Mr. Ellis has preserved up to this time, leaving thus unanswered the note in question, as well as that of the 21st of the same month, in which the undersigned manifested the willingness of the Mexican Government to receive the satisfaction which that of the United States assured Mr. Gorostiza should be given through Mr. Ellis, has induced His Excellency the President to believe that Your Excellency still persists in your resolution to depart, and that you have in fact cut short your relations with the Undersigned. Under this impression His Excellency orders him to assure Mr. Ellis that if at six o'clock this evening no reply should have been received, the Passport which he has asked shall be remitted to him and the escort which he desires to accompany him for his security shall be in readiness—the Mexican Government repeating in this manner the proofs of that consideration which it has constantly manifested towards the United States and their representative in this Capital." [36]

On February 6, President Jackson, disappointed and bellicose after receiving from Ellis full information of his fruitless negotiations to secure Mexican acknowledgment of American claims, and possibly influenced by Gorostiza's action in criticizing American policy by means of a printed pamphlet distributed to members of the diplomatic corps at Washington, promptly notified Congress. He declared that the unredressed claims for Mexican injuries, "independent of the recent insults by the late extraordinary Mexican Minister, would justify in the eyes of all Nations, immediate War"; but, instead of war, he suggested an act authorizing reprisals by a naval force if Mexico still refused a naval demand for adjustment. The Senate (on February 27) voted to give Mexico another chance by presentation of a new demand, accompanied by a statement of injuries with proofs, and leaving the method to be determined by the President; and the House, recommending that the last appeal should be presented by a diplomatic official of the highest grade, put in the appropriation an item for the salary and outfit of a minister to Mexico to be used whenever the President should decide that intercourse could be honorably renewed.

Van Buren, to whom Jackson left the appointment of a new minister, on March 6 nominated Ellis, the previous American chargé at Mexico, who was promptly confirmed by the Senate but whose commission was withheld by the President until Mexico could decide to disavow the conduct of Gorostiza. By authority of the President, Secretary Forsyth sent for the archives of the American legation in Mexico and from its records prepared a list of 57 unadjusted claims which seemed free from doubt. He decided first to present these claims through a special messenger, Robert Greenhow, the interpreter of the department who, on May 27, was instructed to invite "for the last time" the serious attention of the Mexican government to the long-standing complaints of injuries and insults, to make a solemn demand for redress, and to ask for an explicit and unequivocal disavowal of Gorostiza's act in circulating the objectionable pamphlet. Greenhow, after presentation of these demands in July, returned to Washington in August with the reply to the Mexican secretary, Cuevas, (dated July 29) stating that Mexico was ready to consider each claim promptly with a view to speedy adjustment (by agreement or arbitration). Although F. P. Martinez, the new Mexican minister, reached Washington by November 18, and presented an answer of

Mexico to a few cases which it had decided after the visit of Greenhow, he found that, through carelessness of Mexican officials, he had brought with him a report on the wrong list of claims. Therefore, the President, in his message of December 5, reporting continued delay on most of the cases, suggested that to Congress now belonged the duty to decide the mode and method of redress. The Senate failed to act, probably agreeing with its Committee on Foreign Relations (as reported by Senator Buchanan) that the House should take the lead in coercive measures. In the House, decisive action was probably prevented by a minority report favoring indulgence of errors and delays resulting largely from revolutionary changes, and possibly also in part by sympathy at the time of the French expedition to enforce claims at Vera Cruz and other Gulf ports of Mexico by "pacific blockade"—which was followed in November and December by the bombardment and surrender of Vera Cruz (resulting in a convention of March 9, 1839, signed by Secretary Gorostiza for the payment of the French indemnity and also in the final adjustment of claims of the British bondholders by Mexican act of August, 1841). In the debates, ex-President J. Q. Adams intemperately declared that the purpose of the American administration was war with Mexico in order to annex Texas. Meantime, in April, 1838, Forsyth accepted from Martinez a proposal to begin negotiations for settlement of claims by arbitration. On August 28, he received from Martinez a memorandum proposing the plan of procedure and scope of the arbitration. By September 3, he had reached an agreement on a convention for settlement of individual claims which was signed on September 11. He declined Martinez's proposal of September 3 to submit all complaints, claims and differences to the King of Prussia—explaining that the President was of the opinion that certain causes of complaint affecting the national character (such as the American attitude toward Texas) did not admit of compromise. As this convention became ineffective by the failure of Mexico to authorize exchange of ratifications within the prescribed period, a new convention to replace it was concluded on April 11, 1839, ratified by the United States Senate on March 17, 1840, and made effective by acts of Congress approved on June 12, 1840, and September 1, 1841. Under the convention of 1839, the commission—two Mexicans and two Americans and a Prussian umpire—met late in 1840 and terminated its duties on February 25, 1842 (according to provision of the convention). Its work was delayed, first by the late arrival of the Mexican commissioners at Washington and later by various controversies concerning oaths of the Mexican commissioners and methods of procedure—the order of the examination of claims (alphabetical or chronological), character of the commissioners' functions (whether judicial or diplomatic), and especially whether claimants had the right of immediate access to the board. By loss of time in discussions, when the last day for action arrived the commission left unsettled several questions which necessitated subsequent correspondence. It decided 30 of the 84 claims cases presented and awarded $2,026,149 of the $6,648,812 demanded. The American government, accepting as final and conclusive the decisions rendered, determined to enter into negotiations for the adjustment of the unfinished business. Already, in May, 1839, Ellis, whose commission had been withheld by the President until Mexico disavowed the conduct of Gorostiza, had been instructed to go to Mexico as envoy extraordinary and minister plenipotentiary to discuss with Mexico, with conciliatory language and deportment, remaining subjects not included in the arbitration —such as the outrage upon the American flag by seizure of the schooner *Texas* on the high seas, the firing upon the brig *Paragon*, the question of the investigation of the case of the *Hannah Elizabeth*, the question of apology for seizure of the *Fourth of July* at Vera Cruz, etc.[37]

After 1839 new sources of irritation arose. In the spring of 1840, Mexican authorities began to arrest American citizens in California and in the following year appeared much alarmed at reported emigration from the United States to California. On July 2, 1840, Ellis requested specific instructions on the question of the arrests. In February, 1841, suggesting the need of a suitable American consul at Monterey on the Pacific, he proposed the appointment of Thomas O. Larkin, who later proved a useful official in making reports to Washington. A few months later, before the arrival of his successor, Waddy Thompson, in April, 1842, he entered into a prolonged and irritating negotiation for the release of American citizens who, as traders or travelers, unfortunately had accompanied the ill-fated Santa Fé expedition from Texas in June, 1841. In this he encountered much difficulty, and, following the first news of Mexican cruelties to the prisoners, his retirement was requested by Americans who desired a more vigorous minister.[38]

REFERENCES

1. G. L. Rives, *The United States and Mexico*, I, p. 185.
2. Van Buren MSS. in Library of Congress. On Butler, see J. Q. Adams, *Memoirs*, XI, 350, and *Atlantic Monthly*, XCV, p. 220, Feb., 1905; Butler, before the War of 1812, had settled in Kentucky and had become a friend of John J. Crittenden whose sister he apparently married.
3. Van Buren MSS., Aug., 1829; Jackson MSS., Aug.-Oct., 1829; *1 Secret Instructions*, p. 39, Aug. 25, 1829; *House Exec. Document 42, 25-1; House Document 351, 25-2; 1 Communications from Agents of Mexico*, Montoya to Van Buren, Oct. 17, 1829.
4. *14 American States Instructions*, No. 6, Apr. 1, 1830; Rives, *The United States and Mexico*, I, pp. 196-204.
5. E. C. Barker in *Am. Hist. Review*, XII, p. 788.
6. *5 Mexico, Despatches*, Apr. 7 and May 21, 1830; Jackson MSS., Apr., 1830, and Oct., 1831.
7. *14 American States Instructions*, p. 252, (No. 25) Feb. 27, 1832; *5 Mexico, Despatches*, (No. 32) July 16, 1832; *House Document 351, 25-2*.
8. *5 Mexico, Despatches*, No. 32, July 16, 1832.
9. *Ib.*; also *House Document 351, 25-2*, pp. 442-.
10. Jackson MSS., Library of Congress; *14 American States Instructions*, pp. 292-93, No. 37, March 20, 1853.
11. *6 Mexico, Despatches*, (No. 50) Aug. 5, 1833, (Private to President) Feb. 26, 1835, and (No. 86) March 31, 1835; Jackson MSS., 1833 and 1834; *15 Mexico, Instructions*, (No. 58) Jan. 13, 1834; *House Exec. Document 42, 25-1*, and *House Document 351, 25-2*.
12. *6 Mexico, Despatches*, No. 86, March 31, 1835.
13. *Ib.*, June 17, 1835.

14. *15 Mexico, Instructions,* pp. 49-50, (No. 94) July 2, 1835; *Ib.,* p. 53, (No. 100) Aug. 6, 1835; *House Exec. Document 42,* 25-1, p. 18.

15. *House Document 351,* 25-2, p. 719; *15 Mexico, Instructions,* p. 58, (No. 104) Dec. 16, 1835; *6 Mexico, Despatches,* (No. 2) Dec. 27, 1835.

16. *8 Mexico, Despatches,* No. 36, Nov. 5, 1836.

17. *15 Mexico, Instructions,* No. 22, Nov. 16, 1836.

18. *6 Mexico, Despatches,* March, and No. 49, July 26, 1833; *House Document 351,* 25-2, pp. 470-71.

19. *15 Mexico, Instructions,* No. 70, May 26, 1834; *6 Mexico, Despatches,* July 13, 1834.

20. G. L. RIVES, *The United States and Mexico,* I, Chaps. XI-XV; *Sen. Doc. 1,* 24-2; *6 Notes to Mexico Legation,* pp. 46-47, July 12, 1836.

21. *Sen. Doc. 84,* 24-2; *Sen. Doc. 1,* 24-2.

22. *Am. Hist. Review,* XII, p. 808; *Texan Diplomatic Correspondence,* I, p. 180.

23. *House Doc. 256,* 24-1, p. 36.

24. *15 Mexico, Instructions,* pp. 57-58, (No. 103) Nov. 9, 1835; *Ib.,* pp. 62-65, (No. 2) Jan. 9, 1836; *House Doc. 256,* 24-1, pp. 40, 42 and 46-48; *House Doc. 351,* 25-2, pp. 773-83.

25. *House Doc. 256,* 24-1, pp. 43 and 31; *6 Notes to Mexico Legation,* p. 34, Apr. 20, p. 35, Apr. 26, p. 37, May 3, pp. 38-43, May 10, 1836, pp. 49-50, Aug. 1, p. 53, Aug. 31 and Oct. 13, 1836; *3 Notes from Mexico Legation,* Apr. 28, Oct. 15, 1836; *Sen. Doc. 1,* 24-2, pp. 93 and 95; *Sen. Doc. 1,* 25-2, p. 114.

26. *15 Mexico, Instructions,* p. 90, No. 24, Dec. 10, 1836.

27. *8 Mexico, Despatches,* No. 45, Dec. 27, 1836 (Enclosure).

28. *6 Notes to Mexico Legation,* pp. 44-45, May 27, 1836; *15 Mexico, Instructions,* p. 85, No. 20, Aug. 16, 1836.

29. *Texan Diplomatic Correspondence,* I, pp. 100, 157 and 201; *Sen. Exec. Journal,* IV, p. 631.

30. *Texan Diplomatic Correspondence,* I, pp. 151-54 and 169; *House Doc. 40,* 25-1, pp. 11-13.

31. *15 Mexico, Instructions,* No. 5, May 18, 1839.

32. *Ib.,* pp. 106-17, No. 3, May 3, 1839.

33. *Ib.,* pp. 31-32, (No. 75) June 24, 1834; *Ib.,* pp. 62-65, (No. 3) Jan. 29, 1836; *6 Mexico, Despatches,* (No. 56) Oct. 25, 1833; *House Doc. 61,* 23-2; *House Doc. 351,* 25-2.

34. *Ib.,* pp. 591-92, Ellis to Forsyth, May 28, 1836; *Sen. Doc. 160,* 24-2, pp. 133-36; *15 Mexico, Instructions,* pp. 106-17, No. 3, May 3, 1839.

35. *Sen. Doc. 160*, 24-2, pp. 138-43, 153, 156 and 167-69; *8 Mexico, Despatches*, No. 40, Dec. 6, 1836.

36. *8 Mexico, Despatches*, (No. 41) Dec. 14, (No. 42) Dec. 21, and (No. 43) Dec. 22, 1836 (Enclosure).

37. J. B. MOORE, *International Arbitrations*, Vol. 2, pp. 1214-17, and p. 1244; *15 Mexico, Instructions*, pp. 106-17, (No. 3) May 3, 1839, and p. 225, (No. 30) March 3, 1843; *Sen. Doc. 1*, 25-2, pp. 105-08; *Cong. Globe*, Apr. 1 and July 7, 1838.

38. *9 Mexico, Despatches*, (No. 24) June 9, 1840; *10 Mexico, Despatches*, (No. 41) Feb. 25, and (No. 43) May 20, 1841.

CHAPTER IV

AMERICAN TEXAN AND CALIFORNIAN POLICY UNDER TYLER

AMERICAN foreign policy under President Tyler was successively under the immediate direction of three prominent secretaries of state: Daniel Webster, from 1841 to May 9, 1843; Abel P. Upshur, from May, 1843, to March, 1844; and John C. Calhoun, from April 1, 1844, to March 6, 1845. Both Webster and Calhoun were men of large public experience and both were known as national leaders. Upshur had served as a judge in Virginia, but was not widely known. The American ministers to Mexico in this period, after the return of Ellis, were Waddy Thompson (to March 9, 1844) and Wilson Shannon (from August, 1844, to May, 1845). Thompson, before his appointment, had served as a member of Congress for six years (1835-41), and Shannon had been governor of Ohio for four years (1838-40 and 1842-44). Shannon later served in Congress (1853-55) and as governor of Kansas Territory (1855 and 1856). For a brief period in 1844, Thompson's secretary, Benjamin Green (son of Duff Green), served as chargé d'affaires. The Mexican minister at Washington for this period was General Juan N. Almonte, reputed son of General Morelos, the patriot priest who had continued the revolution begun by Hidalgo.

While unsatisfactory Mexican relations were further complicated by correspondence on Mexican cruelties to certain Texan prisoners, the question of the American annexation of Texas, which had remained dormant and doubtful since the summer of 1837, again arose in 1841, following the end of the rather extravagant Texan administration of the non-annexationist

Texan, Governor M. B. Lamar, who was succeeded by Governor Houston (in December, 1841). Texas had remained secure only by the continued postponement of the threatened Mexican reconquest—similar to the earlier threatened Spanish expeditions for reconquest of Mexico. No longer apprehending danger from attack, its government began to plan for the extension of its authority to the Rio Grande. In June, 1841, without legislative authority, Governor Lamar sent an ill-advised, preposterous and inadequately equipped "caravan" expedition of about 350 men northwestward over an unmarked route, ostensibly to open trade with Santa Fé and, incidentally, to offer to the dissatisfied people of New Mexico the blessings of Texan government. It was an unfortunate event which steadily embittered Mexican-American relations in a series of later events. Every member who reached Mexican territory was captured there, and surviving prisoners were taken on the long march by way of El Paso and Chihuahua to the City of Mexico, where many lingered in military prison until June 16, 1842—creating in the United States, late in 1841, considerable agitation for American unofficial diplomatic intervention. Early in 1842 Webster directed Ellis to demand the release of any American citizens who had accompanied the expedition as traders or as travelers—a demand which was granted promptly. In March, 1842, following the news of an unexpected retaliatory Mexican demonstration or raid under General Woll against San Antonio, which at first was wrongly suspected as part of a Mexican advance for conquest of Texas, at a time when President Houston had no money to equip an army, American hostile excitement against Mexico temporarily rose high, and Secretary Webster apparently expected the President to order a military force to restrain the Indians near the border.[1]

Following the first news of Mexican cruelties toward the Santa Fé prisoners, Webster was urged to select a more efficient minister to replace Ellis in Mexico, preferably Waddy Thompson, who had served as a Whig member of Congress from 1835 to 1841 and was an ardent friend of Texas. In March, the President appointed Thompson, who, by Webster's instructions of April 15, was directed to demand the release of the Americans confined with the Santa Fé prisoners, but who later reported that the Americans entitled to release had been surrendered before the arrival of these instructions. Leaving his family at home, Thompson, on April 2, sailed from New Orleans and on April 10 entered the harbor of Vera Cruz, where he found yellow fever raging. He arrived at Mexico City on April 16, in an American-built stage driven by an American over the thief-infested road. At the capital his first official act was a visit to Kendall and other Texans who were imprisoned with lepers—a visit which was promptly reported at the palace and probably resulted in hastening his first visit to Santa Anna, whose wife was at the point of death. He was able to exert an influence which resulted in the release of the Santa Fé prisoners by Santa Anna on June 16, 1842.*

Thompson found that the Mexican authorities were greatly displeased and angered by the news of the American popular hostile feeling which had resulted from Mexican treatment of the Santa Fé prisoners and from the captures at San Antonio. The intensity of Mexican feeling found expression on May 31 in an unusual circular letter of Bocanegra, the Mexican Minister of Relations, to the diplomatic corps, submitting an official statement of Mexican grievances against the United States for official toleration of aggressions against the territory of Mexico contrary to international law and treaties, and against the protests of the Mexican government. In it he mentioned American public meetings to aid the Texan "adventurers," recruiting of American volunteers for Texas and shipments of arms and munitions of war to the Texans. After the statement of grievances, he significantly added: "His Excellency the Provisional President, desires, in consequence of what has been here set forth, and with regard to the future, that the nations with

---

* The Santa Fé prisoners, when released, were furnished money for expenses home, but, after a wait in Vera Cruz for a vessel on which to leave, they needed additional money, which was furnished by an American merchant, L. S. Hargous. Thompson later stated that the amount advanced was $10,000 to $15,000, and that he had told Hargous that he had no doubt that he would be reimbursed by the American government. (Thompson's *Recollections of Mexico*, p. 10.)

which the Mexican Republic happily maintains the strongest friendship, should be made well aware of these facts; and should know that Mexico, though not wishing to disturb the relations which she still preserves with the said United States, will assert and maintain the justice of her cause which she considers to be based on the Law of the Nations, by doing all that is imperiously required for her honour and dignity." [2]

To the new documentary contest thus begun by this extraordinary and astonishing circular, Thompson, although he at first planned to refer the matter to Webster for reply, after some reflection fired a warm return shot—a counter circular of June 6 asserting the right of public meetings and freedom of speech, explaining the difference between emigration and enlistment of organized military bodies, stating the right of trade in contraband by private citizens of neutrals on their own account and at their own risk, and denying any American violation of treaties or international law. In justification of his decision to reply he said: "Whilst I am very sure that the Government of the United States recognizes no tribunal to which it holds itself responsible but the enlightened publick opinion of its own people, yet a just regard for the opinions of the world may require a reply to, and refutation of the very harsh charges, which are equally harshly made by the Mexican Government." Referring to the "uniformly kind and forbearing" conduct of the United States, he declared: "Not only have we never done an act of an unfriendly character towards Mexico, but, I confidently assert, that from the very first moment of the existence of the Republick, we have allowed to pass unimproved no opportunity of doing Mexico an act of kindness. I will not now enumerate the acts of that character both to the Govt. of Mexico, and its citizens publick and private. If this Govt. chooses to forget them, I will not recall them." In hoping that the Mexican government would review its opinions, he concluded as follows: "I am not restrained from the expression of this hope by the language of apparent menace which has been used in the communications to which I have alluded. I am very sure that no one who is familiar with the past history of my country will attribute these feelings to fear on her part. They proceed from a very different source. Whilst we are at all times prepared to meet, as becomes us, collisions with other countries, we do not deem it discreditable to say that we hold war, in all its forms as one of the greatest of human calamities, and a causeless war as the very greatest of publick crimes." [3]

Bocanegra, in another circular of July 6, stated that the public meetings to which he objected were those whose sole purpose was to excite citizens "to arm and leave the country in order to usurp the territory and rights of a friendly nation," and that the emigration to which he objected consisted of emigrants supplied with munitions of war with the unconcealed purpose of war against a neighbor nation. [4]

Meantime, on June 29, Webster, who on June 9 had instructed Thompson to propose mediation between Texas and Mexico for termination of a war which was useless and hopeless, and injurious to both parties, and likely to become annoying to other commercial nations, received directly from Bocanegra, "through the agency of Mr. Velezuez de Leon of New York," a communication dated May 12, similar in nature to the circular of that date, criticizing the attitude of the American government in regard to Texas and lauding Mexican forbearance and sacrifices for the sake of peace, charging that American citizens had been aiding Texan rebels in arms against the lawful authority of Mexico, stating that American proceedings could not have been more hostile if war had actually existed between the United States and Mexico (and that insurgents of Texas could have had no more effectual cooperation), and practically threatening a declaration of war. Webster, in his reply of July 8 through instructions to Thompson, denied the justification of the Mexican complaints, demonstrated that the conduct of the American government had been especially marked by moderation and forbearance, reviewed the general facts relating to the settlement and revolt and independence of Texas, and the strict neutral policy of the American government in the Mexican-Texan contest, and reminded Bocanegra that Texas appeared to be as independent and as stable as Mexico and that trade and emigration were not violations of neutral duties under international law. Referring to Bocanegra's theoretical veiled threat of war and expressing the hope that Mexico would "not inconsiderately and needlessly hasten into an experiment" to prove the truth or fallacy of Bocanegra's sentiments, he closed with a sophomoric warning which included the following:

"The efficiency of American hostility to Mexico has never been tried; the Government has no desire to try it. It would not disturb the peace for the sake of showing how erroneously Mr. de Bocanegra has reasoned; it trusts that a just hope may be entertained that Mexico will not inconsiderately and needlessly hasten into an experiment, by which the truth or fallacy of his sentiments may be brought to an actual ascertainment. . . . Every provision of law, every principle of neutral obligation will be sedulously enforced, in relation to Mexico as in relation to other powers. . . . But the continuance of amity with Mexico cannot be purchased at any higher rate. If the peace of the two countries is to be disturbed, the responsibility will devolve on Mexico. . . . The United States . . . desire peace. . . . Yet no fear of a different state of things can be allowed to interrupt its course of equal and exact justice to all nations, nor to jostle it out of the constitutional orbit in which it revolves." [5]

Immediately after mailing his letter of July 8, Webster received Bocanegra's second letter (of May 31) and also copies of his first circular to the diplomatic corps, Thompson's circular in reply, and Thompson's dispatch of June 6 and his private letter of June 21. He suspected that Mexico was seeking an excuse to avoid payment of the awards of the claims commission. On July 13, stating that Bocanegra's second letter, written before he could reasonably expect an answer to his first, was regarded by the President as highly exceptionable and offensive, by imputing to the American government in the most unjust and indecorous manner violations of honor and good faith, he instructed Thompson to inform Bocanegra by note: "That the President . . . directs that no other answer be given than to declare that the conduct of the Government of the United States, in regard to the war between Mexico and Texas, having been always hitherto governed by a strict and impartial regard to its neutral obligations, will not be changed or altered, in any respect, or in any degree. If for this the Government of Mexico shall see fit to change the relations at present existing between the two countries, the responsibility rests with herself." [6]

Bocanegra, without entering into discussion of "the harshness of some of the expressions" of Webster, closed the correspondence by stating his reliance on Webster's assurances of strict neutrality.

Later, American sympathy was further enlisted for the Texans by another Mexican force of advance which, under General Woll, suddenly in September, 1842, seized 53 Texans at San Antonio, including a judge and several lawyers, and marched them to Mexico City as prisoners. It was further enlisted by the Mexican treatment of 226 prisoners captured late in December from a body of Texans who without authority had crossed into Mexico to attack the town of Mier and had surrendered under written assurance of liberal treatment. These prisoners, escaping en route to Mexico, had been recaptured and decimated. The survivors were marched to the fortress near Mexico City where some escaped or died, some were executed, and others were finally released in September, 1844, through the unofficial intervention of the American minister, Waddy Thompson—who, by threatening through Bocanegra to involve in the war a much more powerful enemy than Texas, induced the Mexican government to countermand the order for further executions.*

In response to President Houston's complaint of the marauding character of the warfare waged by Mexico, and to his request (of October, 1842) for the interposition of the American and English governments to require Mexico either to make peace or to conduct war by the established rules of international

---

* On October 29, 1843, Thompson reported that a Mr. John Bradley had been released on recommendation of a letter from General Jackson, that Mr. Calhoun would be released in a few days, and that in connection with his departure for home the others might be released by Santa Anna, with whom he was on good terms. (*11 Mexican Despatches* No. 31, October 29, 1843.) On October 3, Upshur had forwarded to Thompson a letter of Chief Justice Taney, seeking release of a relative, John Taney, who apparently was one of the Texans taken at Mier. (*15 Mexican Instructions* No. 48, October 3, 1843.)

law, Webster, in December, 1842, informed the new Texan minister, Van Zandt, that he had already respectfully warned the new Mexican minister, General Almonte, that Mexico must cease the predatory method of warfare recently conducted against Texas. Later, in January, 1843, he instructed Thompson to mention the subject to the Mexican government in a friendly conversation, admitting Mexico's right to resubjugate Texas by lawful means of war, but asserting the interest of the neighboring United States in the restoration of peace and "also in the manner in which the war shall be conducted, if it shall continue," and adding a warning that the American government contemplated a more formal remonstrance at an early date unless Mexico consented to make peace with Texas, or at least showed the disposition and ability to prosecute the war with respectable forces. On March 14, Thompson, reporting the performance of his duty at a time when the treatment of the prisoners of the Mier expedition was under consideration, and before the end of the excitement resulting from the mistaken seizure and brief occupation of Monterey, California, by an American naval officer (Commodore Jones), wrote Webster that Bocanegra declined to listen to suggestions from other governments concerning prisoners captured in her "rebellious province" and therefore subject to treatment as rebels. Later, in June, 1843, American neutral policy was illustrated by the action of Captain Cooke of the United States dragoons on the Arkansas River (in southern Kansas) in dispersing a body of 200 Texans who, under a commission from Houston, had started to capture "enemy property" from Mexican merchants on the Santa Fé trail.[7]

After the Texans had discovered their inability to invade Mexico or to secure a permanent peace without the aid of the United States or some other foreign power, the American government was again confronted by the question of Texan annexation. Secretary Webster, by October, 1841, following the resignation of the Clay Whigs from the cabinet, had learned from President Tyler that the acquisition of Texas by treaty was contemplated, and in November and December the administration newspapers indicated that plans for annexation would be revived; but the project was not favored by Webster, nor by J. Q. Adams, the Chairman of the Committee on Foreign Affairs in the House. In July and in December, 1842, after Houston had succeeded Lamar as President of Texas, and had seen no hope of a satisfactory adjustment with Mexico which still threatened invasion, President Tyler informed the Texan minister of his readiness to negotiate a treaty of annexation as soon as he could feel sure of the cooperation of the Senate, and on March 3, 1843, J. Q. Adams and others signed and distributed a document asserting that the Southern states had determined upon a speedy execution of the plan of annexation, even at the risk of a dissolution of the Union; but the vacillating Houston, while he looked forward to future annexation, felt uncertain of Tyler's ability to secure the approval of his policy and first sought to appeal to European powers, England and France, to aid in securing from Mexico the peace which he thought was so essential to Texan security and prosperity. Both before and after the failure of the proposed "triple interposition" of Great Britain, France and the United States (in October, 1842) to secure peace between Mexico and Texas, Tyler probably shared the unbounded suspicions of other Americans that the British government intended to aid the Mexicans against Texas. By the summer of 1843, he was displeased with the news that certain peace negotiations for an armistice arranged between Mexico and Texas, as a result of earlier unofficial amateur negotiations of one John W. Robinson with Santa Anna, might involve a return of Texas to Mexican allegiance as an independent department of Mexico.[8]

In selecting a successor of Webster, the President, after a brief interregnum service of Hugh S. Legaré, finally decided to appoint Upshur of Virginia. The latter strongly favored the annexation of Texas, but he delayed negotiations until he was convinced that Great Britain under Aberdeen, influenced by the mission of Elliot, contemplated efforts for the abolition of slavery in Texas in connection with a policy of inducing Mexico to recognize Texan independence to prevent American acquisition of Texas—an acquisition which, it was feared, might result in American acquisition of the Bay of San Francisco. Influenced in part by newspaper rumors and expressions of the feeling of suspicion and distrust of British activities in Texas, and the later confirmation of these rumors and reports by London letters of "General" Duff Green * erroneously stating that the British government was disposed to support a Texan loan to prevent annexation to the United States, Upshur, on August 8, 1843, wrote William S. Murphy (the American chargé in Texas) that the United States had a high interest to counteract any attempt of Great Britain to aid the abolition of slavery in Texas, which might establish a British controlling influence there. Two days later he assured Van Zandt (the Texan representative at Washington) of American interest in Texas and stated that American interests could best be served by promotion of Texan interests. On September 22, after receiving further evidence in confirmation of the English purpose to encourage abolition of slavery in Texas, he nervously and confidentially instructed Murphy that the American government desired to aid Texas, although support by the people in this policy was still doubtful, and that Texas should yield nothing to the counsels or influence of Great Britain which was already claiming an ascendency on the Gulf. Without waiting for denials or explanations from London, he urged President Tyler to authorize the opening negotiations for annexation, and notified Van Zandt that the American government had changed its attitude and was ready for early action in arranging a treaty to submit to the Senate. On October 16, 1843, referring to "recent occurrences" at London and possibly influenced by the belligerent tone of Mexico as to the proposed annexation, he again announced to Van Zandt his readiness to open negotiations. He was doubtless somewhat disappointed, although not surprised under the circumstances, by the decision of Houston and the Texan government (announced by its instructions of December 13) declining to negotiate for a treaty of annexation at that time when speedy settlement of Mexican difficulties through

* Duff Green's daughter, Margaret, had married a son of John C. Calhoun.

the good offices of other powers was expected, and when the attitude of the American Senate toward the proposed treaty was uncertain. About a month later, in reply to an unauthorized inquiry from the sympathetic and anxious Van Zandt, who had withheld full information of the Texan refusal to negotiate, he gave verbal assurance that the President was ready to agree to offer naval and military protection to Texas following the signing of a treaty of annexation, which Houston feared might prove the signal of an invasion by Mexican forces; and, about the same time (January 16, 1844), he confidentially instructed Murphy that there was no longer any doubt that a clear constitutional majority of two-thirds in the Senate would favor the treaty if negotiated, and he urged the importance of annexation as a measure deeply involving American and Texan destiny—by preventing causes of irritation which might possibly result in a war between the United States and Texas, involving an American contest with other powers and the disturbance of the peace of the civilized world.[9]

Murphy, agreeably surprised that the Houston government (even before it had definitely abandoned its armistice negotiations with Mexico) had finally decided to begin preliminary negotiations, assumed the responsibility of giving in writing (on February 15, 1844) the requested assurance that the American government would aid in the protection of Texas against Mexico pending the proposed negotiations—an assurance which Tyler thought was beyond his constitutional power, although he was willing to concentrate forces in the Gulf and on the border as a prudent precaution.

Meantime, Mexican opposition and protests had continued. On August 23, 1843, Bocanegra sent to Thompson an offensive statement that the Mexican government would regard as a declaration of war an act of the American Congress incorporating Texas into the United States—a statement which Thompson apparently regarded with unperturbed serenity. Thompson promptly replied that such threats of war were calculated to excite a war feeling where none existed, and, if intended for intimidation, could have no effect and should not be repeated.

Later, on October 20, he was instructed by Upshur to demand promptly the withdrawal of any subsequent letter of such offensiveness or to request an apology. In concluding this instruction, considering Texas as an independent, sovereign power competent to treat for herself, Upshur said: "If war should ensue, Mexico herself will be the aggressor and will alone be responsible for all the evils which may attend it." Suggesting the necessity of using a tone of decision with Mexico, which was assuming toward the United States an attitude of superiority, he declared: "In the transaction of business with that Government it will be proper to present as soon as possible your ultimatum and to insist on a direct and positive answer. . . . Unreasonable delays are to be met by an urgency on your part which shall show at once the disposition of the United States to render full and prompt justice to Mexico and to insist on receiving like treatment from her." On November 18, unable to see any excuse for the conduct of the Mexican government in protracting discussion as to Texas and American claims, he notified Thompson that American relations with Mexico must speedily be settled on a basis which would ensure proper respect for American rights and security of American interests, and authorized him to state that he expected a speedy decision on the convention for settlement of all unadjusted claims.[10]

Upshur considered the business of the legation so important that he would not consent to Thompson's wish for a visit to the United States. On September 27, 1843, to Thompson's request for a leave of absence for a visit, he stated that in the delicate state of relations he did not feel free to grant the request, and four days later he added, at the President's request, that in case the proposed leave was urgent he should at once inform the Department in order that his successor might be provided promptly. On November 27, he notified Thompson that the President was reluctantly compelled to permit his return to the United States and to appoint his successor.

Meantime, on October 29, Thompson, before he received Upshur's instructions of October 20, and when he thought Mexico really desired to maintain friendly relations which were

so much to her interest, wrote Upshur that he was entirely satisfied that the Mexican communication as to the annexation of
Texas "was solely intended for political effect and to operate on
approaching elections." [11]

A few days later the discussion was renewed at Washington
by a belligerent note of November 3 from General Almonte,
who, expecting that Congress would consider the question of
annexation of Texas, stated that such a measure could not be
considered in any other aspect than as an aggression. By order
of his government Almonte protested, and threatened in advance the termination of his mission and a Mexican declaration
of war if the United States "in defiance of good faith and justice
should commit the unheard of act of appropriating an integral
part of Mexican territory." To this note, Upshur, after denying
that the American government had ever done anything inconsistent with the just claims of Mexico, but without mention of
plans as to Texas, stated that the President, with full reliance
in the wisdom and justice of Congress, saw no reason why its
policy should be affected by threats of the Mexican government
or should not receive the hearty cooperation of the executive,
and reminded Almonte that his admonishments as to the duty
and reputation of the United States were quite unnecessary.
Refusing to disclaim any intention of Congress to annex Texas,
he declared that Texas was an independent nation, fully competent to manage its own affairs (as proven by its successful
resistance to Mexico), and with which the American government could properly conduct business without the necessity of
consultation with any other nation. Almonte, reassured by an
interview with J. Q. Adams, was still hopeful that Congress
would not undertake annexation.[12]

President Tyler, in his message to Congress on December 5,
1843, which was accompanied by Upshur's correspondence with
Almonte, especially complained of Mexican prohibitions against
foreign retailers in Mexico and of Mexico's predatory method of
conducting the war against Texas, hinted at British interference
in Texan affairs, and declared that Mexico should be informed
firmly that the war with Texas must cease.

In January, 1844, Upshur mentioned to Almonte the wish of the American government to acquire Texas by purchase from Mexico; and, on February 16, a few days before his death, explaining the American fear of British influence in Texas against American interests and peace, and stating his wish to remove all cause of annoyance or conflict with Mexico, he again proposed the Mexican cession of Texas for adequate compensation and urged upon the interested Almonte that such a cession would prove advantageous alike to the treasury and the honor of Mexico. The proposition appealed to Almonte because he regarded it as a recognition of Mexico's rights to Texas and as a means of diverting or delaying any American attempt to use force to secure the territory. Upshur, in a long memorandum of the conference, closed with the statement that Almonte had agreed, in the views presented, that he had expressed a hope that in case of the annexation of Texas by the United States the matter might be amicably settled between the United States and Mexico and that he had declared that he had long been of the opinion that the nations of America ought to have a policy of their own, that a good understanding was of course necessary to this, and that he would take great pleasure in communicating the substance of the conversation to his government.[13]

John C. Calhoun, Upshur's successor in the Tyler cabinet and the active guardian of slavery, had favored annexation of Texas since 1836, but his leadership in urging the measure in 1844 was expected to increase the opposition in the Senate. Tyler hoped to complete the treaty before Calhoun's arrival from South Carolina at the end of March but was unable to arrange it. Calhoun, after a conference with the two Texan representatives (Van Zandt and Henderson), promptly notified Almonte that the treaty was under consideration, and suggested a provision in it for a compensation to Mexico to prevent a breach. Obtaining in reply a suggestion to offer negotiations directly with Mexico for the purchase, and a threat to demand passports if the Texan treaty should be approved by the Senate, he resumed his conferences with the Texan representatives and (on April 11) notified them that the President had ordered a concentration of forces in the Gulf and on the frontier and would use all his constitutional power to protect Texas from foreign invasion "during the pendency of the treaty." On the following day the proposed treaty of cession was signed, the United States assuming the public debts and liabilities of Texas whose boundary was not specified. On April 17, Calhoun told Almonte that it was largely due to fear of English policy, stating that it should not be regarded as a cause of offense. Again suggesting some offer of compensation (possibly $5,000,000) to Mexico for renouncement of its pretensions and acceptance of boundaries planned, he even proposed to send a special messenger to offer compensation before submitting the Texan treaty to the Senate.[14]

Although Almonte—feeling that his government had been "ignominiously treated" by failure to consider its dignity—refused to lend his cooperation or countenance to the proposed Mexican negotiations, Calhoun, desiring to forestall criticism in the Senate, promptly sent a special messenger, Colonel Gilbert L. Thompson, with instructions (of April 19) to Benjamin E. Green, the American chargé in Mexico (and the brother of his son's wife). In these he explained that the Texan treaty had been forced on the United States in self-defense against British policy and was not intended as an act of disrespect or indifference to the honor or dignity of Mexico, and directed Green to inform the Mexican government of the wish to settle with it all related questions including that of a satisfactory boundary. Three days later, he received from Almonte a note complaining that American newspapers had "studiously endeavored to inculcate the idea" that he (Almonte) had declared that his government would conform to the explanation or indemnification which the government of the United States might choose to give to secure assent to the incorporation of Texas with those states—a report which he characterized as an invention "highly offensive to the dignity of Mexico" whose government he said adhered to the protests addressed to the American government on August 23 and on November 3, 1843, against the annexation of Texas. He promptly replied that such statements and speculations were based on no intimation of his and had received no countenance from him. Possibly he had not read Upshur's memorandum of February 16, which may have been the basis of the newspaper articles.

At the same time, in reply to a British note of February 26 to Upshur, and possibly influenced by Waddy Thompson's report that Santa Anna expected Great Britain to furnish aid to prevent American annexation of Texas, Calhoun wrote Pakenham a note (probably intended primarily as an argument for the Senate) presenting fully the reasons which forced the United States to annex Texas. Although pleased with the British disclaimer of any purpose to disturb the internal peace of the southern section of the United States, or to interfere by domination or compulsion to abolish slavery in Texas, he feared the British policy of promoting abolition of slavery throughout the world, especially if successful in Texas, would endanger the safety of the United States. Therefore, he said, restating his earlier views of 1836-37, the American government, non-aggressive, without any responsibility for the circumstances in Mexican relations and British relations which had forced new problems upon American consideration, had concluded the Texan treaty as a duty of self-defense.[15]

President Tyler, in presenting the treaty and accompanying documents to the Senate on April 22, emphasized the national importance of the annexation, especially the "reclaiming" of territory claimed under the Louisiana treaty of 1803 and contributing to the perpetuation of the Union by protection and security of the South against foreign efforts to disturb its institution. He soon found that, partly under influences of the approaching presidential campaign, the treaty was already discredited by the Whig opposition and especially by Clay's Raleigh letter of April 17 against annexation (for reasons of expediency), and also by Van Buren's letter of April 20 agreeing with Clay that annexation might result in a war with Mexico which would be inexpedient to attempt. On June 8, after all the presidential nominating conventions had been held, the treaty failed in the Senate by a vote of 35 to 16—short of the required two-thirds. The President and Calhoun, however, after consultation with the Texan representatives, had already planned (on May 5) to secure annexation by a majority vote of Congress if the required two-thirds could not be obtained in the Senate. On June 11, just preceding the adjournment of Congress, Tyler published an appeal to Congress and the people, expressing confidence in the popular wish for expansion of territory, and submitting to the House the responsibility of finding a constitutional way to accomplish the important national object which he had unsuccessfully sought to achieve by treaty, and which he declared would give a new and important impulse to every industrial and commercial interest of the Union. He urged the annexation as a useful protection to an exposed frontier.

Relations were further disturbed by other difficulties. The negotiations for a new claims treaty were complicated by the Texan question and the poverty of the Mexican treasury, which made necessary a new convention to provide a specific arrangement for the payment of awards rendered under the convention of 1839. Finally, Thompson concluded with Mexico a new convention of January 30, 1843 (proclaimed March 30), which provided for payment of the settled claims in equal quarterly installments beginning on April 30 and continuing for a period of five years. At the same time, Mexico agreed to the future negotiation of another new convention for the settlement of all undecided claims, both American and Mexican. On October 29, 1843, Thompson reported a fair prospect to conclude the proposed new claims convention with certain features proposed by Upshur. In this negotiation he reported that he was favored by Mexican apprehension of collision with England which he suggested might furnish him an opportunity to interpose officially with good offices. At that time Upshur was still in doubt, and, on November 18, disgusted with the Mexican policy to protract discussion, he instructed Thompson to say that he expected a speedy decision on the convention for the settlement of all unadjusted claims. On November 20, just before the early termination of his mission was decided upon, Thompson concluded with Mexican plenipotentiaries a convention, which he thought secured all the points which had been regarded as most material by Upshur, and provided that the commission under it would meet at Mexico City convenient to the archives. This convention, however, in addition to a provision for the settlement of individual claims, also contained a stipulation for governmental claims (Article XV) which the American government declined to approve and which the American Senate struck out. Thus amended, it was presented to the Mexican government which withheld its ratification. Among the large and exaggerated claims which were still unsettled was one of W. S. Parrott, who, after practicing dentistry in Mexico, had become a merchant there and by luxurious living had become a bankrupt, and who later (in 1845) was sent as an American secret agent to ascertain whether Mexico would reopen diplomatic relations.[16]

The difficult negotiations to induce Mexico to ratify the amended claims treaty were conducted through Benjamin E. Green (son of Duff Green), who was commissioned secretary to the American legation in Mexico on May 24, 1843, and became chargé d'affaires *ad interim* from March 9, the date of Thompson's departure, to September 1, 1844. After conferring with Bocanegra, who said no action on the amended convention could be taken before the arrival of news from General Almonte, he reported to Calhoun on April 8 that the new administration, using the convention of 1839 to throw odium upon the Bustamante administration and to divert attention from itself, and anxious to throw all claims into the hands of the umpire, refused to listen to friendly argument, and was attempting to satisfy the people by the assertion that Mexico had claims against the United States sufficient to balance the American claims against Mexico. Suggesting that Santa Anna (who had told Thompson that Mexico needed a foreign war to develop her resources) probably wanted a war with a view to resumption of dictatorial powers, and, considering the questionable ability of Mexico to pay the installments under the previous claims treaty, he said the American government had nothing to gain by quarreling unless it could end by getting California. On April 30, 1844, the Mexican government, without admitting that it had no money, failed to pay the fourth quarterly installment due under the convention of January 30, 1843. Three months later it failed to pay the fifth, and soon, thereafter, following a change in the government, it suspended payment of all orders on the treasury. At the same time, it continued to postpone consideration and conclusion of the proposed new convention for liquidation of claims, on the pretext that it was waiting for some documents of the old commission. On July 24, Green sent to Monasterio a note protesting most solemnly against the non-payment of the installment which had been due on April 30, and which Monasterio on May 6 had said would be paid on the following day.[17]

In Mexico, Calhoun's instructions (of April 19, 1844) to Green resulted in a spirited although fruitless and goalless contest of six weeks between Green and the Mexican government in May and June, involving American plans to interfere with any Mexican expedition against Texas. On the arrival of the special messenger (Colonel Thompson) on May 22 with the instructions, Green promptly (May 23) notified Bocanegra that President Tyler sent assurances that the American government intended no disrespect to Mexico by the treaty with Texas, that it would have been glad to act in concurrence with Mexico in the annexation, that it had taken every precaution to make the terms of the treaty as little objectionable to Mexico as possible, that it wished to settle all questions between Mexico and the United States, and invited Mexico to open boundary negotiations through the Mexican minister at Washington (with the understanding that the United States would pay an indemnity for any Mexican territory acquired). On May 28, he received from President Santa Anna a request that Colonel Thompson's departure be postponed until after a conference between the President and Green on the proposed negotiations—a conference at which Colonel Thompson was present and which seemed to indicate that the course of the Mexican government would be based upon the impression that the American Senate would reject the treaty and upon the expectation of American internal dissension in regard to slavery. Santa Anna, reelected to the presidency notwithstanding the unpopularity of his dictatorship, and seeing an opportunity to regain his waning popularity, declared that Mexico was resolved to maintain its rights over its revolted territory and refused to favor any suggestions of pecuniary compensation. Bocanegra, in a long reply (of May 30) to Green, severely criticizing the American government, declared that signature of the Texan treaty of annexation would lead to consequences most serious and result in great injury for which Mexico would be entitled to satisfaction. He concluded by saying that approval by the American Senate would place upon Mexico the duty to act in accord with international law and as threatened in repeated protests. In regard to the proposed new boundary treaty with the promise of indemnity for any Mexican territory which the United States might acquire by the treaty, he asked "What rule or what data will serve to distinguish Mexican territory from that of the United States." In the later correspondence, Bocanegra, on June 12, contended that "to the mother country alone pertains the recognition which produces independence." In reply Green attempted to end the discussion by recalling the inconsistent fact that Mexico, although its independence was not recognized by Spain until December 28, 1836, had officially (and properly) refuted for 24 years the doctrine that Spanish recognition was necessary to Mexican independence.

In June, and for several months thereafter, the American government was in doubt concerning Santa Anna's intentions toward Texas, against which he threatened a new expedition, although a few months earlier the Minister of War had acknowledged to General Thompson that the reconquest of Texas by Mexico was impossible and the clergy "with their usual sagacity" were opposed to a renewal of the war. On June 10, 1844, the new Mexican Minister of War (Reyes) told the Mexican Congress that $4,000,000 would be necessary to undertake an immediate campaign against Texas. On June 19 General Woll sent President Houston a declaration of war, causing Houston's government, on August 6, to request the American government to interpose with military aid to Texas; but Green reported that Santa Anna's proposal to make war on Texas was only a pretext to get an increase to the army to aid his own ambitions for power. A few days later, on June 24, after a request through Bocanegra to state clearly and explicitly whether troops which Mexico might send against Texas would be opposed by land or sea by forces of the United States, as rumored in the public press, Green replied that he had no communications on the subject, but that he expected early dispatches which might enable him to give the desired information. Then he added the following tantalizing paragraph: "In the mean time, the undersigned, actuated by a sincere & frank desire of giving to H. E. all the information he possesses, begs leave to call to mind a note, addressed to the late Minister of the U. S., Mr. Thompson, on the 23d of August last; in which H. E. Mr Bocanegra himself first originated with this legation the question of the annexation of Texas to the U. S., accompanying his communication with a direct threat of war, in case the U. S. should determine on the measure referred to. That measure is now the subject of consideration in the Senate of the U. S.: and the undersigned has reason to believe, that it is true, that forces have been prepared by his Govt., both by land & sea, to meet any contingency which may arise; all which however, as the undersigned believes, has been done, as a defensive precaution, made necessary by the oft repeated threats, with which H. E. Mr Bocanegra, in the name of the Mexican Govt., has thought proper to menace the U. S." [18]

The later purpose of Santa Anna and the failure of his plans may be briefly sketched. In August, after receiving from the Mexican chargé at London the assurance (of May 29) that if Mexico would acknowledge the independence of Texas, Great Britain and France would probably arrange a joint guarantee of Texas to prevent annexation to the United States—a proposition which, if adopted, might have resulted in a war to enforce the Monroe Doctrine—he was still appealing unsuccessfully to Congress for money. Later, by October, 1844—after Great Britain, dropping the plan of joint guarantee, had given warning that it could promise no help in any plan for invasion of Texas—the Mexican government returned to the plan of recognition to prevent American annexation. Santa Anna, disappointed by the hesitation of Congress to support his plans, retired to his country estate in September for a rest, and in his absence he was blamed with the loss of Texas and steadily lost public confidence, Finally, a revolt, begun at the end of October and led by Paredes, soon resulted in the loss of his remaining popularity, a mock procession headed by his amputated foot which had been resurrected from the cemetery, his impeachment (in December), and finally his expulsion from Mexico with his young wife (on June 3, 1845) and a temporary residence at Havana.

To replace Thompson who (deciding to support Clay) had resigned his place as minister, Tyler chose Wilson Shannon, an Ohio lawyer who had served two terms (four years) as governor of that state, and had been an unsuccessful candidate for the United States Senate in 1842. Calhoun in his general instructions of June 20, 1844, to Shannon, after reviewing various causes of complaint—non-payment of installment due under the claims convention of 1839, and promulgation of certain recent obnoxious Mexican decrees restricting the retail trade of foreigners and ordering the expulsion of American citizens from Mexican territory of California, Sonora, Sinaloa, and Chihuahua—especially directed him to avoid any controversy in regard to the Texas treaty (which had "violated no prior engagement or stipulation with Mexico"), and with proper dignity to ignore the provocative and unwarranted menaces and offensive language officially used by the Mexican government. On September 10, 1844, he assured the Texan government that the President would later recommend to Congress the adoption of measures to protect Texas pending the question of annexation, and that meantime he would protest against the renewal of the war in the savage manner which Mexico had proposed. At the same time (September 10), he issued through Shannon the protest against Mexican plans to renew the war with savage ferocity in order to defeat annexation, and also a warning that the President, while the question of annexation was pending, would be compelled to regard the invasion of Texas by Mexico, to force it into a foreign and unnatural alliance, as highly offensive to the United States. A few days later American orders were issued to restrain Indians on the frontier, and, if necessary for that purpose, to occupy places in Texas (with permission of Texan authorities).[19]

Shannon arrived by August 28, after being robbed on the way, and was received on September 1, 1844. On October 14, he promptly presented to Rejon (the new Minister of Relations) the full force of the protest and warning as required by Calhoun's instructions of September 10, stating that the United States while annexation was pending could not permit either the conquest of Texas or the forced formation of other connections less acceptable than American annexation which, he indiscreetly said, had been a cherished American policy for 20 years. The contents of the note soon became known outside of official circles and produced quite a sensation. Rejon, rejecting the protest, was rather offensive and violent in his long reply of October 31, which, together with the Mexican revolt against the administration of Santa Anna, probably hastened annexation measures in the United States. On November 4, Shannon stated that he could hold no communication unless in terms respectful to himself and to the government and people which he represented. He demanded the withdrawal of Rejon's note on the ground that, by repeatedly charging the government and people of the United States with "falsehood, intrigues and dishonorable designs and barefaced usurpation," it manifested a purpose of deliberate insult.

This demand Rejon characterized as a pretext to avoid a reply to his "true and unconfused" statement of the Texas question, and he refused to withdraw his note, partly attempting to justify the discourteous language by the counter-charge that Shannon in his note of October 14 had often called the Mexican government "barbarous," and by the assertion that (while showing consideration to the majority of the American people) he had referred to "important facts which proved the bad faith of two administrations and of the Southern people."

"Therefore," said he, "the Government of the undersigned, far from finding a reason to withdraw the note which it addressed to the American Legation on the 31st of October last, the more it considers it the more it is convinced of the necessity of allowing it to remain in the terms in which it was transmitted, regretting only that the opportunity has not been given it to amplify the facts which it has discussed to show to the world that system of deceit which has been followed toward Mexico for the last 20 years, and which the American Legation's note of the 14th of October has just confirmed.

"Therefore the undersigned is directed to repeat it in its entirety and at the same time to repeat that if on account of Mexico's acting on her rights the present Government of the United States should break off the friendly relations which the Government of this republic has tried and will try in good faith to preserve, the Mexican administration, accepting the hard terms which it is forced to adopt, will repel any unjust aggression against it, placing on the Government of President Tyler the responsibility for all the evils resulting from such change." [20]

On November 8, Shannon replied, stating that the American government during the 69 years of its successful operation had discharged its international duties and performed its obligations to its own citizens with a fidelity, honor and integrity which commanded the confidence and respect of all the governments of the civilized world. "If the Govt of Mexico constitutes an exception to this truth," said he, "the Govt of the U. S., to whom the undersigned will refer the notes of H. E. Mr Rejon, knowing what is due to its own character, can & will correct the erroneous opinion, which is the misfortune of Mexico, by means more efficient than any written refutation by the undersigned of the calumnies made and reiterated in the notes of Mr Rejon, would be." Referring to Rejon's charge that the American government had followed toward Mexico a system of deceit in regard to Texas, he said there had been no time during the whole period mentioned, that the government of Mexico did not know the American desire to acquire Texas. Announcing that Rejon's notes would be immediately referred to his government for further instructions he unwisely declared that "unless they are withdrawn, all further intercourse between the undersigned and the Government of Mexico must be suspended until those instructions are received." *

After considering Mexican intentions to recover Texas, the causes of hostility to the United States and the unpaid installments past due under the claims convention, on November 12 he declared that forbearance toward Mexico was unwise. With his official dispatch of November 12 to Calhoun, forwarded by Mr. (Benjamin E.) Green, he also sent the following private note of the same date:

"The insolence of this Government is beyond endurance and if it is submitted to in one case it will only give encouragement to its repetition. I think we should take high ground with Mexico and let her distinctly understand that she must retract her insults and do us justice in all matters of complaint which we have against her. I am fully convinced we can do nothing with Mexico as to the settlement of any of the difficulties we have with her until we either whip her, or make her believe we will do so. So long as she thinks we will confine our complaints to diplomatic notes she will treat them with an indifference amounting to insult. I think we ought to present to Mexico an *ultimatum.* My last note to Mr. Rejon may appear rather severe but I think it was called for and that a more mild note would (have) produced no effect, on this people. I will wait with some solicitude your further instructions." [21]

Later, on January 16, 1845, after the end of the revolution and the flight of Santa Anna to the coast, Shannon suggested that the new administration would probably be better disposed toward the United States and that questions growing out of the proposed annexation of Texas could be amicably adjusted

* Shannon's hasty action in assuming the high responsibility of suspending all diplomatic intercourse without previous authority of his government was disapproved several months later, early in Polk's administration, by Secretary Buchanan, who favored a policy of "firmness of action accompanied by moderation of language," and suggested that nothing could have been more agreeable to the Mexican government than his note of November 8 by which he had unfortunately placed himself in such a position that he had never since been able to press upon Mexico the numerous claims—thus relieving Mexico from these demands while American citizens continued to suffer from the delay. [15 *Mexican Instructions,* No. 10, March 29, 1845.]

—a prediction which was not verified or justified by later events.[22]

Meantime, in October, coincident with a Mexican political crisis, Duff Green, who (on September 12) had been appointed American consul at Galveston, had arrived in Mexico City from Galveston on some sort of private mission involving a report to Calhoun on political conditions. He was in close touch and sympathy with Shannon by whom he was detained because of "the importance of events transpiring" and who felt "greatly indebted for his aid and advice." On October 28, when the brig *Lawrence* was at Vera Cruz awaiting his orders to convey him to Galveston, he reported to Calhoun his conviction that to obtain the consent of the Mexican government to the cession of Texas or other territory was impossible. Although concluding that there was nothing to hope from Mexico, he suggested that the American government could get all its desires in *one* way—upon which he reserved his views for personal explanation after his visit to Texas. On November 12, in a private note to Calhoun, he summarized his view of the Mexican situation as follows:

"I have been detained here much longer than I anticipated and refer you to Governor Shannon's dispatches for the causes. Benjamin's letters to you will have prepared you in some measure for events here. They are now hastening to a crisis. There is great dissatisfaction with Santa Anna. . . . There is not a dollar in the treasury. . . . There is no confidence in those who are opposed to Santa Anna. . . . I see no prospect of his overthrow. Therefore apparently you will have to deal with him. Any successor will be compelled to take as strong or stronger ground against the United States. . . .

"You can not adjust the Texan question by consent of Mexico. Santa Anna rather than adjust that question will prefer angry negotiations which serve as a pretext for keeping up his army, but he knows he can not sustain himself by a war.

"Yet you can not have peace with Mexico without a war. They have so long bullied, insulted and plundered us that they have lost all respect for us as a nation. . . . Even the English would be glad to see them whipped. On these matters I refer you to my son who has many facts in confirmation of what I say.

"It seems to me that the United States has no alternative. . . .

They must demand a withdrawal of the insolent charges and imputations contained in Mr. Rejon's notes, and an immediate adjustment of all our claims against Mexico. This will not be done and a war must be the consequence.

"Governor Shannon was at first resolved to demand his passports, indeed he had written his letter demanding them and he was only prevented from sending it by a belief that the course which he adopted would relieve the Government from the charge of wishing to place the United States which would necessarily lead to war.

"By suspending his official relations until he can receive instructions from you, he enables the President to place on Congress its just responsibility. . . . Indeed the time has come when we have no alternative but to punish Mexico. . . .

"We have no means of regaining the trade of Mexico but by chastising them into decent behavior, and the advantage of a war with Mexico will be that we can indemnify ourselves while reinstating ourselves in the estimation of other nations. . . . You know that I am for peace and that I would be one of the last to advise a war . . . but we have gone so far that I see no means of avoiding a conflict with Mexico. . . ."

A few days later "General" Green sailed for Galveston, carrying copies of the diplomatic correspondence in relation to Texas which Shannon was forwarding to the American chargé in Texas. On November 29, in a private note from Galveston to Calhoun, enclosing a memorandum of "important facts," indicating that the political contest in Mexico was a struggle of Santa Anna to place himself at the head of an absolute despotism, he wrote as follows: "It is not for me to advise, but I do not believe that you can accomplish any thing with Mexico unless you seize upon Vera Cruz, and my opinion is that the best way of taking the fort is to take the town, and that this may be done with a very small force if it is done promptly. Santa is an able man, and he has resolved to fall back on Vera Cruz, and this fort, but he is compelled to call off his whole force to meet Paredes and cannot supply new troops for some two or three months. If we take the town and fort they should not be given up, as they are the keys to the commerce of Mexico. . . ."

On December 8, a day before the close of Houston's term as President of Texas, Green wrote Calhoun from Washington, Texas, as follows:

"I have now been here several days and have conversed with many of the most influential members of Congress. I find that upon the question of Annexation there is little or no difference of opinion . . . General Houston has had other views. If he were left to himself he would put on foot an offensive war. All his arguments go to show that his mind is occupied with the Conquest of Mexico and the establishment of a new Republic. He goes freely into the comparison of the two propositions, Annexation and Conquest. All his remarks are appeals to the passions and interests which he desires to enlist in the Conquest of Mexico. . . .

"In the meantime, as the only serious impediment to annexation is to be found in the ulterior Aspirations of General Houston, I deem it fortunate that Major Donaldson came when he did. Armed as he was by letters from General Jackson, knowing Houston and his early history, he has used arguments and urged considerations which no one else could have done with the same effect and neutralized if he has not eradicated the purpose of Mexican Conquest. General Houston will leave here in a few days, and has declared himself in favor of annexation, saying that Texas can do nothing, but await the action of the United States. . . . In the meantime I am by no means sure that it will be for the interest of the United States or of Texas that the question should be closed *now*. . . ." [23]

Meantime, in the American presidential campaign, Texas was the chief issue. Annexation sentiment was probably increased by the report that Aberdeen in June had discussed with the Mexican and Texan representatives in London a project for an Anglo-French joint guarantee against American aggression if Mexico would recognize the independence of Texas—although the project was postponed in July. The chances of the success of annexation were also increased by the reunited democracy under Polk, resulting from the withdrawal of Tyler from the four-cornered contest (on August 22), and also by Clay's somewhat indefinite letter of July 27 which, seeking to attract Southern votes, expressed a personal willingness for annexation under certain circumstances, "without dishonor, without war," and without injection of the subject of slavery. The election of Polk was regarded as a popular mandate for annexation, which no outside influence could prevent. Calhoun, through an "Unofficial-Private" dispatch of October 31 from A. D. Mann from Bremen, was assured that America need fear no danger from Europe. "The 'protests' of certain powers of Europe and the manifest opposition of others against the annexation of Texas," said he, "should be regarded by our Government in the light they are intended, *as mere scare crows*. No nation dare go to war with us. Rothchild holds the purse strings and he will never untie them for the purposes of war anywhere. . . . If any state should become involved in war with America, revolution would succeed revolution in Europe." [24]

President Tyler, in his exultant message of December, 1844, declared that his Texan policy had been fully sustained at the November elections and recommended to Congress immediate annexation by joint resolution on the terms as agreed by the two governments concerned; and possibly he felt more certain of success after Houston was succeeded by Jones as President of Texas, on December 12. In the House the support of the joint resolution was led by Ingersoll who advocated *re-annexation* as a great national measure, and by Douglas who strategically credited President J. Q. Adams with originating the project of annexation. Adams closed the discussion by distinguishing between his early proposition for "purchase" and the contemplated proposition for "burglary." The chief objections offered were extension of slavery and lack of constitutional power to annex a foreign state by the method proposed. The resolution was finally adopted by the House on January 25, 1845, by a majority of 118 to 101, and by the Senate on February 26, by a majority of 27 to 25. As amended in the Senate, the resolution was approved by the House on February 28, by a majority of 132 to 76, and signed by President Tyler on March 1. After a cabinet meeting on March 2, and especially on the urgent recommendation of Calhoun, it was promptly submitted to the Texan government through instructions of March 3 to Donelson, the American representative in Texas. On March 6, 1845, General Almonte, the Mexican minister at Washington, after a solemn and vigorous protest in compliance with his instructions—pronouncing the annexation illegal and a most unjust aggression against the friendly nation which claimed the territory as a province of Mexico—announced to Calhoun the termination of his mission and demanded his passports.[25]

President Polk promptly adopted the Texan policy of Tyler and Calhoun. Buchanan, whom he selected as the successor of Calhoun as Secretary of State, assumed office on March 10, and immediately wrote Donelson to confirm Calhoun's instructions of March 3. At the same time, in reply to Almonte, he expressed the President's regret at the offense taken by the Mexican government at a reasonable action which, having been irrevocably decided, could not be reopened to further discussion, and proposed to use his efforts toward an amicable adjustment of all causes of complaint between the two governments. On March 29, informing Shannon that, in order to restore peace and harmony, it would be necessary to employ some other agent against whom the Mexicans had no prejudice, he said: "Should Mexico commence hostilities against us, we shall be prepared to maintain the interests and honor of the United States, but nothing short of hostilities or plunder and imprisonment of our citizens will induce the President to depart from the tone and language of conciliation." [26]

In Mexico, Cuevas, the Minister of Relations under the new administration of Herrera, in his report to Congress written about February 15, admitted that Texas completely separated from Mexico was independent and could not be recovered except by a long and costly war; but he declared that the very existence of Mexico was involved in the question of annexation to the United States, which he hoped to prevent by a plan of recognition with the support of England and France (for which there was no longer any chance). On March 21, on receipt of Almonte's dispatch of February 28, he became much excited, but was somewhat calmed by the advice of the British and French ministers. On March 28, in a note of somewhat moderate tone, he informed Shannon that diplomatic relations could not be continued since the "grave offense" which the United

States had inflicted and which Mexico had endeavored to fore-stall. In this note he repeated the protest against annexation, and stated that Mexico, confident of the justice of its cause, would "oppose with all the earnestness which becomes its honor and sovereignty" and at the cost of all its power and resources. He also addressed a note to the members of the diplomatic corps at Mexico City, protesting against the American action. Shannon (before the arrival of official information of the final action of his government on the question of annexation) replied on March 31, stating that the United States, having given friendly assurances of a wish to adjust amicably all questions including that of boundary, and regretting the refusal of the Mexican government to arrange difficulties in order to preserve peace, left to Mexico the determination of whether friendly relations should be preserved, or disturbed by injurious conflict. On April 2, Cuevas, in a brief note, stated that he had nothing to add—that he abstained "from entering on new discussion which the present interrupted relations do not admit of."

Shannon, in a dispatch of April 6 to Buchanan, reporting that he was preparing his baggage for the first caravan to Vera Cruz and would be detained about two weeks, while hoping to receive news from Washington (from which he had received nothing since November), stated in conclusion: "It is utterly useless to think of arranging our difficulties with Mexico in an amicable way for the present. All here are clamorous for *war*." On May 8 he requested Cuevas to furnish the required pass-port so that he could leave Mexico, stating that since the gov-ernment of Mexico had discontinued all diplomatic intercourse, his further stay could be no longer useful to his country. On the following day he received the passport with information that the Minister of War had been requested to order an escort for May 14.

Already the President, through Secretary Buchanan, disap-proving Shannon's course in the Rejon correspondence of the preceding October and November, regretting his lack of mod-eration of language and his assumption of the high responsibil-ity of suspending all diplomatic intercourse with the Mexican government without previous authority of his own government, and desiring a friendly adjustment of all questions in dispute, had granted him (on March 29) a leave of absence to return home and thus had prepared the way for the selection of a more suitable minister for the delicate negotiations required.[27]

Meantime, steps had been taken to complete the annexation of Texas and its organization into an American commonwealth. A. J. Donelson, the American minister, who had known something of Houston's shifting views, probably had reason to doubt whether President Jones, under the influence of the English and French project for settlement of difficulties with Mexico (to forestall annexation) would prefer the proposed annexation to independence. That "General" Duff Green had met with some difficulty in efforts to influence the situation after December 8 is indicated by the following dispatch of Donelson to Calhoun under date of January 27, 1845:

"When I reached Washington on the 4th. Jany. General Green's Exequatur [as consul at Galveston] had been revoked, and the worst possible feeling existed between him and the President. The Secy of State, Mr. Allen had prepared a statement of the case to be transmitted to his agent at Washington city. I immediately sought an interview with the President, and suggested to him the course which was adopted, of stating the circumstances to me, and of permitting the explanations to pass through me to you. My first object was to remove the impression that General Green was authorized to commit his Government in any manner; and then to relieve him of the charge that he had sought to corrupt and menace the President, for you will perceive that the statement of Mr. Allen makes this charge distinctly, and thus created a personal issue which under the circumstances could not have failed to injure the character of the General.

"I consider the General, although out of his sphere, and not defensible as a Consul, as not obnoxious to the severe imputation cast upon him. He was full of zeal in the cause of annexation, and mistaking the sense in which the members of Congress heard his project for the defence of the Western frontier and the invasion of Mexico, approached the President too familiarly, but without a doubt of his disposition, if not to concur in his views, at least to consider them in a spirit of kindness. Whereas in truth his movements were watched with suspicion from the beginning, and before he was aware of it, he was involved in the responsibility of measures, contemplating a serious change in the policy of the Republic, employing the Indians of the U. States and Texas in the invasion of Mexico and revolutionizing the country from the Rio Grande to the Pacific under the flag of Texas.

"You will see that in my note to Mr. Allen of the 6th inst., whilst I expressed my disapprobation of such projects, I treated the affair as not involving the United States, and reaching to no higher importance than what was due to private character and opinion. In this point of view it has been settled, and after a full disclaimer on the part of Gen Green of all intention to approach the President in the manner charged, the personal imputation on his character has been withdrawn to an extent that ought to be satisfactory to him. . . ."[28]

On April 28, and again on May 6, Donelson wrote that the Texan people considered the question settled in favor of annexation. On June 15, in reply to Donelson's urgent requests for troops, Buchanan wrote that if the Texan Congress favored annexation by a nearly unanimous majority the President would feel obligated to repel a Mexican invasion which, however, Texas ought to repel if necessary before the action of the convention. On the same day, Secretary Bancroft ordered General Taylor from Fort Jessup to the Sabine in preparation for advance to the Rio Grande after annexation had been accepted by the Texan convention. By the end of July, Taylor, embarking his infantry at New Orleans, was encamped at Corpus Christi, just west of the Nueces River. President Jones of Texas declared that Donelson, and Captain Stockton (in command of the United States naval forces off the Texan coast) were trying to force a war with Mexico and that Taylor's advance to Corpus Christi was not justified by any serious danger to Texas from Mexico. On June 16, Jones submitted to a special session of the Texan Congress the alternatives of annexation or independence on the basis of the Mexican agreement of May 19 (which had been received through the French and British legations). On June 21, the joint resolution was adopted unanimously and the proposed preliminary treaty with Mexico was rejected. On August 28, the Texas convention unanimously adopted a state constitution which was subsequently adopted by popular vote (in October, 1845); and on February 16, 1846, the new state government was inaugurated.[29]

Whether the annexation would result in war depended largely upon the decision and action of Mexico concerning the final settlement of the much disputed question, and concerning the adjustment of unpaid American claims which, together with a disputed boundary, now furnished a basis of American expectations for acquisition of California.

Associated with problems of Texas and of claims, in Tyler's administration, was the new problem of California resulting in part from increasing American interests in the Pacific and in Oregon.

American interest in California, which had begun a half century earlier, largely increased in the decade before 1845. At a very early date, California harbors attracted American traders who were engaged in the fur trade between the Northwest coast and China. The American ship *Columbia,* which sailed from Boston and in 1789 collected furs along the Northwest coast, attracted the attention of Spanish officials in Mexico who instructed subofficials in California to seize the vessel with its crew if it should arrive at the port of San Francisco. In October, 1796, a fur-trading vessel from New England arrived at Monterey and began a trade which was continued thereafter, and early in the nineteenth century New England whalers began to visit California harbors for supplies for the homeward journey. As early as 1799 American whalers who visited the California coasts were a source of complaint of the local governor, because of their "arrogant boldness." Among the early American participants in the coast fur trade was William Alden Gale who established the first business house in Monterey in 1824 and married into a California family. In 1826, Jedediah S. Smith of the Rocky Mountain Fur Company led the first overland expedition into California, starting from near Great Salt Lake and reaching the Pacific at San Diego. Later, Americans, as other foreigners, in violation of the Mexican decree of May 1, 1828, which required a passport for entrance to Mexican territory, entered California first as trappers or hunters, or traders, or possibly as deserters from foreign ships, and later as settlers. By 1830, the arrival of trappers and adventurers over the passes of the Sierras, although small in number, alarmed the suspicious Mexican officials who suspected plots to seize the port of San Francisco. Later, in the revolution of "native sons" of California against Mexican policy in California, the American foreigners were used to support the local cause—as in 1836. In 1836-37, American residents and sailors, led by Isaac Graham, a native of Tennessee, who had a "moonshine" distillery near San Juan, supported a successful revolution led by Alvarado and Castro against Governor Gutierrez at Monterey. For their service, which was possibly given with the hope of transferring California from Mexico to the United States, they received lands and cattle.[30]

In August, 1835, probably at the suggestion of American whaling interests, the Jackson administration unsuccessfully planned to negotiate with Mexico for acquisition of northern California, including San Francisco Bay. After August, 1839, wandering Americans found a refuge at the interior frontier camp or fort established on the Sacramento by the German-Swiss adventurer, Sutter, who as a naturalized Mexican citizen obtained a large grant of land in June, 1841, and soon was regarded as a possible leader in making California a second Texas—for he had little respect for the Mexican rulers. In 1840, about 100 other Americans and Englishmen were arrested in the seaports and imprisoned, with plans for banishment, and about 50 were sent to San Blas; but following complaints of the American and British ministers in Mexico, many of them, including Graham, were allowed to return by July, 1841.

American interests were further increased under Tyler's administration. By 1841 companies of overland immigrants, American frontiersmen influenced by economic distress resulting from the panic of 1837, or attracted by rumors of climate and soil, began to arrive; and for the next five years their number was increased, largely by the overflow from the Oregon trail. Early in 1841, after Mexico had become alarmed at reported emigration of Americans to California and had shown a disposition to arrest them, the American government, at the suggestion of Ellis at Mexico, decided to appoint a consul at Monterey on the Pacific and selected an American citizen named Thomas O. Larkin. Waddy Thompson, in his first dispatch, under date of April 29, 1842, after announcing that the Texan prisoners would probably be released soon, repeated to Webster the suggestion of the appointment of a consul at Monterey. At the same time he suggested to Secretary Webster that Mexico might be willing to cede with Texas the Californias, upon which both France and England had their eyes, which was all that the American government could expect to get for American claims, and which would give America the ascendency on the Pacific where it had large whaling and commercial interests. In his enthusiasm he proposed to take an excursion to California in the following summer if he could get Webster's approval. Stating that California with harbors far better than the Columbia River "would furnish places of refuge for the numerous American fishing vessels and that no doubt by internal communication with the Arkansas and other western streams it would secure the trade of the Indias and the whole Pacific," he added as other inducements for the acquisition: "California is destined to be the granary of the Pacific. It is a country in which slavery is not necessary, and, therefore, if that is made an objection, let there be another compromise. France and England both have had their eyes on it. The latter has yet. She has already control of the Sandwich Islands, of the Society Islands, New Zealand, etc., and through the agency of that embryo East India monopoly, the Hudson Bay Company, she will ere long have a monopoly of the commerce of the Pacific and not an American flag will float on its coasts. . . . I would like to be instrumental in securing California."

On July 30, reporting that Santa Anna was making "preparations" for the invasion of Texas and Yucatan and was expecting British aid in case of a war with the United States, and that an agent of the Mexican government was in England with plans for a mortgage or sale of Upper California, he expressed the hope that England would not be allowed to engage in any of the wars on this continent as a party; and, expecting instructions on the subject of claims, he suggested that, as Mexico was anxious to avoid collision with the United States, the time was most favorable for proper settlement. On August 16, following new cases of injuries to Americans and after the appointment of General Almonte as minister to Washington, he recommended that negotiations for settlement of pending difficulties should be conducted at Mexico City in order to avoid excuses for delay, and suggested that under existing "doubt as to our probable movement" the time was propitious to bring differences to a point. Both then and again on November 8, he suggested the expediency of a pacific policy.[31]

Webster, with the approval of the President, authorized Thompson to negotiate with Mexico a treaty providing for payment of her debt by cession of California, and also took steps to sound the British government concerning its views on the proposition. When he received Thompson's suggestion, he was in the midst of negotiations with Ashburton from whom he obtained an opinion that England would make no objection to the proposed American acquisition from Mexico of territory from 42° southward including the port of San Francisco. Hoping to secure San Francisco through the good offices of the British government, in a letter (of January 29, 1843) to Everett relating to the Oregon boundary, he suggested a tripartite arrangement between Great Britain, Mexico and the United States, and expressed the view that Mexico must cede Upper California to the United States for a sum sufficient to pay claims of American citizens and British citizens against Mexico. He also sounded the Mexican minister at Washington, and again renewed the proposal for a cession at the date of the ratification of the claims convention, March 29, 1843, after news from California concerning the hasty action of Commodore Jones at Monterey had lessened the chances of the success of further attempts at negotiation.[32]

The action of Commodore Jones—which embarrassed Webster and furnished him another problem on Mexican relations (his last one)—arose from Bocanegra's rash distribution of his extraordinary circulars to the diplomatic corps on May 12, 1842, and their publication in the Mexican newspapers, creating the popular impression that war might soon follow. Jones, in command of a small squadron of the American navy on the west coast of South America, early in September, 1842, at Callao, received from John Parrott, the American consul at Mazatlan, a newspaper clipping of one of the circulars and a statement that American pressure of claims might result in a break in diplomatic relations. At the same time, a day before a British squadron suddenly left Callao, he received a clipping from a Boston newspaper which erroneously stated that Mexico would cede California to Great Britain as payment for the British debt. After a conference with the American minister to Chile, he sailed to Monterey, California, imprudently demanded the surrender of the Mexican fort there, and on October 20 took possession—in order to prevent a British attempt at occupation of the territory (!). Learning from the American consul, Thomas O. Larkin, that the rumors had no basis, he properly lowered the American flag and evacuated the place. On December 19, Bocanegra, in a note to Thompson, demanded reparation. The latter replied that the act of Jones, for which the Mexican menacing circular was partly to blame, was not authorized by the American government which would promptly disclaim the action and make the proper reparation. In January, 1843, Webster issued through Thompson a disclaimer and regret; but, feeling that the over-zealous Jones had intended no insult to Mexico, he refused to agree to the punishment which the angry Almonte demanded—although Jones was temporarily relieved from his command after his return home late in 1844.[33]

That the Americans, seeking a maritime outlet from the interior, would eventually obtain possession of San Francisco, whatever the fate of Monterey, was predicted by Sir George Simpson in his narrative of his visit to California in 1842.

Meantime, the Santa Anna government (which had succeeded that of Bustamante in 1841) at the suggestion of Vallejo, an able California leader, had sent (in 1842) a military governor, the boastful Micheltorena, in command of 300 convicts to enforce the Mexican laws in California and to prepare to repel American invasion in case of war with the United States; but the experiment was unsuccessful,* and by the close of 1844 American immigration (without Mexican passports and neither aided nor hindered by the American government) was increasing, while the Mexican government, without money, awaited the outcome of the Texan question. A Mexican decree of July 14, 1843, directing the expulsion of native Americans from California, Sonora, Sinaloa and Chihuahua, was first delayed by the prompt and vigorous protests of Waddy Thompson, and was never published or applied in California. Thompson, who, late in December, 1843, first heard of the order, promptly presented protests in an angry correspondence, demanded prompt replies, and finally got the order rescinded by resort to "ultima ratio" of diplomacy (on December 30), demanding his passports (which he was afraid would be sent to him). In his note of December 31 to Bocanegra, admitting Mexico's unquestionable right to punish or prevent sedition clearly proven, but denying the right to make arrests on vague and unfounded suspicion, he declared that Mexico must be held responsible "to make good" the charges made against American citizens, or to repair whatever damages might be suffered.[34]

In October, 1843, Thompson welcomed an opportunity to sound Mexican policy concerning California. On October 3 he had a long interview with Santa Anna, who seemed to anticipate collision with England and said that the only damage expected was a blockade which he regarded as the best possible thing for Mexico (because Mexico had no need of commerce!).

* In November, 1844, Micheltorena, after falsely promising the rebellious native Californians under Alvarado and Castro to discharge his convict troops, enlisted the aid of Sutter and a body of American and English frontiersmen and drove the native rebel forces from San José. Following them southward he, with his native Mexican troops, surrendered to Alvarado's troops at Cahuenga, near Los Angeles, on February 20, 1845, and returned to Mexico, resulting in the change of the capital from Monterey to Los Angeles, where Castro became military governor. The customhouse at Monterey was placed in charge of Alvarado. In 1845, American immigrants were still received by the careless Mexican authorities of California with great friendliness. (Bancroft, *California*, IV, 604.)

At the close of the interview, he suggested that if war occurred England would probably seize some portion of their territory, California perhaps, and retain it. "Oh," said he, "your Government will not permit that, will it?" Thompson replied that he was not authorized to speak on the subject, but that "we should not like to see California pass into the hands of any great maritime power." Unable to obtain any definite result in negotiations for a new claims convention, or to obtain prompt payment under the earlier convention, he still said "we must not press them too hard." A few days later, reporting another conversation with Santa Anna in which the latter had stated his intention to sell California to the United States in case of any danger of British seizure of the province, he asked for instructions to guide him in case a prospect should occur.[35]

Plans for the proposed negotiation for California, which had been spoiled in Mexico by the news of Commodore Jones' seizure of Monterey in 1842, were revived in connection with the question of claims in April, 1844, and in consideration of the American-Texan treaty of annexation of April, 1844, which designedly left undefined the boundaries of Texas. On April 8, 1844, Ben E. Green, encountering great difficulty with Mexico in the negotiations concerning American claims, and doubting the wisdom of a mild and conciliatory tone, declared to Calhoun: "However, we have nothing to gain with her unless we should end by getting California and thereby secure a harborage for our shipping on the Pacific and one of the finest countries on the globe." [36]

One cause of Green's interest in California at that time is indicated by the following extract from a private letter which he wrote to Calhoun three days later (on April 11): "Mr. [Lansford W.] Hastings of Ohio [a leader of emigration to Oregon in 1842] who about three months ago passed through here on his return to the United States, told me *in confidence* that California is on the point of following the example of Texas, and declaring for independence. The whole project has been well digested and reduced to a systematized plan. . . . A German named Suter [Sutter?] is at the head of the movement and the execution of his plans is only delayed for the return of Hastings with a reinforcement of settlers. . . . Nor is California

the only portion of Mexican territory in danger. Sonora has been for
2 years the theatre of civil war, and will probably join with the
movement in California. The provinces bordering on Texas have long
envied the freedom from forced loans and martial law enjoyed by
their neighbors. New Mexico has been on the eve of a revolution
ever since the Santa Fé trade was closed, and there is reason to believe
that Tamaulipas were it not for her exposed position would at once
throw herself into the arms of Texas." [37]

In the following October, Duff Green, who had been appointed consul at Galveston and was in Mexico City advising
and aiding Shannon in negotiations there, in a private note to
Calhoun wrote as follows:

"I am convinced that it is *impossible* to obtain the consent of this
Government to the cession to the United States of Texas, California
or any other part of the domain of Mexico. I will proceed to give you
my reasons. The policy of Santa Anna since the time of Poinsett,
has been to foster a prejudice against the United States (as to apprehension of invasion) and make his countrymen believe that he alone
can protect them. . . . He left here September 12 on belief that the
army would pronounce against Congress and make him Protector for
life. . . . When I arrived a crisis had been reached and a pronunciamento was expected. Santa Anna whose old wife was not yet a month
in the grave had married a young girl of 16 by proxy whom he was
to leave to save the country whenever the army should pronounce
against Congress and call him from his retirement. . . . In such a
state of party division, it is regarded as treason to sell any part of
the public domain. I have learned too that Mexican bond holders
in England hold a mortgage on the Californias to secure the payment
of 26 millions of deferred debt. . . . The war against Texas is the
pretense on which both parties are seeking office. Any party (in power)
selling Texas or California to the United States would be driven
from office. . . . I believe there is but one way by which our Government can get all it desires—and more, but I reserve my views for
personal explanation until after I have visited Texas. . . . It is important that you should obtain a copy of the British deed of mortgage
on the Californias subject to foreclosure in 1847—as the possession of
California will necessarily command the settlements on the Columbia.
. . . We have nothing to hope from Mexico." [38]

The American policy was doubtless influenced by the renewed rumors (late in 1844) of a possible transfer of Upper

California to Great Britain through some arrangement with British holders of Mexican bonds, and to prevent its occupation by any other power as a result of Mexico's neglect and weak hold upon it. These rumors resulted from suggestions or proposals of British naval officers, or consuls or traders; but the British government under Aberdeen, however much it would have been displeased with a transfer to any other power, did not countenance the proposals for the establishment of a British protectorate, and James A. Forbes, British consul at Monterey in 1845, told Larkin, the American consul, that the rumored British negotiations were false and that he had been reprimanded by the British government for introducing the subject in September, 1844.[39]

REFERENCES

1. *Texan Diplomatic Correspondence*, I, p. 546, and II, p. 737, (Rp. Am. Hist. Ass'n., 1908); *Sen. Doc. 325*, 27-2, pp. 3-8.
2. *11 Mexico, Despatches*, No. 2, June 6, 1842 (Enclosure); Pamphlets, *Political American*, Vol. 117, No. 9, Library of Congress.
3. *11 Mexico, Despatches*, No. 2, June 6, 1842.
4. Pamphlets, *Political American*, Vol. 117, No. 9, Library of Congress.
5. *15 Mexico, Instructions*, pp. 179-82, (No. 9) June 9, 1842; *Ib.*, pp. 182-200, (No. 10) July 8, 1842; *Webster's Works*, VI, pp. 445-57.
6. *15 Mexico, Instructions*, pp. 200-201, No. 11, July 13, 1842; *Webster's Works*, VI, p. 459.
7. *House Doc. 271*, 28-1, pp. 69 and 71; *15 Mexico, Instructions*, p. 221, No. 26, Jan. 31, 1843.
8. *Texan Diplomatic Correspondence*, I, pp. 567 and 633; *Niles' Register*, LXIV, p. 97.
9. *House Doc. 271*, 28-1, pp. 18-22, 25, 37, 43-48, 80 and 95; *Texan Diplomatic Correspondence*, II, pp. 232 and 239-43.
10. *15 Mexico, Instructions*, pp. 264-67, (No. 51) Oct. 20, 1843; *Ib.*, pp. 268-73, (No. 53) Nov. 18, 1853; *Sen. Doc. 341*, 28-1, pp. 89-94.
11. *15 Mexico, Instructions*, pp. 261-62, (No. 46) Sept. 27, and (No. 47) Sept. 23, 1843; *11 Mexico, Despatches*, (No. 31) Oct. 29, 1843.

12. *4 Mexico, Notes* (to the Department), Nov. 3, 1843, and Dec. 11, 1843; *Sen. Doc. 341*, 28-1, pp. 94-103.
13. G. L. Rives, *The United States and Mexico,* I, pp. 599-602; *4 Mexico, Notes* (to the Department), Feb. 16, 1844.
14. *House Doc. 271,* 28-1, p. 96; G. L. Rives, *The United States and Mexico,* I, p. 607.
15. *House Doc. 271,* p. 54; *4 Mexico, Notes* (to Department), Apr. 22, 1844; *6 Notes to Mexico Legation,* Apr. 2, 1844; *Rp. Am. Hist. Ass'n, 1899,* II, pp. 578-79; *House Doc. 271,* 28-1, pp. 50-53.
16. *15 Mexico, Instructions,* p. 225, (No. 30) Mar. 3, 1843; *Ib.,* pp. 268-73, (No. 53) Nov. 18, 1843; *11 Mexico, Despatches,* Nov. 20 and Nov. 30, 1843; *House Docs. 19 and 158,* 28-2.
17. *15 Mexico, Instructions,* (No. 39) June 9, 1843; *12 Mexico, Despatches,* Apr. 8, (No. 5) May 30, and (No. 15) July 30, 1844.
18. *Ib.,* (No. 5) May 30, (Private) June 17, (No. 8) June 21 and June 25, 1844; *Rp. Am. Hist. Ass'n, 1899,* II, pp. 960-61 (Calhoun Correspondence); *Sen. Doc. 1,* 28-2, pp. 52-89.
19. *15 Mexico, Instructions,* pp. 297-305, No. 1, June 20, and No. 6, Sept. 10, 1844; *Sen. Doc. 1,* 28-2, pp. 23 and 29.
20. *12 Mexico, Despatches,* Aug. 28, (No. 2) Sept. 21, (No. 4) Nov. 12, 1844; *Sen. Doc. 1,* 28-2, pp. 48-52; *House Doc. 19,* 28-2, pp. 8- .
21. *12 Mexico, Despatches,* No. 4, Nov. 12, 1844 (Enclosure); *Niles' Register,* LXVII, 262-65, Nov. 8, 1844; *Rp. Am. Hist. Ass'n,* II, p. 995 (Calhoun Correspondence).
22. *12 Mexico, Despatches,* No. 8, Jan. 16, 1845.
23. *Ib.,* No. 4, Nov. 12, 1844; *Rp. Am. Hist. Ass'n, 1899,* II, pp. 975-80, 991-95, 1003 and 1006-07 (Calhoun Correspondence).
24. *Ib.,* pp. 982-86.
25. *Sen. Doc. 1,* 29-1, pp. 32 and 38; *4 Mexico, Notes* (to the Department), March 6, 1845.
26. *Sen. Doc. 1,* 29-1, p. 39; *15 Mexico, Instructions,* No. 10, March 29, 1845.
27. *12 Mexico, Despatches,* (No. 10) Apr. 6, and (No. 11) June 23, 1845; *15 Mexico, Instructions,* pp. 324-26, No. 10, March 29, 1845.
28. *Rp. Am. Hist. Ass'n, 1899,* II, pp. 1019-20.
29. *Sen. Doc. 1,* 29-1, pp. 40, 42 and 56; *House Doc. 60,* 30-1, p. 80.
30. H. H. Bancroft, *History of California,* I, p. 445; *Ib.,* II, p. 32; *Ib.,* III, pp. 151-52; Cardinal Goodwin, *The Trans-Mississippi West,* Ch. XIII; T. H. Hittell, *History of California,* II, pp. 73, 74; *Sir George Simpson's Narrative,* I, pp. 326-27.

31. *10 Mexico, Despatches*, (No. 41) Feb. 25, and (No. 43) May 20, 1841; *11 Mexico, Despatches*, (No. 1) Apr. 29, (No. 4) July 30, (No. 5) July 30, and (No. 7) Nov. 8, 1842.

32. *Am. Hist. Review*, XVI, Jan., 1911, p. 293; *11 Mexico, Despatches*, No. 1, Apr. 29, and May 9, 1842; J. Q. ADAMS, *Memoirs*, XI, p. 347; *Webster's Writings*, XIV, pp. 394-96.

33. *15 Mexico, Instructions*, p. 220, No. 25, Jan. 17, 1843.

34. *11 Mexico, Despatches*, No. 38, Jan. 4, 1844 (and enclosures); WADDY THOMPSON, *Recollections of Mexico*, p. 227; *Sen. Doc.* 390, 28-1; BANCROFT, *California*, IV, p. 380.

35. *11 Mexico, Despatches*, Oct. 3 and 14, 1843.

36. *12 Mexico, Despatches*, Apr. 8, 1844.

37. *Rp. Am. Hist. Ass'n, 1899*, II (Calhoun Correspondence).

38. *Ib.*, pp. 975-80, Oct. 28, 1844.

39. JAMES ALEXANDER FORBES, *California*, p. 146; EPHRAIM D. ADAMS, *British Interests and Activities in Texas, 1838-1846*; H. H. BANCROFT, *History of California*, V, p. 70.

CHAPTER V

POLK'S POLICY: ACQUISITION OF CALIFORNIA

Polk, although nominated for the presidency as a "dark horse," was already well known by his public service. He had been a member of the lower house of Congress from 1825 to 1839 and had served as speaker from 1835 to 1839. For a term of two years, 1839-41, he was governor of Tennessee. As President he appointed for the office of Secretary of State a man of wide experience, James Buchanan—who had served as a member of the lower house of Congress (1821-31), minister to Russia (1831-34), and as a member of the United States Senate (1834-45).

The Polk administration, after adopting the policy of Tyler and Calhoun as to the annexation of Texas, recognized that its chief foreign policy was the peaceful acquisition of California by which it planned to adjust all difficulties with Mexico. With the hope of peaceful adjustment, it first sought to reestablish diplomatic relations, which had been suspended by the withdrawal of Almonte and discontinuance of communication with Shannon in March, 1845. To convince Mexican authorities of its interest to restore friendly relations, and to ascertain whether they would receive a new minister, it sent as confidential agent on a peace mission William S. Parrott, long a resident of Mexico (first as a dentist and later as a merchant), who sailed from New York (on April 3) on the ship which carried Almonte and family back to Mexico. The nature of Parrott's mission is indicated by his instructions of March 28, in which Secretary Buchanan said:

"Your success may mainly depend upon your perfect command of temper in all situations and under all circumstances, and upon your

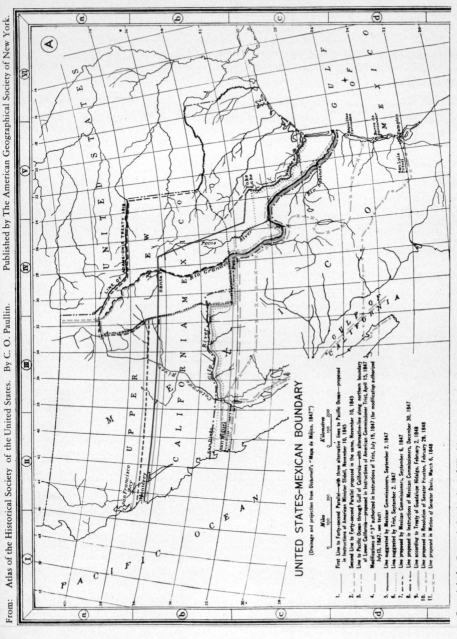

UNITED STATES-MEXICAN BOUNDARY

(Drainage and projection from Disturnell's "Mapa de Méjico. 1847")

1. ———— First Line to Forty-second Parallel—with three alternative lines to Pacific Ocean—proposed in Instructions of American Minister Slidell, November 10, 1845
2. ———— Second Line to Forty-second Parallel proposed in the same, November 10, 1845
3. ———— Line to Pacific Ocean through Gulf of California—with alternative line along northern boundary of Lower California—proposed in Instructions of American Commissioner Trist, April 15, 1847
4. ———— Modifications of "3" authorized in Instructions of Trist, July 19, 1847 (for modification authorized July13, 1847, see text)
5. ———— Line suggested by Mexican Commissioners, September 2, 1847
6. ———— Line suggested by Trist, September 2, 1847
7. ———— Line proposed by Mexican Commissioners, September 6, 1847
8. ———— Line proposed in Instructions of Mexican Commissioners, December 30, 1847
9. ———— Line according to Treaty of Guadalupe Hidalgo, February 2, 1848
10. ———— Line proposed in Resolution of Senator Houston, February 29, 1848
11. ———— Line proposed in Motion of Senator Davis, March 6, 1848

prudence in refraining from the least intimation that you are a Government agent, unless this should become indispensable to the success of your mission. The trust confided to you is one of a delicate and important character and may involve the public peace. . . . You will proceed without delay by the most expeditious route to the City of Mexico, and will there ascertain the temper and tone of the present Mexican Government towards the United States. Such previous knowledge is necessary to enable you to decide upon the manner of approaching the chief officers of that government. . . . The great object of your mission and that which you will constantly keep in view in all your proceedings, is to reach the President and other high officers of the Mexican government and especially the Minister of Foreign Affairs, and by every honorable effort to convince them that it is the true interest of their country, as it certainly is, to restore friendly relations between the two Republics. Should you clearly ascertain that they are willing to renew our diplomatic intercourse, then and not till then you are at liberty to communicate to them your official character and to state that the United States will send a Minister to Mexico as soon as they receive authentic information that he will be kindly received. . . . Whilst you ought not to conceal that the reunion of Texas with the United States is already decreed and can never under any circumstances be abandoned, you are at liberty to state your confident belief that in regard to all unsettled questions, we are prepared to meet Mexico in a most liberal and friendly spirit. . . . If upon your arrival at Vera Cruz you should find that the government of Mexico have commenced open hostilities against the United States, you will return immediately. In that unfortunate event we shall be prepared to act promptly and vigorously. . . ." [1]

On May 22, 1845, Parrott reported that the weak government of Herrera, after learning of President Jones' call for a Texas convention, had summoned a special session of the Mexican Congress to meet on July 1. At this session, Cuevas, Minister of Relations, on July 16, reported the failure of the British plan of settlement by negotiation of the Texan question, the expectation that the Texan people would ratify the action of the Texas Congress on the question of annexation to the United States, and the surprising news that American troops under Taylor would advance from Fort Joseph by way of New Orleans and Galveston to the Rio Grande. On July 21, he proposed to Congress a resolution that, following the Texan acceptance of annexation or American invasion of Texas with troops, "it

shall declare that the nation is at war with the United States
. . . for the purpose of saving the integrity of Mexican territory within its ancient limits." Herrera, although his administration was severely opposed for its willingness to bargain for
the independence of Texas, was elected President for Santa
Anna's unexpired term (to February 1, 1849), and on September 14 appointed a new ministry. His new Minister of Relations
was Pena y Pena, an able lawyer of moderate means, who, according to Parrott, was expected to favor an amicable arrangement with the United States, but who soon found it expedient
to join in protests of non-forgiveness of the "unparalleled offense" of their "perfidious" neighbors. On August 16, and again
on August 26 and August 29, Parrott reported to Buchanan
that he had reason to believe that the Herrera government, embarrassed by the insubordination of Paredes which threatened
a civil war, would welcome an American minister.[2]

President Polk, who doubted whether he could rely upon the
support of Congress in a war which was threatened by existing
conditions, was greatly pleased with the prospect of a satisfactory adjustment of all pending problems—claims, boundaries
and California—by negotiation. On September 16, with the
unanimous approval of the cabinet, he decided that the reopening of diplomatic relations was expedient, and, at the suggestion
of Buchanan, appointed as envoy extraordinary and minister
plenipotentiary, John Slidell of New Orleans, who, by his
knowledge of Spanish and his courtesy, moderation and prudence, was regarded as well qualified for the secret mission—the
chief purpose of which was to secure a permanent boundary by
the purchase of Upper California and New Mexico for fifteen
to twenty million dollars if possible, or for forty millions if
necessary. The mission was delayed by the decision first to learn
officially whether the Mexican government would receive a
minister to negotiate for the *amicable* adjustment of all causes
of complaint and the cultivation of friendly relations. On September 17, stating that the President was "anxious for peace,
although prepared for war," Buchanan instructed Black, the
American consul in Mexico, to ascertain officially whether the

Mexican government would receive an envoy "intrusted with full power to adjust all questions between the two governments," and he stated that such an envoy would immediately be sent if Mexico agreed to receive him.[3]

Meantime, influenced by information received from Mexico through Parrott in April and May, and from Texas through Donelson in June, Polk regarded the situation as critical. General Taylor was ordered to be ready to march from Natchitoches. On June 24, Bancroft confidentially informed Commodore Sloat of the Pacific fleet of the President's policy to secure a peaceful settlement with Mexico, and instructed him to avoid any act which might be regarded as one of aggression. On July 11 he had sent similar instructions to Commodore Conner of the Gulf fleet. In preparation for compulsion, if necessary, however, the administration had ordered Taylor, in May, 1845, to cross the Sabine to protect Texas, and later (in June) he ordered Conner in case of war to take possession of Tampico and (if his force was sufficient) the castle at Vera Cruz, and also ordered Sloat to seize San Francisco Bay and other Pacific ports.[4]

Several months later, on October 17, 1845, before the departure of Slidell for Mexico, and after receiving from Thomas O. Larkin (the American consul at Monterey, California) a report (of June 6 and June 10) that the people of California were apathetic and (in some cases) disloyal to Mexico, and that possibly France and Great Britain had designs on the provinces, Secretary Buchanan suddenly became more active in regard to California. Notifying Larkin of his appointment as a confidential agent in California, he also furnished him a clear statement of the American policy to acquire California without war but with the spontaneous wish of its people, and to secure the cooperation and good will of the Californians without compulsion or improper influence and with the hope that they would resist any attempt to transfer California (without their consent) either to Great Britain or France. Duplicates of the instructions to Larkin, and others to Sloat, were forwarded on November 1 through Mexico by way of Vera Cruz by a special messenger,

Lieutenant A. H. Gillespie of the United States Marine Corps, who had secret instructions to communicate promptly with Sloat at Mazatlan and with Larkin at Monterey, and to assist the latter in executing his instructions concerning the peaceful policy in California.

The substance of Larkin's instructions appears in the following extracts:

"The future destiny of that country is a subject of anxious solicitude for the Government and people of the United States. The interests of our commerce and our whale fisheries on the Pacific Ocean demand that you should exert the greatest vigilance in discovering and defeating any attempts which may be made by foreign governments to acquire a control over that country. In the contest between Mexico and California we can take no part, unless the former should commence hostilities against the United States, but should California assert and maintain her independence, we shall render her all the kind offices in our power, as a sister Republic. This Government has no ambitious aspirations to gratify and no desire to extend our federal system over more territory than we already possess, unless by the free and spontaneous wish of the independent people of adjoining territories. The exercise of compulsion or improper influence to accomplish such a result would be repugnant both to the policy and principles of this Government. But whilst these are the sentiments of the President, he could not view with indifference the transfer of California to Great Britain or any other European Power. The system of colonization by foreign monarchies on the North American continent must and will be resisted by the United States. It could result in nothing but evil to the colonists under their dominion who would naturally desire to secure for themselves the blessings of liberty by means of republican institutions, whilst it must prove highly prejudicial to the best interests of the United States. Nor would it in the end benefit such foreign monarchies. On the contrary, even Great Britain, by the acquisition of California, would sow the seeds of future war and disaster for herself, because there is no political truth more certain than that this fine Province could not long be held in vassalage by an European Power. The emigration to it of people from the United States would soon render this impossible. . . . Whilst I repeat that this Government does not, under existing circumstances, intend to interfere between Mexico and California, it would vigorously interpose to prevent the latter from becoming a British or French Colony. In this they might surely expect the aid of the Californians themselves. . . . You will not fail by every safe opportunity to keep this Department advised of the progress of events in California and the disposition of the authorities and people towards the United States and other Governments. We should, also, be pleased to learn what is the aggregate population of that province and the force it can bring into the field. . . ." [5]

Gillespie also carried a message to Captain John C. Fremont, a native of Georgia, who, through the influence of Joel Poinsett, had been appointed an officer in the United States corps of topographical engineers, and who, after his marriage to one of Senator Benton's daughters, had been appointed (1842) to command the expedition to improve communications with Oregon. In June, 1845, Fremont had started on his third government trans-Rocky expedition by way of Great Salt Lake and the region later named Nevada, and, by the end of October, was encamped at Walker Lake from which he crossed the Sierra Nevada to Sutter's Fort in January, 1846.

Nearly a month after the October instructions to Larkin, another step was taken to restore diplomatic relations with Mexico. On November 10, Buchanan received through Parrott, in person, the written reply of Pena y Pena of October 15 stating that, although Mexico was "deeply injured by the United States through the acts committed by them in the department of Texas, which belongs to this nation," his government, while it had a "firm decision to exact adequate reparation" for its injuries, was "disposed to receive [from its 'adversary'] the commissioner [of dignity and prudence] . . . who may come to this capital with full powers to settle the present dispute in a peaceable, reasonable and honorable manner"—provided the United States would withdraw the naval force from near Vera Cruz. At the same time he received Black's statement that Pena y Pena had orally asked him to explain that the expressions referring to the grievances of Mexico were used only to reconcile the opposition which was ready to condemn every act of the government.[6]

The President, evidently pleased, promptly notified Slidell to await instructions at Pensacola. On the same day (November 10) Buchanan sent the secret instructions which had been drafted several weeks earlier (on September 22), and approved by the cabinet on November 8, and which mentioned as the chief purposes of the mission: (1) The speedy and satisfactory settlement of American claims which had so long been evaded and delayed, and which probably could be satisfied only by American assumption in return for Mexican agreement to the Rio Grande as the boundary of Texas (an additional $5,000,000 was proposed for a boundary which would include all of New Mexico); (2) The acquisition of Upper California, which was only nominally dependent upon Mexico, and might be subject to the designs of Great Britain and France, and for which the President was willing to pay an additional $25,000,000 (or $5,000,000 for the northern part with a boundary north of Monterey). On November 19, Buchanan sent additional instructions urging that negotiations should be hastened and brought to a conclusion without delay, to enable the President to submit the question of claims to Congress before the close of its next session—so that, in case of failure, the administration could adopt prompt and energetic measures to redress injuries sustained by American citizens. Soon thereafter the American ships of war were temporarily withdrawn from before Vera Cruz.[7]

Slidell, followed by Parrott, who had been appointed secretary of the legation and who was accompanied by Lieutenant Gillespie en route to Monterey with dispatches for Larkin and Sloat, reached Vera Cruz on November 29 and Mexico City on December 6, 1845. He learned through Black that Pena y Pena was much disturbed by his early arrival, fearing that his appearance at the capital might cause the opposition to start a revolution against the Herrera government which was regarded as too willing to proceed with the negotiations with the American government for adjustment of difficulties. His "secret" plans were announced in opposition broadsides which declared that his reception by Herrera would be an act of treason. Following his prompt note presenting his credentials, he encountered the usual delays; and finally, on December 20, was officially informed by the Minister of Relations that, according to the decision of the government council, he could not be received under his commission as envoy extraordinary and minister plenipotentiary, and that he should get new credentials as a mere "commissioner." Through the British minister, Bankhead, he was informed that the Mexican government, if it succeeded against the Paredes revolt, would attempt to renew diplomatic relations. Although surprised at the "bad faith" and excuses of the Mexican government, he avoided any word or act which might furnish an excuse for ending the efforts at adjustment by peaceful negotiation.

While awaiting further instructions, Slidell reported to his government the political situation which, before he left the capital (in January, 1846), resulted in the successful revolt of Paredes—under the plan of San Luis, largely based on the protest against the consent of the peace-planning cabinet to the presence of Slidell who was accused of designs to buy Mexican independence. He saw little hope for any change in policy by the new cabinet, of which Castillo y Lanzas was Secretary of Relations and General Almonte was Secretary of War (and general leader). He saw no hope unless the cabinet should be disappointed in its expectations of war between the United States and England or feel the pressure of financial embarrassment. At Jalapa, to which he retired by January 20, he awaited further instructions for renewal of negotiations. Directed by Buchanan to refuse to restrict his negotiations to adjustment of Mexican claims to rights over Texas, to insist upon the connection of American claims with boundary adjustments and to demand his passports if Mexico refused to receive him, on March 1 he made a last effort to preserve peace by asking Castillo to receive him under the credentials presented. Receiving a final negative reply (of March 12) which, influenced by domestic politics, repeated previous reasons or pretexts for declining to receive him or to discuss a settlement at that time, on March 17 he repeated the American defense of its Texan policy and demanded his passports—which Castillo promptly enclosed on March 21 with a parting statement of the needlessness of further discussion of historical arguments as to Texas which had already been "successfully refuted." [8]

From his note of March 17 to Castillo the following is quoted: "As it is the intention of the Undersigned, in conformity with his instructions, to return to the United States with the least possible delay, embarking at Vera Cruz, he has now to request that he may be furnished with the necessary passports, which he will await at this place.

"As Y. E. has advanced no new arguments in support of the refusal to receive the undersigned as Envoy Extraordinary and Minister Plenipotentiary he will abstain from commenting upon that portion of the note of Y. E. which with a mere difference of phraseology presents, substantially the same reasoning as that urged by Mr Pena y Pena in his note of 20th December last. . . . The United States can confidently appeal to the history of the events of the last twenty years, as affording the most conclusive refutation of the charges of usurpation, violence, fraud, artifice, intrigue and bad faith so lavishly scattered through the note of Y. E."

In his dispatch to Buchanan, on the following day, he said:

"The Mexican Government cannot shift the responsibility of war upon the United States, by assuming that they are the aggressors. A plain unanswerable fact responds to all the subtleties and sophistries by which it is attempted to obscure the real question. That fact is, the presence in Mexico, of a Minister of the United States, clothed with full power to settle all the questions in dispute between the two nations, and among them that of Texas. . . . With what reason does Mexico attribute to the United States the desire of finding a pretext to commence hostilities? . . . With these avowed intentions on the part of Mexico . . . with what fairness can she complain of precautions having been taken by the United States to guard against the attacks with which they have been menaced, so far at least, as their very moderate peace establishment, would permit them to do so. Are they patiently and meekly to abide the time when Mexico shall be prepared to strike with due effect the threatened blow?" [9]

The stubborn attitude of Mexico, which seemed unreasonable, seems to have had no basis in expectations of foreign aid. Mexico, after 1844, found little hope in its efforts to secure foreign assistance in case of a war in which it would risk a loss of more territory. On February 20, 1845, Gorostiza, the Mexican minister at Madrid, informed his government that the Spanish government, although its attention had been attracted by the "ambitious tendencies" shown by the "dishonorable conduct" of the Washington government, could not be expected to undertake any effective action to prevent the "usurpation which is projected." From London, Tomas Murphy, in the following August, was disappointed that Lord Aberdeen advised Mexico to refrain from declaring a war which he feared would result in the American conquest of the Californias. In the following October, he reported that Great Britain, fearing the dangers of war with the United States, was unwilling to take any bold stand unless with complete understanding with France whose people were not willing to support British policy. He said that Aberdeen, whom he had expected to attract by a British colonization scheme in California, had become increasingly unwilling to intervene in any way between Mexico and the United States (and especially not before the amicable adjustment of the Oregon dispute).[10]

Possibly Mexico still had some reason for expectation that the Oregon controversy would result in an Anglo-American war. In July, 1845, the British minister at Washington declined the American proposal to settle the Oregon question by extension of the line of 49° to the Pacific. Polk refused to propose or to invite any other proposition and in December, in a message asserting his adherence to a new Monroe Doctrine forbidding European interference with American annexations on the American continent, recommended to Congress that notice should be given for termination of the joint occupation treaty of 1827— a resolution which, after much debate, the House approved by a vote of 163 to 54 on February 9, 1846, and which the Senate finally adopted by a vote of 40 to 16 on April 16, 1846, resulting in a joint resolution of April 23, 1846. Thereafter, however, Anglo-American adjustment came quickly. The draft treaty submitted on June 6 by Pakenham was (on June 10) submitted by Polk to the Senate which on June 12 advised its acceptance. On June 15 it was signed, indicating that the United States was now free to settle its problems with Mexico and to obtain California.

At Washington, Polk was preparing for more aggressive action toward Mexico. In his annual message of December to Congress, after referring to Almonte's protest and the consequent rupture of relations with Mexico which had since continued an attitude of hostility threatening war, he stated the steps which he had taken to protect and defend Texas from invasion, and the efforts to ascertain the real designs of the Mexican government and whether it was disposed to adjust in a friendly way the pending differences by renewal of diplomatic negotiations. On January 13, 1846, a day after the arrival at Washington of the first news of Slidell's failure, Taylor was ordered to advance from Corpus Christi to the Rio Grande and Commodore Conner was ordered to return with his fleet to waters near Vera Cruz; and Slidell was promptly notified by Buchanan that the President would be prepared to act with vigor whenever he obtained authority of Congress.

A month after the first news of Slidell's failure, American policy was influenced by an unusual and interesting incident. On February 13, the President had a call from a Colonel Alexander A. Atocha, a naturalized American citizen who had long resided in Mexico, who had just returned from a visit to his ambitious old friend Santa Anna * and represented that the latter, who was in constant communication with his friends in Mexico and had sanctioned the Paredes revolution, might soon return to power in Mexico and that he was favorable to a treaty ceding to the United States the Mexican territory east of the Rio Grande and north of San Francisco for $30,000,000 (with $500,000 in hand)—but indicated that any settlement

---

* Before the United States "board of commissioners" under the treaty of Guadalupe Hidalgo, Alexander A. Atocha, friend of Santa Anna, presented a claim for alleged wrongful expulsion from Mexico (against the protest of the American minister, Shannon)—a claim which the commissioners rejected. Failing later to secure a reversal of the decision before a committee of the United States Senate, he continued to appeal to Congress until he finally obtained the passage of an act, in February, 1865, to refer his case to the Court of Claims, which in 1873 rendered in favor of his administratrix a judgment for $207,852.60. [Moore, International Arbitrations, Vol. 2, pp. 1264-65.]

with the Mexican government could be affected only after a show of strong American force, and that Slidell should withdraw from Jalapa and, from an American vessel, make his demands for payment of claims. On this confidential communication, proposing that Santa Anna would cede territory for American assistance in securing his return to Mexico and recommending a vigorous military policy, Polk based a large part of his later plans. To his cabinet he proposed that Slidell should be instructed to request an immediate reception by Paredes and, if refused, should be authorized to demand from aboard an American vessel of war off Vera Cruz the immediate settlement of all claims—after which the President should be authorized by Congress to obtain redress by aggressive measures. On March 12, the date on which the Mexican government rejected Slidell's new demand to be received, Buchanan, who had opposed the adoption of Atocha's advice and had managed to delay action, finally sent new instructions directing Slidell to press Paredes for his final decision, but before terminating his mission to inform him discreetly of the willingness of the American government to relieve any financial embarrassment of his administration upon the assurance of the negotiation of a treaty for the settlement of boundaries. Slidell had left Mexico before he received these instructions.[11]

On April 7, 1846, the President received the news of the final Mexican refusal to receive Slidell and obtained consent of the cabinet to submit to Congress a message in favor of war-like action—which, however, was twice prudently delayed, first to await news of Slidell's departure from Mexico, and then to await news from England.

Already the conditions on the Rio Grande threatened to result in an early military clash. Taylor, on March 28, 1846, had reached the Rio Grande opposite Matamoros, which soon showed considerable signs of hostility. On March 20, he had been met about 20 miles east of the Rio Grande by a small party of Mexican cavalry which warned him to stop but retreated without opening fire. On April 12, he received from General Ampudia a letter threatening war, and demanding his prompt retirement to the Nueces during the negotiation of the pending question. Declining to discuss international questions, he replied that he was obeying orders, and that "the responsibility for war would rest with those who rashly commenced hostilities." [12] Soon thereafter he ordered a blockade at the mouth of the river, against which Ampudia protested, and which resulted (on April 23) in a proclamation of a "defensive war" by Paredes who claimed that hostilities had been begun by the United States on the Rio Grande and were threatened at Monterey in Upper California. On the following day, he was formally notified by Arista (Ampudia's successor) that hostilities were begun; and with the Mexican troops who crossed the river his scouting party had a skirmish resulting in its capture on April 25. He promptly (April 26) notified Washington by messenger that hostilities had begun. His messenger reached the President on May 9, the day of the battle of Resaca de la Palma, and was promptly presented to the cabinet which agreed that a war-like message should be sent to Congress.

On May 8, in a conversation with Slidell, Polk agreed with the latter's statement that the only remaining course for the United States toward Mexico was to act with promptness and energy in demanding redress for wrongs and injuries, and said he would soon submit the matter to Congress. On May 9, with plans to communicate with Congress on May 12, he asked the cabinet whether he should then declare war for which there was ample cause, and received an affirmative reply from all except Bancroft who preferred to await an act of hostility by Mexican forces. On the following day, after the arrival of the news of the Mexican advance across the Rio Grande and the skirmish with Taylor's troops, he took advantage of the lucky psychological moment to prepare his war message to inform Congress that "war exists by act of Mexico."

On May 11, he submitted to Congress his skillful war message, which, after reviewing the unsuccessful mission of Slidell for reconciliation, and referring to the wrongs unredressed, stated that Mexico, by invasion of American territory and shed-ing of American blood on American soil and by proclamation of hostilities, had begun war, and requested Congress to put at his command the means of prosecuting it with vigor in order to hasten the restoration of peace and the renewal of negotiations for amicable adjustment. In his message, which was accompanied by certain correspondence of Slidell in regard to unpaid claims, he declared that "the grievous wrongs perpetrated by Mexico upon our citizens throughout a long period of years remain unredressed, and solemn treaties, pledging her public faith for this redress, have been disregarded." In the correspondence submitted, he included Slidell's note of December 24, 1845, to the Mexican Minister of Relations, complaining that the Mexican government, in considering the amended but unratified convention of November 20, 1843, had "interposed evasions, difficulties, and delays of every kind," and had never decided to accept it, although pressed by the American government to do so, and that meantime additional claims had reached the "enormous aggregate of $8,491,603." The authority and means requested by his message the President promptly obtained by a bill approved by the House on May 11, by a vote of 173 to 14 and by the Senate on May 12, by a vote of 42 to 2. The President's action and that of Congress doubtless met with general approval on the ground that war was justified by the delinquencies and hostilities and obstinacy of Mexico. The President had correctly reached the conclusion that the British government, which had decided to accept the American proposal for the settlement of the Oregon question, would refuse to interfere in favor of Mexico which had persisted in a dangerous and unreasonable policy against friendly British warnings.

Suspecting that England or France might join Mexico to prevent American acquisition of Mexican territory, Buchanan (on the day war was declared) drafted a circular letter to American diplomatic agents announcing that conquest was not the purpose of the war, although Polk clarified his mind by the statement that America, in making peace, would, if practicable, obtain California and other Mexican territory "sufficient to indemnify our claimants on Mexico and to defray the expenses of the war."

Although, on May 21, 1846, General Scott, on the basis of information received from Colonel A. Butler and J. T. Mason concerning the rainy season in northern Mexico, wrote Marcy that there was no advantage in beginning military operations before October, the administration promptly prepared for military movement. The cabinet decided that New Mexico and Upper California should be seized at once, and for this purpose Colonel S. W. Kearney was ordered to move from Fort Leavenworth over the Santa Fé trail with five companies, later followed by additional force. By confidential orders of June 3, he was directed to proceed, after the occupation of New Mexico, by way of the Gila River to the Pacific coast to take possession of California. On June 12, Taylor, who on June 4 had been instructed to conciliate the Mexican people by a proclamation asserting that their institutions and rights would be protected, was ordered to advance beyond the Rio Grande "toward the heart of the enemy's country"—on lines including the "high road to the Capital of Mexico," which, however, Taylor did not think should be included in the operations from the northern frontier (to cut off the northern provinces). By the end of August, Bancroft was still undecided as to the possibility of landing an expedition at Vera Cruz to advance against Mexico City.[13]

Promptly after his message, the President, through Bancroft, (on May 13) confidentially ordered Conner of the American naval force near Vera Cruz to allow Santa Anna to enter Mexico freely if he attempted to do so. Early in June (in the presence of Slidell) he sent Slidell's nephew, Commander Alexander Slidell Mackenzie, to Havana with secret instructions to communicate with Santa Anna—to sound him and to notify him of the American determination to prosecute with vigor the war "to resist the attack of the intrusive military Government of General Paredes," but to terminate hostilities speedily and to "bring all matters of dispute to an early and amicable adjustment." He also directed Mackenzie to say that the President, hoping for the overthrow of the military despotism of Paredes which had risen by cherishing hostility to the United States, would be glad to see the restoration of Santa Anna to power in Mexico and would consent to a suspension of active hostilities provided Santa Anna should announce his readiness to treat through an American minister of full powers who would be ready to offer liberal terms in ready money for the establishment of a natural permanent geographical boundary advantageous to both countries—ceding to the United States territory which was probably already in American military possession. Mackenzie arrived at Havana June 5; and, on June 7, at a long conference, he read the views of Polk to Santa Anna who expressed appreciation for the order allowing him to return to Mexico, recalled pleasant memories of General Jackson in Washington, regretted the errors of his past administration, and finally agreed to enter into negotiations to arrange a peace as proposed by means of a treaty of limits. To attain the object desired, Santa Anna proposed that General Taylor should advance to Saltillo, and urged the importance of a seizure of Vera Cruz. The military suggestion Mackenzie reported to Taylor about July 20, and his full report of the conversation reached Washington on August 3.[14] In accord with Polk's orders, Santa Anna was allowed to pass the American blockade.

Meantime, Polk, who after his visit from Atocha (and before hostilities) had consulted with several members of Congress concerning the proposed offer of an immediate payment of a half million or a million dollars following the treaty of peace, had adopted Benton's policy of negotiations combined with military force. On July 27, 1846, in accord with Webster's advice in his speech to the Senate on June 24, and with the approval of Benton, he sent through Buchanan to the Mexican Minister of Relations a note proposing to send to Mexico a minister with full powers to conclude a treaty of peace for adjustment of all questions in dispute; but, at the same time, he notified Commodore Conner, through whom the note was transmitted, that acceptance by Mexico should not result in the suspension of the blockade at Vera Cruz.[15] On August 4, without any mention of Atocha or Mackenzie, in a confidential message he urged the Senate to consider the proposal for compensation to be paid immediately on the signing of the proposed treaty. The Senate, after a secret debate, approved the general plan for the appropriation by a vote of 33 to 19.*

The administration awaited with interest the political news from Mexico which indicated the return of Santa Anna to power. Paredes, who had become temporary President under the plan of San Luis Potosi, and whose chief unofficial adviser was believed to be Lucas Alaman of known monarchist tendencies, was very unpopular by March, 1846, resulting in the resignation of Gorostiza as Secretary of the Treasury, and of Almonte, Secretary of War, soon thereafter. The revolution in favor of Santa Anna was opened on May 20 at Guadalajara and completed at Mexico City on August 4 by General Salas, who assumed the executive power until the arrival of Santa Anna. The latter, following his reception as a hero at Vera Cruz, sent to the capital Rejon and Almonte, who had accompanied him from Havana. In the new cabinet which was immediately formed Rejon returned to his old place as Minister of Relations and Almonte became Secretary of War. Although by August 16 Santa Anna was President *ad interim* of Mexico and in command of the Mexican forces, he declined the offer of peace negotiations proposed by Buchanan's note of July 27 which was submitted to him promptly after his arrival at the Mexican capital. The most urgent problem of the new coalition cabinet was the policy in regard to war, for which Mexico had not prepared. Almonte, as minister at Washington in the spring of 1844, had created false hopes of security by confidentially assuring his government that parts of the United States could not be relied upon to support a war against Mexico. The Mexican government, "long" on faith in Mexico and "short" on knowledge of American conditions, was not yet ready to nego-

---

* On October 8, two days before the date set for adjournment of Congress, Polk sent to both houses a proposal for an appropriation of two million dollars for the purpose proposed. In the House the bill, amended by the Wilmot Proviso, was approved by a vote of 85 to 79, but in the Senate a vote was prevented by the debate on the Wilmot Proviso which continued until adjournment.

tiate openly for peace, especially not on the basis of refraining from discussion of the causes of the war. Therefore, Rejon wrote Buchanan, on August 31, that it had decided to submit to the next session of the Mexican Congress Buchanan's note of July 27.

Buchanan, with no intimation of loss of confidence in Santa Anna's earlier assurances, replied on September 26, two days before the capture of Monterey, and twenty-five days after the arrival of the news of the American occupation of California, that Polk would "wait with patience and with hope"; but he also gave notice that until the Mexican government offered terms of peace the war would be continued with vigor. On October 11, the entire cabinet refused to approve Taylor's agreement to an armistice, which had been made on the basis of Ampudia's statement that Santa Anna had declared himself favorable to peace; and, on October 13, Marcy directed Taylor to give notice that the armistice would cease at once.[16]

Polk, on September 19, on reading Rejon's reply of August 31 (to the overtures of peace) indicating that the assurances of Santa Anna were not reliable and that peace could be gained only by conquest, decided that Tampico should be seized at once and proposed that Taylor, instead of paying for supplies, should levy contributions (a plan which Taylor found impracticable). Soon he began to plan an expedition to Vera Cruz, against which Conner had maintained a strict blockade. On November 14, Tampico was peaceably occupied by Conner's forces. On November 7, following the election, Polk was urged by Benton to seize Vera Cruz immediately, preparatory to a bold and rapid movement from there to attack Mexico City by way of the old Cortez route with peace commissioners at army headquarters ready to act promptly whenever needed.[17] On November 19, he offered the command of the Vera Cruz expedition to General Scott who promptly accepted.

The decision upon the campaign from Vera Cruz toward Mexico City was probably influenced by news of Sloat's occupation of northern California and of Castro's retreat which reached the Washington government on September 1. For this occupation Fremont had helped to prepare the way by his surveying expedition. From Sutter's Fort about January 15, 1846, with a small party of his men without passports, he went by water by way of San Francisco Bay to Monterey to obtain consent of the Mexican authorities to visit the settlements in order to refit and obtain necessary supplies for his corps of armed geographical surveyors while they were resting. Encountering no objection from Commanding General Castro and other officers, whom he visited in company of Larkin, and to whom he explained the purpose of his government survey—to determine (in the interest of science and commerce) the nearest practical route from the United States to the Pacific—about February 20 he collected his men near the site of San José from which he marched them to the Pacific near Santa Cruz and thence southward along the shore to the Salinas. On March 5, he was ordered by Castro to retire northward at once to the uninhabited region of the San Joaquin. Refusing to obey, he began to build a log fort on the summit of Gavilan Peak, almost within sight of Monterey—causing much excitement there and great anxiety to the American consul, who promptly notified the American consul at Mazatlan (John Parrott) and also Secretary Buchanan. Later, threatened by a superior force, he retreated "growlingly" eastward, reaching Sutter's Fort by March 21. From Sutter's Fort, moving northward, by May 8 he reached Klamath Lake, Oregon, where he was overtaken on May 9 by Lieutenant Gillespie who on April 17 had arrived at Monterey by way of the Sandwich Islands from Mazatlan and on April 28 had reached Sutter's. Apparently he received from Gillespie a secret message from Washington—possibly from Senator Benton who, by invitation, had held a conference with President Polk on October 24, 1845, on the application of the Monroe Doctrine in California.[18] Returning with Gillespie, he reached the American settlements on the Sacramento, north of Sutter's, by May 24, apparently with the intention of returning home by way of the Colorado—an intention from which he was diverted by the influence of Gillespie's persuasions or by the wishes and hopes of the suspicious American settlers who encouraged him to defy Castro. Here, while he was contemplating the humiliation of his recent retreat from a Mexican force, his camp soon became a center for alarming rumors of an impending attack by troops under Castro, who was really planning to attack the Spanish Governor Pico at Los Angeles. Early in June, with his knowledge and consent, an adventurous American party under Ezekiel Merritt captured a large number of horses which had been obtained for Castro from Vallejo at the inoffensive Mexican settlement of Sonoma. On June 11, another party under Merritt, again starting from Fremont's camp (and either by his permission or his direction), captured the village; and, after a long debate, it declared California independent and raised the "bear flag." Expecting the approach of Castro, who believed that he had aided the insurgents, Fremont joined the insurgent force at Sonoma on June 23, and by July 4 planned to conquer all of California. The complications which might have arisen from the action of the Americans at Sonoma were averted by the arrival of Commodore Sloat. Until June, Sloat, at Mazatlan, had not considered that the news from the Rio Grande would justify his occupation of any part of California under instructions of June 24, 1845. In explanation he said: "Neither party have declared war." On June 7, however, learning of the American blockade of Vera Cruz, he sailed for Monterey which he reached on July 2 and occupied on July 7 by landing 250 men, raising the American flag, and proclaiming the annexation of California to the United States. Under his orders the shores of San Francisco Bay were occupied on July 8 (three weeks before he was succeeded by Stockton), resulting in the abandonment of the "Bear" republic at Sonoma and, also, in the retreat of Castro to Los Angeles. The dramatic entrance of Fremont into Monterey at the head of his 160 frontiersmen was witnessed and reported by Admiral Seymour of the British navy who was making a friendly call there. Stockton, who succeeded Sloat on July 23, took Fremont and his men into the service of the navy and ordered them to Los Angeles. Near the latter village, on January 13, 1847, by the so-called treaty of Cahuenga, Fremont received the surrender of the entire native force. This treaty, which divorced California from Mexico and resulted in the flight of Castro and Pico to Mexico, Stockton reluctantly confirmed; and, on August 17, at Los Angeles, he proclaimed the authority of the United States and appointed as commandant Lieutenant Gillespie who, although soon driven northward by a local revolution, was regarded as the local authority until the arrival of Colonel Kearney from San Diego on January 10, 1847.[19]

Two days after the appointment of Scott to command the Vera Cruz expedition, Polk, anxious to smooth the way to peace, authorized Buchanan to appoint as confidential agent to Mexico the owner of the New York *Sun*, Moses Yale Beach, who after leading in the establishment of various means to increase the rapidity of news service, including the New York Associated Press, had decided upon a trip to Mexico with plans to improve the transmission of military and other news. In his instructions of November 21, Buchanan said:

"You are well aware that the President had resorted to every honorable means to avoid the existing war; and whilst prosecuting it with vigor, he has been anxious, ever since its commencement, to make peace on just and honorable terms. It is known that you entertain the same desire in all your conduct and conversation in Mexico, you ought to keep this object constantly in view.

"The trust thus confided to you is one of great delicacy and importance. In performing the duties which it imposes, great prudence and caution will be required. You ought never to give the slightest intimation to any person, either directly or indirectly, that you are an agent of this Government, unless it may be to Mr Black, our Consul at Mexico, or to some high officer of that Government, and to the latter only after you shall have clearly discovered that this may smooth the way to peace. Be upon your guard against their wily diplomacy and take care that they shall obtain no advantage over you." [20]

The errand of Beach was halted (in March, 1847) by a false report that Santa Anna had defeated General Taylor.

By March, 1847, Polk felt more certain of the support of his policy by Congress. Late in December, 1846, he received from Calhoun a warning that he would not vote to ratify any treaty of peace with Mexico which contained a restriction upon the

extension of slavery to the territory acquired by the treaty.
To avoid or postpone a controversy or a discussion on this subject Senator Berrien of Georgia proposed a self-denying amendment (to the appropriation bill) declaring that the war against
Mexico "ought not to be prosecuted with a view to the dismemberment of that republic" or with a view to the acquisition or
conquest of any portion of its territory—a resolution which
Webster supported but which never reached a vote. For this
amendment Cass proposed a substitute declaration that the war
should be vigorously prosecuted and that a reasonable indemnity
should be required of Mexico. Calhoun, who opposed an invasion
into the heart of Mexico, proposed a policy of the establishment
of a new "defensive boundary line" to which all military operations should be restricted. A bill for the proposed appropriation
of $3,000,000 "to enable the President to conclude a treaty of
peace, limits, and boundaries" on liberal terms of adjustment
was reported in both houses of Congress in January, 1847, and
was approved by the Senate on March 2 by a party vote of 29
to 24, and finally by the House on March 3 (a day before adjournment of Congress) by a vote of 115 to 82 after elimination of the proposed Wilmot Proviso. This approval was coincident with the retreat of Santa Anna southward from Buena
Vista toward San Luis Potosi and toward the Mexican capital
which was disturbed by a contest of factions. It was also coincident with the occupation of Chihuahua by Doniphan, and
the sailing of Scott for the anchorage off Vera Cruz (from
which he occupied the city and the castle on March 29).

Meantime Polk had received new "evidence" that Mexico was
ready for peace negotiations. On January 12, 1847, Buchanan,
at a cabinet meeting, reported that Colonel Atocha with
friendly letters from Santa Anna, and from Almonte and Rejon, had again visited Washington, apparently to restate the
views of Santa Anna and to open the way for negotiations by
suggesting boundary terms (the Rio Grande with a neutral
zone eastward to the Nueces, and upper California for fifteen
or twenty million dollars), and to propose a suspension of the
blockade at Vera Cruz during the negotiation of peace com-

missioners. Polk, although unwilling to favor the Mexicans by raising the blockade or by relaxation of military movements before the conclusion of a treaty, and refusing to agree to the proposed neutral zone east of the Rio Grande, suggested Walker's view of a boundary due west from near the mouth of the Rio Grande, on the parallel of 26°, to the Pacific. He approved, and probably directed, Buchanan's draft of a letter of January 18 to the Mexican Minister of Relations submitting a more specific peace plan than the earlier proposition of July, 1846, proposing that each government send to Havana, or to Jalapa, one or more distinguished commissioners with full powers to conclude peace, and providing for suspension of hostilities and blockades at the discretion of the American commissioners. Finding that the cabinet approved the plan, but was opposed to the suggestion to send Senator Benton in command of the army and also with full diplomatic power, he proposed to send Buchanan as commissioner to conduct the negotiations.[21] By March 20, Atocha, who carried to Mexico City Buchanan's note and a statement of the American conditions of peace, returned to Washington with Minister Monasterio's reply requiring as a preliminary condition of negotiations for adjustment the raising of the blockade and complete evacuation of territory, and also the understanding that Mexico would maintain the independence and integrity of the republic.

Polk, although disappointed at the reply brought by Atocha from Santa Anna's government, was encouraged by the military news from Buena Vista and Vera Cruz to renew with his agreeable cabinet (on April 10) a discussion of proposed preparation for negotiations for peace by sending a commissioner to army headquarters on the road to the Mexican capital. Embarrassed by different factions of his party, he found impossible the appointment of any prominent suitable man, except Buchanan, without offending others. He would have appointed Buchanan as sole commissioner if he had received from Mexico any assurance of probable early and speedy negotiation which would have shortened the time of his attendance at army headquarters. Buchanan, recognizing the difficulties, suggested as a compromise or substitute commissioner, with special and well-defined instructions, the loyal chief clerk of the Department of State, N. P. Trist, a student of law under Jefferson and the husband of Jefferson's granddaughter, for a time private secretary of President Jackson and later American consul for eight years at Havana where he learned Spanish and, incidentally, was accused of aiding the slave trade. He obtained consent of the cabinet to send Trist secretly with a project of a treaty prepared by Secretary Buchanan and approved by the cabinet, and with authority to offer it to the Mexican government for signature with the understanding that, if it was not accepted, Buchanan would probably go as commissioner later. This project of April 15 was similar to the earlier instructions to Slidell: a boundary by which the United States would obtain all of New Mexico and both Upper and Lower California and a grant of the right of transit across the Isthmus of Tehuantepec similar to that obtained across Panama by treaty with New Granada of 1846. For this the maximum payment authorized by Polk (besides the assumption of American claims) was thirty million dollars (or twenty million dollars for New Mexico and Upper California alone, without Lower California and the Tehuantepec transit which were estimated at five millions each).[22]

Three months later, learning that the boundaries of New Mexico were uncertain, Buchanan sent Trist additional instructions concerning the boundary west of the Rio Grande:

"The more I reflect upon the subject," said he, "The better am I convinced of the importance of running the boundary line between the Rio Grande and the Gulf of California along the thirty second parallel of North Latitude. We cannot learn that the boundaries of New Mexico have ever been authoritatively and specifically determined, and the difficulties might hereafter arise between the two Governments in ascertaining where the south western angle of New Mexico is situated. A conversation with Major Emory since the date of my last despatch, has convinced me still more of the importance of this modification. . . . It is not intended that you shall make the parallel of 32°, instead of the River Gila, a sine qua non; but yet it is deemed of great importance that you should obtain this modification, if it be practicable.

"If lower California cannot be obtained, then the line on the parallel of 32° might be extended to the Pacific ocean, taking care, in that event, to secure to our citizens, in accordance with your original instructions, 'in all time to come, a free and uninterrupted access to and from the ocean through the Gulf of California from and to their possessions north of the said division line.' " [23]

On April 15, Buchanan, with cabinet approval, delivered to Trist his credentials, including letters to General Scott and the commander of the Gulf naval force, requesting them to facilitate the mission and to suspend hostilities if a treaty should be concluded. On the following day Trist departed by way of New Orleans on his "profoundly secret" mission, news of which, however, soon leaked through the *National Intelligencer* and other federal papers"—resulting in great vexation to the President.[24]

Scott, who on April 6 had prepared to move inland from Vera Cruz, on April 18 captured the summit of Cerro Gordo (twenty miles east of Jalapa) at which Santa Anna had concentrated his forces after leaving Mexico on April 2, following his assumption of the presidency with extraordinary powers to raise money for his support, but without any authority to alienate national territory. He captured useful supplies and dispersed the panic-stricken Mexican army, opening the road to Mexico City. On May 11, he published at Jalapa a conciliatory manifesto stating the pacific desires of the American army, creating there a favorable impression. On May 15, part of his force under Worth took possession of the peaceable city of Puebla after a skirmish with a body of cavalry commanded by Santa Anna who on May 11 had arrived from Orizaba, and on May 18 returned to Mexico City where he found that the terrified and impotent Congress while giving him unlimited power in the conduct of the war had restricted his power to make peace or to enter into communication with the American government.

At Jalapa, Scott received from Trist a letter (dated at Vera Cruz on May 6) enclosing orders of the War Department of April 14 stating that the President had commissioned him to be in readiness at military headquarters for convenience in receiving expected Mexican proposals for peace. He also received a sealed note from the Department of State to the Mexican Minister of Relations to be forwarded by flag of truce, but which furnished him with no explanation of the real objects of the Trist mission except the statement that "Mr. Trist is clothed with such diplomatic powers as will authorize him to enter into arrangements with the Government of Mexico for the suspension of hostilities" and to notify General Scott for the President "whenever he should decide that the contingency had arisen." With his suspicions aroused and pride wounded by what he regarded as a degradation, he promptly declined to forward the sealed communication to the Mexican government. On May 21, a week after Trist's arrival at Jalapa, Scott, upon whom he had not called, received from him a tactless and abusive criticism of the refusal to obey orders and a renewal of the demand to forward the note. On May 29, he replied from Puebla, where he had begun a long wait for reinforcements, expressing doubt of Trist's authority to negotiate a treaty and adding his thanks to the President "for not degrading me by placing me in any joint commission with you." On June 4, in a letter to Marcy, he asked to be recalled.

The President was much displeased with the controversy. He privately threatened to remove Scott from the chief command. Through Marcy and Buchanan, he promptly (June 15) reminded the irascible gentlemen disputants of the folly and public danger of the personal quarrel (which delayed for six weeks or more the possibility of negotiations with Mexico).[25]

Meantime, on June 6, Trist sent from Puebla a letter to the British minister, Bankhead, at Mexico City, asking him to inform the Mexican Minister of Relations of his presence at Scott's headquarters on a diplomatic mission and to deliver Buchanan's note. Bankhead promptly sent Edward Thornton, an attaché of the British legation, on June 10. In separate interviews with Trist and Scott (who were not yet on speaking terms), Thornton referred to the conditions affecting the desired peace negotiations. He promptly returned and delivered

Buchanan's note to Bankhead. The latter, after learning that Santa Anna would be pleased to receive the letter, and knowing that there was a large peace party in Congress, delivered it through Ibarra (the new successor of Baranda as Minister of Relations) who courteously replied that the subject would have the early attention of Congress (at a special session). This reply Thornton delivered to Trist at Puebla on June 24. The action of Trist, invoking the aid of the British minister, Buchanan later approved as justified under the circumstances. Trist, with whom Scott had become happily conciliated by June 26, received from secret agents of Santa Anna the suggestion that the appointment of peace commissioners for official negotiations could be facilitated by a *secret* payment of a million dollars at the signing of the treaty and ten thousand on account *at once* to overcome opposition in Congress. This suggestion of a way to open negotiations to end the war without further march on Mexico appealed to Trist and also to Scott who, from his secret-service fund, immediately paid the ten thousand dollars—an act for which he and Trist were later rebuked by their superior officers in the government, but which Scott justified as a purchase of information or of services voluntarily tendered. Santa Anna, however, fearing that he could not at that time control Congress in proposed peace negotiations for which it refused to assume any responsibility, suggested that he must first allow the American army to advance to a position near the capital before he could undertake negotiations for peace.[26]

Scott, therefore, prepared to advance on the capital with a view to some new victory or advantage which would lead to peace. After the arrival (on August 7) of Franklin Pierce with reinforcements from Vera Cruz, he severed all communications with his base at Vera Cruz and, like the earlier conquistadors, advanced boldly with his enthusiastic army and well-organized staff to the conquest of Mexico. Among the many members of his staff were Captain Robert E. Lee, Lieutenant P. G. T. Beauregard, and Lieutenant George B. McClellan, and others of later distinction. In three days his army reached the summit of the mountain pass from which it suddenly obtained a spectacular

view of the valley of Mexico. On August 11, it halted at Ayotla
in front of the Mexican lines. On August 20, it won by flank
attack the great victory at Contreras (or Padierna) resulting
in the successive occupation of San Angel, Coyoacan, San Antonio and Churubusco (on the same day) and, also, resulting
in the flight of Santa Anna to the palace in despair with a disposition to open negotiations for an armistice.

On the evening of August 20, Scott was visited by Thornton, attaché of the British legation, accompanied by Macintosh,
the British consul general, who had long lived in Mexico and
who held a Mexican concession for the Isthmus of Tehuantepec
and other interests which made him eager for peace for which
he evidently sought to prepare the way. Late on the same night,
Pacheco, the new Minister of Relations, requested the British
minister, Bankhead, to transmit to Trist a note expressing the
anxiety of Santa Anna to discuss preliminaries of the establishment of relations and to receive Trist at once as a plenipotentiary for that purpose. The skillfully worded note was cleverly
put in the form of a reply to Buchanan's note of April, and
it stated that Santa Anna, with a view to a definite treaty
within a year, had decided to hear the mutually advantageous
proposals which Trist had been instructed to make. On the following day the note was delivered by General Mora y Villomil
through General Scott, who, with an unimaginative mind and
with little knowledge of Santa Anna's character, saw in the
written proposals a fulfillment of the assurances received by him
at Puebla and was glad of the opportunity to halt his victorious
corps at the gates of the capital, although he had no written
request for an armistice.[27]

In an imprudent note to Santa Anna, Scott himself, before
the arrival of Mora, had proposed an armistice which became
effective August 24. This note he now sent without mention
of Mora's later oral proposals. "Too much blood has already been
shed in this unnatural war," he said. "In order to open the way
. . . to enter into negotiations, I desire to execute on reasonable terms a short armistice." Santa Anna, replying with insolent tone through Alcorta, his Secretary of War, said: "The

proposition of an armistice to end this scandal has been acceded to with pleasure." The resulting armistice, which was arranged at the Macintosh residence without any requirement of material guarantees from the defeated Mexicans, and with provision for continuance during the period of negotiations, proved entirely futile. At the beginning, the Mexican government contemplated negotiation on a basis of Mexican victory(!).[28]

The gullible Trist at first expected Santa Anna promptly to agree to a treaty and to omit no effort to secure its ratification by Congress—which had already been called into special session by Santa Anna on August 21, but evidently had dispersed to prevent a quorum, leaving the executive to assume undivided responsibility. On August 27, he promptly presented to the Mexican commissioners (whose selection had caused some delay) the project of a treaty which he had brought from Washington. Pacheco countered (on August 29) by instructing the Mexican commissioners (1) to ask the motives and objects of the war, the basis of the demands, and the basis of American retention of Texas, and (2) to demand, as a *sine qua non,* the natural Nueces boundary, indemnity for Texas, no other cession, release from all American pecuniary claims, restoration of all fortifications, and withdrawal of all American troops immediately following the signing of the treaty, and (3) to suggest the American payment of the expenses of the war (!). These impossible requirements were cancelled by order of Santa Anna to prevent the resignation of the Mexican commissioners which would have resulted in the termination of the armistice. In an informal conference of September 2, finding that the chief difference was the boundary, Trist proposed to abandon Lower California and the Tehuantepec transit in order to secure an agreement for a cession of New Mexico with Upper California for a pecuniary consideration; and he also made the surprising offer to submit to the Washington government the question of the Nueces. These terms Santa Anna promptly rejected, probably by the advice of General Tornel and Señor Pacheco and possibly of Rejon and others. On September 6, the

Mexican commissioners made a counter proposal offering to grant California territory north of 37° and suggesting an invitation to Great Britain to guarantee the faithful performance of the treaty.

The reason advanced for refusing a territorial cession beyond Texas is interesting:

"The Mexican Republic, willing to agree in consideration of the proper indemnity, to the claims of the Washington Government to the territory of Texas, has done away with the cause of the war and the war must cease since there is no longer any title for continuing it. No right has until now been alleged by the Republic of North America to the other territories coming within Article 4 of Your Excellency's draft, neither do we believe it possible that any can be alleged. It, therefore, could not acquire those territories except by title of conquest or from the result of cession and sale which Mexico might now make. But, as we are satisfied that the Republic of Washington will not only absolutely dismiss but will despise the first of those titles; and since on the other hand, it was a new experience inconsistent with any ideal of justice to wage war on a people on the only ground that that people refuse to sell territory which a neighbor would buy from them; we expect from the justice of the Government and people of North America that the broad changes which we have the honor to submit as to the cession of territory (outside of that of the State of Texas) which is claimed in the said Article 4, shall afford no ground for continuing a war which the worthy General of the North American troops has justly styled 'unnatural.' "

Trist, on September 7, in a long reply of eight closely written pages, closing with an excellent summary of the reason for the demand as to boundary, expressed his view of the cause of the war as follows:

"It was commenced, not by the United States to acquire Texas; but by Mexico, to subjugate Texas, after her national existence had become irrevocably blended & identified with that of the United States. . . . This invasion [by Mexico] was repelled; and the war thus forced upon the United States became soon a war of invasion on their part; a war of invasion, but not of aggression; for they had remained passive until struck, and until the pertinacity of the Mexican Government in maintaining its attitude of hostility had made it manifest that no good consequences could result from further forbearance, and had precluded all doubt that the only hope of the restoration of peace between the two Countries rested upon a vigorous prosecution of the war by the party assailed."

Closing with a reference to the proposition of the American government to retain a part of the territory which it had been reluctantly compelled to occupy after exhausting every other means to preserve peace and for which it generously offered to Mexico a pecuniary relief far more important to her than the recovery of remote and uninhabited districts over which she had exercised only a nominal and sterile authority, he consistently and promptly announced the end of negotiations. Thus the blundering armistice also ended, although Scott preferred to terminate it on the ground of its violation by Mexico—making charges which furnished Santa Anna an opportunity to display his forensics.[29]

On September 4, 1847, speaking to his cabinet, President Polk asserted that, if Mexico should obstinately continue to refuse to negotiate, the American government should insist on more territory than that named in Trist's instructions; but he was not yet ready to accept a suggestion for recall of Trist. On September 14, he regarded the news of the armistice with considerable anxiety. He received his first definite news of the conferences, on October 1, from a Mexican document containing the official correspondence published at the end of the armistice. After a long discussion in the cabinet, feeling the insult of the insincere Mexican counter offer, he promptly ordered Trist's recall in order to discourage false Mexican views of American anxiety for peace on Mexican terms—views which had also been influenced by Polk's series of peace overtures and notes. He again determined to prosecute the war with greater energy, declaring that "Mexico must now sue for peace." Marcy dismissed with contempt the well-intentioned but unwise proposals that all American troops should be withdrawn from Mexico before the conclusion of a treaty of peace—proposals which, if adopted, would have resulted in an indefinite prolongation of a state of quasi-war. He believed that the successes of the American army had "opened the way to act upon and influence those who probably can, if they will, put an end to hostilities." "By making them suffer the usual calamities of war," he said, "they must be made to desire peace." On October 6 he ordered Scott to take the capital and to live on the country, and expressed confidence that he would conduct the war to secure its main object —Mexican "consent to such terms of peace as we have a right to ask and expect." Buchanan, on the same day, directed Trist to return to Washington, leaving the Mexican government to transmit any future overtures to Washington through the American commanding general—a policy which, if followed, would doubtless have prolonged the war and extended the problems of territorial occupation. By November, Buchanan, influenced by changes in public opinion, favored seizure of additional territory—including Tamaulipas, and all of the region east of the Sierra Madre Mountains. He and the cabinet agreed that if Mexico should obstinately continue to refuse to negotiate, the President in his message of December, 1847, should assert the American policy to "continue to occupy Mexico" with troops and to encourage and protect the friends of peace in Mexico to establish and maintain a republican government able and willing to make peace, and if necessary "fulfill that destiny which Providence may have in store for both countries." Polk, however, denying his intention to make any permanent conquest of Mexico or to annihilate its separate independent existence, limited the results of continued occupation to "taking the full measure of indemnity into our own hands" and enforcement of "terms which our honor demands." Already, in October, in Lower California, Eugene Gillespie had announced the proclamation of Commodore Shubrick pledging the good faith of the American government to the inhabitants who espoused the American cause and declaring that the United States would never again relinquish the Californias.[30]

Polk's message of December, 1847, to Congress was disappointing to many who had expected an early peace. Announcing the recall of Trist, it offered no promise of peace. It stated that no further overtures of peace would be made, although it admitted readiness to receive and consider overtures which Mexico might decide to make. It indicated that American de-

mands for territory would be increased and that the enlargement of American boundaries would be determined by the
measure of Mexican obstinacy. For nearly three months, while
the administration was withholding the olive branch and waiting for Trist to return, the message furnished the basis for warm
and wandering debates in Congress, including much criticism
of the administration and especially much discussion of the
status of expected territorial acquisitions as to slavery. Calhoun,
fearing that Polk's policy would result in the annexation of all
Mexico, offered an opposing resolution which the Senate politely laid on the table, but which he later asserted had turned
the tide of public sentiment and caused the defeat of Polk's
plans to conquer and annex all Mexico and compelled the acceptance of the later Trist treaty.[31]

Meantime, on November 16, when the instructions of October 6 reached Scott and Trist, the situation in Mexico had
greatly changed since the end of the armistice. Scott had captured Molino del Rey (on September 8) and the formidable
Chapultepec (on September 13) and with his staff had entered
the palace of Mexico City and hoisted the American flag, on
September 14—several hours after the retreat of Santa Anna
and the Mexican army toward Guadalupe Hidalgo. Here, on
September 16, Santa Anna, by advice of Pacheco and Alcorta,
resigned the office of President in order to lead an attack on the
American rear garrison at Puebla—an attack which proved unsuccessful. On September 27, he was temporarily succeeded in
the presidency at Queretaro by Pena y Pena, the presiding judge
of the Supreme Court. The latter appointed to the position of
Minister of Relations Don Luis de la Rosa, an advocate of
peace. On October 7, he issued an order relieving Santa Anna of
his command and ordering him before a court of inquiry to
answer for his conduct in the campaign which had resulted in
the loss of the capital. Later, in hasty flight, and probably regretting that he had accepted the invitation to leave Havana,
Santa Anna sought to enter Oaxaca but, being refused by the
governor, Benito Juárez, he left Mexico (on April 5, 1848)
under an American safe-conduct and went to Jamaica where he

wrote a defense of his conduct in the war—and prepared for a
later return to rule.

Trist, who believed that the new government had triumphed
over the intrigues of Almonte, on October 20 sent through the
British legation to Rosa a note dated September 7, a reply to
the last note of the Mexican commissioners before the end of
the armistice. In it he indicated his wish to proceed with the negotiations. From Rosa on October 31 he obtained a promise of
the early appointment of new commissioners to continue the
negotiations. On November 11, Pena y Pena became Minister
of Relations by appointment of the new President *ad interim*,
Anaya, chosen by Congress and sustained by a conference of
governors. On November 22, six days after Trist had received
his recall, and also after the knowledge of the recall had reached
the Mexican government through Thornton, he announced to
Trist (by note sent through Thornton) the appointment of
commissioners to continue the conferences, and urged him to
remain for the negotiations which he had expressed his readiness
to renew. To the Mexican commissioners he said Trist could not
now withdraw since he had offered to renew negotiations and
his offer had been accepted—that the American government
must continue conferences begun in due season by its own
agent and accepted forthwith by the Mexican government. Also
urged by members of the Mexican commission and by General
Scott, who felt confident that his treaty would be ratified at
Washington to prevent a continuance of the war, Trist, after
announcing officially on November 24 his recall and the revocation of his powers and after preparations for his departure,
changed his mind by December 3 and decided that his duty was
to withdraw his notice of revocation and to remain to assume
the responsibility of a treaty on the basis of the American territorial demands of his instructions, believing that if he did not
promptly seize the opportunity "all chances for making a
treaty *at all* will be lost for an indefinite period—perhaps forever." To Thornton he wrote (on December 4): "I am resolved to carry home with me a treaty of peace, if the Mexican
Government feels strong enough to venture upon making one

on the basis, as regards boundary, of the project originally presented by me. . . . If they do not feel thus able, let them surrender at once to the Puros, and dismiss forever all thoughts of a treaty." On December 6 he wrote Buchanan a long dispatch of rather insolent tone, announcing and explaining his intention to disobey orders and disguisedly intimating that the President now wished to annex all Mexico.[32]

Although formal negotiations were delayed by Pena y Pena upon the pretext that the new commissioners required the approval of the new Congress which would meet in January, Trist made some progress in December by private conferences, and on December 29 he reported to Buchanan that a treaty would probably be signed in a week and ratified early in January. On January 2, 1848, he attended the first official conference, following the arrival of Pena y Pena's instructions of December 30, suggesting the immediate retirement of the American army north of the Rio Grande and the Gila and the arbitration of American pretensions by a Congress of representatives of American nations or by a friendly power, and indicating the main features of the proposed treaty. He resisted attempts to deviate from the basis of the project already presented. To the Mexican proposal for a compensation of $30,000,000 for cessions he refused to pay more than $15,000,000. To the renewed suggestion of the line of the Nueces and a line from the Gila to the Pacific north of San Diego, he insisted upon the line of the Rio Grande and thence to the Pacific south of San Diego. This ultimatum he asserted again after January 8 when Rosa succeeded Pena y Pena as Minister of Relations. He did not press the proposed concession for right of transit across Tehuantepec * which Mackintosh, the British consul, proposed to sell to the United States.[33]

---

* Clayton later considered that the Mexican rejection of Trist's overture concerning the Tehuantepec transit was in some respects fortunate.

"Had its fate been different," said he, "it is at least doubtful whether the Senate would have deemed the privileges sought worth the price which was authorized to be stipulated for them. If the Senate had refused to sanction a treaty embodying them, this might have been the means of prolonging the war and of leading to the incalculable evils which must have resulted from it." (*16 Mexico, Instruction*, No. 1, Clayton to Letcher, Sept. 18, 1849.)

Trist's position in the negotiations was doubtless much strengthened by the knowledge of his recall which enabled him effectively to threaten to terminate negotiations if his demands were ignored, and was also influenced favorably by the army of Scott who, although he contemplated no immediate hostile action, had refused to agree to another armistice pending negotiations.

After the form of the treaty was completed by the commissioners (by January 24), Trist was disappointed by the conditions which Rosa attached (January 26) to the authorization of its signature: including the requirement that Lower California should remain connected with Sonora by land, that invaders should withdraw from the capital immediately on the signature of the treaty, and that an advance payment should be made to enable the government at Queretaro to maintain itself against possible anarchy or civil war following the conclusion of the treaty.

To Thornton he declared, on January 28, that he would terminate all negotiations and leave unless the Mexican signatures to the treaty could be obtained at once. On the following day he confidentially planned to send an official note breaking off negotiations—a note which he wished to withdraw if the commissioners were ready to sign the treaty by February 1. Scott planned to march troops against Queretaro to disperse the provisional government. The Mexican commissioners, confidentially informed of Trist's intentions (by Doyle, the British chargé) and impressed with the gravity of the situation, hastened a courier to Queretaro to urge a definite decision at once, stating that the provision for a military convention to arrange cessation of hostilities would accomplish the same purpose as the proposed evacuation of the capital, and suggesting that a demand for payment of money before the signature of the treaty was not decorous. Urged by the British chargé, the provisional government under President Pena y Pena surrendered its views and concluded the negotiations, and Rosa sent a fast rider with a note authorizing the commissioners at Mexico City to sign the treaty in the form agreed upon, in order to end calamities and to check the "projects of annexation of Northern America." By the wish of the Mexican commissioners, the ceremony of signing occurred at the neighboring town of Guadalupe Hidalgo, the seat of a famous shrine.[34]

Meantime, in January, 1848, following a report that Scott and Trist had contemplated bribery in the unofficial negotiations at Puebla, and a report of some later trouble between Scott and two of his generals in regard to the distribution of military merit in the war, Polk and his cabinet decided to replace Scott with General William O. Butler, who was next in rank, and to order a court of inquiry to consider all charges— a court which sat in Mexico from March 16 to April 28, 1848, and later in the United States. During the first week of January Polk received the first intimation that Trist would disregard orders and continue negotiations. On January 15, he received from Trist definite information to this effect in a long letter which he regarded as "impudent, insulting to the Government, and personally offensive to the President," and which he suspected was written at Scott's dictation. As a rebuke, he asked Marcy to direct Major General Butler to order Trist from army headquarters and to "inform the authorities of Mexico that he had no authority to treat"—an order, however, which was not forwarded to Butler by Marcy until January 26, and did not reach Butler until after Trist had completed the treaty of negotiations and started home. Polk received his first intimation of Trist's final success from a private letter of Atocha to Buchanan, soliciting money to bribe the Mexican Congress to ratify the treaty of peace, but not stating whether the treaty had been signed. On February 19, he received, by Trist's messenger, the treaty which in its essential provisions followed the instructions of April 15, 1847. Besides provision for a compensation of fifteen million dollars (one-fifth payable immediately) for the territory acquired, the United States agreed to assume payment of all unpaid claims of American citizens against Mexico as decided under the conventions of April 11, 1839, and January 30, 1843, and all other such claims which had arisen before February, 2, 1848.* Among other provisions were: a military convention for cessation of hostilities, American control of marauding Indians, revival of the treaty of commerce of 1831 for eight years, arbitration of future differences, and rules applicable in case of another war.[35]

Although two members of the cabinet (Buchanan and Walker) advised rejection of the treaty, Polk, on February 21, announced his decision to submit it to the Senate, stating his fear that the administration could not be sustained if it rejected its own terms. He submitted it without commendation, leaving the entire responsibility to the Senate, but he and all the cabinet agreed that Article X as to Mexican land grants should be rejected. After a few days of delay, resulting from the death of John Quincy Adams, the Senate Committee on Foreign Relations, by vote of Webster, Benton, Mangum and Hannegan, decided to report adversely and to recommend the appointment of an imposing commission of three or five members to Mexico to negotiate a new treaty—a proposition which Polk regarded as "worse than an idle ceremony." In an executive session of the Senate the committee finally reported without recommendation, but Webster followed with an unsuccessful motion to recommend the commission and Houston unsuccessfully urged rejection of the Trist treaty on various grounds. Webster's policy, which aimed at peace without territory, would have resulted in prolongation of the war and more territory (which was Houston's purpose). A radical proposal of Jefferson Davis to amend the boundary, to include in the cession all of Coahuila and the greater part of Tamaulipas and Nuevo Leon and much of Chihuahua, was defeated by a vote of 44 to 11. With two omissions and minor modifications, but no change in the leading or important features, the treaty was finally ratified on March 10 by a vote of 38 to 14.

To explain the seven amendments made by the Senate and

* By act of August 10, 1846, Congress had appropriated $320,000 to pay claimants the fourth and fifth installments due under the convention of January 30, 1843, and by act of July 29, 1848, it authorized the payment of all liquidated but unpaid claims against Mexico under the conventions of 1839 and 1843. (Moore, *International Arbitrations*, p. 1248.)

to persuade the Mexican government by personal conferences to accept the changes and to ratify the treaty, the President, on March 14, appointed Senator Sevier, chairman of the Committee on Foreign Relations, as commissioner plenipotentiary to go to Mexico with the treaty. Buchanan, in his instructions of March 18, indicated that if the war should be renewed the United States would be compelled to appropriate, without pecuniary compensation, enough territory to indemnify for all expenses of the war. On March 18, the President appointed, as associate commissioner, Nathan Clifford (the Attorney-General). The latter reached Mexico City April 11, four days before Sevier, who was delayed by illness. He found that on February 18, General Scott had been superseded by General Butler with whom the Mexican government had arranged a general armistice which had gone into effect five weeks after the signature of the treaty and had practically conferred on Butler the authority to suppress all Mexican attempts at revolution. The stern pressure of facts had prepared the way for approval of the treaty. Opponents of ratification had been answered by the Mexican negotiators, who especially emphasized the fact that the treaty ceded only part of the territory lost by war and was "more exactly an agreement of recovery than an agreement of cession." Fortunately the news of the discovery of gold on the American River in California did not reach Mexico until several months later (August). Clifford and Sevier found a general expectation of early ratification, but that no leader wished to assume responsibility. They remained at Mexico City to await the preliminary action of Congress which assembled at Queretaro on May 3. After the Chamber of Deputies approved ratification on May 19 by a vote of 51 to 35, they were invited to Queretaro where they arrived on May 25, an hour after the Senate had approved ratification by a vote of 33 to 4. After exchange of ratifications on May 30, four days before the inauguration of President Herrera as the successor of Pena y Pena, they returned to Mexico City to make the first payment of three million dollars and to arrange for retirement of the American troops—resulting in the withdrawal of the American flag from Mexico City on June 12 and from Vera Cruz on July 30. There was some delay in American delivery of maritime customshouses at certain ports. At Guaymas and in Lower California questions arose in regard to restoration. On July 13, Commodore Jones sent to Clifford a memorial from inhabitants of Lower California who, following the proclamation of Commodore Shubrick in October, 1847, had espoused the cause of the United States in the war and had expected that territory to be annexed to the United States.* When he abandoned the peninsula he received on board about fifty families, fugitives who abandoned their property. The emergency consul, Eugene Gillespie, appointed by Jones' recommendation, had great difficulty in protecting unfortunates who were bold enough to remain, and was in danger of assassination from those who had been led to believe that the United States would never relinquish the Californias. In August, after the news of the discovery of gold in California, Clifford reported that the Minister of Relations objected to the Coahuila route selected by Colonel J. W. Washington for his journey to California.[36]

Although Sevier took leave June 4, Clifford, who was commissioned envoy extraordinary and minister plenipotentiary on July 28, presented his new credentials on October 2, thereby completing the resumption of friendly relations under Trist's treaty. In his instructions of August 7, concerning the importance of able representation at Mexico in the new period of relations, Buchanan stated the chief objects of his mission: to soothe irritations, to counteract the injurious machinations of foreign governments, and to persuade the Mexican government

* Late in April Polk submitted to Congress, without recommendation, the question of Yucatan which had resumed its sovereignty on January 1, 1846, had refused to aid Mexico in the war against the United States and, on April 3, 1848, fearing English interference, had offered to transfer its sovereignty to the United States. Although the question stimulated considerable debate, it was satisfactorily adjusted by Yucatan on May 17 without the necessity of further American consideration. Later, on May 30, the date of the exchange of ratifications of peace with Mexico, Polk, with views of a Caribbean policy influenced by the events of the recent war, presented to the cabinet the question of a "fair purchase" of Cuba and on June 17 sent through Buchanan "profoundly confidential" instructions to Saunders to begin negotiations for that purpose. (*14 Spanish Instructions*, p. 253, No. 21.)

to abandon its absurd and unreasonable tariff. He also explained that the President was reluctantly constrained "to decline, at least for the present," the Mexican request for 3,000 or 4,000 American troops for use against Mexican Indians, beginning with those of Yucatan. This request had been presented verbally on August 3 to the Department of State by Señor Arrangoiz and had been submitted to the President in cabinet council which decided the plan impracticable, as it would have necessitated a treaty which probably at that time could not have obtained the approval of the necessary two-thirds vote in the Senate, and was also contrary to the American established policy against interference in the domestic concerns of foreign nations. In later instructions of August 15, Buchanan offered the following significant suggestion: "The Mexicans are captious and verbose writers, and if you get into a discussion with them on any subject, it will have no end. Accomplish, therefore, as much as possible by conversation. Indeed, this is a good rule in diplomatic intercourse." [37]

Meantime the presumptuous Trist, the official bearer of the olive branch, and successful negotiator, who had hastened peace by the continuation of negotiations after his recall, found his salary and allowances cancelled and the doors of the State Department closed to him. Unable to secure a hearing, he sought redress and the impeachment of Polk, through a letter (of August 7, 1848) to the Speaker of the House who referred it to the Committee on Foreign Affairs which buried it in the basement cemetery. Long he talked without reward for his efforts. Long forgotten, he was finally vindicated by an appropriation of $14,560 from Congress in 1871 through the influence of Senator Sumner.

REFERENCES

1. *1 Special Missions,* March 28, 1845.
2. Parrott to Buchanan, May 22, Aug. 16, 23 and 29, and Sept. 23, 1845.
3. *House Doc.* 60, 30-1, p. 12.
4. *Ib.,* pp. 231-33.

5. *1 Special Missions*, Oct. 17, 1845.
6. *House Doc.* 60, 30-1, p. 13.
7. *16 Mexico, Instructions*, pp. 1-22, (No. 1) Nov. 10, 1845; *Ib.*, pp. 23-26, (No. 3) Nov. 19, 1845.
8. *House Doc.* 60, 30-1, p. 37; *12 Mexico, Despatches*, (No. 2) Nov. 30, (No. 3) Dec. 17, (No. 4) Dec. 27, 1845, (No. 7) Jan. 14, (No. 8) Feb. 6, (No. 11) Mar. 18, and (No. 13) Apr. 2, 1846.
9. *Ib.*, No. 11, March 18, 1846 (with Enclosure).
10. G. L. RIVES, *The United States and Mexico*, II, pp. 90-95.
11. *Polk's Diary*, Feb. 17, 1846; *16 Mexico, Instructions*, March 12, 1846.
12. *House Doc.* 60, 30-1, p. 139.
13. *Sen. Doc.* 378, 29-1, pp. 6 and 11; *House Doc.* 60, 30-1, p. 326.
14. JESSE S. REEVES, *American Diplomacy under Tyler and Polk*, pp. 299-307.
15. *Webster's Works*, V, 157; *Sen. Doc.* 107, 29-2, pp. 2-3.
16. *Cong. Globe*, Appendix, 29-2, p. 24; *House Doc.* 4, 29-2, pp. 43-44; *House Doc.* 60, 30-1, pp. 355-59.
17. *Polk's Diary*, II, pp. 221-23 and 108.
18. *Polk's Diary*, I, pp. 83 and 68-72.
19. G. L. RIVES, *The United States and Mexico*, II, Chap. XXXIV.
20. *1 Special Missions*, Nov. 21, 1846.
21. *Sen. Doc.* 1, 30-1, p. 36.
22. *Sen. Doc.* 1, 30-1, p. 37; *Polk's Diary*, II, 465-75, *passim* Apr. 10-13, 1847; *16 Mexico, Instructions*, p. 46, Apr. 15, 1847.
23. *Ib.*, pp. 72-74, No. 4, July 19, 1847; *House Doc.* 359, 71-2, pp. 442-43.
24. *Ib.*, p. 46, Apr. 15, 1847; *Sen. Doc.* 52, 30-1, pp. 81-89; *Polk's Diary*, pp. 483-84; *House Doc.* 60, 30-1, p. 940.
25. RIVES, *The United States and Mexico*, II, 432-33; *House Doc.* 60, 30-1, p. 996; *Polk's Diary*, III, p. 58.
26. *16 Mexico, Instructions*, (No. 4) July 19, and (No. 7) Dec. 21, 1847; *14 Mexico, Despatches*, July 23, July 29, and (No. 10) July 31, 1847.
27. *Ib.*, No. 12, Aug. 22, 1847 (Enclosures); *Sen. Doc.* 52, 30-1, pp. 187-89.
28. *Sen. Doc.* 52, 30-1, pp. 308-50.
29. *Ib.*, pp. 190-91, 195, 315-16, 378, 383 and 203; *14 Mexico, Despatches*, (No. 14) Aug. 29, (No. 15) Sept. 4, (No. 16) Sept. 27, and (No. 19) Oct. 31, 1847; *House Doc.* 359, 71-2, pp. 447-71.
30. *Polk's Diary*, III, pp. 172, 186 and 215-18, Nov. 9, 1847; *House Doc.* 359, 71-2, pp. 443-46; *16 Mexico, Instructions*, No. 5, Oct. 6, and No. 6, Oct. 25, 1847; *Sen. Doc.* 52, 30-1, pp. 91

and 138-40; RICHARDSON (Ed.), *Messages and Papers of the Presidents*, IV, pp. 544-45; *38 Mexico, Despatches*, No. 118, Sept., 1869.

31. *Cong. Globe*, XVII, pp. 96-100; *Rp. Am. Hist. Ass'n, 1899*, II, p. 75 (Calhoun Papers).

32. *14 Mexico, Despatches*, (No. 18) Oct. 25 and Oct. 31, (No. 21) Nov. 27, and (No. 22) Dec. 6, 1847; *Sen. Doc.* 52, 30-1, pp. 231-66 and 266-68.

33. *14 Mexico, Despatches*, (No. 25) Dec. 29, 1847, and (No. 26) Jan. 12, and (No. 27) Jan. 25, 1848 (and Enclosures); *House Doc.* 359, 71-2, pp. 472-79; *Sen. Doc.* 52, 30-1, pp. 275, 278 and 280.

34. *14 Mexico, Despatches*, No. 28, Feb. 2, 1848; G. L. RIVES, *The United States and Mexico*, II, pp. 608-13.

35. *House Doc.* 60, 30-1, pp. 1040-46; *Polk's Diary*, III, pp. 300, 310, 313-17, 329, 347, 350 and 365.

36. *House Doc.* 50, 30-2, pp. 47-52; *13 Mexico, Despatches*, (No. 17) July 6, (No. 24) Aug. 11, and (No. 25.) Aug. 21, 1848; *38 Mexico, Despatches*, No. 118, Sept. 22, 1869 (Enclosure; Eugene Gillespie to Thomas H. Nelson); *House Exec. Doc.* 5, 31-1, p. 105.

37. *16 Mexico, Instructions*, pp. 100-04, No. 2) Aug. 7, 1848; *Ib.*, pp. 105-10, No. 4) Aug. 15, 1848.

CHAPTER VI

THE TEHUANTEPEC TRANSIT NEGOTIATIONS, 1848-53

AMERICAN diplomacy of the period 1849-53 was injuriously affected by frequent changes in the office of the Secretary of State and by the untrained ministers who were sent to Mexico. Secretary John M. Clayton, who had been trained by service in the Senate from 1829-35 and 1845-49 and who adopted a foreign policy which strictly regarded American obligations and rights and sought to promote commerce, was succeeded on July 23, 1850, by Daniel Webster who, after his retirement from the office in 1843, had served continuously in the Senate since March, 1845. Webster, following his death late in October, 1852, was succeeded (on November 6) by Edward Everett who, after experience as a pastor, and as a professor at Harvard (1819-26), had served his state in Congress for ten years (1825-35) and as governor for four years (1836-40), had declined a commission to China in 1843, and had served as president of Harvard from 1846-49. The American ministers in Mexico for the period were: Robert P. Letcher of Kentucky who had served his state in Congress from 1823 to 1841 and as governor in 1840-44, and Judge Alfred Conkling of New York who had served a term in Congress, 1821-23, and as a United States district judge from 1825 to 1852. Letcher, who replaced Clifford in August, 1849, and continued as minister until August, 1852, was especially temperamentally unfitted for his post, resulting in quarrels both with the Mexican government and with Webster. His successor, Judge Conkling, added very little to American prestige in Mexico in his brief term of one year as minister. Mexico, although troubled by revolt, sent to the United

States its best trained diplomats: Luis de la Rosa, a distinguished statesman who had been Secretary of Relations in the cabinet of Pena y Pena; Manuel Larrainger; and Juan N. Almonte who had been Mexican minister to the United States under the Tyler administration.

From the settlement of old problems arose new difficulties which later threatened another war. One of the most important and irritating and critical questions in American policy relating to Mexican relations in the first half decade after 1848 was that of the Tehuantepec isthmian transit which at that time was regarded as the most practicable route for a transcontinental railroad communication between California and the East. American interest in this route arose early in the Mexican War. In April, 1847, Polk and his cabinet agreed that this free transit was worth five million dollars, and authorized Trist to include it in his negotiations and to pay as high as fifteen million dollars. The Mexican commissioners declined to consider the question, explaining that Mexico in 1842 (by decree and compact of Santa Anna), had granted the concession, with title to all unoccupied lands for ten leagues on each side of the route, to José de Garay, a private contractor—whose enterprise had first been delayed by the revolution of 1844 which overthrew Santa Anna and alarmed the capitalists, and who later, in 1847-48, with consent of Mexico, transferred it to English subjects, Manning and Macintosh. The latter in 1849 transferred their concession to American citizens, the Hargous brothers of New York, who promptly invited the attention of the American Senate to the project, especially in connection with the consideration of contracts to carry the mail to California, and suggested that Congress should not commit itself in favor of the Panama or any other route.[1]

The American government, quick to patronize a grant which bestowed greater privileges than those sought by the instructions to Trist, apprehensive of the attitude of the Mexican government to the transfer of the Garay privilege to American citizens whom it was determined to protect, instructed Nathan Clifford, the American minister in Mexico, to say that the

American executive would regard any annulment of the grant as a violation of the treaty of 1831 and wholly at variance with pacific relations and would view with dissatisfaction any infringement of rights of American citizens obtained as a result of confidence in pledges of Mexican decrees (issued at a time when Congress was dissolved and dispersed by revolution). In reply to his note of June 20, 1849, to the Minister of Foreign Relations, Clifford was assured that the Garay grant had not been annulled, but he was frankly informed that the question of its validity or of forfeiture for non-compliance with obligations under it was exclusively a Mexican affair which must be decided by Mexican law and authority. Soon thereafter (on September 18, 1849), in order to encourage capitalists by suitable protection in undertaking an enterprise of such large importance to the world, Secretary Clayton instructed Robert P. Letcher, the successor of Clifford, to negotiate for a convention of guaranty for the protection of the rights and property of American citizens who might engage in the construction of a highway, railway, or canal across the isthmus. Clayton in proposing this guaranty said: "This the President is willing to bestow in view of the importance of the undertaking to the world and of the large and special interest which the United States have in its success. He does not covet, however, and will not stipulate for any rights of sovereignty over the country through which communication may pass, nor will he guaranty such rights to Mexico. He desires that she should maintain them herself." After a brief summary of the advantages which Mexico might expect from the enterprise, to the success of which the proposed convention was necessary to inspire confidence among those who dreaded the evils arising from the caprice and instability of the governments and the general Spanish-American antipathy to foreigners—he added the explanation that the American government would not undertake a guaranty of Mexican sovereignty similar to the guaranty of the sovereignty of New Granada at Panama by the treaty of December 12, 1846, which the Senate had hastily approved in 1848. To allay any unfounded expectation (of such a guaranty) which might spring from an apprehension of ambitious American designs, he continued: "We could derive no advantage from such an acquisition and are not willing to incur the risks or to bear the burthens which it would entail. Our sole desire is that the sovereignty of that region should remain entire in the Mexican Republic, or subject to those limitations only which she has herself voluntarily imposed in the charter to Don José de Garay. The guaranty in the Treaty with New Granada is a conspicuous exception to our usual cautious and wise policy. That treaty was concluded without instructions from this Department. There is reason to believe that it was reluctantly submitted to the Senate. It was approved by that body without full examination, and passed at the very close of the session of 1848. It cannot be deemed a safe precedent. There certainly is no disposition to be guided by it in our course with reference to Tehuantepec." [2]

The chief points of the proposed treaty were indicated as follows: For the purpose of protecting the rights and properties of the grantees throughout the period of construction and after completion, either party had the liberty to employ any necessary military and naval force which should be hospitably received in the harbors of the isthmus or allowed to occupy the line of the work or the adjacent region so far as indispensable complaints of non-compliance with the terms of the grant were to be decided by an arbitrator; in case of a decision of forfeiture, the property of the grantees was to be sold at public auction only to private individuals (not to a foreign government or corporation); transportation rates for American citizens or officers or their goods were not to exceed rates for Mexican citizens or officers or their goods.

At the end of October, about six weeks after the instructions to Letcher, Clayton instructed the American minister at London that American policy as to Tehuantepec was the same as that relating to Nicaragua. "Tell Palmerston," said he, "that we encourage and shall certainly protect all routes, whether by canal or railroad across the American isthmus, and that we invite Great Britain to occupy the same ground, she to enjoy equal benefits with us and *we* all the benefits of the most favored nation." On April 23, 1850, after learning through Letcher that the British minister in Mexico had intimated that Great Britain desired to join in the guaranty of the integrity of the isthmus, Clayton authorized an invitation to other nations to join in the proposed treaty for guaranty of the neutrality of the route.[3]

The treaty which Mr. Letcher concluded in January, 1850, although it contained no express reference to the Garay grant, appears from its terms to have been intended to protect the interests of the holders of that grant. One article (the twelfth), stipulated that the actual holder of the privilege should give his consent in writing before the treaty could be submitted to the Senate of the United States or the Mexican Congress. The purport of several articles, however, was deemed so obscure, that it was thought advisable to return the draft to Mexico for amendment. Few of the desired amendments were obtained, however, and a storm of opposition was excited in Mexico against any treaty with the United States on the subject—later resulting in the repeal of the Garay grant by the Mexican Congress, following elaborate committee reports against the grant.[4]

On June 22, 1850, Letcher signed with Pedraza a new convention which contained several changes from the original draft but seemed the best obtainable at that time.

It limited American aid in protection only as required by Mexico, provided for reduced tolls (20% less) on Mexican products, required American cooperation in maintenance of the neutrality of the route including the adjacent country for a distance of ten leagues on each side of the route, and permitted other nations (by joining in the guaranty) to share in the privileges. It also required the consent of the holder of the Garay grant.

With the unpopular treaty Letcher transmitted to Clayton the following explanatory note: "It is not such a treaty, in every particular, as I desired to make; but is the best that could be obtained. It is the same, with the exception of a very few verbal alterations, which was agreed upon on the 3d Inst., five days before the arrival of your instructions of the 23d of April in answer to my dispatch of the

16th of March, No. 8. After receiving your instructions, whether to sign the treaty or not became a question of the most perplexing character.

"To refuse my signature to the treaty, after having agreed to it, would be to put an end to the negotiation and, as a matter of course, to place me in a position altogether embarrassing. Viewing the subject in all its aspects and consequences, believing that your instructions would not be violated in the spirit, knowing that further delay would be fatal to all hopes of a treaty in future, and impelled also by other considerations of expediency and policy, I have ventured to accept and sign it as it is.

"You will see that I have been careful to exclude all idea of a guarantee, on our part, of the *sovereignty* to Mexico; confining our eventual interference, only to the *protection of the route, and the territory immediately adjacent,* and that only in the case of a summons from Mexico. With regard to the admission of other nations to the same advantages, there can be no possible doubt or difficulty; as Mexico is ready, at any moment, to allow all the nations of the commercial world to enjoy the same privileges, upon the same terms, as those conceded to the United States, if application should be made to her Government; but she considers it due to herself, that such application should be addressed to her directly." [5]

Hargous, to whom Webster on August 12 submitted the convention for criticism, desired greater protection from his government, especially urging the need of authority to repress or repel Mexican officials, the need of an American commissioner on the line of construction and an equal voice with Mexico in fixing or changing transportation rates, and also some assurance of protection of the company's property from unjust compensation and violence. Definitely assured by Webster that the American government would protect American investments in the enterprise by remonstrance against invasions of their rights or by other means, if necessary, he consented to the convention on August 26, only with the expectation that the American government would extend its protection if the Mexican government failed to protect. Soon thereafter, he interested in his project several New Orleans residents who formed a temporary organization for a stock company to finance the company, in December sent surveyors to the isthmus, and in the following

March began to sell lands and woods in the twenty-league strip —resulting in an increased opposition to the grant and steps to interfere with the vessels of the New Orleans company whose actions were misinterpreted as the beginning of another scene in the drama of aggressive absorption.[6]

Meantime, on August 24, Webster, before submitting the treaty to the Senate, instructed Letcher to make overtures for modifications suggestive of an American protectorate; and, in case the overtures were rejected, he threatened to act independently and to withhold payments due under the treaty of 1848. From Letcher's reply of October 22, he learned that both the Mexican Minister of Relations and the Mexican President (and his council) courteously but firmly declined to accept the amendments which they said would infringe upon Mexican sovereignty if adopted, but which he said probably would be rejected unanimously by Congress and result in the overthrow of the administration. Pedraza explained that the government had already been severely censured for agreeing to the treaty, and that he had been denounced as a vile traitor. After being given several chances for reflection and reconsideration he still remained impervious to argument, persuasion and appeal by which Letcher sought to induce him to change his obstinate opinion and his persistent objections, but he seemed pained by the situation. When incidentally informed that, if Mexico refused to enter into a fair treaty for the protection of the enterprise, the American government in justice to its citizens was determined to take the affair into its own hands, he replied (substantially): "Your government is strong. Ours is weak. You have the power to take the whole, or any portion of our territory. . . . What is required of us we can not grant. If Mr. Webster knew our exact condition, if he knew the precarious tenure by which we hold power, the violence and strength of the opposition, the refractory spirit of the states, and the peculiar prejudices of our people, *surely* he would not exact such terms." Later, in reporting the unanimous rejection of the chief two proposed amendments by the President and cabinet, he said (substantially): "I hardly have the heart or

courage to make known to you the decision of last night . . .
Mexico with the strongest desire to maintain the most intimate
relations . . . is unable to concede the two amendments you
have insisted upon with so much earnestness." President Arista
manifested the deepest concern and seemed exceedingly uneasy,
and members of the cabinet expressed their regret. Letcher's
only answer was that Mexico had committed a great error.[7]

Webster, following the receipt of Letcher's report of his
unsuccessful negotiations, after expressing regret sought a compromise. In his instructions of December 4, he said: "Inasmuch,
however, as you represent that they entertained decided and
insurmountable objections to the 4th and 11th Articles of that
draft, it has been deemed expedient to confer with the holders
of the grants with a view to instruct you to sign the Treaty
without insisting upon those Articles. The result has been an
acquiescence by them in this course of proceeding. If therefore
you should not be able to obtain more favorable terms, you may
embody in the Treaty the 4th and 11th Articles as they originally stood in the instrument signed by you on the 2nd of
June, last." The result was a new treaty of January 25, 1851,
which, although practically the same as that of June, 1850, received the consent of Hargous and was ratified by the American
Senate.[8]

From subsequent despatches Webster learned that violent
opposition to the treaty had developed in Mexico, from almost
every quarter except from President Arista. From the American chargé, Buckingham Smith, he received a despatch of April
1 (during the absence of Letcher on a visit to the United
States), stating that with the strong opposition against an
American foothold which it was feared might result in the
seizure of additional territory, ratification of the treaty by the
Mexican Congress did not seem possible. Aroused by the statement of Rosa (the Mexican minister at Washington) that the
original Mexican grants to Garay might be forfeited by the
Mexican government, he vigorously declared (on April 30) that
such action or the rejection of the treaty would prove a serious
calamity to American citizens who had "embarked their for-

tunes upon their reliance on the good faith of both governments" and who were expending large sums in sending a large
surveying force "with the express permission and under the
sanction of the Mexican government." A few days later he had
new cause for complaint, indicated in his instructions of May
5, with which he enclosed the President's ratification of the
treaty of January 25: "You will also receive, herewith," he
said, "a copy of a letter addressed to the Department by J. P.
Benjamin, Esquire, of New Orleans, from which it appears that
the Mexican Consul there has refused a clearance to a schooner
bound to the Coatzacoalcos River with stores for the surveying
party. As that party proceeded to the Isthmus with the express
consent of the Mexican government, and cannot easily subsist
there without supplies from home or reach the United States
on their return except by direct communication, the act of Mr.
Dabelsteen referred to has created much surprise. It may be
true that no port of entry has been established on the Coatzacoalcos River, and this objection would have been valid against
the voyage of the schooner thither, if it had been for trading
purposes. As its object, however, was merely to receive the surveying party, the technical objection of the Consul to granting
her a clearance, has an unfriendly aspect, but we will not believe, without further information, that he had any special instructions upon the subject. All difficulty in regard to the
intercourse between New Orleans and the Isthmus would at
once be removed, if the Mexican government would establish
ports of entry there, say one at Minotiblan on the Coatzacoalcos and another at Salinas or Ventosa on the Pacific. That
government has recently recognized a Consul of the United
States at Tehuantepec, which is very near to Ventosa, and this
act may be considered as implying that commerce between the
United States and the Isthmus may be rightfully carried on.
There can be no doubt that if the ports referred to were made
ports of entry, a trade across the Isthmus highly advantageous
to Mexico would at once arise. If, however, that government
should not think proper to adopt this measure, you will inform
the Minister for Foreign Affairs that it is trusted no further

impediment will be interposed to the free communication between New Orleans and San Francisco and the surveying party
on the Isthmus." [9]

On the following day he wrote Smith concerning the treaty: "It is
to be hoped that the adverse sentiment of the Mexican Congress
of which you speak, will undergo a change, and that the treaty will
ultimately be ratified. It is difficult to comprehend the ground for the
apprehension to which you refer, that the Isthmus, if made a highway
for our citizens between the two oceans, would be lost to Mexico as
Texas has been. There is not the slightest resemblance between the
two cases, and if the treaty were to go into operation there would
not be, even if the Isthmus were coterminous with United States
territory, for the treaty would compel us to arrest by force, if necessary, not only the hostile designs of foreign powers upon the Isthmus,
but of such citizens of the United States as might be disposed to
defy the sovereignty of Mexico. If the Report of the Committee of
the Mexican Senate to which you refer should be published, you will
at once send a copy to the Department. It is desirable to know why
General Salas had less authority for any of the acts of his administration than for that by which Santa Anna and Herrera were subsequently
placed at the head of the government." [10]

Learning from later news that the Mexican government had
refused to allow foreign vessels to enter ports of the Tehuantepec isthmus, that the Mexican Congress (on May 22, 1851)
had nullified the Salas decree (of November, 1846) by which
the Garay grant had been extended, and that the Minister of
Relations had given orders to suspend the survey of the isthmus
and to expel the laborers who excited suspicions of a possible
attempt to gain possession by force, Webster, on August 18,
1851, sent through Letcher a solemn protest against the constitutionality of the rash action of the alarmed Congress and
urged him upon his return to Mexico to make prompt efforts
to secure ratification of the Tehuantepec treaty—within the
time limit which was later postponed until April 8, 1852, by
protocol. Recognizing the difficulty of the task by judging
from the tone of opposition to the Garay grant, he advised that
any questioning of accuracy of the prevalent adverse opinion
should be done prudently and not offensively. "It will occur

to you," he suggested, "that as the grant authorizes the grantee to associate foreigners with him in the prosecution of the enterprise, it shows that the grantor had the sagacity to perceive that it could not be completed without their agency. Foreigners, however, could not be expected to embark their capital in such an enterprise in a country ravaged by both a foreign and by civil wars, as Mexico has been almost ever since the grant was made. For the purpose of mitigating party feeling against the expediency of the grant on account of its origin, you may also invite attention to the fact that it is in the nature of a charter . . . Mexico cannot expect her resources to be developed without the aid of foreign science, enterprise and capital. These will never seek employment there without assurances of protection from the mutability of its government and that hostility towards strangers which is a characteristic of the Spanish race." [11]

On September 14, 1851, before the return of Letcher to Mexico with Webster's instructions of August 18, Smith reported that no Mexican Congress would ever ratify the treaty, that the Mexican government would remain firm against every intimation of force, and that the Mexican people, although not blind to the consequences of war, would consider resistance as a point of honor even if it should result in the extinguishment of their nationality. Soon thereafter, Smith was removed from office by President Fillmore on the basis of information that he had no good will toward the treaty and had done everything in his power to defeat it.[12]

Letcher on his return found that the treaty had no support from any quarter. Wishing to avoid a unanimous rejection in order to gain time for improving its chances before the next Congress, he "was forced to resort to the expedient of agreeing, or rather seeming to agree, to reopen the negotiation . . . to furnish the Minister of Relations with a proper apology for disobeying the demand of Congress" (to submit the treaty). Writing to Webster on October 29 concerning the pending negotiations, he said that much of the opposition to a treaty on the subject of Tehuantepec was due to the absurd but "confident expectation that its rejection may lead to a rupture between the two countries" which was hoped to result in annexation of Mexico to the United States. He found, however, much prejudice against the Garay grant upon which the proposed treaty was predicated, and especially against the New Orleans corporation—which had dared to threaten war against Mexico in case it should reject the treaty, and had avowed the determination to take forcible possession of the Isthmus and construct a railroad in defiance of Mexico. He also stated that his negotiations had been embarrassed by the recent revolt (of Carvajal) on the Rio Grande which was another cause of hostility to the treaty. He reported that President Arista, who had been accused of being a stockholder in the New Orleans company, but who, since the outrageous behavior of the company, had ceased to express any concern in regard to the treaty, felt a deep sense of heavy responsibility and had recently said: "Mexico must be lost in a short time unless the United States should extend to her a helping hand. This is our only salvation." [13]

A month later, Letcher attributed part of the strong opposition to the feeling that rejection of the treaty would be popular in the United States. An influencing factor was the opposition of certain American interests against the Tehuantepec interests. In August, 1851, the New York *Herald* had favored the plans of Vanderbilt in Nicaragua. On December 14, as an illustration of interference of Americans who were interested in the Panama or Nicaragua routes or other routes through Mexico, Letcher mentioned the letter which Jonas P. Levy, who was interested in a steamer line to Mexico, had written to President Arista on November 7, warning him of the danger of a loss of the territory of Tehuantepec. A copy of this letter was used by Webster to secure the arrest of Levy under the old Logan law of 1798, prohibiting an unauthorized person from meddling in negotiations with foreign powers. Although Levy was indicted by the grand jury at Washington, his trial was prevented by the refusal of Arista to deliver the original letter which was needed for evidence.[14]

On December 22-23, 1851, following the Mexican irritation

in connection with the Carvajal revolt on the Rio Grande and the news that the Mexican Senate planned to transfer to Great Britain the Tehuantepec concession, Webster instructed Letcher to inform the Minister of Relations that the United States "could not see with indifference that isthmus . . . under the sway of any European state" and that failure to ratify the treaty within the time limit "would lead to serious consequences." In the following March (on March 19), after the arrival of Letcher's report (of February 14) of the probable Mexican aim to reject the treaty and of his probable inability to secure an acceptable new treaty or satisfactory changes, President Fillmore, with approval of Webster, and evidently wishing to avoid a war to gratify the wishes of a private company, addressed directly to the President of Mexico an unofficial note earnestly urging him to adjust the Tehuantepec controversy in order to prevent probable international difficulties— which might result if Mexico should break her plighted faith in the grant to Garay and thereby cause heavy losses to American citizens who would appeal to their government for enforcement of their rights. On March 22, 1852, he instructed William M. Burwell to go to Mexico as special confidential agent with a copy of the letter to Arista with the hope that he could reach Mexico before the expiration of the extended time limit for ratification of the treaty—the limit having been extended from January 25 to April 8 by protocol signed by Letcher and Ramirez on January 21—and that he could aid in effecting a change of sentiment among public men in Mexico as to indemnity, and as to expectation as to release from the 11th article of the treaty of 1848. To Letcher he wrote that the special and confidential agent was sent "with the hope that the Mexican government may before it is too late be induced to pause in its unnecessary and unwise opposition to the Garay grant." [15]

Meantime Letcher, who in January, 1852, had asked Minister Ramirez to extend the time for ratification of the treaty from January 25 to June 25, but had only been able to secure an extension to April 8 on condition that no attempt at reconnaissance or operations on the Isthmus would begin during the extended period of negotiations, had not been pleased with the conferences of February and had finally suggested a suspension of conferences in order to give the Mexican minister the repose and time necessary to conclude for publication a report on the rights of Garay. Letcher left with the Mexican minister the impression that he considered the negotiations concluded, as his government refused to change the terms of the treaty. On April 2, following the publication of this report as a circular, communicated to the diplomatic corps in defense of the Mexican refusal to recognize the Garay grant, he wrote Ramirez a vigorous note—expressing surprise at the publication which he characterized as "improper and unheard of in the annals of negotiations," criticizing the capricious resistance of the Mexican government to the execution of a great enterprise and requesting him to submit the treaty to Congress. On April 6, Ramirez, in reply, suggested that under strict diplomatic usage the personalities of the note would have justified its return, and denied Letcher's right to "take to task" the Mexican minister for his supposed deliberations with Congress to whom he now transmitted the treaty and Letcher's note without explanation (in compliance with Letcher's wishes and thus terminating the negotiations). Letcher, in a note of April 7, regretting that the minister had "permitted himself to be so excited," declared that he "had no motive or design to wound the sensibility" of any one, characterized as "gratuitous and unjust" the insinuations that he wished to give offense to Mexico, and availed himself of the occasion "to assure his excellency that, let him be in enjoyment of prosperity or oppressed by adversity, whether in good or bad humor, he will always ardently desire the welfare and happiness of his excellency." Even this explanation Ramirez found "clothed in the same dress as the anterior note," and he still thought the words used by Letcher transcended the rules by descending to personalities. In his reply of April 11 suggesting that the discussion should be stopped, he expressed his expectation that Mexico, without refusing foreign assistance and cooperation, would apply her resources to the opening of the desired communication for the commerce of the world, that under less adverse auspices all difficulties would be removed and all interests reconciled and that the measure proposed would meet the approbation of Letcher and thereby facilitate the arrangement of other questions pending. The request of Letcher to submit the treaty to Congress, which was so promptly granted, resulted in almost unanimous rejection by that body—a rejection which under the circumstances the Committee on Foreign Relations of the American Senate in the following August reported as a discourtesy requiring a review of all existing relations with the Mexican government.[16]

On April 25, following the rejection of the treaty and the visit of Burwell, Letcher wrote Webster: "Since the rejection of the Tehuantepec Treaty, I have held no intercourse with the Minister of Foreign Relations. I am satisfied however, that the Administration and Congress are anxious to escape from the consequences of the act which they have perpetrated, and that they will adopt some plan of Legislation, by which the right of way will be granted. I think I may say, they are determined on this course. . . . It was stated in Congress and confirmed by the Administration that all the requisitions in regard to Tehuantepec, contained in the annual message of the President of the United States, should be complied with. . . . I have learned from a reliable source that Mr. Maman, the leader of the Conservative party, declared yesterday, that he could do anything except to recognize the Garay grant, to relieve Mexico from her present perilous position, and that Congress should not, with his approbation, adjourn until adequate measures shall have been adopted to secure that object.

"I ought to add, that in consequence of your instructions and of the interest which the Government of the United States has manifested in the success of the Treaty, I have gone very far, both in my official correspondence and conferences, to excite *the apprehensions* which now exist. I have not hesitated, before and since the rejection of the Treaty, to express the opinion, that the most serious consequences might result to Mexico, on account of the flagrant violation of her engagements. It is also proper to state, that I have not allowed myself to be consulted, with regard to any new schemes, which are now pending before Congress." [17]

Among the plans of legislation proposed in the Mexican Congress, that relating to the project of A. G. Sloo, an American citizen, met with the most favorable consideration, and later a new concession was granted to Sloo and associates for $600,000 and without the provisions of the Garay grant to which Mexico objected.

In May, President Fillmore received President Arista's prompt reply of April 15, 1852, stating that the Tehuantepec question should cause no international friction, if the obstinate New Orleans company, instead of urging the validity of the Garay grant, would apply directly to Mexico for a new concession as he had proposed to Letcher before the latter, by demanding the submission of the treaty to Congress, seemed to see "occasion to bring the two countries into a conflict." With it he received a copy of the Ramirez memorial which Arista approved and a notice that Don Manuel Larrainger had been sent to Washington with instructions to explain the Mexican position of non-recognition of the assignees of the Garay grant—and to maintain that position. On May 19, 1852, Webster wrote Fillmore that he feared Mexico would provoke the United States to take another slice of territory on the plan of compensation to the Mexican government.[18]

The Senate in July, 1852, asked Fillmore for the correspondence relating to the Tehuantepec negotiations; and, on August 30, a day preceding adjournment, it considered the resolutions submitted by the Committee on Foreign Relations against further negotiation and in favor of remedial action to protect American rights if Mexico should fail to reconsider her position. The debate, resulting in the tabling of the resolutions, indicated that the Tehuantepec interests were strongly opposed by the supporters of rival routes and that the situation was not as critical as Mexican newspapers feared. In the fall of 1852, articles of Ben E. Green in the New York *Herald* opposed the New Orleans company which had been favored by Webster.[19]

Meantime Letcher, who in May had expressed a desire to be recalled, had been succeeded in Mexico by Alfred Conkling of New York who was informed that the most important question pending was that of the Tehuantepec transit, negotiations concerning which were fully reviewed. Conrad, acting as Secretary of State during Webster's last illness, adopted a more moderate

tone towards Mexico in his instructions of October 14 to Conkling—directing him to learn Mexico's objections to the Garay
grant, and, if he found recognition of it could not be obtained
even in modified form, to sound the government upon the question of a direct cession to the American government of a right
of way which might obviate the difficulty (of pride) encountered by a direct recognition of the Garay grant. "Mexico having
rejected the Convention and repudiated the grant, and having
made no proposition whatever either to our Minister there or
through her Representative here," said he, "this government
cannot consistently with a due regard to its own dignity, make
any overtures to renew the negotiation. Nevertheless, this government anxiously desires that some arrangement should be made
whereby the communication across the Isthmus may be established, and would listen to any reasonable proposition for that
purpose. If, therefore, any such proposition should be made, you
will receive and transmit it without delay." [20]

Conkling on his arrival late in November, reported that the
New Orleans company was supposed to be exerting its influence
to defeat any new project. A month later (December 24) in a
despatch to Secretary Everett, he referred to British covert designs and intrigues to prevent the adjustment of the Tehuantepec question which was regarded as a danger to British designs
to appropriate Yucatan, and he stated that Mexico would never
release the United States from Article XI of the treaty of
1848. In connection with the discussion of insurrections in
Sonora and Guadalajara he had informed the Foreign Minister
(Levasseur) that "it was vain to expect any change for the
better until the government of the country should be placed in
other than Mexican hands"; and, apparently not apprehensive
of discords between powers of diverse interests, he had suggested
that "it might not be amiss for the great commercial nations to
consider whether it would not be both just and expedient for
them by compact between themselves to assume, so far at least
as relates to commerce, the government of a country whose pretensions to any capacity for self-government were so clearly
preposterous." At the same time he had declared that the United

States, with a settled policy to prevent European powers from extending their domains on the American continent, would never allow England to appropriate Yucatan. On January 1, 1853, referring to the unstable conditions, he reported that he had declined a proposition of the Mexican President that the ministers of the United States, Great Britain and France unite in a treaty arranging to order their naval forces to Mexico for protection of foreign commerce. Six days later he announced the defeat of the government forces, the resignation of President Arista, the succession of Ceballos and the remonstrance of the foreign ministers against violence and bloodshed by the victorious party.[21]

On February 2, 1853, following the resignation of President Arista, Conkling reported that Ceballos, who had succeeded to the presidency with extraordinary powers conferred by Congress, had expressed confidence that the United States could arrange an adjustment of all difficulties. Referring to the probability of a contract between Mexico and the Sloo interests and evidently without observing the limit placed on his power by his instructions of October 14, he said, "I shall venture to engage in any proffered negotiations without waiting further instructions." On February 7, he reported the prospect that Ceballos would for a long time maintain his position and that the Sloo contract was favorably regarded by the public. On the following day, he reported that as a result of a sudden political change Ceballos was down and that General Sombardini had become President under the "Italisco plan" which proposed the centralization of power and the recall of Santa Anna. On February 22, he announced the probable election of Santa Anna and that the anxiety of the Mexican government to treat with him indicated a propitious opportunity for negotiations of a Tehuantepec treaty.[22]

On March 21, without waiting for instructions and full powers, he signed with Mexico a convention recognizing the Sloo grant and forbidding the conveyance of armed forces across Tehuantepec without express authority of the Mexican government. One provision, giving the United States a qualified right to withdraw protection and guaranty, he said met with determined opposition from the Mexican negotiators but was finally yielded. Convinced that the Garay grant could be enforced only at the point of the bayonet, he said, "If I had shrunk from the weighty responsibility of signing this convention without delay . . . the United States would have lost an opportunity more favorable than it would ever have again." This convention, although regarded as a way of escape from a critical situation which had arisen under the Whig administration, did not meet the approval of the Democrat administration of Pierce which promised a more vigorous policy in regard to Tehuantepec, and also in relation to other problems of the Caribbean and Central American region.[23]

Throughout the period from 1848 to 1853 American policy and American relations with Mexico were influenced or conditioned by chaotic conditions in Mexico, by new American claims for damages, by certain filibustering raids from American territory into the northern frontier of Mexico, by Indian depredations along the international border and by disagreement concerning the southern boundary of New Mexico. In the latter part of the period another factor was an increasing eagerness to annex additional Mexican territory for various reasons (including economic convenience or need and prevention of European intrusion). On January 4, 1853, Lane of Oregon declared in Congress that the sooner the Mexican states joined the American union the "better for them and for the rest of mankind." On February 4, Senator Douglas expected early Mexican conditions which would demand intervention from combined motives of humanity and national security.

The earliest prominent American claims after the treaty of 1848 were those of the tobacco dealers who were required to pay heavy duties for goods imported into Mexico before the end of the period of American occupation. Others were for various commercial irregularities, robberies, breach of contract, and personal injuries including false imprisonment (such as the case of the American consul, Francis W. Rice, at Acapulco in 1852).

Mexico, while disturbed by filibustering expeditions planned against Cuba, and especially by the second Lopez expedition (of 1851) which was coincident with the threatened invasion of Mexico by the Louisiana Tehuantepec Company, felt more deeply the dangers from invasions across the international boundary beginning with emigrant gold seekers of 1849. These expeditions, which the American government was apparently unable to restrain satisfactorily, seriously affected negotiations for transit and other concessions. Among the chief border invasions were: the Joseph C. Moorehead filibustering expedition from southern California to Mazatlan and La Paz with plans for a descent upon Sonora, in March-August, 1851; the combined insurgent-filibuster expeditions resulting from cooperation of Texan merchant-smugglers with a revolution in Tamaulipas, and led by José Maria Carvajal, across the Rio Grande from Texas in 1850-52 and later; the unsuccessful expeditions of Raousset de Boulbon (a French soldier of fortune) from San Francisco to Sonora in 1852-53, beginning as a mining and colonization scheme and developing into open rebellion in favor of an independent Sonora—with which there was considerable sympathy at San Francisco, especially expressed in the later and more famous expeditions of William Walker to Lower California and Sonora in 1853-54.[24]

In the case of the Carvajal expeditions the American government, in September-October, 1851, acted promptly by instructions to military commanders and a proclamation of warning. On December 22, 1851, Webster wrote Letcher that although the government had acted according to its duty, the military authorities had been rendered somewhat helpless by desertions of troops to join Carvajal. In the spring of 1852, one raid was suppressed by General Harney, by the arrest of Carvajal who, however, was released on bond and began preparations for another invasion which might possibly have been prevented if Congress had enacted a more stringent neutrality law as recommended by the President. Letcher, who on October 29, 1851, had complained that his negotiations were embarrassed by the earlier movements, reported that the third invasion by

Carvajal had awakened a feeling of intense Mexican "prejudice against everything connected with American interests." [25]

The American responsibility for the control of the various wild Indian tribes along the boundary of the newly acquired territory—which the United States from necessity assumed under Article XI of the treaty of 1848, chiefly to make the treaty acceptable to Chihuahua and the other northern border states of Mexico—proved a heavy and difficult task. From it the American government soon sought to be released, after a period of groping toward the formulation of a definite and consistent policy under the conditions of rigid economy imposed by Congress and the resulting inefficiency of the frontier military force. American officials, unable to manage the complicated problems satisfactorily, sometimes (and perhaps without good reason) blamed the Mexican government for lack of cooperation in efforts to defend its own territory against the destructive Indian depredations. Mexican complaints against the American government for failure to comply with its treaty obligations were frequent. In February, 1851, President Arista seemed ready to propose a union of Mexican and American troops on both sides of the boundary. In July, 1851, the Mexican government proposed tentatively for reference to Washington a reciprocal crossing of the border. Webster, on August 19, authorized Letcher to propose, in the interest of harmonious relations, a release from Article XI of 1848 and also from Article XXXIII of 1831, which, however careful the American government might be, was liable to result in charges of bad faith and in exaggerated or fraudulent claims. For this release he proposed a pecuniary consideration, provided part of the amount could be applied to satisfy unpaid installments under the claims convention of 1843 and to pay American claims which had arisen against Mexico since 1848. Finding that Letcher's negotiations for release from the Indian obligation encountered various obstacles and proceeded very slowly, and that the Mexican government had been advised that the American government would probably be willing to pay ten million dollars for the release, Webster, in response to Letcher's request of January 24, 1852, for instructions to increase the offer, authorized an offer of an additional two millions. He soon learned that Letcher, disheartened by Ramirez's demand for twelve millions, had closed the negotiation, which, however, was unsuccessfully resumed by his successor (Conkling) and later continued by Gadsden.

Relations were considerably disturbed after 1850 by various difficulties connected with the survey of the new international boundary as provided by the treaty of 1848. The delay in marking the boundary was partly due to partisan policies in Congress resulting in limited funds for the survey and later changes in the survey commission, and partly to geographical questions which arose in connection with the survey.[26] From the Rio Grande the boundary was described as "westerly, along the whole southern boundary of New Mexico which runs north of the town called Paso to its western termination; thence, northward, along the western line of New Mexico, until it intersects the first branch of the river Gila; (or if it should not intersect any branch of that river, then to the point on said line nearest to such branch, and thence in a direct line to the same;) thence down the middle of said branch and of the said river, until it empties into the Rio Colorado; thence across the Rio Colorado, following the division line between Upper and Lower California, to the Pacific Ocean" (one league south of San Diego). The joint commission met at San Diego (in July, 1849) as required by the treaty. It determined the initial point on the Pacific on October 10, and the point of junction of the Gila and the Colorado in January, 1850. Instead of continuing the survey eastward up the Gila and beyond, it adjourned to meet at El Paso in November. Already a member of the commission (Major Emory) had suggested that the prospective Gila branches, starting in the Sierra Madre south of the southern boundary of New Mexico, probably disappeared in the sand long before they reached the Gila and yet might properly be considered affluents of the Gila. In view of the inaccuracies of the Disturnell map, he had thought that the commission might adopt the parallel of 32° to the San Pedro, or even a more southern parallel west of the Rio Grande, in order to secure a good practical route for a railway under American jurisdiction. Meantime the American commissioner, John B. Weller, had been dismissed, and, in June, 1850, he was replaced by John Russell Bartlett (after the place had been offered to John C. Fremont). At El Paso, where the work of the survey was resumed in December, 1850, before the arrival of the American surveyor, A. B. Gray, the first question was the determination of the initial point on the Rio Grande. Here arose a dispute, resulting from errors in the Disturnell map by which the position of El Paso on the Rio Grande was located a half degree too far north and two degrees too far east. By a compromise the southern boundary was run three degrees west of the Rio Grande on parallel 32° 22'—seven minutes north of El Paso as it appeared on the Disturnell revised map of 1847. This compromise was regarded by some as a surrender of territory best adapted for a practical route for a railroad which had been contemplated in the negotiations of the treaty of Guadalupe Hidalgo (Art. V). Therefore, Gray, upon his arrival, refused to sign. The result was a series of quarrels between the American commissioner and his subordinates. These quarrels delayed the survey and led to further changes in the personnel. They also possibly contributed to later charges against Bartlett which discredited the commission before it was finally legislated out of existence in 1852—partly under the influence of Senator Weller who after his release from the commission had been elected to the United States Senate from California. In January, 1852, La Vege, the Mexican minister at Washington, protested to Webster against the delays resulting from the absence of the American surveyor, the changes in the American commission and lack of harmony among its members; and he urged better organization to prevent confusion. Although in the appropriation bill of March, 1853, provision was finally made for funds to complete the survey of the Rio Grande, the dispute concerning the southern boundary of New Mexico remained unsettled until the administration of Pierce. With it were involved two grave problems: (1) the loss or gain of a practicable southern route for a railway to the Pacific; and (2) the attitude of the people residing in the

region of the disputed territory—including along the Rio
Grande the fertile strip, Mesilla, which seemed to prefer American jurisdiction. The latter influenced the governor of New
Mexico, W. C. Lane, on March 13, 1853, to claim jurisdiction
over the entire contested region, following the news that Congress had repudiated Bartlett's compromise line if it should be
found to be located farther north of El Paso than the southern
boundary of New Mexico as indicated in the Disturnell revised
map of 1847.[27]

Many Southern leaders, who had expected to obtain a larger
cession of territory from Mexico in 1848, were still hoping for
an opportunity to get an additional cession "to maintain the
balance of power" with the North. Clayton, who opposed this
policy, on March 14, 1853, in a speech defending the Clayton-
Bulwer treaty of 1850, expressed the view that "the true policy
of this government is to build up Mexico as a republic, to sustain and cheer her by good offices, and to teach her by our
example the science of self-government—not to annex a ring-
streaked and speckled people who can never be incorporated as
states of the United States." [28]

REFERENCES

1. *16 Mexico, Instructions*, No. 1, Sept. 18, 1849; *15 Mexico, Despatches* (General observations of W. Hunter, preceding Letcher's
   despatch No. 100 of Dec. 1, 1851); *Sen. Misc. Doc. 50*, 30-2;
   Sen. Exec. Doc. 97, 32-1, pp. 132-33; J. FRED RIPPY, *The United
   States and Mexico*, pp. 48-52.
2. *Sen. Exec. Doc. 97*, 32-1, pp. 7-8; *16 Mexico, Instructions*, pp.
   132-33, (No. 19) Apr. 30, 1849, and (No. 1) Sept. 18, 1849;
   15 Mexico, Despatches (General observations of W. Hunter).
3. *16 Great Britain, Instructions*, p. 70, Oct. 31, 1849.
4. *15 Mexico, Despatches*, June 20, 1853 (General observations of W.
   Hunter).
5. *14 Mexico, Despatches*, (No. 29) June 24, and (No. 30) July 13,
   1850.
6. *Sen. Exec. Doc. 97*, 32-1, pp. 23-35, 57, 81; *De Bow's Review*,
   Jan., 1851, p. 94; PIERCE BUTLER, *Judah P. Benjamin*, p. 125.
7. *16 Mexico, Instructions*, pp. 207-24, (No. 42) Aug. 24, 1850;
   14 Mexico, Despatches, (No. 33) Oct. 22, 1850.

8. *16 Mexico, Instructions,* No. 47, Dec. 4, 1850.
9. *14 Mexico, Despatches,* No. 49, Apr. 1, 1851; *16 Mexico, Instructions,* No. 62, May 5, 1851.
10. *Ib.,* No. 63, May 6, 1851.
11. *Ib.,* (No. 70) Aug. 16, and (No. 71) Aug. 18, 1851.
12. *14 Mexico, Despatches,* No. 85, Sept. 14, 1851; *15 Mexico, Despatches* (Observations of W. Hunter, preceding Letcher's No. 100 of Dec. 1, 1851).
13. *14 Mexico, Despatches,* No. 97, Oct. 29, 1851, *Sen. Doc. 97,* 32-1, p. 101.
14. *15 Mexico, Despatches,* (No. 100) Dec. 1, and (No. 101) Dec. 14, 1851, and (No. 3) Apr. 4, 1852.
15. *Sen. Exec. Doc. 97,* 32-1, pp. 109-11; *16 Mexico, Instructions,* pp. 317-25, No. 90, Mar. 22, 1852, to Letcher and special of March 22 to Burwell.
16. *15 Mexico, Despatches,* No. 3, Apr. 4, 1852; *Rp. of Com. on Foreign Relations, U. S. Senate,* IV, pp. 83-95, Aug. 30, 1852.
17. *15 Mexico, Despatches,* No. 5, Apr. 25, 1852.
18. *Sen. Rp. 355,* 32-1, pp. 14-19; *6 Notes from Mexico Legation,* July 10, 1852; *Webster's Works,* XVIII, pp. 531-33.
19. *Cong. Globe,* pp. 32-1 and 32-2.
20. *16 Mexico, Instructions,* No. 4, Oct. 14, 1852.
21. *16 Mexico, Despatches,* (No. 7) Dec. 24, 1852, (No. 9) Jan. 1, and (No. 12) Jan. 7, 1853.
22. *Ib.,* (No. 14) Feb. 2, and (No. 16) Feb. 3, (No. 20) Feb. 7, and (No. 23) Feb. 22, 1853.
23. *Ib.,* No. 26, March 24, 1853.
24. J. FRED RIPPY, *The United States and Mexico,* Chaps. IV and V; *6 Notes from Mexico Legation,* Oct. 23 and Nov. 13, 1851; *16 Mexico, Instructions,* p. 273, (No. 76) Sept. 24, 1851; *14 Mexico, Despatches,* (No. 92) Oct. 5, 1851; *16 Mexico, Despatches,* (No. 5) Nov. 30, and (No. 7) Dec. 24, 1852.
25. *Sen. Exec. Doc. 97,* 32-1, pp. 100-02 and 109-11.
26. *Sen. Exec. Doc. 52,* 30-1, pp. 176 and 293; *14 Mexico, Despatches,* (No. 45) Feb. 16, and (No. 74) July 12; *15 Mexico, Despatches,* (No. 101) Dec. 14, 1851, and (Private) Jan. 19, 1852; *16 Mexico, Instructions,* (No. 72) Aug. 19, 1851, and (No. 4) Oct. 14, 1852.
27. PAUL NEFF GARBER, *The Gadsden Treaty,* pp. 11-17; J. FRED RIPPY, *The United States and Mexico,* Chap. VI; *Sen. Exec. Doc. 34,* 31-1; *Sen. Doc. 119,* 32-1; *Sen. Exec. Doc. 41,* 32-2; *Cong. Globe,* 32-1, pp. 2270-71, 2402-04 and Appendix, p. 776.
28. *U. S. Review,* I, pp. 1-11, Jan., 1853; *31 Cong. Globe,* 32-3, Vol. 27, Appendix, p. 270.

CHAPTER VII

THE GADSDEN PURCHASE AND RELATED ISSUES UNDER PIERCE

PRESIDENT PIERCE, although nominated for the presidency as a "dark horse," had already had considerable valuable experience in public service—as a member of the lower house of Congress, 1833-37, as a member of the United States Senate from 1837 to 1842 (when he resigned), and as an officer in the Mexican War (reaching the rank of brigadier general in March, 1847). After first offering the office of Secretary of State to John A. Dix, to whom extreme Southern leaders objected, he finally selected for this high office William Learned Marcy, an astute New York politician of long experience in public service—as state comptroller (1823-29), associate justice of the state supreme court (1829-31), United States senator (1831-33), governor of New York (1833-39), Mexican claims commissioner (1839-42), and United States Secretary of War (1845-49). For Secretary of War he selected Jefferson Davis who had a large influence on the policies of the administration and was especially influential in the selection of the American minister to Mexico in 1853. For the Mexican mission he chose a South Carolinian, James Gadsden, who had served with distinction in the War of 1812, had later served as confidential aide-de-camp with Jackson in the Florida campaign of 1817-18, had been interested in Florida politics from 1825 to 1838, and, returning to Charleston in 1839, had been elected in 1840 as president of the Louisville, Charleston & Cincinnati Railroad (later the South Carolina Railroad)—a position which he held until 1850 and which stimulated his interest in a transcontinental railroad. Gadsden's successor, John Forsyth, whose father was Secretary of State

From : Atlas of the Historical Society of the United States. By C. O. Paullin.

Published by The American Geographical Society of New York.

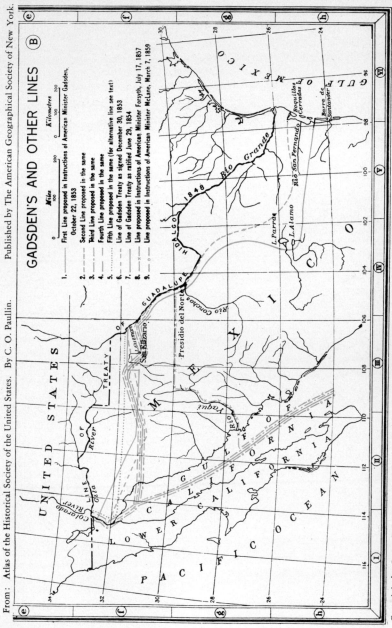

GADSDEN'S AND OTHER LINES (B)

Miles
0   100   200   300

Kilometres
0   100   200   300

1. First Line proposed in Instructions of American Minister Gadsden, October 22, 1853
2. Second Line proposed in the same
3. Third Line proposed in the same
4. Fourth Line proposed in the same
5. Fifth Line proposed in the same (for alternative line see text)
6. Line of Gadsden Treaty as signed December 30, 1853
7. Line of Gadsden Treaty as ratified June 29, 1854
8. Line proposed in Instructions of American Minister Forsyth, July 17, 1857
9. Line proposed in Instructions of American Minister McLane, March 7, 1859

from 1834 to 1841, had served in the Mexican War and had been editor of the Mobile *Register* since 1853.

The beginning of the Pierce administration was coincident with a change in the Mexican administration. The resignation of the friendless Arista on January 5, 1853, a result of the Guadalajara revolt which started the previous July, prepared the way for the return of Santa Anna who was installed in the presidency April 15, 1853, and who, following the death of Secretary Alaman early in June, appointed Bonilla as successor to the office of Minister of Relations. The Mexican minister at Washington for the larger part of the period (July, 1853, to February, 1856) was General Almonte who was well known by his previous period of diplomatic service at Washington, 1842-45. He was succeeded by Manuel Robles Pezeula in April, 1856.

Pierce evidently expected to direct a "brilliant foreign policy" which had been lavishly predicted and advertised by his campaign managers. In his inaugural address he indicated that his policy contemplated alterations in the map by further territorial expansion important for national protection. In practice it was expressed by a Canadian reciprocity treaty and efforts for protection or extension of American trade everywhere, the improvement of the diplomatic and consular service, and protection of the rights of naturalized citizens. It included plans for the opening of South American rivers and the free use of the Danish Sound, and interesting adventures in the Pacific (in Japan, China, Hawaii and Ecuador) and in the Caribbean (in Cuba, San Domingo, Colombia, Central America and Mexico).

At the opening of his administration, President Pierce sought a peaceful settlement of the critical dispute concerning the southern boundary of New Mexico which was complicated by problems of destructive Indian raids from the United States into Mexico and American desire for release from responsibility for these Indian depredations under Article XI of the treaty of 1848, the old question of claims, American interest in Tehuantepec, and the ebullitions of "manifest destiny." Desiring to avoid a dispute on territorial limits, Marcy, on May 18, disapproved a letter which Conkling had sent to Governor Lane early in April at the request of the Mexican Minister of Relations—a letter in which, while disapproving Lane's course, Conkling had assumed a position tending to impair the American claims to the territory in dispute. While he considered that the southern boundary of New Mexico had not yet been determined under the treaty, and agreed that neither government should undertake to occupy the disputed area and instructed Governor Meriwether (Lane's successor) to this effect, he planned to merge the boundary issue into a negotiation for acquisition of additional territory—a negotiation which may have had its "origin in the fertile imagination of Jefferson Davis," as the New York *Herald* later charged.[1]

Believing that Mexico, again under the direction of Santa Anna and in need of funds, would be willing to cede additional territory in connection with the negotiation of a treaty for satisfactory boundary adjustment and settlement of all other difficulties with its neighbor, in May Pierce appointed to conduct the negotiations the somewhat unscrupulous James Gadsden, a South Carolinian politician and railway promoter, who, through his friend Jefferson Davis, had become especially interested in the plans for a proposed Southern Pacific railway involving an effort to secure a more practical route south of the Gila River—a route which he had designated at the Memphis Convention in 1845 and for which, in the same year, he had recommended a western terminus at Mazatlan on the Gulf of California. Marcy, in his instructions of July 15 to Gadsden, stated that the President was not yet prepared to announce his course of duty concerning the Garay grant or the proposed convention of Letcher for the guaranty of the recent Sloo grant which was in direct conflict to the earlier grant, but he approved the earlier position asserting that the United States had fulfilled its obligations under Article XI of the treaty of 1848, and especially emphasized the importance of securing an alteration of the boundary proposed in Article VI of the treaty in order to facilitate the purpose of the negotiators concerning the construction of a canal or a railroad. As a canal was now considered impracticable by that route, a feasible route for a railroad was sought.[2]

"It is difficult to tell, without an actual survey, the extent of the alteration required for such purpose," said he. "It would be important particularly to the interests of Mexico that such a rail-road should connect with the navigable waters of the Gulf of California. For this purpose it is desirable that the true line—as we contend—the line commencing on the Rio Grande a few miles north of El Paso—should be continued for a considerable distance west beyond the treaty line, then run south about 30' and then again west to that Gulf. Should Mexico be unwilling to make so large a cession of country as such a line would require she might agree to have the line on the southern border of New Mexico continued until it shall strike the River San Pedro and thence down that river to its junction with the Gila. . . . Should you find Mexico disposed to treat for a new line," he continued, "you are instructed not to press a discussion of our claim—after having clearly stated it—for the disputed territory. It is probably the expedient way of disposing of that question to let it be merged in the negotiation for an alteration of the boundary. With this negotiation for a change of the line it may also be proper to embrace the settlement of the claims of our citizens against Mexico and the pretended claims of her citizens against the United States arising under the 11th Article of the Treaty of Guadalupe Hidalgo."

Although he apprehended that the Mexican government, influenced by hostile feelings engendered by the period of war, was not favorably disposed to a fair adjustment and might embarrass the negotiations, he hoped that prejudices might be removed by the President's liberal course and by the American desire for amicable relations and free commercial intercourse.

Gadsden, who had accepted his appointment on May 19, left for New Orleans on July 23, arrived at Vera Cruz by August 4, and had an audience with Santa Anna by August 17. In July, before he left Charleston, he urged the importance of a survey of the Gulf of California and the adjacent regions as an aid to discreet and intelligent negotiations for a satisfactory boundary which would not need further revision, and later he felt that his success would have been promoted if the government had heeded his request to send a surveyor (A. B. Gray) with him. By September, after considering the problems of

Mexican finances and politics, he requested supplementary instructions as to the amount of territory desired; and, evidently influenced by the views of Jefferson Davis, he suggested the acquisition of the five frontier states by a liberal offer at the psychological moment, aided by a contingent fund for application to immediate pressing necessities of the Mexican government and by increase of border and naval forces for an impressive effect. A few days after his arrival, in answer to a complaint of Bonilla concerning some disorderly acts of Americans on the Chihuahua border, possibly in connection with preparations to establish a new post opposite El Paso, he explained that the new governor of New Mexico had been accompanied to his post by a force large enough to preserve order. On September 9, in reply to Bonilla's complaint of the increasing destructiveness of "incessant incursions of savage Indians" resulting from "nonfulfillment of engagements . . . contracted" by Article XI of the treaty of 1848—and for which numerous claims had recently been submitted at Washington—he denied that the American government had been delinquent in its international obligations or that the Mexican government could properly claim indemnity. At the same time he offered to receive from Bonilla any proposals as to a method of settlement—an offer to which Bonilla refused to respond. On September 18, expecting a proposal which would lead to the settlement of all difficulties by acquisition of territory, he wrote Marcy that the natural line from the standpoint of restraining Indian incursions was not north of 31° but might be found south of it. To influence or facilitate peaceful negotiations he favored a show of force on the frontier, and later proposed a call to Washington for a "private and confidential conference with the President." [3]

Following the refusal of Bonilla to answer his note of September 9, he obtained a conference (of September 25) with President Santa Anna who agreed to negotiate for a new boundary involving the sale of Mexican territory. On October 3 he reported a personal interview with Santa Anna, who agreed that the disputed territory should remain in *statu quo* and that Mexico would negotiate for a new boundary and also accorded a permit for reconnoitering frontier areas; but he found that Santa Anna, apparently impervious to Gadsden's arguments in favor of anticipating manifest destiny of the frontier states south of the Rio Grande, refused to consent to the alienation of territory beyond the amount actually needed for the proposed railroad. In a conference of October 2, Gadsden had suggested a cession of a large tract in order to obtain a natural mountain and desert boundary such as he had suggested in 1848. A few days later he forwarded to General Garland a permit for exploration of the Gila region. Still awaiting the expected supplementary instructions, on October 17, after reporting the progress of negotiations with Bonilla, who was apprehensive of the American explorations south of the boundary, he mentioned the necessity of embracing all issues in the proposed adjustment. On November 3, reporting no further progress, he mentioned the extravagant expectations of the Mexican government as to claims under Article XI of the treaty of 1848 and the proposed cession of the Mesilla Valley. Later, on November 17, he reported more encouraging prospects of adjustment, although later negotiations were influenced by a filibustering expedition from San Francisco to Lower California which he reported.[4]

Meantime Marcy, apprehending a critical emergency which might induce Santa Anna to make a liberal cession of territory for immediate pecuniary means, and possibly influenced by conditions in Sonora and Lower California which invited filibustering expeditions, had sent by special messenger, C. L. Ward, confidential supplementary instructions bearing date of October 22. By these secret instructions, which Ward was directed to communicate orally to Gadsden, the latter was authorized to negotiate a single treaty providing for acquisition of new territory, release from Article XI of the treaty of 1848, and settlement of claims. He was authorized to pay a maximum of fifty million dollars (including an attractive cash payment) for release from claims and from obligations under Article XI of the treaty of 1848 and for the most desirable boundary—beginning on the Gulf far south of the Rio Grande at a point midway between the Boquillas Cerradas and the Barra de Santander, thence westward along the ridge between the San Fernando and Santander rivers to the coast range, thence across the range and along the heights to a point south of Lake Parras, thence northward veering westward along the highlands between the Sabinas and Conchos and to the "parallel of San Eliasario," thence westward south of Lake Guzman along the highlands to 111° W., thence directly to the Gulf of California at 31° N., thence down the middle of the Gulf and around the point of Lower California and northward along the western coast to the United States boundary on the Pacific. In case of failure to get this boundary he was authorized to accept one of four alternates (for smaller sums) with the release from claims for damages under Article XI of the treaty of 1848: (1) From the Gulf at a point midway between the Rio Grande and the Rio San Fernando, and along the highlands until they were intersected by the river, thence along the river to 31° N., thence from the cañon and along the mountain range near the river to the "parallel of the Presidia San Eliasario," thence westward as before to the middle of the Gulf of California, thence northward to the American boundary on the Colorado (for thirty-five million dollars); (2) Along the Rio Grande to the cañon, thence along the mountain range to the parallel of the Presidia San Eliasario, and thence westward, etc., as in the first proposal, including Lower California (for thirty million dollars); (3) Same as second alternative to the middle of the Gulf of California, thence northward to the American boundary on the Colorado (for twenty million dollars); (4) From Frontera on the Rio Grande, at 31° 48', west to the Gulf of California, or from the Rio Grande west on 32° —neither of which was regarded as a good boundary, although each furnished a good route for a railroad. (For this boundary the sum of fifteen million dollars was authorized.) [5]

With these instructions Marcy handed Ward the following note in cipher to present to Gadsden: "This accredits to you Christopher L. Ward who is sent by the President as special messenger fully possessed with his views in regard to the negotiations of a new line with Mexico. His verbal communications on that subject you will regard as instructions from this Department." [6]

Ward, before he left the shores of the United States, returned to Marcy by mail the written instructions, and, on November 14, in Mexico City, he furnished Gadsden in writing his recollections of the memoranda to which, however, he added a specific direction urging the protection of the holders of the Garay grant in which he seemed much interested. Stating that the President was determined to support the claims of the Garay group in every proper way short of war and to repudiate the Conkling treaty, he urged Gadsden to arrange in one treaty at once all points of difference if possible to do so without delaying the boundary question. That Ward was not authorized to urge the inclusion of the Garay grant, but that he was directed to caution Gadsden not to embarrass or clog his negotiations with it, was stated in a later instruction of Marcy who regarded that grant of "very indifferent character" but prudently feared that the release of the claim would subject the American government to a demand of a very large sum by the assignees of that grant.[7]

Gadsden, offended by the advice and presumptuous attitude of Ward, on November 20 sent Marcy a long protest urging that the injection of the question of a grant which the Mexican government had repeatedly repudiated, together with the reduction of the financial consideration by introduction of claims, might endanger the success of his negotiations. At the same time he intimated that the President might have a contingent or secret-service fund which could be used to advantage in facilitating a difficult negotiation. In reply, Marcy sent to Gadsden the exact written instructions to Ward and the statement that the latter was authorized to direct Gadsden not to embarrass the negotiations by the Garay grant; and he also stated that the secret-service fund for the year had been expended, and that an application to Congress for an immediate large increase of the fund for the proposed purpose would be indiscreet—by submitting the subject to a debate which would defeat the purpose of facilitating the negotiation. In a later letter, written after the negotiations were completed, he explained that his desire to disconnect the negotiations from the Tehuantepec grants was partly due to the apprehension that persons interested in the grants had in Mexico agents who had "extraordinary facilities for getting information" and would use all possible means in order to influence the negotiations to forward their own interests.[8]

Meantime, Gadsden promptly prepared a project for a treaty in which he included the Garay claims and obtained from Santa Anna a promise to appoint a commission at once to confer concerning the settlement of all questions. Suspecting recent Mexican appeals to Europe, and European opposition to his negotiations, on November 29 he informed Bonilla that European interference would only hasten the inevitable American absorption of a large part of northern Mexico including Lower California and urged the cession of the region in order to secure a "natural boundary" of mountain and desert which would prevent causes of future border troubles. On December 10, he began with Bonilla and the other two commissioners the difficult negotiations which, after six sessions, finally terminated in a treaty on December 30. He repeatedly urged the cession of a large area of territory, against the repeated refusal of the Mexican representatives to cede more than the minimum necessary for the proposed railroad. At the close of the second conference, disturbed by speculators, by the Walker filibusters, by Mexican extravagant demands and mistaken hopes, and by the attempt to transfer part of the issues to Almonte at Washington, he threatened to terminate the negotiations—and probably also threatened a resort to force, for which he had no authority.* In a note to Bonilla he made an offer to purchase Lower California, consideration of which was promptly declined by Bonilla—possibly due in part to the influence of the inopportune Walker expedition upon Santa Anna. Entering the third conference at the request of his antagonists and with the hope that

* Although instructed to avoid any collision with Mexican military or civil authorities, General Garland, probably influenced by a later order to be prepared for any Mexican aggression, on December 27 wrote Gadsden that he had arranged his troops "ready to attack, or repel, whichever may be necessary."

they might revise their "extravagant estimates of the value of worthless domain," in the fourth he finally consented to negotiate on the Mexican territorial basis (after the failure of his final attempts to obtain access to the Gulf of California and to secure Lake Guzman), but he continued to resist Bonilla's extravagant demand of eight million dollars as compensation for past damages and future relief from American responsibility under Article XI of the treaty of 1848 which Gadsden refused to admit. In the fifth (of December 24), he persistently but unsuccessfully pressed for Mexican recognition of the Garay grant, even offering three million dollars, but was finally forced to accept Bonilla's suggestion to include the Garay claim among those which the United States proposed to assume as part of the compensation to Mexico for territory or concessions. The agreement on compensation was a compromise. Gadsden offered a total of seventeen million dollars, twelve millions to Mexico and five millions to American citizens for claims against Mexico, but finally agreed to pay fifteen millions to Mexico (one-fifth on exchange of ratifications and the remainder in four monthly installments) and five millions for the private claims.[9]

Thus, by the treaty of December 30, Santa Anna, who had proclaimed himself Perpetual Dictator on December 16, found a way to finance his despotic career by funds received from the sale of the Mesilla Valley—a sale which fomented discontent against him and led to the demand for his removal under the plan of Ayutla of March 1, 1854, and to his final resignation and his exile on October 9, 1855.

On December 16, Gadsden had complained to Marcy that the Mexican extravagant pretensions and expectations were based on erroneous information from Washington, evidently from Almonte. This complaint resulted in an interesting conference of Marcy with Almonte whom he assured that the American government could not pay an enormous sum for barren land needed for a railway in the vicinity of the Gila, and could regard only incidentally the Tehuantepec grants which must not be permitted to embarrass the negotiations. To Almonte's suggestion that the negotiations had been embarrassed by American requests for large areas of territory Marcy replied that beyond a feasible route for a railroad the American government wanted no territory except what was incidentally necessary in securing a safe and easily-defended boundary in which Mexico was concerned more than the United States.[10]

The treaty which was signed at the American legation on December 30, after six conferences with Bonilla, contained ten articles. Article I defined the boundary, which, between the Colorado and the Rio Grande, was as follows: from the intersection of the previous boundary with the Colorado, down the middle of the stream to a point two marine leagues north of the beginning of the Gulf of California, thence by right line to the intersection parallel of 31° N. with meridian 111° W., thence by right line to the Rio Grande at parallel 31°, 47' and 30"— including a new area which was considerably reduced by the amended boundary proposed in the American Senate. Article II annulled Article XI of the treaty of 1848 without giving the United States a complete release from obligations concerning the conduct of the border Indians. Article III stated the compensation for territory, and American claims against Mexico (including claimants under the Garay concession). Article IV provided for organization of a claims commission. Article V granted to the United States free navigation of the Gulf of California to and from its neighboring territory. Article VI applied to the ceded territory and persons and property therein, all the provisions of the eighth, ninth, sixteenth and seventeenth articles of the treaty of 1848. Article VII placed restrictions for determining the validity of Mexican land grants in the ceded territory. Article VIII provided for reciprocal cooperation in the suppression of "lawless enterprises" across the border (filibuster raids). Article IX provided for peaceful adjustment of future differences, reaffirming Articles 21 and 22 of the treaty of 1848. Article X placed a time limit of six months for exchange of ratifications.

At Gadsden's suggestion, the signers of the treaty agreed to keep secret the stipulations of the treaty until ratification. A copy of the document was promptly forwarded to Washington by C. L. Ward who presented it to President Pierce on January 19, 1854, coincident with Gadsden's arrival at Charleston, South Carolina, by way of New Orleans, and a day before a summary of the treaty appeared in the New York *Herald* which evidently had some source of inside information.

Pierce, who was inclined to reject the treaty because of its provision as to the Tehuantepec grants, immediately submitted it to the cabinet for discussion. On February 14, on the recommendation of four members of the cabinet, he submitted it to the Senate (in confidence) for its advice, recommending three changes: (1) making reciprocal the obligations imposed by Article II; (2) rejection of the provision of Article III for assumption of American claims against Mexico under the Garay grant; (3) modification of the promise of mutual cooperation to suppress filibustering expeditions. In the Senate, which on February 13 had confirmed the appointment of Gadsden as minister to Mexico, consideration of the treaty was delayed by the debate on the Kansas-Nebraska bill and the absence of Senator Mason, chairman of the Committee on Foreign Relations. On March 3, it was reported from the committee, which accepted two of the President's proposed amendments but retained the provision in favor of the Garay claimants. Although consideration was in executive (secret) session, the proceedings leaked into the newspapers. Debates occupied much time until April 25, resulting in a demand for all correspondence and documents connected with the negotiations—including even a copy of the Conkling convention which Pierce had refused to submit for ratification, and all the correspondence of Ward.[11]

The struggle for confirmation of the treaty was first led by Mason (until April 6), and then by the conciliatory Rusk (of Texas), and, after failure on April 17, was finally forced through the Senate on April 25 under the leadership of Dawson (of Georgia) and Jones (of Tennessee) immediately following their return from an enthusiastic commercial convention at Charleston, South Carolina, in which Polk and Gadsden had participated. The chief opponents to confirmation were the large anti-slavery group led by Seward (and Sumner, Fish, Chase and

Wade), a smaller group who wanted a larger cession of territory and a port on the Gulf of California (Gwin, Weller and
Shields), and a group who urged recognition of the Sloo grant
as a *sine qua non* (Bell, Clayton and Bayard). Another impediment to confirmation was the disclosure (on March 27) of
Ward's activities in favor of the Garay grant. Shields' proposed
amendment of April 4 to extend the boundary farther south
in order to get a port on the Gulf of California was rejected by
a vote of 21 to 20. Gwin, who favored a line across Mexico from
30 miles south of the mouth of the Rio Grande to 30 miles south
of Mazatlan, on April 5 offered a resolution to extend the
boundary to 31°—which was defeated by a vote of 26 to 12.
On April 10, Rusk, who desired only enough territory for the
proposed railroad route, sought to conciliate two opposition
groups by an amendment reducing the amount of territorial
cession (which was approved by a vote of 32 to 14). Two days
later, he offered a similar amendment for a new boundary which
also was accepted (beginning on the Rio Grande at 31°, 47′,
thence west 100 miles, thence south 30 miles, thence west to the
meridian 111°, thence directly to the Colorado 20 miles south
of the junction of the Gila). The latter was slightly changed
on April 25 by Mason's article defining the boundary as finally
established by the revised treaty ("thence south 30 miles" being
changed to "thence south to the parallel of 31°, 20′ "). On
April 12, Rusk obtained consent to substitute for Article II
the simple declaration that Article XI of 1848 was abrogated.
He also proposed substitutes for Articles III and IV, reducing
to seven millions the sum payable to Mexico and omitting any
mention of private claims (including those of Hargous, the successor of Garay). These substitutes were accepted by a vote of
30 to 13. Gwin's motion to reject Article VIII concerning cooperation in suppression of filibustering expeditions was adopted.
On April 17, Bell offered a new article providing for recognition of the Sloo grant by both governments and protection
of any company formed under it—an article whose final defeat
by a vote of 28 to 18 (less than the required two-thirds) was
a large factor in the immediate defeat of affirmation of the

treaty by a vote of 27 to 18 (three less than the required two-thirds).

Immediately following the vote against ratification of the amended treaty, Pierce, while declaring that he also would have rejected it, announced that the responsibility for a war which might result from failure of the treaty would rest upon the Senate. On April 18, a vote to reconsider the rejected treaty prepared the way for the final contest. Mason's proposal to place the boundary slightly further south than that proposed by Rusk (but securing 9,000 square miles less territory than would have been secured by Gadsden's treaty provision) was approved (with only 11 negative votes). The proposal to increase to $10,000,000 the compensation to Mexico was also approved. Bell's amendment for the promise of protection by both governments to the work of the Sloo grantees was accepted by a vote of 30 to 14. Finally, on April 25, ratification of the amended treaty, establishing a boundary line considerably different from that to which Gadsden and the Mexican agents had agreed, was recommended by a vote of 33 to 12. Apparently its fate was determined by its provision relating to the Tehuantepec transit —Article VIII, containing the principles of the Conkling draft convention which Pierce had refused to submit to the Senate. Another determining factor was the reduction of the extent of the territorial cession.[12]

Possibly the greatest mistake of the treaty, as of that of 1848, was its failure to secure a more logical and more convenient boundary which would have prevented later difficulties—especially its failure to secure enough of Sonora to furnish a suitable land connection with the Gulf of California, needed for the development of Arizona and the Southwest. Before the ratification of the treaty, migrating Americans who were under the impression that Sonora was embraced in the new acquisition were arrested in the spring of 1854 for landing in Mexico without passports, and a year later Almonte in a note to Marcy remonstrated against the occupation of the Mesilla Valley by American troops. The treaty left unsettled several questions which caused later trouble—especially the question of American claims which Gadsden had sought to settle by American payment as a part of the compensation for Mexican concessions, and the question of preventing lawless expeditions or raids across the border. As a settlement of the Mexican question it proved unsatisfactory. It became a basis for new diplomatic issues (especially concerning transit routes and border troubles), and partly determined the Mexican policy of the Buchanan administration to acquire additional territory and transit routes and to assume a temporary protectorate over border territory of Mexico.[13]

Pierce, although he did not favor government interference to protect private companies in foreign countries, and was much annoyed by the amendment which appeared in Article VIII, and even considered the question of reopening negotiations for another treaty, finally decided to accept the amendments and ratify the treaty only because it would remove the most threatening of the many difficulties with Mexico. Marcy, therefore, forwarded a copy of the altered treaty to Mexico by a special messenger of the Mexican legation with the assurance that President Pierce would ratify it if Santa Anna should agree to the amendments. On May 6, informing Mr. Cripps (the American chargé in Mexico) of the "outdoor opposition" to the treaty which might possibly result in certain American efforts to influence rejection of the treaty by the Mexican government, he urged efforts to secure prompt ratification by the Mexican government on the ground that it could obtain nothing better for Mexico, and that, if resubmitted to the American Senate for any alteration, it would be in danger of unfavorable action. To Gadsden, who was at Washington, he explained that the continuation of negotiations with a view to further modification was useless, because there was no hope of approval by the Senate. Gadsden, who was asked to return to his post, reached Mexico City on June 4; and in a dispatch of June 9 he reported that the Mexican government, although it disliked the "one-sided treaty" offered by the United States, had delegated full powers to General Almonte to exchange ratifications.[14]

The approval of Congress for the expenditure of the money

involved was not obtained until June 28. In the House the debate, on the proposed appropriation required for the execution of the provisions of the treaty, extended from June 21 to June 28. The opposition was led by Benton who especially objected to the stipulation for acquiring from Mexico for Robert J. Walker and others, at big expense, a far distant and desolate desert railroad route to San Diego—a route which he regarded of little use in comparison with the "good national route" already under American jurisdiction. Finally, on June 28, the appropriation was approved by a vote of 103 to 62. On June 29, the altered treaty was ratified by signature of President Pierce; and, on June 30, ratifications were exchanged with Almonte at Washington, and the treaty was proclaimed. On July 1, a few days before Santa Anna granted to his friend Alejandro José Atocha a concession for a railway and telegraph line from Presidio del Norte (or Piedras Negras) to Guaymas, the American government handed to Almonte a check for $7,000,000, the first installment under Article II of the treaty.[15]

Several months later, Marcy administered a conciliatory criticism to Gadsden who in June, while preparing to negotiate an extradition treaty, had continued to reflect upon the defects of his "emasculated" treaty and to record his dissent—especially in regard to boundaries and lack of reciprocity. Although he agreed that the boundary negotiation by Gadsden was better than that arranged by the Senate, he could not agree with other objections of Gadsden and of Mexico nor assent to the startling inference that "any change of circumstances would authorize and justify repudiation" of the treaty by Mexico—for whom he regarded it as an advantageous contract, and who had been free to accept or reject it. He especially expressed surprise that the Mexican government objected to Article VIII which embraced objects accepted by Mexico in the Conkling draft treaty. In closing he said: "The President is confident your individual views will not abate your zeal or efforts in urging on Mexico the scrupulous fulfilment of the obligations imposed by the treaty." In the following January, when there were several new subjects of complaint and irritation between the two governments, he received from Gadsden a dispatch of January 5 explaining his motive for reviewing the action of the President and Senate upon the treaty, complaining of the reopening of issues which crippled the negotiations of the legation for adjustment, and at the same time proposing to adjust American claims by negotiation of another strip of territory which (according to rumors) Mexico was willing to sell * and which he said had no alternative except the sword.[16]

Aware of the danger of arousing further the anti-cession sentiment of Mexico which had led to the expulsion of Santa Anna, and possibly influenced by the recent failures to secure Cuba and Hawaii, the Pierce administration hesitated to propose negotiations for more Mexican territory. After the negotiation of the Gadsden treaty, however, there were various sources of friction and irritation which, while they threatened to arrest the progress of American expansion in the Southwest, also encouraged expectations of new territorial cessions to which no Mexican government could ever have been induced to agree after the troubled experience of Santa Anna. Seeing no chance to effect an arrangement involving a pecuniary liquidation of claims, Gadsden wrote to Marcy in the spring of 1855 that, "if property, extension of territory, or other grants or commercial privileges are not acceptable as a means of settlement, resort must be had to the sword, which will end in the absorption of the whole Republic." [17]

During the remainder of his mission Gadsden persistently pressed upon Bonilla the question of claims but without success. Apparently his failure was largely due to the disturbed conditions of Mexico, encouraging filibustering and also especially resulting in outrages which furnished to Gadsden new causes of complaint and to President Pierce new irritations to test his forbearance and his firmness in a policy of moderation.[18]

The Mexican government still nursed the memories of recent American filibustering raids—of Moorehead from California to

---

* Gadsden mentioned rumors that a proposition from the American government for extension of domain would be favorably received—and that they were coupled with a suggestion that Yucatan might be acceptable in American supposed designs on Cuba.

La Paz and Sonora in 1851, of Carvajal and his followers from Texas against Camargo and Matamoros in 1851-53, of the Raousset de Boulbon adventurers as invaders from San Francisco in 1852, and of the William Walker adventurers from San Francisco to Lower California and Sonora in October, 1853, to May, 1854—raids which the American government had been unable to restrain, although it had shown its good intentions by the orders issued to its military forces and by the arrests of Carvajal in 1852 and of part of Walker's band near San Diego in May, 1854. It was apprehensive of future American invading expeditions, which soon materialized as protective measures against Indian raids from Mexico and to recover fugitive slaves. Such an expedition, which possibly also aimed at the occupation of territory needing a government, was that of Texan Rangers under the command of J. H. Callahan and W. R. Henry. This expedition precipitated a crisis in October, 1855, by crossing the Rio Grande near Fort Duncan and by marching southward until it encountered an ambuscade of Mexicans. Then, retreating to escape the treacherous Mexican attack, it pillaged and burned the Mexican town of Piedras Negras before it recrossed the river near Fort Duncan. In his reply to the complaint of Almonte, Marcy defended the action as a legally justifiable exercise of the pursuit of an enemy into neutral territory, and as an act of self-defense. Another expedition of a different character was that of 90 Frenchmen under command of J. N. Zerman, which sailed from San Francisco in October, 1855, to La Paz, to aid the revolution of General Alvarez by blockade of Mexican ports. It was promptly captured by officials of the Santa Anna government, resulting in 108 claims for indemnity for imprisonment. In January to March, 1856, Henry A. Crabb, a Tennesseean who had migrated to California, and who was influenced by the news of the success of William Walker in Nicaragua, and by encouragement of Mexican revolutionists (who expected annexation to the United States) in Sonora, led an unfortunate expedition of about 100 men (the "Arizona Colonization Company") to Sonora where, after an ambuscade, its survivors surrendered and were promptly shot—resulting in 93 cases of claims for indemnity for murder besides another wave of indignation, and a series of retaliatory disorders and counter border raids (both American and Mexican) which hindered the development of that part of the southwestern frontier and threatened southern communications with California. Late in 1856, another source of irritation arose in Texas from local expulsion and murder of Mexicans, from San Antonio and southward, by bands of masked men for alleged aid to runaway slaves, and for underbidding Texans in the transportation trade with the coast. In October, the Mexican minister at Washington complained to Marcy who promptly started an investigation through Governor Pease of Texas. Although the lawless bands, who later turned their attention to indiscriminate robberies, were finally dispersed and suppressed by neighborhood lynch law, they incited a bitterness which later contributed to the development of the lawless raids led by the notorious Mexican outlaw, J. N. Cortina.[19]

In his message of December, 1856, Pierce informed Congress that the forbearance of the American government toward Mexico was due only to a recognition of the restricting influence of internal disorders and difficulties upon the policy and action of the Mexican government. On February 5, 1857, Marcy in a note to Pezeula at Washington, complained of the many un-redressed Mexican injuries to American citizens in Mexico. He declared that, although he had resisted American appeals for aggressive counter-action, the American government had a right and a duty to adopt measures to protect American citizens from invasion of their rights by Mexican authorities. An additional irritation, after 1853, resulted from the attempt of the Mexican government to set up pretended counter-claims against the United States for non-fulfilment of Article XI of 1848 before its abrogation by Gadsden's treaty of December, 1853. In May, 1856, when Pezeula renewed at Washington the Mexican demand for indemnities claimed under Article XI, Marcy rejected the claim for reasons which were later accepted by the American-Mexican Claims Commission in 1873.[20]

From the middle of 1854, Gadsden saw no hope for Mexico,

except through revolution or American protection or protectorate. On August 1, reporting the progress of the Mexican revolution and the blockade of Acapulco against the revolutionists who had seized the town, he suggested the necessity of an American naval force on the Pacific coast. On September 2, a half month following his protest against Mexican decrees restricting liberty of speech, he repeated the suggestion in a dispatch referring to the growing distrust of the United States and the indisposition of the Minister of Relations to treat with respect and attention the business of the American legation. On September 5, referring to frontier disturbances and increasing hostility to the United States at the Mexican capital, he declared that American troops should march into the country. On September 19, referring to American sympathy with the revolutionists at Acapulco, he urged the importance of an American naval force on both Mexican coasts. On October 16, promising to press American demands for redress in the various unsettled questions and referring to frontier disturbances on the Rio Grande and to semi-official newspaper attacks on American institutions and policy, he declared: "The Government at Washington ought to sustain Mexico against the usurpation of absolutism which threatens her existence." On February 5, 1855, reporting the Mexican denial of any American unadjusted claims against Mexico, the Mexican extraordinary assertion that Mexican claims under Article XI of the treaty of 1848 had not been released by its abrogation, and rumors of an apprehended invasion of Sonora from California, he said that the United States must either come into collision with Mexico or reconcile more completely the disturbing issues. On May 18, three months before the abdication of Santa Anna, disgusted with the duplicity of the Mexican government and suspecting an alliance between Mexico and England and France and Spain, he favored American coalescence with Mexican revolutionists "to dispose the usurper" and recommended an American protectorate over Mexico. Already, on February 19, after threatening to suspend intercourse, he had suggested that the American payment of the additional three million dollars as provided by the treaty should be withheld. On July 3, nearly six weeks before the abdication of Santa Anna, referring to the unfriendly attitude of "Santa Anna and his Pharisaical premier," and their failure to notice his repeated presentation of claims and grievances, he announced to Marcy that diplomatic intercourse was suspended. On September 18, a month after the abdication of Santa Anna, and immediately following the abdication of Carrera, whom he had refused to recognize, when Alvarez was marching from the north to preserve order, he mentioned his support to the revolution which had verified his predictions and suggested the advantage of offering the three million dollar installment to the revolutionary party.* Through Alvarez, who was elected President *ad interim* on October 4 and entered Mexico City on November 15, he sought to democratize Mexico—by active influence with Liberal (revolutionary) leaders—in order to secure friendlier relations with the United States and to reduce European activity and influence in Mexico. His hopes soon vanished —after the resignation of Alvarez on December 8, and the appointment of his substitute, Ignacio Comonfort, who soon became a conservative and unfriendly to Gadsden. The latter on December 5, stating that all governments of Mexico were influenced by fear or money (and could be conquered by the first and purchased by the last), advised Marcy to withhold the payment of the installment of three million dollars—which however was paid in February, 1856, to the holders of Mexican drafts against the wishes of Gadsden. Although relations were improved by a more liberal Mexican tariff of January 31, Gadsden, who negotiated a postal convention which was not ratified by either country, was unsuccessful in his efforts to negotiate a commercial treaty.[21]

Suspicion concerning European influence was a prominent factor in Gadsden's later negotiations. After the negotiations of the Gadsden purchase, the dispatches from Mexico were full of

---

* Apparently there was prevalent rumor that the revolutionary generals intended to claim the protectorate of the United States. On September 22, Gadsden, through the press, issued a denial of a secret treaty of alliance and protectorate, but stated that some of the Conservatives had made suggestions favorable to an American protectorate. (New York letter in London *Times* of November 6, 1855.)

rumors of projected or impending interventions or a discussion of the conditions which might invite foreign intervention and the establishment of a protectorate. The necessity of intervention in Mexico and the establishment of a protectorate was considered on both sides of the Atlantic. The idea of a protectorate to remedy the political conditions of the republic had earlier been discussed by the French and American ministers in Mexico, soon after the *coup d'état* by which Louis Napoleon became Emperor of France—as early as the latter part of 1852, at the time of the revolution in Sonora. Early in the following year, Senator Seward opposed a resolution for enforcing the Tehuantepec grant, on the ground that Mexico in meeting the demands of the grant would become dismembered and disorganized and would necessarily fall to the United States. After the beginning of the brief dictatorship of General Santa Anna who had been recalled by the revolutionists in 1853 to take the place of President Arista, who had resigned his office to prevent civil war, there was a growing distrust of the United States which was fostered by the official paper. Gadsden, who had just negotiated for the strip south of the Gila, urged that his government should make some naval and military demonstration "to create an impression that in the obligations and policy of the United States the Monroe doctrine is no abstraction." [22]

Early in 1855, during the Crimean war, when the Mexican Minister of Relations "injected anti-slavery sentiments into his official correspondence," Gadsden, writing that European influence was preparing for "possible alliance of Mexico with those European interferences in Cuba threatening to take part in the political adjustments of the Americas," said that if further territory or other grants were not acceptable as a means of the settlement of the American claim against Mexico, the United States must again resort to the sword and direct a war which would end in the absorption of the entire republic—a consummation which he said "the European allies had better encourage than resist in their sensitive interference to arrest the progress of the American system on its own domain." He stated that the monarchical influence (of the Triple Alliance) on the reigning government was so strong that it had "even dreamed of the restoration of the legitimacy in one of the royal families of Spain, and had received no check except from Santa Anna who in spite of their secret diplomacy had opposed their design to make Mexico the exponent of the monarchical European element in America, antagonistic to liberal progressive government and for readjustment of national balance." "It is imperative," he urged, "that the United States anticipate possible events in the East which may leave the allies at liberty to concentrate their power in the American seas and relieve the Mexican rule from apprehension of a premature alliance in designs not limited to one continent." Six weeks later, writing that Santa Anna was drifting into an alliance with England, France and Spain on the Cuban issue and to check the growth of the United States, he advocated that the United States as the exponent of liberal government in the Americas should coalesce with the liberals whose government had been violently expelled by a "one man military despot" and interpose to prevent alliances hostile to the American system and to save Mexico to the Americas. After Santa Anna's brief dictatorship was succeeded (in August, 1855) by the new liberal government which had "American predilections," Gadsden informed Secretary Marcy that the allies were doubling their energies to win the new government in favor of the "Europeanization" of Mexico, and that it might falter and succumb to European influence if the United States failed to interpose for its rescue. "I feel obliged," said he, "to reaffirm that another crisis at this capital is threatened which may give a triumph to European recolonization and expel American influences from Mexico until recovered by another revolution and the sword." From London in the following summer, Dallas wrote Marcy: "The rumored Spanish movement against Mexico —a movement which should put General Gadsden and our home squadron on the alert—involves an ulterior purpose of Louis Napoleon either to send a scion of his imperial house to the hall of the Montezumas . . . or so to involve Spain and Mexico in war as to furnish to the former a plausible reason for transferring Cuba to England." [23]

In his valedictory dispatch at the time of his recall, near the close of the Pierce administration, Gadsden, writing to complain that his dispatches had been treated with indifference and that fleets from France, England and Spain threatened to visit Vera Cruz in a few months to adjust issues with Mexico by a threat of war, still urged that French diplomacy, in the ascendency in Mexico, was in close affiliation with British and Spanish diplomacy to consolidate and perpetuate the Mexican executive in one absolute head, and was planning an alliance with Mexico to check the progress of American ideas in Spanish America, to control Tehuantepec, to guarantee Cuba and return Santo Domingo to Spain, to place Haiti under the protection of France and to oppose various objects of American foreign policy. Early in Buchanan's administration, writing to Cass from Charleston, charging that the retiring administration had interfered with his mission, and offering suggestions as to the policy of the United States toward Mexico which he said had "never since the revolution reposed on a legitimate government," he again asserted that the threatened expedition against Vera Cruz was a diplomatic deception and a part of long-meditated plans to bring Mexico into harmony with European ideas and repudiated political dogmas, and to antagonize American progress.[24]

In his valedictory dispatch, written to exonerate himself from all responsibility for the impending loss of Mexico, Cuba and the Gulf, Gadsden attributed his recall to the energy with which he had watched and reported European designs which threatened to check the progress of America by the formation of an alliance of Spanish America against the United States. According to the Mexican government, however, his recall was first requested through General Almonte "for official and offensive conduct in the opinions and spirit" of his correspondence— "extravagant pretensions, inopportune discussions, tergiversation of ideas," general hostility in starting questions of international political policy and incessant disputes on frivolous grounds, distortion of facts, disregard of legitimate channels of communication, and insulting language—especially illustrated by a note (on Article XI of the treaty of 1848) which was regarded as an insult to the government and to the whole Spanish race, and by a circular in which he had authorized his fellow citizens to disobey a law of Mexico. Bonilla's request of October 3 was (on October 23) submitted to Marcy, who, surprised by the charges, on December 19 forwarded to Gadsden a copy of Almonte's note and asked for information for use in an appropriate reply.[25]

On receipt of Marcy's request with its enclosure, Gadsden promptly, on January 29, 1855, in a note to Bonilla, after stating that the correspondence in question was "invariably in response to communications which in their spirit and temper invited corresponding rejoinders," suggested that "there would seem to be a propriety of suspending *all official correspondence,* until the will of the President in this affair can be made known; or His Excellency, by a withdrawal of his excited remonstrances and complaints, shall renew the amicable and cordial relations, which the Undersigned, until a late hour of this day, had relied on as existing, and as particularly manifested in recent interviews, encouraging the expectations that the two Governments were approximating to a reconciliation of disturbing issues, on a basis more conciliatory and permanent than that which now appertains when most unexpectedly undeceived by the confidential communication." Bonilla, to sustain his request for recall, sent, as evidence against Gadsden, additional documents which Almonte submitted to Marcy on May 14 with the following statement: "Both previously as well as subsequently, several communications were addressed to the government of the Undersigned by the gentleman aforesaid, upon matters pending before the Courts of Justice, in which, therefore, the Executive could not interfere, wanting the Mexican Government to take upon itself the settlement of these matters, although beyond its Jurisdiction, and to set at liberty persons accused of crime who are imprisoned. Mr Gadsden being thus placed in an attitude of antagonism towards the authorities of the country and seeking to set its institutions at naught, which he wishes to have assimilated to those of the United States, however dissimilar may be their circumstances and condition, the

Secretary of State will easily perceive that it is impossible to maintain harmony and good relations with the American government, however sincere and incessant may be, as they are, the efforts of H S H, the President of the Mexican Republic, if the aforesaid gentleman continues as Minister in Mexico." [26]

On March 14, 1855, supposing from Gadsden's dispatch of February 19 that he had suspended diplomatic intercourse because of Bonilla's complaints against him—Marcy, recognizing an embarrassing situation and regretting that a rupture of intercourse had preceded the reply to the request for his recall, instructed Gadsden that he "should have made some reply to the complaints of the Mexican Government against him before requiring them to be withdrawn and suspending diplomatic intercourse till that request be complied with." On September 19, Gadsden, in a dispatch requesting an early leave to visit the United States, mentioned the rumors of his intrigues with different parties in Mexico. A month later, following the election of Alvarez to the Mexican presidency, he announced that relations had been reopened. On March 3, 1856, stating that he had received no recent instructions, he complained that the silence of Marcy might seriously affect the relations between the two countries. On April 18, complaining that he had not been entrusted with the adjustment of the three million dollars installment as stipulated in the treaty and that his influence had been weakened by the Department of State, he protested against being held responsible for any failure of his mission. A month later, he wrote from Charleston, South Carolina, announcing the signing of a postal convention and his hasty departure from Mexico under orders of a physician, but he returned to Mexico on August 3, when he acknowledged receipt of Marcy's instructions of June 30 recalling him, following the repeated request of the Mexican government. The final demand for his removal, presented to Marcy on May 9 in a note from Pezeula, was based on grounds of meddling in domestic affairs, improper censures of the Mexican government and other irritating acts interfering with pacific relations. In yielding to the Mexican request, President Pierce and Marcy were probably also influenced at Wash-

ington by a lobby of American speculators, especially representatives of the Hargous and Sloo interests in Tehuantepec, whom
Gadsden charged with the domination of the policy of Marcy
toward Mexico and who, after the abdication of Santa Anna,
had become more hostile to Gadsden because of his refusal to aid
them in Mexico.[27]

Gadsden in his "valedictory" dispatch of October 4, while
awaiting the arrival of his successor, complained that he had
been embarrassed by the non-arrival of instructions necessary
to the public interests in connection with relations with Comonfort—the "usurped Executive of a one-man will . . . disposing
of himself to the highest bidder." He took occasion again to
reaffirm the danger of European alliance with Mexico which he
had "photographed in almost every dispatch since he was
accredited in this capital." Later, on March 23, 1857, in a post-
mission dispatch to Secretary Cass, he advised the Buchanan
administration to offer to Mexico a new treaty—including readjustment of the boundary (by locating it at 31° N.) and
American control of the Tehuantepec transit—and advised it
simultaneously to station troops and naval forces at strategic
points.[28]

Three months before Gadsden left his post, John Forsyth, of
Alabama, received his commission as envoy to Mexico, with
instructions from Marcy to allay all suspicions that the United
States had sinister designs on Mexico, but to urge trade reciprocity, revision of the Mexican tariff, a postal convention, and
fair indemnities to adjust American claims which could be properly sustained by proof. He arrived at Mexico City by October
23, before the departure of Gadsden, who, a month earlier, had
threatened to leave the legation in the hands of Mr. Cripps, the
secretary, whom he expected to return from California. After
viewing the conditions, he reported that there was little hope of
stability for Mexico except through a proposed alliance with the
United States by the infusion of Americans into the Mexican
army. On February 10, 1857, stimulated by a rumor of the
prospective arrival of a British fleet to enforce British demands
against Mexico, he negotiated four treaties which he thought

would strengthen the Mexican government and remove the danger of European interference, and which also would have made important changes in the internal relations of the two nations. One treaty, not authorized by instructions, provided for a loan of fifteen million dollars, of which three millions were to be withheld for payment of claims of American citizens and four millions were to be applied on the British convention debt. The seven millions for these claims and debts were to be secured by 13% of the Mexican import duties and the remainder of the loan (eight millions) was to be extinguished by a reduction of 20% in duties (both import and export) on trade between the two countries which was to be stimulated by reciprocity on stipulated articles. The loan was regarded by Forsyth as "a floating mortgage upon the territory of a poor neighbor" which he could not acquire at that time, but which might later be obtained by a peaceful foreclosure with consent of Mexico. With this were combined a postal convention, a reciprocity treaty, and commercial arrangements to open Mexican markets to American manufactures. The President had weighty objections to some of these treaties, and especially to the stipulation that all must be accepted conjointly (that the rejection of one would involve the rejection of all), and decided not to submit them to the Senate so near the close of his administration.[29]

REFERENCES

1. *16 Mexico, Instructions*, (No. 20) May 18, 1853; *16 Mexico, Despatches*, (No. 31) Apr. 9, 1853; N. Y. *Herald*, Jan. 30, 1854.
2. *DeBow*, III, pp. 447 and 485, May and June, 1847; *16 Mexico, Instructions*, No. 3, July 15, 1853.
3. *18 Mexico, Despatches*, July 12 and 19, (No. 1) Aug. 17, (Private) Sept. 5, (No. 4) Sept. 18, and (No. 6) Oct. 3, 1853.
4. *Ib.*, (No. 6) Oct. 3, (No. 10) Oct. 17, (No. 12) Nov. 3, (No. 13) Nov. 17, (No. 14) Nov. 19, and (No. 15) Dec. 5, 1853.
5. *1 Special Missions*, p. 38, Oct. 22, 1853; *Secret Service*, p. 647.
6. *16 Mexico, Instructions*, p. 435, Oct. 22, 1853.
7. *Secret Service*, p. 655, Nov. 14, 1853; *16 Mexico, Instructions*, pp. 436-64, No. 19, Dec. 22, 1853.

8. *18 Mexico, Despatches*, (Private) Nov. 20, 1853; *16 Mexico, Instructions*, (No. 19) Dec. 22, 1853, and (No. 20) Jan. 6, 1854.

9. *18 Mexico, Despatches*, No. 16, Dec. 16, 1853, and March 20, 1854.

10. *Ib.*, (No. 16) Dec. 16, 1853, and (No. 20) Jan. 4, 1854.

11. *N. Y. Herald*, Jan. 20, Feb. 9 and Feb. 15, 1854; *Sen. Exec. Journal*, IX, pp. 235-39, 241, 247, 264 *et seq.; Cong. Globe*, 33-1.

12. *Sen. Exec. Journal*, IX, pp. 238-316 *passim; Cong. Globe*, 33-1; *House Doc. 359*, 71-2, pp. 243-50; PAUL N. GARBER, *The Gadsden Treaty*, Chaps. V and VI; J. FRED RIPPY, *The United States and Mexico*, Chap. VIII.

13. *17 Mexico, Instructions*, No. 29, May 29, 1854; *8 Notes from Mexico Legation*, May 10, 1855; *18 Mexico, Despatches*, (No. 31) June 9, and (No. 32) June 17, 1854.

14. *17 Mexico, Instructions*, (No. 25) May 6, (No. 27) May 11, (No. 31) June 9, and (No. 32) June 17, 1854.

15. *Cong. Globe*, 33-1, Vol. 28, Part 2, pp. 1476, 1536, and 1564-65.

16. *17 Mexico, Instructions*, pp. 20-25, (No. 37) Oct. 13, 1854; *18 Mexico, Despatches*, (No. 32) June 17, 1854; *19 Mexico, Despatches*, (No. 52) Jan. 2, and (No. 53) Jan. 17, 1855.

17. *19 Mexico, Despatches*, No. 60, Apr. 3, 1855.

18. *Ib.*, (No. 55) Feb. 5, and (No. 57) Feb. 19, (No. 61) Apr. 17, (No. 63) May 18, and (No. 66) July 3, 1855; *17 Mexico, Instructions*, (No. 44) March 14, 1855.

19. *19 Mexico, Despatches*, (No. 76) Nov. 17, and (No. 78) Dec. 5, 1856; *7 Notes to Mexico Legation*, Jan. 23, 1856; W. O. SCROGGS, *Filibusters and Financiers*, pp. 308-16.

20. *7 Notes to Mexico Legation*, Feb. 5, 1857; *19 Mexico, Despatches*, (No. 55) Feb. 5, and (No. 57) Feb. 19, 1855; *17 Mexico, Instructions*, No. 44, March 14, 1855; J. B. MOORE, *International Arbitrations*, III, pp. 2444-47.

21. *18 Mexico, Despatches*, (No. 36) Aug. 1, (No. 37) Aug. 16, (No. 38) Sept. 2, (No. 41) Sept. 5, (No. 43) Sept. 19, and (No. 46) Oct. 16, 1854; *19 Mexico, Despatches*, (No. 55) Feb. 5, (No. 57) Feb. 19, (No. 63) May 18, (No. 66) July 3, (No. 71) Sept. 18, (No. 77) Nov. 25, (No. 78) Dec. 5, and (No. 79) Dec. 17, 1855, and (No. 88) May 18, 1856.

22. *17 Mexico, Instructions*, (No. 2) Apr. 6, 1861; *Seward's Works*, Vol. 3, pp. 626-27 and 645; *16 Mexico, Despatches*, No. 7, Dec. 24, 1852; *18 Mexico, Despatches*, (No. 33) Aug. 16, and (No. 38) Sept. 2, 1854.

23. *19 Mexico, Despatches*, (No. 57) Feb. 19, (No. 60) Apr. 3, (No. 63) May 18, (No. 77) Nov. 25, 1855, and (No. 82) Jan. 18,

1856; G. M. Dallas, *Letters from London*, Vol. I, p. 46 (No. 22) June 6, 1856.

24. *19 Mexico, Despatches*, No. 97, Oct. 4, 1856; *20 Mexico, Despatches*, March 22 and 23, 1857.

25. *19 Mexico, Despatches*, (No. 97) Oct. 4, 1856; *7 Notes from Mexico Legation*, Oct. 23, 1854; *17 Mexico, Instructions*, No. 41, Dec. 19, 1854; *8 Notes from Mexico Legation*, May 10, 1855, June 27, 1856.

26. *Ib.*, May 14, 1855.

27. *17 Mexico, Instructions*, pp. 33-39, (No. 44) March 14, 1855; *Ib.*, (No. 65) June 30, and (No. 94) Aug. 3, 1856; *19 Mexico, Despatches*, (No. 72) Sept. 19, and (No. 73) Oct. 19, 1855, and (No. 88) Apr. 18, 1856; *8 Notes from Mexico Legation*, May 9, 1856; *N. Y. Herald*, Apr. 10, 1856.

28. *19 Mexico, Despatches*, No. 9, Oct. 4, 1856.

29. *17 Mexico, Instructions*, pp. 81-87, (No. 2) Aug. 16, 1856; *Ib.*, (No. 11) March 3, and (No. 12) March 11, 1857; *19 Mexico, Despatches*, (No. 100) Oct. 23, (No. 5) Nov. 8, and (No. 14) Dec. 19, 1856; *20 Mexico, Despatches*, (No. 24) Feb. 10, and (No. 29) Apr. 4, 1857; J. M. Callahan, *The Mexican Policy of Southern Leaders Under Buchanan's Administration* (Rp. Am. Hist. Ass'n, 1910, pp. 133-51).

CHAPTER VIII

BUCHANAN'S MEXICAN POLICY: NEGOTIA-
TIONS FOR TERRITORY AND TRANSITS

JAMES BUCHANAN, who after his period of service as Secretary of State under Polk had served as minister to Great
Britain from 1853 to 1856, was as President largely influenced
by the views and policies of Southern leaders who had been
a prominent factor in determining his election to the presidency. For Secretary of State he chose a well-known citizen,
seventy-five years of age, Lewis Cass, who had reached the rank
of brigadier general in 1813, and thereafter had served his
country in various offices—as governor of Michigan Territory
(1813-31), Secretary of War (1831-36), minister to France
(1836-42), and United States Senator (1845-48 and 1849-
57). For minister to Mexico Cass first retained John Forsyth
who had been appointed by Pierce in 1856, but who demanded
his passports and withdrew from the American legation on
October 20, 1858, and finally resigned on February 7, 1859.
Later, on March 7, 1859, he appointed, as Forsyth's successor,
Robert Milligan McLane (of Maryland) who, after a period
of service in the army (1837-43), had served two terms in
Congress (1847-51) and as commissioner to China (1853), and
whose father, Louis, had twice served as minister to Great
Britain (1829-31 and 1845-46) and for a brief period as
Secretary of State (1833-34). McLane's successor was John B.
Weller who had served in Congress from Ohio in 1839-45, had
attained the rank of colonel in the Mexican War, had been a
member of the American-Mexican Boundary Commission in
1849-50, a United States Senator from California, 1852-57,
and governor of California, 1858-60. The Mexican ministers at

Washington for the period were M. R. Pezeula (to July 31, 1858), and J. M. Mata (April 28, 1859, to August 11, 1860). The secretary of the Mexican legation, Matias Romero, acted as chargé after August 11, 1860 (until May, 1863).

At the beginning of his administration Buchanan was confronted with the question of the Mexican mission and American-Mexican problems and policy. Apparently he was inclined to concur with the advice of his friend Robert Toombs who, while planning for himself the English mission by which to aid the American acquisition of Cuba, recommended for the Mexican mission Judah P. Benjamin. The latter, like Toombs, had a special interest in the plans of Hargous in the Tehuantepec transit route, and also in plans for a charter for a railroad from the Rio Grande to Tiburon preparatory to the purchase of Sonora, which many regarded as necessary to the development of the region of Arizona and to secure proper protection to the Southern mail route to California, and which some later advocated partly from the desire to avenge the murders of the members of the Crabb expedition. Whatever his inclinations, Buchanan decided to undertake negotiations through Forsyth, although he, like Pierce, did not approve the four treaties submitted by him in February. Cass so informed Forsyth on March 11.[1] Several months later, in connection with renewed negotiations, he stated the reasons:

"In the four treaties which you negotiated last winter, and which were all dependent upon each other, provision was made for a generous loan of money to Mexico, without any other equivalent than was to be found in certain commercial arrangements of which, in this way, the United States were to become practically the purchasers. If these arrangements had been far more valuable than they really were, it would still have been a dangerous departure from our established policy to have given for them a pecuniary equivalent. A treaty of commerce, in every just view of the subject, should rest upon the basis of reciprocity, and commercial privileges in the one country should be paid for by commercial privileges in the other country. If the contrary rule should prevail, and the nations of the earth should go about bidding against each other for the monopoly of commerce, the laws of trade would be virtually abrogated, and the longest purse would buy the richest market. Such a doctrine belongs to a past age of the world, and wherever else it may be sanctioned, can meet no favor in a republic like ours—whose interests demand the most liberal competition and the freest trade." [2]

Forsyth, explaining to Cass the obstacles which prevented the execution of his instructions to buy territory and which induced the formulation of the treaties of February 10, said that his pacific policy was one sanctioned by reason and demanded by the overruling necessities of the case, and that it was one which the American government would be forced to accept as the alternative to very grave evils in its future relations with Mexico. Impressed with the political importance of his negotiations in the establishment of a definite Mexican policy, he said: "The land will come to us without hurry." Much disappointed by the disapproval of these treaties by the Buchanan administration, early in April he urged upon Cass the importance of securing a guiding influence in the counsels of Mexico whose riches had attracted the gaze of other nations which were ready to act on Mexican appeals if the United States declined. "Believe me, sir," said he, "we cannot play the dog in the manger with our Monroe Doctrine. Mexico cannot afford to perish . . . because we choose not to be the physician . . . I can see a hundred contingencies that will make Mexico the battle ground for the maintenance of American supremacy in America—the theatre for the practical illustration of the value of the Monroe Doctrine." He continued to report the danger of war between Mexico and Spain and the alleged complicity of France and England in the complications, and to suggest the policy that the United States should pursue in her relations with Mexico. Contemplating the possibility of war between Spain and Mexico, he early wrote to Cass: "There are many eventualities to such a contest once begun of which the United States can not be indifferent spectators. The triumph of Spain here would be the triumph of principles, opinions and purposes wholly at variance with the interests and settled policy of the United States. With that moral and financial support which she can only get from the United States, there is room to hope that Mexico might emerge from a successful conflict with her old oppressor, improved and strengthened by the ordeal." Soon thereafter he reported that new clouds of revolt were gathering and thickening around the Comonfort government and that Santa Anna was exerting all his energy to ferment troubles and to solicit aid from Spain. "What Mexico wants," said he, "is a firm and good master to hold her destinies in his hands and to save her from herself. Mexico can not furnish such a master and may welcome one from abroad. It is high time for the United States to take present means to provide for her future stake in the destinies of this country." Again, two months later, referring to the swift, recurring revolutions which were increasing the dangers of European intervention in Mexican politics, and especially the recent solicitation of Santa Anna for Spanish aid, he wrote: "Mexican institutions are crumbling to pieces and interposition, to gather up the wreck, from some quarter, is as certain as it is indispensable." [3]

Meantime, on June 18, after reading Forsyth's memorandum of a conversation of April 21 with Montes (the Mexican Minister of Relations), in which was expressed the supposition that new treaties would be negotiated on the basis of those concluded in February, Cass promptly sent instructions correcting the supposition and stating that the President agreed with his predecessor. At the same time he promised early instructions in regard to renewal of negotiations which were regarded as "most important," but proved to be based upon a policy determined by the President instead of that proposed by Forsyth.

A month later the Buchanan administration, largely under the influence of Senator Judah P. Benjamin, who was the attorney for the new Louisiana Tehuantepec Company, resumed negotiations for territory and transits which were desired in a single treaty. On July 17, two months before the time set for the termination of the extraordinary power of President Comonfort, of Mexico, the President, through Secretary Cass, sent to Forsyth new instructions—which were handed to him by

Emile La Sère, president of the Louisiana Tehuantepec Company, who went to Mexico with Benjamin to secure a modification of the Sloo grant with a view to construction of a railroad by the united interests (Garay, Hargous and Louisiana Tehuantepec Company). These authorized him to conclude a treaty with Mexico for the acquisition of Lower California, nearly all of Sonora, and part of Chihuahua north of 30° and the Rio Chico (or whatever else Mexico might will to sell), and the confirmation of the right of way or transit in perpetuity, under American guarantee of neutrality and Mexican sovereignty, on any route of commerce which should be constructed across Mexico from ocean to ocean. The reasons which might induce Mexico to cede the territory were suggested as follows: "Lower California is so separated . . . so distant from the seat of government that the authority of Mexico over it is little more than nominal, and it is really of no value to that republic. The other territory described besides being remote, also, from the city of Mexico, is occupied to a considerable extent by savage tribes of Indians, whose incursions extend frequently to the more civilized parts of the country. The more rapid settlement which would inevitably attend its acquisition by the United States would gradually remove this danger, and thus add to the security of the remaining Mexican provinces." The compensation authorized was four or five million dollars for Lower California, and eight or ten million for the Sonora and Chihuahua territory—with a provision for retention of two million to pay personal claims of American citizens against Mexico (but not contract claims). At the same time, Forsyth was instructed to aid Benjamin and La Sère, and was authorized, if expedient, to employ their services in obtaining the cession of territory which would entitle his name to be enrolled on the list of America's "most distinguished diplomatists." [4]

Forsyth, whose previous dispatches had reported the impracticability of any attempt to negotiate a new boundary treaty with a government which had strongly pledged itself by manifesto of March 4 not to alienate, cede, exchange, or hypothecate any part of the national territory, hesitated to undertake negotiations which contemplated the acquisition of so much territory at a price far below the exaggerated Mexican estimates of its value, and which offered no pecuniary compensation or equivalent for the franchises giving privileges of right of way across Tehuantepec in extension of the concession of 1853. He complained that his instructions had placed him in an untenable position. Although he considered that any attempt to negotiate for territory was hopeless from the beginning, he carefully approached President Comonfort, and later Lerdo de Tejada, who declined to consider the subject. He then warned them that the United States would not yield a jot of rights acquired by the Gadsden treaty. Meanwhile, beyond the courtesy of an introduction, he had declined to cooperate with Benjamin and La Sère, known in capital papers as the "American negotiators," whose presence he felt had tended to degrade the legation and who (on September 7) secretly concluded a private contract with Mexico to which Forsyth objected on the ground that it annulled the Sloo grant, put in jeopardy all American interests on the isthmus, gave the United States no benefit, and was not in conformity with the terms and conditions of Cass's instructions. Considering the attitude of these "negotiators" and their position in the public thought, he felt "compelled by self-respect to decline to advise them," but at the risk of a rebuff he undertook to inform President Comonfort of Cass's instructions that the grant must conform to certain stipulations of the Gadsden treaty of December, 1853. He especially resented the pretensions of Benjamin, who he felt had been largely responsible for the failure of his treaties of February 10, who boasted that he carried the Buchanan administration in his pocket, and whose Mexican acquaintances of the banking and capitalistic class openly remarked that he had secret and ample powers which placed the United States legation in temporary abeyance.[5]

On their return to the United States, the smooth Benjamin and La Sère, in a note to President Buchanan, attacked Forsyth's integrity and honor as a gentleman, blaming him for his course regarding their transit negotiations which had caused them to lose a million dollars, and accusing him of favoring the cause of Soulé, the representative of the Sloo interests, who was in Mexico City at the same time to oppose the plans of Benjamin and La Sère. The inquisitive and dominating Benjamin "acting as a spy" evidently had kept a diary in which he had made full notes of all Forsyth's daily life and actions.[6]

The irate Forsyth declared that he was assailed because he had not been a pliant tool of the clique of Tehuantepec speculators who for ten years had kept the legation in hot water and had "vaunted" its ownership of more than one American minister to Mexico. In his defense he said his instructions had not required him to subordinate, to the interests of a company seeking lucrative railway privileges, any of the public questions involved in his negotiations—including the proposition to transfer the sovereignty of an empire. At the same time he declared that (before the arrival of Benjamin), by negotiations not complicated with attempts to get territory, he could have obtained a satisfactory treaty which would have secured to the United States the virtual protectorate and military occupation of the Tehuantepec transit and a cession of a right of way for a railroad transit across the northern part of Mexico (with the same privileges as at Tehuantepec), almost on the line which the Buchanan administration had proposed as a new boundary, together with grants of alternate leagues of land which, in addition to use as a fund for the construction of the road to Guaymas, "would have fenced off and consecrated to American use, and ultimately to American ownership, the very territory" which he had been instructed to purchase. He desired authority to open negotiations for a treaty of transits and commerce on this basis for which he proposed to pay $12,000,000—$6,000,000 for commerce, and $3,000,000 for each of the transits, or $8,000,000 for commerce and $4,000,-000 for the two transits; and he warned Cass that if the American government could not consent to such a basis "then the only alternative is to adopt the higher tone and compel Mexico to respect her obligations to us as a neighbor."[7]

The American government did not approve Forsyth's project for a treaty, and especially declined to contribute money to relieve Mexico "unless it could get a consideration equally valuable in return." President Buchanan could not concur either in the proposed purchase of commercial privileges by payment of a pecuniary consideration for a right of way across Tehuantepec, or across Sonora, for which an ample equivalent was provided by the proposed American guaranty and protection of the route. Cass, therefore, instructed Forsyth to make his official action conform to the deliberately adopted policy of the administration even if he continued to disapprove it. On November 17, Cass, in a long reply to Forsyth's report of the failure of his negotiations and to his complaints that his opinions had been disregarded in the instructions of July, administered a rebuke both for his presumption and his indiscretion.

"Your position was that of an agent," said Cass, "and you were quite right in supposing that it was your duty to carry into effect the instructions of your principal, both in their letter and their spirit, whether you fully approved them or not. Any other doctrine than this would make the foreign policy of the Government dependent on the individual opinions of its respective ministers, and would compel the President, instead of controlling the action of our public agents, himself to receive their instructions, and regulate his conduct by their views. If the negotiation confided to you was 'hopeless from the beginning,' as you declare it to have been, you had the consolation of knowing that you were not responsible for it, and if, in obeying the wishes of your government, you had received 'an official rebuff,' no blame for the indignity could possibly have rested on you. I regret, therefore, that you should have received your instructions of July 17th with so much distrust of their wisdom, as to make you unwilling to give them the usual chances of success, by urging them upon the attention of the Mexican Government through its Minister of Foreign Affairs. You avoided this course, you inform the Department, because you were unwilling to subject your own Government 'to the certainty of an official rebuff,' and deeply impressed with the hopelessness of your mission, you sought an interview with President Comonfort, and laid before him the wishes of your government, 'with such arguments as delicacy would allow me [you] to use to a man whose opinions I knew, and who knew also, that I was perfectly aware that he had declared those opinions unalterable.' It is not surprising, perhaps, under these circumstances, that you received informally from the President that 'rebuff,' of your proposal, which you had so anxiously deprecated in an official form from the Minister of Relations. It is somewhat remarkable, however, that having thus in a personal interview committed the President to a decisive opinion against the possibility of your success, you should have, then, thought it wise to make a formal application to the Minister of Relations, in order to receive that very 'official rebuff' which in the beginning you seemed anxious to avoid. Than such a reply nothing else, you say, was to have been expected, because by any different one President Comonfort would have violated his pledges, as well as the organic law upon which he entered into power. The Department was not unaware of the public declarations on this subject to which you refer, but if under a change of circumstances the Executive of Mexico had found it necessary to change its views, also, with respect to any alienation of its territory, this would not be the first instance in the history of the Mexican Affairs, where such a change had taken place. And if any thing could justify the change, it might possibly be justified by the pecuniary necessities under which you describe the Mexican Government as now laboring." [8]

On November 18, Forsyth, reporting that the clouds of revolution were gradually gathering and thickening around the Comonfort government which was without money, and which he desired to sustain with pecuniary aid, wrote that he was trying to inspire the confidence of the bankers who were afraid to make a proposed loan on the unpledged receipts of the customhouses. In the proposed steps taken to aid the government, he later explained that he had contemplated no infringement of the rule of "non-intervention with the domestic policies." Apprehending a crisis in which Comonfort might be driven by emergencies to cede territory, he earnestly advised Cass to enlarge considerably the limits of price previously authorized and to empower him at the critical moment "to offer an irresistible temptation to the President and to Congress"— on the ground that it is "better to be liberal than to force a hard bargain through Mexican necessity"—but he was promptly informed that the maximum price already offered could not be extended. A month later, on December 17, following the *coup d'état* of Comonfort which made him master of Mexico, he suggested that the new dictator, if able to sustain himself, would have the power to dispose of territory. Early in January, 1858, when Comonfort was besieged in his palace, referring to the latter's great need of money, in a private note to Cass he expressed confidence that he could have obtained the signature to a treaty of cession if he could have had the ready cash; and, expecting other opportunities, he urged that $1,500,-000 should be placed at his disposal to be applied as part payment immediately on the signing of the treaty. Again, on January 30, after the fall of the Comonfort government and his recognition of the Conservative government of Zuloaga, still feeling the pulse of the new government for indications of a cession, he reported that the symptoms were favorable and advised an extension of the limit of price for territory—stating that Senator Benjamin had told Comonfort that the United States ought to give fifty million dollars for Sonora (!), and declaring that twelve or fifteen millions were insufficient to enable the Mexican government to justify the alienation of the territory for redemption of the country from its financial difficulties.[9]

On February 13, 1858, on receipt of Cass's letter of rebuke of November 17, Forsyth explained that his only purpose in opening the negotiations for territory was to secure in writing the refusal of the Mexican government in order to place the matter beyond dispute. Denying any presumption to set his views against those of the President, he said: "I merely desired to vindicate my intelligent comprehension of the Mexican situation . . . I was anxious to make it clear that the purchase of commercial privileges was contemplated, and in fact desired, merely as a means to a political end—that end being to sustain Mexico and to keep her from falling to pieces, perhaps into the hands of Foreign Powers, until such a time as we were ready to 'Americanize' her." Heartily concurring in the desire to execute the President's wishes, he reported that the question was "now warm upon the anvil of discussion" and that the consent of the President of Mexico and two members of his cabinet had been gained. On March 1, he reported that the President of Mexico and his cabinet were unanimous in the opinion that a treaty of cession was necessary but that they lacked the courage to act and would probably procrastinate. On March 18, he announced to Cass that events had opened the way for treaty negotiations and that the favorable moment had arrived.[10]

Encouraged by the reports of his ecclesiastical agents who had sounded both Zuloaga and Minister Cuevas, on March 22, 1858, in a note to Cuevas, he formally and tactfully proposed prompt negotiations for a change of boundary and for transits. On the proposition for cession of territory, his argument was the doctrine of "manifest destiny" supported by the inevitable, unchangeable and inscrutable laws of the Creator. He stated that without prophetic eye he could see that under the steady operation of natural causes and inevitable laws, and the inscrutable wisdom of their author, the tenure of Mexico would be weakened on the regions of waste territory north of 30° and the Yaqui (and Lower California) which the American government now sought to acquire by fair purchase. On April 3, while still awaiting a reply to his note, he urged upon Cass the necessity of American cruisers on Mexican coasts to facilitate his business with the Mexican government. Cuevas, on April 5, politely declined to cede territory and clearly stated his reasons. Attributing the rejection to timidity and "a paroxysm of political cowardice," Forsyth withdrew his proposition by a brief note stating that the generosity of the United States would be vindicated in the fullness of time, and emerged from the brief diplomatic contest with the firm conviction that Mexico needed another government. In a dispatch to Cass, deploring the lack of American foreign policy since the Mexican War, he urged that the plain and obvious duty of the United States was to resort to the argument of compulsion to induce Mexico to meet her obligations, and incidentally to enable the United States to secure territory. "You want Sonora?" said he. "The American blood spilled near its line would justify you in seizing it. . . . You want other territory? Send me power to make an ultimate demand for the several millions Mexico owes our people. . . . You want the Tehuantepec transits? Say to Mexico, 'Nature has placed that shortest highway between the two oceans, so necessary to the commerce of the world. . . . Give us what we ask for in return for the manifest benefits we propose to confer on you for it, or we will take it.' " Such language, he said, would result in good to both countries. Considering the possible decision of the American government to accept a protectorate for Mexico, he urged that the selection of a worthy head of the new Mexican government should be an essential condition. He doubted the wisdom of selecting Juárez and he proposed to eliminate Comonfort. He especially commended the clever Miguel Lerdo de Tejada, who had lost all hope in his country and was thoroughly converted to the "doctrine that an American protectorate was the only recourse." He also favorably mentioned Osollo, to whom he suggested a conference with Lerdo whom he regarded as the real Liberal leader. "If these two men choose," said he, "I believe they will have the power to change the government in 24 hours." [11]

As the fury of civil war increased, he ruffled the composure of the palace by presenting cases for consideration and by the belligerent stand which he took in protesting against forced loans and contributions to which he advised foreigners not to yield unless confronted by armed force. He was finally summoned (about June 9) to a private interview by Zuloaga, who stated that as a last resort he had decided to make the sacrifice of territory for the good of his country and for his own salvation, but the rising hopes thus produced were suddenly lowered again by the vacillation of Zuloaga two days later. Assured that the Buchanan administration was satisfied with the manner in which he had performed his negotiations, and receiving no further special instructions during the remainder of his stay, Forsyth assumed an attitude of active opposition to the Zuloaga government—and especially of antagonism to Cuevas, who had, he learned, requested his recall. He confidently reported that the government would either be overthrown or be forced to negotiate with him a treaty of cession. At the close of an undignified and undiplomatic correspondence in June, he suspended diplomatic relations until he could learn the pleasure of his government.[12]

This suspension was the immediate result of the expulsion of an American citizen, Solomon Migel, for his refusal to pay a special tax, levied by decree of May 15, 1858, against which Forsyth had protested on the ground that it was a forced loan. The language of the protest Cuevas characterized as "vehement and offensive," and stated that the "tone of acrimony in current affairs," even if it had accompanied a break of diplomatic relations, would have been inexcusable. Although stating his conviction that his reply would have no effect except to furnish Forsyth an opportunity to write a still more offensive note, he ventured to say: "The undsd. has never heard that a foreign Minister had the power to tell the subjects of his nation, not to obey the laws of the country in which they live. It would appear that H. E. Mr. Forsyth, believes the contrary & that he wishes to convert his official representations as Minister of the U. S. into a government opposed to another government; forgetting that, as foreign Minister, he can only shield his countrymen through the protection accorded by the laws of the land." The attitude of Forsyth on the reception of this note is indicated by the following extract from his dispatch of June 19 to Cass: "I shall immediately reply to this note, & after carefully & fully refuting its positions & carrying the war a little into Africa, for the purpose of showing that the whole course of Mr. Cuevas since he assumed the portfolio of States, has been reckless of right & justice towards the U. S. & calculated, if not designed to embroil the two countries. I shall conclude by informing him that the relations of this Legation with the Govt. of Mexico will be suspended until the pleasure of my Govt. can be made known to me." [13]

To Cuevas Forsyth wrote (on June 21):
". . . This is not the first time that the truths which the dilatory & evasive system of the Dept. of Relations, has reluctantly compelled the Und. to force upon its attention, have been met with the im-

putation of 'offensiveness.' It will avail now, no better than it has before. The Und. was sent here to deal with facts, to demand & to have justice, to speak the truth. He knows how to do all this with as much good breeding & propriety as any Mexican Minister of State can teach him, either by precept or example, & he knows also when it is necessary to drop courtly & unmeaning phrases to grapple with grave & serious facts. . . . Mr. Cuevas has consistently worked upon a fixed design to embroil the two countries in unnecessary difficulties, or else, relying upon the long-forbearing magnanimity of the Govt. of the U. S., to insult its dignity & refuse justice to its citizens with impunity. . . . This consistent perversity of action in some cases & of studied contempt in others, has forced the Und. to believe either that the Min. of Rs. seeks a breach of friendly relations with his Govt. or that he disdains its claims for justice as unworthy of his thoughts. And in dwelling upon this subject, the Und. has been unable to forget that it was H. E. the Minister of Rs. who conducted the Diplomacy of the Mex. Govt. which resulted in the war between the two countries, eleven years ago; nor can he divert his mind of the idea, that . . . he is treading the same path, inevitably leading to the same unhappy end, which he so pertinaciously followed in 1845. If therefore, out of the question involved in this correspondence, an interruption of the pacific relations between the two nations should grow, the Und. charges upon H. E. the Minis. of Rs. the responsibility of all that may follow, as its active, persistent and principal instigator & author. . . . Despairing therefore, after repeated efforts & failures of bringing the Govt. of Mexico, by mild and persuasive measures to a sense of its duties to the U. S. & seriously apprehensive that the Min. of Res. has listened to busy and interested counsel to provoke a rupture with the U. States, the grave & widespread consequences of which he seems to have too lightly considered, the Und. has to announce to H. E. the Min. of Rs. that he suspends from this date the political relations of this Legation with the Govt. of Mexico until he learns the pleasure of his Govt. & until that period limits his official action to whatever may be necessary for the protection of his countrymen in Mexico. . . ." [14]

Nearly a year later, M. D. Bonilla, when protesting against the American recognition of the Juárez government, stated that Forsyth, after the rejection of his proposals for territory and transits, completely changed his policy—beginning to place obstacles in the way of the administration by provoking disagreeable questions, wounding the national pride, pressing exaggerated claims in caustic and offensive language, and counseling disobedience to the government in order to provoke coercive measures with a view to suspension of relations.[15]

While awaiting a reply from Washington, Forsyth kept in close touch with the enemies of the Zuloaga government and informed his own government that he saw the signs and preparations of an almost matured revolution under the leadership of Lerdo, who, after several recent changes of domicile to avoid arrest, had become a guest under the roof of the American legation, and had confided his plans to the American minister. Learning that the Mexican authorities had discovered Lerdo's retreat and might attempt to take him by force, he prepared arms and ammunition and 30 Americans to defend his "castle." In August, when he received instructions sanctioning his suspension of relations and directing him to take the steamer which had been sent to Vera Cruz to carry him home, he replied that his private interests would not permit such precipitate haste, and remained two months longer to vex the Mexican government, whose downfall he hoped personally to witness. Finally, the discontented minister, who had so often held out straws of hope to encourage his government at Washington, pronounced Mexico a hopeless wreck ready for the wreckers, sent a caustic parting note to the new Minister of Foreign Relations, and without waiting for a government escort angrily departed with his family on October 20 for Vera Cruz, from whence he soon reached Mobile.* From Castillo, whose inadequate offer of escort he had not accepted, he received a note stating the "sincere regret" of the government that his "anxious desire . . . to set out as soon as possible could not be gratified at once." En route to Vera Cruz he and his party, armed to protect themselves, encountered a band of robbers

---

* In his parting note of October 20, Forsyth wrote Castillo: "I shall go, preferring to brave the chances of robbery and assassination on the road to remaining in Mexico subject to the insults and slanders of the servile n. p. organs of the government, to exposing my friends to the vengeance and prisons of the government, to having my house surrounded by government spies as if I were a malefactor and my own servants converted into spies within my dwelling. I prefer to deal with the robbers in the highway. These at least will assail me openly, with arms in their hands; and I can in the same manner resist them." [Enclosure in 22 Mex. Desps., No. 91, Nov. 22, 1858—written at Mobile, Alabama.]

whom they gallantly defeated and from whom they rescued thirteen stolen mules—feats which he suggested should prove to the Zuloaga government their ability to take care of themselves.[16]

Summoned to Washington by the President, Forsyth resigned on February 7, to take effect on March 2, 1859. In May, he published in the Washington *Constitution* extracts of his correspondence, justifying himself on grounds of self-defense against various newspaper attacks. In the following June, assuming undivided responsibility as editor of the Mobile *Daily Register,* and devoting himself to the work of "recovering rights in the Union lost by southern supineness—or, in default of that, of preparing the southern mind for that serious alternative which the South may be forced to adopt for self-preservation," he said that his personal differences with President Buchanan would in no wise influence his course of duty to the Democratic Party. "Let bygones be bygones." [17]

Meantime, President Buchanan, referring to the weak Mexican local governments and consequent disorder along the international boundary, and recognizing the futility of attempts to secure from Mexico money indemnity for claims, contemplated the possible necessity of asking authority to resort to reprisal by occupation of portions of Mexican unsettled territory "to be held in pledge" to guarantee the redress of injuries. In his annual message of December to Congress, he proposed as a remedy for frontier troubles the establishment of a temporary protectorate (with military possession) over the northern part of Chihuahua and Sonora. Later, on February 18, 1859, in a special message, he requested authority to use land and naval forces for protection of American citizens and their property in transit across the isthmus routes—a request which was largely approved by Southern leaders, but which Congress, after considerable debate, refused to grant.[18]

Late in December, 1858, with a view to opening diplomatic relations with the Juárez government in case it should prove able to adjust questions at issue between the two republics, Buchanan sent to Mexico a special confidential agent, William

M. Churchwell. Two months later, he received from this agent a confidential report (of February 22) enclosing a memorandum signed by Ocampo, Secretary of Relations of the Juárez government, indicating a willingness to negotiate various treaties, including a cession of Lower California and perpetual rights of way across the isthmus of Tehuantepec and over other transit routes from the Rio Grande to Mazatlan and Guaymas, on the Gulf of California, but not including the much-desired territories of Sonora and Chihuahua in the basis for negotiations for cession.[19]

The nature of Churchwell's report of February 8 to Cass, recommending the recognition of Juárez as the legitimate President of Mexico, is indicated by the following extracts:

". . . As Juárez is the Constitutional President in virtue of the office which he held at the time Comonfort vacated the Presidency, and as Miramon is but the successor of Zuloaga who was himself an usurper, no valid reason can be alleged why we should not establish relations with Juárez at Vera Cruz, just as though he were at the city of Mexico, and treat with him accordingly. In this connection I have had repeated informal interviews with Juárez and his cabinet, of a satisfactory nature. The maintenance of the Liberalists in power is an object worthy of the ardent moral co-operation of our Government. . . . If we shall manifest a generous interest in their welfare, when it is so much needed; if we shall satisfy them that we are not inclined to despoil them of their territory; . . . then will they adopt us as their virtual Protector and, profiting by our advice leave no effort untried to emulate that of our example which is good. . . . A new phase in Mexican nationality is now a positive necessity, and that phase, if we are not utterly deaf to the dictates of common sense, must be of our own creation and of great moment. . . . The present condition of affairs in Mexico affords the best and it may be, the last opportunity which will ever be presented to the United States to form a Treaty with this Republic that will secure to them not only the sovereignty over a country which recent disclosures and the most authoritative accounts respecting its soil and mineral resources represent as being even more valuable than Upper California—but also the perpetual right of way from El Paso to Guaymas on the Gulf of California and from a point on the Rio Grande to some point on said Gulf, together with vast cessions of territory to such companies in the United States as may obtain the sanction of the Government to build a rail-road through the States of Sonora and Chihuahua, etc.; and also the same perpetual right of way through the Isthmus of Tehuantepec. . . . In my opinion, although it may be an experiment, we have no alternative left but the immediate recognition of the Juárez Government. The occasion is one which should be improved without the intermission of a single hour of unnecessary delay." [20]

The President decided to send a minister to Vera Cruz. On March 7, Robert M. McLane, of Maryland, was appointed envoy extraordinary and minister plenipotentiary, with authority (1) to recognize the Juárez government after verifying the report of Churchwell as to its political condition and its attitude toward proposed adjustments and without undertaking to intervene in its behalf, (2) to negotiate a satisfactory treaty of commerce and limits—including an offer of $10,000,000 for the cession of Lower California and the grants of transits, $2,000,000 of which was to be retained to pay the claims of American citizens against Mexico.[21]

On his arrival in Mexico, McLane, in order to assure himself that the representations of Churchwell were well founded, promptly opened communication with Ocampo on April 1. The latter manifested much uneasiness in regard to several of the points suggested for adjustment after the establishment of regular intercourse, and was especially uneasy in regard to the proposed cession of Lower California. Apparently he had become somewhat distrustful by unrealized expectations of earlier establishment of intercourse through Mata at Washington from which was expected negotiations for loans and war materials. McLane explained that propositions submitted for future negotiations had been presented before and could not be regarded as a consideration exacted by the American government as a compensation for the act of political recognition. On April 5, finding Ocampo still reluctant to bind himself to any actual cession of territory, he "held him to his implied obligations to give us Lower California if we desired it," and secured from him a written statement that Churchwell had truly reported to the President that the Mexican government had the "political right to an adjustment in an honorable and satisfactory manner of the questions which were pending when the relations between the two countries were suspended" and that later events had not changed its power or its "perfect willingness to settle amicably and loyally the questions at issue." His conclusion, by April 7, to recognize the constitutional government was largely determined by "the very large interests already involved in the rights of way over Tehuantepec" and the American interests in Sonora which were threatened by a contest with the central government in regard to its public domain in that state. His negotiations were doubtless rendered more difficult by the protest (of April 14) of the central conservative government at Mexico City, which, although promptly notified that the American government would maintain a neutral policy, declared through Bonilla that the United States had recognized the Juárez government in order to despoil Mexico of her national territory, and proceeded to pronounce void all treaties and agreements between the two countries.[22]

In the negotiations which followed, the chief obstacle was the proposition for the cession of Lower California, which was especially opposed by Lerdo, the Minister of Finance, and which other members of the Juárez government believed would be repudiated by the northern and central states of Mexico. Ocampo, although "reluctant to engage himself to any actual cession of territory," finally avowed the readiness of Juárez to cede it. Doubting, however, whether the Congress which was to be elected in October could be induced to ratify such a provision, he proposed that it should be placed in a separate treaty. In reply to the suggestion that there should be two separate treaties and a distinct division of the $10,000,000 between territory and transits (five millions for each, or seven for territory and three for transits), President Buchanan adhered to the belief that both should be included in the same treaty, which he thought would be more likely to be ratified.[23]

On the question of protection of transits the two countries could not agree. Ocampo declined to agree to the right of the United States to protect the transit across Tehuantepec, although he was inclined to be more liberal in regard to the concession of transit from Guaymas to Tucson by which

McLane thought that the adjacent state of Sonora was likely to be Americanized even before Arizona could be admitted as a state. He recognized the obligation of Mexico to protect the routes, and he agreed that, if Mexico should fail, the United States, with previous consent of the former, might employ armed forces, but should submit them to the laws and authorities of Mexico in all things not relating to the internal government of the troops and should exercise no act of jurisdiction over the inhabitants or passengers except to suppress crime in the act of being committed. Cass could not accept this article unless it could be modified so as to make previous consent of Mexico necessary "except in cases of sudden emergency." [24]

At the same time a combination of conditions and events— the pecuniary distress of the Juárez government, the discontent in the party that supported it, the atrocities committed in territory over which it had no control, and the apprehension of European intervention at Vera Cruz—suggested the idea of an Americo-Mexican alliance which would give protection and order to Mexico and enable the United States to protect the lives and property of American citizens in Mexico, "by chastising any power there which should presume to violate sacred treaty obligations and the common law of humanity." In June —a month after McLane and Consul Black recommended the immediate occupation of San Juan de Ulua by the United States (with consent of the Juárez government) to prevent its seizure by England or France—Ocampo submitted a project of a treaty of alliance providing for protection and security to rights of way granted to citizens of the United States, and making it "obligatory on either of the two Republics to aid in maintaining order and security in the territory of the other" upon request of a legitimate and acknowledged government (obeyed by the majority of the nation and democratic in tendency). This proposition McLane declined to consider, regarding it as an attempt at diversion from his plans for a cession of territory, and basing his objections largely on traditional grounds which were approved by Secretary Cass. At the same time, although he was opposed both to Lerdo's proposed guarantee of territorial integrity and Ocampo's more general proposition for the support of republican institutions, he always agreed that, after a satisfactory treaty relating to transits and the cession of Lower California, the United States could be expected to enter into some arrangement which would give steadiness and security to the mutual interests thus established, and which "could be extended with propriety to the maintenance of law and order in the entire Republic." Although he could not agree to obligate the United States by treaty to intervene at the call of the Mexican government, he suggested to Cass that an article authorizing the United States to exert its military power to enforce the stipulations embraced in the general treaty, and to chastise and punish, if necessary, would secure the ascendency of American influence and American commerce in Mexico and establish a government of constitutional freedom there.[25]

The administration was finally forced to abandon its instructions for negotiations on a basis of acquisition of territory. From the beginning McLane confessed that he saw the impracticability of negotiating for the acquisition of Lower California unless the ratification and the purchase money could be promptly secured, enabling the government to distribute a share of the money to the states which sustained the treaty. At one critical time, he encouraged his government by the announcement that Lerdo, who in the cabinet had strenuously opposed any cession except at the exorbitant price of $30,000,-000, had unexpectedly modified his views enough to favor a reconsideration on the basis of $15,000,000; but, with little hope of success, he suggested that his government should thereafter leave the territorial question to his discretion.* At least,

* Lerdo went to the United States at this time on a mission to raise money on confiscated church property. "If he should succeed," wrote McLane, "there is no probability of acquiring Lower California. If he fail, I think he will advocate the cession." [23 *Despatches, Mexico*, No. 26, July 12.] Two months later Consul Black wrote McLane that it was currently reported that Lerdo had completely succeeded in his negotiations at Washington and that Sonora and Lower California had been sold to the United States for $30,000,000. The report, however, was incorrect. [24 *Despatches, Mexico*, No. 38, Sept. 24.] Lerdo failed to negotiate a loan. [24 *Despatches, Mexico*, No. 49, Nov. 6, 1859.]

he thought that the proposed maximum price should be increased from $10,000,000 to $12,000,000. Doubting the wisdom of negotiating for a transfer of territory at a time when two opposing governments were in conflict for possession of the empire, he hoped President Buchanan would authorize him to sign a treaty without reference to Lower California, and to pay $2,000,000 or $3,000,000 in consideration of the other stipulations. While the President was extremely unwilling to sanction any convention in which the cession was not embraced, he finally authorized as a last resort the acceptance of transits and other rights at a stipulated payment of $4,000,000, of which the sum of $2,000,000 was to be reserved for the claims of American citizens.[26]

In the later negotiations conducted with Fuente, the new Minister of Relations, who adhered closely to the defense of Ocampo's project, McLane was unable to overcome the objections to the discretionary power of military force by the United States for the protection of the transits. The Juárez government, urging that it must maintain its sovereignty over the transit routes, proposed for the protection of the transits an agreement to keep a fixed military force in commission which would obviate the possible contingency of any sudden emergency which might render necessary the military force of the United States without previous consent of Mexico. There was still another obstacle which had already been suggested by both Ocampo and Lerdo. Fuente urged the necessity of an immediate payment of the pecuniary consideration and declared that his government, unless it could receive money at once to increase its power, could neither make the concession relating to Lower California nor that relating to the discretionary power of the United States to protect the transits without danger of exciting an opposition which would lead to the overthrow of the government before ratifications could be exchanged.[27]

After closing negotiations, McLane suggested that the weak Juárez government, which still adhered to Ocampo's project of alliance, might be induced to accept a ·matured proposition from the United States. In an unofficial dispatch of October 31, he proposed to sustain the weak Juárez government by some sort of a military alliance.[28]

This proposed military alliance the American government regarded as a wide departure from previous American policy and disapproved—because it was intended, not for a temporary emergency, but as a part of a general treaty, and also because it endangered the acceptance of any treaty with which it might be connected. The President, however, with a view to satisfaction of claims and prevention of foreign interference with the government of Mexico, decided to authorize the negotiation of a treaty providing for intervention in Mexican affairs incidental to transits and commerce. In his annual message of December, 1859, he approved and accepted a recommendation, made by McLane two months earlier, that the President should "ask Congress the power to enter Mexico with the military forces of the United States, at the call of its authorities, in order to protect the citizens and treaty rights of the United States." He considered this a neighborhood duty and a wise precaution to prevent the future necessity of interference for the maintenance of the established American policy against intervention of European nations in American political affairs.[29]

At the same time American policy was influenced by the depredations of J. N. Cortina, a lawless Mexican bandit, who, at the head of a band of armed Mexican desperadoes, had defied the authorities of Brownsville, Texas, and of the state of Texas, since July, and who, by November, emboldened by his triumph over a body of Texans and Mexicans who had stormed his stronghold near Matamoros, had begun preparations for vengeance with a program for redemption of Mexicans in Texas. The American government began to send troops to the lower Rio Grande to drive from American soil the banditti who had established their camp there, and to prevent further incursions. On November 18, Secretary Cass, by order of the President, with a view to the adoption of necessary and proper measures for security of the frontier, sent the venerable Duff

Green on a private and confidential mission to the region of
these disturbances to make a thorough investigation of the
situation—the number of persons engaged in the "irruptions,"
the nature of their organization, their proposed object and
actual designs, and the attitude of Mexican federal or pro-
vincial authorities toward their incursions of murder and
pillage. He also invited Green's opinion (after careful observation) "of the probability of obtaining the necessary security
without marching a force into Mexico, not only to capture
these marauders if possible, or to drive them off if they cannot
be apprehended, and also to retain possession of the Country
till a stable government is established possessed of the requisite
power and disposition to perform their duties towards the
United States, and to prevent the recurrence of similar outrages." Later, near the close of December, Cortina was driven
from his camp by a force of American regular troops and Texas
Rangers under Major Heintzelman who overtook and defeated
him near Rio Grande City from which he and his survivors
escaped into Mexico without arms. Soon thereafter, he established a new camp on the south side of the Rio Grande about
35 miles above Brownsville. Attempting to seize a vessel on
the river on February 4, he was defeated by Texas Rangers
who crossed the river. Later he was driven into the mountains
40 miles from the frontier by a Mexican force, at the suggestion of Robert E. Lee who was placed in charge of the
United States Military Department in Texas with instructions
to secure the dispersal of Cortina's band by demand upon
Mexican authorities, or, if that failed, by crossing into Mexico
with the American forces.[30]

Meantime, McLane, returning to Vera Cruz in November,
after a vacation of two months, found the conditions more
favorable for negotiating a treaty of transits and of commerce
and intervention. Unable to secure the loan which Lerdo had
been sent to negotiate in the United States, and too weak to
maintain order and enforce treaty stipulations, the Juárez
government accepted the only alternative—to conclude the
negotiations for a treaty on the basis of McLane's later instruc-

tions. Fuente, again refusing to accept any modifications of
Ocampo's project, promptly retired from the government.
Ocampo, who resumed the post of Minister of Relations, was
assured by McLane that he had no desire to press the views
of his government nor to resume negotiations except on the
American basis previously proposed. He promptly and fully
conceded the views of President Buchanan in regard to the
protection of transits and agreed to modify other articles to
suit the views of the American government. The most difficult
task was to induce the constitutional government to recognize
its obligation to seek the aid of the United States whenever
it should be unable effectually to perform its proper functions
as a government in the enforcement of treaty stipulations and
the maintenance of order. This was finally accomplished by
emphasizing the fact that sooner or later the United States
would act, without reference to the constitutional government
or any other government or authority, in defense of treaty
rights and to protect its citizens. While emphasizing the fixed
policy of his government to avoid all interference in the domestic administration of Mexico, McLane "insisted that it was
the recognized duty of the United States to interfere when its
own security, or what is due itself in the abstract or in virtue
of treaty stipulations, required such intervention." [31]

The resumption of negotiations promptly (by December 15)
resulted in a treaty of transits and commerce, conceding valuable privileges for which the United States agreed to pay
$4,000,000. Of this amount, $2,000,000 were payable on the
exchange of ratifications and $2,000,000 were to be retained
by the United States for the payment of claims of American
citizens against Mexico. The privileges included the rights of
way under the sovereignty of Mexico across the Isthmus of
Tehuantepec and also from the lower Rio Grande at Matamoros or Camargo by way of Monterey to Mazatlan and from
Rancho de Nogales to Guaymas by any kind of road, together
with a port of deposit at each terminus of the route and free
and unrestricted passage of merchandise and of mail in closed
bags across Tehuantepec. The United States also was given the

right to transport troops, military stores and munitions of war over the Isthmus of Tehuantepec and from Guaymas to some suitable place on the boundary in the vicinity of Rancho de Nogales.[32]

The McLane-Ocampo draft treaty of December 14 provided that both the United States and Mexico should protect the transits and guarantee their neutrality. It stipulated that Mexico should use her military forces if necessary to protect persons and property passing over any of the routes; but that, upon her failure to act, the American government, with the request and consent of the Mexican government, or of the Mexican minister at Washington, or of the competent and legally appointed local authorities, might employ military force for the same purpose (but for no other). In case of imminent danger to the lives and property of American citizens, the American government was authorized to act with military force for their protection without obtaining previous consent of Mexico.

Remarkable convention articles to enforce treaty stipulations departed radically from the traditional policy of the United States in their provision for direct intervention under certain conditions. The provisions of Article 1 were as follows: "If any of the stipulations of existing treaties between Mexico and the United States are violated, or the safety and security of the citizens of either Republic are endangered within the territory of the other, and the legitimate and acknowledged Government thereof may be unable from any cause to enforce such stipulations or to provide for such safety and security, it shall be obligatory on that Government to seek the aid of the other in maintaining their due execution, as well as order and security, in the territory of that Republic where such violation and discord occur; and in every such special case the expense shall be paid by the treasury of the nation within whose territory such intervention may become necessary; and if discord shall occur on the frontier of the two Republics the authorities of the two Republics nearest the place where the disorder exists shall act in concert and cooperation for the arrest and punishment of criminals who have disturbed the public order and security of either Republic, and for this purpose the parties guilty of these offenses may be arrested within either Republic and delivered over to the authorities of that Republic within which the crime may have been committed; the nature and character of such intervention, as well as the expense thereof, and the manner of arresting and subjecting to punishment the said criminals, shall be determined and regulated by an agreement between the executive branches of the two Governments."

Other articles relating to commerce provided for reciprocity of trade in certain products and guaranteed exemption from forced loans, and freedom of worship.

The extraordinary nature of the convention was recognized, and it was justified only as a measure which might prevent serious international complications. Consul Black, hoping it would "turn out best in the end," wrote: "Our country has a solemn duty to perform—to itself, to the world, to the cause of humanity and to that of freedom and human rights—from which it will never shirk." The convention was regarded as the only hope left to the constitutional government. In urging ratification by the Senate, McLane said that if the United States should decline the responsibility of the convention, the continuation of anarchy in Mexico would result in direct intervention from some quarter and perhaps expose the United States to the "responsibility of a general war and a conquest that few would desire to undertake or consummate." If the President could secure ratification and authority to use the naval and military power of the government in the Gulf and the Pacific to establish the constitutional government in Mexico and enforce treaty stipulations, he expected the prompt submission of the Miramon government, which in spite of his assurance of continued neutrality had published a vigorous and offensive protest. "When it is ratified," said he, "I can easily dictate terms to the Miramon government, obtain redress, and pacify this country. If it is rejected, anarchy will be the order of the day, and American influence will cease here." A month later, desiring to anticipate any possible action of the protesting Miramon which might embarrass the situation, he urgently requested authority to adopt a decisive policy and to act as though the treaties had already been ratified. "Let us take the constitutional government firmly by the hand," said he, "and we will in a twelve-month drive out of Mexico every anti-

American element and pave the way for the acquisition of Cuba." Two days later he left on a visit to New Orleans. On March 30, returning to Vera Cruz which was invested by Miramon's forces, impatient with the slowness at Washington, and apprehensive of European intervention which unless counteracted by his government would make his position humiliating, he advised withdrawal from all active responsibility and diplomatic intercourse with Mexico in case Congress should fail to sustain the Mexican policy of the administration.[33]

Meantime, on January 4, 1860, President Buchanan submitted the proposed treaty to the Senate. The Senate, after considering it in executive session * several times, finally rejected it on May 31 by a vote of eighteen (fourteen Southerners) to twenty-seven (twenty-three Northerners). Although, on June 27, it voted to reconsider, it postponed further discussion until the next meeting of Congress in the following December. On May 24, Cass, in announcing to McLane the failure of the Senate to approve, wrote that if the Senate should adjourn without placing relations with Mexico on a basis proposed by the treaty, American affairs there would assume a grave aspect and would receive the careful consideration of the President.[34]

The President, although deferring all consideration of McLane's proposal of withdrawal, probably foresaw that an attempt of the French government to colonize any part of Mexico would almost necessarily involve the United States in a war with France to vindicate the Monroe Doctrine; and he was as much disappointed as McLane with the failure of the Senate to approve the treaty and with the refusal of Congress to give him power to use military force in Mexico, by which, he later said, "European Governments would have been deprived of all pretext to interfere in the territorial and domestic concerns" of that country and the United States relieved from the obligation of resisting European attempts to deprive a neighboring Republic of portions of her territory—"a duty

* Through some leak the full draft of the proposed treaty appeared in the *National Intelligencer* of February 18, 1860.

from which we could not shrink without abandoning the established and traditional policy of the American people." [35]

While the treaty was before the Senate, the Spanish government, seeking to prevent an American preponderance or protectorate, had unsuccessfully increased its efforts to induce France and Great Britain to join in an intervention in Mexico. In July, when Lord Lyons, the British minister at Washington, submitted to the Department of State a proposition inviting the United States to join France and Great Britain in addressing an identical note to Miramon and Juárez advising a call of a national assembly to settle their domestic difficulties, Assistant Secretary Trescot stated that the general policy of the United States was opposed to any interference of other powers in the domestic affairs of an independent nation—and especially in Mexico where the President had recognized the Juárez government as a constitutional one. [36]

Later in the summer, while McLane was absent from Mexico on a visit to the United States, Cass received from Elgee, the American chargé at Vera Cruz, the information that, following a peremptory demand (ultimatum) upon the Juárez government by the Spanish naval commanding officer, he had been asked by the Minister of Relations "if the United States could lend any assistance to Mexico in the event of the prosecution of hostilities." Cass, recognizing that "our wishes can not regulate our duties," soon directed a full explanation of the views of the American government in order to prevent expectations of cooperation which could not be fulfilled. Although the American government increased its naval squadron at Vera Cruz (to sixteen vessels) with a view to the protection of American citizens who might be placed in danger by threatened hostile operations, it instructed the commanding officer not to resist the Spanish force in legitimate war operations which might ensue. [37]

Near the close of the summer, in a conference with Cass at Washington, McLane, probably at the suggestion of Juárez, requested authority to make to the European ministers in Mexico some reliable statement of policy which would limit

their operations in Mexico and at the same time encourage the
Juárez government and increase the influence of the United
States there. Embarrassed by the effect which the failure of
the treaty might have on his subsequent influence in Mexico,
at a time when England, France and Spain had given notice
of their determination to intervene to restore peace and enforce
demands for redress, he suggested that he should confer with
the English, French and Spanish ministers at his own discretion
and opportunity in order to advise them that he would use
his best offices to facilitate all efforts for the restoration of peace
on a fundamental basis of the right of the people of Mexico
to establish and regulate their own government and political
destiny, and that the enforcement of demands for redress of
wrongs subject to international reparation must not be exercised capriciously as a pretext to change and control the political destiny and institutions of the country. Cass replied that
notwithstanding the President's good wishes and desire for the
exemption of Mexico from all foreign possession or control,
the American government without authority of Congress could
not lend the aid requested by the Juárez government; that
France, England and Spain knew our policy and had disavowed
any design to act in opposition to it, and that the department
had no information to confirm McLane's opinion that they
meditated projects incompatible with that policy; that the
United States would not oppose advice by the European powers
to induce the contending parties in Mexico to enter into an
amicable arrangement and establish a stable free government
sustained by a majority of the Mexican people; but that, if
they should undertake to extort assent and establish European
ascendency, the United States would meet the attempt by
armed action—in case Congress should adhere to the policy
which had so long been avowed and publicly proclaimed; that
while the policy embodied in the rejected treaty and recommendations of McLane, for empowering the executive to act
with vigor, would have placed our relations with Mexico in a
most satisfactory situation, and although the executive was
disappointed in his expectation of Congress, there should be

no abandonment of watchfulness of American interests in Mexico; and that McLane should return to Vera Cruz without delay, establish friendly relations with the Juárez government, ascertain what objects the foreign powers had in contemplation, give them to understand that the United States would adhere firmly to its policy against foreign intervention, and to be guided by circumstances as they should occur.[38]

McLane, who returned to Vera Cruz as directed, reported in the following November that the Spanish minister had confirmed previous disavowals of any desire or intention to hold possession of any part of the country or to control its destinies. At the same time, stating that President Juárez had steadily resisted all suggestions for signing a supplemental article for extending the time for exchanging ratifications of the treaty, he resigned and recommended the withdrawal of the mission. His resignation was accepted by the President, who approved his course, but who continued the mission by the appointment of a successor in the person of John B. Weller, of California. Before his return, declining an invitation to cooperate with the European powers in favor of mediation, McLane sent Mr. La Reintrie as a special agent on a mission to the interior to deny the allegations that the United States desired a continuance of civil war in Mexico, and to declare both to the Liberals and to foreign representatives the policy of the United States in regard to foreign intervention. In his special communication to the ministers of all foreign powers in Mexico, sent from San Angel (near Mexico City) on December 20, a week before the capture of the capital by the forces of Juárez, La Reintrie, after reviewing the situation in Mexico and the failure of mediation by the English and subsequently by the French and Spanish, made a statement of American policy. In it, although not denying the right of European powers to wage warfare for a sufficient cause, he declared that in case the European powers should interfere directly or indirectly with the political independence of the republic of Mexico, the United States would "to the extent of its power defend the nationality and independence of said Republic"—a declaration to which

Seward was unwilling to commit his government eight months later.[39]

Weller, the new American minister, arrived at the City of Mexico, in January, 1861, with many claims of United States citizens to press. After presenting his credentials to Juárez, he wrote that the United States and England should interpose to secure a permanent government under the constitution of 1857 with which the people were satisfied. A month later, he referred to the confidence of the masses in Juárez who had just been re-elected to the presidency. He felt that it was an auspicious moment for the negotiation of treaties with a view to the encouragement of immigration.[40]

In the meantime, events in the United States rendered improbable any reconsideration of the McLane treaty by the Senate. The secession of South Carolina started a movement which turned public attention to new questions and soon took from the Senate almost all the members who had voted for the treaty.

The sequel to the story of persistent negotiations which terminated in an unratified treaty may be found in the Confederate policy to form an alliance with Mexico or to absorb it, the French policy of intervention in Mexico, and the American policy under Seward to prevent the execution of both Confederate and French policies and to preserve the integrity and independence of Mexico.[41]

REFERENCES

1. *Correspondence of Robert Toombs* (Rp. Am. Hist. Ass'n, 1911), II, Toombs to Burwell, March 30, 1857; *17 Mexico, Instructions*, (No. 11) March 3, and (No. 12) March 12, 1857.
2. *Ib.*, No. 33, Nov. 17, 1857.
3. *20 Mexico, Despatches*, (No. 29) Apr. 4, (No. 40) June 1, (No. 43) July 2, 1857; *21 Mexico, Despatches*, (No. 51) Sept. 26, (No. 52) Sept. 29, and (No. 58) Nov. 25, 1857.
4. *17 Mexico, Instructions*, p. 149, (No. 28) July 17, 1857; also, (No. 27) July 17.
5. *21 Mexico, Despatches*, No. 48, Sept. 15, 1857 (Enclosures: Forsyth to Lerdo, Sept. 5 and 15, and Lerdo to Forsyth, Sept. 12); *Ib.*, (Private) Jan. 14, 1858.

6. *Ib.*, No. 57, Nov. 24, 1857.

7. *Ib.*, (No. 48) Sept. 15, (No. 51) Sept. 26, and (No. 52) Sept. 29, 1857.

8. *17 Mexico, Instructions*, pp. 169-81, No. 33, Nov. 17, 1857.

9. *21 Mexico, Despatches*, (No. 56) Nov. 18, (No. 62) Dec. 17, 1857, and (Private) Jan. 14, (No. 66) Jan. 29, (No. 67) Jan. 30, (No. 69) March 1, and (No. 71) March 18, 1858.

10. *Ib.*, (No. 68) Feb. 13, and (No. 69) March 1, and (No. 71) March 18, 1858.

11. *Ib.*, (No. 71) March 18, (No. 72) Apr. 3, (No. 73) Apr. 8, Apr. 16, and (Private) Apr. 15, 1858; *23 Mexico, Despatches*, (No. 12) May 7, 1859 (Enclosures).

12. *17 Mexico, Instructions*, (No. 46) May 19, 1858; *22 Mexico, Despatches*, (No. 77) June 1, (No. 78) June 17, (No. 79) June 19, and (No. 80) June 25, 1858. Forsyth reported that M. de Gabriac, the French minister to Mexico, was at the bottom of a movement against the American legation. [Also see enclosures in *23 Mexico, Despatches*, (No. 12) May 7, 1859.]

13. *Ib.*, (No. 80) June 25, and (No. 79) June 19, 1858.

14. *Ib.*, No. 80, June 25, 1858 (Enclosure); *9 Notes from Mexico Legation*, Aug. 1, 1858 (with enclosures from Cuevas).

15. *23 Mexico, Despatches*, No. 10, Apr. 30, 1859 (Enclosure).

16. *22 Mexico, Despatches*, (No. 81) July 1, (No. 90) Sept. 18, (Private) Oct. 1, (No. 98) Nov. 22, 1858.

17. Mobile *Daily Register*, May 18 and 24 and June 12, 1859.

18. RICHARDSON (Ed.), *Messages and Papers of the Presidents*, V, pp. 221 and 538-40; *Senate Journal*, 35-2, p. 343.

19. *17 Mexico, Instructions*, Dec. 27, 1858; *23 Mexico, Despatches*, (Tel.) Apr. 7, and No. 1, Apr. 7, 1859.

20. *21 Special Agents*, pp. 780-98, No. 2, Churchwell to Cass, Feb. 8, 1859.

21. *17 Mexico, Instructions*, No. 2, March 7, 1859.

22. *23 Mexico, Despatches*, (No. 1) Apr. 7, (No. 5) Apr. 21, 1859; J. M. CALLAHAN, *The Mexican Policy of Southern Leaders Under Buchanan's Administration* (in Annual Rp., Am. Hist. Ass'n, 1910, pp. 133-51); J. M. CALLAHAN, *Evolution of Seward's Mexican Policy*, pp. 7-10.

23. *23 Mexico, Despatches*, (No. 1) Apr. 7, (No. 10) Apr. 30, (No. 12) May 7, 1859; *17 Mexico, Instructions*, (No. 9) May 24, 1859.

24. *23 Mexico, Despatches*, (No. 5) Apr. 21, (No. 20) June 22, (No. 23) July 10, 1859; *17 Mexico, Instructions*, (No. 16) July 30, 1859.

25. *23 Mexico, Despatches*, (No. 8) Apr. 2, (No. 12) May 7, (No.

22) July 10, and (No. 23) July 10, 1859; *17 Mexico, Instructions*, p. 242, (No. 14) July 8, 1859.

26. *23 Mexico, Despatches*, (No. 23) July 10, (No. 26) July 12, and (Unofficial) June 25, 1859; *17 Mexico, Instructions*, No. 16, July 30, 1859.

27. *24 Mexico, Despatches*, (No. 30) Aug. 27, and (No. 33) Aug. 31, 1859.

28. *Ib.*, No. 31, Aug. 28, 1859.

29. *Ib.*, (Unofficial) Oct. 31, (No. 31) Aug. 28, 1859; *17 Mexico, Instructions*, (No. 21), Nov. 4, 1859; *Buchanan's Works*, X, pp. 335-56 and 367.

30. *House Exec. Doc. 81*, 36-1, p. 2; *House Rp. 701*, 45-2, pp. v and 75-82; *3 Special Missions*, Cass to Duff Green, Nov. 18, 1859; *13 Special Agents*, Green to Cass, Nov. 29, 1859, to Feb. 20, 1860; *House Exec. Doc. 52*, 36-1; *House Exec. Doc. 81*, 36-1.

31. *24 Mexico, Despatches*, (No. 56) Dec. 9, and (No. 57) Dec. 15, 1859.

32. *Ib.*, No. 57, Dec. 15, 1859.

33. *Ib.*, Dec. 9, (No. 65) Dec. 30, (No. 57) Dec. 15, (No. 63) Dec. 22, 1859; *25 Mexico, Despatches*, (No. 66) Jan. 7, (Private and Confidential) Jan. 21, (No. 68) Jan. 21, (No. 72) March 30, 1860; *26 Mexico, Despatches*, Memorandum of McLane's conversation with Cass, Aug. 20, 1860.

34. *Senate Exec. Journal*, XI, pp. 115—; H. L. Wilson, *President Buchanan's Proposed Intervention in Mexico* (in Am. Hist. Review, V, pp. 687—).

35. *17 Mexico, Instructions*, (No. 32) Apr. 28, (No. 34) May 26, (No. 36) June 30, 1860; *Messages and Papers of the Presidents*, V, p. 646.

36. *17 Mexico, Instructions*, (No. 38) Aug. 8, 1860; *26 Mexico, Despatches*, (No. 99) Sept. 17, 1860.

37. *17 Mexico, Instructions*, No. 39, Sept. 20, 1860.

38. *26 Mexico, Despatches*, Sept. 1, 1860; *17 Mexico, Instructions*, pp. 306-38, No. 39, Sept. 20, 1860; *Messages and Papers of the Presidents*, V, p. 646.

39. *26 Mexico, Despatches*, (No. 104) Nov. 5, (No. 106) Nov. 12, (No. 113) Dec. 21, 1860; *17 Mexico, Instructions*, (No. 42) Nov. 20, 1860; *House Exec. Doc. 100*, 37-2, Vol. 8, pp. 17-18, Apr. 14, 1862.

40. *26 Mexico, Despatches*, (No. 2 Elgee) Jan. 1, (No. 2 Weller) Feb. 18, (No. 3) March 18, 1861; V. W. KINGSLEY, *French Intervention in America* (N. Y., 1863, 22 pp.).

41. J. M. CALLAHAN, *Evolution of Seward's Mexican Policy.*

CHAPTER IX

SEWARD'S MEXICAN POLICY

SEWARD, the fortunate choice of Lincoln for Secretary of State, somewhat familiar with the questions which had arisen on both sides of the Atlantic for several years, was fully alive to the possibilities and dangers of European intervention in American affairs—both those of the United States and those of the other countries of the continent.[1] By his experience in the United States Senate since 1849, and by his industry and his faith in his country in a period of national crisis, and by his faith in republican government, he was well fitted for the diplomatic duties of his new position—a position which he held for eight years. With Mexico he conducted relations, successively, through six American diplomatic representatives: Thomas Corwin, of Ohio, as minister, from March 22, 1861, to April 27, 1864; William H. Corwin, as chargé *ad interim*, from April 27, 1864, to November 22, 1865; Lewis D. Campbell, of Ohio, as minister, from May 4, 1866, to June 16, 1867; Marcus Otterbourg, of Wisconsin, as chargé, from April 21, 1866, to August 20, 1867, and as minister (appointed July 1) to September 7, 1867; Edward Lee Plumb, of New York, as chargé *ad interim* from August 15, 1867, to December 10, 1868; William S. Rosecrans, of Ohio, as minister, from July 27, 1868 (to June 26, 1869). John A. Logan, of Illinois, who was commissioned as minister on November 14, 1865, declined. Thomas Corwin (born 1794) had served as a member of the lower house of Congress (1831-40 and 1859-61), as governor of Ohio (1840-42), as a member of the United States Senate (1845-50), and as Secretary of the Treasury under President Fillmore (1850-53). Campbell had been a Whig mem-

278

ber of Congress in 1849-57 and from 1857 to May 25, 1858, when he lost his seat in a contest with C. L. Vallandingham, and he had served as a colonel in the Civil War, 1861-62. Rosecrans had served in the United States army as an engineer in 1842-54, and, after a period of industrial experience in the Kanawha Valley of western Virginia, had reentered the army at the opening of the Civil War, and by his military ability in important campaigns had attained the rank of major-general by March, 1865. As minister to Mexico he especially urged the need of railway construction and other forms of American enterprise and industrial leadership as a solution to the Mexican question.

At Washington, Seward kept in close touch with Mexican affairs through conferences with Matias Romero who ably represented the Juárez government, first as chargé (to May 8, 1863) and later as minister (from October 29, 1863, to July 13, 1868). For a brief time Ignacio Mariscal, secretary of the Mexican legation, acted as chargé (October 31, 1867, to April 6, 1868).

Apprehensive that the attempts of Spanish authorities in Cuba to introduce Spanish authority in San Domingo was a step in a policy of armed intervention in Spanish America, on April 2, 1861, Seward wrote Tassara, the Spanish minister at Washington, that if such attempts had the sanction of the Spanish government, the President would be "obliged to regard them as manifesting an unfriendly spirit toward the United States, and to meet the further prosecution of enterprises of that kind in regard to either the Dominican republic or any other part of the American continent or islands with a prompt, persistent, and if possible, effective resistance." At the same time, he wrote to the ministers of Mexico, Guatemala, Salvador, Nicaragua, Costa Rica, Honduras and New Granada, confidentially enclosing a copy of his note to Tassara to the end that their governments might adopt such measures in this exigency as the safety and the welfare of the respective states on the American continent might seem to require. On April 4, he received Romero's written reply: "I flatter myself with the hope that in Mexico the attitude taken by the United States on this occasion will be considered as a frank declaration of the matured and firm resolution of the government of the United States to oppose the increase on this continent of any European influence which would do so much prejudice to the progress of the systems of republican government, in the preservation and development of which all humanity is interested." [2]

The Lincoln administration, though it found the archives full of complaints against Mexico, desired to give that unhappy country time to establish order and security to enable it to maintain its complete integrity and independence against the dangers from foreign powers, and against the visionary aggressive schemes of the filibustering confederates who while seeking to destroy the union had conceived designs "to effect either a partial dismemberment or a complete overthrow of the Mexican government with a view to extending over it the authority of the newly projected Confederacy." It promptly took steps to show its friendly feeling for the unfortunate country. It commissioned as envoy extraordinary and minister plenipotentiary to that country Thomas Corwin who, on February 11, 1847, had delivered a famous speech in the Senate in opposition to the war against Mexico. It exercised prompt vigilance to prevent Confederate filibustering expeditions which Romero feared might attack Lower California and Sonora. Seward, in his instructions of April 6 to Corwin, deprecating the chronic reign of disorder in Mexico, and, referring to its influence in producing the contention which led to the secession movement in the United States, declared that the President had no sympathy with the schemes of foreign powers to intervene in Mexico to establish a protectorate, nor with those of the Southern discontents to prepare some further revolution in Mexico with a view to a protectorate or other control. "The President . . . is fully satisfied," said he, "that the safety, welfare, and happiness of Mexico would be more effectually promoted by its complete integrity and independence than by dismemberment with transfer or diminution of its sovereignty, even though thereby a portion or the whole of the country or its sovereignty should be transferred to the United States themselves." Later, after receiving information of fresh Confederate designs to gain possession of Lower California and parts of northern Mexico, Seward wrote Corwin that the United States, though she desired no part of Mexico, would buy Lower California to save it from the Confederates, if Mexico would name the price, and sent him full powers to treat; but these instructions were later superseded.[3]

The constitutional government of Mexico authorized Mr. Romero to express to Mr. Seward its good disposition to negotiate a political treaty which would guarantee the existing boundaries of Mexico and the integrity of its territory and prevent the introduction or spread of slavery into it—which the Confederates might seek to accomplish either by open war or filibustering expeditions.

Corwin on his arrival in Mexico promptly reported the situation—that in its disorder it sought the help of other nations, and was greatly in need of money to meet the demands of England, France and Spain for payment of debts, and to establish a permanent government that could prevent disruption. Fearing that European intervention would overthrow the constitutional government and substitute another which would be the mere instrument of the intervening parties, and perhaps result in a dissolution of the Mexican states and new combinations which would be highly prejudicial to the United States, he declared that the American government was bound to sustain Mexico. He suggested that the purchase of Lower California, which might become indispensable to the Pacific possessions of the United States, would save Mexico from partition or subjugation by Europe—and at the same time terminate the secession movement, secure American interests, and promote successfully the cause of human progress on the entire continent. A month later, after the Juárez government had suspended payment of all indemnities for a period of two years and England and France had both terminated diplomatic intercourse, and when England was preparing to resort to a distress by seizure of the customhouses at the ports of Tampico and Vera Cruz, he urged that it was the duty of the United States to prevent the aims of European powers in regard to intervention in American affairs; and he recommended that the American government, with proper pledge of territory as a guarantee, should arrange to negotiate a loan to pay the interest on the Mexican debt for five years. By this plan he said that the United States, destined to be the only safe guardian of the independence and true civilization of the continent, would be benefited in all time to come.[4]

Seward, although recognizing that it was not prudent to provoke debates with foreign countries by formal reassurances of the American policy in relation to foreign nations, and not willing to commit his government to all the opinions which La Reintrie by direction of McLane had expressed in his circular (of December 20, 1860) to representatives of foreign powers in Mexico, did not hesitate to affirm the American desire for Mexican independence and freedom from all foreign political interference or control, nor did he doubt that the United States would be willing to take decided measures favoring that independence. Regretting that, as a result of the secession movement started by "infatuated" leaders, all Spanish America was threatened with the evils of past centuries, and alluding to the increasing responsibilities which prevented the United States from intervening to aid the reorganization of Mexico, he wrote Corwin: "We may perhaps prevent her extensive territories . . . from falling into the possession of powers which it is only reasonable to expect would manage them for their own aggrandizement, inconsistent equally with the principle of government there and with our own dignity and even our own safety." With this purpose, and by direction of President Lincoln, he authorized Corwin to negotiate with Mexico a treaty by which, provided the European powers would consent to forbear from resort to hostilities in Mexico on account of its refusal to pay the interest on its debts, the United States would agree to pay the interest (at three per cent) on the funded debt of Mexico ($62,000,000) for five years from the date of the decree by which payments had been suspended, on condition that Mexico on her part would pledge the reimbursement by a lien on the public lands and mineral rights in Lower California, Chihuahua, Sonora and Sinaloa, which would become the property of the United States at the end of six years in default of reimbursement. This seemed to him to be the best course to guard against the extinction of the Mexican republic.[5]

In taking this step to strengthen the Juárez government, the Lincoln administration was doubtless influenced in part by a desire to circumvent the plans of the government of the Southern Confederacy which, taking advantage of the divided condition of Mexico, had been ready and willing to recognize any and every government, state or national, and ready to make treaties with governors or with presidents to suit the exigencies of the occasion—and had endeavored especially but in vain to induce the constitutional government to refuse to grant permission for the transit of United States troops from Guaymas to Arizona, and to reconsider its refusal to entertain any proposition which might seem to recognize the Confederate States in any way except as a part of the United States.[6]

Pickett, whom the Confederate leaders sent to secure an alliance with Mexico, and who sought in vain to open communications with the Juárez government, in an unofficial communication threatened an invasion of the northern states of Mexico. He especially sought to prevent any treaty arrangement which would relieve the embarrassment of Mexico and prevent the foreign interference which would furnish the opportunity for filibustering in northern Mexico; and, in the vain endeavor to interfere with Corwin's negotiations, he warned the constitutional government of Mexico that the Confederates would never consent to any sale or hypothecation of lands to any government not in amity with the Confederacy. In a letter to Toombs he suggested that the Confederates should take military possession of Monterey and hold all that region until all questions with the United States were amicably adjusted. "Such an occupation," said he, "would ensure to us the permanent possession of that beautiful country." While threatening retaliation, Pickett proposed to Mexico to recede Upper California and New Mexico on condition that the Mexican government would agree to negotiate a treaty of free trade with the Confederacy. Smarting under the pain of his complete failure, and confident that the Confederate revolution had emasculated the Monroe Doctrine, he made friendly approaches to the Conservatives who favored the restoration of Spanish rule; and, acting more like a bully than a diplomat, he apparently endeavored to force the Juárez government to recognize him as a pernicious intriguer who was anxious to precipitate a crisis that would give the Confederacy an opportunity to form a "natural" alliance with Spa·n which would secure the partition of all Mexico and "tend to check the expansion of the North"(!). After serving a brief period in jail for a brutal attack on an American citizen, he withdrew, reaching Vera Cruz with the French minister in December, in time to witness its occupation by Spain. In leaving, he delegated the duty of furnishing the Confederacy reports of passing events in Mexico to John S. Cripps (of South Carolina), who soon reported that the Mexican government had become full of animosity toward the Southern States.[7]

In the meantime, Seward, hoping to satisfy foreign creditors, had kept in close touch with the situation. Late in September, hearing rumors of the proposed tripartite expedition against Vera Cruz to make demands on Mexico, he wrote Dayton that the United States, desiring peace in "this hemisphere," looked with deep concern on the threatened expedition and was not unwilling to tender its good offices to prevent it. Although he was informed that the French government, in its conference with Dayton, disclaimed all idea of territorial acquisition, he was still anxious to prevent further complications. Hearing that Spain meditated a demonstration against Mexico, he instructed Adams to ask Earl Russell whether the United States could make to Spain any proposition which would receive the favorable consideration of Great Britain. However, when Corwin proposed that the United States should advance five or ten million dollars to the Mexican government to relieve the threatening situation, he declared this plan impossible even if it were wise, and he confined his efforts to the proposition which seemed to him more feasible—a loan to pay the interest on the Mexican debt.[8]

Before negotiating the proposed treaty he sought to obtain from the English and French governments an agreement to refrain from operations against Mexico until the President could submit the treaty to the Senate and obtain its ratification. He promptly and informally communicated his plans to both these governments, neither of which approved—probably fearing that the plan was "preliminary to an entry for foreclosure" rather than an effort to maintain the abstract principle announced in the Monroe Doctrine. Thouvenel thought France ought not in any way to recognize the transaction. Lord Lyons suggested to Seward that the difficulty and the dangers of intervention might be most satisfactorily met by the cooperation of the United States, Great Britain and France with Spain in some distinctly defined policy.[9]

Soon, Spain and France and Great Britain signed a convention exacting from Mexico the performance of its obligations, but disclaiming any purpose to seek acquisition of territory or to control the internal affairs in any such way as to prejudice the rights of Mexico to choose and constitute freely the form of its government. Agreeing to begin demonstrative operations as soon as their combined forces could unite in the vicinity of Vera Cruz, they invited the cooperation of the United States. On December 4, Seward declined to cooperate with the European powers, stating several reasons: inexpediency of seeking satisfaction at that time; traditional policy confirmed by experience; and the desire to cherish good will toward a neighboring republic on the American continent. He also referred to his plan to aid Mexico by a loan which would enable it to meet its obligations to the European allies and avert the war which they had agreed to wage and which Romero said was planned with the object to establish a monarchy in Mexico.[10]

When the Spanish fleet arrived at Vera Cruz in December and seized the port as a pledge in a demand for payment of the Spanish debt, Corwin, realizing the seriousness of the situation and still hoping to obtain permission to make the loan, was anxious to know whether the American policy was to join the three powers against Mexico. Believing that both Spain and

France had covetous eyes on the Spanish American republics and that Spain desired the reconquest of her lost colonies, he urged Seward (in a dispatch forwarded by Mr. Plumb) to take measures to secure the representation of every South American republic in Mexico to meet the Spanish and French while they were making their first demonstration.[11]

Later, on February 19, 1862, at Soledad, the ministers of Spain, Great Britain and France signed with the Secretary of State of the Juárez government a preliminary convention recognizing the government and disclaiming all designs against the sovereignty and integrity of the Mexican republic, and agreeing to negotiate at Orizaba a settlement of their claims. Corwin expected affairs to be settled favorably to Mexico; but, believing that the allies (who said they had come to establish order and restore peace) were waiting only for a plausible reason or pretext to aid one party or the other, and fearing that they might decide to set up a church party and hold Mexico as a European colony, he urged that he should be authorized to furnish the Juárez government financial aid at once pending the negotiations. "The conditions on which I am instructed to aid Mexico," said he, "will forbid me to do anything which Mexico can accept, because if the allies are to be satisfied and to leave before the desired aid is given, the public lands must be given to the allies as security, leaving the United States no security for the loan."[12]

Early in April the situation was changed by the dissolution of the triple alliance after a stormy conference at Orizaba, each of the allies announcing a resolution to adopt separate action. Both England and Spain soon withdrew their troops from Mexico. The French government, now free to pursue its own policy, though it emphatically assured the United States that it had no designs on the independence of Mexico and no intention to establish Maximilian on the throne of a Mexican monarchy, proceeded to reinforce the Mexican expedition, placed General Forey in command to conduct the advance against the Juárez government and pushed forward the preparations which were to end in an attempt to establish a monarchy.[13]

Corwin was certain that it had become the Mexican policy

and duty to give the allies no further pretext for seizing the country and for dictating its government. "I trust our government will remonstrate firmly against all idea of European conquest on this continent," he wrote, "and in such tone as to have its influence on the position of France in Mexico." Referring to the dangers to the Pacific possessions of the United States, he urged that to prevent the threatened occupation of Mexico would be less expensive than to secure the necessary dislodgement thereafter.

Seward had already formulated a clear expression of the views of the administration in the form of a circular letter. At the close of January, at the request of Peru (who had recently initiated a Spanish American movement toward founding a union or league for mutual protection against European attacks upon their independence), he had been invited confidentially by Romero to authorize the American minister at Lima to "agree to a secret pact in relation to the defensive attitude that it is convenient for all the American republics to take with a view to avoid that the Europeans be overlimited in this continent." He prepared no written reply, but a few weeks later, after Romero had written him again in regard to the designs of the French, he submitted to him confidentially a copy of the resolutions of the Committee of Foreign Relations of the Senate on Mexican affairs, and later showed his interest and concern by submitting extracts of Dayton's correspondence.[14]

On March 3, at the close of the first year of the Lincoln administration, he addressed to the several American legations abroad a letter containing the following extracts:

"The President has relied upon the assurance given his government by the Allies that they were in pursuit of no political object, but simply the redress of their grievances. . . . Nevertheless the President regards it as his duty to express to the Allies, in all kindness and candour, that a monarchical government established in Mexico, in the presence of foreign fleets and armies, occupying the waters and the soil of Mexico, has no promise of security or permanence; in the second place, that the instability of such a monarchy would be enhanced if the throne were assigned to a person alien to Mexico; that in these circumstances the new government would instantly fall unless sustained by European alliances, which, under the influence of the first invasion, would be practically the beginning of a permanent policy of armed intervention by monarchical Europe, at once injurious and inimical to the system of government generally adopted by the American continent. . . . There can be no doubt that in this matter the permanent interests and the sympathies of our country would be on the side of the other American republics. . . . It is enough to say that in the opinion of the President the emancipation of the American continent from the control of Europe has been the principal characteristic of the past half century. It is not probable that a revolution in the opposite direction can succeed. . . ."

He promptly informed Dayton of reports from the United States consul at Havana which indicated that France aimed at the subversion of republican institutions (the American system) in Mexico. Later he received Thouvenel's explanations and disclaimers and promptly communicated them to Romero.[15]

On April 6, Corwin had finally negotiated a treaty granting to Mexico a well-secured loan, of which $2,000,000 was payable at once—a treaty which he said was "to manifest to European powers that we are the friend of Mexico and resolved to use all peaceable means to prevent forcible intervention" which might result in the acquisition of Mexican territory. The United States Senate, however, had already declined (February 25) to approve any policy that would require the assumption of any part of the Mexican debt (principal or interest) or the concurrence of the European powers, and the President decided that it would be useless to submit for ratification a treaty providing for a loan to Mexico made at the time when the French forces occupied a portion of the territory of Mexico.[16] Thanking Seward for the "ability and sagacity" displayed by him in the management of our European difficulties, Corwin continued to urge the "imperative necessity" of securing the ratification of his treaty as the only means left to prevent helpless Mexico from falling into the hands of France (and England). Romero also continued to press his fears that the purpose of the European intervention was to establish a monarchy.[17]

Seward, after stating that he approved Corwin's negotiations, and informing him of the final decision of the Senate against

his treaty, at the same time mentioned the friendly assurances
with which France had disclaimed any designs which had been
attributed to her. He soon found reason to hint politely that
Napoleon's assurances were contradicted by his actions. From
Romero he continued to hear that France was using the question of claims as a mere pretext and that the real purpose was
conquest and the establishment of a monarchy in Mexico, and
he was urged to consider the advisability of a general congress
for mutual defense on the ground that the blow aimed by Napoleon against Mexico would later be extended to the whole
continent.[18]

The government at Washington, bending every energy to
preserve the Union, endeavored to pursue a policy of strict neutrality in the Franco-Mexican war; but naturally this policy
did not relieve it from criticism. For a while, as the French advanced, the Mexican cabinet, observing the export of mules,
wagons and other supplies from the United States for the use
of the expedition, directed Romero to make complaints of par-
tiality—which were made the subject of inquiry by the Senate at the beginning of 1863 and again in 1864. In January,
1863, the Juárez government viewed with apprehension the report that Seward in the summer of 1862 had invited the advice
and cooperation of the governments of Great Britain and
France concerning the request of the Granadian government for
enforcement of the American guarantee of the neutrality of the
Panama transit route under the treaty of 1846.[19]

About the same time, efforts were made to induce the administration to adopt a bolder, more belligerent policy. On
January 19, McDougall, a Democrat of California, presented
resolutions in the Senate in favor of sustaining the Monroe Doctrine by rendering assistance to Mexico. On February 3, they
were taken up for consideration, by a vote of 29 to 16, against
the opposition of Sumner who counseled prudence in our foreign relations and urged that "the suppression of the rebellion"
was the first step to arrest the return of empire in Mexico, New
Granada and San Domingo. Although, after an executive session, the resolutions were laid on the table by a vote of 34 to 10,

they promptly attracted the attention of the watchful eye of Napoleon, who expressed a hope that there was no danger in them.

Seward, undiverted by criticism and calmly confident of a friendly future, watchfully kept his bearings in a middle course. Careful to avoid any unnecessary action which might give offense to France, he had occasion to disapprove an unauthorized and unofficial remark of Koerner, the American minister at Madrid, suggesting later American belligerent action to drive the French from Mexico. He steadily adhered to the policy of non-intervention and neutrality in American affairs, as he consistently declined the invitation to cooperate with France, England and Austria in an appeal to Russia in regard to affairs in Poland.

In midsummer, after the crisis in the American Civil War had been safely passed, Seward was confronted by news of the romantic establishment of the new Franco-Mexican empire which, by many, was regarded as a rude shock to the Monroe Doctrine. For this establishment he was blamed on the ground that he had failed to make a firm and fearless reaffirmation of the Monroe Doctrine in 1861, and that he had maintained "the silence that gives assent." General Forey, just before his occupation of the Mexican capital, had organized a temporary government for Mexico. The French minister selected thirty-five Mexican citizens to form a supreme junta. These chose an executive composed of three regents (of whom Almonte was at the head), and then chose 215 citizens of Mexico to associate with themselves to form an assembly of notables (245 in number and nearly all enemies of Juárez) to which was assigned the authority to establish a permanent government. On July 11, the day after the occupation of the capital, this assembly voted in favor of an empire-monarchy, and decided (with only two votes in the negative) to offer the crown to Maximilian of Austria and his descendants, or, in case he should not accept, to any other Catholic prince whom Napoleon should indicate for the Mexican nation. There was reason for apprehension that this Franco-Mexican empire, conceived as a direct blow at the

Monroe Doctrine (at a time when Napoleon supposed the United States was ruined), might ally with the weakened Confederacy in order to erect a counterpoise to the growing strength of the United States and proceed to extend French dominion southward from Mexico to the gateway of the isthmus where it might construct a canal and lay tribute upon the commerce of the world, essentially modifying the possible preponderance of the American union on the continent.

Seward promptly instructed Corwin not to address the new provisional government inaugurated under the protection of French forces, and granted him leave of absence. At the same time, he instructed Dayton to ask Lhuys for information in regard to the intentions of the Emperor in his latest military interference with the rights of the people of Mexico, and in regard to his designs on the adjoining territory of the United States. Dayton had already been assured that France, having had enough colonial experience in Algeria, contemplated only temporary intervention, and, departing after her grievances were satisfied, would leave no puppet behind her. He promptly presented Seward's inquiry to Lhuys who again disclaimed all intention to hold permanently, or to colonize, any part of Mexico, or to interfere with the right of the people to choose or maintain their own form of government, or to interfere with the United States or its adjoining territory; but, remembering Talleyrand's famous *bon mot,* and attaching little importance to the disclaimers, he wrote Seward: "Our *power* is our security, and that only." * A week later, speaking with Lhuys in regard to the report that the United States only awaited the end of the war to drive France from Mexico, he frankly stated that although the United States, relying on the constant assurances of France, had made no formal protest and had no purpose to interfere in the quarrel, yet she had not concealed her earnest solicitation for

* "These intimations by France amount to but little," said Dayton, "for she can easily manage to get up an apparent expression of public sentiment in Mexico. Yet Mexico proposes, if France consents, to accept Maximilian." [*53 Fr. Desps.,* No. 342, Sept. 7, 1863.] "You very correctly intimate," replied Seward, "that French explanations do not afford a reliable guarantee for the future. . . . As you say she will be largely influenced by her estimate of our power. You may make discreet explanations of our strength." [*16 Fr. Instrs.,* p. 451, No. 406, Sept. 26, 1863.]

the well being of Mexico and her sensitiveness of foreign intervention.[20]

Whether he had determined to drive France from Mexico at the first favorable opportunity, Seward was frank to say that the introduction of a monarchical form of government supported by French arms would threaten the continuance of free republican institutions in America which were required for the safety of the institutions of the United States, and therefore might lead to war between the United States and France. He wrote Dayton that, relying on the assurances of France that her occupation was not permanent, the United States continued to be neutral; but aware that many in the United States and in Mexico doubted the French assurances that the occupation would be only temporary, and finding it hard to secure rigid observation of the neutrality laws, he urged that the interests of the United States and France required an early solution of the complications on a basis of the unity and independence of Mexico. At the same time, he disclaimed any desire of the United States to control or annex any part of the country. Again, although stating that the United States practiced non-intervention in Mexico as elsewhere, he said: "This government believes that foreign resistance or attempts to control American civilization must and will fail before the ceaseless and ever increasing activity of the material, moral and political forces which peculiarly belong to the American continent. Nor do the United States deny that . . . their own safety and the cheerful destiny to which they aspire are intimately dependent on the continuance of free republican institutions throughout America." Still recognizing that the Emperor's purposes might change, he suggested that the American government was not likely to neglect provision for its own safety.[21]

Feeling sure of the future vindication of the supremacy of republican institutions upon the American continent, for the time he was willing to pursue a policy of "masterly inactivity." Although he knew that normal opinion in Mexico favored a republican government, and although he admitted the war between France and Mexico had continued longer than he had expected, he said the United States, adhering to the principles of neutrality, had "neither the right nor the disposition to interfere by force in the internal affairs of Mexico, whether to establish or maintain a republican (or even a domestic) government there or to overthrow an imperial or foreign one if Mexico should choose to establish or accept it." To Motley, who had reported (August 17) that Austria was recruiting troops to accompany Maximilian to Mexico and had suggested the enforcement of the Monroe Doctrine to prevent it, he replied that, as Austria had neither explained that she had any interest in the subject nor expressed any desire to know the American views, he did not consider it necessary for the representative of the United States to engage in a political debate which the unsettled aspect of the war had elicited. Later, he added that the Monroe Doctrine had no application in the cases of recruiting which Motley had mentioned.[22]

Though not apprehensive of the rumored intentions of France to seize Texas or to form an alliance with the Confederates, Seward, pointing out the danger of collision between France and the United States (and other American republics) which might result from the adoption by France of a policy in Mexico antagonistic to American opinions, stated that the American government, "not unobservant of the progress of the events," would not likely neglect such protective measures as every sovereign state should provide for use "when nations . . . cease to respect their moral and treaty obligations." Though instructions were issued (November 23, 1863) to the army in the Southwest enjoining forbearance from intervention in Mexico, Seward suggested that the Emperor should make a reliable guarantee of the informal statements of Lhuys. Consistently adhering to the policy of neutrality, and the Monroe Doctrine, which would leave the destinies and sovereignty and independence of Mexico in the keeping of her own people, he still maintained kind relations with the Juárez government in the face of its misfortunes and its increasing weakness, and did not expect an easy and permanent establishment of monarchy in Mexico. When he received Lhuys' intimation that the recognition of the

proposed empire by the United States would hasten the withdrawal of the French troops, he declined to accede to the proposal—preferring to err on the side of strict neutrality in
marked contrast to the authorities at Richmond who, bold and
inventive in their political expedients, on January 7, 1864, appointed Preston envoy extraordinary and minister plenipotentiary to the government of Maximilian with the vain hope of
new conditions or complications which would enable him to secure some sort of recognition.[23]

At the beginning of 1864, there was considerable popular agitation in favor of a more aggressive policy against the French in
Mexico. Romero and ardent spirits in Congress were disappointed that Lincoln entered into no discussion of the Monroe
Doctrine in his annual message of December, 1863, and thought
that Seward had not been vigilant enough. Romero, at a dinner
in New York (on December 16) expressed his surprise that
Napoleon, whose plans were aimed against the United States
as well as against Mexico, had been allowed to collect his large
army and navy in the Gulf "without any remonstrance, without any protest, or even without any demonstration of interest
or concern on the part of the United States." Early in 1864, he
complained that the United States was not observing strict neutrality between the parties to the war in Mexico.[24]

Congress in the meantime had been assuming a more restless
attitude. In the Senate, on January 11, 1864, McDougall of
California had renewed his resolution declaring that "the occupation of a portion of the territory of Mexico by armed forces
of the government of France is an act unfriendly to the republic of the United States of America," and that it was the
duty of the United States government to demand withdrawal.
Though this resolution was never reported from the Senate
Committee on Foreign Relations to which it was referred, the
House Committee on Foreign Affairs—possibly influenced in
part by the rumor that Mercier in Paris pretended to have the
assurances of President Lincoln that the United States would
recognize the Maximilian government in Mexico if France would
not recognize the Confederate government at Richmond—re-

vived the question of directing foreign policy by the legislative assembly. On April 4, H. W. Davis reported from the committee a resolution which was accepted by the House (yeas 109) without a dissenting vote, declaring against the policy of acknowledging "any monarchical government in America under the auspices of any European power." The same resolution was offered in the Senate, but it was referred to the committee where Sumner allowed it to sleep.

Seward, who had often warned France that American popular opinion was opposed to the French policy in Mexico, and who was alert in preventing any American diplomatic representative from entering into intercourse with any revolutionary government in Mexico antagonistic to the Juárez government, was somewhat embarrassed by the resolution. In response to a note from Geofroy (the French chargé) requesting an explanation * of it, he instructed Dayton to inform the French government that, although the resolution was a true interpretation of the unanimous sentiment of the people of the United States, the action of the House alone could not determine the policy of the government—and that France would be seasonably notified of any change of policy which the President might think proper to adopt in the future. For this instruction he was severely criticised: (1) by a report of the House committee, written by Mr. Davis, which presented historical precedents of the rights of the House, and declared the right of Congress to prescribe the foreign policy of the United States; and also, a few months later, (2) by a resolution offered by Mr. Davis, asserting (a) the right of Congress to a voice in the recognition of new powers as well as in other matters and declaring (b) that "the propriety of any declaration of foreign policy by Congress is sufficiently proved by the vote which pronounces it, and that such a propo-

* On April 3, Geofroy, desiring to avoid complications on the frontier, where he feared invasion by General Banks, informed Seward that French troops had been sent to Sonora to prevent occupation by immigrants from California under grants from Juárez. Without assuming to judge the effect of the war upon titles to land, Seward promptly informed Banks of the French purpose, and enjoined him to observe the instructions of November 23, 1863, requesting him to forbear from any form of intervention, but also informed Geofroy that peaceful emigration from the United States was free from all restraint. (*Dip. Cor. 1865-66*, Vol. 3, p. 357.)

sition while pending and undetermined is not a fit topic of diplomatic explanation with any foreign power.[25]

On April 10, at Miramar, near Triest, Maximilian formally accepted the crown offered by the Mexican deputies; and, with an agreement from Napoleon to uphold him with French troops for five years, accompanied by his wife he promptly departed for Rome en route for Mexico. In reporting to Seward the acceptance of Maximilian, Dayton, who had already said: "We cannot afford a war with France for the quixotic purpose of helping Mexico," now declared: "Nothing has happened since I came here which so much foreshadows the future differences with France. . . . France has not kept faith with us, but it is needless to complain now—not till we are able to enforce reparation. France knows the conditions on which we have announced to her our policy of non-intervention." A few days later, after he had explained to Lhuys the meaning of the House resolution which he said contained nothing more than the basis of the previous statements of policy submitted to France, he wrote Seward: "This Mexican question is the point of danger between the United States and France." [26]

Seward, after the news of Maximilian's acceptance, referring to the "new duties" which would "devolve upon us," wrote Dayton: "I remain now firm, as heretofore, in the opinion that the destinies of the American continent are not to be permanently controlled by political arrangements that can be made in the political capitals of Europe." Although clubs were formed, and other efforts were made, to urge the government in favor of a more active policy in the maintenance of the Monroe Doctrine, he knew that intervention against France in Mexico at that time would have been dangerous to the safety of the United States. Writing to Adams (May 3) in regard to the Mexican situation and the European jealousy of the United States, he said: "I know no way but to contemplate the situation calmly, do our duty faithfully and meet every emergency as it rises. Domestic perils crowd out the consideration of foreign and remote dangers now." Two days later, confident of the remedial virtues of time, he wrote confidentially to Bigelow, consul-general at Paris: "I might say to you confidentially, if it were entirely wise to say anything unnecessary, that those who are most impatient for the defeat of European and monarchical designs in Mexico might well be content to abide the effects which must result from the ever-increasing expansion of the American people westward and southward. Five years, ten years, twenty years hence, Mexico will be opening herself as cheerfully to American immigration as Montana and Idaho are now. What European power can then maintain an army in Mexico capable of resisting the martial and moral influences of emigration?" Later, he wrote Adams that the belief that all the European powers except Russia had agreed to recognize the Mexican government had induced the President to think it "proper to practice especial circumspection in regard to the war between France and Mexico"; but, fully informed of South American apprehensions of the designs of other European powers, and cognizant of the general discontent manifested in the United States against his forbearance, he informed Koerner that a demand of public opinion for reconsideration of the American policy of neutrality might produce complications which would endanger the peace of nations.[27]

France soon had an opportunity to observe new indications that the presence of her troops in Mexico was irritating to the American people. The Radical Republican convention (at Cleveland on May 31) declared that "the national policy known as the Monroe Doctrine has become a recognized principle and that the establishment of any anti-republican government on this continent by any foreign power can not be tolerated." On June 7, 1864, the platform of the Republican national convention at Baltimore approved the views of the government—"that the people of the United States can never regard with indifference the attempt of any European power to overthrow by force or to supplant by fraud the institutions of any republican government of the Western Continent, and they will view with extreme jealousy, as menacing to the peace and independence of their own country, the efforts of any such power to obtain new footholds for monarchical governments, sustained by foreign

military force in near proximity to the United States." Lincoln
in his letter of acceptance (June 27) construed this resolution as
an approval of the course that Seward was then taking—and
had been taking for some time, as indicated by a large volume
of correspondence submitted to the Senate on June 16. On July
14, Seward, still considering the various and uncontrollable consequences of the American Civil War abroad, wrote (to Motley): "All that can be done in regard to them is to practice
prudence and good faith in our foreign relations, and at the
same time make preparations for self defense, if, notwithstanding our best efforts, we find ourselves involved in new complications." Benjamin, who was urging General Preston to send Mr.
Ford from Havana to Mexico to induce the Maximilian government to signify a desire to open intercourse with the Confederacy without waiting for a response from the overtures made to
the United States government, on June 23, writing Slidell of
the indications of "an entente between the cabinets of Washington and Paris," said that the unanimous determination in the
United States to overthrow the French schemes in Mexico indicated that "the safety of the new empire is dependent solely
upon our success in interposing a barrier between Northern
aggression and the Mexican territory." [28]

In December, just after the arrival of Lincoln's annual message which contained the Monroe Doctrine "coiled up for a
spring," John Bigelow, who had succeeded to the duties of the
American legation in Paris, and who carefully guarded the interests of the United States and conducted the delicate and difficult negotiations for the next two years, was anxious to secure "a reconciliation of the national policies" of France and
the United States on the Mexican question. One of his first
duties was to ask explanations in regard to the reported plan of
Maximilian to cede Sonora to France. He was assured that the
proposition, upon which no action had been taken, had contemplated only a lien on the mineral products of Sonora as security
for the Mexican debt to France; and, early in February, the
Emperor, through the *Moniteur*, officially denied the cession.

Meanwhile, Seward had received from Romero a formal and

explicit protest against the proposal of Maximilian to settle the
French claims against Mexico by a cession of Lower California
and the northern states of Mexico (north of the Yaqui on the
Pacific and the Panuco on the Gulf) to France—who had objected to the hypothecation to the United States in April, 1862,
and whose purpose was to establish in it a military colony. On
February 25, he notified Romero that the protest had been filed
in the archives "for such uses and purposes as future events may
render it necessary to apply it to." On February 7, he promptly
instructed Bigelow that "such a cession, or even creation of a
lien upon the mineral resources of Sonora could not be regarded with favor by the people of the United States." At the
same time, referring to the recent projects of the Confederates
to suspend or end the war of secession by a combined war
against France,* he said that the United States preferred to
fight the Civil War to end on previous lines in case no foreign
state should interfere in behalf of the insurgents.[29]

While the Confederate fortunes were rapidly waning, Bigelow, assured that Napoleon had abandoned the hope that the
American Union would be dissolved, and informed by the
French Minister of Finance that Mexico was the only possible
remaining source of war between the United States and France,
at first endeavored to disarm apprehensions that the United
States was destined to be a dangerous neighbor to the Franco-

---

* In the Confederate Congress, in November, 1864, and again in January, 1865,
at a time when there were plans for an armed immigration of Confederates into
northern Mexico to sustain Maximilian [Dip. Cor., 1865-66, Vol. 3, pp. 498-9] and
probably for the purpose of inducing Napoleon to take some action favorable to the
Confederacy, resolutions were offered in opposition to European intervention in
Mexico and to all apparent violations of the Monroe Doctrine. [McPherson, political
History of the United States During the Great Rebellion, pp. 617-18.] On December
27, 1864, Benjamin, declaring that the Confederacy was fighting the battles of
France and pitifully appealing to France to name the terms or conditions upon which
she might be able to recognize the Confederacy, pointed out the "contemptuous dis-
dain" and "insolent irony" with which Lincoln had referred to France in his recent
message and solemnly predicted that Lincoln, after success against the Confederacy,
would not long delay the inevitable aggressive war with France which would result
from the execution of the platform principles on which he had been elected. An
editorial in the Richmond Enquirer declared that the Confederacy, if it should yield,
would join the North in applying the Monroe Doctrine from Bering Strait to the
Isthmus of Darien. [Callahan, Diplomatic History of the Southern Confederacy,
p. 254.] On February 3, at the Hampton Roads Conference, Stephens favored an
arrangement for a joint invasion of Mexico. (Ibid., p. 257.)

Maximilian empire—by assuring Lhuys that the Americans never had much interest in Mexico, were disinclined to wage any war on account of wounded pride or anything except for national existence, and would have no difficulty in disbanding the large armies which were completing the work of suppressing secession. Impressed with the conviction that, but for the Mexican entanglement, the insurgents would receive very little countenance or sympathy from the French government, he wrote Seward in substance: "I do not know your views as to the policy to pursue toward Europe. Our only hostile act will be to withhold recognition of Maximilian and perhaps we may later even recognize him. Mexico is to be conquered by immigration and not by the sword. No nation can afford to be so indifferent as ours to the efforts of Mexico to found an empire. We have nothing to do but to set the example of a good popular government. All else shall be added to us. . . . The propagation of these views in the United States will lead to more pleasant relations with the European powers." A few days later, after an interview with Napoleon in regard to the recent Hampton Roads Conference ("negotiations"), he reported that the Emperor, fearing above all a reunion of the secessionists with the unionists to sustain the Monroe Doctrine, evidently expected the United States, at the close of her civil strife, to use her arms in Mexico, where he (Napoleon) declared that the honor of France was engaged to support Maximilian. Later still, in March, he said that the North could not afford to risk war with France who was determined not to leave unfinished the work begun by Napoleon III in Mexico.[30]

Seward was not yet ready to take a more aggressive stand. He had just obtained possession of a dispatch of a Confederate emissary in Canada which seemed to indicate that the Confederate authorities proposed the Hampton Roads Conference, at which they suggested alliance as a basis for sustaining the Monroe Doctrine, as a bait in order to induce the French government to offer immediate assistance or recognition to the Confederacy, and that they expected that Napoleon "would punish any attempt on the part of the United States to pursue the Monroe Doctrine," and that he might decide to recognize the Confederacy as a nation. Early in March, two days after Lincoln's second inauguration, while expecting "important things" to be effected by a change at Richmond, he wrote Bigelow a private note which contained the following: "Congress has adjourned, and the policy of this government toward Mexico as hitherto made known by the President remains unchanged. It rests with France to decide whether this is satisfactory. If we have war with her, it must be a war of her own making either against our ships or upon our territory. We shall defend ourselves if assailed on our own ground. We shall attack nobody elsewhere. All subordinate and collateral questions ensuing out of the war are left by us to the arbitration of reason under the instructions of time. Forbearance and liberality toward the United States in Europe will relieve the situation."

On March 13, after the Maximilian government had taken steps to obtain recognition from the United States through a confidential note of Luiz de Arroyo (Maximilian's Secretary of State) to Mr. Corwin, Seward promptly stated that it was the American government's "fixed habit to hold no official intercourse with agents of parties in any country which stand in an attitude of revolution, antagonistic to the sovereign authority in the same country with which the United States are on terms of friendly diplomatic intercourse," and "to hold no unofficial or private intercourse with persons with whom it can not hold official intercourse." At the same time he wrote Bigelow that Maximilian might be informed through the French government that no exclusion of American consular agents from Mexico would have any influence in inducing the United States to change its political attitude toward Mexico.[31]

Four days later (March 17), Seward analyzed the American policy on the Mexican situation more fully and more carefully. Though he had striven to be neutral, he held that the United States could not renounce the doctrine, which was a living sentiment of the people, that the continuance of free republican institutions throughout America was required for the safety of the institutions of the United States.

Replying further to Bigelow's suggestion of February 14, he said: "This government foresaw the present embarrassment and expressed itself frankly to the imperial government before it intervened in Mexico. It is that embarrassment which now affects the political situation in regard to that country. . . . The Emperor's persistence implies that he yet believes it to be certain what we have constantly told him that the people of the United States, reasoning upon preconceived sentiment and national principles, can not even apprehend to be possible. . . . It would seem that all parties must abide the trial of the experiment, of which trial it will be confessed that the people of Mexico must ultimately be the arbiters. This government has not interfered. It does not propose to interfere in that trial. It firmly repels foreign intervention here and looks with disfavor upon it anywhere. . . . I remain, however, of the opinion I have often expressed, that even this vexatious Mexican question in the end will find its solution without producing any conflict between the United States and France. The future of Mexico is neither an immediate, nor even a vital question, for either the United States or France. For both of them it is a foreign affair, and therefore time and reason may be allowed their due influence in its settlement. . . . So long, however, as France holds us to be a divided nation, so long will it be apprehended by portions of the American people that the policy of France in setting up an imperial system in Mexico is not confined to that unfortunate country, but embraces the overthrow of republican institutions here and throughout the American continent. . . . France, while she can not have the sympathies of this country in regard to Mexico, has no ground for that reason to apprehend hostility in any form from this government. It remains for France to decide for herself whether by manifesting her acceptance of the integrity of the American Union and the indivisibility of the American people as facts established, she will once more come into the friendly relations which were mutually cherished . . . until the breaking out of the civil war." [32]

One week later (March 28), informed by Bigelow that the future American attitude toward Mexico was a source of anxiety in Paris, Seward promptly replied that the United States, though seeking its national rights and consistent in its political convictions, sought no ulterior national advantages or aggrandizement and desired no occasion for retaliating in any form of hostility against any foreign state.[33]

A week before the instructions of March 17 were written, and perhaps even later, Bigelow, still uncertain what course affairs might take, was inclined to place some credence in the reports that President Lincoln might decide to recognize the Maximilian government. After the reception of Seward's instructions, and after the news of the evacuation of Richmond (which reached Paris by April 18), he still felt doubtful of the future position of the United States on the Mexican question. In May, in connection with a conversation with the French Minister of State on the subject of the withdrawal of belligerent rights from the Confederates, he made some reference to Mexican affairs which was misapprehended favorably to the Maximilian government by the French minister and required later explanation. On June 9, M. Rouher, in the French Assembly, after referring to the declarations of Rosecrans at Boston in regard to the alleged recruiting of American soldiers for the Mexican army, asserted that Bigelow, while stating the American preference for republican government, had said to Lhuys: "We understand that Mexico, which has long been governed by the monarchical form, may desire to return to that state of things, and we are not going to make war upon a question of form of government." Bigelow promptly (June 12) informed Lhuys that this was an erroneous interpretation of his conversation and asked him to correct it.[34] His despatch to Seward contained the following passage which indicated his opinion at the time: "What I stated that may have given the impression which has misled the minister of state was this, in brief—that now the experiment had been begun the Americans wished it to be fully tried under the circumstances best calculated to determine finally and forever whether European systems of government suited the Mexican people best; if it should appear that they did, and public tranquillity was restored, no nation was more interested in such a result than her immediate neighbors. I added that the success of republican institutions in the Spanish American states had thus far not been such as to encourage us to attempt the propagation of them there otherwise than by example, and that whatever government was acceptable to the Mexican people would be satisfactory to us."

When Seward returned from a visit to Auburn, New York,

on July 3, he promptly wrote Bigelow as follows: "It is thought that the argument which you have recited in the passage thus extracted is not warranted by the instructions of this department. It will be well at your convenience to make this explanation to Mr. Drouyn de Lhuys. So far as our relations are carried, what we hold in regard to Mexico is that France is a belligerent there in war with the Republic of Mexico. We do not enter into the merits of the belligerents, but we practice in regard to the contest the principles of neutrality as we have insisted on the practice of neutrality by all nations in regard to our civil war. Our friendship toward the republic of Mexico and our sympathies with the republican system on this continent, as well as our faith and confidence in it, have been continually declared. We do not intervene in foreign wars or foreign politics. Political intervention in the affairs of foreign states is a principle thus far avoided by our government. I attach no great importance to this matter. It is right and proper nevertheless that the French government should not misunderstand the case and so be suffered to fall into a belief that we have entertained any views favorable to it as an invader of Mexico, or that we at all distrust the ultimate success of republican systems throughout this continent." [35]

Still anxious that Napoleon should be given no reason to believe that the United States had changed its views expressed to France—in reply to which the latter had repeatedly disclaimed all purpose of interfering with the government or sovereignty of Mexico—and, at the same time, apprehending that a war to drive France from Mexico might strengthen Napoleon by enlisting the French national spirit, Seward decided that peace and time with a series of diplomatic negotiations would secure the best settlement of all questions without reviving the danger of American disunion. Though still confident of the ultimate success of republican institutions in Mexico and still hoping to secure by peaceful diplomacy what others were anxious to obtain by active military intervention, he was stimulated by the course of events to reiterate, then to emphasize, and finally boldly to insist upon what he had so often hinted or suggested before—the necessity of the withdrawal of the French from Mexico.

For several months after the close of the war by the defeat of the Confederates, circumstances indicated a growing demand in some quarters to find or to make a *casus belli* with a view to the solution of the political situation in Mexico. As early as the middle of April, General Carvajal, the newly appointed governor of Tamaulipas, whom Juárez had authorized (November 12, 1864) to accept the services of 10,000 foreigners and to provide for their equipment, arrived in New York (at the suggestion of General Lew Wallace) on a fruitless mission to negotiate a loan with which to provide men and means for the enforcement of the Monroe Doctrine and for raising the credit of the Juárez government. General Grant, the self-confident soldier, favored forcible measures to drive the French from Mexico, and perhaps was anxious to provoke hostilities that would have made war with France unavoidable. In May, Grant had sent General Sheridan to Texas with orders to assemble a large force on the Rio Grande; and later, in order to prepare for the possible future necessity of acting against the French army in Mexico, General Schofield was given a leave of absence for a year with permission to go beyond the limits of the United States—where it was expected he would organize an army from disbanded United States soldiers and Confederate soldiers, who by orders from Grant were to be supplied with arms by General Sheridan, who was anxious to use his army on the Rio Grande for driving the French from Mexico. The policy of enforcing the American doctrine was urged by many other prominent men—notably in the speeches of General Wright at Sacramento (June 11), General Lew Wallace at Washington (June 15), General Banks at New Orleans (June 4), Montgomery Blair at Hagerstown (July 12), Secretary James Harlan (of the Department of the Interior) at Washington (July 13), and in the farewell order of General F. P. Blair at Louisville (July 11). The last issue (August 16) of the *Index*, a Confederate organ published at London, referred to these utterances as "official declarations" of American policy.

The danger from those who sought a *casus belli* was aggravated by reports that the French authorities at Matamoros had received into their service a "large detachment of the late rebel soldiers with their arms." On July 12, Seward received from the War Department information that General Meijia (the commander of Maximilian's forces at Bagdad on the Rio Grande) had encouraged a new secessionist movement in Texas by stating that he considered the Confederates in Texas a "recognizable power" and that these Confederates who still intended to continue the contest against the United States were the friends of the Imperial Government of Mexico and cooperating with it. He also received information that the imperial government was endeavoring to get the support of the people of west Mexico by creating the impression that Texas would be annexed or that a protectorate would be extended over it. Ten days later he instructed Bigelow promptly to notify Lhuys and ask the proper explanations.[36]

Seward, desiring to allay apprehensions and prevent difficulties, promptly asked Bigelow to suggest prudence to the French government and to state that the encouragement of Dr. Gwin's schemes by either Maximilian or Napoleon would tend to produce the impatience of the American people who would regard the schemes as a menace to the United States. "Nor can it be necessary to say," said he, "that after having expelled the insurgents from our own borders, the United States government could not look with satisfaction upon their reorganization as martial and political enemies on the opposite banks of the Rio Grande." On August 1, Bigelow brought these speculations to the attention of Lhuys and stated that the American government, refusing to discredit the disclaimers made by France at the beginning of the war with Mexico, confidently expected "in some form an assurance that all the pretences of Dr. Gwin, and his associates, are destitute of any sanction from the Emperor of France." Lhuys (on August 7), betraying considerable sensitiveness in regard to what he called "vague allegations based on documents of a dubious character," and stating the resolution of France to observe in all the internal questions which may agitate or divide the Union an impartial and unscrupulous neutrality, significantly added: "We have nothing to offer as pledge of our intentions but our word, but we deem the word of France a guarantee which will satisfy any friendly power (in spite of certain recent manifestations) as we ourselves are satisfied with the words pledged to us by the Federal government to remain strictly neutral with regard to affairs in Mexico." In the meantime, Seward had information from Mexico indicating that the schemes and speculations had altogether failed; but he continued to receive information of the policy of Maximilian to encourage immigration into Mexico from the states which had recently been in insurrection against the United States, and notified Romero that measures had been adopted to meet the exigency and that the subject would receive the proper attention later.[37]

In the meantime another unsuccessful effort had been made to induce Seward to recognize the Maximilian government. A prominent New York paper, in its issue of July 4, contained a contributed article which, after justifying the interference of France in Mexico and stating that Maximilian was really elected by the people, closed with the following: "The Monroe doctrine has in no way been concerned in the recent history of France, Mexico and the United States, and the frank, temperate policy of the United States is based on this policy." Two weeks later, Seward, having been informed by Marquis de Montholon that a special agent of Maximilian had arrived at Washington with a letter for the President, promptly replied that the President declined to receive the letter or the agent, stating that the United States was on friendly terms with the republican government of Mexico. Early in August, he assured Romero that the reception of commercial agents of the Maximilian government was not regarded as a recognition of the Maximilian government.[38]

At the same time, Seward was informed of various private enterprises organized professedly to develop the resources of Mexico by immigration and "to enforce the Monroe doctrine." Late in July, 1865, General Carvajal, claiming authority from the Juárez government and encouraged by General Lew Wallace, surprised Romero by entering into a contract with Daniel Woodhouse, the financial agent of the somewhat shadowy and unknown company pompously called the "United States, European and West Virginia Land and Mining Company," receiving from it an agreement to negotiate the sale (at not more than 60 per cent discount) of interest-bearing bonds with a face value of $50,000,000, secured by 106,800 acres of select mineral lands in Tamaulipas and San Luis Potosi, and by 80 per cent of all federal and state revenues from port dues, imposts and taxes aggregating about $3,000,000 per annum, and also granting the company 500 square leagues of vacant agricultural land in Tamaulipas and San Luis Potosi with privileges of colonization, and the right of way and accompanying privileges for the construction of a double track steam railway from Matamoros to the western limit of San Luis Potosi, and branch lines. On August 6, Carvajal, stating that Seward had "offered no objection," submitted the general terms of the contract to Romero, who, refusing to ratify it, promptly wrote his government a dispatch stating that Carvajal had exceeded his powers and that the contract was invalid.[39] Romero, after receiving further instructions (August 18, 1865) from his government authorizing him personally and exclusively to negotiate a loan of $100,000,000 by pledging all the revenues of the nation, took steps to prevent the delivery of the Carvajal bonds to Woodhouse, resulting in the fiasco of the Woodhouse scheme. In the meantime, Carvajal had opened negotiations with John W. Corlies and Company for a second contract, which after some objection from Romero was signed (on September 11) with the consent of Romero with whom Carvajal, by order from the Mexican government, consented to act in concert— although he still claimed powers plenipotentiary as an agent of the supreme government equal to the powers of Romero. This contract contained no grant of privileges for railways, telegraphs and colonization, and thus differed from the first (Woodhouse) contract which, under various reorganizations of the Woodhouse company, continued to be an obstacle to the success of the new plan for a bond issue, and a source of trouble even after the French had evacuated Mexico.[40]

Interpreting the pulse of the American people through public speeches and the press, forseeing the large attention which Congress probably would give to foreign affairs, and anticipating the dangers which might arise from the irritations and annoyance liable to be produced by the military forces confronting each other across the Rio Grande, Seward saw that France in the interests of future peace should not long delay her withdrawal from Mexico. Anxious that the French government should "not be suffered to fall into the belief" that the United States government while practicing neutrality between belligerents had entertained any views favorable to France as an invader of Mexico, or had in any degree changed its friendship toward the Mexican republic in which it had continually declared its faith and confidence (in a private note of August 7), he again asked Bigelow to make such explanations as might be necessary to remove any misapprehensions or hopes which Lhuys might have obtained from the interview with Bigelow in the previous May and which the latter had never yet had an opportunity to correct.

In reply he received from Bigelow a long "unofficial" dispatch, written at Dieppe on August 21, which was substantially as follows: "I have had no opportunity to see Lhuys for four weeks to transact business—nor am I likely to have one for three weeks to come (as he expects to be absent from Paris). . . . I shall leave upon his mind a distinct impression of our future policy toward the interventionists in Mexico, as your instructions authorize. In absence of anything more explicit from you I shall feel it my duty to avoid saying anything which would commit our government to extreme measures in any contingency: (1) because I do not understand that the President had determined to abandon the policy of a passive for one of an active armed resistance to French intervention in Mexico in any emergency; and (2) because I am unable to see how such a policy can commend itself to his judgment hereafter. . . . I have no evidence at all conclusive that the people are more disposed now than ever before to depart from their traditional policy of non-intervention in the affairs of foreign states—nor do I see more signs of coveting Mexico than in 1847. . . . I think you will find, when the question is raised in practical shape . . . that . . . opposition to the extension of European influences in the Western Hemisphere is a sentiment which they cherish but not a policy for which they will fight. A war for such a purpose would become unpopular. The abstract folly of making ourselves the armed champions of all or any of the Spanish American states whose people . . . have been trained under social and political institutions having very little in common with those of the United States, would be aggravated now by the state of our finances. . . . The Spanish race in our hemisphere will require for many years a much more centralized government than we can offer them under our present constitution, and, therefore, it is hardly worth our while, under pretext of defending republican institutions, to get ourselves into a war with one and perhaps several of the most powerful states of Europe. I doubt if there is a power in Europe that would formally sustain our pretensions under what is called the 'Monroe doctrine'. . . . The mere apprehension of such pretensions would impair our credit in Europe, postpone our reduction of tariff and check European emigration to America. In a war . . . to redress the wrongs of Mexico or to propagate republicanism by the sword, we would in my opinion be likely to fail. Such a contest would accomplish for the Emperor of France what he has sought in vain to accomplish hitherto. . . . Our government is based on the will of the people, who will not prosecute an expensive war for soi disant republics. . . . My notion of my duty here as I understand it to be now prescribed to me is substantially this: to say nothing and do nothing which would require us in honor to compel France to leave Mexico if she does not choose to yield to peaceful arguments and on the other hand to avoid saying or doing anything which would lead the Emperor to suppose we would not resort to force if ultimately necessary for the liberation of Mexico.

"I had, and . . . have still, a somewhat different view of our policy towards France. Short of recognizing Maximilian I would give France every possible evidence of our friendship. . . . Of course he [Napoleon] will fail. . . . If he is to fail we do not need the credit of having caused his failure. Mexico will get emigrants from the United States anyhow and finally become annexed to the United States

"Though by my policy the United States can improve her credit and strengthen her position with all Europe . . . I assume from the tone of your recent notes that this policy does not commend itself to the public men of the United States. I bow to their superior wisdom, and shall endeavor to carry out your instructions with fidelity. . . . I beg you will not forget that the American people have never seriously considered the question we are now discussing as a live, practical question. . . ." [41]

Before his dispatch of August 21 had reached Washington, Bigelow had written another dispatch (August 31) reporting the details of a conversation in which he had corrected the views of Lhuys, who in return had freely stated his opinion of Seward's recent instruction of July 3 and had objected to the expression of sympathy for the Juárez government.[42]

Seward, who in the meantime had information that Maximilian felt that his prospects were discouraging, replied to Bigelow at length, and in a more decided tone, in confidential instructions of September 6—significantly stating that the United States, no longer troubled by civil war, might be expected to devote considerable attention to foreign problems, the chief of which was relations with France connected with the Mexican policy. These instructions, a copy of which were to be read or given to Lhuys in case the latter should request explanations of President Johnson's opinions or policy, contained the following views:

"On this subject [relations between the United States and France as affected by Mexico] this government does not think itself called upon to volunteer opinions, counsel or advice, or gratuitously to offer explanations to the governments of Europe; on the contrary we have been content to stand upon what we have already very frequently set forth, while every proper care has been taken to prevent or allay irritations which might tend to bring about unexpected and undesired collisions. It is possible nevertheless that the French Government may think it proper to ask you for explanations, to some extent, of the President's opinion and policy. . . . [After referring to the character of the United States constitution and the state constitutions, and to the belief that surrounding American nations should have the same peculiarities of government] . . . I think it not improper to add that although the constitution of this government, and the habits of the American people formed under it, disincline us from political propagandism, and, although they still more strongly disincline us from seeking aggrandisement by means of military conquest—yet that the nation has, at various times since its organization found necessity for expansion, and that the like necessity may reasonably be expected to occur hereafter. . . . To these two facts may be added the general one that peace and friendship between the United States and other nations on this continent, and consequently the advance of civilization in this hemisphere, seem to us more likely to be secured when the other American states assimilate to our own. . . . France appears to us to be lending her great influence with a considerable military force to destroy the domestic republican government in Mexico and to establish there an imperial system, under the sovereignty of an European prince who until he assumed the crown was a stranger to that country.

"We do not insist or claim that Mexico and the other states on the American continent shall adopt the same political institutions to which we are so earnestly attached, but we do hold that the people of those countries are entitled to exercise the freedom of choosing and establishing institutions like our own if they are preferred. In no case can we in any way associate ourselves with the efforts of any party or nation to deprive the people of Mexico of that privilege.

". . . I have next to remark that this government finds itself neither less obliged nor less disposed at the present moment than it has hitherto been to adhere to its settled policy—which depends on public opinion and therefore is probably essential to the safety and welfare of the Union.

"The intense popular interest which was awakened by the prevalence of a civil war of vast proportions, during a few years past, has tended in some degree to moderate the solicitude which the situation of foreign affairs was calculated to create; but that interest is now rapidly subsiding, and it may be reasonably anticipated that henceforth the Congress of the United States, and the people in their primary assemblies, will give a very large share of attention to questions of extraneous character, and chief among these is likely to be that of our relations toward France with regard to Mexico.

". . . It is perceived with much regret that an apparent if not a real, a future if not an immediate, antagonism between the policies of the two nations seems to reveal itself in the situation of Mexico. . . . The United States have at no time left it doubtful that they prefer to see a domestic and republican system of government prevail in Mexico rather than any other system." [43]

Napoleon injected into the negotiations for withdrawal a proposition for a basis of *quid pro quo*. In August, Lhuys expressed a strong desire to withdraw the French troops "as soon as circumstances would allow it," and in September he said that the United States could greatly facilitate the departure of the troops by adopting toward the Maximilian government "an amicable attitude, which would aid to the consolidation of order, and give evidence of security for the interests which had induced France to cross the Atlantic." Late in September, Bige-

low, after a conversation in regard to the withdrawal of the
French troops, wrote to Seward that Lhuys was satisfied with
Montholon's report of the disposition of the United States and
promised that the reduction of French forces would go on as
fast as possible—the Emperor being anxious to retire as soon as
French interests in Mexico could be properly protected. Two
weeks later, he submitted the explanation of the French position which Lhuys had furnished in reply to Seward's dispatch of
September 6. After another two weeks he sent (October 19)
a confidential note stating the views of Lhuys, who admitted
that the Mexican question could be simplified by the withdrawal
of the French troops and suggested a peaceful basis by which
the withdrawal could be secured. At the same time Lhuys sent
(October 18) to Montholon instructions which he said were
in reply to a question by Bigelow in his own name (and without prejudging the opinion of his government) "whether the
recognition of the Mexican empire by the United States might
facilitate and hasten the recall of the French troops." Lhuys
had wished the United States to recognize the Maximilian government as a preliminary to the withdrawal of France. Bigelow,
however, had said clearly that American recognition of any
government in Mexico, so long as it was sustained by foreign
arms, was impossible. He had asked whether Maximilian would
be able to sustain himself without aid of France if his authority
were recognized by the United States. Though he had suggested
the possibility that Maximilian might determine to press the
return (withdrawal) of the French soldiers if the United States
showed a disposition to recognize his government after the
French evacuation, he had in no way compromised the position
of the Washington government.[44]

In the meantime, Seward had kept himself informed of the
serious conditions in Mexico which he had foreseen would result
from the establishment of an exotic government upheld by a
European power. Maximilian issued two decrees, one of which
probably shortened his tenure of office, and the other his tenure
of life. The one encouraged the immigration of Confederate
planters into Sonora with their slaves under plans of Dr. Gwin

(and others) to colonize the frontier as a hostile barrier, which with the cooperation of French troops would prove formidable in resisting all attempts against Maximilian from the Texas side of the Rio Grande where the United States troops still hovered. The other, issued several months later (October 3) and aimed directly against the forces of the Juárez government which the United States recognized as the constitutional government, ordered that in the future "all persons belonging to armed bands, not legally organized, whether they proclaim or not any political principles" should be tried by court-martial and condemned to decapitation "within twenty-four hours following the sentence." The American government could never recognize the dangerous and desperate government which issued these decrees. To whom, then, could it protest or apply for redress in case of future violations of American rights? Could it present its case through France? Lhuys replied, "Go to Juárez with your griefs." [45]

Still mindful of Napoleon's earlier promises to evacuate Mexico, Seward continued to grow bolder in extending to France a courteous and friendly, but persuading, invitation of exit from Mexico, couched in pressing and admonishing language which the Emperor was finally induced to accept. While planning the adjustment of the Mexican question by moderate but vigilant policy through pacific diplomacy, he found his line of action threatened by more aggressive plans which promised a rupture with France. In the summer of 1865 he had opposed a proposition, apparently favored by Romero, to direct American emigrants to Mexico and to organize them into an army in Mexico under the command of a prominent officer of the United States army. After General Grant obtained from the President a leave of absence for General J. M. Schofield, who had agreed to undertake the proposed command in Mexico, and had directed General Sheridan, of the army of observation along the Rio Grande, to cooperate with the plan by diversion of ordnance supplies to Schofield, Seward (in August, 1865) found an opportunity to prevent the plan by diversion of its chief actor from military motives to the honors of an innocent special "diplomatic" mission. In order to thwart General Grant's project for organizing an American army in Mexico, he authorized General Schofield to sail from New York (on November 19) on a trip to Paris to ascertain (in a private capacity) whether there was any way by which to induce Napoleon to withdraw his troops in order to prevent the possibility or necessity of their expulsion by force.[46] With a firm decision against the suggestion of Lhuys that the American government might favor or assist the Emperor's desire to withdraw by giving some assurance that the United States would recognize the *de facto* government of Mexico, and stating that "political relations at present supersede those of commerce in the consideration of the American people," he instructed (November 6) Bigelow that the President adhered to the views expressed two months before.* "French authority in Mexico is in direct antagonism to the policy of this government and on basic principles," said he, "the United States have hitherto practiced frankness and still regard the French effort to establish permanently a foreign and imperial government in Mexico as disallowable and impracticable. Therefore they can not compromise their previous position. They are not prepared to recognize any political institutions in Mexico which are in opposition to the republican government with which we have so long, and so constantly, maintained relations of amity and friendship." [47]

When Bigelow read this instruction to Lhuys at the close of November, the international situation indicated that the expulsion of the French from Mexico was necessary for the development and security of the Americas. It was the evident purpose of France by operations in Mexico, and Spain by operations in South America, to limit Anglo-Saxon influence and assert the right of the Latin to expand to the New World.

* It appears that General James Watson Webb had gone to Paris at the solicitation of the Emperor Napoleon and that at an interview (on November 10) he received from Napoleon a secret agreement, subject to the approval of the President, providing for the withdrawal of the French army in twelve, eighteen and twenty-four months and also proposing the purchase of French Guiana by the United States. The President approved the withdrawal from Mexico, but proposed to negotiate for the purchase of Martinique or St. Pierre instead of French Guiana. [*Sen. Exec. Doc. 52*, 43-1, p. 204.]

Lamartine had just asserted, in a published article, an anti-American pronunciamento in contradiction to the Monroe Doctrine, that the continent of America was the property of Europe—an article that attracted the attention of the American press.[48] In his interview with Bigelow in regard to the instruction of November 6, Lhuys seemed much displeased with Seward's frank expression. He regarded it as a "menace to the authority which France was trying to establish in Mexico for the benefit of the world." "The language practically claims that the whole American continent belongs to the United States," said he, "and that governments and institutions there must correspond to your wishes. You feel strong now and assert erroneous pretensions which you have not given to the world before." Asserting that France was not timid, nor much accustomed to flinch from a policy once begun, he said, "If you mean war why not say so frankly?" Bigelow replied that, although Seward had not threatened armed intervention in behalf of Mexico, his instructions had asserted that the effort to establish a foreign and imperial government in Mexico was "disallowable and impracticable" and therefore that he could not compromise his previous position by recognizing political institutions in Mexico which were in opposition to republican government. "The United States has not changed position," said he, "nor been wanting in its ingeniousness in discussing it with the Imperial government." Lhuys said it was not fair to say that France had imposed a government on Mexico. Urging that France should follow the Golden Rule in diplomacy and look at the question from the American standpoint, Bigelow stated that, while the United States desired to continue the friendship with France, the American national feeling was "opposed to a government founded on our borders for the avowed purpose of limiting the diffusion of the Anglo-Saxon race on the American continent," and that it was "idle to contend against national feeling." Lhuys replied with a smile that Napoleon's letter in regard to limiting the Anglo-Saxon was designed for home rather than for foreign consumption. In reporting the conference with Lhuys, Bigelow said: "He would probably consider it a relief if we could find some adequate pretext to take Mexico off the end of their spear with our own. Though he spoke with warmth, he seemed to imply that if we insisted, it would be the end of their Mexican experience—that he would not attempt to defend Mexico in a war with the United States." [49]

In his interpretation of the Monroe Doctrine, the President, in his annual message of December 4, precisely reflected the feeling of the nation. A foreign monarchy forced on a sister republic on the American continent, and at the time chosen, was regarded as an insult and a standing challenge to the United States.[50]

A few days before Congress met, Montholon had furnished Seward a confidential instruction (November 29) stating that, if the United States by opening diplomatic relations with the Maximilian government should furnish assurance that she had no intention of impeding "the consolidation of the new order of things founded in Mexico," France "would see no difficulty to enter in arrangement for the recall of troops within a reasonable period." [51] In his reply of December 6, explaining the causes of American sentiment on the Mexican question, Seward said:

"The Emperor suggests that France is willing to retire from Mexico as soon as she may; but that it will be inconvenient unless the United States first give assurances of a friendly and tolerant disposition to the Maximilian government. . . . The chief cause [of the discontent prevailing in the United States in regard to Mexico] is not that there is a foreign army in Mexico; much less does that discontent rise from the circumstances that the foreign army is a French one. . . . The real cause of our national discontent is, that the French army which is now in Mexico is invading a domestic republican government there which was established by her people, and with whom the United States sympathize most profoundly, for the avowed purpose of suppressing it and establishing upon its ruins a foreign monarchical government, whose presence there, so long as it should endure, could not but be regarded by the people of the United States as injurious and menacing to their own chosen and endeared republican institutions.

"I admit that the United States do not feel themselves called upon to make a war of propagandism throughout the world, or even on this continent, in the republican cause. We have sufficient faith in the eventual success of that cause on this continent, through the operation of existing material and moral causes, to induce us to acquiesce in the condition of things which we found existing here, while our own republic was receiving its shape and development. . . . We should think it wrong as well as unwise, on the part of the United States, to attempt to subvert by force monarchical governments in Europe for the purpose of replacing them with republican institutions. It seems to us equally objectionable that European states should forcibly intervene in states situated in this continent to overthrow republican institutions and replace them with monarchies and empires." [52]

Seward saw that Congress was preparing to take action in directing the national policy in regard to Mexico. On December 11, the Senate called for information concerning the "barbarous decree of the so-called Emperor of Mexico (of October 3) ordering all Mexicans who bravely defend the sacred cause of their independence to be shot without form of trial." It also requested correspondence relative to the occupation of Mexico by French troops and the establishment of monarchy. At the same time, Van Horn of Missouri offered to the House the following resolution which was referred to the Committee on Foreign Affairs: "Resolved, That the Committee on Foreign Relations be instructed to inquire into and report what measures and means may be necessary on the part of the United States to restore to the Mexican people the free and unrestricted right to choose their own form of government, and of giving effect to the unanimous voice of the people of this nation that no foreign power shall impose despotic government upon any state or people of this continent." Mr. Orth, by unanimous consent, also offered a resolution requesting the President to furnish correspondence showing the "steps taken at any time by the so-called Emperor of Mexico" to obtain from the United States a recognition of the "so-called empire of Mexico" and the action of the administration thereon.[53]

Seward hastened to utilize the legislative situation to facilitate his diplomatic negotiations. In fresh instructions to Bigelow, approving his remarks to Lhuys and declaring that the United

States could not agree to recognize the Maximilian government, he requested him to inform the French government that the American legislative department in session was also "interested and concerned in the question whether the present condition of things shall be continued in Mexico" and was "authorized by the constitution to direct by law the action of the United States in regard to that important subject," and to say that the policy of the United States executive to continue friendship with France "would be brought into imminent jeopardy, unless France could deem it consistent with her interest and honor to desist from the prosecution of armed intervention in Mexico, to overthrow the domestic republican government existing there, and to establish upon its ruins the foreign monarchy which has been attempted to be inaugurated in the capital of that country." [54]

In the meantime, Schofield, whose presence in Paris attracted considerable newspaper comment, in unofficial conversations which were reported faithfully to the Emperor, had found an opportunity to make known to Prince Napoleon and high officers of the Emperor's staff the views and purposes of the United States. He found that, although the Mexican policy of France was unpopular, the national pride hesitated to withdraw under menace. [55]

Bigelow, considering the different aspects of the French policy and desiring to facilitate French withdrawal, had already (December 14) in a private note suggested the presentation (in Congress) of an admonitory resolution relating to the repugnance of the American people toward monarchical institutions on the American continent, and inviting the Emperor to leave Mexico. A week later (December 21), stating that the President's message had placed the American government and policy before the world in an attitude of command and respect, he announced that France, anxious to solve the Mexican question, had determined to leave; and he recommended that Congress should occupy itself with domestic questions. He felt sure that the President's reference to American relations with France and Mexico, if properly interpreted by the French government, would result either in an early change in relations between France and Mexico or in a still graver change in relations of France with the United States.[56]

The Emperor, assured that the United States would not deviate from its traditional policy of non-intervention unless forced by the aggression of European powers, was considering the feasibility of a plan to adjust the Mexican question satisfactorily by personal correspondence between himself and the President. Though through Bigelow, who took Christmas dinner at the Palace, he was informed that the President seemed resolved to do nothing that would embarrass him, he had some anxiety in regard to the appointment of General Logan as minister to Mexico. He also made inquiry in regard to the status of General Schofield. The Empress, though satisfied with the President's message, feared what the American people or Congress might do. On January 4, 1866, Bigelow received from Lhuys a proposal for a plan of adjustment providing that, as a condition of the French withdrawal, the United States should (1) secure as an equivalent the payment of the French debt in Mexico, (2) allow France to hold Sonora and sell it to the United States to indemnify herself, and (3) agree not to interfere in Mexican affairs. Though he could not see why the American government should secure the French debt, nor how it could recognize the legality of a title given through Maximilian, he asked for a memorandum of the last proposition—stating that the United States had no disposition to interfere with any authority which was acceptable to the Mexican people. This memorandum he received (January 10) from Lhuys who agreed, on receipt of assurance of scrupulous neutrality on the part of the United States, to make known the result of negotiations with Maximilian for guarantees which were to complete the purpose of the French expedition, but who declined to specify exactly what guarantees he hoped to obtain from Mexico, or the form of the assurance which he expected from the United States. Though Bigelow doubted whether a formal covenant was consistent with the dignity of either nation, he decided to request Seward to send fresh instructions on the American policy of intervention which might be read to Lhuys as a possible means of getting the two governments to a point where they could begin to act in concert for stopping hostilities in Mexico between Juárez and Maximilian. On January 11, he proposed to Seward to test the sincerity of the Emperor's offer to withdraw his forces, by agreeing to observe strict neutrality between the Juárez and Maximilian governments with the understanding that Maximilian would form his army entirely from naturalized Mexicans, and that the French troops and flag would not be replaced by those of any other nation.[57]

Two weeks later, Bigelow wrote that, as soon as he could receive instructions giving assurances of non-intervention by the United States in Mexico, he expected to receive a report of negotiations between Napoleon and Maximilian in regard to French withdrawal. He also proceeded to give two reasons why the Emperor erred in desiring an American promise of neutrality: (1) the Emperor had desired his retirement to appear to be entirely voluntary; (2) no private engagement with France could add strength to those already announced to the world to respect all independent nationalities.

At the same time, in another dispatch to Seward, he wrote:
"I told Lhuys there were some objections to our giving a formal assurance that we would not disturb the status quo of Mexico on the withdrawal of the French army. I closed by informing him that United States in the ninety years of their existence had never attempted by arms to interfere with or modify the government of any other nation; that our first President on laying down his office made a parting request, the wisdom of which none of his successors has ever questioned, that as a government we should avoid all unnecessary responsibility for the political institutions of other countries; . . . and finally that no prominent statesman in the United States had ever advocated a policy of intervention in the government of other independent states. In view of these facts and in view of the language held by you during the last four years in your correspondence with the diplomatic representatives of the United States, I thought that the Emperor would find every assurance he would require of our disposition to respect the independence and nationality of Mexico. Lhuys replied that he would look through the correspondence . . . and if he could find the assurances . . . he would submit them to the Emperor." [58]

In the meantime, negotiations had been transferred to Washington. Surrounded by difficulties, and observing that the French people (who were still ignorant of recent negotiations) did not question the propriety of the American demand and showed much solicitation concerning the rumors afloat, the Emperor wrote (January 15) to his commander in Mexico that he had concluded to recall all troops within a year. At the same time, in maturing his new plans he was resolved to continue diplomatic negotiations with Seward for the purpose of securing every advantage possible. On January 9, in a dispatch which was carefully prepared by direction of the Emperor in reply to Seward's instructions of December 6 (and which reviewed the French policy in Mexico and attempted to justify it), Lhuys directed Montholon to assure Seward: (1) that the French expedition, to establish a regular Mexican government which would be disposed to keep its engagements, had in it nothing hostile to the institutions of the New World and still less to the United States; (2) "that the French army in entering Mexico did not carry monarchical traditions in the folds of its flag." He also instructed Montholon to endeavor to overcome antagonism to the monarchical government of Maximilian by citing the monarchy of Brazil with which the United States was holding friendly relations. On January 29, a copy of Lhuys' instructions was submitted to Seward by Montholon.[59]

On February 12, in a note reviewing the Mexican question and the United States policy, and inviting the Emperor to give definite information of the time when the French operations in Mexico might be expected to cease, Seward replied to Montholon. He plainly stated that the United States did not reproach Mexico on account of her past calamities. Referring to Lhuys' denials, he said: "Nevertheless, it is my duty to insist that, whatever were the intentions, purposes and objects of France, the proceedings which were adopted by a class of Mexicans for subverting the republican government there, and for availing themselves of French intervention to establish on its ruins an imperial monarchy, are regarded by the United States as having been taken without authority, and prosecuted against the will of the

Mexican people. . . . The people of the United States have not seen any satisfactory evidence that the people of Mexico have spoken and have called into being or accepted the so-called empire. . . . I can not . . . properly exclude the observation that, while this question affects by its bearings, incidentally, every republican state in the American hemisphere, every one of these states has adopted the judgment which, on the behalf of the United States, is herein expressed. . . . France is acquainted with the relations of the United States toward the other American states to which I have referred, and is aware of the sense that the American people entertain in regard to the obligations and duties from them to those other states." While declining to be drawn into a discussion in regard to Brazil, he said: "Where the people of any country, like Brazil now, or Mexico in 1822, have voluntarily established and acquiesced in monarchical institutions of their own choice, free from all foreign control or intervention, the United States do not refuse to maintain relations with such governments, or seek through propagandism, by force or intrigue, to overthrow those institutions. On the contrary, where a nation has established institutions, republican and domestic, similar to our own, the United States assert in their behalf that no foreign nation can rightfully intervene by force to subvert republican institutions and establish those of an antagonistic character." [60] On the following day a significant resolution of sinister views, and suggesting that the President solicit an alliance of all the republics of the continent to enforce it, was offered in the House but was not considered. [61]

Meantime, the Emperor had shown a disposition to calm the American people by his speech at the opening of the French legislative chambers. He had also eased the public mind in France by publishing (January 29) recent correspondence in regard to the Mexican problem, including Lhuys' instructions of January 9. On February 22, he made the first general announcement of his purpose to withdraw his troops from Mexico, at the same time expressing his hope that it would allay the emotions in America. His decision indefinitely announced, Napoleon saw that he must not long delay a definite program. Van Horn of Missouri introduced in the House a resolution (which was referred to the Committee on Foreign Affairs) accepting the Emperor's declaration of his purpose, insisting as a guarantee for its fulfilment that the French troops in Mexico should be used only to preserve the *status quo* until the period of withdrawal, and asserting that the use of the troops for further conquests should be regarded as a violation of the pledge. In spite of the "imperialistic" views of Marshal Forey, the French government could not counteract the useful influence which the American treatment of the Mexican question was exerting in Europe.[62] By March 6, M. Rouher informed the *corps législatif* that the Emperor would soon withdraw.

The reply to Seward's note (of February 12) Lhuys furnished in his instructions to Montholon under date of April 5. Abstaining from the prolongation of the discussion of assertions on points of doctrine or history, and confiding in the assurances of non-intervention which he regarded as a sufficient guarantee, he said France was ready to adopt measures for the return of the army—in three detachments, November, 1866, March, 1867, and November, 1867. On April 5, the *Moniteur* definitely announced that the troops would be withdrawn in the three detachments (as stated by Lhuys), and a week later Napoleon directed Bazaine to that effect.[63]

Seward, vindicating his policy, expressing his great satisfaction that an agreement had been reached, and hoping France possibly might "find it convenient and consistent with her interests and honor" to abridge the time limit, frankly suggested that, as even the continuance of the intervention would "necessarily be regarded with concern and apprehension by the masses of the people and perhaps by Congress," the United States "army of observation must also be continued in some proportion on the southern bank of the Rio Grande." At the same time, he was endeavoring to prevent Austrian aid to Maximilian. Hearing that the French troops were to be replaced by volunteers from Austria, levied by the Emperor's brother with Austria's consent, he instructed Motley to inform the Austrian government that the United States could not engage to remain silent and neutral spectators of such hostilities. Motley hesitated to act on what seemed to him a departure from Seward's earlier policy; and, in a dispatch which he showed to the Austrian Minister of Foreign Affairs, questioned the right of the United States to protest against these proceedings—which he said were clearly within the sovereign rights of Austria. On April 30, Seward, promptly disapproving Motley's delay, directed him to file the protest and "at once to withdraw from Vienna" in case Austria, without discussing the matter with the United States, should permit the departure of the volunteers. In the meantime, the recruiting had become languid; and, after Motley presented Seward's protest, the Austrian government (preparing for the approaching war with Prussia) promptly replied that necessary steps had been taken to prevent the departure of troops.[64]

Seward's increasingly persistent attitude met with general popular approval. Although he had reaffirmed the purpose of the United States to adhere strictly to the principles of non-intervention and neutrality, there was still a strong feeling in favor of some more effective expression of the warm sympathy felt for the republican government of Juárez, which it was feared might be crushed out by the intrusive empire of Maximilian while we waited. The popular demand was partly satisfied (on May 4) by the appointment of L. D. Campbell as minister to the Juárez government to fill the vacancy which had remained unfilled since the withdrawal of Corwin and the subsequent refusal of General John A. Logan to accept the place. In Campbell's instructions of October 25, 1866, Seward, desiring to favor the Mexicans in the resumption of the conduct of their own affairs and disavowing any territorial designs, suggested that the American government, if desired by the Juárez government, might favor and advance the pacification of the country by some disposition of American land and naval forces with a view to usefulness in the restoration of law and order and republican government without interference with the jurisdiction of Mexico. Radicals still wished to make the moral power of the United States felt among nations by prompt, energetic maintenance of the Monroe Doctrine. Stevens, in the House, on the ground that France was no longer a belligerent in Mexico, and in order to give practical force to the American policy called the Monroe Doctrine, proposed to the Committee on Foreign Affairs "to inquire into the propriety of loaning to the republic of Mexico, on proper security (a mortgage of Lower California, Sonora, Sinaloa, or Chihuahua), $20,000,000 to enable said republic to prevent the overthrow of its government and the establishment of a monarchical government on the continent of North America." Though he said such a measure could no longer be a breach of neutrality at which France could take offense, he agreed that it "might be justly considered by Maximilian as a cause of war, for which we would be responsible to him," and to him alone. "If it should provoke a war with Maximilian," said he, "I suppose no one would be much alarmed; it would give the great republic an opportunity to vindicate her honor, which has become dim under the Micawber policy of our foreign secretary. By vindicating that honor we should increase and consolidate the strength of the nation." [65]

In the meantime, new complications were threatened. Santa Anna, who in 1864 had returned to Mexico but had not been allowed to stay, was watching for an opportunity to try new projects. Arriving in New York in the summer to solicit aid for a new military scheme, he soon formed an alliance with one of the Fenian factions of the city, and endeavored to obtain resources to further his plans by issuing a series of bonds ($750,000) secured by a mortgage deed of trust upon what he considered his personal property—378 square miles of land in Vera Cruz, and two palaces, one on Saint Thomas Island and the other in Turbaco, New Granada. It appeared that his agent (according to Hiram Barney, ex-collector of the New York customhouse) was Daniel Woodhouse. On June 19, 1866, the New York *Herald,* which had previously favored the cause of Santa Anna, published a letter representing that General Ortega as lawful President of Mexico was acting in concert with all the governors of the states and with the chiefs of the national powers, that he was animated with the best desires to make a treaty with the United States highly advantageous to the latter, and that he had submitted his plans to President Johnson and General Banks. In August, in response to an inquiry, Seward declined to receive Santa Anna who was contemplating a visit to Washington.[66]

For a time, Maximilian was inclined to believe Napoleon's decision had been announced for diplomatic reasons and would soon be modified, but he was soon disillusioned. In vain did his wife, the youthful, energetic Princess Carlotta, go to Paris to plead his cause. Already mourning the loss of her father, Leopold of Belgium, and shocked at the crushing defeat of the Emperor of Austria, she completely failed in her mission to France and soon became insane while negotiating with the Pope at Rome. Napoleon, unable to retreat from what he had promised under pressure of simple, patient, frank and optimistic American diplomacy, and at the same time disturbed by prospects of trouble on his eastern frontier where Prussia was preparing to dispute with France the position of arbiter of Europe, politely but coldly and obstinately refused to sustain the pleading prince whom he had lured into the turmoils of Mexico. In the early autumn, he sent his aid, Castelnau, to Mexico to express his decision that the limit of French sacrifice had been reached. At the same time, he notified the American government that he would do nothing to persuade Maximilian from abdication in case the latter should consider it impossible to overcome all difficulties with his own resources.[67]

Seward anxiously observed the situation in Mexico where new complications were threatened by the attempts of General Santa Anna and Chief Justice Ortega to organize armed expeditions in the United States for the overthrow of the national government of the republic of Mexico, the constitutional term of Juárez having ended in December, 1865. Hearing that there were doubts in some quarters whether the French troops would be withdrawn at the time stipulated, and contemplating the possibility of some disposition of the United States forces which "would be useful in the restoration of law, order and republican government . . . without interfering within the jurisdiction of Mexico or violating the laws of neutrality," he prepared fresh instructions for Campbell—who had not yet started on his mission, and who it was now determined should be accompanied to Mexico by General Sherman in order to render the formal recognition of Juárez more impressive. Stating that the United States desired not the future conquest of Mexico, but only to see her relieved from all foreign interference, he directed Campbell to go to Chihuahua or to any other place in Mexico (not occupied by the French) where he might be able to find Juárez, to ascertain whether the latter desired the good offices of the United States to aid in the restoration of order, to forward all news that could be obtained, and to await further orders. Two days later, he wrote additional instructions giving his views of the Monroe Doctrine and the American policy in Spanish America.[68]

In November, Campbell, accompanied by Sherman, sailed from New York, and arrived at Brazos by December 13, but, finding that the main Gulf ports of Mexico were still held by the French, went to New Orleans to watch developments from a distance. In a later attempt to find Juárez or his government, they were unsuccessful until April 21, 1867, when a messenger sent by Campbell reached San Luis Potosi by way of Matamoros and saw Lerdo de Tejada, Secretary of Relations.[69]

On November 23, Seward, having received from Bigelow a dispatch stating that the French evacuation had been postponed until spring, promptly sent a copy to Campbell, and seeking more definite information cabled a protest to Paris. "The United States expects an early withdrawal of France from Mexico," said he. "Delay would seriously conflict with the plans of the United States." General Dix, who had received appointment (on September 24) as successor of Bigelow, on December 11 reported his arrival in Paris and the satisfactory state of the Mexican question. The Emperor had agreed to withdraw all his troops in the spring, and had advised Maximilian to abdicate. He also made a proposition (which Seward declined on January 18, 1867) that a new provisional government should be formed, excluding both Maximilian and Juárez. On January 8, Seward telegraphed Campbell: "We wish you to remain at New Orleans while events ripen in Mexico. It now seems that it may be so long as March. But we can not anticipate events. It may be much shorter." [70]

Napoleon withdrew more quickly than he had promised. The departure of troops, begun in December, continued regularly until March 12 when the last detachment was withdrawn, while the stage was rapidly being prepared for the last tragic act of the drama of the Mexican empire.

It only remained to be seen whether the exotic monarchical government of Maximilian, which Seward had regarded as dependent on the support of French bayonets, would now "vanish like chaff before the wind" as the Americans had predicted. It was after some hesitation that the unfortunate prince decided to remain after the withdrawal of the last foreign forces. He soon discovered that the intolerant, conservative, clerical party which had clamored for the restoration of the confiscated church property, was powerless to uphold him. His tottering empire went to pieces in two months and a week. Seward, foreseeing the early collapse of the empire, promptly telegraphed Campbell to transmit to Juárez the hope that captured prisoners would receive humane treatment. The special messenger whom Campbell sent returned with a reply which intimated that Maximilian and his leading supporters, if captured, would be executed in retaliation for the harsh decrees which they had proclaimed. On June 1, hearing that they had been captured on May 15, and in response to the appeals of Austria, France and Great Britain to endeavor to avert the execution of Maximilian, Seward telegraphed Campbell to hasten to Mexico and earnestly to urge Juárez to adopt a policy of clemency. Under various pretensions, including lack of transportation, Campbell delayed his departure from New Orleans until June 15, when Seward telegraphed for his resignation and requested Romero to notify his government promptly that the United States, seeking no undue advantage in Mexico and apprehending no future

European intervention there, strongly recommended clemency toward Maximilian who had developed into a Mexican partisan chieftain. On the same day the Juárez government confirmed the court-martial sentence of death upon Maximilian, who was promptly shot four days later, and whose remains after some delay were surrendered to his relatives and carried to Vienna where the funeral was celebrated in great pomp in the cathedral, on January 18, 1868. In failing to commute Maximilian's sentence, doubtless Juárez was influenced by the passions of the army and by certain views connected with the future security of the country. In subsequent cases he practiced clemency which was gratifying to Seward.[71]

The French empire never recovered from the shock of the expensive Mexican failure. After eating the pie of humiliation and defeat which Seward's shirt sleeves diplomacy prepared for him, the Emperor continued to lose prestige in Europe. Urged along slippery paths by fame-seeking generals and ambitious Jesuits, and finally by his wife, the Empress Eugénie, in 1870 he entered into a war against Prussia which resulted in his defeat and capture at Sedan, the collapse of his empire, the shattering of the Napoleonic legend, and the establishment of the French republic.[72]

The subsequent government of Mexico, although it faced many difficulties and was long restricted by internal disturbances and prejudices toward foreigners, was immediately successful beyond all expectation. The Liberal forces soon crushed all armed opposition and reestablished the constitutional government. Santa Anna, who returned to Mexico in the *Virginia* in the early summer to promote an insurrection, was arrested after his feeble, futile attempt and sent into banishment, from which he was finally allowed (1874) to return to the Mexican capital where he died in poverty and obscurity in 1876. On July 15, Juárez entered Mexico City which had been occupied by Diaz, his main commander. Elected President (on October 12), he inaugurated policies which started Mexico on a new era of development, and which after his death in 1872 were continued by Lerdo until 1876, and later by Diaz, who had headed a rebellion against both Juárez (1871) and Lerdo (1876) and who after 1884 served as President continuously until 1911. Plumb, the American chargé, who arrived at the Mexican capital on October 6, found that the Juárez government, receiving congratulations on the triumph of republican institutions, was entirely satisfied with the policy of the United States, though there was a lingering prejudice against all foreigners.[73]

To the Juárez family and to M. Romero, Seward extended unusual courtesies. On June 10, 1867, through Romero, he offered to place at the disposal of Mrs. Juárez and family a man-of-war for transportation to Mexico. Accepting the offer on June 17, Mrs. Juárez with her family (of fifteen, including three servants) left Washington by way of Cincinnati to New Orleans where the American public vessel *Wilderness* awaited her orders (about July 6). On October 7, Seward offered to Romero and his friends the use of the same vessel for passage from Charleston to Vera Cruz (leaving Charleston on October 14). Romero, accepting the courtesy and returning to his country with two invited friends, Senator O. P. Morton and Hon. N. P. Banks, expressed to Seward his deep gratitude in the statement that he would "do all possible to promote the best understanding between the two republics." [74]

Though there had been predictions that the expulsion of Maximilian would result in the "grateful annexation of Mexico" to the United States, or the satiation of the expansion ambitions by acquisitions beginning with the purchase of Lower California and Sonora,[75] Seward continued to adhere to his declaration that the United States desired to see the Mexicans relieved from all foreign military intervention to the end that they might assume the conduct of their own affairs, and desired no aggrandizement by conquest of Mexico or by purchase of land or dominion. He evidently expected that the future of Mexico would be largely influenced by a gradual process of Americanization through slow and peaceful emigration of citizens and capital and development of transportation and trade —by economic infiltration or percolation. As a special relief to the Juárez government, whose consolidation of republican institutions he did not desire to hinder, he generously waived for a time the presentation of claims of American citizens. In adopting this friendly policy he was looking forward to the negotiation of a claims convention for the mutual adjustment and settlement of all claims (since 1848) without the necessity of pressure, and was not disappointed by the reciprocal responses which included the granting of privileges of transit of military supplies from Guaymas overland to Arizona and of naval coaling facilities at La Paz and an agreement to a claims convention of 1868. In August, 1867, in his instructions to Otterbourg, from whom he had learned of the pretensions of many American citizens congregated at Mexico City, he wrote: "You will be careful not to take part in any of the projects and speculations now said to be maturing in Mexico, nor will you present nor urge these speculations upon the Government, in any case, unless directly and especially instructed by this Department." From Edward L. Plumb, who became American chargé in Mexico in October, 1867, he learned that the Juárez government was satisfied with American policy in the long, critical period since 1861, and had agreed to follow the advice to be more lenient with political prisoners, but a few months later he was somewhat surprised by Plumb's report of a widespread Mexican feeling of hostility against foreigners to which Americans formed no exception, and later by the report of provisions in a proposed Mexican law to prevent foreigners from obtaining railway concessions or other similar concessions.[76]

Partly with a hope of helping to remove Mexican prejudices against Americans, in the fall of 1869, after his term of office had expired, Seward visited Mexico, traveling by way of San Francisco with his wife and son (F. W.) and several friends. On his visit he made several public addresses which interpreted the significance of past events and were full of optimism for the future of the nations and peoples of the American continent.

At Colima (on October 12) he said: "One additional principle remains to be adopted, to secure the success of the republican system throughout the continent: . . . That the several American republics, just as they constitute themselves, while mutually abstaining from intervention with each other, shall become, more than ever heretofore, political friends through the force of moral alliance. This, in short, is the policy which I have inculcated at home, and which . . . I shall commend, as far as possible, to the republics of Mexico, Central America, and South America." On November 30, in a speech at Mexico City to the President of Mexico and the assembled people, he closed as follows: "The people of the United States . . . comprehended better than even their government has ever yet done, the benignant destinies of the American continent, and their own responsibility in that important matter. They know and see clearly that although the colonization in all parts of the continent was assigned to European monarchical states, yet that in perfecting society and civilization here, every part of the continent must sooner or later be made entirely independent of all foreign control and of every form of imperial or despotic power—the sooner the better. . . To the people of the United States the universal acceptance of republicanism is necessary, and happily it is no less necessary for every nation and people on the continent." [77]

Although in Mexico he was gratefully received and hospitably entertained by the authorities as the guest of the nation, he was apparently unable to allay the prejudice and distrust of the enemies of the two governments who especially sought by malicious means to injure the government of Juárez—by charging it with selling Sinaloa to the United States and subserviency to the American government in its domestic and foreign policy and by criticizing it for the displays in honor of Seward who was surreptitiously charged with ulterior motives connected with the disintegration of Mexico and whose movements were carefully watched (!).[78] For the next decade the prejudice and distrust remained prominent.

REFERENCES

1. *17 Mexico, Instructions*, No. 2, Apr. 6, 1861.
2. *7 Notes to Mexico Legation*, pp. 200-04; *17 Mexico, Instructions*, pp. 156-58, Apr. 2, 1861; *9 Notes from Mexico Legation*.
3. *17 Mexico, Instructions*, (No. 2) Apr. 6, 1861; *9 Notes from Mexico Legation*, Apr. 1 and Apr. 3; *17 Mexico, Instructions*, (No. 2) Apr. 6; *28 Mexico, Despatches*, (No. 1) May 29, and (No. 9) June 15, 1861; Letter of May 3, 1861, from Thomas Sprague who had been a commercial agent of the United States.

4. *9 Notes from Mexico Legation,* May 4 and May 6, 1861; *28 Mexico, Despatches,* (No. 2) June 29, (No. 3) July 29, (No. 4) Aug. 28, and (No. 5) Sept. 7, 1861.

5. Dayton feared a break with France at that time. Among other reasons for seeking to secure the continuation of the friendly feeling of France, he suggested the danger of a French attempt to set up a protectorate over Louisiana. [*50 France, Despatches,* (No. 29) Aug. 19, 1861]; *17 Mexico, Instructions,* (No. 16) Aug. 24, (No. 15) Aug. 24, and (No. 17) Sept. 2, 1861.

6. CALLAHAN, *Diplomatic History of the Southern Confederacy,* p. 76; *28 Mexico, Despatches,* (No. 4) Aug. 28, (No. 5) Sept. 7, (No. 6) Sept. 29, (No. 7) Oct. 29, (No. 2) June 29 (Enclosure "D"), and (No. 3) July 29, 1861. Dayton reported to Seward a conversation with General Almonte in relation to the effort of John S. Cripps of South Carolina to arrange with the Mexican party in power to agree to the union of Mexico and the Confederate states as one power or some other basis of intimate relations against the United States. [*50 France, Despatches,* No. 17, July 11, 1861.]

7. *28 Mexico, Despatches,* (No. 3) July 29, (No. 4) Aug. 28, (No. 5) Sept. 7, and (No. 7) Oct. 29, 1861; *Confederate Correspondence,* Package 44, Pickett's (No. 12) of Oct. 29, (No. 13) of Nov. 29, and (No. 14) of Dec. 24, 1861; *Ib.,* Package 50, Cripps' No. 1 (from Mexico), Apr. 22, 1862.

8. *16 French Instructions,* p. 57, (No. 60) of Sept. 24, and p. 83, (No. 79) (in reply to Dayton's No. 62 of Oct. 16); *50 France, Despatches,* (No. 51) Sept. 25; *18 Great Britain Instructions,* (No. 99) Oct. 10; *28 Mexico, Despatches,* (No. 7) Oct. 29; *17 Mexico, Instructions,* (No. 23) Oct. 2, 1861.

9. *16 France, Instructions,* p. 61, (No. 67) of Oct. 11, 1861; *House Exec. Doc. 100,* 37-2, p. 201; *28 Mexico, Despatches,* (No. 14) Jan. 26, 1862; *50 Br. and For. State Papers,* p. 375.

10. *28 Mexico, Despatches,* No. 8, Nov. 29, 1862; *House Exec. Doc. 100,* 37-2, pp. 136-37, 187 and 190; *9 Notes from Mexico Legation,* Nov. 28, 1861.

11. *28 Mexico, Despatches,* No. 11, Dec. 24, 1861; *52 Br. and For. State Papers,* p. 381.

12. *Sen. Exec. Doc. 11,* 38-1, Vol. 1, pp. 178, 146 and 159; *28 Mexico, Despatches,* (No. 17) Feb. 22, (No. 18) March 20, (No. 19) March 24, 1862.

13. *28 Mexico, Despatches,* No. 21, Apr. 16, 1862; *House Exec. Doc. 54,* 37-3; *Sec. Exec. Doc. 11,* 38-1, Vol. 1, pp. 291 and 294-96.

14. *France, Despatches,* Apr. 22, 1862; T. M. J. in *Merchants' Magazine,* June, 1864; *28 Mexico, Despatches,* No. 21, Apr. 16,

1862; *10 Notes from Mexico Legation*, Jan. 28, Feb. 16 and Feb. 21, and Apr. 17, 1862; *7 Notes to Mexico Legation*, p. 188, Apr. 11, 1862.

15. *House Exec. Doc. 100*, 37-2, p. 218; *16 France, Instructions*, p. 125, (No. 126) March 10, p. 135, (No. 135) March 31, and p. 164, (No. 158) May 12, 1861.

16. *28 Mexico, Despatches*, (No. 22) Apr. 28, and (No. 21) Apr. 16, 1862; *6 Sumner's Works*, pp. 365-75.

17. *28 Mexico, Despatches*, (No. 22) Apr. 28, (Private) May 22, (No. 23) May 5, (No. 25) May 28, and (No. 32) Aug. 28; *10 Notes from Mexico Legation*, May 10, June 2, June 8 and June 18, 1862; also, *House Exec. Doc. 54*, 37-3, (802 pp.), Feb. 4, 1863. In reply to a resolution of the House, President Lincoln (on Apr. 14, 1862) submitted 434 pages of correspondence [*House Exec. Doc. 100*, 37-2] but later (May 27) he stated that it was inexpedient to comply with the request for further correspondence.

18. The resolution against the Mexican negotiations carried by a vote of 28 to 8. Some feared that a loan would result in annexation of Mexico in whole or in part—a result which many thought ought never in any contingency to be favored. Others desired to treat with no foreign power on the subject. [*17 Mexico, Instructions*, No. 50 (Confidential) June 24, 1862]; *28 Mexico, Despatches*, No. 34, Oct. 27; *12 Notes from Mexico*, Sept. 6, Oct. 2 and Oct. 20, and Dec. 27, 1862. Romero's note of Oct. 2 on the historic background of French intervention (in reply to the discourse of M. Billault in the French legislative body on June 26, 1862) forms an entire volume in the manuscript archives at the Department of State. A reprint of it from the *Diario Oficial* contains 259 pages: Historia de las intrigas europeas que ocasionason la intervencion francisca en Mexico [*Mexico*, J. M. SANDOVAL, 1868].

19. *12 Notes from Mexico Legation*, Dec. 10, Dec. 27, 1862, Jan. 14, March 9, 19 and 20, 1863; *28 Mexico, Despatches*, (No. 38) Jan. 27, 1863; *Sen. Exec. Doc.* (No. 24) 37-3, (No. 47) 38-1; also, *Sen. Exec. Doc. 33*, 38-2, Vol. 1, Feb. 4, 1865; *El Continental*, Jan. 1, 1863; *2 Notes from New Granada*, June 26; *16 France, Instructions*, (No. 180) and (No. 205) of Aug. 25; *Great Britain, Instructions*, (No. 296) July 11; *Sen. Exec. Doc. 112*, 46-2, Vol. 4, p. 4; *3 Communications from Agents of U. S. of Colombia* (Herran), Jan. 6, 1863; *6 Notes from U. S. of Colombia*, (No. 141) Jan. 12, 1863; *7 Notes to Mexico, Legation*, March 20, 1863.

20. *17 Mexico, Instructions*, p. 452, (No. 82) Aug. 8; *16 France, In-*

structions, (No. 382) (Confidential), Aug. 8, 1863; *Sen. Exec. Doc. 11,* 38-1, Vol. 1, p. 461; *53 France, Despatches,* (No. 336) Aug. 21, (No. 345) Sept. 14, 1863.

21. *16 France, Instructions,* p. 406, (No. 400) Sept. 21, and pp. 451-8, (No. 406) Sept. 26, 1863; *5 Works of Seward,* pp. 339 and 402.

22. *Sen. Exec. 11,* 38-1, Vol. 1, pp. 451-83; *Switzerland, Despatches,* (No. 50) Oct. 2; *1 Austria, Instructions,* (No. 31) Aug. 17, (No. 41) Sept. 11, and (No. 45) Oct. 9, 1863. At the same time he reported rumors of an impending recognition of the Confederacy by the new Mexican government, and an arrangement of the French government with the Confederacy to obtain Texas—possibly with the desire to precipitate with the United States a war which would give France an opportunity to interfere in favor of the Confederacy. [*Austria, Despatches,* (No. 34) Sept. 21, 1863; *Dip. Cor. 1865-6,* Vol. 3, pp. 784-86.] Copies of the instructions of October 9 (No. 45) to Austria were sent by Seward to the American ministers at Paris, Madrid and Brussels [*The Nation,* Jan. 5, 1882, and Jan. 30, 1896].

23. *30 Mexico, Despatches,* (No. 48) Oct. 26; *53 France, Despatches,* (No. 361) Oct. 9; *16 France, Instructions,* p. 466, (No. 417) Oct. 23; *1 Austria, Instructions,* (No. 41) Sept. 11; *17 Mexico, Instructions,* p. 464, (No. 93) Feb. 20, 1863; *5 Works of Seward,* pp. 410-11.

24. M. ROMERO: *The Situation in Mexico* (12 pp.), N. Y., 1864; *Sen. Exec. Doc. 11,* 38-1, p. 402; *Sen. Exec. Doc. 47,* 38-1, May 28, 1864; *66 Cong. Globe,* pp. 3339 and 3359, Jan. 28 and 29, 1864.

25. *C. S. A. Corres.,* Mason to Benjamin, March 16, and Slidell to Benjamin, May 2, 1864; *64 Cong. Globe,* Apr. 4, 1864, p. 1408. Seward, seeing that popular opinion was against France [*16 France, Instructions,* p. 513, (No. 468) Feb. 1, 1864], when the resolution was first offered wrote Dayton: "May these impressions not prepare the way for France to consider it wisdom to end the hopes which are the main support of the Confederates?" [*16 France, Instructions,* p. 504, (No. 456) Jan. 12, 1864]; *Spain, Instructions,* (No. 81) Apr. 7, 1864; *16 France, Instructions,* (No. 525) Apr. 7, 1864; *House Rp. 129,* 38-1, Vol. 2, June 27, 1864; *Dip. Cor., 1865-6,* Vol. 3, p. 357 *et seq.; 67 Cong. Globe,* Dec. 19, 1864, p. 67.

26. *54 France, Despatches,* (No. 442) March 25, (No. 454) Apr. 22, and (No. 461) May 2, 1864.

27. *France, Instructions,* (No. 538) Apr. 30, 1864; *3 Dip. Cor., 1865,* p. 759; *5 Works of Seward,* p. 124; BANCROFT's *Life of*

Seward, p. 429; *19 Great Britain, Instructions*, p. 307, (No. 965) (Confidential), May 28, 1864; Spain, Instructions, (No. 95) (Confidential), May 19, 1864.

28. *Sen. Exec. Doc. 11*, 38-1 (496 pp.); *C. S. A. Corres.*, Benjamin to Preston, (No. 6) June 20; *ib.*, Benjamin to Slidell, (No. 40) June 23, 1864.

29. *N. Y. Times*, Jan. 25 and 27, 1865; *56 France, Despatches*, (No. 8) Jan. 20, 1865; *Notes from Mexico Legation*, Feb. 6, 1865; *France, Instructions*, (No. 33) Feb. 7, 1865; *Dip. Corres.*, *1865-66*, Vol. 3, pp. 363 and 500.

30. *56 France, Despatches*, (No. 30) Feb. 14, (No. 29) Feb. 14, (No. 30) Feb. 14, (No. 37) (Confidential) Feb. 23, (No. 52) March 10, and (No. 55) March 14, 1865; *Dip. Cor.*, *1865-6*, Vol. 3, p. 380 *et seq.*

31. *56 France, Despatches*, (No. 65) March 28; *17 France, Instructions*, pp. 275-77, (Very Confidential), March 1, and pp. 277-99, (Private) March 6, and (No. 70) March 13, 1865; *Dip. Cor.*, *1865-66*, Vol. 3, pp. 484 and 378.

32. *5 Works of Seward*, p. 27; *17 France, Instructions*, pp. 300-03, No. 71, March 17, 1865.

33. *56 France, Despatches*, No. 55, March 14, 1865; *Dip. Cor.*, *1865-66*, Vol. 3, pp. 380-86 and 388.

34. *56 France, Despatches*, (No. 52) March 10, (No. 63) March 21, (No. 88) May 5, (Private) May 19, (No. 107) May 26, and (No. 117) June 13, 1865; *28 Notes Fr. Leg.*, May 5; *Italy, Despatches*, (Marsh) (No. 119) May 15, 1865; *Dip. Cor.*, *1865-6*, part 3, pp. 144 and 394-97; *17 France, Instructions*, p. 392, (No. 184) June 26, 1865.

35. *17 France, Instructions*, pp. 393-5, No. 187, July 3, 1865; *Dip. Cor.*, *1865-6*, Vol. 3, p. 389.

36. *17 Mexico, Instructions*, June 17, and No. 205, July 22, 1865; *House Exec. Doc. 33*, 40-1, July 10, 1867; *Dip. Cor.*, *1865-66*, Vol. 3, pp. 404-05.

37. *Dip. Cor.*, *1865-6*, Vol. 3, pp. 518-35; *17 France, Instructions*, (No. 195) July 13, and (No. 231) Aug. 24; *56 France, Despatches*, (No. 157) Aug. 10; *Notes from Mexico Legation*, Oct. 20 and Dec. 31, 1865.

38. New York *Times*, July 4, 1865. The *Times* continued to advocate the policy of "peace and time" for the settlement of the Mexican problem [*Ibid.*, Aug. 26 and Dec. 4, 1865], and to declare that a policy of propagandism for the spread of republicanism throughout the world was not in harmony with the principles upon which the United States government was founded.

[*Ibid.*, Aug. 2, 1865]. MOORE, *International Law Digest*, Vol. I, p. 238.

39. *18 Notes from Mexico Legation*, Apr. 20, 1867.

40. *House Exec. Doc. 33*, 40-1, July 10, 1867, pp. 32, 41, 43, 49, 56-65, 78-81, 85, 110-11, 129 and 132-67; J. M. CALLAHAN, *Evolution of Seward's Mexican Policy*, pp. 64-66.

41. *58 France, Despatches*, part of No. 158, Aug. 21, 1865.

42. *58 France, Despatches*, No. 166, Aug. 31, 1865.

43. *Mexico, Despatches*, (No. 12) Aug. 15; *17 France, Instructions*, pp. 432-37, (No. 259) Sept. 6, 1865 (*5 Works of Seward*, pp. 422-24).

44. *Dip. Cor.*, 1865-6, Vol. 3, pp. 416 and 811-12; *58 France, Despatches*, (No. 177) Sept. 21, (No. 180) Oct. 6, (No. —) Oct. 19, 1865, and (No. 268) Feb. 9, 1866; *17 France, Instructions*, (No. 405) March 2, 1866.

45. *Mexico, Despatches*, (No. 10) July 11, (No. 11) July 22, (No. 13) Sept. 10, (No. 14) Oct. 28; *14 Notes from Mexico*, July 8, Oct. 5 and Nov. 4, 1865.

46. J. W. ROBINSON in *N. Am. Review*, July, 1866.

47. *Dip. Cor.*, 1865, p. 429; *17 France, Instructions*, pp. 467-69, (No. 300) Nov. 6, and (No. 332) Dec. 16, 1865.

48. *La France*, Nov. 19; *59 France, Despatches*, (No. 199) Nov. 21, and (No. 212) Dec. 5; *17 France, Instructions*, (No. 333) Dec. 16; N. Y. *Times*, Dec. 12, 1865; *Dip. Cor.*, 1865-6, p. 430.

49. *59 France, Despatches*, No. 209 (18 pp.), Nov. 30, 1865.

50. N. Y. *Times*, Dec. 7, 1865.

51. See Lhuys to Montholon, Oct. 18, 1865. (*Dip. Cor.*, 1865-6, p. 449.)

52. *5 Works of Seward*, p. 426; *Dip. Cor.*, 1865-6, pp. 450-1. Seward's note of Feb. 12 (1866) to Montholon appears in *House Exec. Doc. 73*, 39-1, p. 549.

53. *Sen. Exec. Doc. 5*, Vol. 1, 39-1, Dec. 13, 1865, (20 pp.); *Sen. Exec. Doc. 6*, Vol. 1, 39-1, Dec. 21, 1865, (100 pp.); *69 Cong. Globe*, 39-1, Part 1, Dec. 11, 1865, p. 20 and p. 172; *ib.*, Dec. 18, 1865, p. 70.

54. *17 France, Instructions*, No. 332, Dec. 16, 1865. (*Dip. Cor.*, 1865-6, p. 429.)

55. *Ib.*, p. 465, (Confidential) Nov. 4, 1865.

56. *59 France, Despatches*, No. 228, Dec. 21, 1865. (*Dip. Cor.*, 1865-6, Vol. 3, p. 725.)

57. *Ib.*, (No. 228) Dec. 21, (Private) Dec. 29, and (No. 229) Dec. 26, 1865, (No. —) Jan. 5, (No. 240) Jan. 11, and (Private) Jan. 11, 1866; *60 France, Despatches*, (No. 272) Feb. 15, 1866.

58. *60 France, Despatches*, (No. 247) Jan. 25, and (No. 251) Jan. 25, 1866.

59. *Dip. Cor.*, *1865-6*, Vol. 3, pp. 805-8.

60. *5 Works of Seward*, pp. 428-43; *House Exec. Docs. 73*, p. 549, March 20, and 93, p. 27, Apr. 23, 1866; MOORE's *International Law Digest*, Vol. 6, pp. 502-3.

61. *69 Cong. Globe*, 39-1, Part 1, p. 811, Feb. 13, 1866.

62. *60 France, Despatches*, (No. 255) Feb. 1, (No. 248) Jan. 25, (No. 253) Feb. 21, and (No. 269) Feb. 9, 1866; *Dip. Cor.*, *1865-66*, Vol. 3, pp. 368-69 and 805; *70 Cong. Globe*, 39-1, Part 1, Feb. 27, 1866, pp. 1067-8.

63. *60 France, Despatches*, (No. 270) Feb. 12, (Private) Feb. 23, (No. 282) March 6; *Notes from France Legation*, Apr. 21, 1866; *Dip. Cor.*, *1865-6*, Vol. 3, p. 828; SCHOULER in *North American Review*, Apr., 1866.

64. *103 North American Review*, Oct. 1866, p. 498; *Notes to French Legation*, April 15 and 25, 1866; *Dip. Cor.*, *1866*, Vol. 1, p. 378; MOORE, *International Law Digest*, Vol. 6, p. 503; *1 Austria, Instructions*, pp. 187 and 189, (No. 167) and (No. 169) of March 9, and p. 292, (No. 173) Apr. 6; *ib.*, p. 302, (No. 181) Apr. 30; *House Exec. Doc. 73*, 39-1, Part 2, pp. 583, 587, and 589; *Sen. Exec. Doc. 54*, 39-1, pp. 13, 18 and 20.

65. *Nat. Quart. Rev.*, June, 1886, pp. 114-37; ("The S. A. Republics and the Monroe Doctrine"); *72 Cong. Globe*, 39-1, June 16, 1866, p. 3917.

66. *59 France, Despatches*, No. 240, Jan. 11, 1866; *House Exec. Doc. 33*, 40-1, pp. 88, 91 and 212; *74 Domestic Letters*, p. 27, Aug. 16, 1866.

67. *61 France, Despatches*, (No. 337) June 14, and (No. 358) Aug. 17, 1866; *Dip. Cor.*, *1866*, Part 1, p. 387.

68. *House Exec. Doc. 17*, 39-2, Vol. 6, Dec. 20, 1866, (179 pp.); *59 France, Despatches*, (No. 240) Jan. 11, and (No. 391) Dec. 13; *18 France, Instructions*, p. 34, (No. 545) Oct. 9, and p. 493, (No. 3) Oct. 23, 1866; *5 Works of Seward*, pp. 470-73; *Foreign Relations, 1867*, Part 2, p. 334, (No. 6) Dec. 13, 1866.

69. *House Exec. Doc. 16*, 39-2, pp. 377-85; *Sen. Exec. Doc. 30*, 40-1, July 11, 1867.

70. *17 Mexico, Instructions*, (No. 4) Nov. 23, 1866, and p. 108, Jan. 8, 1867; *18 France, Instructions*, p. 38, (No. 550) Nov. 23, p. 42, (No. —) Nov. 27, 1866, and (No. 11) Jan. 18, 1867; *62 France, Despatches*, Dec. 11, 1866.

71. *17 Mexico, Instructions*, Apr. 6, and (No. 10) Aug. 8, 1867; SCHOULER in *N. Am. Rev.*, Apr., 1866; *Dip. Cor.*, *1867*, Part 2, p. 560; M. ROMERO's "Correspondence de la Legacion en

Washington durante la intervencion extranjera, 1860-68"
[*Mexico, 1870-85*] Tome IX.

72. *Dip. Cor., 1867*, pp. 598-613 and 624-65. (Speeches in the French
Corps Législatif, on July 9 and 10, by Thiers, Favre and
Rouher.)

73. *Ib.*, Vol. 2, pp. 557-84, 613-20, 668 and 684; *31 Mexico, Despatches*, Oct. 9, 22 and 23; *Notes from Mexico Legation*, Oct.
4, 1867.

74. *Foreign Relations, 1867*, Part II, p. 558.

75. *Fortnightly Rev.*, Jan., 1866; Phila. *N. Am. Gazette*, Apr. 12,
1867; *House Exec. Doc. 177*, 40-2, Feb. 17, 1868.

76. *Ib., 1868-69*, Vol. 2, p. 433 (No. 87, Plumb to Seward, March
12, 1868), and p. 446 (No. 53, Seward to Plumb, Apr. 13,
1868); *17 Mexico, Instructions*, p. 536, (No. 10) Aug. 8, 1867;
31 Mexico, Despatches, (No. 11) Oct. 9, 1867; *33 Mexico,
Despatches*, (No. 131) May 20, 1868; *34 Mexico, Despatches*,
(No. 198) Oct. 2, and (No. 211) Oct. 22, 1868.

77. *17 Mexico, Instructions*, p. 493, (to Campbell) No. 3, Oct. 23,
1866; *38 Mexico, Despatches*, (Nelson) No. 165, Jan. 28, 1870;
5 Works of Seward, pp. 579-83.

78. *37 Mexico, Despatches*, (No. 113) Nov. 20, 1869; *38 Mexico,
Despatches*, (No. 165) Jan. 28, 1870.

CHAPTER X

A DECADE OF AMERICAN POLICY RELATING TO FRONTIER TROUBLES

THE new era of Mexican constitutional government for which Seward had prepared the way was disappointing to the American government which had hoped for the stability and prosperity of the neighboring nation. For a decade after the withdrawal of the French, Mexico was disturbed by domestic contentions, accompanied by serious border lawlessness which at times impaired good relations and severely tested American patience. The situation, precipitating troublesome difficulties and questions of policy, reached an acute stage after November, 1876, when the constitutional government of Mexico, which the United States had continuously recognized without interruption for seventeen years (since 1859), was overthrown by the successful military revolution of General Porfirio Diaz.

Under President Grant's two administrations, a difficult period of transition, from 1869 to 1877, Hamilton Fish, whose appointment to the office of Secretary of State was a surprise, served as the directing agent in efforts to solve the Mexican situation. Although he had been a member of the lower house of Congress (from 1843 to 1845), governor of New York (1849-50), and a member of the United States Senate (1851-57), he entered the cabinet with no experience in diplomatic affairs; but, as an observer abroad, he had learned something of foreign affairs and by long experience he had learned the value of caution and patience in steering a course of policy, and, besides, in facing serious or complicated questions he sought advice from others of more experience. The American ministers to Mexico for the period were: (from 1869 to 1873) Thomas

341

Henry Nelson (of Kentucky) who had previously served as minister to Chile (1861-66) and (in 1864-66) had been an active mediator in the war between Chile and Spain; and Nelson's successor, John W. Foster, who had been colonel of an Indiana regiment in the Civil War and later a newspaper editor, but who began his useful career as a diplomat by accepting the Mexican mission. The Mexican minister at Washington was Ignacio Mariscal who had previously acted as chargé (from October, 1867, to April, 1868).

The American government, while sympathizing with a neighbor nation struggling for the success of republican government, and countenancing every effort toward the attainment of a steady rule of law, each year encountered a duty to complain of trans-boundary invasions by lawless bands of Mexicans from Tamaulipas and Indians from Coahuila, whom the Mexican government professed its inability to control or punish, and who, after committing depredations and crimes, found a safe asylum by recrossing the Rio Grande into Mexico. For the depredations and crimes committed it presented just demands for redress which the Mexican government treated with indifference and apathy, and for protection of its citizens and the punishment of the lawless invaders it proposed cooperative measures and treaty stipulations to which the Mexican government refused to agree. The border troubles included raids of cattle thieves from Tamaulipas across the lower Rio Grande to Texan counties below Laredo, raids of savage Indians from Coahuila and the "unknown" part of Chihuahua across the upper Rio Grande above Laredo (and especially from Piedras Nogales and Eagle Pass to El Paso) to northwestern Texas and southeastern New Mexico and, also, from Sonora across the international boundary to Arizona. They also included smuggling and other disorders incident to the Mexican Free Zone (of the lower Rio Grande) which had been granted as a special privilege to Tamaulipas.

This Mexican Free Zone, which was closely associated with the cattle raids and regarded as a contributory cause to the raids, was a belt six miles wide along the entire length of Tamaulipas on the Rio Grande into which goods could be imported free of duty. It had originated in March, 1858, in a revolutionary decree of Ramon Guerra (the acting governor of Tamaulipas), issued in accord with an act of the legislature—in violation of the Mexican Constitution and hostile to other Mexican ports of entry. It had been established with a view to prevent the decay of towns of the northern frontier of Mexico (by the movement of local Mexican trade to Texan towns). After 1865, it had served as a base for smuggling into the United States. It authorized the introduction of foreign goods into Matamoros, Laredo and other towns on the Rio Grande (below Laredo) free of all import duties. It gave to merchants of these towns an advantage which made competition of American merchants on the Texan side of the river impossible, and facilitated smuggling from the belt across the long unguarded lines through the wilderness. In 1861 it had been formally ratified by the Mexican Congress which, in 1870, following an attempt of Tampico and Vera Cruz to secure a revocation of the obnoxious law, voted to extend the limits of the zone but failed in the proposed extension by non-concurrence of the executive.[1]

In December, 1866, Plumb, on a visit to Brownsville and Matamoros, obtained information indicating that a considerable part of the business of those places consisted in the illicit introduction into the United States of European merchandise landed at Matamoros free of duty under the Free Zone arrangement of 1858. In the following June, he wrote Seward that this contraband trade interfered with legitimate American trade with Mexico; and he suggested that the remedy was to secure from the Mexican government a "revocation of the disposition which created this free zone," by representations that the policy was injurious to both countries. In November, 1868, in response to a request of Secretary Seward of the previous September, he urged upon Lerdo de Tejada the propriety of terminating the free zone arrangement which was a serious detriment to the United States and a question of mutual concern; and, in December, he reported to Seward that the Mexican government already had the subject under consideration and would probably suppress the arrangement unless some political object should intervene. He found that the Mexican government and the Mexican Congress, anxious not to offend the Mexican frontier region, hesitated to take any action against the belt of free territory—although its discontinuance had already been recommended by a Mexican commission and was later urged by Romero, Mexican Minister of Finance, on the ground that it was unconstitutional and was no longer needed to prevent migration from Tamaulipas to American neighboring towns.[2]

American policy concerning the zone was somewhat aimless and wavering. In 1868, Congress failed to act upon a House resolution of James G. Blaine concerning the unfriendly character of the zone by its interference with American commercial rights. In 1870, and in each annual message thereafter for several years, the President mentioned the evil of the zone as a base for smuggling across the boundary into American territory. A committee of the Senate in May, 1870, reported that honest merchants, unable to compete with the smugglers, had been compelled to abandon the country or to engage in illicit trade, and that communities on both sides of the river had become so thoroughly demoralized that they regarded smuggling as a legitimate and honorable business. Irritated by the report of the Mexican extension of the unfriendly zone over two more Mexican states, and stating that the hope of successful negotiation seemed to have been exhausted, it impatiently recommended as a measure to counteract the evils of the zone a proposed bill to repeal all existing laws (of August, 1852) authorizing the transportation of foreign merchandise in bond to the frontier of Mexico, overland or by inland waters, and it suggested the possible necessity of other protective measures "to induce Mexico to regard the comity of nations." Possibly this committee recommendation stimulated the Mexican Congress, in the following November, against the wishes of President Juárez and Romero, to approve the zone on the ground that its establishment had saved Tamaulipas from depopulation, and to extend it to the Coahuila and Chihuahua frontiers and to the northern part of Nuevo Leon. Don Ramon Guzman, on October 27, in a speech in favor of the zone, said: "Ought we not to remember that the colossal power, which has located eight custom-houses, with bonded warehouses, along the desert line of only eighty leagues, intends to build up its own settlements at our expense? . . . I propose no aggression. . . . I wish for a reciprocity of interests in our relations, and especially upon our northern frontier; and as we endured for twelve years while they maintained in front of us their ports of deposit, let them now endure the continuance of the Free Zone; and if the competition should be pursued, let us, in turn, endure their establishment of free ports." [3]

President Grant, in his message of December 5, 1870, regretting that American representation as to the injurious effects of the Mexican policy had been fruitless, suggested to Congress the expediency of serious consideration of proper measures for countervailing that policy. In his annual message of December, 1875, he complained that the injurious zone still remained in full operation, defrauding American revenue and checking honest commercial enterprise. Probably the wavering and aimless or indefinite action of the American government encouraged the Mexican government to adopt a policy of sullen inactivity in meeting any American demands on the subject.

The cattle raids from Tamaulipas, on the Lower Rio Grande below Laredo, which since 1848 had caused trouble in the Texan region of fine pasturage between the Rio Grande and the Nueces and had become prominent in the remarkable incident known as the Cortina war in 1859-60, had declined during the American Civil War as a result of the conditions which made Matamoros an important market and gave its population a temporary brisk, remunerative trade. They were renewed at the close of the campaign against Maximilian, and, accompanied by murder and robberies, increased greatly (tenfold) and steadily after the return of the criminal Cortina to the border as governor and military commander in 1870. They were facilitated by a numerous class of vagrant population who visited the Texan ranches to obtain temporary employment, were largely caused by the ease with which criminals could escape to an asylum in Mexican territory in which there was no punishment for the crimes committed, and were intimately connected with the collateral question of the condition of the free zone along the Mexican side of the Rio Grande and the subject of extradition. Through these raids, cattle stealing from Texas, in whose profits the entire local Mexican community shared, became a chief occupation of an increasing number of organized Mexicans whose leader became more powerful than any other authority in Tamaulipas, local or national, and, in fact, determined the selection of local authorities friendly to the raiding operations. They culminated in the Corpus Christi raid of March 26, 1875, which, by its murders and seizure of prisoners and its influence in producing the reign of terror which followed, attracted the attention of the American government to the precarious position of Americans along the Rio Grande border.[4]

A contributory cause of the trouble, according to a report of 1875 by a permanent committee appointed at a meeting of citizens at Brownsville, was the fact that the great mass (about nine-tenths) of the population between the Rio Grande and the Nueces were of Mexican origin and had retained their Spanish language and customs, had continued their intercourse with Mexicans and were not prompt in furnishing information against the raiders. Another difficulty arose from the Mexican squatters who, in order to secure land or a certain degree of immunity, had made a declaration of intention to become citizens—and who, after committing a crime, took refuge in Mexico and claimed exemption from the provisions of the treaty of extradition on the ground that they were not American citizens.[5]

From 1871 the raids became more serious and threatening. On August 2, General McCook of the United States army reported that the Mexican system of cattle stealing on the frontier threatened disaster to the stock-raising interests of Texas and the precipitation of a local predatory war which might eventually result in an international conflict. On March 25, 1872, the grand jury of the United States circuit court for the eastern district of Texas in a report to the court said:

"A reign of terror is proven to exist between the Rio Grande and the Nueces. Mercenary bands of marauders, Mexican officers and soldiers, and Mexican outlaws and bandits, have been, for about seven years, holding a saturnalia of crime, violence, and rapine upon the soil of Texas. They have pronounced the penalty of death against any who may become informers. . . .

"The evidence submitted justifies the declaration that a predatory war has existed on this frontier since 1865; that it has been waged by men organized in Mexico, by Mexican soldiers acting under the orders of a Mexican general, and commanded directly by officers of the Mexican army; that the authorities of Mexico, civil and military, have countenanced, legalized so far as the acts of Mexican officials could legalize murder, robbery, and other criminal outrages; that the markets of Mexico have been used openly, publicly, and shamelessly to effect the sale of property robbed from the people of Texas; that Mexican officials, merchants of that and other nationalities, and all classes of Mexicans, have bought and sold cattle, hides, horses, and other property, stolen from the people of Texas, and they have done so knowing they had been dishonestly obtained; the custom-house and municipal authorities of Mexico have profited by the piratical acts of Mexican soldiers and highwaymen, and a tax has been levied upon cattle which they knew had been taken by armed bands from the rightful owners; that the people on the Mexican side of the Rio Grande consider and treat the Americans as enemies; they claim the country between the Nueces and the Rio Grande, and express a determination to drive the Americans from it. . . .

"It is believed from the evidence and from other reliable authority that since the close of the civil war in this country there has been an average of five thousand cattle stolen from Texas monthly, and driven into Mexico, and this estimate is confined to the Lower Rio Grande. The total number is estimated at four hundred and twenty thousand, and the actual value at six million three hundred thousand dollars. This does not include losses accruing from the depredations of the Kickapoo Indians, naturalized citizens of Mexico. . . ." [6]

American commissioners, appointed under a joint resolution of Congress (of May 7, 1872), to investigate the frontier depredations, reported in December, 1872, that, according to evidence examined, the number of cattle, which in 1870 was near 200,000, had been reduced between two-thirds and three-fourths since 1866 and that the loss to the cattlemen was nearly $28,000,000. They recommended a larger cavalry force for the Rio Grande border, but Congress neglected to take further action. Concerning the delinquencies of Mexican officials, they said: "The Mexican local authorities, as a rule, civil and military, have been cognizant of these outrages, and have (with one or two honorable exceptions) protected the offenders, defeated with technical objections attempts at recovery of the stolen property, assisted in maintaining bands of thieves, or directly and openly have dealt in the plunder or appropriated it to their personal uses." In conclusion they stated that the frontier troubles were "traceable directly to an unwise system of legislation regulating the commerce of the right bank of the Rio Bravo, which has made that frontier a rendezvous for the lawless, and a base of operation for an illicit traffic with the interior of Mexico and the United States detrimental alike to commercial prosperity of the two governments and to the unorganized condition of society on the two banks of the Rio Grande, its natural sequence." [7]

In a second report, on June 30, 1873, the commissioners stated that they had taken 736 depositions in 1873, making a total of 1090 which were submitted in support of 321 petitions filed in 1873 and 102 in 1872.

The Mexican commission of 1873 reported that American losses had been exaggerated and were largely due to Texan thieves, who were also accused of stealing Mexican horses, that the few guilty Mexican thieves had been taught to steal by Texans, and that Americans, in making complaints of Mexican raids and the Free Zone, were seeking a pretext for annexation of Mexican frontier territory.

Following the increase of robberies and murders in 1874, Governor Coke organized three companies of minute men for frontier defense to supplement the inadequate federal force; and, evidently influenced by the act of Colonel Mackenzie in crossing the upper Rio Grande with federal troops in pursuit of Indians, he ordered pursuit of Mexican marauders into Mexican territory when in close pursuit. In a letter vindicating his order he said:

"No state has surrendered the right of defense of its people in its own way against aggressions from neighboring states of people. . . . I apprehend that international courtesy, comity and amity have never been required by the law of nations, carried to the romantic extent of surrendering the great natural right of self-defense against the constant infliction of serious, permanent and wrongful injury upon the people of one nation by those of another, although the attacks may be unauthorized by the government of the territory from which it comes." [8]

In March, 1875, a joint select committee of the Texas legislature reported that the small herds of cattle which remained were only about ten per cent of the former vast herds. After reporting the extent of Mexican border troubles—the incursion of large parties of armed and defiant Mexican raiders and freebooters extending a hundred miles from the Rio Grande—which had resulted in 105 murders, incalculable losses to the cattle interests without any redress, and had produced a general feeling of insecurity, it declared that the American government had neglected or disregarded its duty and obligation of protection of its citizens and recommended prompt and suitable measures for state protection with the hope of later necessary action of the American federal government in extending protection and securing indemnity for losses.[9]

A few days later occurred the "Corpus Christi" raid of March 26, 1875, named for what was supposed to be the main objective of the raiders, which began near Tule Lake with the capture of horses which the captors (about twenty) rode without saddles or bridles until they obtained equipment and clothes by robbery of a store a few miles from Corpus Christi. It was characterized by various robberies and destruction of stores accompanied by several murders and the seizure of citizens who were driven like sheep. It was followed by petitions of terrified Texan citizens to the Texan legislature and to the American government and Congress, asking for protection of life and stating that under the recent increasing troubles they had ceased to complain of pecuniary losses from the stealing of cattle.[10]

On March 30, 1875, Governor Coke, fearing that the increasing depredations threatened the depopulation of Texas along the lower Rio Grande, wired an appeal to President Grant for protection. On March 30, and again on May 29, 1875, he wrote to the President concerning the continued forays of the foreign robber bands which were becoming bolder in execution and more extensive in their proportions. On May 29 he said:

"I have two companies of State troops on duty in that country, but they, as well as the forces of the United States, are powerless as long as the Rio Grande River is an inviolable line, beyond which the invaders cannot be pursued. There is, in my judgment, no efficient mode of defending the Texas border other than through retaliatory measures on the territory and people west of the Rio Grande. The information I give you as to the deplorable condition of that country, and the imminence of a sanguinary border-war, is corroborated fully by General Ord, in his correspondence with me. Necessity for prompt action exists, and must be taken by the State authorities unless the arm of the General Government is interposed in our defense. I respectfully but earnestly ask that relief be given, and the State authorities relieved of the responsibility of dealing with this subject, which pertains properly to the national administration." [11]

On May 24 he wrote:

"These invasions have been occurring so regularly, have been so bold, and have been marked with such impunity that the Texas Mexicans, who are simple people—many of them very ignorant—peculiarly exposed as they are to the depredations of these robbers, have been led to doubt the ability of our government to give them protection, and through ignorance and fear for the safety of themselves and property rather than sympathy for the marauders, have, in some instances, given them aid and comfort. If assured of protection against the vengeance of these bandits, they are well disposed and loyal to our government, and will perform their part in expelling them from the country. . . . Impunity has emboldened the invaders, and has subjugated a large portion of the Mexican population on this side to the passive acquiescence in their raids. If terror were stricken into the invaders, and their insignificance demonstrated by prompt action on the part of our government, the Mexican citizens on this side would be relieved of their fears, and feeling assured of the ability as well as the will of the government to protect them, would need no other stimulus to a discharge of their duties as citizens.

"No force that the United States Goverment will probably keep on the Rio Grande can prevent the invasions which disturb that country. Peace cannot be secured by confining the operation of troops to this side of the river. As long as the west bank of the river is an inviolable sanctuary for the marauders, they will depredate on us as heretofore. . . .

"Whenever Texas is successfully defended against the invaders, it must be done through retaliatory measures upon the people and territory west of the Rio Grande. In my judgment, as long as the Mexican Government is unable or unwilling to control her lawless population, there is no other mode of defense."

On April 27, 1875, the American consul at Monterey, in a report to Assistant Secretary Hunter following the Corpus Christi raid, declared that no frontier Mexican was disposed to censure the acts of the raiders and that the only practical remedy was American occupation of a strip of Mexican territory north of a line drawn from Matamoros to Laredo in order to defend Texas from Mexico and restrain Mexicans by a hand ready to strike.[12]

Meantime the American government, absorbed in its domestic difficulties relating to the period of reconstruction and indulgent in its attitude toward the government of Mexico, had continued a temporizing, neglectful policy which permitted the growth of the border evils, although Secretary Fish had repeatedly warned the Mexican government that American troops must cross the border in case Mexico could not stop the raids. Finally, in 1875, it sent additional troops to the border and armed vessels to the mouth of the Rio Grande, inducing President Lerdo of Mexico to recall (and subsequently to arrest) Cortina—who, however, later escaped, issued a pronunciamento against Lerdo and, with his raiding bands, aided General Porfirio Diaz in his successful revolution launched on the Texan side of the Rio Grande.[13]

Following the news of the Corpus Christi raid, Secretary Fish promptly instructed Foster that the American government expected the Mexican government to omit nothing in its power to prevent such raids and to secure punishment of the raiders. After complying with this instruction (on April 14), Foster, in a later interview (on May 3), took occasion to say to Minister Lafragua that one of the most fruitful causes of the border troubles was the favor shown the marauders by the Mexican local authorities, especially referring to the bad reputation of General Cortina and suggesting the need of his removal from the frontier (where he was acting as mayor of Matamoros). When Lafragua in his reply stated that his removal although desirable would embarrass the Mexican government because of his personal troubles with Governor Canales, Foster remarked that the Mexican government might face the necessity "to decide whether the objection to his removal . . . would outweigh the embarrassments likely to arise with the Government in case of his retention and continued complicity with the raiding and outlawry in Texas." On May 20, Secretary Fish, in reply to Foster's dispatch of May 4, and evidently influenced by the embarrassment of the Mexican government (from fear of desertion and lack of funds), and also by the increasing American public sentiment in favor of an aggressive and vigorous policy, and by the suggestion of the American consul at Monterey, instructed Foster to sound the Mexican Minister of Relations on the disposition of his government on the question of allowing the American government to cross the boundary and occupy temporarily the territory in which the raids originated—say north of a line drawn from Matamoros to Laredo.[14]

With full knowledge of all the facts of the Corpus Christi raid, and after receiving from Foster the Mexican official statements suggesting that the raid was made by residents of Texas and that other Mexican raids were probably the result of similar Texan raids into Mexico, Secretary Fish on May 20, 1875, replied that "to seek to justify the hostile incursions into our territory on the ground of retaliation for similar incursions from this side . . . may be regarded as frivolous." No charge of a robber raid from Texas into Mexico was ever substantiated by evidence.[15]

On June 26, 1875, Foster had a long but unsatisfactory interview with Mr. Lafragua, the Mexican Minister, who insisted that his government, under the existing political and financial situation, had done everything possible by instructions to the frontier authorities. After stating the American expectation that the Mexican government would adopt more energetic measures and that promises and assurances alone were insufficient, he suggested that American feeling resulting from the continuance of the raids was encouraging a strong American public sentiment in favor of an aggressive and vigorous policy and that the Mexican government's admission of its inability to restrain the lawlessness of its citizens would furnish a strong argument to any Americans who might advocate the further acquisition of territory. Stating that the American government, with the approval or consent of Mexico, had power to provide a remedy without violation of Mexican sovereignty, he proposed that the Mexican government should grant permission for the regular American troops "to follow the raiders across the border when in close pursuit, or, what would be still more efficacious, permission to temporarily occupy certain points on the Mexican side where the Mexicans are accustomed to cross the river." In reply, Lafragua said the executive had no authority to grant such permission without consent of Congress and could not prudently ask its consent for what the sentiment of the country would not approve.[16]

In a dispatch to Fish, on the same day, reporting that Mexican troops which should be guarding the frontier were guarding the elections in various states, Foster said that an occupation of the Mexican frontier by American troops would be regarded by Mexico as akin to cession of territory and as a national humiliation which would not be permitted; and he suggested that any embarrassing American demands on the Mexican administration at that time might precipitate a state of anarchy there. Early in July, in response to the Mexican Minister's acknowledgment of inability to send troops to cooperate with those of the United States in suppressing the raids, Foster declared that if the Mexican government could not protect American citizens in Texas from the Mexican raiders the American government would protect them. On July 12 he reported the arrest of Cortina by the

Mexican government, an act which he regarded as the most decisive step yet taken toward the restoration of order.[17]

On June 3, 1875, Brigadier General E. O. C. Ord, who had taken command of the Department of Texas in April and had ordered federal troops to cross into Mexico on a fresh trail of the raiders, reported that the marauders were practically in control of the country on the east bank of the Rio Grande and that the remaining Americans there were in constant dread. He recommended to his superior officer that a regiment of white cavalry should be placed at his disposal for service on the lower Rio Grande at once and that light-draft ironclad vessels should be sent to aid in the patrol of the river. On September 10, following the American order for a movement of the naval force to the Mexican border and the later order of the Mexican government for the arrest of Cortina, he sent to his superior officer a report in which, after referring to the intimidation of American inhabitants by frequent murders and threats by the Mexican raiders and their vagrant allies, he said:

"Throughout the valley of the Rio Grande, from the mouth for a distance of two hundred miles up the river, and for a hundred and forty miles back from it, crops and herds have been abandoned; people dared not travel except in armed parties; civil law outside of the towns was suspended, and sheriffs and judges reported to me that it was unsafe to attempt to execute processes of law outside of the towns, unless the officers of the law were accompanied by soldiers to protect them. Under these circumstances, the governor of the State applied through me, and directly, for a sufficient United States military force to protect the frontier, stating his inability to do so with the means at his disposal. I was directed to inform him that it is 'the duty of the troops on the Rio Grande frontier to protect all the officers of the general government, and, as far as possible, aid the State authorities in protecting the people against organized bands of marauders from any quarter,' which I did; at the same time I called attention to the grave character of the invasion, and the importance of prompt and decisive measures by the Government of the United States."

Ord urged that "some more effectual means must be adopted than simply sending troops and sailors to look on while our people are being despoiled and murdered, for it is evident that

the sailors and soldiers, however willing, can do nothing if confined to this side of the river, and an order to make reprisals
with the means to carry out the order has sometimes resulted in
indemnity as well as security." Although he quoted the opinion
of the Catholic bishop, of the disturbed region, that "there
would be no peace in that country for our citizens until the
Sierra Madre should be made the boundary line," he still believed that the United States would be "able to enforce a proper
regard for its own soil without extending its limits." [18]

By the latter part of 1875 conditions were no better. In
December, Captain McNally, in command of the Texas state
troops, reported evidence that the stealing operations of the
raiders continued on a large scale. In November, 1875, Captain
Randlett, of the United States forces, authorized by instructions
from Fort Brown to catch a band of thieves and if in hot pursuit to follow them into Mexico, overtook a band of the cattle
thieves at the Las Cuevas crossing. There, after brief hostilities
interrupted by darkness, he opened negotiations with the Mexican village authorities for the return of the stolen cattle and
planned to cross with his troops on the following morning, but
was further delayed by an order to await reenforcements. There,
also, he arranged to protect the return of Captain McNally, of
the Texas Rangers, who had joined in the pursuit and impatiently crossed the river with his small force and engaged in a
skirmish with a much larger Mexican force. He soon crossed
to aid McNally, but following a truce was ordered to withdraw
by his superior officer who arrived from Fort Brown.[19]

On November 24, 1875, the constitutional convention of
Texas in a resolution and memorial invited the attention of
Congress to the Mexican depredations and atrocities in Texas
and the evil influence of the Mexican Free Zone, with a view to
the interposition of the American government to obtain future
security of persons and property. Following a report of the committee of the Texas legislature recommending an increase of
state forces to protect the cattle and people from the desperate
raiders, the lower house of Congress, suggesting that the government at Washington should assume the duty of furnishing more

adequate assistance for protection, appointed a special investigating committee which, in February, 1876, reported an intolerable border situation of terrorism which was growing worse.[20]

Before this committee on Mexican border trouble General Ord testified on February 12, 1876, and stated that the only way to protect and recover American property and prevent the raids was to send troops across the river whenever they found a fresh trail which indicated a prospect of overtaking the thieves. He, therefore, recommended a sufficient force to maintain itself on the Mexican side of the river for a short time if necessary. In justification of this proposed action he said that the Mexican local authorities, under the influence of the lawless population and of its leaders who sometimes participated in the cattle raids, were averse to restoration of stolen property, and that the Mexican central government was unable to enforce its own laws, or even to protect its own property. He suggested that effective plans for stopping the raids could easily be arranged if the governor of Tamaulipas could be influenced by the same motives as those which had already induced the governors of Sonora and Chihuahua to agree to cooperate in the capture of the Indian raiders. In his testimony he explained that a difficulty which seriously complicated the question of the capture of raiders was the uncertainty of the Rio Grande River, which had frequently changed its bed since the date of the treaty which designated it as the boundary, and which in some places was no longer regarded as the boundary. Mexican laws were enforced in the *bolsas* or pockets of the bend of the river which had been left on the American side by changes in the location of the river channel, and here the raiders could rendezvous under Mexican jurisdiction.[21]

In its report of February 29, 1876, the special committee of the House declared that the American government, by its inactivity and its international politeness, was responsible for the increase of the number and power and contempt of the Mexican robber clans and that it must now send a larger defensive force than would have been required a few years earlier. In this report, after considering the reports of American officers on the border, and with a desire to avoid a war of retaliation which might precipitate complications, it was reluctantly forced by facts to reach the conclusion that prompt federal protection by increased force and by authority to cross the Rio Grande in hot pursuit of robbers with stolen property, and the adoption of necessary measures for recovery of the property, was justified. In justification of this policy it summarized the failures of past efforts: the appeals from Texas had been earnest and oft repeated; Governor Coke had addressed urgent calls to the federal authorities; the Texan legislature and the constitutional convention had memorialized Congress; the representations of Mr. Fish to the Mexican government had been earnest and persistent; the Mexican government was utterly powerless to prevent or check the evils, and through its embarrassment and pride could not be expected to agree by formal treaty to the right of continued pursuit and punishment of the robbers as the only means of efficient defense.[22]

Congress, however, acting in a spirit of moderation in marked contrast with the excitement in Mexico, failed to act upon the recommendation of its special committee, thus leaving in operation the border conditions which had impressed the necessity of the measures recommended. On April 29, Foster, in a dispatch to his government, advised against the passage of this proposed resolution by Congress, stating that it was bitterly condemned by the Mexican press and interpreted as an unfriendly contemplated infringement upon Mexican sovereign rights.[23]

President Grant, in his annual message of December, 1876, expressing the hope of ultimate adjustment of the border difficulties, considerately offered the explanation that the increase of the frequency of acts of violence and the difficulty of adjustment was due to changes in the course and bed of the Rio Grande, placing on either side of the river "portions of lands which by existing conventions belonged to the jurisdiction of the government on the opposite side of the river"—an explanation which had been mentioned by General Ord merely as a serious complicating difficulty.[24]

Above the town of Piedras Negras on the Rio Grande the

Mexican Indian tribes of Lipans and Mescaleros, located in Coahuila, had long engaged in predatory warfare on the scattered Texan settlements. The Kickapoos, who in 1863 had migrated to the wilder frontier of Santa Rosa, Mexico, from their American reservation in Indian Territory, had later begun a series of frequent raids into Texas, stealing between the Rio Grande and San Antonio many horses which were sold to Mexicans. Against these raids the American government began to present protests to the Mexican government as early as 1869 or 1870. In 1869, and for several years thereafter, it unsuccessfully sought the cooperation of the Mexican government in efforts to arrange for the return of the Kickapoos.

Secretary Fish, on December 12, 1870, following the authorization of military operations against bands of Texas Indians (located in the Guadalupe Mountains) who had committed depredations upon the settlements in the region of El Paso, authorized Nelson to request the cooperation of the government of Chihuahua by permitting any necessary crossing of American troops into Mexican territory and by use of Mexican troops to intercept the Indians in their flight. Through Nelson's reply of January 10, 1871, he learned that President Juárez, on recommendation of Lerdo, Secretary of Relations, had authorized the governor of Chihuahua to cooperate by use of Mexican forces to intercept the flight in Mexico but had not the power without the consent of Congress to grant American troops permission to follow the Indians into Mexico. Later, in April, he learned after discreet inquiry that Juárez had concluded that the time was not favorable for submitting the proposition to Congress. On June 26, 1871, after receiving through Nelson a report of William Schuchardt (United States commercial agent at Piedras Negras) concerning frontier depredations by bands of Indians from Mexico (Kickapoo, Lipan and Mescalero tribes) and their safe escape into Mexico where their acts seemed to have the approval of Mexican accomplices and other influential Mexicans, Fish forwarded the following instruction: "You may say . . . unofficially that it may become our duty at least to weigh the expediency of pursuing the hostile Indians into Mexico, without consent of the government, if it shall not adopt measures toward checking the robberies." From Nelson's reply of August 30 he learned Mariscal's unofficial opinion that the Mexican government, although it had no power, without consent of Congress, to permit foreign troops to cross into Mexico, would not seriously complain of such crossing in pursuit of savage and hostile Indians in case of imperious necessity.[25]

In March, 1872, after the investing of Juárez with extraordinary powers and the establishment of martial law in Coahuila and Nuevo Leon, Nelson, in accord with his instructions from Fish, submitted to Mariscal a statement of the evils and perils resulting from the incursions of the Kickapoos. Referring to his antecedent notes (since July, 1869) on the subject, and urging the absolute necessity of vigorous measures for suppression of the outrages, he again proposed, as the most efficacious measure, cooperation in the American project of removal of the Indians to their reservations and solicited permission for American troops to cross the Mexican frontier. From Mariscal, on April 23, he received promise of efficient cooperation in the American plan of removal, by furnishing a Mexican military escort to the frontier, in case the Kickapoos should freely consent to the emigration.[26]

In January, 1873, Secretary Fish, after reading a recent dispatch of the American commercial agent at Piedras Negras relative to the predatory Indian incursions, instructed Nelson that sooner or later, if the Mexican government should remain apathetic or powerless to prevent the raids, the American government would have no other alternative but "to endeavor to secure quiet on the frontier by seeking the marauders and punishing them in their haunts, wherever these may be." [27]

United States commissioners, appointed under the joint resolution of Congress approved May 7, 1872, made a second report on June 30, 1873, based upon a large amount of general evidence and observations on a visit to territory exposed to the raids of Kickapoos, Lipans and other Mexican Indians. After examination of the evidence submitted, showing that the raids were aided by Mexican accomplices, degraded merchants and spies, and had resulted in the loss of an astonishing number of Texans, it declared:

"The grave responsibility of the Mexican Government cannot be overlooked when the continued protection given to marauders by its frontier authorities, the illicit trade with the Indians carried on by its degraded merchants, who are justly suspected of furthering outrages on Texas, and the fact of a friendly shelter being given to the retreating raiders laden with the spoils of a friendly territory, are considered. . . . The laxity of the Mexican Government is the great cause of these raids." [28]

A Mexican commission of 1873 complained that the Indians who had committed the depredations on the American side of the boundary had been driven into Mexico by the American policy of driving them to the frontier, and that from their out-rages Mexicans had suffered more than the Americans. This statement had some basis so far as it may have referred to the Kickapoos.

Unable to obtain permission for military pursuit of the hostile Kickapoo Indians across the line in a hot chase following their damaging depredations in American territory, the American government, in 1871, and again in 1872, in accord with the Mexican central government, sent agents (Miles in 1871) to arrange for a removal from Mexico; but their purpose was de-feated by opposition and interference of local Mexican author-ities, who were influenced by the local beneficiaries of the profitable trade connected with the raids. In 1872, Secretary Fish, by urging Mexican responsibility for the acts of the Indians, induced Mariscal to offer aid to prevent any further local Mexican interference against removal. In 1873, Nelson obtained from Lafragua the assurance of measures to insure the aid of Mexican governors of the frontier states in the proposed removal. Finally, Mexican action was hastened by the action of Colonel R. S. MacKenzie who, with Lieutenant Bullis, in May, 1873—following a suggestion of Secretary Fish that the Ameri-can government might resort to an invasion of Mexican terri-tory in hot pursuit in order to disperse marauding bands of

Indians—trailed a band of the horse thieves to the Indian village in Coahuila, killed nineteen of the band, captured forty, and recovered over sixty stolen horses. This expedition was soon followed by the removal of over 400 Kickapoos from Mexico to the United States. This removal resulted in a period of rest and peace for that part of the border until late in 1876 when, following a decrease of cattle from Tamaulipas, the remaining Kickapoos and the Mescalero and Lipan Indians renewed the raids, resulting in many murders of American settlers.[29]

Efforts for further removals were continued. On April 12, 1875, Secretary Fish, informing Foster of the embarrassments which Henry M. Atkinson had experienced in his mission to remove remaining Kickapoo and Lipan Indians from Mexico, and the apparent local Mexican opposition to the removal, said: "This Department is reluctant to believe that the authorities at Mexico are insincere in their professions of good will in this matter, but it is hoped that they may have control enough over the frontiersmen to cause their orders to be respected. It is difficult to see what substantial advantage Mexico can expect from keeping those Indians." Foster, on June 25, reported that Lafragua attributed the origin of the local opposition to the "harsh judgment of Texan newspapers and citizens against the Mexican people and authorities of the frontier and to their projects of invasion and acquisition of territory," but stated that the governors had been instructed to remove any obstacles to a later attempt at removal of the Indians. Reviewing the various earlier proposals which the American government had made, Lafragua explained that the Mexican government had no constitutional power to expel the Indians by force and could not consent to their removal by American troops—especially not at a time when the Mexican frontier localities were influenced by irritations and suspicious fears engendered by Texan suggestions of invasion and annexation. The American proposal for removal by extradition he said was not authorized by Mexican laws nor by treaty. He said the Mexican government had consented willingly to the final American proposal of removal by an arrangement between American commissioners and the

Indians for transportation to their reservations in the United States, and had given orders to facilitate the removal in that way and would continue to cooperate to the extent of its duties and powers. Foster, while expressing his gratification for the new Mexican instructions, courteously expressed his opinion that the Mexican government had erred in the decision that it could not compel the return of Indians who were refugees from the authority of the United States. He also suggested that the losses and suffering so long borne by Texans from raiding bands of Mexican outlaws, some of which were reported to be led by a general of the Mexican army, and all of which found a safe refuge and protection in Mexico where they disposed of their plunder without fear of punishment there, was sufficient to create in Texas a public opinion unfavorable to the justice of Mexican authorities and the consequent threats of counter invasions and reprisals and occasional proposals to place the Mexican frontier under the authority of the United States.[30]

On November 16, 1875, convinced that the central Mexican government could not control the frontier Indians, Ord, in a telegram to his superior officer, recommended an immediate notification to the governor of Coahuila that unless the local government could stop the outrages "we must protect ourselves by attacking the Indians wherever we find them." In February, 1876, he arranged with the governor of Chihuahua an understanding similar to one which, when in command of another division, he had earlier arranged with the governor of Sonora— an understanding by which troops could cross the border in pursuit of marauding Indians from either side, and under which Mexican troops actually cooperated with American troops in American territory for several weeks.[31]

Meantime, on November 16, 1875, Secretary Fish, in accord with the recommendation of Secretary Chandler of the Department of Interior, instructed Foster to consult the Mexican government with a view to plans to remove to the interior of Mexico the remnants of the Kickapoo and Lipan tribes of Chihuahua who would not agree to return to the United States. On February 1 and March 8, 1876, Foster reported that the Mexi-

can government had arranged to remove these remnants to
Mapimi, a point distant from the frontier. In the preceding
month he had reported that Colonel Thomas G. Williams, the
American special commissioner for removal of the Mescalero
Apaches, had agreed with the Mexican commissioner to approve
an agreement of the Chihuahua government with these Indians
for removal to Mexican reservations far from the frontier and
to recommend its approval by the Mexican central government.
This arrangement Williams regarded more satisfactory than the
original plan to obtain consent of the Indians to return to their
American reservations. On February 29, 1876, a special committee of the House (appointed under a resolution of January
6) reported that the Indians, whose robberies had been checked
by a severe chastisement by General Mackenzie, had been removed, and that disturbed conditions had been replaced by
comparative peace and amicable intercourse. Foster later reported to his government that the Lerdo administration, occupied with the revolution, had not removed the small bands
as promised, but that he hoped the new administration
after the establishment of official relations would execute the
plan.[32]

The Indian raids across the border, however, were not ended.
In May, 1876, Colonel W. R. Shafter, acting under orders of
General Ord, decided to pursue a band of Lipan Indian murderers into Coahuila and sent Lieutenant Bullis across the river
to find their camp. In July, he and Bullis crossed about twenty-
five miles above the Pecos, and, after a southward march of
several days, Bullis attacked and destroyed a Lipan camp and
recovered nearly a hundred horses. In the following January,
Bullis with his company, aided by about 200 negro cavalry,
advanced about 125 miles into Mexico in pursuit of a body of
Lipans and Apaches who, however, eluded them. On March 19,
1877, a few days after the inauguration of President Hayes,
General Sheridan, learning from Shafter that the Indian raiders
found refuge in Mexican towns where they sold stolen property,
recommended measures to compel the Mexican government to
prevent the Indian incursions. In May, after receiving reports

of another raid, he renewed his recommendation which was repeated by General Sherman.[33]

In January, 1876, a new source of trouble appeared in the new revolution of General Porfirio Diaz against the Lerdo administration in Mexico—a revolution which became more widespread than that of 1871-72 against Juárez and resulted in martial law and forced loans and suspension of communication with Vera Cruz and other points. For a time American neutrality was threatened by Diaz, who established headquarters at Brownsville, Texas, where he, with his companion-adviser, Manuel Gonzales, developed plans until his supporters were ready to assume hostilities. The American government felt relieved when (in disguise) Diaz took passage on an American mail steamer from New Orleans to Vera Cruz. On February 3, 1876, Foster suggested to his government that measures should be taken to prevent violation of American neutrality by operations of the revolutionists. On March 21, he reported Mexican press complaints of the absence of American measures against the plans of Diaz in Texas.[34]

On April 22, Foster notified Fish that Diaz (late in March) had crossed from Texas to Mexico and on April 2 had easily captured Matamoros which gave him the key to the frontier and enabled him to obtain foreign military supplies. Apparently, however, the revolutionary operations of Diaz, which were planned on American soil in Texas, promised no hope for improvement of border relations which had produced an increased anti-American attitude in Mexico. To further his cause he used the Mexican feeling of hostility and accepted the aid of lawless leaders of Tamaulipas. Among the latter was Cortina who, after escaping from the "excessive surveillance" of the police of Mexico City following his release from prison on May 18, 1876, issued a pronunciamento to the nation—protesting against the "outrages" committed upon his person by "the arbitrary government of Lerdo de Tejada" and inviting all Mexicans "who in other times have fought with me in defense of liberty" to rally around the flag unfurled by the "well-merited General Porfirio Diaz." [35]

By the beginning of 1877, Diaz, who had proclaimed himself

provisional President in November, 1876, was in undisputed possession of power in Mexico. On November 16, 1876, Foster reported the complete defeat of the Mexican government forces by Diaz in a decisive battle at Tecoac (about 75 miles east of Mexico City). When the latter occupied the capital on November 23—following the flight of Lerdo, who, like Iglesias, soon took refuge in the United States—Foster suggested to the diplomatic corps the decision to await subsequent events and instructions before the recognition of any new government. On December 14, after Matamoros had passed temporarily to the control of the Iglesias faction, he suggested that in case of the continuation of the contest for power American intervention for protection of Americans on the Rio Grande frontier might become necessary. Influenced largely by the accidental November victory at Tecoac by which Diaz had obtained possession of the capital, he supposed that the early recognition of the Diaz government would be a practical question although dependent upon many elements of future trouble. On January 20, 1877, asking for instructions, he suggested to Secretary Fish to delay recognition while awaiting the result of the Mexican popular election and, meantime, to give attention to prospective adjustment of pending questions. In an unofficial interview he had just been assured by Diaz's Minister of Relations that the American reception of the first installment on the awards of the Claims Commission would not involve the question of recognition, and was also informed that Diaz would do everything possible to stop depredations on the Texas frontier and would nullify only the illegal contracts of the Lerdo administration.[36]

Meantime, Secretary Fish, on December 19, after reception of Foster's dispatch of November 28, had authorized personal intercourse with the officials of the Diaz government, and, on January 19, he authorized recognition of the new government, subject to the discretion of Foster, especially with a view to its payment of the installment of indemnity which would soon be due. On February 12, approving the views of Foster, he instructed the latter to impress upon Mexican public men the idea that the United States before deciding upon official recognition would expect Mexican repeal of the law creating the *Zona Libre* and the institution of measures to prevent raids—although he admitted that these conditions might not be urged finally.[37]

On February 19, following the reception of instructions of January 19 from Fish, Foster expressed his intention to recognize the *de facto* government of Diaz. By March 3, expecting the election of Diaz, he established unofficial relations with the government and assured it that the American government would not allow American territory to be used as a base of operations against Diaz and would not interfere in the internal affairs of Mexico. Although satisfied with Diaz's expressions concerning the preservation of order, he doubted whether the new government would want to meet the opposition which might result from the attempt to repeal the *Zona Libre*.[38]

The American government for the time avoided the question of recognition by the accommodating spirit of the Diaz government which, realizing the embarrassing situation concerning the payment of the first installment of the award of the Claims Commission of 1868 (due on January 31, 1877),* agreed with

---

* Under the Claims Commission Convention of 1868 for adjustment of mutual claims, a commission was duly organized at Washington July 31, 1869. Its powers were extended by convention of April 19, 1871, and again by a convention of November 27, 1872. A mutual arbitration provided by the treaty gave a balance of about $4,250,000 to American citizens. The claims submitted under it were remarkable both in number and in amount—those presented by the United States aggregating one thousand and seventeen, and those of Mexico nine hundred and ninety-eight, while the total amount claimed on one side and the other exceeded half a billion dollars. Nearly one-third of the award against Mexico was for two claims (the LaAbra and the Weil claims), which the Mexican government alleged were fraudulent and which after an investigation by act of Congress in 1878, and an attempt to arrange a rehearing in 1882 were finally (in 1892) submitted to the jurisdiction of the American Court of Claims at Washington. In 1897 the court decided that fraud had been employed in the LaAbra case and forbade payment to the claimants. In 1900 the United States returned to Mexico the undistributed balance of the awards already paid and in 1902 appropriated $412,572.70 for repayment to Mexico of installments previously distributed to the fraudulent claimants.

The famous Pious Fund case, first presented for adjustment to the Mexican Claims Commission in 1870, was subsequently referred to the umpire, Sir Edward Thornton, who, in 1875, awarded to the United States $904,700.99 as interest on the fund at 6% from 1842 to 1868. Mexico, in paying the award, stated that the amount was in full, but the United States claimed a continuation of a yearly interest after 1868. This difference was finally settled under a protocol of 1902, submitting it to the Permanent Court of the Hague (the first case before the court) which, in October, 1902, rendered an award in favor of the United States for $1,428,682.67 in Mexican currency for the period from 1868 to February 2, 1902, and also an annual interest of $43,050.99 thereafter.

Foster to make the payment through Señor Mariscal who had
been accredited by the Lerdo administration as Mexican minister
at Washington. By this decision the pressing issue of recognition
and the related issues of border raids were postponed for consideration of the succeeding American administration.[39]

REFERENCES

1. *House Rp. 701*, 45-2, Apr. 25, 1878, pp. xix-xx.
2. *Ib.*, Appendix C, pp. 291-93 and 303-13; *Dip. Cor.*, *1868-69*, Vol. 2, pp. 594 and 627.
3. *House Rp. 701*, 45-2, App. C, pp. 298-301, and 313-16; *Sen. Rp. 166*, 41-2, p. 7; *For. Rels.*, *1870*, p. 497, and 1871, p. 608; RICHARDSON, *Messages and Papers of the Presidents*, VII, 146.
4. *House Rp. 701*, 45-2, App., pp. 117, 190.
5. *Ib.*, App. B, pp. 194-95.
6. *Ib.*, pp. 85, 92.
7. *Ib.*, pp. 98-99, 109 and 113; *Sen. Rp. 39*, 42-1.
8. *Ib.*, p. 161; *House Rp. 343*, 44-1, pp. 161-67.
9. *House Rp. 701*, 45-2, App. B, pp. 115-16.
10. *Ib.*, pp. 164-65.
11. *Ib.*, pp. 117 and 131.
12. *Ib.*, p. 121; *House Rp. 343*, 44-1, p. 147.
13. *House Rp. 701*, App., pp. 144 and 198.
14. *19 Mexico, Instructions*, (No. 206) March 29, (No. 207) March 31, (No. 228) May 20, 1875; *54 Mexico, Despatches*, (No. 279) May 4, 1875; *For. Rels.*, *1875*, pp. 909 and 924.
15. *House Rp. 701*, 45-2, App. B, pp. 156, 158.
16. *Ib.*, 128-29; *For. Rela.*, *1875*, p. 943; *54 Mexico, Despatches*, No. 308, June 26, 1875.
17. *54 Mexico, Despatches*, (No. 309) June 26, (No. 317) July 7, 1875; *For. Rels.*, *1875*, p. 946.
18. *House Rp. 701*, 45-2, App. B, pp. 133, 181-83.
19. *Ib.*, p. 115; *House Exec. Doc. 13*, 45-1.
20. *House Rp. 343*, 44-1, p. 171; *House Rp. 701*; 45-2, pp. 148-62.
21. *Ib.*, pp. 174-77 and 181; *House Rp. 343*, 44-1.
22. *Ib.*, p. 151, 159-60; *House Rp. 343*, 44-1, pp. 161-62; *For. Rels.*, *1876*, p. 398.
23. *56 Mexico, Despatches*, No. 405, Apr. 29, 1876.
24. RICHARDSON'S *Messages and Papers of the Presidents*, VII, p. 404.
25. *For. Rels.*, *1871*, pp. 607 and 610 and 655; *House Rp. 701*, 45-2, App. B, pp. 199, 203-04 and 206.

26. *Ib.*, pp. 209-11 (and *For. Rels.*, *1872*, p. 394).

27. *Ib.*, pp. 214-15.

28. *Ib.*, pp. 218 and 221.

29. *Ib.*, p. 205; *For. Rels.*, *1870*, pp. 649 and 416, 1871, pp. 635, 647-55 and 662, and 1873, p. 643; *House Exec Doc. 64*, 45-2, p. 187; *House Exec. Doc. 1*, 43-1, Part 1, p. 716.

30. *House Rp. 701*, 45-2, App. B, pp. 227-31.

31. *Ib.*, pp. 231 and 176.

32. *Ib.*, pp. 232-35, 155 and 238; *55 Mexico, Despatches*, No. 375, Feb. 1, 1876.

33. *House Misc. Doc. 64*, 45-2, p. 188; *House Exec. Doc. 13*, 45-1.

34. JOHN W. FOSTER, *Diplomatic Memoirs*, I, pp. 75-76; *55 and 56 Mexico, Despatches*, No. 379, Feb. 3, and March 1, 1876.

35. *House Rp. 701*, 45-2, App. A, p. 52, and App. B, p. 198; *For. Rels.*, *1876*, p. 396.

36. *58 Mexico, Despatches*, (No. 477) Dec. 14, 1876, and (Unofficial and Confidential) Jan. 20, and (No. 487), Jan. 16, 1877.

37. *19 Mexico, Instructions*, (No. 356) Dec. 19, 1876, (No. 366) Jan. 19, and (No. 370) Feb. 12, 1877.

38. *56 Mexico, Despatches*, (No. 496) Feb. 19, (No. 502) Mar. 3, (No. 503) Mar. 3, 1877.

39. FOSTER, *Diplomatic Memoirs*, I, p. 86.

CHAPTER XI

RELATION OF MEXICAN PROBLEMS TO THE AMERICAN RECOGNITION OF DIAZ

THE dangerous breach in relations of amity, threatened by the conditions on the land frontier which the Mexican government had failed to remedy because of certain obstacles in the way of efficient measures, was for a time widened by the delay of the American government (under President Hayes) to recognize Diaz, whom the period of revolution and politics in Mexico had placed in power in November, 1876—and whose new minister (sent to Washington soon after the establishment of the revolutionary government) the American government would not receive. Formal recognition was deferred for almost a year after recognition had been accorded (in May, 1877) by the several Latin American governments and European governments then represented at Mexico City. This delay was first due to a prudent hesitation to acknowledge authorities emanating from a revolution which subverted the established constitutional order and endangered the existence of republican government, and to a desire to be assured that his election was approved by the Mexican people and to ascertain whether his administration had stability and a disposition to comply with the rules of international comity and the obligations of treaties. Subsequently, it was due to a refusal of the government of Diaz to enter upon any settlement of various pending questions which involved the rights and protection of American citizens—and especially to the continuation of irritating occurrences on the Rio Grande border which created doubts as to the ability and disposition of the new government to fulfill the "obligations of treaties" and to perform the duties of "international friendship."

Although General Diaz after his accession to power, anxious to secure the recognition of the American government, made exertions to quiet the border conditions, he was hampered by pre-election promises and connections and the problems of internal consolidation. The great difficulty in relations with Mexico was the wide difference between the professions of the Mexican government and the performance of its international duties—a difference largely due to weakness of the government resulting from uncertain tenure and the compromises required to prevent cause or pretext of new revolts (especially in states along the northern frontier which was regarded as the most dangerous locality in which to originate Mexican revolutions).

The border conditions which had induced American forces to cross the frontier in hot pursuit more than once in President Lerdo's administration, continued under Diaz, whose officers also pursued revolutionists across the river into Texas where Lerdo's Minister of War had established himself near the border and was directing his adherents in the organization of a counter revolution against Diaz. The turbulent conditions finally induced the American Secretary of War, on June 1, 1877, in self-defense and against the protest of Diaz, to issue an order authorizing federal troops if necessary to pursue Mexican marauders across the frontier and to arrest and punish them on Mexican soil.

William M. Evarts, who directed the foreign policy under Hayes, was selected for the place against the opposition of Senator Conkling of New York and other machine politicians of New York and Pennsylvania in the Senate—especially Simon Cameron who was chairman of the Senate Committee on Foreign Relations. He was the acknowledged leader of the American bar. He was United States Attorney-General from July, 1868, to March, 1869, had defended President Johnson in the great impeachment trial, had been United States counsel in the Geneva arbitration of 1872 and had represented the Hayes interests before the Electoral Commission. By temperament and social gifts he was well qualified for the duties of a diplomat. In directing American policy in Mexican relations he confronted disturbing situations which severely tested his patience; and, against his denials, he was charged with plans of annexation of Mexico by many opponents, including James G. Blaine, who became his successor in office. By his vigorous and unrelenting insistence upon the protection of the lives and property of Americans he sought to induce the Mexican government to recognize and to observe its moral and international obligations. For the conduct of negotiations at Mexico City he retained John W. Foster who, after his promotion to the Russian legation, was succeeded (in March, 1880) by P. H. Morgan of Louisiana—who had served as a first lieutenant in the Mexican War, had remained loyal to the Union (by going to England) and had later served successively as United States district attorney (1866-73), judge of the Louisiana supreme court (1873-76) and judge of the international tribunal at Alexandria, Egypt (1876-80).

The Hayes administration which inherited from the previous administration all the border problems—the raids by Mexican banditti, the ravages of Indians and the smuggling annoyance of the *Zona Libre*—sought satisfactory solution of all as a preliminary to the American official recognition of the Diaz government. This policy was already foreshadowed by the presentation of the latest instructions of Secretary Fish whose earlier instructions had seemed to indicate a policy to recognize Diaz, and who, on January 19, had entrusted the decision of the question to Foster who advised against haste.[1]

On March 24, Foster reported that the Mexican government intended to recall Mariscal from Washington and to replace him with Mata (who had sailed from Vera Cruz for Washington on January 21 with coin to pay the first installment of the awards of the commission under the treaty of 1868). On April 24, he reported the intimation of the Minister of Relations that the Diaz government if recognized could enter into an arrangement for cooperative military forces for the repression of disorders. Four days later, in a private dispatch, he presented arguments in favor of American recognition of Diaz—whose autograph letter of March 4 to President Hayes had not yet been answered, and whose government was embarrassed by having at Washington no official representative in whom it could repose confidence.

On May 7, he requested instructions on the subject. In his private ("Unofficial and Confidential") dispatch of April 28, referring to his own embarrassing official position and inclining to the opinion that the recognition of the *de facto* government of Diaz was expedient, he said: [2]

"In the present condition of affairs, I regard General Diaz as the only hope of the country, from within itself, much as I deprecate his revolutionary conduct. If he has not the capacity and popularity to maintain a government, the danger is that the nation will fall into anarchy. Mr. Lerdo's restoration to power would only be the signal for outbreaks in all directions and a ceaseless guerrilla warfare. At the best the prospect is gloomy enough. . . . I do not know whether the question, often discussed in American newspapers, of a protectorate over this country has any support in the councils of President Hayes; but in the absence of all knowledge on that point, I venture the suggestion that the only pressure or influence we ought at present to exert in the internal affairs of this country is that which will secure the peace and good order of our frontier and the protection of American citizens and their interests in this Republic. . . . Should the President and you think it opportune to make a formal recognition of Diaz, and should deem it advisable to entrust to my discretion, under such instructions as you may see proper to give, the adjustment, concurrently with the act of recognition, of some of the pending questions of most interest to our Government, I probably would be able to bring about an earlier settlement of them than otherwise. I refer especially to the Texas Border questions, the removal of the Indians to the interior of Mexico, and the Mazatlan and Acapulco difficulties. It might also be well in this connection to inform me of the views entertained by our Government concerning the crossing of the Rio Grande by Col. Shafter, which is undoubtedly regarded by Mexico as a violation of its territory and an indignity to the nation."

Later, on April 30, he added: "A point not noticed in my letter may be worthy of consideration. Is not recognition important in order to fix upon Mexico responsibility for the claims, of various kinds, of American citizens against the Diaz government. . . ."

On March 27 Secretary Evarts approved Foster's course in establishing unofficial relations with the *de facto* government of Diaz, but advised him to await progress of events and the action of Congress before taking further steps toward formal and official recognition of Diaz as the lawful President of Mexico. On May 16, following new border outrages, he sent additional instructions, through Assistant Secretary F. W. Seward, directing Foster to inform the Minister of Relations unofficially that the United States would defer recognition of the Diaz government while awaiting more evidence of its permanence, friendly disposition and intentions concerning the performance of treaty obligations.

In these instructions Seward said: "The Government of the United States in its dealings with the Mexican Republic has aimed to pursue not merely a just but a generous and friendly course. While earnest to guard and protect the rights of its own citizens and the safety of its own territory, it does not seek to intervene in political contests or changes of administration. It is accustomed to accept and recognize the results of a popular choice in Mexico, and not to scrutinize closely the regularity or irregularity of the methods by which presidents are inaugurated. In the present case it waits before recognizing General Diaz as the President of Mexico until it shall be assured that his election is approved by the Mexican people, and that his administration is possessed of stability to endure and of disposition to comply with the rules of international comity and the obligation of treaties.

"Such recognition, if accorded, would imply something more than a mere formal assent. It would imply a belief that the government so recognized will faithfully execute its duties and observe the spirit of its treaties. . . . There have been raids and depredations upon the Texan frontier; theft, murder, arson, and plunder; violation of post-offices and custom-houses; incursions by armed men to destroy life or property; cattlestealing has become a profitable occupation; military officials posted to protect the frontier are said to have protected the robbers; forced loans have been demanded, and American citizens have been compelled to submit to unjust and unequal exactions. Within the past few weeks the guides of an American commander have been seized and carried into the interior, with threats of summary execution; and a consul of the United States, in gross violation of international comity, has been imprisoned. For each and all of these acts, many of them committed, if not with sanction, at least in the name of the Government of Mexico, not one single man, so far as is known to this government, has been punished. . . . It is natural that Mexican statesmen should urge upon you the argument that the restoration of official relations between the two governments would open the way toward such an adjustment. But it is natural, on the other hand, that the

Government of the United States should be disposed to believe that some guarantee of such an arrangement should be made the condition precedent to any recognition, rather than to trust to the possibility that it may ultimately follow." [3]

Negotiations were embarrassed and delayed by Mexican excitement and irritation resulting from the American orders of June 1 authorizing General Ord to cross the Rio Grande in hot pursuit of Mexican border raiders. On March 31, 1877, Secretary Evarts—after reading reports of many recent Indian marauding parties, and Colonel Shafter's opinion that the only way to check the atrocities was by pursuit of the delinquents into Mexico in order to attack them in their lairs—instructed Foster that the President might soon consider seriously the expediency of entering Mexico to punish the wrongdoers wherever found, and suggested that he informally "intimate these views to persons of importance" at the Mexican capital. On April 23, Foster frankly mentioned these views to Vallarta of the Mexican Foreign Office; and, in the conversation which followed, he recalled to him that recent occurrences on the frontier fully confirmed his recent strong suggestion, immediately following the establishment of the Diaz government, that a sufficient border force of regular Mexican federal troops under a high military officer of character and tact was essential to the maintenance of cordial relations. To this Vallarta agreed, but suggested that to make fully effective the cooperation of such a force with American military authorities the restoration of official relations was first desirable. [4]

On May 5, 1877, General Sheridan, in view of the difficulty of protecting the long frontier from marauding incursions, recommended that the proper authorities take steps to require the Mexican government to aid in the protection of the frontier. President Hayes promptly ordered American military authorities on the Rio Grande to exercise the utmost vigilance in suppression of the raids, and in the punishment of the guilty parties and the recapture of the property stolen by them. By his orders General Ord was directed to invite the cooperation of the Mexican authorities and to notify them of American determination to stop the invasions, even, if necessary, to cross the border in hot pursuit in order to punish the lawless invaders. On May 28, following information from the Secretary of War (George W. McCrary) concerning another thieving raid resulting in the theft of two hundred head of cattle, Secretary Evarts wrote Foster:

"It is apprehended that the Mexican Government is not well aware that, although for a heavy pecuniary consideration it has released the United States from the obligations in respect to predatory incursions of Indians from this country into Mexico, the obligations of that government in respect to similar marauders from that country into the United States are entire, as provided for both by public law and by treaty. The duty of that government, therefore, at least to aid in restraining its savages from depredations upon us, seems to be clear. If this duty shall continue to be neglected, we may be compelled in self-defense to disregard the boundary in seeking for and punishing those bandits." [5]

Finally, on June 1, in response to renewed appeals and apparently with almost unanimous approval of the American press, the Hayes administration through Secretary of War McCrary directed General Sherman to instruct General Ord to invite the cooperation of the local Mexican authorities to suppress the long-continued lawlessness and to inform them that if the Mexican government continued to neglect its duty to suppress the outrages the duty would then devolve upon the American government which would perform it, even, if necessary, to cross the border occasionally with troops. At the same time, it directed Ord at his discretion, when in close pursuit or on a fresh trail of a band of marauders, to follow them across the Rio Grande and to overtake and punish them and retake stolen property.[6]

Meantime, late in May, Foster had discussed with the Mexican government the problems of American neutrality and the Mexican duty to establish order on the Rio Grande. On May 24, 1877, in reply to Vallarta's complaint of the immunity extended to the Lerdist chief, Valdez, by the American authorities in Texas following the latter's "hostile crossing," he said that he presumed that the American authorities were pursuing

toward the partisans of Lerdo the same course observed the
previous year toward General Diaz—who had been permitted
to remain undisturbed in Brownsville for considerable time
while the revolution, of which he was the recognized head, was
developing in Mexico, and who after being driven from Mexico
was allowed to return there without molestation of American
officials. On May 28, however, he promptly suggested to his
government that the American authorities should be enjoined
to observe strict impartiality in the Mexican conflict and to enforce neutrality. On the same day, he informed Evarts that the
Diaz government, recognizing the importance of the frontier
question, had decided to send a prominent and prudent general
with adequate force and with instructions to act in accord with
General Ord in repressing outlawry on the frontier. On June
9, Evarts wired a reply that the Mexican orders for cooperation
of Mexican troops for suppression of the raids were satisfactory
and gratifying; but twelve days later, protesting against an invasion of Mexican troops by an attack on a party of revolutionists whom they drove to the American side of the Rio
Grande, he demanded disavowal of the act and punishment of
the perpetrators.[7]

The instructions to Ord were used by the Mexican government to create a new national issue, and resulted in a revival of
earlier Mexican newspaper charges, previously refuted, that the
raids and depredations had been mutual. Following the publication of the American orders, Diaz increased the tension and
rallied to his support all Mexican parties by instructions of
June 18 to General Treviño of the frontier forces. He directed
Treviño immediately to locate his troops with a view to the
protection of the Mexican frontier and to the prevention and
punishment of border robberies, to pursue robbers within Mexican limits and deliver captives to competent courts, to invite
the cooperation of American military authorities if necessary
but without crossing the boundary and, in case of any invasion,
"to repel force with force"—acting with prudence but with due
energy. This Mexican order, Foster, on June 21, forwarded to
his government after a verbal protest to the Mexican govern-

ment. On the following day, he forwarded various newspaper articles showing the public temper against the policy of the Hayes administration—one of which reflected the Mexican view that the purpose of President Hayes was "to withdraw public attention from the irregularities of his election and to provoke a war that will permit him to maintain an army sufficiently respectable to meet every emergency." He was especially irritated by a hostile article in the *Diario Oficiel* arraigning the American government for insulting the Mexican government by the Ord orders, and charging American intentions to acquire Mexico. Recognizing the volatile and childish character of the people and their incapacity to treat a great public question with calmness and without prejudice, he promptly prepared in reply a long historical memorandum on the following points: (1) The American instruction to General Ord is not the announcement of a new measure; (2) The depredations of the past four years have not been common to both sides of the frontier; (3) Mexico has taken no adequate or vigorous measure to prevent the depredations or punish the outlaws; (4) Mexico has frequently acknowledged its inability to discharge its duty on the Rio Grande frontier, giving as a reason its internal dissensions; (5) The instructions to General Ord are misinterpreted by the Mexican government; (6) In view o the foregoing facts, the official declarations of the Mexican Minister of War that the instructions to Ord are in contradiction to treaties and international law and civilized practice are unwarranted. On June 23, after expressing to Villarta his surprise and regret concerning the statements in the official journal misrepresenting the American executive and his cabinet and the order to General Ord, he submitted to him the memorandum with a request for its publication in the *Diario Oficiel*. He was disappointed that, although the *Diario Oficiel* published a brief explanation, the publication of his memorandum was not approved by the cabinet and President. Yielding graciously to the desire of President Diaz he withdrew his request for publication —especially with a feeling of the importance to his government that he should keep on good terms with Diaz and his ministers who, chafing under the delay of recognition, under the slightest pretext might seek to make him the "scapegoat" of his government's supposed neglect and hostility.[8]

In the following week, on June 28 and in a private letter of June 30, Foster reported to Washington more fully the bitter newspaper attacks on President Hayes and his cabinet resulting from the publication of the Ord order, which the Mexicans regarded as "utterly without cause or provocation" and as inspired by filibusters and speculators combined with the machinations of ex-President Lerdo and the political considerations of President Hayes; and he again mentioned the Mexican suspicion of American intentions to get a cession of territory by driving Mexico into a war or to establish a protectorate over all Mexico. Confident that the Ord order had not been issued without careful consideration by the American government, but that Diaz would demand its repeal or modification, he suggested, as his opinion, that any yielding in regard to it in the slightest degree was inadvisable "until all pending questions are settled and full assurance and security given for the future." [9]

Meantime, about June 19, Treviño had reported a conference at Piedras Negras with General Ord whose proposition for reciprocal passage of the frontier he had declined; and he had stated his plans to organize a volunteer force from the vicinity of the border, which Foster suggested to Evarts would prove unsatisfactory.[10]

Foster, who was disappointed and embarrassed by his instructions of May 16 but could not intimate to Mexico that the policy was contrary to his recommendation and advice, later admitted (in his Diplomatic Memoirs) that the vigorous policy indicated in the Ord order might be explained by a plan to use pressure upon the Mexican government in order to present the alternatives of hostilities or the sale of the northern states of Mexico.[11]

To the embarrassment of Foster's negotiations, resulting largely from the Ord order, certain self-assumed and "unofficial" missions also contributed. Foster was surprised (about May 1) by a call from Simon Stevens who presented a card of Secretary

Evarts, and, in the private interview which followed, represented himself as an American confidential diplomatic agent by invitation of Secretary Evarts to report and advise upon the Mexican political situation, and who stated that at Evarts' office he had been shown all Foster's dispatches and confidential letters and had been furnished with the Department cipher for use in telegraphing (!). Foster, feeling that Stevens was drawing liberally on his imagination and that his real business in Mexico was his Tehuantepec railroad project, declined to introduce him to President Diaz with whose government the accredited American minister had no official relations. On receipt of this information, Evarts replied to Foster that he would not be expected to rely on oral statements of travelers but would receive specific instructions in writing when his official action was desired.[12]

Already the representatives of a more interesting mission had reached Mexico: two well-known Californians, the visionary General John B. Frisbie and his garrulous father-in-law, General M. G. Vallejo—both of whom had recently lost a fortune by financial reverses. Vallejo, son of a Spanish soldier who had landed in California in 1769, was born at Monterey in 1808. Eighth of a family of thirteen, he reared a family of sixteen. In the home-rule revolt in California in 1836-37, begun by Alvarado and Castro, by appointment of Alvarado he became military commander—a position later confirmed by the weak central government at Mexico City—and as his share of the spoils got the control of the missions of San Rafael and San Francisco de Solano. Frisbie was born at Albany, New York, in 1823. In command of a military expedition, in 1846 he sailed by way of Cape Horn and reached Yerba Buena (San Francisco) in March, 1847, after a voyage of six months. For a time he commanded the fort at El Presidio, and there he married a daughter of General Vallejo, the former commander of Mexican forces. After the disbandment of his regiment in July, 1848, he engaged in business with General Vallejo, managing the latter's extensive estate. Later he purchased from Victor Castro land at Vallejo at which, by securing a favorable recommendation of Commander Appleton P. Jones, he obtained the location of the Mare Island Navy Yard. Later, he connected Vallejo with Sacramento by the California Pacific Railway—a road which was finally absorbed by a rival company, the Central Pacific, headed by C. P. Huntington and his associates, who obtained a controlling interest in 1871. On May 5, 1877, Secretary Evarts had commended to Foster these two well-known Californians who were "about to visit Mexico to get acquainted with conditions there" and to report freely either to Foster or to the Department of State direct as might seem advisable. "In view of the present disturbed situation," said Evarts, "it is deemed not improper to commend them to your special attention. While they have no official powers or functions, they are well informed as to the public affairs and familiar with the relations which exist between the United States and Mexico. They will lay before you some views in regard to this subject, which are deemed not unworthy of consideration. It is quite possible that in their unofficial intercourse with leading persons in Mexico they may acquire information which will be of interest and importance to this government." [13]

On May 28, Foster reported the arrival of Frisbie and Vallejo and stated that every attention would be given them by the legation. A few days later, he introduced Frisbie to Diaz; and on June 18 he reported that he seemed satisfied with his progress. On June 18, General Frisbie reported directly to Secretary Evarts stating that he had had interviews with Diaz in regard to prospective railway concessions and a proposed cession of the northern states of Mexico. [14]

"I find General Diaz a thoroughly practical man," he reported. ". . . He has a high appreciation of our countrymen, and is prepared to make the most liberal offers to induce American immigration. Upon the question of railroads, he is almost an enthusiast. . . . My last interview with him was on the 16th inst. . . . I remarked that if his government had applied the proceeds of the territory ceded to the United States to the construction of railroads, his country would now be in a prosperous condition, and . . . intimated that Mexico still had much more territory than she could possibly utilize and would be stronger without than with. He seemed to assent to the proposition, but said that the great body of the Mexican people were exceedingly jealous of their boundary lines and disliked to contract their limits. Yet this sentiment might be overcome, and a transfer of territory made popular, if it was apparent that it would secure the improvements all had so much at heart. He then enquired if I thought the United States government was inclined to treat for the Northern States of this Republic. I replied that the possession of them would in my opinion be of advantage to it, and I believed that a reasonable proposal for their transfer would be favorably received. As I was taking leave of him, he said that he was greatly impressed with the subject of our interview and desired that I should call upon him again this evening."

This letter was received by Evarts on June 28 and was read by him to the President early in July.

Meantime, however, Frisbie, confronted by indignant assertions of the Mexican government which denied that it had ever been approached or that it would ever entertain any such unpatriotic proposal, found reason to disavow the unofficial mission, rumors of which, by his indiscreet interviews before he left the United States, had reached the Mexican newspapers through the American newspapers. On July 9, Foster reported that the mission was impracticable at that time because of recent occurrences; and, on July 30, he reported that the mission had failed —possibly as a result of the alarm caused by the New York *Herald* publication of a detailed project for the cession of the northern states of Mexico and the bad feeling caused by the representative character assumed by N. S. Renau and Simon Stevens in the interest of railroads. On October 6, he reported that Frisbie had returned to the United States, and that he, actuated by personal motives, would present a recommendation for recognition of Diaz—which Foster urged the Department not to accept. He doubtless suspected that Frisbie had been successful in obtaining from Diaz certain concessions—concessions which in 1878 led him to move to Mexico City where he became a patriarch of the American colony of successful industrial promoters, first in mining and railway construction, and later (after 1901) in sugar production (in Guerrero) and an electric (light and power) plant in which he was still interested as late as 1910.

N. S. Renau, who had personal affairs in Mexico City, had suggested to Evarts that his acquaintance with prominent men in Mexico would enable him to obtain useful information for Foster to whom he offered to bear official dispatches from Washington. He had been entrusted as a dispatch bearer on June 1 by Secretary Evarts who, however, had taken the precaution to warn Foster that "He has no other official character or instructions . . . and his functions and compensation as bearer of dispatches will cease after his arrival at the Legation." [15]

On July 30, Foster reported that he was embarrassed by the general feeling of Mexican distrust toward the United States resulting from "irresponsible reports of American newspapers and the self-assumptions of individuals"—reports of extra-official and confidential missions to Mexico and of American designs on northern Mexico hidden under cover of the Ord order and reports which, in the opinion of many Mexicans, had been confirmed by recent events. In submitting the facts to Secretary Evarts, he especially mentioned the activity of the New York *Herald* in circulating stories which had been given general currency in the Mexican press, much to the alarm of timid and suspicious Mexicans. He also mentioned a letter of a Diaz agent declaring the rejection of the proposition for a cession of territory, and also the rumor that N. S. Renau of Washington had told Diaz and his ministers that until a desired railroad grant was confirmed the Diaz government "never would be recognized by the American Department of State." In conclusion he significantly said:

"Although Mexican politicians are not very intelligent in regard to our governmental affairs and practice, I have not thought it proper or sufficiently important even in a private manner to say to them that our government is not likely to be influenced in its policy or action towards Mexico by the reception given by the latter to the private business interests of Americans, neither that its custom is not to entrust important matters of state policy to private citizens in the manner indicated." [16]

Meantime, early in June, Foster, following the reception of his instructions of May 16, although he was disappointed, submitted to the Mexican government a memorandum of subjects for negotiation: a reciprocity treaty, a postal convention, abolition or modification of the Free Zone, protection of American investments and interests by joint guaranty and by exemption of American citizens from forced loans, the establishment of a commission or court of claims for settlement of all claims, an agreement for reciprocal crossing of the border, modification of the extradition treaty of 1861, and a more definite agreement concerning the property rights of citizens of each country residing in the frontier territory of the other. On June 19, he especially submitted the policy of the Hayes administration in regard to the question of recognition and prepared to press Vallarta for negotiation of a treaty to cover all matters of difference and to place commercial intercourse on a better footing. His instructions, which reviewed the Rio Grande troubles and other causes of complaint, he read to Señor Vallarta. In a notable interview characterized by great intensity of feeling, Vallarta insisted that his government possessed all the conditions of recognition required by international law and practice, cited the recognition by all other nations which had diplomatic representatives in Mexico, urged that the adjustment of complaints and claims should properly follow recognition, charged that according to information from New York the Hayes administration had changed the policy of the American government through the influence of certain American schemes for war and annexation of Mexican territory which the Ord order was designed to accomplish, and declared that an absolute declaration of war would have been more considerate. To Vallarta's arguments Foster replied that every nation must judge for itself as to the time and manner of recognizing a new and revolutionary government, and that Secretary Evarts had confirmed the assurance already given that the American government did not seek to intervene in the internal politics of Mexico but that it felt an interest in the stability and responsibility of whatever government it might recognize.[17]

"If the government of General Diaz has not up to the present time been recognized by that of the United States," said he, "it is owing to its own neglect of plain duties. Mr. Vallarta will remember that six months ago, soon after entering the foreign office, I called his attention to the critical condition of affairs on the Rio Grande frontier, and stated that they more seriously threatened the peace of the two countries than any and all other matters. I referred to the raids into Texas by Mexican banditti, the ravages of the Indians, and the annoyance of the *Zona Libre*. There had been no change of policy on the part of the Government of the United States with the change of administration, as he (Mr. Vallarta) unjustly, and I thought inconsiderately, asserted. . . . The records of the Mexican foreign office will show that the present policy of my government as to the frontier is the same as that assumed or foreshadowed during all my residence in Mexico. Early in March last I conveyed to him the contents of a dispatch from Mr. Fish, in which the impression was expressed that the United States, prior to deciding in favor of official recognition of the Diaz government, would expect that efficient measures would be taken toward checking inroads into their States and territories, and toward the repeal of the *Zona Libre*. . . . I have been assured of the good intentions of General Diaz's government, but up to date of the order of Secretary McCrary absolutely nothing had been done in that direction, so far as I was informed."

Within the next week, Foster reported to Evarts that the spirit of the Mexican government was not much better than that of the people who were influenced by the anti-American attacks of the press—such as the official journal of Diaz, which charged that the Hayes administration was influenced by Lerdo de Tejada and by E. L. Plumb and others who were favoring Lerdo with the hope of securing valuable concessions through him. Through Romero, the only member of the ministry who showed equanimity, Foster, who preserved his serenity, was enabled partially to pacify the officials of the government. On June 30, after long conferences, he received from Vallarta, in a long memorandum of replies to the various points, a statement that the Mexican government, after a conscientious study of the unpleasant frontier difficulties which at times had been the motive for conflict, had decided to transfer negotiations to its plenipotentiary at Washington (Mata) with instructions to propose measures for a satisfactory solution. On the same day, in a dispatch referring to the discourteous treatment which he had received from the Mexican government in regard to negotiations for settlement of pending questions, he requested that such negotiations should not be opened at Washington with Mata whose acceptance by Evarts was planned as an effort to get recognition of Diaz. Feeling that his official character as the diplomatic representative of the United States had been called into question (by the proposed transfer of negotiations to Mata) he expressed to Evarts the wish that he (Foster) be formally empowered to act on all questions and that he be advised in detail concerning the views of the administration on each question. In July, although inclined to reply to some of Vallarta's "fallacious inferences," he wisely refrained from continuing a discussion upon questions for whose adjustment the Mexican government had expressed a desire to undertake treaty negotiations.[18]

Meantime, on June 21, Evarts requested Foster to remonstrate with the officers of the Mexican *de facto* government against a recent violation of American territory by troops of Diaz which, after defeating forces of Lerdo on Mexican soil, had continued the pursuit into Texas and had attacked and dispersed them there. He was directed to say that the American government expected "a prompt disavowal of the act with reparation for its consequences and punishment of its perpetrators." On July 7, Foster made the formal demand as requested. Two days later, he obtained a prompt and satisfactory reply from Vallarta, who, also, expressed satisfaction that the later orders to Ord authorized pursuit across the frontier line "only under a grave emergency" and also the hope that the orders would be withdrawn completely. By telegram, of July 20, he recommended steps to prevent violation of American neutrality by Lerdist partisans who were organizing a revolution against Diaz.[19]

Later, in instructions of August 2, after considering Foster's various reports of interviews with Vallarta and the informal memoranda of Mata at Washington concerning the points upon which he could be empowered to negotiate a treaty if the Diaz government should be officially recognized, Evarts suggested that the proposed treaty must not be limited to the single ques-

tion of border irritations but "must deal explicitly and clearly
with the question of the use of military force to pursue offenders and recapture stolen property even beyond the territorial
limits of the United States" if no other way could be found,
and should include a clear understanding in regard to other
questions besides border depredations. He stated that the President, although desirous of terminating the period of suspended
relations, was especially desirous that the basis for renewed relations should be just and amicable (in order to be permanent).
He instructed Foster to continue unofficial intercourse in order
to learn the precise terms to which Diaz would accede—stating
that a conference on these points must necessarily precede any
recognition of the government of General Diaz, in order to determine whether it deserved recognition. "By acceding to terms
which will secure the protection of the lives and property of
American citizens, the safety of American ships, and the security of American territory from unlawful depredations," said
he, "the government of Diaz will give proof of its strength and
stability, and will therefore be legitimately entitled to be regarded as the government of the Mexican Republic." [20]

On the arrival of the Department's instructions of August 2
directing renewed negotiations for the settlement of difficulties,
Foster found unfavorable conditions resulting from (1) the recent conviction that the American government aimed at annexation, from (2) the firm opposition to any reciprocal arrangement for crossing the Rio Grande (which was regarded as
a concession to the United States), and from (3) the belief that
the United States (especially because of strikes) was completely
occupied with the preservation of its internal peace. The insist-
ent demand for a stipulation to allow hot pursuit across the
border proved the chief difference in the negotiations for adjustment of the border questions. In reporting to Mr. Evarts his
first conferences with Mr. Vallarta, the Mexican Minister of Foreign Affairs, however, Foster stated that assurances of a proper
settlement were expected on the following points: The Rio
Grande frontier trouble; the *Zona Libre*; the proper disposition
of the Indians in Coahuila and Chihuahua; the rectification of

the boundary of the Rio Grande, or the recognition of rights rendered uncertain consequent on the changes of the channel of said river; the abolition of the law which prevents American citizens from holding real estate in Mexico on the frontier; the exemption of American residents in Mexico from forced loans; the recognition and adjustment of claims of Americans arising from the Diaz revolution in 1871-72; the complaints for the seizure of the American vessels *Dreadnaught* and *Montana* at Mazatlan and outrages at Acapulco (including the imprisonment of Consul Sutter). On August 31, he reported the Mexican indisposition to adjust any questions except the border troubles, especially mentioning strenuous opposition to a treaty stipulation for reciprocal crossing, refusal to exempt Americans from forced loans, inability to abolish the *Zona Libre* and denial of responsibility for certain claims.[21]

Foster (on September 4), after an interview with General Diaz and six prolonged conferences with Vallarta at which were discussed all the important questions between the two governments, reported that no single question had been satisfactorily adjusted, although several had been postponed with hope of some acceptable arrangement or from habit of procrastination. The proposed repeal of the Free Zone, although considered constitutionally desirable, was declined on grounds of political expediency. Questions postponed were the disposition of the Indians, changes in the Rio Grande channel affecting the boundary, the right of Americans to hold real estate on the Mexican frontier, the recognition and adjustment of American claims arising from the Diaz revolution of 1871-72, and American complaints concerning certain recent outrages at Acapulco. In the conferences the Rio Grande frontier troubles received most of the attention and approached more nearly to an agreement, although (chiefly because of the question of reciprocal crossing of the border) no adjustment was reached. The American proposal for a reciprocal crossing of troops in pursuit of raiders, regarded as a *sine qua non* by Foster, was resisted by the Mexican government at every step. In the second conference, Vallarta suggested that President Diaz would be "willing to agree to the crossing of troops in pursuit of wild Indians, or in the desert and unpopulated regions of the frontier, upon condition that the instructions to General Ord (of June 1) would be withdrawn and disavowed and that reparation be made by the government of the United States for armed invasion of Mexican territory." Foster replied that no such disavowal or reparation could be made and that, if demanded, the conference should terminate at once. Declaring that the instructions to General Ord were completely justified by the circumstances and not satisfied with the proposed limited permission to cross on the upper Rio Grande, he suggested that the objections of Mexico could be met by two limitations on the crossing at any point: (1) when troops of the other nation were stationed on the opposite bank ready to continue the pursuit and (2) when the police and civil organization of the larger towns on the Mexican side was sufficient to render capture probable. He declined to accept the new counter proposition of Diaz to confer on the executives of the two countries the power to concede and regulate the permission by mutual consent, because it avoided and postponed the main issue. In the final conference he was promised a later written proposition which Vallarta thought would prove satisfactory and acceptable.[22]

The question of widest difference in the conferences was the proposed reciprocal exemption of citizens from forced loans or other arbitrary exactions. Foster, who urged the wisdom of the adoption of a reform policy recognizing and enforcing the principle of the illegality of forced loans in line with the recent decision of the Mexican supreme court, encountered the objection that the exemption would place foreigners in a condition superior to natives and that Mexico should not be expected to enforce constitutional guarantees as strictly as the American government or other older governments. Two months later, he reported that Vallarta had more plainly taken the position that a government is not responsible for damages sustained by foreigners during a revolution or insurrection—a defense which Foster said was used by Diaz and his officials to avoid responsibility for their own acts.[23]

Thus, according to Foster's dispatches, the Diaz government not only refused to give any assurances as to any of the points presented, but even disavowed the apologies and the salute of the American flag at Acapulco by local authorities for the outrage of the imprisonment of the American consul at that port, stating that their act was extra-official.

Although American considerations of prudence dictated the delay in the first steps toward American recognition, the refusal of the Diaz government to enter upon any settlement of the questions pending between the two countries (questions involving the rights and protection of American citizens) was responsible for the subsequent delay.

On September 10, Foster, feeling that his government misapprehended the Mexican situation and the spirit of the Diaz government, suggested a leave of absence of twenty days to visit Washington to confer with President Hayes and Secretary Evarts at the Department of State, but the latter did not approve the visit at that time. Strained relations continued—but fortunately without a clash on the Rio Grande frontier. On September 11, interpreting the Mexican attitude, Foster expected the rejection of all American terms. Two months later (November 12), he reported a growing bitterness and a general belief that the American policy aimed to provoke a conflict and that war was almost inevitable. Referring to the hostile feeling of Mexico, which was due in part to American delay in recognizing Diaz and had increased after the recent crossing of Lieutenant Bullis and Colonel Shafter, and especially from the belief that the latter had shown a disposition to battle with the Mexican troops, he reported to Evarts that the Mexican Senate would ratify no treaty resulting from conditions precedent to recognition. On November 17, he announced the apparent resolution of the Diaz government to make no concession and asked whether he should modify any of the American positions. On November 28, after further conferences which were embarrassed by the Mexican refusal to agree upon the frontier questions until after an American disavowal of Colonel Shafter's act in crossing the border, he wired that the Mexican government declined to consider any question until after official recognition which was demanded as a right with no condition precedent, and that it had assumed a more hostile attitude and had sent two thousand troops to Matamoros. He was almost tempted to indulge in undiplomatic personalities. To the Minister of Relations, who had spoken bitterly against the course of the Texan government in border matters, he retorted in kind by referring to the reckless conduct and character of the governor of Chihuahua who was known as an habitual drunkard. On December 1, he announced that Diaz, probably in response to newspaper demands for alliance with Spanish America, had submitted to Congress a proposed law establishing a mission to the South American republics.[24]

Meantime, in the United States, the Hayes administration was accused of plans to provoke war with Mexico in order to divert attention from domestic affairs and with a view to annexation of the northern states of Mexico. The special session of Congress which met at the call of the President in October, 1877, showed considerable hostility to the Mexican policy of the President, forcing Secretary Evarts to appear in defense before the House Committee on Foreign Affairs and to call Foster from Mexico to testify on the situation. Although Evarts admitted he might find necessary the abandonment of his efforts to obtain an understanding as a prerequisite to recognition, he expected a diplomatic break if the Mexican government continued to neglect the border and to oppose American military crossing of the border in hot pursuit of raiders.[25]

President Hayes, in his annual message of December 3, 1877 —although he admitted that the general American custom in cases of previous changes of government in Mexico had been to recognize the *de facto* government as soon as it had the approval of the Mexican people and showed a disposition to adhere to treaty obligations and international friendship—stated that official recognition of the Diaz government had been deferred by the continuance of border disorders on the Rio Grande, which he regarded with some solicitude and which necessitated the constant employment of a military force in that vicinity. While he did "not anticipate an interruption of friendly relations with Mexico," he looked with "some solicitude upon a continuance of border disorders as exposing the two countries to initiations of popular feeling and mischances of action which are naturally unfavorable to complete amity." On December 4, in reply to the Mexican protest against the recent crossing of Colonel Shafter into Mexico, Evarts stated that General Ord would investigate and would prevent the crossing of American troops except when in hot pursuit or on a fresh trail of marauders. Two days later, at the Department of State, he conferred with Zamacona, who appeared as a confidential agent of Mexico with a letter of introduction from Foster, to endeavor to remove prevailing American erroneous impressions as to the hostile intent of the movement of Mexican troops on the border. On January 2, he informed Foster that the recent manifestation of cooperation of Mexican troops with American troops under Lieutenant Ward (in December) in following the trails in pursuit of hostile thieves into Mexican territory was gratifying and that such cooperation if continued would tend not only to repress depredations but to the renewal of diplomatic intercourse; but he later learned from Foster's dispatch of January 17 that the Mexican Minister of War had taken steps to punish the subaltern officer of the Mexican troops who had cooperated with Ward (in what was regarded as a new invasion of Mexican territory) and had repeated the Mexican orders of June 18 "to repel force with force" to prevent the crossing of American troops—orders which Foster, in a note informing Vallarta of his expected departure for Washington, took occasion to characterize as "highly inopportune." [26]

Before the end of the year, Foster, whose course concerning recognition was approved by Evarts, foresaw a possible modification of the policy of the Hayes administration. On December 14, after reading a newspaper report that the American Secretary of War and General Sherman before the House Military Committee had expressed themselves adverse to the proposed stipulation for reciprocal crossing which had been the chief obstacle to the success of all his negotiations and had embarrassed him personally, he suggested to Evarts that if this stipulation and the question of forced loans should be waived he could probably reach an agreement for the settlement of the other questions. Finally, late in January, 1878, in response to a summons of January 5 to appear before the House Committee on Foreign Affairs which was investigating conditions on the Rio Grande frontier, he went to Washington under Evarts' instructions (of December 31) and testified concerning the frontier situation, the stability of the Diaz government and its disposition toward Americans and American enterprises. On February 9, during his absence, Richardson, who was left in charge, reported that Diaz, who had been elevated to the presidency by the almost unanimous vote of Mexico and had shown more energy than any other Mexican President in preserving order on the Rio Grande, would not give guarantees for the performance of international obligations—because such guarantees would be virtually a purchase of recognition.[27]

Foster in connection with his evidence, desiring to discourage Mexican hopes of American public condemnation of the Hayes policy, advised against any appearance of criticism of the executive by Congress or any action directing the President to recognize the Diaz government except by his own voluntary act based upon his judgment and discretion. He admitted that recognition was desirable in the interest of the development which the Mexican government was anxious to foster, and he hinted that it should not be determined by Mexican neglect of the Rio Grande frontier disorders—a neglect which he said was caused by inability rather than by indisposition. Apparently he greatly influenced the policy of Evarts who instructed him upon his return to Mexico to extend recognition, in order to relieve the embarrassment of the Diaz administration in its pre-recognition discussions of pending differences, but directed him to follow the action by vigorous efforts to obtain from the new government a consideration of permanent measures to prevent frontier lawlessness, to protect American interests in Mexico and to settle various other subjects of American complaint.[28]

Secretary Evarts in his oral instructions to Foster probably discussed the possibility of war which the written instructions sought to avoid. He thought that the continued cattle-stealing raids from Mexico and the apparent indifference of Mexican troops, which seemed unable to suppress them, justified the American consideration of plans for more effective pursuit and capture of the Mexican marauders. This possibly explains the instruction of Assistant Secretary F. W. Seward of April 10, 1878, inclosing a letter of the Secretary of War requesting that Foster procure printed maps of the Mexican border states and Lower California.[29]

Following the decision of the administration to recognize the Mexican *de facto* government, the House Committee on Foreign Affairs at Washington, while admitting the right of the Mexican people to determine their government, approved the tardy policy of the American government in deciding the question of the recognition of successful leaders of a revolution which threatened "the downfall of republican constitutional order in Mexico." In justification of the long delay it said: "One of the conditions entitling a *de-facto* government to recognition is that it demonstrates its power in its own country. General Diaz may have had, and no doubt did have, power in the greater portion of Mexico, but where it was most material for us that power should be exercised, that is, on our border, it was certainly demonstrated that he did not have it." Considering the annoyances and sufferings and spoliations to which American citizens had been subjected in Mexico, and which remained unredressed, it had urged that the American government, in response to the needs of American foreign markets and other expanding interests, should adopt a more decided and a more active and intelligently directed policy, especially in the protection of American citizens abroad. It declared that the Mexican government must either give to the citizens of other nations the protection of its laws or be held responsible for its indifference or neglect of duty.[30]

In its lengthy report of April 25, 1878, the Committee recommended an adequate military force on the border in Texas, the continuation of the order to cross the boundary if necessary in pursuit until a suitable treaty stipulation could be obtained for equally efficient protection, the negotiation of a treaty providing a method of indemnification for American losses for which the Mexican government was responsible, a treaty provision for the abolition of the Mexican Free Zone, and an amendment to the extradition treaty or some other arrangement to secure speedy trial and punishment of criminals (who resided on either side of the boundary) in courts within whose jurisdiction the crimes were committed, and also treaty stipulations for exemption of Americans in Mexico from forced loans and other illegal exactions there. It declared that recent events had clearly demonstrated that a permanent military force on the border was the only guaranty of peace. It especially condemned the Mexican manner of plundering merchants by forced loans which, although declared illegal by the Mexican supreme court, was still exacted by the Diaz government contrary to the constitution and the laws.[31]

That the American government was embarrassed and its activity restricted by the provisions of its extradition treaty with Mexico was commonly recognized. According to the committee report, "one of the worst causes of the crimes committed by Mexicans in Texas" was the easy escape of the criminals to an asylum or sanctuary where they were free from punishment and from which they were not extraditable under the extradition treaty then in force. In theory the Mexican government punished Mexican citizens for crimes committed outside of Mexican territory, but in practice crimes committed by Mexicans in Texas were not punished. The Mexican local courts, regarding such crimes as international and under treaty provisions, took no cognizance. The Mexican extradition officers in reply to demands for extradition of criminals explained that the treaty was not applicable to Mexicans who were accused of committing crimes in Texas. In one case (the Corpus Christi raid), Foster reported that the criminals were arrested; but, later, he reported that they were released without punishment. By proving Mexican citizenship they escaped trial and punishment, the means by which society is protected. General Ord testified that the practical effect of the extradition treaty was to serve as an excuse to shield criminals from punishment. The situation seemed to justify active hot pursuit of the criminals into Mexican territory as the only hope for an immediate practical remedy.[32]

In considering whether a commercial treaty could increase American facilities for trade with Mexico, the House committee reported adversely—partly because of the objections of Congress to Romero's proposition for American abatement of the duty on sugar, and partly because of the Mexican fear that the American purpose in negotiating such a treaty was "peaceable conquest . . . by the industrials, the merchants, by millions of immigrants." It regarded as far more practical the increase of facilities for communication with Mexico by government encouragement of the regular steamship lines to Vera Cruz, and especially, and far more promising, the extension of one or more American railways into Mexico along the high tableland region from Mexico City to the Rio Grande—a natural route with not a noticeable river to be crossed. It suggested, however, that treaties should secure the safety of capital invested in such enterprises by providing for protection by the American government in case of the inability or failure of the Mexican government to furnish proper protection. It renewed the suggestion whether American trade would not be increased by abolishing the facilities for transit of foreign goods under bond across American territory into Mexico.[33]

Foster, who, during his absence at Washington, and who, while using his efforts there to convince the President and Secretary Evarts that further delay of recognition was not expedient or advisable, had been attacked by Mexican newspapers as the only obstacle to American recognition. He returned to Mexico with Secretary Evarts' instructions of March 23, which authorized him to recognize the Diaz government and to enter into negotiations for the settlement of all pending questions. On April 11, promptly after his arrival at the Mexican capital, he opened official relations. Immediately after recognition, he was honored by a banquet given by President Diaz to celebrate the event which marked the beginning of a new era of friendly relations and gave to the American minister a more pleasant social position in Mexico. Official recognition at Washington, deferred by occurrences on the Rio Grande frontier, was finally announced by Secretary Evarts early in May, 1878, when a formal reception was accorded to the new Mexican minister, Zamacona, appointed by Diaz on April 11. Later, at his legation home, Foster introduced to President Diaz the charming young lady who, although the daughter of Diaz's former political foe (Señor Romero Rubio), became the popular Mrs. Diaz, the "first lady" of the land, whose influence on the soldier-president and his administration was undoubted.[34]

In his efforts to execute his new instructions from Evarts, Foster encountered the usual Mexican delays incident to diplomatic negotiations and, also, new complications resulting from Mexican irritation aroused by Lerdist revolutionary activities in Texas and the crossing of the border by American troops in hot pursuit of marauders. Finally, he was presented with a Mexican demand to the American government for withdrawal of the Ord order before the resumption of further negotiations.

One of Foster's earliest acts after recognition was to inform his government that Mexican insurgents in Texas were preparing to invade Mexico and to suggest the necessity of prompt military action to preserve neutrality. He promptly began conferences on frontier affairs, especially on an arrangement for the crossing of troops. Mexico countered with a request for indemnity for past violations of territory and a withdrawal of Ord's instructions—to which Foster could not accede. On May 2, he recommended a firm policy as to the crossing with the expectation that Mexico would accede. On May 23, he reported that Diaz had asked the Mexican Senate to authorize a stipulation for reciprocal crossing. A week later, he announced the Senate's approval; but further action was postponed by the adjournment of Congress (on May 31) and a change in the office of Minister of Relations. On June 27, he reported the new Mexican proposition of Mata for reciprocal crossing in pursuit of Indians upon condition that the American government first withdraw the Ord instructions; and, on July 15, he forwarded the Mexican protest against the crossing of Shafter on June 17 as tending to defeat the American negotiations for settlement of pending difficulties, and also announced the Mexican intimation of a possible break of negotiations.[35]

In July, in protesting against the reasons alleged by Mata for breaking or changing the course of negotiations for a peaceful solution, Foster made a reference to President Diaz which was mistakenly regarded as a diplomatic impropriety.

"It may be true, as your excellency set forth in your note," said he, "that to a limited extent bands of Mexican revolutionists have crossed over from Texas into Mexico with the object of overthrowing the existing government of this country, and after their reverses have fled to the territory of the United States in order to cross again to their own country to continue their attacks upon the existing order of things. But in setting forth so minutely the alleged state of recent events on the Rio Grande, your excellency, unintentionally perhaps, has described with perfect accuracy the experience and treatment had by the present chief of the Mexican Republic on the same frontier only two years ago. . . . He fully understands how a Mexican leader can successfully organize a revolutionary movement in American territory without violating the neutrality laws, and how difficult it is for the government to prevent such movements." Continuing he said: "It is well known that the revolution carried on by General Diaz occasioned several grave complaints on the part of the Government of the United States. . . . Ever since the success of the revolution and the establishment of its government, I have been using constant and persistent efforts to secure a settlement of all these disagreeable and serious complaints. But I have been met by delays, postponements, denials of justice, or absolute rejection of the just demands of my government, and up to the present date I have not been able to obtain a satisfactory settlement of a single one of these questions." [36]

Early in August, Mexico was alarmed by rumors of American hostile intentions and probable rupture of diplomatic relations which indicated that the prospects of the settlement of pending questions seemed more remote than ever; but, by August 15, the *Diario Oficiel* stated that recent explanations of Secretary Evarts at a cordial conference with the Mexican minister at Washington justified the expectation of amicable settlement. Later in August, in a conference with Mata and President Diaz concerning the critical situation on the border, Foster proposed a joint expedition against the Indians which was peremptorily rejected by Diaz except on condition of the revocation of the Ord order. In his interview, he referred to the Mexican government's proposition of July, 1851, for the reciprocal crossing of troops—a proposition on which Diaz said he would be ready to conclude a convention subject to the revocation of Ord's instructions. On September 19, coincident with the retirement of Mata, Foster reported that he had received from the Mexican Foreign Office an offer to agree to such an executive convention upon the precedent condition of withdrawal of the Ord instructions—which was regarded as a *sine qua non*.[37]

Mexican hostility had reached another climax. Even Señor Matias Romero, who had so long been friendly to the American government and people, in a semi-official paper declared that the American administration was hostile to Mexico and seeking motives or pretexts for the creation of difficulties in relations. On September 15, at the Mexican anniversary celebration at the theater, Foster witnessed the excited, unthoughtful and discourteous reading of a fierce anti-American poem which aroused the thoughtless audience to a frenzy of anti-American shouts. The incident, although disapproved by Diaz, furnished the press an opportunity to circulate alarming rumors—including the rumors of a break of diplomatic relations and charges of an American policy to seek hostilities with a view to annexation or a protectorate. On September 23, and in October, he reported the general Mexican expectation that the situation would result in war—and, apparently, the supposed danger of a foreign war restrained internal revolution against Diaz.[38]

On September 26, in declining Avila's invitation to make further suggestions with a view to Mexican action for prevention of injuries to the United States from the existence of the Free Zone, Foster, after reviewing the dilatory and evasive course of the Diaz government on the question, declared:

"When it is remembered that year after year, for ten years past, assurances have been given by the Mexican Executive that at the earliest convenient opportunity the subject would be presented to

Congress; when your honor's department has so unequivocally pronounced against the expediency of the existence of the zone; and when the present minister of finance, to whose department the subject belongs, has for years past been publicly known as a decided opponent of the *Zona Libre*—when these facts are called to mind, the continued delay of the Executive in proposing to Congress its abolition greatly strengthens the conviction, so prevalent in the United States, that the Mexican Government does not possess the requisite ability or disposition to discharge its international obligations on the Rio Grande frontier."

In his dispatch of October 14 to Evarts he stated that no question in Mexican international relations more clearly illustrated the incapacity of the Diaz government to discharge its plain duty toward the United States.[39]

Foster, feeling that the original question of recognition was becoming a contest for the control of American public opinion, urged his government to continue its policy of firmness. In refutation of Mexican claims of American prospects for trade relations with Mexico, he published a letter of October 9 in which he presented the obstacles to American trade development resulting from Mexican prejudices against American enterprise in Mexico and from lack of Mexican protection to American citizens and American capital. At the close of October, with not a single pending question satisfactorily adjusted since the recognition of the Diaz government, which had been extended in response to hopeful suggestions and promises, and with most of the American demands unconditionally rejected, Foster prepared an abstract of pending business and announced his belief that the contemplated time had come "for use of plain language and vigorous measures" to prevent further prolongation of the unsettled condition of questions—especially of the two which appealed to American national honor and duty. He expressed the hope that the President in his message would treat the Mexican question with vigor and in a way to reach a settlement. In his abstract he mentioned the Mexican refusal of cooperation with American troops while awaiting acquiescence in the demand for the unconditional withdrawal of the Ord order, the Mexican failure to comply with the promise to repeal the Free Zone law, the neglect to repeal injurious Mexican laws which prohibited American citizens from acquiring lands in the Mexican border states, the refusal of the Diaz administration to recognize the important right of American citizens to exemption from forced loans, rejection or delay of American claims for reparation of damages (in various cases of arrest, imprisonment, or seizure) and the Mexican requirement of matriculation for foreign residents who sought to plead their foreign nationality in the Mexican courts or executive departments.[40]

Early in September, Foster had informed Secretary Evarts that secret Mexican agents were operating in the United States in hostility to the policy of President Hayes and to create sentiment in favor of Diaz. Later, on October 3, he wrote that General John B. Frisbie, opposed to the Hayes policy, would endeavor to influence the American Congress at its next session to revoke unconditionally the Ord order and to establish a joint American-Mexican commission for the settlement of all pending questions. On October 26, he furnished detailed information concerning the activities of W. T. Pritchard and C. E. Lester as secret agents of Mexico in the United States. Later, on December 16, he reported that the letter of attack on the Mexican policy of Evarts, which had been published in the New York *Sun*, was apparently prepared in the Mexican Foreign Office and submitted to the *Sun* by the Mexican minister at Washington. Later, in February, 1879, at Mexico City, members of a commercial excursion party from Chicago made irresponsible representations of Evarts' hostility which were willingly seconded by General Frisbie, and by Romero, the Mexican Minister of Finance, who, seven weeks before his resignation, published a statement charging that the Hayes administration was hostile to Mexico and seeking pretexts for difficulties.[41]

Evarts, meantime, had remained firm in his course. On August 13, after regretting the refusal of the Mexican government to modify the law establishing the troublesome Free Zone, and its failure to repress or to punish the Mexican raiders, he declared to Foster that the American government, although it sought no acquisition of Mexican territory and would prefer to be relieved of the necessity of pursuing Mexican raiders across the boundary, must act to repress the destructive raids if Mexico could not do so. Although he gratefully recognized signs of improved relations in the Mexican supreme court decision in favor of extradition of Mexicans to the United States by Mexico, in the aid of the alcalde of Las Vegas in the recovery of stolen cattle by United States troops, and in the later declarations of President Diaz's message, he soon found cause for new complaints in the report of an August raid led by one Ariola with cognizance of the commander of the Mexican troops. He instructed Foster to say that, in view of the ceaseless border turmoil, mere indemnification for actual losses would not be regarded as satisfactory reparation. At the same time, he was also disturbed by reports of the murder of an American citizen, Walter Henry, at Saltillo and the seizure of his effects by Mexican authorities—which he regarded as an indication of the inability of the Mexican authorities to protect life and enforce law on the Mexican side of the boundary. Later, he was disappointed by Foster's report of October 29 that not a single pending question had been adjusted since his recognition of the Diaz government, that most of the American demands had been unconditionally rejected, and that the time had now come for the use of plain language and vigorous measures. Nettled by the unsatisfactory Mexican reply that the Mexican government disavowed any accountability for the crimes of cattle stealing, he wrote the disheartened Foster: "Surely it does not mean to deny responsibility for acts committed by persons in its service." In November, he instructed Foster to take steps to prevent the proposed Mexican policy to make Bagdad the only port of entry in the *Zona Libre*.[42]

The President, in his message of December 2, 1878, naturally avoiding any direct admission that he had been defeated in the negotiations with Diaz, stated that, although no agreement had been reached with Mexico in regard to border troubles, much had been done by frontier forces to remove the sources of dispute and that at the earliest opportunity consistent with his duty he would recognize the ability of the Mexican government to restrain effectively violations of American territory. On the same day, however, Foster, after a prolonged diplomatic discussion on the subject of forced loans which discouraged the investment of foreign capital and which Americans regarded as a subject for diplomatic intervention, and after presentation of an abstract of the other questions pending, stated that the situation was "most unsatisfactory." By December 10, he declined further discussion of forced loans as fruitless; and, on December 20, considering the disturbances and public insecurity and the failure of the Mexican Congress to approve American railway enterprise, he regarded the outlook as gloomy. He doubtless realized that the Hayes administration had been defeated in the vigorous diplomatic contest with the determined Diaz.[43]

In the early part of 1879, the difficulties of the situation concerning pending questions unadjusted were increased by new irritations. On March 26, Evarts asked Foster to protest against the Mexican prohibition on the admission of American citizens to the island of Ciare (in the Gulf of California) as a violation of the treaty of 1831. He declared that the Mexican law forbidding American citizens from holding real estate in Mexico was a discrimination incompatible with the spirit of the treaty. Later, in the American Congress, a proposition for a commission to negotiate with Mexico a treaty—a proposal which was approved by Foster who submitted subjects which should be embraced in the treaty—was introduced by a joint resolution which, however (in July) failed to pass either house. In February, 1880, in response to Foster's recommendation, the Navy Department stationed war vessels on the coasts of Mexico to observe the progress of affairs and to guard the interests of American citizens there.[44]

Before the close of Diaz's first administration, relations became more cordial. Although for a time the American government declined to recall the Ord order, no conflict of forces occurred and the crossing of American troops ceased with the better Mexican guarding of the frontier. Early in 1880, Evarts regarded as a valuable and hopeful precedent the trial and execution of Zeferino Avalos, a Mexican, in Mexico for a murder committed in Texas. When Foster visited Matamoros in the latter part of 1879, he was entertained by Mexican festivities which were attended by General Ord and he saw no evidences of the old border hostility. Returning to the capital by way of Vera Cruz, which he reached on a Mexican gunboat, he was honored by a dinner given by the President in the national Palace. He promptly reported the good disposition of the President on the frontier and in regard to restoration of order and peace. Before his departure to the Russian mission, to which he was appointed on January 19, 1880, he participated in the festivities to General Grant and his party, who, after a tour of the world, visited Mexico in March, 1880, as the guests of the Mexican government, and he returned by steamer to the United States with the Grants.[45]

Finally, the American government, satisfied with the improvements in the Diaz administration and the general prevalence of order, withdrew the Ord instructions of June 1, 1877, for crossing the border. Although Foster at the close of December, 1879, had recommended that the Ord instructions should remain in force, the Hayes administration soon thereafter decided otherwise. On February 19, 1880, Secretary Evarts in an interview with Zamacona, who in the previous May had sought a withdrawal of the orders, informed him that they would probably be withdrawn in a few days. On March 1, 1880, he informed Foster that the orders had been declared inoperative. On March 10 they were withdrawn.[46]

In the following July or August, Evarts learned from Foster's successor (Morgan) that the Mexican Minister of Relations had reiterated a desire to negotiate for an arrangement for crossing the border in pursuit of hostile Indians. In September, he saw reason for prompt action following an attack on American troops by a band of savage Indians (under command of Victoria), which after the attack had escaped into Mexico from American territory (but were finally dispersed by the combined and harmonious action of the military forces of the two nations). Assistant Secretary Hunter, by a cipher telegram, instructed Morgan to offer Mexico the alternative of permission for American troops to follow Victoria across the border or Mexican assumption of all responsibility arising from noncompliance with this request. Morgan promptly asked, as a courtesy, the consent to pursue the savage murderers, urging the necessity of action. He obtained an interview with President Diaz who said that Congress had authorized him to enter into a convention for reciprocal crossing of troops but that any arrangement for entry of foreign troops without consent of the Senate was prohibited by the constitution. In the following month, after learning from Mariscal that Diaz had favored a reciprocal consent for pursuit for ninety days, he reported opposition in the Senate which prorogued for three months the authority granted to the President in May, 1878. He suggested the hope that the Indian raids might be terminated by the extension of railways and a consequent current of immigration to populate the deserts. A satisfactory adjustment of the Indian question was not finally reached until July 29, 1882, when, by an agreement between Secretary Frelinghuysen and Romero, the American government obtained a temporary provision for reciprocal right to pursue savage Indians across the respective boundaries—based upon Mexican terms which Secretary Frelinghuysen accepted. This agreement was later modified by another of September 2, 1882, and was renewed by later agreements.[47]

Before the close of 1880 other sources of controversy arose. In June, 1880, in a letter of May 10 from the governor of Texas, Secretary Evarts encountered a new source of Texas complaint—the diversion of the waters of the Rio Grande by Mexicans. To this was soon added another—the impressment of American citizens (Texans) into Mexican military service, and the requirement that they could be released only by application to the Mexican courts. In October and November the impressment question reached a critical stage. On October 27, Morgan, in accord with his instructions from Washington, demanded the immediate release of several Texas citizens (of Mexican names) who had been impressed into the Mexican army, and he requested a reasonable pecuniary indemnity for their detention and also measures to prevent such impressments in the future. To the response of Fernandez that the courts of Mexico were open to consider such complaints, he replied (on November 5) protesting against the doctrine that release from unlawful duress could be obtained only by the ordinary process of law. He declared that the case, involving the comity of nations and fulfilment of treaty obligations, was one which necessitated diplomatic intervention. On December 22, a new American complaint, concerning the harsh or unjust enforcement of Mexican customs regulations by the revenue authorities at La Paz, was presented as a subject of public policy by Acting Secretary John Hay.[48]

At the same time, improved relations were influenced by the improvement of Mexican political conditions in the latter part of the first administration of Diaz, who determined the choice of his successor, General Manuel Gonzales, according to the forms of law. The freedom from revolution by 1880, resulting from the fact that the chief revolutionists were in power, gave freedom from forced loans. Diaz—after serving under the peaceful administration of Gonzales, first as Minister of Fomento (until May, 1881) and for a time (in 1882) as a member of the supreme court and, also, as senator—visited the United States early in 1883. Escorted by General Foster, he was received in triumph as the guest of the nation. In November, 1884, he was reelected to the presidency in which he continued to serve his country as a master director of its policies for over a quarter of a century thereafter, during which conflicts with the American government were adjusted before they reached a crisis and the peaceful penetration of American economic interests was encouraged by the Mexican government.[49]

REFERENCES

1. *For. Rels.*, *1877*, p. 410; *House Rp. 701*, 45-2, App. C, p. 316; *59 Mexico, Despatches*, (Unofficial and Confidential) Apr. 28, and June 20, 1877.
2. *Ib.*, (No. 511) March 24, (Unofficial) Apr. 28, 1877.

3. *19 Mexico, Instructions,* (No. 377) March 27, (No. 390) May 16, 1877; *For. Rels., 1877,* p. 403; *House Rp. 701,* 45-2, App. G, p. 447.

4. *Ib.,* App. B, pp. 235-38; *House Exec. Doc. 13,* 45-1, pp. 4 and 14-15; *For. Rels., 1877,* p. 401; *19 Mexico, Instructions,* p. 328, No. 379, March 31, 1877.

5. *House Rp. 701,* 45-2, App. B, p. 240, and App. A, pp. 65 and 239; *House Exec. Doc. 13,* 45-1, p. 12; *19 Mexico, Instructions,* No. 392, May 28, 1877.

6. *House Rp. 701,* 45-2, p. xvi, and App. B, p. 241.

7. *Ib.,* App. A, p. 63, and App. B, p. 253; *House Exec. Doc. 13,* 45-1, p. 14; *For. Rels., 1877,* p. 405; *19 Mexico, Instructions,* p. 350, June 9, and June 21, 1877.

8. *House Rp. 701,* 45-2, App. B, pp. xvi, 242-52, and 257-62; *59 Mexico, Despatches,* (No. 552) June 21, (No. 560) June 23, (Confidential) June 30, and July 24, 1877.

9. *Ib.,* (No. 560) June 28, and (Confidential) June 30, 1877; *House Exec. Doc. 13,* 45-1, p. 28.

10. *For. Rels., 1877,* p. 419; *House Rp. 701,* 45-2, App. B, p. 263; *59 Mexico, Despatches,* July 13, 1877.

11. Foster, *Diplomatic Memoirs,* I, pp. 92-93.

12. *59 Mexico, Despatches,* (Confidential and Unofficial) May 16, 1877; *19 Mexico, Instructions,* May 29, 1877.

13. H. H. Bancroft, *History of California,* III, p. 750; Thomas J. Gregory, *History of Solano and Napa Counties; World's Work,* Feb., 1909; *19 Mexico, Instructions,* p. 334, (B. Confidential) May 5, 1877.

14. *59 Mexico, Despatches,* May 28, 1877; *Misc. Letters,* June, 1877, Part II.

15. *19 Mexico, Instructions,* p. 543, (B) June 1, 1877.

16. *60 Mexico, Despatches,* (Unofficial) July 30, 1877.

17. *For. Rels., 1877,* p. 410; *House Rp. 701,* 45-2, App. G. pp. 448-50; *59 Mexico, Despatches,* No. 550, June 20, 1877 (Enclosure).

18. *Ib.,* June 28, and (Confidential) June 30, and July 24, 1877; *House Rp. 701,* 45-2, App. B, pp. 257-62.

19. *19 Mexico, Instructions,* (No. 395) June 21; *59 Mexico, Despatches,* (No. 572) July 9, 1877; *House Exec. Doc. 13,* 45-1, pp. 13 and 15; *House Rp. 701,* 45-2, App. B, pp. 254-57.

20. *Ib.,* App. G, pp. 450-51 and p. xxxix; *19 Mexico, Instructions,* pp. 354-58, No. 407, Aug. 2, 1877.

21. *60 Mexico, Despatches,* Aug. 19; *61 Mexico, Despatches,* (Unofficial) Dec. 14, 1877; *House Rp. 701,* 45-2, p. xxxix.

22. *Ib.,* App. G, pp. 451-54; *60 Mexico, Despatches,* Nos. 597 and 598, Sept. 4, 1877.

23. *Ib.*, (No. 599) Sept. 4, (No. 626) Nov. 8, 1877; *House Rp. 707*, 45-2, App. G, pp. 454-57.

24. FOSTER, *Diplomatic Memoirs*, I, p. 94; *19 Mexico, Instructions*, Sept. 10, 1877; *60 Mexico, Despatches*, (No. 629) Nov. 12; *61 Mexico, Despatches*, (Nos. 635 and 636) Nov. 28, (No. 637) Nov. 29, and (No. 639) Dec. 1, 1877.

25. C. R. WILLIAMS, *Life of R. B. Hayes*, II, pp. 209-10; *House Misc. Doc. 64*, 45-2; *61 Mexico, Despatches.*

26. *House Rp. 701*, 45-2, App. A, pp. 64-65; RICHARDSON, *Messages and Papers of the Presidents*, VII, 468; *19 Mexico, Instructions*, (No. 430) Dec. 4, 1877, and Jan. 4, 1878; *29 Notes from Mexico*, Dec. 6, 1877; *61 Mexico, Despatches*, (No. 662) Jan. 17, 1878; *For. Rels., 1878.*

27. *19 Mexico, Instructions*, (No. 436) Dec. 14, and (No. 437) Dec. 31, 1877, and (Tel.) Jan. 5, 1878; *61 Mexico, Despatches*, (Unofficial) Dec. 14, 1877, and Feb. 9, 1878; FOSTER, *Diplomatic Memoirs*, II, p. 95.

28. *For. Rels., 1878*, p. 544 (Foster to Evarts, Mar. 23, 1878).

29. *19 Mexico, Instructions*, p. 404, (No. 462) Apr. 10, and p. 411, (No. 473) May 31, 1878.

30. *House Rp. 701*, 45-2, Apr. 25, 1878, pp. xxxvii and xxxviii.

31. *Ib.*, pp. xli and xlii, xix and xxvii.

32. *Ib.*, pp. xxii and xxiii and App. G, p. 461.

33. *Ib.*, pp. xxiii-vi.

34. *61 Mexico, Despatches*, (No. 678) Mar. 14; *62 Mexico, Despatches*, (No. 689) Apr. 11, and (No. 691) Apr. 12, 1878; *19 Mexico, Instructions*, (No. 457) Mar. 23, and p. 408, May 8, 1878; FOSTER, *Diplomatic Memoirs*, I, p. 95; *For. Rels., 1878*, p. 675.

35. *62 Mexico, Despatches*, (Tel.) Apr. 28, (No. 708) May 23, (No. 714) May 30, (No. 735) June 27, (No. 740) July 15, 1878.

36. *For. Rels., 1878*, Vol. I, p. 558 (Enclosure in Foster's No. 740 of July 15).

37. *63 Mexico, Despatches*, (No. 750) Aug. 6, and Aug. 12, (No. 767) Aug. 24; *64 Mexico, Despatches*, (No. 785) Sept. 19, 1878; *For. Rels., 1878*, p. 608.

38. *64 Mexico, Despatches*, (No. 787) Sept. 21, (No. 806) Oct. 10, 1878; FOSTER, *Diplomatic Memoirs*, I, pp. 101 and 103.

39. *64 Mexico, Despatches*, No. 807, Oct. 14, 1878; *For. Rels., 1878*, pp. 654-57.

40. FOSTER, *Diplomatic Memoirs*, I, p. 115; *65 Mexico, Despatches*, (No. 822) Oct. 29, (Confidential and Unofficial) Oct. 30, 1878.

41. *63 Mexico, Despatches* (No. 775) Sept. 5, and (Personal) Sept. 9; *64 Mexico, Despatches*, Oct. 3, (No. 810) Oct. 26, 1878; *66 Mexico, Despatches*, Feb. 8, and (No. 888) Feb. 15, 1879.

42. *19 Mexico, Instructions*, p. 425, (No. 494) Aug. 10, (No. 495) Aug. 13, (No. 497) Aug. 16, p. 436, (No. 502) Aug. 31, (Unofficial) Nov. 12, (No. 514) Sept. 20, (No. 509) Sept. 14, (No. 550) Nov. 10, and (No. 537) Nov. 15, 1878; *65 Mexico, Despatches*, (No. 822) Oct. 29, and Oct. 30, 1878.

43. *19 Mexico, Instructions*, (No. 548) Dec. 2; *65 Mexico, Despatches*, (No. 850) Dec. 10, and (No. 859) Dec. 20, 1878.

44. *19 Mexico, Instructions*, (No. 609) Mar. 26; *20 Mexico, Instructions*, (No. 655) July 17, 1879, and (No. 721) Feb. 19, 1880.

45. FOSTER, *Diplomatic Memoirs*, I, pp. 105, 135-41; *20 Mexico, Instructions*, p. 73, (No. 713) Jan. 23, 1880; *69 Mexico, Despatches*, (No. 1078) Dec. 27, 1879; *For. Rels.*, *1880*, p. 726.

46. *Ib.*, p. 735; *20 Mexico, Instructions*, No. 727, Mar. 1, 1880.

47. *For. Rels.*, *1880*, pp. 764, 768 and 774, 1881 (No. 121, Morgan to Evarts, Oct. 16, 1880), and 1882 (No. 309, Acting Secretary Davis to Morgan, Aug. 18, 1882); *70 Mexico, Despatches*, (No. 63) July 24; *71 Mexico, Despatches*, (No. 102) Sept. 21, 1880; *20 Mexico, Instructions*, (No. 271) June 6, and (No. 349) Dec. 15, 1882.

48. *Ib.*, (No. 25) June 12, (No. 80) Dec. 8, and Dec. 22, 1880; *71 Mexico, Despatches*, (No. 125) Oct. 27, (No. 133) Nov. 13 (Enclosures), 1880; *For. Rels.*, *1880 and 1881*, pp. 752-53.

49. *73 Mexico, Despatches*, No. 254, Morgan to Blaine, (Confidential) Aug. 13, 1881.

CHAPTER XII

ADJUSTMENTS OF THE DIAZ ERA IN MEXICO

In American-Mexican relations the three decades from 1880 to 1911 were marked by a rapid improvement of border conditions coincident with a steady growth of centralized power under Diaz, greatly aided by American economic influence—especially in the construction of railroads—and resulting in a growth of friendly relations between the governments, and a growth of commerce. A reciprocity treaty was signed in 1882, the troubles from the Free Zone and extradition were treated with respectful consideration, the southwestern boundary was re-marked in 1891-96, the California Pious Fund controversy was arbitrated by the Hague Court in 1902, difficulties resulting from the shifting of the Rio Grande and the Colorado were partially adjusted and a good understanding between the governments was manifested in various other ways.

In Mexico, Diaz, after dictating President Gonzales as his temporary successor for four years, from 1880 to 1884, served as president continuously from 1884 until his resignation, in 1911, to avoid bloodshed from revolution. In this long period he was favored by the long tenure of Ignacio Mariscal as Minister of Foreign Affairs (1871-72, 1880-83 and after June, 1885) and the long service of M. Romero in directing the Mexican legation at Washington (from 1882 until his death on December 30, 1898). In the United States, for practically the same period, from 1881 to 1913, the government was successively conducted by seven different executives under whom foreign policies were successively directed by twelve different secretaries of state, and the American legation in Mexico was successively under the direction of eleven different American diplomatic representatives of higher rank—serving with the rank of minister until December, 1898, and with the rank of ambassador thereafter.

The twelve American secretaries of state in this period, in the order of their service, were James G. Blaine (1881), Frederick T. Frelinghuysen (1881-85), Thomas F. Bayard (1885-89), Blaine (1889-92), John W. Foster (1892-93), Walter Q. Gresham (1893-95), Richard Olney (1895-97), John Sherman (1897-98), William R. Day (1898), John Hay (1898-1905), Elihu Root (1905-09), Robert Bacon (1909) and Philander C. Knox (1909-13). Two of these (Foster and Hay) had previous diplomatic experience. Five had previous service in the cabinet: Sherman as Secretary of the Treasury (1877-81); Gresham as Postmaster General and as Secretary of the Treasury under President Arthur; Olney as Attorney General (1893-95); Root as Secretary of War (1899-1904); and Knox as Attorney General (1901-04). Five had served in the United States Senate: Blaine (1876-81), Frelinghuysen (1866-69 and 1871-79), Bayard (1869-85), Sherman (1861-77 and 1881-97) and Knox (1904-09). Two had served in the lower house of Congress: Blaine (1863-76—as speaker in 1871-76) and Sherman (1855-61). Two had previous service as Assistant Secretary of State: Day (1897-98) and Bacon (1905-10).

The eleven American representatives who successively served at the American legation in Mexico City from 1880 to 1913 are here named in order of service with a brief statement of their larger previous achievements or services:

P. H. Morgan of Louisiana (born 1825) had studied law in Paris in 1841-46, had served in the Mexican War with the rank of lieutenant, had remained loyal to the Union in the Civil War (by residing in England) and had considerable legal experience—including membership of the Louisiana supreme court (1873-76) and a position as judge of the International Tribunal at Alexandria, Egypt (1876-81);

Henry R. Jackson of Georgia (born 1820) had served as a colonel in the Mexican War, as a judge of the superior court of Georgia (1849-53), as American minister to Austria (1853-58) and had been a brigadier general in the Confederate army;

Thomas C. Manning of Louisiana (born 1831) had three times been appointed as justice of the Louisiana supreme court 1864, 1877 and 1882—once (1877) as chief justice;

Edward S. Bragg of Wisconsin (born 1827) had served as a brigadier general in the Civil War and later as a member of Congress (1885-87). At the Democratic national convention of 1884 he had seconded the nomination of Cleveland;

Thomas Ryan of Kansas (born 1837) had served as a captain in the Civil War and later as a member of Congress (1877-89).

Isaac P. Gray of Indiana had been a colonel of cavalry in the Civil War and had served his state successively as president of the Senate, Attorney General (1880-81) and governor (1885-89).

Matt W. Ransom of North Carolina (born 1826) had served as a major general in the Confederate army and later in the United States Senate (1872-95).

Powell Clayton of Arkansas (born 1833) had attained the rank of brigadier general in the Civil War and had later served as governor of Arkansas (1869-71) and as a member of the United States Senate (1871-77).

Edwin Hurd Conger of Iowa (born 1843) had served as a captain in the Civil War and later as a member of Congress (1885-90), and had been in diplomatic service since 1890 (as minister to Brazil, 1890-93, and as minister to China, 1898-1905).

David E. Thompson (born 1854) had been successively a railroad employee, a manager of industrial institutions, and a journalist and banker, and had served as minister to Brazil (1902-05).

Henry Lane Wilson of Washington (born 1857), after experience as editor and lawyer and banker, had served as minister to Chile (1897-1905) and as minister to Belgium (1905-10). He had become active in politics in 1880 and was a delegate to the Republican national convention in 1896.

Blaine, who became Secretary of State in 1881, had been a colleague of Garfield in Congress for many years and had been a large factor in determining his selection for the Republican presidential candidate in 1880. Although without previous diplomatic experience, for nearly eighteen years as a member of Congress he had been in touch with national and international problems and policies whose study largely determined his own foreign policy, especially in relations with Mexico and all other Latin American countries—a policy to prevent wars and to cultivate cooperation and friendly commercial relations. Although ignorant of international law and diplomatic history, he had qualities of a diplomat and a rising interest in diplomatic problems. Regarding earlier American policy as too largely one of drift and watchful waiting, resulting perhaps chiefly from American isolation and aloofness from world politics, he planned to undertake a policy of more purposeful direction and encouragement of foreign enterprise in diplomacy. In the Mexican policy he began with suggestions in regard to tariffs, the evils of the Mexican Free Zone, trade relations of a reciprocal nature, and the questions of forced loans and prompt and impartial administration of justice—and, also, concerning friendship in American crises. To these suggestions Morgan replied that he had already expressed to Mexican officials the American views of these subjects so far as formal intercourse and the limited opportunities of social intercourse with the government had permitted, but that concerning them he had been unable to overcome Mexican prejudices and an unfriendly press. From his long dispatch, the chief purpose of which was to enable him "to appreciate the difficulties" of obtaining information and of impressing American views, Blaine received little encouragement.[1]

After instructions of June 1 and 16, outlining the general American-Mexican policy in regard to American enterprise in Mexico and in regard to the detailed applications of this policy to capital and commerce (which are treated in another chapter), Blaine directed attention promptly (1) to the removal of any Mexican suspicions of American disposition to obtain a cession of Mexican territory and (2) to the American desire fo: peace in Mexico and on the entire continent.

On June 16, feeling some concern about a dispute between Mexico and Guatemala in regard to boundaries and territorial jurisdiction which Guatemala brought to his attention, he suggested that America—by its friendly and frank policies and its recognized impartiality, and by its position as founder (and in some sense as the guarantor and guardian) of republican principles on the American continent—would be warranted in the tender of amicable counsel to the disputants to preserve tranquillity. On June 21, after further news of the dispute, he stated that the established policy of the American government, in

accord with the continental policy of the American republic to
refrain from territorial acquisition, and its enlarged policy of
interest in all Central American republics, gave it a right to use
its friendly offices to discourage any movement of any neighboring state which might tend to disturb the balance of power
between them. In this policy he asked the cooperation of Mexico
and suggested that a frank avowal of Mexican policy toward
neighboring states would fortify good feeling. He was especially
apprehensive that Guatemala, if hard pressed by Mexico, might
cede Soconusco to some European power which had recently
seemed anxious to get a footing on the Pacific.[2]

On July 9, when Morgan explained to Mariscal that Guatemala had requested the good offices of the American government, he was told that there was no necessity for arbitration,
that a convention to fix the boundaries had been signed, and
that Guatemala was responsible for any delay in the appointment of the commission. He found that Mexico was in no
humor to arbitrate the dispute. On July 15, while awaiting a
formal reply and when angry feeling seemed to threaten a war
which the American government desired to avoid, he obtained
a second interview at which in a conciliatory tone and manner
he firmly presented the American view: that a war once started
would probably become a war of conquest for Mexico which,
through a demand for the expenses of the war, might inaugurate
a further movement with the possible result of absorption of
all Central America and extension to the Isthmus of Panama;
that such a war would affect adversely the many vast schemes
of public improvement, transportation and communication
which were in progress of construction in Mexico and in which
the United States felt a natural interest; that such a conquest
of neighboring territory would greatly harm Mexico and set a
bad example to the world; and that the American government,
the pioneer of republican institutions, must view such territorial
changes with disfavor and must interpose to prevent actions
which threatened the common interests. He was told by Mariscal, in reply, that Mexico, after causing the evacuation of the
territory occupied by Guatemala troops without authority, and

after replacing the destroyed "monuments," would be ready to renew negotiations for a commission to survey the boundary. Early in August, he reported that the chief Mexican objection to arbitration was the disposition of Chiapas. A few days later, he reported that the Guatemala representative, Herrera, had queered the proposed arbitration by suggesting to Mariscal a settlement on the basis of a cession of Chiapas and Soconusco to Mexico on condition of the Mexican payment of an indemnity therefor. He also reported the rumor that the Mexican government was furious at the arbitration proposal, which was regarded as an insult, and that Mariscal had declared that his government, even at risk of war, would not accept it. On September 22, following an interview with Mariscal on September 21, he wrote Blaine:

"We parted on the best of terms but he left me more than ever convinced that nothing would prevent a war between Mexico and Guatemala unless a positive position is taken by the United States and I venture to suggest that unless the United States Government is prepared to announce to the Mexican Government that it will actively if necessary preserve the peace it would be the part of wisdom on our side to leave the matter where it is. Negotiations on the subject will not benefit Guatemala and . . . what we have already done in this direction has not tended to the increasing of cordial relations which I know it is so much your desire to cultivate."

On November 2, when the subject of the American proposal of arbitration was under general discussion in Mexico outside the Foreign Office, Morgan informed Blaine that since his residence in Mexico no other occurrence had excited so much bad feeling.[3]

In reply to Morgan's dispatch of September 22, Blaine, on November 28, wrote him as follows:

"It would be a matter of gravest disappointment if I found myself compelled to agree with you in your conclusion after your conversation with Mariscal. . . . To leave it where it is is impossible for it will not remain there. To put aside such an amicable intervention as an unfriendly intrusion or to treat it, as I regret to see the Mexican Secretary for Foreign Affairs seems disposed, as a partisan manifestation on be-

half of claims which we have not examined can certainly not contribute 'to the increasing of the cordial relations.' Moreover, 'to leave
the matter where it is' is to leave Mexico and Guatemala confronting
each other in armed hostility with the certainty . . . of leading to
actual collision . . . and another lamentable demonstration on this continent of the so-called right of conquest, the general disturbance of the
friendly relations of the American republics and the postponement
for an indefinite period of that community of purpose and unity of
interest upon the development of which depends the future prosperity
of these countries."

In reply to Mariscal's suggestion that General Barrios, President of Guatemala, was planning to get the influence of the
United States in order to further his ambition to become president of a unified Central America, Blaine declared that American interest in the union of Central America, which had been
urged upon Central America for many years, should certainly
not render unwelcome the proposal for friendly intervention.

"The United States has a sincere and deep interest in the prosperity
of the Spanish American republics," said he, "and is influenced by no
selfish considerations in its earnest efforts to prevent war between
them. It will continue its policy of peace even if it can not have the
great aid which the cooperation of Mexico would assure; and it will
hope at no distant day to see such concord and cooperation between
all the nations of America as will render war impossible."

Finding that the Mexican government was not inclined to
accept his offer of good offices for arbitration, Secretary Blaine
determined to repeat the offer.

"Press on Mariscal the views already submitted," said he, ". . . and
if Mexico refuses to join in establishing the principle of friendly arbitration for international differences on this continent I am compelled to
declare that the United States will consider a hostile demonstration
against Guatemala for the purpose of weakening her power as an act
not in harmony with friendly relations between the United States and
Mexico and injurious to the best interests of all republics of this continent." [4]

On November 29, 1881, the day following his instructions to
press the offer of arbitration in the Mexican dispute with Guate-

mala, and also following negotiations with the parties to the war of the Pacific, Blaine issued to Mexico and to the other independent states of America an invitation to attend at Washington on November 22, 1882, a congress to devise means for settlement of disputes without resort to arms and for mitigation of the horrors of war. Mariscal in his reply through Morgan, although he referred to the difficulty of finding a practical method to end war, approved the purpose of the proposed congress, eulogized the attitude of the American government, and announced that Mexico, no longer embarrassed by difficulties and serious inconveniences which had prevented participation in the congress recently projected by Colombia (with Chile, etc.), accepted with pleasure—regarding it compatible with national interest to send representatives.[5]

Meantime, Blaine in his enforced retirement (in December, 1881) resulting from the accession of Arthur to the presidency, felt keenly the partial abandonment of his foreign policy—until in 1889 when he welcomed the opportunity to vindicate that policy.

Frederick T. Frelinghuysen, who, under President Arthur, succeeded Blaine on December 19, 1881, had larger experience and a more conservative attitude than his immediate predecessor and conformed naturally to the regular traditions of the Department of State, leading him to reverse certain policies which Blaine had adopted with enthusiasm. He had represented New Jersey in the United States Senate in 1866-69 and in 1871-77. He had escaped experience in the diplomatic service by declining the honor of minister to Great Britain for which President Grant nominated him in July, 1870—a nomination which the Senate approved after much opposition from Sumner and Wilson.

Frelinghuysen modified considerably the policy of Blaine. He recalled the invitations to the proposed congress at Washington. He refrained from pressing upon Mexico the principle of arbitration in the Mexico-Guatemala dispute. Early in his period, however, in August, 1882, the Mexican and Guatemalan ministers at Washington signed a convention with basic stipulations for the final settlement of the boundary substantially in accord with the Mexican contention, but providing for arbitration by the President of the United States in case of disagreement concerning the delimitation of the boundary. Nearly three years later, when the Guatemala minister was again apprehensive of a war of conquest by Mexico and requested American influence to prevent it, the American government tendered its good offices in favor of peace between the American republics.[6]

Already, on July 29, 1882, a partial relief from the border lawlessness of the previous decade was sought in an agreement with Mexico (later renewed yearly for several years) providing for crossing the border by armed forces of either country in pursuit of Indians. Further relief was sought by a convention for the establishment of the international boundary by surveys conducted by reconnaissance parties and by an International Boundary Commission to erect proper monuments of stone and iron, to replace destroyed markers and to establish new ones, from the Rio Grande to the Pacific. In 1882-83 Frelinghuysen conducted with Romero at Washington much correspondence concerning Indian incursions across the border from the United States into Mexico—especially from San Carlos reservation to Sonora—and also concerning reciprocal passage of troops across the border and restoration of booty in possession of the raiders when captured. In connection with the Indian border troubles, Secretary Frelinghuysen in June, 1883, forwarded to Morgan a letter of General John C. Fremont, governor of Arizona Territory (to the Secretary of the Interior), proposing an arrangement with Mexico to remove the frontier Indians to Lower California. Without stating his own views, he asked Morgan to submit the suggestion to the Mexican government for its views thereon. In accord with his instructions, Morgan, on August 25, 1883, mentioned the proposed plan to Mariscal who seemed favorably inclined and agreed to mention it to President Diaz.[7]

At that time, the American government had considerable interest in parts of Lower California—due in part to American immigration. In February, 1883, Frelinghuysen instructed Morgan to apply to Mexico for permission to establish an American coaling station at Magdalena Bay; and, on March 27, he asked for the recognition of James C. Hale as consular agent there. In June, he reported to Morgan that the authorities of Lower California had given permission to land coal there free of duty, and announced that Hale (the consular agent) was also permitted to engage in business.[8]

On the lower Rio Grande, as a result of the Diaz system of keeping order, the American government was practically free from the embarrassments of Mexican raids into Texas and from the defiant attitude of lawless men across the river. In the case of Pedro Garcia, whose extradition was requested for his habit of abusing Texan officers from his retreat on the Mexican side of the river, the Mexican government agreed to stop Pedro's bad habits.

On the Rio Grande boundary, in 1884, arose several incidents which eventually resulted in a boundary-line treaty. In April, Frelinghuysen presented the American claim to jurisdiction over the island of Morteritos, one of the Rio Grande frontier islands on which Texan citizens complained that Mexican customs officers had recently seized their cattle. In July Frelinghuysen, reporting the failure of Congress to make an appropriation for the re-survey of the boundary line, stated that a request for an appropriation would be presented at the next session in time to authorize the completion of the work within the time fixed by the convention. At the same time, he instructed Morgan to ask for the withdrawal of the Mexican claim to Morteritos Island (in the Rio Grande) which according to the original survey belonged to the United States, and informed him that after the adjustment of this dispute the American government would consider the proposed convention to settle the ownership of other islands in the Rio Grande. On August 14, 1884, he sent additional instructions to press for the settlement of claims of American citizens against Mexico for the value of cattle seized by Mexican customs officials on the Rio Grande islands, refusing to allow reference of the claims to Mexican courts. By October 16, he was able to announce the Mexican renunciation of claim to Morteritos, although without adjustment of American claims for cattle seized there by Mexican officials (claims which were later pressed by Secretary Bayard), and at the same time he considered favorably the renewed request (of October 10) of the Mexican minister at Washington for a proposed convention for adjustment of the boundary made doubtful by changes in the bed of the Rio Grande.[9]

Among the American-Mexican questions which remained pending in an unsatisfactory condition in August, 1882, was the matriculation required by Mexico for alien residents before they were allowed to assert certain rights which according to Secretary Freylinghuysen were determined by international law. In September, Morgan presented to Mariscal a full statement of the American view that the rights of an alien under international law are inherent and can neither be created nor destroyed by Mexican law. Later, near the close of the Arthur administration, Frelinghuysen still found reason to deny the right of Mexico by municipal regulations to refuse to allow diplomatic intervention, although he recognized the Mexican right to place reasonable restrictions on foreign residents.[10]

Much of the correspondence of 1883 was in regard to cases of American claims, imprisonments, fines and extradition. In October, 1882, convinced of the failure of justice in the Mexican courts in the case of the murder of Walter Henry, and feeling that the report of the case by the Mexican government was unsatisfactory, Frelinghuysen had applied through Morgan for copies of papers showing the investigation proceedings in the case. Morgan, after considerable correspondence in which the Mexican government denied that the case was one for American diplomatic intervention, reported Mexican agreement to consider a complaint based on a charge of denial of justice. He finally received a report exonerating Mexican officials, and he announced that his duties on the case were ended by the willingness of Secretary Frelinghuysen to abide the action of the Mexican courts. Later, in 1885, Secretary Bayard complained of the delay of the Mexican government in submitting a statement of the court proceedings. Without further investigation and report, he was unable to reconcile the Mexican conclusion that there had been no failure of justice.[11]

A useful and significant incident in President Arthur's administration, in the spring of 1883, was the unusual reception to the successful General Diaz who, for a brief time released from public duties in Mexico, decided to embrace the opportunity to visit the United States. At the request of Secretary Frelinghuysen, General John W. Foster, postponing his departure on a mission to Madrid, met the distinguished visitor at the frontier to invite him to become the guest of the nation and to escort him and his wife and her parents to Washington where, after various attentions en route (via St. Louis, Chicago, Buffalo and New York), he and his party were the recipients of generous hospitalities by the American government—hospitalities which had a salutary effect in removing any remaining bitterness resulting from the American policy of delay in recognizing the revolutionary government of Diaz.

Steady improvement in relations was also greatly aided by extensions of railway communication to the frontier by 1881, and to the interior of Mexico by 1883-84, constructed with American capital—and also by connection of the telegraph systems of the two countries through the completion of a submarine cable in March, 1881.

Even before the opening of railway communications, many had believed that the geographic and political relations between the two countries, as well as their commercial welfare, justified mutual concessions in customs duties to improve trade conditions. On January 29, 1876, Foster, reporting that Mexico approved the general policy of reciprocity, had suggested that the time was opportune to open negotiations on the subject. On November 30, 1881, Blaine had received from the Mexican minister at Washington a note denouncing the treaty of 1831. His successor, Frelinghuysen, on January 11, 1882, resisting the termination of the treaty, instructed Morgan to furnish a memorandum of the Mexican objections to the treaty and to suggest that its provisions should remain in force until the conclusion of a new and improved treaty. On March 17, he telegraphed instructions to make a formal request for the prolongation of the old treaty until July 14. Favoring a reciprocity policy, on November 16, 1882, he inquired by wire whether Mexico would appoint commissioners to negotiate a new commercial treaty. As a result, on January 20, 1883, at Washington, special commissioners of the two governments—U. S. Grant, William H. Trescot, M. Romero and A. Cañedo—signed a treaty providing that certain merchandise from the United States would be admitted into Mexico free of duty and that certain products from Mexico would be admitted free into the United States. This treaty, negotiated by a Republican administration, was a significant departure from a policy of commercial exclusion—which, however, already had a precedent in the treaty of 1876 with Hawaii, although the object was different. After modification (especially by the insertion of the word "steel"), it was finally approved by the American Senate on March 11, 1884, and ratified by the Mexican Senate on May 18 without any change and with authority to extend the time for exchange of ratifications. It was ratified by President Arthur on May 20 and proclaimed on June 2. Through the opposing influence of specially protected American interests, however, the American Congress failed to enact the legislation necessary to make the treaty effective; and, although the limit of time was twice extended by diplomatic negotiations, the treaty ceased to be operative on May 20, 1887. Although the earlier openings of railways across the boundary frontier had stimulated a policy of reciprocity, the later establishment and multiplication of international railway communications, revolutionizing commercial conditions and giving the United States a great predominance in the trade of Mexico, largely supplanted the need of a reciprocity treaty which Romero continued to advocate in 1889.[12]

Meantime, under an act of Congress of July 7, 1884, a commission had been appointed to visit Latin American countries to ascertain the best methods of promoting more intimate international and commercial relations—a policy resulting from the need of more adequate markets, and from the desire to prevent the temptation of American neighbors to seek with European powers embarrassing engagements or guaranties or antagonistic alliances. In Mexico, Commissioner Thatcher, acting upon instructions from Frelinghuysen, in a personal interview asked the views of President Diaz concerning the practicability of holding a Pan-American congress, and received from him a favorable reply indicating his belief that the movement would make peace permanent in the Western World. On questions of trade, he found that Diaz, agreeing with Romero's views, expressed his readiness to consider favorably the immediate renewal of the treaty of commerce, navigation and consular rights. He, also, obtained a satisfactory response to proposals to agree upon a common silver coin to pass current in all countries of the hemisphere, to make effective the recent Mexican-American reciprocity treaty by enactment of necessary legislation in each country, and to insert into a renewal treaty of commerce and navigation a clause (concerning the coasting trade) which he thought would tend to the encouragement of a merchant marine in each country. Commissioner Reynolds proposed that future treaties should have sufficient guaranties of protection to American capital invested in Mexico—to which Diaz responded that American capital legitimately invested was adequately protected under Mexican laws, although he admitted that methods of enforcing the laws, resulting from the prejudices of local judges, should be remedied in both countries by extension of the jurisdiction of the federal courts in cases of complaints of aliens. The American commissioners mentioned complaints of American citizens who had been detained in custody for crimes for which they had been unable to secure trial —to which Diaz replied that the courts were usually speedy in disposing of charges and that he was anxious for complete protection for aliens in their rights of person and property in order to encourage investment of foreign capital and development of resources. Thatcher presented the arguments against the Mexican Free Zone along the northern frontier—to which Diaz agreed, but to which he replied that repeal was difficult because of political reasons. He urged the need of the establishment of bonded warehouses in Mexico and more liberal tariff regulations to facilitate increased trade—to which Diaz replied favorably, promising to give early attention to these subjects with a view to removal of obstacles to trade between the two countries.[13]

On November 4, 1884, while awaiting the result of the South American commissions to Mexico, Frelinghuysen sent Morgan full confidential instructions to guide his action with the new Diaz administration on pending diplomatic and commercial questions not included in the partial adjustment of relations by the reciprocity treaty. With these he submitted a brief outline of points upon which Romero thought a comparison of views would be advantageous: (1) a new commercial treaty to replace that of 1831; (2) the problems of the Free Zone; (3) matriculation; (4) rights and duties of consuls on the inland frontier; (5) demarcation of the frontier along the changing Rio Grande below El Paso; and (6) extradition. He instructed Morgan, on his return to his post in Mexico, to confer with Romero who, while in Mexico on leave of absence from Washington, would try to influence his government to examine existing conditions and to consider new ones with a view to facilitating the adjustment of pending questions on diplomatic and commercial relations. Later, on December 19, in accord with a confidential request of Romero who, after a technical resignation from the post at Washington, had decided to return to Washington, he requested postponement of these questions until Mariscal, the new Mexican Minister of Relations, entered upon his duties. Before entering upon actual negotiations of a treaty —which should include provisions for abolition of the laws relating to the Free Zone and restrictions of the domicile of American citizens on the Mexican frontier, settlement of the question of matriculation, a statement of the rights and functions of consuls, and an arrangement for assimilating sea travel to land travel by better treatment of commercial vessels in Mexican ports—he desired first to secure cooperative efforts to remove distrust and create a better understanding which would facilitate negotiations. He already had under consideration a formal treaty, the negotiation of which was proposed by

Romero, to settle all cases of dispute concerning the true de-marcation of the frontier where rendered doubtful by gradual or sudden changes in the channel of the Rio Grande. Questions of extradition and matriculation he had also considered with Romero who had proposed to exercise his influence concerning them on his visit to Mexico.[14]

Thomas Francis Bayard, the successor of Frelinghuysen as Secretary of State, was partly prepared for his new duties by a service of sixteen years as United States senator from Delaware —a position previously held by his father (whom he succeeded) and earlier by his grandfather preceding the latter's service on the peace commission at Ghent in 1813-14. One of his first acts on assuming his duties under President Cleveland was to consider the conditions of trade between the United States and Mexico, especially the defective system of customs regulation, and to suggest to Morgan an attempt to secure revision and increase of trade facilities. On May 1, 1886, he instructed the American chargé (Joseph L. Morgan) to urge the Mexican Min-ister of Relations to authorize the Mexican minister at Wash-ington to agree to an article to extend for another year the time for legislative action required to make effective the reciprocity treaty. On May 6, the conferences of the commissioners were reported to the Senate by Senator Frye, in connection with a favorable recommendation of a bill "to promote the political progress and commercial prosperity of the American nations." Investigations disclosed that public opinion in Mexico was di-vided in regard to the best policy of relations with the United States. The conservatives, or church party, ignoring the political changes since the Mexican War, were afraid of annexation and advocated a policy of isolation and complete non-intercourse— illustrated by the alarm expressed in 1887 in regard to coloniza-tion in Lower California by American companies. The liberal party, properly recognizing the stubborn fact of contiguity of territory, proposed to grant to the United States reasonable advantage which would make annexation useless and even dangerous. In pursuance of the latter policy, the Mexican gov-ernment had made liberal railway grants, and, by 1889, it modified the old Mexican land laws and gave to American citizens liberal mineral and other grants. On December 6, 1886, Cleveland renewed the recommendation of legislation to make the reciprocity treaty effective, and proposed negotiations for a new and enlarged treaty of commerce and navigation to replace the commercial treaty of 1831 which had been terminated.[15]

Other chief subjects of diplomatic correspondence with Mexico in the Cleveland administration, under which Bayard served, were Mexican differences with Guatemala, Mexican discriminations in favor of a Spanish and Central American line of steamers between San Francisco and Panama, the Arizona quarantine against Mexican cattle, the crossing of the border by cattle, the Cutting case in which Mexico claimed extraterritorial jurisdiction, the Mexican seizure of the *Rebecca,* the invasion of Arizona by Mexican troops, Rio Grande boundary questions under the rule of the convention of 1884, Mexican wing dams on the river, the Mexican Free Zone, extradition, matriculation of foreigners, and negligence of the Mexican government in cases of murder of aliens and wrong imprisonment of Americans in Mexico.

Bayard regarded with apprehension the action of Mexico in concentrating forces on the Guatemala frontier in March, 1885, ostensibly to maintain order but apparently with a purpose to intervene in Guatemala—with which Mexico still had a boundary dispute, and whose President, Barrios, had attempted to achieve a Central American federal union by force. He was assured by the Mexican Minister of Relations, however, that Mexico had no ulterior motives. Later, at the request of the Central American Union to prevent apprehended conquest by Mexico, he tendered American good offices in favor of peace between the Spanish American republics.[16]

In May, 1886, following a complaint of export duties unlawfully levied on American cattle by Mexican authorities at Piedras Negras, Bayard proposed a convention for facilitating the passage of cattle across the border (especially for grazing purposes). A convention for the reciprocal crossing of cattle from one country to the other was signed at Washington on

July 1, 1888, and, after amendment by the United States Senate, was forwarded for the consideration of the Mexican government; but it was opposed by the inhabitants of the frontier Mexican states and was still pending before the Mexican Senate in January, 1894, when Congress by a joint resolution authorized the Secretary of the Treasury to permit owners of cattle and horses to pasture them in Mexico and to reimport them free of duty within a period of twelve months.[17]

The most prominent controversy in Bayard's period arose in the case of A. K. Cutting who was imprisoned at Paso in Mexico in July, 1886, for an alleged libelous newspaper article (published in Texas) involving the question of the extraterritoriality of penal laws. His release was promptly demanded by telegram by Secretary Bayard (acting through Jackson) on the ground that Mexico had no right to hold an American citizen in Mexican courts for an act of publication in Texas. Bayard denied Mexican jurisdiction in the case on the ground that it would create a dual responsibility which would result in inextricable confusion, and he protested against the "unendurable" imprisonment in a loathsome jail with insufficient food and covering. On August 13, he instructed A. G. Sedgwick as a special agent acting under direction of the President to investigate the Mexican claim to extraterritorial jurisdiction, which was regarded as novel but was sustained by the Mexican courts. Pending this investigation, undertaken by Cleveland with the hope that the Mexican statute based on a doctrine unknown to American law would be repealed in the interests of good neighborhood of "irrevocable neighbors," Cutting was released—following the abandonment of the complaint by the Mexican citizen.[18]

On November 1, 1887, Bayard instructed Connery, the American chargé, to reopen discussion of the case, to demand indemnity for Cutting and to ask a repeal of the Mexican law as to extraterritorial jurisdiction. He soon learned that further negotiations were embarrassed by the publication of this news in the Mexican press, to which Mariscal had evidently furnished it for political effect. Connery, who acted as American chargé in Mexico following the absence and death of the American minister (Manning) in New York (on October 11), refrained from reminding Mariscal that the place to discuss such a serious question was in the secrecy of diplomatic correspondence. In February, 1888, he wired Bayard that Mariscal declined to indemnify Cutting for his imprisonment, on the ground that he was treated better than other prisoners. Nine days later, against the American argument which had been prepared by J. B. Moore, he reported Mariscal's argument that the claim had no foundation in right, that most nations recognize extraterritorial jurisdiction and that the payment of the indemnity would wound the patriotism of the Mexican people. In acknowledging Connery's dispatch of February 21 (No. 306) inclosing Mariscal's note of February 10, Bayard on May 4 in instructions to Bragg, the new American minister, regretted that the American chief object to secure modification of the Mexican claim of criminal jurisdiction over the territory of the United States did not receive more favorable consideration in the interest of good neighborhood. He explained that the question of pecuniary indemnity was urged only as an incident to the general principle involved which was not affected by the merits of the Cutting case, and he directed that the American views be again presented with the hope that Mexico would see its way to modify its penal code. At the end of May, Bragg reported that the Mexican minister had taken the claim under advisement. Later, President Diaz, in a résumé of his policy and acts in the four years preceding November 30, 1888, stated that the reasons for refusal of indemnity in the Cutting case were "so justifiable that the government at Washington did not insist." [19]

In conducting Mexican relations, Bayard successively acted through instructions to three American ministers in Mexico. H. R. Jackson, who was appointed minister on March 26, 1885, and who after his arrival in Mexico in June found little pleasure in the presentation of various complaints and claims, evidently expected larger interest of the Department of State in his extensive report of the corruption of Mexican officials and the wholesale robbery of the Mexican treasury to which he traced the cause of the Mexican financial crisis. He finally resigned in a letter to President Cleveland on June 30, 1886, stating that he considered his position embarrassing and impotent because of the failure of the Department to press the claims in the case of the *Rebecca* which, bound for a Texas port, had been forced by a storm to stop at Tampico where it had been seized and sold for its failure to observe the rule requiring a manifest of its cargo. In reviewing relations affecting the discussion of pending American claims, he also especially objected to Mariscal's statement that an appeal by an American citizen to the American minister or the American government, from Mexican officials, whether executive or judicial, was a punishable offense. President Cleveland and Secretary Bayard, influenced by the rise of the Cutting case, decided that the time was not an opportune one for the acceptance of Jackson's resignation, the announcement of which might have led to misinterpretation. On August 19, however, Bayard explained that he had neglected to reply further in regard to the *Rebecca* because it was but a single feature in a very long series of correspondence beginning in a former administration. He asserted that Jackson by a short note of request could easily have obtained from the Department an easy explanation which would have removed all possible embarrassment, and he closed by a statement that after long deliberations the President and he had reached the conclusion that "your resignation ought not to be obstructed." On September 4, following correspondence of July and August in the Cutting case and during the period of the special mission of Sedgwick (to investigate the Mexican claim to extraterritorial jurisdiction) which was explained to him by Secretary Bayard, Jackson gave very lengthy reasons for his resignation which Bayard had accepted, and, on October 7, he presented his recall letter. In rehearsing the more salient causes of his resignation he suggested that they might be "grouped into one": Bayard's "indifference to our relations with Mexico." [20]

Jackson's successor, Thomas C. Manning, was appointed on September 8 and went to Mexico under instructions of September 28 and died in New York on October 11, 1887, while Thomas B. Connery was acting as chargé in Mexico. In March,

1887, Manning reported on a case of the invasion of Arizona by Mexican troops who rescued a prisoner in custody of American officials. The Diaz government, although it recognized the right of the American government to demand the return of the prisoner, requested that as a favor the demand be withdrawn. In May, Manning reported that the offending Mexican officers were sentenced to death, but that upon request their lives had been saved by commutation of the death sentence. Later, in April, 1888, his successor reported that the trial of the officers had resulted in affirmation of the death sentence, but that this sentence had been commuted to imprisonment for twenty years.[21]

Edward S. Bragg, the successor of Manning, was appointed on January 17, 1888. Among the claims which he was instructed to press (in February, 1888) was that of the *Rebecca* which had been pressed by his two predecessors and which the American government, in view of the "important principles of international justice and amity involved"—the right of a vessel to enter a harbor by necessity, without blame of its officer who had no wrongful intent—believed should not longer prejudice the best interests of neighbors by further delay. In October, 1888, he was directed by Bayard to revive the case of J. R. Flippin, who was complaining of the delay in the settlement of his old claim against Mexico, and to urge the Mexican Foreign Office to expedite the report promised in the case and previously urged by instructions of July 2, 1886.[22]

By the close of the second term of Diaz, in November, 1888, both governments recognized the need of new conventions to remedy the natural increase of diplomatic complaints which would result from increased facility of communication. In November, 1888, Bayard, in instructions to H. R. Whitehouse, American chargé *ad interim,* opened correspondence with the Mexican government in regard to a dam which the Mexican government had erected across the Rio Grande at Paso del Norte—a construction which he said was evidently a violation of Article III of the convention of 1884 and an invasion of territorial sovereignty. He soon expressed satisfaction, however, concerning promised Mexican cooperation in the matter.

From the Mexican minister at Washington he received a disclaimer of any intention of asserting that the boundary line remained as fixed by the treaty of 1853 regardless of changes in the current of the Rio Grande. On February 28, 1889, he inclosed to Bragg copies of his correspondence with the Mexican minister at Washington concerning the negotiation of a proposed convention for an international commission to settle questions affecting the water boundary between Mexico and the United States—negotiations which were successful, resulting in the boundary convention signed on March 1, 1889, approved by the American Senate on May 7, 1890, and ratified and proclaimed by the President in the following December.[23]

On March 12, 1889, sixteen days before his recall, Bragg inclosed to Secretary Blaine a clipping from a Mexican newspaper charging the new (Harrison) administration with "cherishing designs against Mexico." Apparently this charge had no basis in fact, although Bragg's successor (Ryan) a few months later forwarded a clipping concerning an American movement for annexation of Lower California where American colonization companies had received concessions which had excited some criticism in the Mexican press in 1887. Possibly the charge had its origin in irresponsible projects of certain visionary Californians. On June 28, 1892, after Blaine was succeeded by J. W. Foster in the office of Secretary of State, Ryan, in a confidential dispatch, reported an interview at the legation a week earlier with one W. D. Southworth, who had appeared at the legation two years before, and who—representing himself as a mining engineer engaged in the formation of a San Francisco syndicate to secure necessary capital for mining development in Mexico, and stating that he found capitalists not inclined to risk money in Mexican investments—sought the approval of the American minister to a plan for annexation of Mexican territory by amicable agencies which he said had been considered recently at a meeting of the chief capitalists of the Pacific slope whose fortunes had been made in silver mining. He asserted that the plan had been favored by the governors of Mexican states (and even by Diaz!). Ryan's action, advising abandonment of the "insane project" at once, was promptly approved by the State Department. Although, as late as 1892-93, there was some expression in favor of the annexation of Mexican frontier territory, the American government, recognizing the friendly cooperation of the Mexican authorities in efforts to prevent the occasional disturbances of lawless marauders on the frontier, testified its good will and its purpose to fulfill international obligations and doubtless had no sympathy with a proposal introduced in the Senate with a view to the purchase of Mexican frontier territory—a proposal originating in personal motives of gain for the promoters who had landed interests in the territory.[24]

President Harrison's attitude was apparently very friendly. In April, 1891, before the appointment of commissioners for re-marking the southwest boundary westward from El Paso as defined by the treaty of 1848, he invited President Diaz to meet him at the boundary at El Paso. In his administration, a better understanding between the two governments was expressed by the establishment of the international water boundary commission under the Bayard-Romero convention of March 1, 1889, to study and determine pending boundary questions or those which might later arise from the variation of the course of the Rio Grande and Colorado rivers with a view to execution of the principles of the convention of 1884.[25]

Secretary Blaine, under Harrison, as in 1881 under Garfield, sought to improve friendly relations with Mexico. He welcomed the opportunity again to act upon his views concerning Pan-Americanism and the peace of the continent—to resume duties interrupted as a result of the death of Garfield and the accession of Arthur. In the international American conference at Washington he felt the friendly influence of the able Mexican delegate, Matias Romero, who by his command of English and enthusiasm for inter-American cooperation was one of the most valuable members. In Mexico City his views were faithfully presented by Minister Ryan, who found a friendly attitude in the consideration of the various diplomatic problems.

Chief subjects concerning which Blaine directed diplomatic

correspondence with Mexico were quarantines, tariffs and reciprocity, questions relating to Central America, Chinese immigration through Mexico, Garza's raid and certain claims.

Questions in relation to Central America arose in connection with the war between Guatemala and Salvador in 1890. When the latter requested the friendly offices of the American government in restoring peace, and the Mexican government expressed a readiness to cooperate with the United States in mediation between the belligerents, the American government wired that it would be pleased to cooperate with the Mexican government but preferred independent to joint action. In August, 1890, influenced by apprehensions concerning the war and possibly by the report that Mexico was secretly aiding an invasion of Guatemala, Blaine wired Ryan that the American government desired to offer good offices concurrently with Mexico and had so instructed the American minister to Central America, believing that concurrent independent action was better than joint action. His efforts of 1881 and 1890 found a fitting conclusion in the final adjustment of the Mexico-Guatemala boundary question in 1895.[26]

Earlier in the Harrison administration arose the problem of quarantines. Ryan, in June, 1889, following the Arizona quarantine against Mexican cattle, announced that the Mexican government was willing to cooperate in measures to prevent the spread of contagious diseases, but later he reported sources of complaint—including a Mexican quarantine against American hogs (in January, 1890).[27]

Questions of tariffs and reciprocity were more prominent in the early part of the administration. On July 12, Ryan wired Blaine that the anti-American press in Mexico declared that the American government had determined to discriminate against Mexican trade by additional *ad valorem* duties on goods arriving at New Orleans in Mexican vessels. In September, when Mexico was preparing to send delegates to the international congress at Washington on October 2, he hopefully reported that the pending tariff controversy with Mexico might speedily result in a treaty of reciprocity productive of good to both

countries. Blaine, by his efforts, induced the framers of the
McKinley Tariff Act of October 1, 1890, to insert a reciprocity
provision under which reciprocal trade arrangements were negotiated by John W. Foster with several countries, but which
was repealed by a hostile Congress before it was fairly tested.
In 1891, under this provision, Foster, through negotiations with
the Mexican minister at Washington, reached an agreement
on a reciprocity arrangement which, however, was defeated
by the influence of the same protected American interests
which had prevented Congress from exacting the necessary
legislation to make effective the convention of 1883. In September, 1891, Blaine wired Ryan that the list of articles
proposed for reciprocity was not acceptable and suggested the
desirability of a conference at Washington. On November 25,
he announced that the President would not recommend to Congress any change in the free list and could not change it. He
was disappointed in his hope to reach a reciprocity agreement
before January 1, 1892. However, the Mexican tariff of 1891
was regarded as a step toward the end of the Mexican Free
Zone—which had been extended to the entire frontier, including Coahuila, Chihuahua, Sonora and Lower California, by the
new Diaz tariff of January, 1884.[28]

The Chinese question in Mexican relations first appeared in
October, 1890. Blaine, acting upon a resolution of the American Congress, instructed Ryan to sound Mexico on negotiations
for a treaty to prevent Chinese laborers from entering the
United States from Mexico, whose constitution provided that
every man had a right to enter and leave Mexico freely in any
direction to secure work. Later, on December 1, he forwarded
the complaint of the United States Treasury Department that
the Mexican consul at New Orleans was giving advice to persons who were trying to violate United States laws in regard
to Chinese emigration from Mexico to the United States. On
May 14, 1892, he forwarded instructions that the Chinese exclusion act would not permit Chinese laborers to enter the
United States even if provided with Mexican letters of naturali-
zation. That the evil was difficult to remedy was evidenced by

instructions of the Department of State to Clayton in May, 1905, presenting additional complaints of the smuggling of Chinese across the international boundary and, also, by instructions of May, 1906, to Thompson to request the Mexican government to permit the transportation companies of Mexico to enter into an agreement to cooperate with the Mexican government to avert the growing peril presented by the problem of the menacing immigration of objectionable Syrians who were seeking surreptitious entry to the United States by way of Mexico and across the Texas border.[29]

In connection with Garza's revolution, Blaine, in December, 1891, assured Mexico that the American government, in accord with its duty of neutrality, was using strong measures to break up the Garza raid into American territory. On February 16 he wired instructions to ask the Mexican government whether it was willing to declare that Garza's force had been suppressed and that the railway routes were not in any way endangered by his band.[30]

The most prominent claims case was that of Janet Baldwin for an indemnity for the murder of her husband, Leon McL. Baldwin, in Durango by banditti late in 1887—a claim previously presented to the Mexican government by Secretary Bayard. In April, 1892, Blaine directed Ryan to continue to urge Mexico to pay this indemnity, stating that the case was different from the recent lynchings of Italians at New Orleans. In February, 1893, Ryan reported to Blaine's successor, Secretary Foster, that Mariscal, after an interview with President Diaz, had promised, in deference to the views of the American government and not as an admitted obligation, to determine upon an equitable sum to pay the claimant "as a gratuity" following the final determination of the right of Mexico to the Weil-La Abra fund which was then in the custody of the American government. The case was not finally settled until the next American administration. In the following year, in Cleveland's administration, Gresham had a long correspondence with Señor Romero concerning the payment of the long-discussed claim for which the Mexican government was finally induced to offer a "gratuity" of $20,000 as an act of equity (without recognition of liability). Refusing to accept the indemnity in silver, Gresham finally obtained a promise to pay in gold by reducing the monthly instalment to $1,000. By June, 1895, the Department received the eleventh instalment.[31]

John W. Foster, who under Blaine's second tenure had charge of the negotiation of reciprocity treaties and later was appointed American agent to prepare the American case in the Bering Sea arbitration, became Secretary of State on June 29, 1892. For his position he was well trained by long diplomatic service. For decisions on problems of policy in Mexican relations he was especially fitted by his long period of service as American minister to Mexico from 1872 to 1880. On August 23, 1892, he authorized negotiations with Mexico for a convention on the new problem of the irrigation of arid lands near the Rio Grande, acting in accord with a joint resolution of the American Congress of April 27, 1890, and with subsequent Mexican instructions (of May, 1892) to the Mexican minister at Washington. On questions of American policy in relations with Mexico, which he found were still largely concerned with border troubles—raids from Texas into Mexico to recapture stolen cattle and horses, but sometimes returning with Mexican cattle and horses—his chief service was to induce the American government to take effective steps, by increase of federal forces, to prevent all invasions of Mexican territory. On January 23, 1893, he replied to the views of Señor Mariscal, the Mexican Minister of Relations, who through Romero complained of American inaction in regard to the Garza bandits near Laredo and who on December 31 had proposed a distribution of Mexican and American forces in concert to guard the several fords of the Rio Grande or an arrangement for mutual pursuit across the border similar to that recently made for pursuit of Indians.

He said that the War Department, although it agreed with the general views, found difficulty as to the proposed provisions for reciprocal crossing.[32]

In Cleveland's second administration, foreign policy was directed first by Judge W. Q. Gresham, a Republican of Indiana, and, later, after Gresham's death in May, 1895, by Richard Olney of Massachusetts. Gresham, before a period of service as a United States circuit judge, had served in the cabinet of President Arthur, first as Postmaster General (1882-84) and later as Secretary of the Treasury (1884-85). Olney, a busy corporation lawyer, not active in politics and not widely known to the public, in 1893 accepted the office of Attorney General from which he was transferred to the Department of State.

Early in Cleveland's administration (in May) Secretary Gresham reported to C. Romero greater effectiveness of the American efforts against the border bandits, illustrated by the arrest of several of the Garza bandits, the surrender of Roman Garcia and Jesus Flores, and the later capture of Pedro Garcia and others. In the following summer, in answer to Romero's complaints of August concerning an invasion of Mexican territory by armed Texans under Captain Frank C. Jones in pursuit of Jesus Holguin, he explained that Jones (who had been killed in an affray) had unintentionally crossed the unmarked boundary. He, also, received apprehensive complaints of a "contemplated armed expedition" into Mexico concerning which General Wharton reported that he had no information. In September, 1893, following the seizure of sheep and two Americans by Mexican officials on the Rio Grande, he promptly wired instructions to Gray to demand immediate release and to present a formal complaint; and, four days later, he agreed to a fair Mexican proposal to release on condition that the American government would release two Mexican guards and all Mexican citizens involved, reserving the question of violation of territory to be settled thereafter by the International Boundary Commission.[33]

In September, 1893, Gresham received from Romero Mexican complaints of the recent frequency of American violation of Mexican territory by American officers, including the recent case of the arrest of Jesus Holguin by Texas Rangers who had advanced across the border into Chihuahua. He was asked especially to consider the peculiar case of one Jesus Garcia, a Mexican citizen, who asked an indemnity of $2,000, complaining that John Roberts, deputy sheriff at Nogales, Arizona, had pursued him following a fight with another Mexican in Nogales and had arrested him in neighboring Mexican territory within the limits of Nogales, Sonora, on July 23 and had taken him before a local Arizona justice of the peace who had fined him $60 in the face of the protest of the Mexican consul and his lawyer, who, in opposition to the testimony of Roberts, declared that the arrest was irregular. Secretary Olney later satisfied Romero by an investigation resulting in a report that Jesus had a reputation inconsistent with his name, that he was an habitual lawbreaker, that when arrested he was drunk and, that in a collision with a local baker who attempted to aid in preventing his escape, he had fallen on the line with his head in Mexico but with most of his body in Arizona and that Roberts in making the arrest stood entirely on American soil.[34]

Among other border questions considered by the administration was a proposed arrangement for the convenience of border stockmen. Congress, by a joint resolution of January 15, 1894, authorized the Secretary of the Treasury to permit owners of cattle and horses in the United States for a period of twelve months to pass into Mexico to pasture them and to reimport them without payment of duty; but the Mexican government declined to concur in the execution of the resolution on the ground that a convention signed July 11, 1888, for reciprocal crossing of cattle was still pending before the Mexican Senate and that it had met with considerable opposition among the people of the frontier states.

In 1894, President Cleveland, referring to the improved relations fostered by many interests, and to the restoration of peace along the frontier, recommended the negotiation of a new treaty of commerce and navigation to replace the one which had terminated thirteen years before. In the next year, on March 1, 1895, Congress by a joint resolution suspending the privilege of free transportation in bond across American territory, unsuccessfully attempted to remedy the abuses resulting from the Free Zone.

In August, 1894, Gresham concluded with Romero a convention further extending (for two years) the convention of 1882 for the international boundary survey; and, in October, 1895, Olney signed with him a boundary convention to extend for another year the convention of March 1, 1889. In 1896, by official proclamation, President Cleveland announced that the American copyright law of March, 1891, was extended to Mexican citizens, the Mexican law having met the conditions required by the act.

On June 4, 1896, Secretary Olney signed with Romero an agreement for reciprocal right to pursue Kid's band of hostile Indians across the boundary at uninhabited or desert regions west of a point 52 miles above Piedras Negras, by proper notice to the nearest military or civil official of the country entered and with the condition that withdrawal must be prompt after the time required for chastisement of the Indians.

Among the claims presented through diplomatic intervention in the Cleveland administration was the famous Pious Fund case, a claim of the Catholic Church of California against Mexico, which was not finally settled until 1902. Secretary Gresham, on June 8, 1893, asked Gray to assist Senator Stewart who was going to Mexico in connection with the claim and discreetly to solicit a reply from Mexico.[35]

Several questions of policy under the American Monroe Doctrine arose in this period. In 1894, the American government was somewhat solicitous concerning the report of a treaty negotiation by Mexico with Great Britain to fix the boundary between Mexico and Belize; but it was satisfied by the explanation of Romero that the treaty (which did not seem to enlarge Belize beyond the former British claim) had been withdrawn from the Mexican Senate and would not be re-submitted. President Cleveland's policy, and that of Secretary Olney, on the Venezuelan boundary dispute with Great Britain, and incidentally on the Monroe Doctrine, was apparently well received in Mexico. On December 26, 1895, Butler reported that opinion there was unanimously favorable to the position taken in the President's message. In the following year Diaz suggested the advisability of the Pan-Americanization of the Monroe Doctrine.[36]

At the same time, Americans in Mexico had a high regard for the ability and attitude of Diaz. The American colony in Mexico City in the summer of 1895 showed its esteem and confidence in him by a memorial expressing the hope that he would accept the nomination for another term—a memorial which the American chargé (Butler) was willing to sign before he was reminded by Assistant Secretary Adee that diplomatic agents abroad are forbidden to participate in any manner in political concerns of the country of their residence and that his "observance of this rule could not fail to be entirely understood by the distinguished recipient of the proposed memorial." [37]

Meantime, in 1895, the American government used its good offices to secure a settlement of the Mexico-Guatemalan boundary dispute which had existed for many years and which after two decades of discussion was finally settled peacefully. On January 21, 1895, during the illness of the American minister (Isaac P. Gray)—when war between Mexico and Guatemala was threatened by a new phase of the controversy resulting from Guatemalan obstacles to the execution of the treaty of 1882 and by the later Guatemalan order for destruction of a logging camp belonging to a Mexican citizen—Secretary Gresham wired E. C. Butler, the American chargé, to express the hope that the difficulties would be adjusted by arbitration. On the same date, in order to stop a Mexican rumor that the American government desired to intervene, Señor Romero wired Secretary Mariscal that Secretary Gresham denied that he had expressed any opinion tending to propose that Mariscal should withdraw any of his demands on Guatemala or that he had counseled Guatemala to refuse to accept such demands, and declared that the American government did not propose to interfere in the question by imposing conditions. On February 12, when war between Mexico and Guatemala was threatened, Butler reported that Mariscal had declared (on February 7) that the Mexican government would receive no proposal of Guatemala unless made direct, but would cheerfully entertain any friendly suggestion of the American government. Subsequent negotiations resulted in a convention of April 1, 1895, providing for settlement of the boundary—the Guatemalan government agreeing that for property occupied or destroyed by its agents it would pay an indemnity to be fixed by an arbitrator mutually selected by the two governments.[38]

In connection with the plans for the adjustment of the Mexico-Guatemalan question, Señor Romero proposed an arrangement for settlement which the Mexican government rejected on the ground that it was substantially identical with the American proposal concerning the satisfaction required by Mexico for the Guatemalan invasion of the territory whose ownership was in dispute. On June 7, he wrote a letter to *El Nacional* and other Mexican newspapers to prove that his project was not identical. Following its publication and a resulting attack on the Mexican government which appeared in the *Tiempo,* he received from *El Diario* a severe criticism, expressing regret that "such complete frankness should have become necessary" and resembling a public reprimand which many expected would result in his resignation. Hurt by the attacks of the Mexican press and feeling that Mariscal and President Diaz did not approve his conduct, he tendered his resignation on April 10, 1895, and later went to Mexico City to settle the matter. On July 18, 1896, he again tendered his resignation; but, at the friendly request of Mariscal, he withdrew it and agreed to continue at his post at Washington.

Meantime, in October, 1895, under the convention of April 1, 1895, the American minister, Ransom, was chosen as arbiter and without objection of his government served until his retirement in 1897 when the Spanish minister, the Duke of Argos, was chosen. In the spring of 1898, under the administration of President McKinley, the new American minister, Powell Clayton, reported apprehensions of a Mexican invasion of Guatemala which, however, the Mexican Minister of Relations said were unfounded. For the completion of the labors of the boundary commission, a new convention was signed by Mexico and Guatemala on May 17, 1898, extending the time.[39]

Under President McKinley, the Department of State was conducted, in succession, by three secretaries. John Sherman of Ohio, appointed in 1897 to provide a place in the Senate for Marcus A. Hanna, had served in the Hayes cabinet as Secretary of the Treasury (1877-81). He had also served many years in Congress—six years in the lower house (1855-61) and thirty-four years in the Senate (1861-77 and 1881-97). William R. Day of Ohio, who succeeded Sherman in April, 1898, had served as Assistant Secretary of State in 1897-98. John Hay, who succeeded Day in September, 1898, was well fitted for his new position by a long period of public service—as secretary to President Lincoln, secretary of several American legations in Europe, Assistant Secretary of State (1879-81) and ambassador to Great Britain (1897-98).

Among the early Mexican questions of the new administration was one relating to the application of the Monroe Doctrine. In August, 1897, the attention of the American government was attracted by the ratification of a treaty between Mexico and Great Britain, which aimed "to define what is the Mexican frontier to which Guatemala referred" in its treaty (of April 30, 1859) with Great Britain concerning its limits with the British possessions in the Bay of Honduras and "what are in consequence the boundaries of those provinces with Mexico." Two years later, in September, 1899, Clayton reported by wire to his government that the Colombian minister had sought to induce Mexico to enter a Latin American alliance contemplated by Colombia in a legislative call for a Latin American Congress to consider mutual protection against unfair European demands and in favor of international arbitration.[40]

On questions relating to the Spanish American War, the Mexican attitude was satisfactory. At the opening of the war, although Mexico was neutral, Clayton wired from Mexico to warn his government to watch all vessels departing from Mexican ports to Cuban waters; and in May, he reported apprehensions of a contemplated invasion of the United States by Spaniards in Mexico. In June, he reported by wire several Spanish shipments from Mexico which indicated difficulty in observing neutral obligations there. On May 13, 1898, Secretary Day expressed through Clayton gratification that the Mexican government had taken measures to stop meetings of Spaniards in Mexico to raise money for Spain for use in the war against the United States.[41]

The Mexican Free Zone was still a subject of discussion. In December, 1898, President McKinley suggested to Congress the authorization of an invitation of a joint conference between representatives of the treasury departments of the two countries to consider the subject in all its complex bearings, including the proposed American suspension of the privilege of free shipment in bond across American territory, and to report with recommendations for congressional action.[42]

Among the subjects of occasional controversy under the McKinley administration was extradition. In 1897, the American government still refused to extradite Jesus Guerra, a member of an expedition which about three years earlier had made an attack at St. Ignacio, Mexico, apparently with a motive primarily political and therefore not subject to extradition under the treaty of 1861. Another question of extradition arose in the case of the Indians of Fort Yuba Reservation (in California) who (without being charged with any crime) trespassed on Mexican territory, apparently preferring to live in Mexico and refusing voluntarily to return. In negotiations for a new and more comprehensive extradition treaty, which was concluded (February 22, 1899) with Mariscal, the Mexican Minister of Relations, Secretary Hay instructed Clayton that the United States would not agree to any proposed amendment giving up the right of asylum or including acts connected with political offenses. In the treaty the parties agreed that an "attempt against the life of the head of the government shall not be considered a political offense." On March 4, Hay announced to McCreery the ratification of the treaty by the American Senate; and, on April 25, he announced that it had been proclaimed by the President on April 24. A request for the extradition of Simon Garcia was withdrawn in the following October because the crime had been committed in 1891 and was barred by limitation under the Mexican laws. Later, by a supplementary convention concluded between Clayton and Mariscal on June 25, 1902, the crime of bribery was added to the list of offenses for which extradition might be granted.[43]

In December, 1898, President McKinley informed Congress that the Mexican water boundary commission, established by the convention of 1889 (which had been extended annually by conventions since 1895), had failed to agree on three important cases: the "Chamizal" at El Paso, the proposition for the elimination of the small island "bancos" formed in bends of the Rio Grande and the subject of "equitable distribution of the waters of the Rio Grande."

The Chamizal tract was located between the old bed of the Rio Grande (as surveyed in 1852) and the bed as it existed in 1898, resulting from changes in the river banks and the consequent progressive migration of the stream southward into Mexican territory extending the area of the American city El Paso and correspondingly reducing the area of the Mexican city of Juárez. The American government contended that the changes were the result of a slow and gradual corrosion and accretion which within the meaning of the convention of 1884 determined that the international boundary was in the later channel of the river. The Mexican government contended that the convention of 1884 did not affect or govern a title resulting from previous changes; and it also contended that the changes in the channel had not been the result of slow and gradual erosion and deposit. Under the convention of 1889 the International Boundary Commission was organized on January 8, 1894. On September 28, it was asked by Mariscal to consider the complaint of Pedro Ignacio Garcia who alleged that he had purchased property known as El Chamizal which was formerly on the south side of the Rio Grande but which, as a result of abrupt and sudden changes in the river current (prior to 1884), was now on the north side of the stream. The commissioners carefully considered the claim and the evidence but reported disagreement as to their decision. One considered that the changes had resulted from slow erosion, and the other considered that the erosion had been violent and intermittent. In March, 1898, in the negotiations for arbitration of the El Chamizal question by a boundary commission, Mexico refused to yield to the proposition of a third commissioner and insisted upon arbitration by a friendly nation or by a joint commission.[44]

The later proposition for elimination of the "bancos" was based on a conclusion of the boundary commissioners, of May 30, 1898, that the application of the treaty of 1884 to these separated "bancos" of land was inconvenient and liable to create new difficulties. This conclusion was the result of observations of the various changes in the bed of the Rio Grande—the abandonment of its earlier channel for a new one. On December 26, 1899, although a convention extending for one year the time of the boundary commission was signed four days earlier, Secretary Hay instructed Clayton to press the Mexican government for a convention (proposed on November 15) for elimination of "bancos" which had been formed along the Rio Grande and the Colorado—involving certain changes in the existing water boundary—and on January 5, 1900, in order to remove Mexican objections, he again explained to Mariscal that the purpose was to provide a method of deciding ownership of disputed territory and did not involve the constitutional question of ceding territory as Mariscal had thought when he proposed to defer action until he could confer with the Mexican Senate.[45]

In November, 1900, Hay signed with Aspiroz a water boundary convention indefinitely extending the duration of the convention of 1889 which since 1895 had been annually extended by conventions.

In the autumn of 1900, the American government through Hay, in response to complaints of cattlemen who were refused permission to cross the border, instructed Clayton to propose reciprocal facilities for recovery of strayed cattle. Cattlemen, however, were refused permission to cross the border in pursuit of stray cattle except during the months of November and December.[46]

Friendly relations with Mexico at this period were illustrated by an incident at Mexico City in August, 1899. Ambassador Clayton introduced to President Diaz and his cabinet a committee of Chicago citizens who invited him to attend the ceremonies of laying the corner stone of a United States government building at Chicago on October 9. The members of the committee were impressed by the courtesy and hospitality of the President who promptly agreed to ask Congress for the required consent for the visit, invited the committee and the Clayton family to dine at the Palace, placed at the committee's disposal two of his private carriages and his private street car and his private railway car to Guadalajara and return, and further honored it by sending his chief of staff and members of his family to the station where he also furnished a band of music. President Diaz, although the Mexican Congress on September 20 consented to the proposed visit to Chicago in October and appropriated $100,000 for the expenses of it, was unable to go because of public business and illness of his wife and, therefore, found it necessary to send his personal representative, Mariscal, Minister of Foreign Affairs. In the following year the Mexican Congress appropriated $30,000 for sufferers in the Galveston flood.[47]

In other ways the American government found a Mexican attitude of friendly cooperation. In March, 1900, Secretary Hay successfully directed McCreery, the American chargé, to request permission, facilities and cooperation to continue the hydraulic survey of the coast of Lower California and Mexico for which permission had been originally granted in 1881 and renewed in 1896. Later, in October, 1903, he again obtained permission for target practice in Magdalena Bay by vessels of the American Pacific squadron. McCreery on February 19, 1900, wired that the Mexican Minister of Relations suggested that the time and place of the next conference of the American republics should be determined by the United States.[48]

Clayton, who had been promoted to the rank of ambassador on December 8, 1898, found after 1900 various causes or reasons for complaints which he registered with Secretary Mariscal: long imprisonments, unreasonable delays or lack of action,

grave irregularities committed by the local courts, the expense
and trouble of required appeals to higher courts and apparent
discriminations against American citizens. On April 25, 1900,
discouraged with his failure to accomplish results in diplomatic
business with Mariscal, he reviewed his complaints in "a very
earnest conversation" which he hoped would be productive of
"more expeditious and effective action." His action was approved by Secretary Hay.[49]

Under President Roosevelt, who succeeded to the presidency
at the death of McKinley in September, 1901, Hay was continued as Secretary of State, and in Roosevelt's elective term he
was retained until his death on July 1, 1905, after which he was
succeeded by Elihu Root. Clayton was continued as ambassador
to Mexico only until the beginning of Roosevelt's elective term.
Apparently he was not entirely happy, although his relations
with the Diaz government were pleasant. In May, 1900, he had
complained to Hay of certain discourtesies to his daughters by
local police who were not tactful in calling attention to a violation of parking rules. In December, 1902, he reported the satisfactory termination of an incident involving the diplomatic
immunity of his servant who had been arrested. Somewhat
earlier, in March, 1902, he reported to Hay that he was much
disturbed in mind by certain American press attacks on his son,
who according to reports had been relieved from detail in Mexico because of a Christmas brawl in 1900 and had lost caste
there because of his refusal to accept a challenge of a Mexican
officer to fight a duel for words uttered in an animated argument concerning American policies in the Orient and Antilles—
reports which Clayton characterized as "malicious and menda-
cious," without a shadow of foundation and primarily aimed to
strike the father over the son's shoulders. His dispatch to the
Department was promptly given to the press.[50]

In May, 1902, by a protocol signed by Hay with Aspiroz, the
Pious Fund claims of the Catholic Church of California against
Mexico, which had been the subject of correspondence with the
Mexican government in 1891-92 and again since 1897, were
submitted to arbitration under the provisions of the Hague

convention—resulting in a decision (in October, 1902) in favor of the United States to whom Mexico was required to pay the sum of $1,420,682.67 to extinguish annuities accrued in the period from February 2, 1869, to February 2, 1902, and also a perpetual annuity of $43,050.99 Mexican.[51]

Secretary Hay still sought an adjustment of boundary difficulties arising from the shifting of the Rio Grande and the Colorado rivers. On December 1, 1904, in instructions to Clayton referring to the boundary question in relation to "bancos," he urged the need of a new boundary treaty or demarcation of the boundary under strict construction of the old treaties. On March 20, 1905, Assistant Secretary Adee concluded with Aspiroz, the Mexican minister at Washington, a convention (proclaimed June 5, 1907) providing for the survey and elimination of the fifty-eight *bancos* in the Rio Grande (between Roma and the Gulf of Mexico) from the effects of Article II of the treaty of November 12, 1884, which had declared that the boundary should follow the center of the normal channel in case of alterations of banks and river courses by slow and gradual erosion and deposit of alluvium. This new convention authorized in such cases the transfer of the sovereignty to the nation on whose side of the river the *banco* appeared. It also authorized the commissioners in their future labors on the Rio Grande and Colorado boundaries to be guided by the principle of elimination thereby established—excepting segregated tracts of over 250 hectares, or tracts with a population of over 200. Two exceptions to this arrangement were San Elizario Island (about 30 miles east of El Paso) where a tract of about 13,000 acres of American territory was cut south of the river, and a "banco" near Presidio, Texas, where a tract of about 3,000 acres of Mexican territory was cut north of the river. The San Elizario controversy had been presented on November 4, 1895, and had been decided on October 5, 1896, upon the basis of changes which occurred in 1857-58, and with the approval of the Mexican government.[52]

On March 24, 1905, four days after the signing of the convention concerning "bancos," President Roosevelt, in the performance of a sad duty, communicated directly with President Diaz concerning the death of Ambassador Aspiroz who had signed the convention and whose body was later conveyed to the Mexican border on the American cruiser *Columbia*.

In the following July, at the death of Secretary Hay, Elihu Root of New York was appointed Secretary of State. For the position he was well fitted by his legal training and experience and by a period of service as Secretary of War in 1899-1904 and as a member of the Alaska Boundary Tribunal at London in 1903. He resigned in January, 1909, to serve as United States senator from New York and was succeeded by Robert Bacon who served until March 5.

On May 21, 1906, Secretary Root concluded with Casasus, the Mexican minister at Washington, a convention (ratified and proclaimed on January 16, 1907) providing for the equitable distribution of the waters of the Rio Grande from the head of the Mexican canal to Fort Quitman, Texas, for irrigation purposes, after the completion of a proposed storage dam near Engle, New Mexico. In December, 1906, by order of President Roosevelt, he requested permission of the Mexican government for expensive American plans to control the insurgent waters of the Colorado River which, through a break of levees along the west bank in Mexican territory, threatened ruin to the Imperial Valley in southern California. He promptly received a satisfactory reply, based upon a conference with President Diaz and Minister Mariscal and resulting in negotiations which were interrupted by the revolutionary movement of 1911.[53]

The better understanding between the two governments, indicated by the several conventions and agreements of the period, was also illustrated in 1906 and 1907 by friendly cooperation in regard to Central American affairs. In May, 1906, when the American government received from Guatemala a report that a revolutionary invasion from Mexico was expected, Secretary Root wired Thompson, the American minister at Mexico City, to direct a discreet use of good offices to discourage revolutionary enterprises in the American republics. On May 26, 1906, disturbed by a dispatch from Guatemala indicating that a revolutionary force was gathering on the Mexican border and that hostilities against the Guatemalan government were imminent, he wired in cipher to Ambassador Thompson directing him discreetly in the interest of peace and commerce to use his good offices with Mexico to prevent the hostile demonstration of a revolutionary enterprise which should be discouraged. On June 6, Thompson replied confidentially by wire that President Diaz had gladly agreed to join in anything to stop hostilities and had wired Salvador a warning against ill-advised plans which would be regarded with disfavor and would probably result in failure. In a dispatch of June 8, he forwarded President Diaz's explanation that Guatemala had distrusted Mexico since the date of his opposition to the Guatemalan proposal to compel by force the union of Central America. On June 17-18 the Department (through Assistant Secretary Bacon), in arranging a conference for direct negotiations between the representatives of the belligerents, on the American vessel *Marblehead,* at which American and Mexican representatives would attend in a friendly advisory capacity, made the following statement by cable in cipher to Thompson in Mexico and to Brown in Guatemala: "The attitude of President Diaz in the Guatemalan-Salvadorian affair is precisely the same as that of President Roosevelt, and his desires for the future peace, good government and happiness of the American states are the same." Later, by a telegram of July 14, President Roosevelt was requested by Cabrera of Guatemala to accept the thanks of Guatemala for his proposition of peace and, also, to express to President Diaz grateful thanks "for his most important and friendly influence which has contributed so much toward the happy solution." [54]

In 1907, similar friendliness was shown in the cooperation of Presidents Roosevelt and Diaz in plans tactfully initiated by President Roosevelt for joint mediation (by simultaneous telegrams to the five Central American executives) to maintain order in Central America, and to provide a remedy against future turbulence there by inducing the several states to agree to a conference for adjustment of differences and to agree to treaties and conventions establishing a court of arbitration and looking toward a renewal of a Central American union.

Other incidents of cooperation appeared in the adjustment of sources of friction in American-Mexican relations. After representations as to frauds committed under cover of exemptions from the payment of duties, the American government was finally able to induce Mexico to agree to abolish the Free Zone. American complaints of the depredations of the Yaqui Indians (in Sonora) in 1905 and 1907, and the suggestion that they should be restrained by Mexico, were soon followed by the Mexican removal of these Indians to Yucatan.

In October, 1907, Secretary Root, in response to the hospitable invitation of President Diaz, visited Mexico on a mission of good will which crowned his mission of the previous year to Latin America and which the venerable Mariscal characterized as an event which would leave its impression on the history of Mexico. Accompanied by Mrs. Root and Miss Root, he was met at San Antonio, Texas, by the Mexican reception committee which accompanied him across the border at Laredo. As the guest of Mexico, he was welcomed by President Diaz at a banquet at the National Palace. In his impressive reply to Diaz he contrasted the prosperous and happy Mexico of 1907 with the distressed Mexico which Seward visited thirty-eight years earlier; and to Diaz, whom he characterized as "the most interesting thing in Mexico," he said the world gave the credit for the change. He closed by expressing a sincere tribute to Diaz whom he regarded as one of the world's great men for whose achievements Mexicans owed a debt "of the steadfast loyalty of a lifetime." On October 3, in his reply to Calero, president of the Chamber of Deputies which honored him by a reception, he showed his appreciation of the tasks and services of legislators, requiring wisdom and self-restraint and patriotism, and he especially cited as a worthy example for all the constancy and high courage of their chief magistrate. To the American colony which gave him a luncheon he stated that, while they were loyal American citizens, they should also be loyal Mexican residents. At a banquet given in his honor by Minister Mariscal, on

October 7, with his usual felicity in expressing his grateful appreciation, he paid a deserved compliment to his gracious host— referring to his unvarying courtesy and his genuine and sincere desire for reasonable and friendly disposal of all questions which had arisen between the two countries during his term of office, and stating that as a result of his reasonable attitude in international politics there then existed between Mexico and the United States "no questions which could give the slightest apprehension or cause the slightest concern as to their easy and satisfactory adjustment." After a week of festivities and hospitalities, which gave him an opportunity to estimate the achievements under the leadership of Diaz, he left Mexico with a feeling "that the people of Mexico have joined forever the ranks of the great, orderly, self-controlled, self-governing republics of the world." [55]

In March, 1908, Root concluded with Godoy, the Mexican representative at Washington, an arbitration convention for the pacific settlement of international disputes.

Under President Taft the American Secretary of State was Philander C. Knox of Pennsylvania who had served as United States Attorney-General in 1901-04 and as United States senator in 1904-09. Relations with the Diaz government of Mexico he found satisfactory. In March, 1909, he received from Ambassador Thompson a report of the Mexican decision to extradite Theodosia Jimenez a Mexican citizen—a decision which Secretary Mariscal requested should be communicated as a precedent, in accord with Article IV of the extradition treaty. Later, in July, he received Thompson's report that the Mexican Foreign Office had finally granted the extradition of one Juan de Dios Rodriguez which had been requested first by Secretary Root and later by Secretary Knox, but had been delayed by the difficulty of presenting the required papers within the forty day period of detention.[56]

Although filed with the Mexican dispatches at the Department of State are many letters recommending the retention of Thompson, the latter, at the close of a correspondence with President Taft on the subject, decided to resign. On September

29, 1909, Assistant Secretary Adee, writing him that the President had made known to the Department his desire to terminate his service as ambassador to Mexico on November 30, directed him to turn the embassy over to the chargé on that day—only a few days before the appointment of Henry Lane Wilson to fill the vacancy.[57]

The growing intimacy of relations during the long presidency of Porfirio Diaz, indicated by many international agreements, culminated in a meeting of Taft and Diaz at the international boundary in October, 1909, and the later conclusion of the Knox-Barra convention at Washington in June, 1910, providing for arbitration of the controversy concerning the title to the Chamizal tract at El Paso. On June 25, 1909, President Taft proposed to President Diaz a personal meeting at the border, suggesting at El Paso. Following the acceptance of President Diaz on July 6, Assistant Secretary Adee prepared the program (protocol of arrangements) for the meeting on October 16, 1909—planned to be an informal but conspicuous celebration of the cordial relations existing between the two countries and including an exchange of morning calls and a six o'clock banquet given by President Diaz on the Mexican side of the boundary. Taft good-naturedly allowed himself to be photographed with President Diaz on the international bridge at the boundary line at El Paso. Copies of the photograph, ordered by the Mexican government and carrying the label "Two great Presidents of two great Republics," were distributed widely in Mexico—possibly to the disadvantage of the United States because of the Mexican popular view of the contrast between the plain appearance of Taft with the distinctive military appearance of Diaz.[58]

Already in Mexico opposing forces were planning to terminate the long executive tenure of the dominant Diaz who had successfully established internal order and peace by a system of rural police and municipal gendarmes and had contributed to his country prosperity by encouragement to American enterprise, immigration and investment—by use of American men, money and machinery. A year later, a month after the celebration of the first Mexican centennial, the American government watched with apprehensive interest the rising revolutionary tide which began late in 1910 with the opposition led by Francisco Madero especially aimed against Señor Corral whom Diaz had chosen as the candidate for the vice presidency and who was especially regarded with popular disfavor because he favored the adoption of American ways and sent his children to the United States to obtain their education. In October, 1910, Madero, following his release from prison after the "reelection" of Diaz and Corral, issued his call for revolution under the "Plan de San Luis Potosi," which after seven months triumphed on May 7, 1911, by the fall of Ciudad Juárez, opposite El Paso.

Ambassador Wilson, in summarizing the causes of the opposition to Diaz, mentioned concentration of wealth, objectionable forms of taxation, condition of the lower classes, rising interest of the middle class in public affairs, corrupt judiciary and anti-American feeling. The latter, which he regarded as one of the strongest assets of the revolution, he attributed to a resentment of American commercial aggression and envy of American property and thrift. On November 9, he complained to the Mexican Foreign Office concerning certain anti-American demonstrations which he thought should have been prevented by the police; and, on the following day, he received from Minister Creel assurances that the government would adopt vigorous measures to repress the disorders and to punish the publishers whose incendiary articles were largely responsible for them—assurances which were followed by prompt action. From President Diaz he received the explanation that the real cause of the anti-American demonstrations was a political movement to discredit the Mexican government. With it he received a request of cooperation to prevent unlawful propaganda against his government in the United States. On March 23, 1911, he reported that the situation seemed hopeless, excepting the possible influence of the military precautions of President Taft which were sobering public opinion and modifying anti-American feeling. A change of cabinet, accomplished on March 28, 1911, by Limantour by command of Diaz with the hope that it would prove a palliative to satisfy the popular demand, failed to save the situation.[59]

On April 18, after warning the Diaz government to prevent the firing across the border by the combatants near Douglas, Arizona, President Taft recognized that the situation there would justify an order to American troops to fire upon the combatants across the line or to cross the border to stop the fighting, but he refrained from any such action which might be misconstrued and misrepresented and possibly result in resistance and greater bloodshed, increasing the danger to Americans in Mexico and the pressure for general intervention, and therefore he advised the governor of Arizona (by wire) to direct the people of Douglas to avoid casualty by placing themselves "where bullets can not reach them." On May 8, Secretary Knox wired instructions warning all Americans in Mexico to remain strictly "non-partisan" and directing Wilson to confer with the diplomatic corps on measures to protect foreign life and property in case of a crisis.

Finally, Diaz, under pressure of the mob and tormented by Limantour, resigned on May 25; and on May 26, en route to Paris, he left for Vera Cruz under an escort led by General Victoriano Huerta. De la Barra, who assumed control of the *ad interim* government, on May 26 accepted a new cabinet in which the Madero family was dominant. He soon realized that the executive power was already in the hands of Madero, who was almost unanimously elected President on October 15 and inaugurated on November 6.

In the disorder which followed, the American government sought to observe strictly its international duty. Although it mobilized troops on the frontier, it declined to intervene and with difficulty maintained neutrality—both before and after it recognized the new government of Madero, which was finally overthrown in February, 1913, by Felix Diaz and General Huerta. On January 3, 1912, following the receipt of a note of December 30 from the Mexican minister requesting more vigilant maintenance of neutrality, Secretary Knox informed Attorney-General Wickersham that the department distinguished between enforcement of neutrality and acts which would be equivalent to participation with the Mexican government in suppressing the revolution. On February 12, 1912, he instructed Wilson that the department policy was to allow Americans in Mexico to use their judgment in deciding whether they would remain in Mexico or leave it, but that advice to leave might later be published through consuls. On February 14, following news of Mexican border fears of American intervention and consideration of the questions whether to permit the passage of Mexican troops over American soil and whether to advise Americans to leave Mexico, Assistant Secretary Wilson instructed Ambassador Wilson that the President was disposed to give warning that troops would be sent into Mexico as a police measure—an instruction which was soon followed by a Mexican warning to the American embassy that Americans in Mexico City would be generally massacred if American troops crossed the line at Ciudad Juárez. Following telegraphic news of March 2 from Wilson that the situation was growing worse and that a heavy emigration of Americans from all parts of Mexico had begun, President Taft immediately issued a proclamation warning all American citizens to observe the laws of neutrality (although the Department explained that this was not a declaration of neutrality nor a recognition of the belligerency). When this proclamation was construed as a warning to Americans to leave Mexico, and as indicating a purpose to intervene, the Department promptly denied any such purpose.[60]

President Madero on April 9, 1912, sent to Washington as ambassador Manuel Calero whose successor in the cabinet was Pedro Lascurain. Already, tactlessly refusing advice and losing his "apostolic affability," and unconscious of the impending storm, he was beset by new revolts which finally resulted in his downfall in February, 1913, through the plot of General Huerta whom he appointed as military commandant of the Palace on February 9 at the beginning of the tragic ten days.

The American government viewed the Mexican situation of this period with considerable doubt and watchfulness. On August 2, 1912, following a rumor of Japanese plans to secure a harbor at Magdalena Bay, by a vote of 51 to 4 the Senate adopted the Lodge opposing resolution concerning American foreign policy, which, however, was not a joint resolution and therefore was not submitted to President Taft for his approval.[61]

After several months of conditions which the Department in April, 1912, regarded as intolerable, Wilson, the American ambassador, in a long note of September 15, just after rumors of a possible *coup d'état* against Madero and acting on a telegram from his government, notified Lascurain, the Mexican Minister of Relations, that the Mexican government must either show promptly that it could handle the situation or confess that it could not. In the latter case, he said the American government would consider what steps to take. On November 27, Mr. Schuyler, the American chargé, forwarded to Secretary Knox the long reply (of November 22) of Lascurain, the Mexican Minister of Relations, expressing surprise at the reproaches contained in Wilson's note and the demand for a categorical reply, denying the imputation of hostility to American interests in Mexico and declaring that the Mexican government could not be held responsible for existing conditions, which he intimated were largely the result of the American failure to expel from its territory the leaders of sedition against the Mexican government.[62]

A few days later, on December 19, in reply to Mr. Schuyler's request for instructions on the American policy concerning the Mexican attitude of responsibility toward foreign claims for damages in times of internal disturbance, Secretary Knox declared that the American government could not admit the existence of any unqualified rule of international law excusing a government from all responsibility for damages done to aliens by uncontrolled insurrectionists. Two days later, in New York City, Ambassador Wilson, in an interview with Minister Lascurain who sought to arrange an interview with President Taft and Secretary Knox on January 2, emphasized the necessity of meeting the American demand for justice with ample guarantees and, in response to an intimation from Lascurain, suggested an agreement for the submission of all pending difficulties to an impartial arbitral commission nominated by the usual method.

President Taft, in his annual message of December 3 to Congress, referring to the delicate questions and difficult situations in relations with Mexico in the preceding two years, stated that American policy had been one of patient non-intervention, the recognition of constituted authority and industrious efforts to safeguard American interests resulting from American investments in Mexico.[63]

In February, 1913, during the siege of the capital, Henry Lane Wilson, who was inimical to Madero, urged Lascurain to convoke the Senate, which on February 15, 1913, influenced by inclination and by fear of American intervention, took steps to obtain the resignation of Madero who, however, declined the suggestion. Later, on February 19, Wilson, who had decided that the Madero government no longer existed and who had unsuccessfully asked the diplomatic corps to join in the withdrawal of recognition, again called the members of the diplomatic corps together and, after reading to them Huerta's report that Madero had been arrested, asked them to recognize the new power.[64] On the following day, after the resignation of Madero in prison, Lascurain, as acting President, nominated Huerta as Minister of Gobernacion by which he assumed the presidency *ad interim.* Two days later Huerta reached the beginning of his later downfall through the murder of Madero (en route to the penitentiary)—a murder for which, although he denied complicity, he was held at least morally responsible by the American government (under President Wilson) which refused to recognize him as President of Mexico. Although Ambassador Wilson urged immediate recognition of the Huerta government before the close of the Taft administration, President Taft decided to leave this question of policy to his successor whom he did not wish to embarrass by any hasty action or by any kind of action so near the end of his term of office.

Two important border problems which have been mentioned briefly and which were under consideration by negotiations of the latter part of the period of Diaz and at the beginning of the period of revolution deserve fuller treatment here. One, the Chamizal controversy, had remained unsettled since the negotiations of 1898. The other, the Colorado question, first became prominent in 1906 when the diversion of the waters of the river threatened to convert the Imperial Valley of southern California into a "Salton Sea." On both questions negotiations were terminated in 1913 and both still remained unsettled in 1931 after the adjustment of the oil and land questions which arose in 1917.

A convention of June 24, 1910 (proclaimed January 25, 1911), provided for arbitration of the questions of international difference as to international title to the disputed Chamizal tract of six hundred acres (at El Paso) upon which members of the International Boundary Commission, established by convention of 1889 to execute the principles of the convention of 1884, had failed to agree. By this convention the case was resubmitted to the Boundary Commission (at El Paso, Texas) enlarged by addition of a Canadian jurist as a third commissioner to preside over the deliberations, and the decision, whether by unanimous vote or by majority vote, was to be final and conclusive and without appeal. The Canadian jurist, selected as the third commissioner, was Eugene La Fleur of Montreal.

Under the new convention, the joint commission met on May 15, 1911, heard arguments until June 2 and reached a decision on June 10. On the basis of evidence of earlier Mexican protests, the American plea of right by prescription was dismissed by unanimous vote. The presiding commissioner agreed with the American commissioner that the Rio Grande boundary established by treaties of 1848 and 1853 was not a fixed and invariable line but an arcifinious boundary and, also, that the treaty of 1884 applied to all changes in the river subsequent to the survey of 1852. On the question whether the entire Chamizal tract (as defined in the convention of 1910) was formed by slow and gradual erosion and deposit within the meaning of the convention of 1884 he voted with the Mexican commissioner in the negative and against the American member. He also agreed with the Mexican commissioner that the formation of the tract to 1864 was due to slow and gradual erosion and deposit and that the changes of 1864-68 were not slow and gradual—two questions upon which the American member declined to vote on the ground that he denied the power of the commission to render a decision of segregation which would divide the tract between the two countries. The American member declared that the location of the river in 1864 was wholly obliterated by the flood so that it was impossible to relocate it or to decide what part of the tract was formed after 1864. Against the divided award, based upon the votes indicated, he filed a dissenting opinion.

On August 24, on the ground that the decision of the title to the Chamizal tract had not attempted to locate the boundary line at the tract in dispute and therefore had left for further diplomatic negotiation the differences which it was expected to terminate, the American government through the Secretary of State suggested to the Mexican embassy the negotiation of a new boundary convention at Washington. La Barra, acting as temporary President, and, also, reserving for himself the direction of Mexican foreign relations, insisted that Mexico now had no option but to endeavor to put the award into effect, although he admitted the advantages to be gained by negotiations of a declaratory treaty which he had earlier proposed when at Washington and would not object to new arrangements to overcome any difficulties in the practical application of the points determined by the umpire. The American government, regarding the recent award as absolutely invalid, especially emphasized the opinion "that any attempt to relocate the line of 1864 would not only prove nugatory but would . . . be almost certain to result in seriously embittering the strained conditions at El Paso and Juárez" and suggested that the Mexican government reëxamine the questions with a view to reaching a practical solution satisfactory and honorable to both countries and without prejudice to the position of either on the validity of the award. Further definite action was delayed by disturbed conditions in Mexico and the case remained in *statu quo*.[65]

Influenced by certain American interests and especially by railway needs for terminal facilities in the tract, the American government in December, 1911, again sought some new basis for settlement. The American proposition, based largely upon objections to the difficulties which might arise from incorporating into Mexican domain and jurisdiction a tract which *de facto* was a part of the city of El Paso and which was separated from Ciudad Juárez by the actual water course of the Rio Grande, probably seemed reasonable to the Mexican government which, therefore, agreed to receive and study the plans for adjustment. On March 11, 1912, Ambassador Wilson submitted the question in an interview with President Madero who replied that any reconsideration involving readjustment of the frontier line at that point should also include adjustment of other points of difference on the frontier. Already, on March 9, the Mexican ambassador, Crespo y Martinez, had stated that his government was disposed to consider the American proposal to negotiate further to seek a solution on a basis of mutual convenience or advantage without discussion of the question of the validity of the arbitral award and without prejudice to the position of either government. In the discussions and suggestions which followed, Secretary Knox learned from Martinez that the Mexican government was prepared to effect a settlement by exchange of its claim to the Chamizal tract for a guaranteed supply of water for irrigation purposes—either from the Rio Grande by increase of the amount provided by treaty of 1906, or from the Colorado in connection with the settlement of questions relating to that river, both of which were decided to be impracticable.[66] Finally, on June 28, the Department submitted to the Mexican ambassador a tentative basis for a convention to settle the Chamizal case and other related questions along lines of practical convenience—including a proposition that Mexico receive in exchange for Chamizal the sovereignty of a tract at the artificial bar known as El Horcón and, also, an additional consideration in money if found necessary to render the readjustment equitable. Further negotiations at that time were suspended by the absence of the Mexican ambassador, who assured

Secretary Knox that he expected on his return from Mexico to bring two draft treaties—one for settlement of the Chamizal question and the other for settlement of the Colorado River question; but on his return without the drafts or instructions he vaguely and orally suggested that the Chamizal question could be arranged more advantageously if delayed until the settlement of the Colorado River question. On January 3, 1913, Knox, at the Department of State, held a conference with the Mexican Minister of Foreign Affairs, Lascurain, who at this visit expressed his intention to make a proposal for a prompt adjustment satisfactory to both governments, as soon as he could consult the records in the case, and to permit no further delays in the negotiations. On January 27, the Mexican ambassador submitted a memorandum offering to compromise by accepting for El Chamizal one or more American tracts of equal area on the right bank of the Rio Grande with provision that the American government pay to lawful holders of Mexican titles in Chamizal the value as determined by a proposed special commission of three. On February 28, De la Barra unofficially informed the American ambassador at Mexico that he was prepared to propose to cede Chamizal for the islands of San Elizario and Beaver, near El Paso, the arrangement which, however, could not be carried into effect until Mexican sentiment was prepared for it. This proposition, regarded as inconsistent with the recent negotiations, Knox by telegram (of March 3) promptly rejected as impossible and again proposed to exchange the Horcón tract which the new Mexican government of Huerta (by March 13) accepted as a basis for negotiations at Washington for settlement of the case. The later policy of the new Wilson administration in failing to recognize Emilio Rabasa, whom Huerta had instructed to settle the Chamizal case as the chief object of his mission, prevented further negotiations at the time and caused the Mexican government to give notice of its reservation of all rights to its portion of Chamizal covered by the award.[67]

The Colorado problem attracted wider attention through press dispatches and magazine articles concerning the formation of the Salton Sea in the fertile Imperial Valley by a diversion of the waters of the Colorado through a break in the west bank of the river which had been tapped by an irrigation company. Irrigation of this valley, much of which is below the level of the sea, had been planned in 1891. For this purpose the California Development Company of Los Angeles had been organized in 1896 to divert part of the water of the Colorado. In 1900 it began the work of construction of a diverting channel from the Colorado at a point eight miles south of Yuma by dredging ten miles of the bed of the Alamo River, an ancient channel of the Colorado which for centuries had been almost filled with sand. In June, 1901, through this cut, water was first applied to the Imperial lands, influencing the Mexican government through Aspiroz at Washington to request the American government to consider the question of this diversion of the waters of the Colorado. Later, after this cut became clogged with silt, the irrigation company constructed another intake, farther down stream, which also became clogged. Later, desiring to tap the river at a point farther down stream and within Mexican territory, it sent an agent to Mexico City to obtain, through a subsidiary Mexican company acting under Mexican laws, a concession for an intake fifty feet wide—which was granted on condition that the company employ a Mexican engineer designated by the Mexican government to supervise the work. Into this new intake the company turned the water in the fall of 1904 before the completion of a control headgate which, by criminal negligence, was delayed with expectation of completion before the regular Colorado flood. In the winter of 1904-05, the narrow emergency ditch was rapidly widened and deepened by an abnormal flood resulting from a cloudburst in the Gila basin which suddenly raised the Colorado below Yuma. In May, 1905, the company failed in its attempts to control the insurgent stream by bags of sand and brush. Later, in July, it attempted to divert part of the water by piles in the river—a diversion jetty which was abandoned in August. In October, it tried to form a dam of piles west of an island in the river opposite the intake. Against this dam, which diverted the

THE IMPERIAL VALLEY, THE COLORADO RIVER,
AND THE INUNDATED COUNTRY.

water from the cut, the river in November showed its contempt by hurling against it floods which destroyed it and most of the island below it. Then by a new attack on the intake which rapidly deepened, the uncontrolled waters rushed on to the work of destruction, submerging buildings and railway tracks and pouring into the lowest depths of the valley, 287 feet below the sea level. By the latter part of June the river seemed to have diverted all its waters from the Gulf of California to the new Salton Sea by a canyon which it had cut fifty feet deep in twenty-five days and which by constant widening was endangering the towns along the edge.

Meantime, in the autumn, the company had obtained financial assistance from the Southern Pacific Railway Company. The gigantic desperate struggle, the "battle of the Colorado," waged by 1,050 men and equipment against nature, the men organized by long and expensive preparation, was begun by an all night battle in placing piles and cables as a basis for a dam constructed from both banks until it met in the middle of the breach. This dam was used as a railway track for trains which constantly strengthened it by dumping immense loads of stone and other materials taken from the granite mountains. The terrific contest was finally ended by an all-night battle of November 3 amidst the tumult of the rising masses of stone and gravel and the dreadful roar of the raging flood of the furious river which still hurled scorn at the hissing locomotives' belching smokestacks. Finally, at noon on November 4, the waters subsided and a triumphant shout announced that the victory was won. The Imperial Valley was rescued by the capture of the runaway river at a cost of over three million dollars. After a second break, which occurred on December 7, less than a month after the first one was closed, the American government received from E. H. Harriman of the Southern Pacific a telegram asking government aid in the expensive reclamation service for which he hesitated to advance more money to the California Development Company. President Roosevelt through Secretary Root promptly directed consultation with the Mexican government with a view to plans for permanent measures to prevent a recurrence of the danger; and he wired Harriman that the California company should act promptly without waiting for government action for which he agreed to recommend legislation to provide against repetition of the break and for an equitable distribution of the burden of expense. On December 11, Secretary Root cabled the situation to the American embassy at Mexico and suggested that the American government by cooperation with Mexico should assume management of the entire work of control of the river which had reached beyond the capacity of individuals or corporations to handle, and upon which depended the safety of Yuma and the American government dam at Laguna. He instructed Thompson to urge upon Mexico the necessity of immediate and effective action and discreetly to ascertain whether Mexico would permit American protective operations on Mexican territory covered by a concession of a Mexican company of Lower California which had failed to meet its obligations. From Thompson's reply (of December 16) he learned that President Diaz agreed to American operations on Mexican territory under a permit from the Mexican government but without expense to Mexico for controlling the river, and that the Mexican government agreed to permit the free entrance of all equipment necessary for conducting the work of control. In the second week of January, 1907, President Roosevelt received from Director Walcott of the United States Geological Survey a letter of January 10 suggesting that he should request an appropriation of two million dollars and should obtain from Mexico assurances that the break would be patrolled and guarded at all times and suggesting that Mexico should be asked to prevent any future artificial cutting of the west bank of the Colorado at any point which might threaten to jeopardize American interests. On January 12, 1907, he promptly presented to Congress the alarming situation by stating that if the break remained unclosed until the spring flood of 1907 all property values in the valley, including three hundred miles of canals, would probably be wiped out and that ultimately futher damage would result up the river to Yuma and to Laguna (twelve miles above Yuma). Stating that the Southern Pacific had expended $2,000,000 or more and that it declined to furnish more (although still working on repairs), he urged as a necessity prompt action to secure permanent protective works and suggested that the general plan under the reclamation service should be a comprehensive scheme of development of all irrigable land upon the Colorado. Already the preliminary trestle work for new efforts to close the break had been begun, and on January 27, over trestle work the first train load of stone was pushed. Before the close of February the break was closed.[68]

The new problem of the Colorado had become an international issue. Above the earlier treaty arrangements providing for navigation of the stream, treating it as a highway of commerce (provisions of doubtful value and of no value after the railway reached Yuma), arose the immediately practical and dominating problem of irrigation and the incidental problems of protection from floods, control of the river and equitable division of the waters—problems which were not foreseen in the negotiations of the treaties of 1848 and 1853. Early in 1908, the American government took steps to ascertain an equitable amount of water from the Colorado which should be distributed for irrigation use of each country and whether the use of Mexican territory by the American Reclamation Service might be necessary to the protection of the reclamation works at the Laguna Dam. For this purpose, Mariscal on March 31 agreed to the appointment of commissioners to obtain data as a basis upon which to treat.[69]

For further protection of lands and property of the Imperial Valley against injury from the changes in the Colorado, Congress by joint resolution approved on June 25, 1910, an appropriation of $1,000,000 authorizing the President to use any portion of this sum within the limits of Mexico. The Department of State, through the American ambassador, Henry L. Wilson, promptly obtained from the Mexican government assurance of cooperation in facilitating the necessary surveys and investigations along the Colorado in Mexican territory. In October, 1910, Assistant Secretary Adee, acting for Secretary Knox,

instructed Ambassador Wilson to request the consent of the
Mexican government for erection of a levee twenty-five miles
in length along the west bank of the Colorado on Mexican lands
owned by the Colorado River Land and Water Company of
which General Harrison Gray Otis and his son-in-law, Harry
Chandler, of Los Angeles, were directors. On November 7, by
instructions of the President, he urged the importance of
prompt action. Ambassador Wilson, after emphasizing to Diaz
the necessity for haste, on November 22 reported by telegram
a reply from the Mexican Foreign Office, stating that President
Diaz had no authority to permit the erection of levees or to
grant free entry of materials for the work and suggesting the
negotiation of a treaty at Washington. On November 26, Knox,
in a telegram accepting the suggestion for the appointment of
a joint commission to examine the levee project, again urged
haste, suggested the substitution of some other arrangement for
a treaty and explained that the American government desired
to secure for itself no rights on Mexican territory but only to
protect settlers of American territory from enormous losses.
Five days later, he was informed by the Mexican minister, La
Barra, at Washington, that the Mexican government had telegraphed its agreement to accept a simple exchange of notes at
Washington as sufficient authority for the construction of the
protective works and had proposed certain bases including provisions that the works should be constructed by the Colorado
River Land Company in accord with plans approved by a Mexican inspector, that Mexico assume no responsibility as to the
results and that the American government by its pecuniary aid
would acquire no right of ownership or easement or any other
right over the works constructed on Mexican territory. On December 24, Assistant Secretary Huntington Wilson, in a note
to La Barra, accepted the bases proposed. Secretary Knox, meantime, asking free importation of materials used by the company
in the work of construction, had proposed (on December 9) an
arrangement for accumulation of deferred payment of duties
until the Mexican Congress could remit them by the necessary
legislation.[70]

Knox had expected to arrange later for negotiation of a treaty providing for the maintenance of the levee after its completion, but he accepted the explanation of La Barra (of January 4, 1911) that under the bases of construction by the Mexican company all other agreements must be exclusively arranged between the construction company and the Mexican department concerned and that the defensive works were without any international character.

The American government, after the completion of the international agreement concerning the work of defense from the insurgent river, soon became apprehensive of other threatening dangers of insurgency against which military measures of defense seemed necessary. On February 12, notifying La Barra of the reported operations of Mexican insurgent political leaders who were supposed to plan to raid the grading camps to entice the workmen away and drive the work animals away, Secretary Knox suggested the need of military cooperation to protect the property which was in jeopardy. On February 14, La Barra replied that the Mexican government had given orders for the increase of the Mexican force on the Colorado and would probably not need to have recourse to American forces whose passage into Mexican territory could be authorized only by approval of the Mexican Senate. Three days later, following telegraphic news from California that the region of the Imperial Valley had been left unprotected by the defeat of the Mexican forces by insurgents, Knox telegraphed Ambassador Wilson to reiterate to the Diaz government the suggestion of effective American cooperation with the Mexican government, at least by American police guards without uniform, and on the same day he received Wilson's telegraphic reply that in view of the urgent necessity the Mexican government verbally agreed (without exchange of notes) to authorize the use of the necessary guards on the pay roll of the construction company with the request for the utmost discretion in sending them across the boundary and in preventing publicity in the American press.

With the increase of the revolutionary movements in Mexico, which daily became more menacing to the construction work on the Colorado, Knox found that the plan of protection arranged by agreement with the Diaz government was impracticable. On March 2, he wired the American chargé at Mexico City that the Diaz government, appreciating the emergency which made indispensable a body of American troops to guard the works, should officially request the American government temporarily to protect the levee. From the American chargé (March 4) and, also, from the Mexican ambassador (March 3), he promptly received the reply that Diaz could not act on the question of inviting foreign troops without the sanction of the Senate which was not in session, and that in agreement with Minister Creel, he thought any permit for entrance of American troops would strengthen the revolution by being construed as an admission of the weakness of the government. To the Mexican ambassador's suggestion that Mexico would be disposed to request from the American government the passage of Mexican troops from Lower California by American railway from San Diego to the Colorado, Knox replied (on March 7) that the American government preferred to adhere to its previous policy of neutrality by requiring the Mexican troops engaged in general hostilities to reach their destination over Mexican territory.[71]

Meantime, the Mexican revolution was approaching a more dangerous stage which required greater watchfulness and military precautions both by President Taft and by President Diaz. The latter, on March 21, expressed great satisfaction with the attitude and activity of the American government which seemed to modify anti-American feeling in Mexico. On May 24 and 27, 1911, however, Knox received from the Mexican minister, Zamacona, a complaint that while the Mexican Federal forces had been engaged in protecting the Colorado River works, filibusters had crossed the international boundary to invade Lower California. Knox, on June 6, replied that the American government had been vigilant in police measures to insure observance of international duties and denied the intimation that filibustering attempts had been organized on American territory. A day later he suggested that the movement in Lower California seemed to be the work of a Mexican political party seeking to throw off Mexican authority and to establish a socialistic republic there, and stated that the utterance of their inflammatory propaganda in the United States without any definite act was not an offense against international law nor against local law.[72]

In September, 1911, Secretary Knox was informed by Samuel Adams, Acting Secretary of the Interior, that the Mexican commissioner had suggested that the Mexican permit and privileges granted in 1910 in connection with the construction of the levee and dam on the Colorado had expired and that application for renewal should be submitted to the Department of Fomento. The new application was promptly granted in November.

Connected with the question of permanent control of the river were international questions which could be settled only by an international board. In February, 1912, Secretary Knox received from Secretary Fisher of the Interior Department a suggestion that negotiations should be opened with Mexico for the erection of an entirely new international commission of broad powers, and composed of both engineers and men familiar with legal and diplomatic issues involved, to investigate and report on the proper method of utilizing the waters of the lower Colorado and with authority to submit a basis for adjustment of all questions relating to the conservation and control of the waters. Assistant Secretary H. Wilson (on March 21) instructed the American ambassador, H. L. Wilson, to press the negotiations; and on April 27 the ambassador reported the view of the Mexican government approving the plan for the proposed new commission but recommending for the time the continuance of the existing International Water Boundary Commission with an increase of practical personnel to study and propose arrangements for adjustment of special problems of the Colorado.

On June 14 President Taft, in a message to the Senate, recommending further appropriations for protection from the insurgent waters of the Colorado, referred to the need of a free and full agreement with Mexico as to joint expenditure and joint use before a larger plan of improvements could be submitted to Congress. On September 10, the Acting Secretary of State, H. Wilson, submitted to Ambassador Wilson the draft of a convention providing for a preliminary commission to study and report upon the bases of distribution of the Colorado waters; and, in November, the Mexican Minister of Foreign Affairs submitted a counter draft. On February 8, 1913, Assistant Secretary Adee, acting for Secretary Knox, forwarded a counter draft of the amended convention with which the Mexican Minister of Fomento (on May 3) announced his practical agreement; but later (May 8) Ambassador Wilson wired that General Huerta had refused to consider the Colorado question until after the American government had extended formal recognition of his government.[73]

The long delay in reaching a satisfactory adjustment of the Chamizal and Colorado questions was a natural consequence of the long period of revolutions and economic reforms which followed the retirement of Diaz from the government of Mexico—a new era of a younger generation which began largely as a protest against the increasing cooperation of the Diaz government with the peaceful penetration of Mexico by American enterprise.

REFERENCES

1. 20 *Mexico, Instructions*, (No. 137) June 16, and (No. 156) July 27, 1881; 73 *Mexico, Despatches*, (No. 254 Confidential), Aug. 13, 1881.

2. 20 *Mexico, Instructions*, (No. 138) June 16, (No. 142) June 21, (No. 143, Confidential) June 21, 1881.

3. 73 *Mexico, Despatches*, (No. 232) July 12, (No. 240) July 19, (No. 247) Aug. 5, (No. 253) Aug. 11, (No. 259) Aug. 25; 74 *Mexico, Despatches*, (No. 273) Sept. 22, (No. 297) Nov. 2, 1881; *Foreign Relations, 1881*.

4. 20 *Mexico, Instructions*, No. 198, Nov. 28, 1881 (*For. Rels., 1881*, pp. 766-70).

5. *Ib.*, (No. 199) Nov. 29, 1881; 75 *Mexico, Despatches*, No. 375, March 28, 1882.

6. *For. Rels., 1882*, pp. 332, 437 and 438; 21 *Mexico, Instructions*, (Tel.) Apr. 11, 1885.

7. *Ib.*, (Tel.) July 30, and (No. 626) July 31, 1884; 20 *Mexico, Instructions*, (No. 419) June 16, 1883; 79 *Mexico, Despatches*, (No. 635) May 30, 1883.

8. *20 Mexico, Instructions,* (No. 368) Feb. 6, (No. 384) March 27, (No. 411) June 5, and (No. 427) June 29, 1883.
9. *Mexico, Despatches,* (No. 819) June 2, (No. 853) July 10, 1884; *21 Mexico, Instructions,* (No. 550) Apr. 23, 1884; *21 Mexico, Instructions,* (No. 579) May 22, (No. 608) July 11, (No. 609) July 11, (No. 663) Aug. 14, (No. 672) Oct. 16, (No. 673), Oct. 16, 1884, and (No. 756) Apr. 16, and (No. 775) May 16, 1885.
10. *20 Mexico, Instructions,* (No. 288) July 24, 1882; *21 Mexico, Instructions,* (No. 732) Feb. 17, 1885; *Mexico, Despatches,* (No. 503) Sept. 27, 1882, and (No. 905) Dec. 20, 1884.
11. *20 Mexico, Instructions,* (No. 332) Oct. 24, 1882; *21 Mexico, Instructions,* (No. 772) May 12, (No. 774) May 15, 1885, and (No. 80) Apr. 9, 1887; *Mexico, Despatches,* (No. 574) Feb. 26, and (No. 610) May 2, 1883.
12. *55 Mexico, Despatches,* (No. 373) Jan. 29, 1876; *20 Mexico, Instructions,* (No. 221) Jan. 11, March 17, 1882, (No. 354) Jan. 23, 1883, (No. 381) May 23, and (Tel.) May 18, (No. 601) July 5, and (No. 606) July 11, 1884; *House Rp. 1848,* 48-1.
13. *Reports Sen. Com. on For. Rels.,* Vol. 6, pp. 278-79, 282, 308-11.
14. *21 Mexico, Instructions,* (No. 681) Nov. 4, (No. 697) Dec. 19, (Personal and Confidential) Dec. 19, 1884.
15. *21 Mexico, Instructions,* (No. 736) March 7, 1885, (Tel.) May 1, 1886; *For. Rels., 1886,* pp. vii-ix.
16. *21 Mexico, Instructions,* (Tel.) March 16, (Tel.) Apr. 11, 1885; *Mexico, Despatches,* (Tel.) March 17, 1885.
17. *21 Mexico, Instructions,* (No. 125) Feb. 5, (No. 193) May 28, (No. 200) June 14, 1886; *22 Mexico, Instructions,* (No. 142) Oct. 11, 1888; *23 Mexico, Instructions,* (No. 523) May 25, (No. 536) June 17, (No. 541) July 3, 1891; *For. Rels. 1888 and 1894.*
18. *Mexico, Despatches,* (No. 266) July 8, (Tel.) July 22, (No. 278) July 28, (No. 285) Aug. 5, and (No. 296) Aug. 14, 1886; *21 Mexico, Instructions,* (Tel.) July 19, (No. 221) July 20, (Tel.) July 22, (No. 228) July 27, (No. 231) Aug. 4, Aug. 13, 1886; *Sen. Doc. 224,* 49-1; *For. Rels., 1886, 1887 and 1888;* RICHARDSON, *Messages and Papers of the Presidents,* VIII, pp. 502-03.
19. *22 Mexico, Instructions,* (No. 200) Nov. 1, 1887, (No. 42) May 4, 1888; *94 Mexico, Despatches,* (No. 273) Nov. 16, (No. 281) Dec. 3, 1887, and (Tel.) Feb. 12, and (No. 306) Feb. 21, 1888; *For. Rels., 1889,* p. 551 (Whitehouse to Bayard, Feb. 28, 1889).

20. *87 Mexico, Despatches*, Aug. 13, 1885; *90 Mexico, Despatches*, (No. 256) June 30, 1886; *91 Mexico, Despatches*, (No. 307) Sept. 4, and (No. 332) Oct. 7, 1886; *21 Mexico, Instructions*, (No. 236) Aug. 13, Aug. 19, (No. 304) Aug. 27, and (No. 332) Oct. 7, 1886.

21. *21 Mexico, Instructions*, (Tel.) March 17, (No. 65) March 19, (No. 69) March 26, (No. 74) Apr. 5, (Tel.) Apr. 8, (No. 79) Apr. 9, (No. 96) May 2, 1887; *Mexico, Despatches*, (No. 93) March 21, (No. 116) Apr. 14, (No. 132) May 7, (No. 141) May 13, (Tel.) May 16, 1887, and (No. 28) Apr. 20, (No. 29) Apr. 24, and (No. 30) Apr. 28, 1888.

22. *22 Mexico, Instructions*, (No. 208) July 2, 1886, and (No. 3) Feb. 17, (No. 26) Apr. 11, (No. 147) Oct. 18, 1888, (No. 210) Jan. 17, and (No. 53) Aug. 14, 1889; *Mexico, Despatches*, (No. 15) March 20, and (No. 196) Nov. 24, 1888; *Sen. Exec. Doc. 109*, 49-2.

23. *22 Mexico, Instructions*, (Tel.) Nov. 14, (No. 167) Nov. 15, (Tel.) Nov. 17, (No. 173) Nov. 27, 1888, and (No. 239) March 11, 1889; *Mexico, Despatches*, (No. X) Feb. 28, 1889.

24. *Mexico, Despatches*, (No. 274) Mar. 12, (No. 81) Aug. 27, 1889, (No. 1003, Confidential) June 28, 1892; *23 Mexico, Instructions*, (No. 777) July 15, 1892; *Arena*, March, 1904, p. 476.

25. *Mexico, Despatches*, No. 602, July 28, 1891.

26. *For. Rels., 1890*, pp. 645, 648 and 652; *22 Mexico, Instructions*, (Tel.) July 31, (Tel.) Aug. 7, and (Tel.) Aug. 11, 1890.

27. *Mexico, Despatches*, (No. 8) June 1, 1889, and (No. 205) Jan. 14, 1890.

28. *Ib.*, (Tel.) July 12, (No. 89) Sept. 2, 1889; *23 Mexico, Instructions*, (Tel.) Sept. 21, (No. 625) Nov. 25, (Tel.) Dec. 23, 1891; *N. Am. Rev.*, Vol. 154, pp. 459-71, Apr., 1892.

29. *22 Mexico, Instructions*, (No. 375) Oct. 22, (No. 399) Nov. 19, 1890; *23 Mexico, Instructions*, (No. 631) Dec. 1, 1891, (No. 747) May 14, 1892; *26 Mexico, Instructions*, (No. 1287) May 24, and p. 38, May 25, 1905; *Mexico, Despatches*, (No. 843) Dec. 17, 1891.

30. *23 Mexico, Instructions*, (No. 655) Dec. 29, 1891, and (Tel.) Feb. 16, and (No. 690) Mar. 3, 1892.

31. *Ib.*, (No. 716) Apr. 14, 1892, (No. 37) June 22, 1895; *115 Mexico, Despatches*, (No. 1166) Feb. 4, 1893; *For. Rels., 1894*, pp. 418-24.

32. *23 Mexico, Instructions*, (No. 797) Aug. 23, 1892; *Mexico, Despatches*, (No. 951) May 12, 1892; *For. Rels., 1893*.

33. *23 Mexico, Instructions*, (Tel.) Sept. 6, (Tel.) Sept 10, 1893.

34. *For. Rels., 1896*, pp. 439-55.

35. J. B. Moore, *International Law Digest*, V, pp. 793-94; *For. Rels.*, *1888, 1896*, pp. 438-39, and 1894; *House Rp. 702*, March 11, 1898; *23 Mexico, Instructions*, No. 35, June 8, 1893.

36. *23 Mexico, Instructions*, (No. 267, Confidential) Aug. 31, 1894; *Mexico, Despatches*, (No. 101) Dec. 26, 1895; *Political Science Quarterly*, July, 1924 (Article by J. F. Rippy).

37. *23 Mexico, Instructions*, No. 61, Aug. 2, 1895.

38. *House Exec. Doc. 154*, 48-1; *For. Rels.*, *1895*, II, pp. 979-87 and 993; *23 Mexico, Instructions*, (Tel.) Jan. 21, 1895; *125 Mexico, Despatches*, (Tel.) Jan. 23, (No. 418) Jan. 31, (No. 426) Feb. 6, and (No. 432) Feb. 12, 1895.

39. *128 Mexico, Despatches*, (No. 164) June 29, 1896; *Mexico, Despatches*, (No. 21) June 12, 1897, (No. 400) May, and (No. 553) July 26, 1898.

40. *Ib.*, (No. 74) Aug. 4, 1897, (No. 286) Aug. 15, (Tels.) Sept. 8 and Sept. 25, 1899.

41. *Ib.*, (Tels.) Apr. 22 and 27, (No. 452) June 3, and (No. 534) July 18, 1898; *24 Mexico, Instructions*, (No. 419) May 13, 1898.

42. *House Rp. 702*, Mar. 11, 1898; Richardson, *Messages and Papers of the Presidents*, X, p. 187; *For. Rels.*, *1898*, p. lxxix.

43. *For. Rels.*, *1897*, pp. 388-94 and 405-16, and 1898, pp. 491-511; *24 Mexico, Instructions*, (Tel.) Feb. 8, (No. 74) Feb. 10, (Tel.) Feb. 17, 1898; *Mexico, Despatches*, (Tel.) Oct. 13, 1899.

44. *Ib.*, No. 336, Mar. 21, 1898; Richardson, *Messages and Papers of the Presidents*, X, pp. 187-88; *For. Rels.*, *1910*, pp. 716 and 720, and 1911, pp. 565-605.

45. *25 Mexico, Instructions*, (No. 271) Dec. 16, 1899, (No. 274) Jan. 5, 1900; *143 Mexico, Despatches*, (No. 450) Dec. 23, 1899; *For. Rels.*, *1900*, pp. 790-802.

46. *25 Mexico, Instructions*, (No. 311, Tel.) Feb. 19, and Apr. 27, (No. 412) Aug. 21, (No. 446) Nov. 16, 1900, and (No. 542) July 18, 1901.

47. *141 Mexico, Despatches*, No. 303, Aug. 25, 1899; J. B. Moore, *International Law Digest.*

48. *25 Mexico, Instructions*, (No. 322) March 8, (No. 363) June 1, 1900, (No. 977) Oct. 27, and (No. 1001) Dec. 1, 1903.

49. *Ib.*, (No. 358) May 16, 1900; *145 Mexico, Despatches*, (No. 647) May 2, 1900.

50. *145 Mexico, Despatches*, (No. 660) May 14, 1900; *155 Mexico, Despatches*, March 19, 1902; *25 Mexico, Instructions*, (Nos. 361 and 362) May 26, 1900, (Tel.) March 24, and (No. 815) Dec. 15, 1902.

51. *For. Rels.*, *1902*, pp. 738-85, and Appendix II.

52. *26 Mexico, Instructions*, (No. 1192) Dec. 1, 1904, (No. 1251) Mar. 24, 1905; *For. Rels., 1907*, pp. 837-40.

53. *For. Rels., 1911*, pp. 225-26.

54. *26 Mexico, Instructions*, (Tel.) May 26, (No. 81) June 8, July 15, (Tel.) July 18, 1906; *For. Rels., 1906.*

55. *Mexico, Despatches*, No. 72, Oct. 22, 1907 (Enclosures); *For. Rels., 1907*, pp. 852-70.

56. *For. Rels., 1909*, pp. 431—, and 415—.

57. *86 Numerical Files*, 1906-10, Cases 566 to 573/25.

58. *For. Rels., 1909*, pp. 425 *et seq.; Sen. Exec. Doc. 285*, 66-2, Vol. 1, pp. 1473-74.

59. *Review of Reviews*, Dec., 1905, pp. 724-25; *For. Rels., 1911*, pp. 353-55, 359 and 432.

60. *For. Rels., 1912*, pp. 708, 712, 727, 731-32 and 929-86 *passim.*

61. *Cong. Globe*, Vol. 48, pp. 10045-47; *Sen. Rps.* 996, 640 and 694, 62-2; *6 Am. Jr. Int. Law*, p. 938.

62. *For. Rels., 1912*, pp. 842 and 871-77.

63. *Ib.*, pp. 984 and xiv.

64. *For. Rels., 1911*, pp. 508-10.

65. *Ib.*, pp. 565—, 598-605.

66. *For. Rels., 1912*, pp. 506-07, 964-65; *For. Rels., 1913*, pp. 965 and 970.

67. *Ib.*, pp. 968-76.

68. *Notes to Mexico Legation*, No. 202, Dec. 5, 1901; *Sci. Am.*, Feb. 22, 1906, pp. 467-69; *Eng. Mag.*, Feb., 1907, pp. 800-03; *World's Work*, March, 1907, pp. 8606-10, and May, 1907, pp. 267-69; *Smithsonian Rp.*, 1907, pp. 331-45; *For. Rels., 1911*, pp. 525-26, 526-34, 534-35; *Sen. Doc. 212*, 59-2; *Sen. Doc. 103*, 65-1.

69. *N. Am. Rev.*, Aug., 1910, p. 233; *For. Rels., 1911*, pp. 537, 539.

70. *Ib.*, 541-52.

71. *Ib.*, pp. 553-63.

72. *Ib.*, pp. 432, 490, 494-95, 498-502.

73. *For. Rels., 1913*, pp. 977-93.

CHAPTER XIII

THE AMERICAN ECONOMIC INVASION OF MEXICO UNDER DIAZ

THE largest outstanding fact which influenced American relations with Mexico in the generation after the decline of border disorders and the American recognition of the Diaz government was the extension of American industrial or economic interests in Mexico, slowly at first but gradually increasing in momentum under the growth of a more liberal Mexican policy under the directing hand of the dominant executive who was able to reduce and partially to suppress old prejudices.

In this movement of economic infiltration, Seward was a prophet and precursor. After the close of the American Civil War, and especially after the success of his diplomacy in terminating French intervention in Mexico, he foresaw and favored a policy of peaceful economic penetration of Mexico for the benefit of Mexico by Americans under the leadership of capitalists and captains of industry seeking investment opportunities. With his optimism he probably could not foresee the obstacles and difficulties which such a policy would encounter from those who by their prejudice against foreigners long failed to appreciate the economic advantages offered by the efforts of individuals and captains of American economic enterprise—the pioneers of a new frontier in the extension of railway communication, mines and smelters, assay offices and chemical laboratories, ranches and haciendas, factories and foundries, financial institutions, public utilities, and facilities for oil production.

The first of the important pioneers in the new industrial advance into Mexico were the railway promoters and railway builders. For the railway system of Mexico which has performed

475

an inestimable service by supplanting antiquated and perilous methods of transportation, and by bridges and tunnels opening regions previously inaccessible, Americans, especially American empire builders trained in the West, were largely responsible and deserve large credit. Although in their earliest plans they encountered much opposition and difficulty, those who persisted finally won in the peaceful struggle against personal prejudices and physical obstacles. As early as 1853 Americans sought a concession for a railway from the American southwest border to the Gulf of California. The earliest concession in that region was granted in July, 1854, to Alejandro José Atocha for a railway and telegraph line from Presidio del Norte (or Piedras Negras) to Guaymas. Another early concession for a railway from Presidio del Norte by way of Villa del Paso (or Juárez) to Guaymas was a grant to the American-Mexican Company of New York by Chihuahua in August, 1859, and by Sonora in March, 1861—later (in April, 1865) supplemented by a national concession which was finally forfeited in January, 1873.[1]

Among the earliest promoters in the post-bellum period were E. L. Plumb and General W. S. Rosecrans, both of whom served for a time in the American diplomatic service in Mexico. On December 13, 1867, Plumb, who had first visited Mexico in 1854 when the first ten miles of the railway from Vera Cruz toward Mexico City had been completed (a road which still lacked 128 miles of completion to the capital), mentioned to Seward the necessity of railroads in Mexico which had no rivers, and suggested that the United States, whose railway achievements had attracted the admiration of the world, should furnish the enterprise and energy for their construction. In the following April, his hopes were deflated by the anti-foreign feeling exhibited in a bitter debate in the Mexican Congress resulting in the adoption of a report of the special committee suspending the decree (of November 27, 1867) by which Juárez had revalidated the concession for completing the railway from Vera Cruz to Mexico City. In 1868, however, the Mexican Congress, under the Juárez government, incorporated "The Mexican and United States Railway Company" (including C. C. Douglas, Jesse Hoyt, Cyrus H. McCormick, Anson Bangs, A. H. Barney, and William B. Ogden) to build a railway from Presidio del Norte to a point between Guayamas and Mazatlan, and a connecting line to Mexico City.

On March 10, 1869, General Rosecrans, reporting to Secretary Fish that social and business conditions had been growing daily worse and that new complications had arisen in northern states of Mexico from plans of Cuban monarchists in Tamaulipas, declared that the only hope for the future must be found in exterior aid. He urged the rapid advance of American railways and telegraphs and American enterprise to the northern border; and he especially advised, from a standpoint of national importance, that the southern transcontinental railway should be compelled to locate its route as near as possible to the border. On March 28, still urging the need of American immigration and industrial leadership for the solution of the Mexican question by pacific means, he recommended the American organization of two or three grand trunk railway lines to penetrate to the heart of Mexico and suggested that such enterprises should be encouraged by Mexican offers of pecuniary profit. At the same time, he was seeking to induce the Mexican government to support railway projects to further the economic development of the country. On April 10, after he had been approached confidentially by intelligent leaders of the opposition seeking to know definitely what the United States was willing to do and what would be required of the Mexican government to encourage the development of immigration and railroads, he submitted to Secretary Fish four alternatives in the choice of a policy as to Mexico: (1) To leave the country to disintegrate with all the attendant sufferings and loss and danger to American interests; (2) To attempt to combine Mexican elements to secure a cabinet under Juárez which would adopt measures to enable the government to perform its duties and to direct a career of progress and intercourse; (3) To aid the constitutional party to establish a government founded on the constitution of 1857 and guarantees in a policy which would secure the ends of government and of progress for both countries; (4) To conquer

and occupy the country (an alternative which he could not contemplate without repugnance). Expecting that the "second and third alternatives would be preferred in their order" he recommended (1) the promotion of the purchase and completion of the English railway from Vera Cruz to Mexico City, or an equivalent line from Antonio Libardo to the valley of Mexico by way of Tehuacan by American capital and enterprise, and (2) the American construction of a railway from Tampico, Tuxpan or some part of the Huasteca valley to the valley of Mexico. In order to cure the Mexican "sick man" he also suggested that organized American capitalists, with the consent of the American government, should buy and control the public debt of Mexico and advance the needful means to the Mexican government to enable it to get organized under American auspices and guaranty. In a despatch of May 10, in which he announced evidences of the near approach of a revolution which he expected to result in the adoption of a system of railways, emigration, assimilation and reciprocity of trade, and for which the United States must be prepared, he wrote:

". . . Always hoping the peaceful and progressive solution I have proposed will be adopted, I have stimulated both parties in Congress to grant two concessions for railroads: *one from Anton Lizardo to connect* with the *Tehuantepec Rail Road, and a branch to the Pacific via Tehuacan* and Cuernavaca; the other from Tampico or Tuspam to Mexico, and probably thence to the Pacific, through populous, and fertile lands. I expect also exemptions from taxes &c for a term of years to immigrant settlers on the Company's lands, and a solemn pledge of the national faith to protect their rights. I report these as now under way with no probability of opposition. . . .

"You will observe that my idea of the use of these grants is that while they afford a just foundation for investments, our great Capitalists will have the additional inducements that they will secure the humane industrial and commercial conquest, peaceful development of a great and wealthy country, and save incalculable human suffering, and even innumerable hazards and expenses to our country." [2]

One of the chief obstacles to the realization of the American program of helpfulness to Mexico by immigrations of Americans and American capital and enterprise is indicated by the following extracts from Nelson's dispatch of January 28, 1870, to Secretary Fish:

"The feeling of jealousy and dislike which has existed in the minds of a very large number of the Mexican people for the last quarter of a century, towards foreigners and especially Americans, is probably more intense at this time, than ever before. This is attributable to several causes, independent of the natural antagonism arising from difference of race, language, religions, habits &c. the chief of which, is the use made by the enemies of both Governments of the good understanding and friendship which is known to subsist between the Government of President Juarez and that of President Grant. Some of the opposition leaders and a portion of the press, more for the purpose of injuring the Mexican Government than any other object, constantly denounce the President and his Cabinet, for what they term, their *subserviency* to the United States, going so far as to say, that the pressure of American influence, is felt in every important question of domestic, as well as foreign policy.

". . . It is said and believed by many, that President Juarez has, by secret Treaty, ceded to the United States, a large part of the Northern Territory. Nearly all the recent *pronunciamientos* contain some artful allusions to American influence and designs. Negrete proclaims Juarez a traitor and denounces the punishment of death against him, for selling Sinaloa to the United States.

"You will perceive by reading the reports of our Consuls to this Legation, that the feeling of distrust, excited by these means and in many other ways, towards our country, is increasing in every part of the Republic, and that in some places much apprehension is felt by our countrymen, of popular uprisings, which will imperil their lives and property. The cry of 'Death to the Americans' is by no means uncommon." [3]

On November 17, 1871, Mariscal, Minister of Foreign Affairs, in a speech in Congress, in reply to a young orator of the opposition party who had accused Romero of plans to leave the Treasury Department in order to negotiate at Washington an American protectorate over Mexico, declared that the Mexican President sought no such protectorate and that any danger to the honor of Mexico or to the integrity of its territory could originate only in new revolution and anarchy which might indicate incapability of self-government, result in material ruin and the loss of all hope for needed immigration and foreign industry and capital and encourage projects or filibustering expeditions which might make more critical the situation. Also declaring that the existing American government had no thought to acquire unjustly or by force or by means of diplomacy any part of Mexican territory, he added, "They will certainly not take it by force while we keep a decent peace, and while under the shadow of our government fairly respected, they may be able to realize great roads of communication and other undertakings . . . enriching our country." [4]

Among the liberal-minded Mexican statesmen of this period was Caneda, who, in a speech in the Mexican Congress, after referring to the changes in the United States in regard to territorial extension since 1847 and stating that fears of American conquest were only imaginary, defended a proposed concession in favor of the construction of an American interoceanic railway.[5]

In the spring of 1872, railway promoters became more active. On April 23, General Rosecrans, accompanied by General Palmer, president of the projected narrow-gauge railway, the Denver and Rio Grande, arrived at Mexico City from California by way of Manzanillo and Guadalajara. Two days later Ex-Governor Hunt of Colorado, after a trip overland by way of Chihuahua, arrived with another part of the Rosecrans party. Rosecrans' various railway plans included a transferred concession for a railway from a Gulf point south of Tampico in the region of Tuxpan to the Pacific (at a point between Zacatula and San Blas) which had been granted to an American in December, 1870—a concession which was declared void in 1873. E. L. Plumb was also at the capital representing the railway project of the International Railway Company of Texas and seeking a concession for a railway from Mexico City to the Pacific and to the Rio Grande. Simon Stevens, president of the Tehuantepec Railway and Canal Company, arrived on April 27.

On October 26, 1872, Porter C. Bliss, as an accommodation, transmitted to President Lerdo through the Minister of Relations (to whom he sent an unofficial explanatory note) certain telegrams of Philadelphia capitalists (Colonel Tom Scott and others) relative to a railway project pending before the Mexican Congress. As evidence that the telegrams had been delivered he forwarded a duplicate of the private note to General Rosecrans who, in violation of diplomatic propriety, on October 29 published a Spanish translation of the note in several Mexican papers. Bliss, embarrassed by general impressions that the note was official, and complying with special instructions from Secretary Fish, promptly explained to the Mexican government that the private note was written without orders from Fish. On June 12, 1873, Thomas H. Nelson reported his unsuccessful attempts to negotiate a Tehuantepec treaty for protection of a railway and an interoceanic canal across Tehuantepec. On August 19, 1874, Foster reported little prospect of obtaining from Mexico a treaty guaranteeing the neutrality of the Isthmus of Tehuantepec. On December 23, however, he reported details of subsidies and grants by Congress to the Tehuantepec Railway, the Central Railway, and others.[6]

In May or June, 1873, about five months after the formal opening of Mexico's first railway, from Vera Cruz to Mexico City, Plumb, as agent of the International Railroad Company of Texas, entered into a contract with the Mexican government of President Lerdo de Tejada for the construction of the International Railroad of Mexico, as a standard gauge, from Mexico City by way of Logos to the Pacific (at some point between Manzanillo and Mazatlan) and also from Mexico City by way of Logos to the Rio Grande del Norte to connect with the International Railroad of Texas. The contract providing for a subvention of $9,000 (in customs certificates) per kilometer required construction to begin at Mexico City within nine months. Coincident with the disapproval of this contract, in November, 1873, the Mexican government awarded to a "so-styled" Mexican Company (only part Mexican) contracts for construction of a national system of railways—contracts which were forfeited in May, 1874, by failure of the promoters to secure the required capital in Europe. The action of the executive in granting a concession to Plumb and a later one to the so-called Mexican Company evoked much debate in Con-

gress on the relative merits of American and European enterprises and on the political policy of granting to any American
company a concession to construct railways in Mexico and to
connect the railway systems of the two republics. Ramon
Guzman, who was reputed to have confidential relations with
the Mexican administration, said it was safer to entrust construction to a European company and to avoid rail connections
which might facilitate another invasion of Mexico. He was
answered by Caneda who was intimately and personally connected with American and European affairs, and who, recognizing the great changes since 1846, was unwilling to sacrifice
to groundless fears a development of commercial relations based
on the sound principles of political and commercial convenience.
By December, 1874, the Mexican executive entered into another
contract with Plumb, as agent of the International Railroad
Company of Texas, for construction from Leon to the Rio
Grande by way of Logos, Zacatecas, Durango, San Luis Potosi,
Saltillo and Monterey a railway to connect with the southwest
terminus of the International and also a contract for a railway
from Guaymas to the north frontier of Sonora (in the direction
of Tucson, Arizona). Both were ratified by Congress on May
29, 1875, a few days before the reappearance of the Guaymas
project in the concession to David Boyle Blair for a railway
from Guaymas northward to the international boundary in the
direction of Tucson, Arizona. Following the Diaz retroactive
decree of September 26, 1876, nullifying any contract of his
predecessor "which may result in any burden to the nation"—
a decree which affected the question of the American recognition of Diaz—Plumb abandoned his project and left Mexico.[7]

In May, 1877, Foster had good reason to believe that Simon
Stevens, whom he declined to present to Diaz, attempted to
further the objects of the Tehuantepec project (to secure neutrality of the route) by representing to the Mexican government that he had been sent by Secretary Evarts on a special
confidential mission to report on political conditions relating to
the Diaz government. Apparently some bad feelings in Mexico
resulted from the statements of Stevens, and also from the state-

ments of N. S. Renau who assumed "representative character" while working in the interest of railroads. On July 9, Foster notified Evarts that General Frisbie, who arrived late in May with M. G. Vallejo and whom he had introduced to Diaz in June, had failed in his private mission, which, because of "recent occurrences," had become "impracticable at present." Possibly the "recent occurrences" referred to a recent alarming publication (in the New York *Herald*) of a detailed project for cession of the northern states of Mexico to the United States—a report which Foster suggested "was not without basis." Later in July, Foster, in an unofficial letter to Secretary Evarts, stated that newspaper reports of extra official or confidential missions— reports evidently based on indiscreet assumptions of private Americans who were seeking railway concessions had caused a general feeling of distrust among suspicious Mexicans. Among those who sought to influence the Diaz government by claiming to hold special relations with the Department of State at Washington was N. S. Renau who suggested that the American government would never recognize the Diaz government until the latter had confirmed the grant sought.[8]

After the paralyzing effects of the Diaz revolution and the continued failure of the government to recognize its foreign debt, Foster, feeling that there was an apparent reluctance of foreign capitalists to invest in Mexican public enterprises, announced that to obtain the inauguration of railroad construction on any scale commensurate with the urgent wants of the country would require the adjustment of the debt, a restoration of confidence in a stable government and security and guarantees to foreign capital.

Under the first Diaz administration, plans for Mexican railway development remained largely unrealized. Although the greatest need of Mexico was the construction of railways, which could not be accomplished without American capital, the Mexican Congress in 1878 was strongly hostile both to American corporations and to the proposed connection of the Mexican railway with the American railway system. In November, 1877, the Secretary of Fomento contracted with William J. Palmer and James Sullivan for construction of a railway from the American border to Mexico City, and a Pacific branch to San Blas or Manzanillo which was to be completed before the line to the frontier, but the charter was defeated in the Mexican Congress on the ground that to grant such a privilege to an American company or to establish railway connections with the frontier was a dangerous policy. A contract of October, 1877, with Ferguson and Lymon to construct a line from Guaymas through Sonora to the American frontier to connect with a projected American railway near the border was also defeated. In May, 1878, the Chamber of Deputies voted to confer on the President the authority to contract for an interoceanic railway which was designed to defeat contracts for the proposed railway across Sonora and all other railways projected to connect with those of the United States. On May 22, in connection with the debates resulting in the overwhelming defeat (in Congress) of the proposed concession for a railway from Guaymas to the Arizona border, Alfredo Chavero, in the Chamber of Deputies, in stating the objections to railway connections with the United States frontier and to the American influence which would result, solemnly warned his colleagues that by historical laws border nations are natural enemies, that northern nations necessarily invade those of the south, and declared that his people did not wish to learn nor to open their eyes (!). In the following September, Chavero, elected president of the Chamber of Deputies, claimed that the wisdom of the recent rejection of the American charter had been shown by subsequent events (!).[9]

Apparently the condition of hostility to railway connection with any American system of railways was not improved by the concurrent resolutions offered by Senator J. T. Morgan in the United States Senate on May 8, 1878, with the most friendly disposition proposing, in the interest of permanent peace and free intercourse between republican governments, the adjustment of Mexican-American relations by a treaty guaranteeing the existing boundary, mutually agreeing to protect the borders from predatory raids and to protect the territory of each against the conquest by any trans-oceanic power, and especially providing "for protection and encouragement of citizens of either country who with the consent of Mexico build and equip a railway from Mexico to the Rio Grande in the direction of San Antonio or any point on the border to connect with any line or lines of railway at the boundary and to secure safe transit over such line or lines within the territory of each country." In the Mexican press the latter resolution was denounced as a proposition to establish an American protectorate over Mexico with the ultimate aim of annexation.

Thus, although an American railway from the Pacific (the Southern Pacific) had virtually reached the Mexican frontier at Fort Yuma by 1877, and although another in Texas from the opposite direction had reached San Antonio with plans of early completion to the Rio Grande if encouraged by satisfactory inducements, and although another line was steadily advancing southward through New Mexico to connect the Mexican frontier with American central and northern systems, Mexico still hesitated to cooperate in a policy of encouraging connecting lines in Mexico. The Mexican Congress, with a policy based on a natural jealousy and fear felt by a weak nation in the presence of a strong rival and with hopes of attracting Oriental trade through Mexican ports by an interoceanic railway route across Mexico farther south, considered a railway from Mexico City to the Pacific far more desirable than a railway connection with the Mexican-American frontier.[10]

On October 9, 1878, Foster, in a paper prepared for a Chicago Association of manufacturers, and giving his views of the great obstacles to development of trade with Mexico, declared that no considerable trade with Mexico could be maintained without an international railway to Mexico City, "that the Mexican Government will not consent to any treaty stipulation or other agreement between the two governments for the joint protection of such a road, and that it requires all persons, employes and capital of the company formed for that purpose, to become Mexican for all purposes of the enterprise [to prevent them from maintaining a diplomatic claim as foreigners, even when alleging denial of justice); that the last Congress positively refused to grant a charter for an American company and the present Congress has manifested the same opposition; and that the Mexican Government is absolutely unable, owing to its financial condition, to pay any subsidy for the construction of the road." For any railroad in Mexico, even if completed, he saw no hope of any immediate returns adequate to justify the investment. The creation of trade along the line would be restricted by Mexican methods, by the evil and annoying system of interior duties and by the general disorder and lawlessness, and by the resulting insecurity of property and of life as illustrated by the many recent American cases of complaint which he had presented to the Mexican government without any satisfactory response or redress. On May 31, 1879, he reported the failure of the Mexican Congress to approve the contracts made by the executive for railways to connect with the American frontier and in the following August, reporting the grounds of opposition, he said: "As the tide of immigration in American states and territories rolls nearer the Mexican frontier and our railway system approaches from the North and East, the feeling of restlessness and dissatisfaction with the present poverty, insecurity and backwardness is becoming more and more apparent in the Mexican border states." In the following December he reported that the Rio Grande and the Sonora projects, even with materially modified charters which prohibited diplomatic intervention in matters relating to the railway company, had been unable to obtain favorable consideration of the Congress which terminated on December 15, but that under the Blair charter of 1875 the grantees of the Sonora contract had obtained from the Minister of Public Works authority to proceed with surveys and with the construction of the road from Guaymas to the frontier (for connection with the Atchison, Topeka and Santa Fe).[11]

In a long despatch (of 50 pp.) of June 7, 1880, Morgan, considering the great cost of the railway lines proposed by the various Mexican railway projects which since his arrival in Mexico had largely occupied the public mind and the attention of the Mexican Congress and the President, and doubting whether Americans, if successful with the President of Mexico, would be wise in involving their means "in face of risks when they can make themselves safe by legislation," submitted to Secretary Evarts full information concerning the situation. A year later he mentioned General Grant's acceptance of a concession without subsidy as an evidence to the Mexican government that American parties would be willing to construct Mexican railways "with their own means" and suggested that such concessions without subventions would have an advantage in reducing the Mexican temptation to declare forfeiture of contract for delays beyond the time limit. Later, he observed that the Mexican government had become more reasonable in granting extensions of time for construction.[12]

After the defeat of the American Palmer-Sullivan charter, the Mexican Congress conferred upon Diaz the power to contract with governors of states for construction of railroads within their limits. The result was not satisfactory. From 1876 to 1880 the total railway mileage of Mexican railways increased very little—from 416 to only 674 miles.

By 1880, however, after the failure of attempts to promote railway construction under state concessions, a change of railway policy to a plan of national franchises encouraged by subsidies was adopted, partly as a result of the American recognition of the Diaz government which removed grounds of Mexican prejudice against Americans seeking concessions, and possibly influenced by Foster's published report of 1878 on trade with Mexico which served to bring the question to an issue. On June 1, 1880, the Mexican Congress enacted a law authorizing the President to amend contracts for the construction of inter-oceanic and international railroads and providing that the term of a concession should not exceed 99 years. By law of December 16, 1881, all railroads and telegraph and telephone lines located in the Federal district and Lower California or crossing state lines or touching Mexican ports were subjected exclusively to the national government in matters relative to taxation, enforcement of national laws, forfeiture, expropriation, rates, service, regulations, construction and repairs, safety, accidents, interference of mail service and liens.

The new policy of Diaz and Gonzales, who were able to obtain approval of Congress to several concessions to American railway companies, attracted American capital and enterprise— although the policy was disapproved by opposition journals, which predicted that the American companies would involve the government in disputes which would furnish pretext for American aggression and annexation. Foster's warning concerning the ungenerous terms of Mexican concessions and the hostility of the Mexican Congress did not discourage promoters of American railway lines from St. Louis and Chicago toward the Rio Grande nor counteract the spirit of enterprise which prompted the *railway invasion* of Mexico. Within three years, under the administration of Diaz and Gonzales who represented the new Diaz policy, American interests obtained concessions providing for the construction of five railways aggregating 2,500 miles and subsidies amounting to $32,000,000. Notwithstanding the pessimistic article published by John Bigelow in 1882—on his return from a trip to Mexico made at the request of Samuel J. Tilden who had become interested in railway promotion there—optimism stimulated by an article of M. Romero in 1882 on railways in Mexico, and a pamphlet by Joseph Nimmo on "Commerce Between the United States and Mexico," found expression in the increasing investment of American capital in Mexican railways causing Mexico temporarily to suspend the payment of subsidies in 1885.[13]

The way for the railway invasion of Mexico in the period after 1879 was prepared by rapid extension of American railway lines to the Mexican border in the early eighties. The Southern Pacific, formed in 1870 from consolidation of four earlier short lines (which had been chartered between 1860 and 1870) and completed eastward from the Pacific coast to Fort Yuma, Arizona (729 miles from San Francisco) in 1877, was extended to Deming and El Paso in 1881, and in January, 1883, was opened as a through line to New Orleans. With it, at Deming in 1881 the Atchison, Topeka and Santa Fe established a connection. This road, under the control of Boston capitalists and seeking a terminus on the Pacific, had reached Las Vegas in July, 1879, and Santa Fe on February 9, 1880. Later, after arranging to use the tracks of the Southern Pacific to Benson, Arizona, it built a branch to Nogales, Arizona, in 1882. In 1881 it also completed a line from Rincon, New Mexico, to El Paso. Eastward from El Paso, at Sierra Blanca, Texas, in 1882, the Texas and Pacific established a junction with the Southern Pacific. In the same year, the International and Great Northern, extended to Austin in 1876 by consolidation of two earlier lines and purchased by the M., K. & T. in 1881, was completed to Laredo to which a narrow gauge (the Texas Mexican) was also opened from Corpus Christi. In 1883 the Galveston, Houston and San Antonio was connected with the Southern Pacific and completed a branch to Eagle Pass. Several years later, in 1890, the Rock Island and Pacific was completed to El Paso.

In 1880, under new concessions, the first actual American railway construction in Mexico was begun. The Atchison, Topeka and Santa Fe interests, while advancing the American line toward the southwest, in 1879 (utilizing the Blair concession from Guaymas to El Paso with a branch to the Arizona border) incorporated the Sonora Railway Company, which obtained a subsidy contract with Diaz in September, 1880, and at Guaymas in the same year began the first American railway in Mexico (shipping the equipment around Cape Horn). In October, 1882, after many difficulties, they completed it to Nogales at the Arizona border where it was connected with the tracks of the American line of the A., T. & S. F., but found the projected route up the Sonora River from Hermosillo to El Paso too difficult. Later, the Atchison, Topeka and Santa Fe, finding the Sonora a disappointment as an outlet to the Pacific, extended its main line to the Pacific at San Francisco under terms dictated by the Southern Pacific interests dominated by Collis P. Huntington. In April, 1880, an American company, the Mexican Central Railway Company, of Massachusetts, representing the same interests as those behind the Atchison and Sonora projects, obtained from the Mexican government the forfeited concession for a railway from Mexico City to Leon, originally granted to a Mexican company in 1874 and now amended to provide for extension to Paso del Norte (or Juárez), Laredo and Guadalajara. By purchase of a Guanajuato state concession extending its right from Leon to Celaya, and by support of Ramon Guzman, a banker and promoter of Mexico City, it obtained a decided advantage over competing interests (the Palmer-Sullivan interests, C. P. Huntington interests, and certain Washington interests represented by Nathaniel S. Renau and backed by Jay Gould, Russell Sage and Thomas A. Scott). The concession of Diaz, on September 8, 1880, for construction from Mexico City to Leon and from Leon to Paso del Norte (to connect Queretaro, Celaya, Irapuato, Guanajuato, Zacatecas, Chihuahua and Guadalajara) was confirmed by Congress on November 8. On September 15, 1880, its managers began to lay tracks which were opened to operation from Mexico City to San Juan del Rio in 1881 and to Logos in 1882. On the northern section of the line work was begun in 1881 and regular trains were running to Chihuahua at the close of 1882. The entire line was completed on March 8, 1884, and was in operation by April from Mexico City to El Paso where it connected with the Atchison, Topeka and Santa Fe line. Construction on a line to Tampico, for which a concession was obtained in July, 1881, was begun promptly but not completed until 1890. The Guadalajara line was begun in 1884 (and completed to Irapuato in 1888). The entire Mexican Central, Mexico's greatest railroad, was built by Boston interests as a feeder to the Atchison, Topeka and Santa Fe, but proved a disappointment.

On September 13, 1880, the Palmer-Sullivan interests, operating as the Mexican National Construction Company, obtained from Diaz a concession for the Mexican National Railway (a narrow gauge) over the route from Mexico City by way of Toluca, Acambaro, Celaya, San Luis Potosi, Saltillo and Monterey to Laredo, and from Mexico City by way of Acambaro, Morelia, Zamara, Guadalajara, and Colima to the port of Manzanillo. The main line from Mexico City to Laredo was not completed until September, 1888, after the reorganization of the company under the control of the English bondholders following a sale under foreclosure in March, 1887. From Laredo the line was opened to Monterey in 1882 and extended to Saltillo in 1883. From Mexico City it was opened to Toluca in 1880 and through Celaya to San Miguel de Allenda in 1883, a year before the company defaulted. On the section between Saltillo and San Miguel, work was begun in 1886 and completed two years later. The work on the Pacific line was abandoned after the construction of the section from Acambaro to Patzcuaro in 1886 and from Manzanillo to Colima in 1889. The work of reconstructing the main line as a standard gauge was not completed until 1903 following a second reorganization of the company in 1902 by which control passed to an American company. On June 7, 1881, through General John B. Frisbie, the Southern Pacific interests (dominated by C. P. Huntington) in the name of the International Construction Company, obtained a concession (without subsidy) for a railway from Piedras Negras to Durango and thence by way of Zacatecas and Guanajuato to Mexico City with a branch through Nieves (Zacatecas) to the Pacific at a point between Mazatlan and Zihuatanejos (Guerrero) and another branch through San Luis Potosi to a point between Vera Cruz and Matamoros on the Gulf of Mexico. Construction was begun opposite Eagle Pass following the completion of the Galveston, Houston and San Antonio to that point in 1883, and tracks were laid to Monclovia by January, 1884, but further extension was slow, reaching Torreon in 1888, Durango in 1892, and Tepehuanas in 1902 a year after the Mexican National obtained control following the death of Huntington. Meantime, the Southern Pacific Railroad Company undertook to construct a railroad through Mexico from the Rio Grande—the Mexican International Railroad, which was later put into operation from Ciudad Porfirio Diaz to Durango in 1892, forming a connection with the Southern Pacific Railroad at Eagle Pass, Texas.[14]

General U. S. Grant, who visited Mexico early in 1880, became interested in the construction of railways for the development of Mexican resources. In 1881 in New York he and representatives of the Atchison, Southern Pacific and Gould interests incorporated the Mexican Southern Railroad Company which obtained from the state of Oaxaca, through the agency of Matias Romero, a concession for a line from Anton Lizardo on the Gulf through Tehuacan, Oaxaca and Tehuantepec to Port Angel on the Pacific (later amended to extend to Guatemala), with which (in May, 1883) became affiliated a Gould concession for a line from the Rio Grande through Victoria to the City of Mexico (which, following a receivership in March, 1884, was forfeited). The Mexican Southern project collapsed with the Grant and Ward failure of May, 1884, and the concession later passed to other interests.

By 1884, the Mexican railway mileage increased to 3,682 miles, chiefly American, beginning a period of awakening and of marvelous transformation of wild woods and deserts. Along these railroads, telegraph lines were promptly established. The Mexican Telegraph Company was organized in 1879, and by agreement with the Mexican government submarine cables were laid between 1880 and 1882 from Galveston to Vera Cruz. From the latter point a telegraph line was promptly erected to the City of Mexico. By March, 1886, over 5000 kilometers (over 3,100 miles) of telegraph lines were completed, with 93 offices. By 1888, the total length was over 31,000 kilometers (over 19,200 miles). In February, 1887, the Mexican lines were united with those of Guatemala.[15]

In the Diaz period, Tehuantepec concessions still attracted Americans. The concession of September, 1857, to the Louisiana Tehuantepec Company, which was permitted by the Maximilian government to change its name to the New York-Tehuantepec Steamship and Railroad Company on October 12, 1866, was forfeited following the fall of Maximilian and transferred to the Tehuantepec Transit Company which lost it by forfeiture in 1867. In October, 1867, a new concession was granted to Emile La Sere, acting for the Tehuantepec Railway Company incorporated in Vermont by Simon Stevens of New York. The application of the American government by instructions of June 10,

1869, for revival of the stipulations of Article VIII of the Gadsden treaty, which conferred certain power on the United States as to any roads or railroads constructed under the later grant, was not granted. Under the new concession of 1867, as amended in 1869, the construction of a railroad was begun in 1870; and the construction of a canal was authorized in December, 1870, by another concession which was granted with a view to competition with the Panama route. Both concessions were revalidated in May, 1872, and the Tehuantepec Railway Company was granted a subsidy in 1874, but both concessions were declared void in 1879. In June, 1879, a new concession was obtained by Edward Learned of New York who built about 22 miles of railway (from the Gulf terminal) before forfeiture in 1882 by the time limit. Thereafter, the Mexican government continued the construction by various contracts which finally resulted in the completion of the railroad in October, 1894. On January 30, 1890, Thomas Ryan wired Secretary Blaine in cipher that a resident and a subject of England (Mateo Clark, a native of Chile), who was in close relations with President Diaz, was apparently engaged in private negotiations with the Mexican government for the purchase or control of the national Tehuantepec Isthmus Railway, then under construction by the government; and a few days later he reported that the plan probably included a ship railway and interoceanic canal franchises on the isthmus—seeming to indicate a purpose to forfeit all franchises previously granted. The project of a ship railway across Tehuantepec was a revival of the project for transfer of ships from ocean to ocean on gigantic platforms running on steel rails—a project which Captain Eads had proposed before Mexico was ready for it and at a time when it encountered in America the opposition of interests in conflict with it. In October, 1890, Blaine inclosed to Ryan a letter from the Secretary of War requesting all available data relative to the Tehuantepec railway which had been planned for completion in July, 1889, and also data relative to the interoceanic railway which was in process of construction from Veru Cruz by way of Mexico City to Acapulco on the Pacific. In August, 1892, Ryan wired his government that Americans were apprehensive that the Mexican government was seriously considering a proposition to authorize a European company to complete the railway and to operate it with connecting lines of steamers on both oceans—a project suggestive of possible mischief to American trade interests. Ten years later Clayton complained that Mariscal in the Mexican railway contract of May 16, 1902, with S. Pearson and Company, who completed the reconstruction of the road between 1899 and 1907, discriminated against American citizens by excluding them from the right to form a company for the work.[16]

In 1881, after American railways had reached the Mexican frontier and following the beginning of construction on Mexican lines under American concessions, Secretary Blaine, preceding the formulation of a general Latin American policy and with plans for "negotiations for further definition and extension of the material relations between the two countries which may become necessary hereafter," sought to induce Mexico to adopt a more liberal and farsighted policy in the provisions of American concessions for "extending facilities of communication conducive to the strength and prosperity of Mexico." On June 1, in his instructions to Morgan expressing a hopeful view of relations, he summarized the basis of a general American policy, the nature of which is indicated by the following extracts:

"As the relations between the Government of the United States and that of Mexico happily grow more amicable and intimate, it is but natural that a disposition should in like manner develop itself between the citizens of the respective countries to seek new means of fostering their material interests, and that the ties which spring from commercial interchange should tend to grow and strengthen with the growing and strengthening spirit of good will which animates both peoples. That this spirit exists is one of the most evident proofs that the frank and conciliatory policy of the United States towards Mexico has borne and is bearing good fruit. It is especially visible in the rapidly extending desire on the part of the citizens of this country to take an active share in the prosecution of those industrial enterprises for which the magnificent resources of Mexico offer so broad and promising a field, and in the responsive and increasing disposition which is manifest on the part of the Mexican people to welcome such projects. . . . At this late day it needs no disclaimer on our part of the existence of even the faintest desire in the United States for territorial extension south of the Rio Grande. The boundaries of the two republics have been long settled in conformity with the best jurisdictional interests of both. The line of demarkation is not conventional merely. It is more than that. It separates a Spanish American people from a Saxon-American people. It divides one great nation from another with distinct and natural finality. . . . It has been the fortunate lot of this country that long years of peace and prosperity, of constant devotion to the arts and industries which make the true greatness of a nation, have given to the United States an abundance of skilled labor, a wealth of active and competent enterprise, and a large accumulation of capital, for which its own vast resources fail to give full scope for the untiring energy of its citizens. It is but natural, therefore, that a part of this great store of national vitality should seek the channels which are offered by the wonderful and scarcely developed resources of Mexico, and that American enterprise and capital should tend to find their just employment in building up the internal prosperity of that republic on like firm bases, and in opening new commercial relationship between the two countries. . . . While carefully avoiding all appearance of advocacy of any individual undertaking which citizens of the United States may desire to initiate in Mexico, you will take every opportunity which you may deem judicious to make clear the spirit and motive which control this movement in the direction of developing Mexican resources, and will impress upon the Government of Mexico the earnest wish and hope felt by the people and government of this country that these resources may be multiplied and rendered fruitful for the primary benefit of the Mexican people themselves. . . ." [17]

On June 16, Blaine sent Morgan additional instructions considering the more detailed application of the general policy indicated in his instructions of June 1, so far as it applied to railroad concessions, capital and commerce. The chief points are indicated in the following extracts:

"While liberality in the concessions may give some immediate and material benefit to the concessionaries, a more far-sighted policy should regard as most imperatively needful a guarantee of certain good faith in the execution of the concessions, and above all, the assurance to those who may undertake to fulfill them that they will find prompt and impartial justice whenever, in the ordinary contingencies of this class of undertakings, they may find themselves required to appeal to the courts of Mexico. . . . It is conceived that the Mexican government fully recognizes the importance of extending the facilities of communication between its own component States and with the neighboring countries, as conducive to the strength and prosperity of Mexico. Recognizing this, it should also be aware of the unwisdom of embarrassing, or practically neutralizing, its concessions for the establishment of railways by limitations springing from a narrow and suspicious jealousy of the foreign capital it so greatly needs. Take, for instance, the provisions, which have hitherto been inserted in such charters as the Mexican government has conceded, to the effect that all the capital, stockholders and employees engaged in the enterprise are to be considered Mexican in all matters touching their operations within the Republic, and that they are not to maintain their claims as foreign, even when alleging denial of justice. This limitation would, of itself, be almost a sufficient prohibition of all such undertakings; and, even if accepted by over-sanguine speculators, might only too probably lead to discussions and issues with foreign governments not conducive to the maintenance of that international cordiality so much to be desired."

Stating that the "permanent prosperity for any lines of railway communication, whether between the Mexican States themselves, or as international arteries of intercourse," was dependent upon the development of traffic along their routes, he said that trade development languished for want of adequate facilities, and especially as a result of the "local, complicated and often contradictory tariff regulations which obtain between the different Mexican States themselves." "These local tariffs," he declared, "coupled with the anomalous institution known as the Free Zone, which still further complicates the operation of the interstate tariffs, and sets a premium on smuggling, tend unmistakably to hinder commerce between the United States and Mexico."

"As a parallel consideration," he said, "it may be expedient to suggest that trade regulations of a reciprocal character might, perhaps, with great advantage be adopted between the two countries. . . . This government has no disposition to complain of any revenue laws which may have for their purpose the protection of native Mexican industries. . . . In Mexico, as in the United States, all matters of this class, affecting the revenues of the nation, must in the end be determined by the national legislative power. While, therefore, it is not within the immediate competence of the Executive power of the two countries to adjust the reciprocal questions of the tariff for mutual good, the government of the United States would be glad to confer with that of Mexico in regard to any measures which will enlarge and facilitate the commercial exchanges between the two countries. . . ."

"Besides the wholesome impetus which an enlarged foreign trade must give, not only to the lines of communication, but to the country through which they pass," he continued, "there should be borne in mind the domestic influences which can be created by the introduction of safeguarded capital. Factories whereby the native productions of Mexico may be wrought for home consumption, and with the abundant cheap labor of the country, for export even and mining industries whereby the wealth of the country may be enormously increased almost without effort, are among the most obvious methods of employment sought by foreign capital and foreign trained enterprise. All that I have said before concerning the needed permanence of vested rights and the guarantee of legal protection, applies with equal, if not greater force to this large class of undertakings. To induce their creation and successful operation the security of the capital invested requires to be completely assured, and with this, also, should go the broadest guarantee of the personal rights of the originators of such projects and of the skilled operatives who must resort to Mexico to carry them into profitable execution. . . ."

"My object," he explained, "is that you should be able, from full knowledge of the views of this Government, to impress upon the statesmen of Mexico that, above all things, the United States desires to see its Sister Republic still further develop into a well ordered and prosperous State. Believing that this growth will be aided by the investment of American capital and enterprise in railways, mines and industrial undertakings in Mexico, and by the enlargement of its commerce with the United States, we desire, without undue interference with the domestic legislation of Mexico, to place the relations of the two countries upon such a footing as will most certainly foster this exchange of wealth and industry. . . . It is earnestly believed that the disposition of the Government of Mexico which can best secure to its people the development of their resources in their own interests, is a spirit of trust arising from an intimate conviction that the United States most sincerely desires the progressive prosperity and strength of Mexico itself. It is this disposition which the Government of the United States desires to encourage by the most direct and effective means. . . . While, therefore, this Government does not oppose any needful action of the Mexican Government which it may deem necessary for the preservation of a proper control over the undertakings of American citizens, for the maintenance of that respect and obedience which is due from all strangers to the institutions and laws of the land whose hospitality they enjoy, it hopes to see a cordial welcome extended to them. It confidently looks, in their behalf, for steady and sure protection against marauders, whether they be highway robbers or the pretended authorities of sudden and short-lived revolutions. And, especially, it expects such prompt and impartial administration of justice as will guarantee unfailing remedy for all manner of wrongs. The realization of these hopes will justify the Government of the United States in assuring its citizens that they will be as adequately protected, when within the territory of Mexico, by the power and justice of the Mexican Republic in all that pertains to life, liberty and property, as every Mexican citizen within the furthest territory of the United States is protected by the laws of the land." [18]

Morgan, who replied that he had already submitted to the Mexican government many suggestions which he was gratified to observe were in accord with Blaine's instructions of June 1 and June 16, but which had usually fallen on deaf ears and had failed to remove prejudices and fears fed by foreigners who were doing business there, read the instructions of June 1 to Mariscal who was greatly pleased at the expressions of good will and stated that they were fully reciprocated by President Gonzales. The instructions of June 16, however, he asked leave (by wire on July 7) to withhold until he could submit by mail to the Department his reasons for the prudent suggestion. In his dispatch, five days later, he especially expressed his reasons for withholding at that time Blaine's views against the stipulations of Mexican concessions, making the companies Mexican and their capital and operations and employees subject to the decisions of the Mexican tribunals without the right of appeal from such decisions: (1) That the suggestion to Mexico of a proposal to interfere diplomatically at some future time might appear premature. "Mexico might, with truth, say that no cause of complaint had as yet come up in this matter, and that as to the clauses referred to, they were inserted for the very purpose of precluding any diplomatic intervention in case of non-fulfillment by the concessionaries of the terms of their contracts, without which the concessions would not have been granted, and that these clauses were accepted by the parties in interest; and therefore they should be bound to them under all circumstances;" (2) That the proposal to raise a question as to submission to the terms of concessions already perfected and accepted by the concessionaries might endanger the assent of the next Mexican Congress (in September) to other important concessions (which contained the same stipulations): "one to Mr. J. B. Frisbie in behalf of the 'International Construction Company' to construct a Railroad and telegraph line from this City to the Rio Grande, with branches to the Pacific and Atlantic Oceans; another to Mr. Prida representing the 'Texas, Topolovampo and Pacific Rail Road Company' to build a Railroad and telegraph line from Topolovampo on the Pacific Coast to Piedras Negras, to Alamos in the State of Sonora, and to Mazatlan; another to Francis Deljrese representing the 'International Railway Improvement Company' to build a Railroad and telegraph line from a point on the Rio Bravo between Laredo and Reynosa traversing a large extent of territory to Mexico and to points on the Pacific and Atlantic Coasts; and another with the International Oceanic Telegraph Company to establish telegraphic communication between the United States and Mexico via Cuba and Yucatan." [19]

On August 31, Blaine approved the course of Morgan as reported in the dispatch of July 12, and left to his discretion the question of communicating to the Mexican government the instructions of June 16. Thereafter he devoted his attention largely to plans for pacific settlement of disputes on the American continent.[20]

Morgan suggested that one obstacle to American development in Mexico was the lack of a friendly press there. The French paper, *Trait D'Union,* of June 16 had just published various anti-American extracts, one of which (an editorial from *El Pacifico* of Mazatlan of May 27) regretted the enervating effect of the railroad fever on the Mexican intellect, "which only sees a brilliant future for Mexico through the smoke of American locomotives and smelting furnaces" and apparently sought to engender bad feeling toward Americans whose vast interests were suspected of threatening to control all the vital sources of the nation's independence—railroads, mining, agriculture and manufacturing. The editor of *El Pacifico* said: "The more consideration we give to the grand movement which is taking place in our country, under the shadow of Railroad concessions, the more are we convinced that our Nationality will run great risks. . . . Today, everything is different, the invasion is pacific, and promises happy results for the American sowing his gold broadcast over the entire republic. Railroad enterprises, the purchase of mines and rural property are the means which are employed to cause the autonomy of Mexico to disappear." *El Nacional* of August 25, 1881, applauded the protection given to European capital which was regarded "most efficacious to arrest the influence of the American element." In September, 1881, in a conversation with Mariscal on the Mexican attitude on the Guatemalan question, Morgan took occasion to refer to the offensiveness of the Mexican press articles which had uttered warnings against granting concessions to Americans on the ground that American enterprise would exert a baleful influence on Mexican interests.[21]

Mexican feeling against American employees on the railways was later shown in various arrests of engineers and others in connection with train accidents. The American government, on February 20, 1883, wired authority to intercede for release of a railway engineer named Trimbath who, although blameless, was imprisoned at Matamoros for the death of a Mexican by a moving locomotive, and whose illness in prison threatened to result in death. The intercession was successful. From the increased facility of commerce resulted a natural increase of diplomatic complaints which necessitated remedies through new treaties (especially relating to extradition and postal regulations).[22]

In 1885, when the Mexican government temporarily suspended the payment of subsidies on railway construction—subsidies which had been promised in excess of the capacity of the treasury—American investors were greatly disappointed and very doubtful of adequate returns on their capital. Henry R. Jackson, minister to Mexico under President Cleveland, in a despatch of August 31, 1885, to Secretary Bayard referred to the "notorious financial embarrassment of the Mexican Government" which had resulted from unpunished official "individual peculation" under the administration of President Gonzales and which was "bearing so heavily upon American interests," and especially mentioned the rumor that Gonzales and his brother-in-law, Ramon Fernandez, were the owners of a large part of the old English debt of 1850-51 which had been given "prurient vitality" by a bond issue. He declared that "It is but natural that the Rail Road Companies, which, by their enterprise and their investments, have so largely swelled the national revenue, should be aggrieved by the assimilation of their claims upon a fund of their own creation, to a doubtful preexisting indebtedness. . . ." "The proceeds of the bonds when sold were to be applied partly to the needs of Government, but mainly to the purchase of Mexican Rail Roads built by American capital, the owners of which, disheartened and disgusted by Custom-House annoyances and other embarrassments to which they have been pertinaciously subjected by the Mexican Authorities, would be glad to sell out at a low figure." [23]

An immigration into Mexico which was stimulated by the construction of railroads was begun before the period of the Diaz administration. Americans early found an opportunity to undertake a settlement in Lower California whose administrative affairs in the decade after 1868 were reported as in a sad state, causing the American commercial agent at St. Lucas (Eugene Gillespie) in September, 1869, to suggest that the United States should acquire the territory honorably at the first opportunity. Early in 1871, the Lower California Company of New York, by payment of $100,000 in gold, had obtained a grant of land bordering on Magdalena Bay, under a Mexican contract, made at Saltillo in 1864 and perfected at Washington in 1866, to settle 420 families there before the following May. Wishing to land its families there instead of at La Paz as required by Mexican law, through General Butler it requested the Department of State to ask the desired permission in order to facilitate the establishment of the settlement. According to the later statement of John Bracken, one of the colonists, the company sent about 400 persons in the first vessel, the steamship *Ocean Queen,* by way of Panama, and they reached Magdalena Bay in March, 1871. The managers promptly contracted with William Denton of San Diego to survey the lands included in the grant, and proceeded to expend large sums of money in improvements, especially including houses and artesian wells. According to later testimony, they complied with all conditions, in the face of obstacles interposed by various local Mexican officials. On July 29, 1871, however, the Mexican government through the Minister of Fomento arbitrarily annulled the grant and closed the port which had been opened by a decree of February 24. Its action was influenced by the suspicion that the company was a filibustering scheme to annex Lower California to the United States. Near the close of the year, the colonists, whose number had increased to 800 or 1,000, expressed much fear of violence from the Mexicans and, after the arbitrary seizure of the American schooner *Cina Greenwood* by a Mexican force (claiming to act under authority of the government of Lower California), and following the seizure and imprisonment of many colonists, the larger number, abandoning their business and property, fled from the port to escape outrages and indignities which were inflicted upon the American consul (Colonel Drake DeKay) and other American citizens who remained. In an attempt to adjust amicably the question of claims which threatened to disturb relations, the Mexican government, through Romero, on March 23, 1872, agreed with the company's attorney (William H. Hurlburt) to make a contract by which the company by renouncing all claims under the previous contract was to receive in compensation a six-year lease of all the orchilla on the public lands of Lower California between Cape St. Lucas and 27° N. and the right to establish warehouses at Magdalena Bay which remained a port of entry. In November, 1872, however, General Butler, in a lengthy interview at Washington with John W. Foster, the newly appointed minister to Mexico, sought to enlist his interest in a claim for indemnity. Nearly six years later, the company, through General Butler (its president), still claiming title to the original grant, issued a protest against any action of the Mexican government which in any way complicated or prejudiced or injured the rights or interests of the company—and especially against the reported grants of land and leases or franchises of salt orchilla, and other soil products between 24° 20' and 31° North. In this protest it held Mexico responsible for illegal nullification of the grant, for "destruction of the flourishing business built up under great difficulties in a desert country," for the large amount of capital invested, for the value of property abandoned, for the forcible expulsion and personal violence, and for the value of products appropriated by others after the date of the nullification of the grant. This protest was presented to Secretary Evarts by Drake DeKay with the request that he promptly submit it to the Mexican government. Evarts replied that the subject would be presented after the restoration of diplomatic relations. General Butler continued to trouble the Department of State, urging it to press the claim for indemnity, but he was never able to fix any responsibility on the Mexican government. By 1880, however, there were probably other more important American interests in Lower California. In December, 1879, following a state revolution in Chihuahua which resulted in outrages on American rights there, Foster, with a view to the protection of American interests in other disturbed regions, especially in Lower California and Sinaloa, requested Secretary Fish to send a man-of-war to the Pacific coast.[24]

Later, the Mexican government was attacked by the opposition press for its action in granting colonization concessions to American companies, especially in Lower California, and was warned against the increase of American influence. It was especially criticized for a concession for several million acres of land granted in 1884 to Adolfo Bulle and Louis Huller who, according to report, in 1887, transferred all or part of the grant to an American company of Hartford, Connecticut. In the

United States considerable attention was attracted by an editorial (against government contracts or concessions to American citizens) which appeared in the irresponsible *El Nacional*
of June 15, 1887, warning the Mexican government and people
"to beware of the insidious Americans who are fast getting
possession of the country" by peaceful conquest. Secretary Bayard was gratified to learn that the article did not reflect the
views of the Diaz government, which Manning promptly
informed him "will not be turned aside from its cordial
encouragement of American immigration and invitation of
American capital by an individual who happens to have type
in which to vent his spleen." In reply to the bitter and repeated statements of the opposition press that the nation was in
danger of losing Lower California through colonizing concessions to American companies, the Mexican Department of Public
Works published an official report, in the *Diario Oficiel* of December 8-16, showing that the colonization contracts (with
Hale, Huller, Bulle and others) were supported by the Constitution, that the companies had placed more colonists than
the government could have done without their aid, that a large
majority of the colonists would be Mexicans, that the pacific
invasion by Americans who survey and settle land was neither
expected nor feared, and that the restriction or discouragement
of such legitimate immigration (of foreigners who came in
search of business and livelihood) would injure national industries. The report closed with a full statement of the colonies
on public lands in Lower California, and also in Sonora and
Chihuahua, including the amount and value of the property,
the condition and the prospects.[25]

Apparently Americans, under the liberal policy of the central
government, were able to evade the Mexican law which prohibited them from purchasing real estate near the northern frontier. There a first colony of Mormons apparently led the way
for a migration of small farmers into Chihuahua and Sonora.
In January, 1880, Secretary Evarts, hearing that the Mormons
were negotiating for the establishment of a Mormon state in
northern Mexico, requested Foster to investigate quietly

whether the rumor was correct. By 1902, six fairly prosperous Mormon settlements, each with a population ranging from 250 to 850, were reported in the consular district of Cuidad Juárez. By 1912, the number of these Mormon settlements had increased to ten, seven in Chihuahua and three in Sonora, and other American immigrants had settled in the more distant states of Mexico. Among the earlier large acquisitions of Mexican land was that of George F. Hearst who, after obtaining large landed interests in California, negotiated for a Mexican ranch (just across the American border) which had gone to ruin as a result of the periodic raids of Geronimo, the Apache chief. Learning of the latter's capture before the news was generally known, he was able to purchase the tract of 200,000 acres at twenty cents per acre.[26]

In 1891, American colonists who had emigrated with the Chiapas Company, which forfeited its concessions, were seeking titles to Mexican land in that region which by 1910, through increasing American enterprise and investments, felt new American influences.

In 1883, Morgan reported various colonizing contracts of Mexico which usually stipulated for immigration of colonists from non-American countries. In April, writing of the prospects for American immigrants, he said:

"There is a large investment of American capital here in Railroads and in Mines, but the number of our citizens who come here is small. Those who do, come in search of employment on the Railroads, or in the mines, or as clerks; and if I may judge by the number of these who apply to this Legation and to the American Benevolent Association for assistance to enable them to return home, I should say that coming to Mexico had not bettered their fortunes. . . .

"Upon principle, I see no reason why the government, or people, should feel suspicious of, or be unfriendly to, Americans who come to Mexico with the sole purpose of bettering their fortunes, at the same time that they are assisting to develop the resources of the country, thereby adding to its wealth, and increasing its population. But this can only be ascertained, in so far as the government is concerned, by actual experiment. The experiment would be primarily tested by some citizens of the United States proposing to make a contract similar in terms with one of those I have referred to. Its solution could only be obtained after the contract with the government had been granted, and after Americans had been colonized thereunder.

"I do not very well see how the Mexican Government could object to enter into such a contract with an American, in view of the contracts which it has made for obtaining a large immigration from other countries. . . . The refusal, on the part of the Mexican Government to make a contract for American immigrants, would only affect any subsidy which might be asked to assist in the colonization, for the laws of the country not only authorize but invite immigration, without respect to the nationality of the immigrants. By the laws, as they now exist, foreigners are permitted to purchase lands anywhere within the limits of the Republic except, in so far as Americans are concerned, they be situated twenty leagues from the boundary thereof. I do not see, therefore, what could prevent a citizen of the United States from purchasing a tract of land in the country, within the limits prescribed by law, and colonizing it with Americans, if he sees fit, and has the means, to do so." [27]

Immigration of aliens was restricted by a Mexican matriculation law and the Mexican doctrine of involuntary change of allegiance. On these subjects the American government had a long controversy with the Mexican government. In July, 1882, Secretary Frelinghuysen, instructing Morgan on the subject of the matriculation law which required registration of aliens as a prerequisite for the assertion of international law rights, declared the right to protect American citizens in rights which were inherent and could neither be created nor destroyed by international law. Later, in December, 1884, he denied the right of Mexico, acting under municipal regulations, to refuse to allow diplomatic intervention. Although he recognized the right of Mexico to place reasonable restrictions on foreigners residing there, he could not accept the Mexican theory affecting relations between Americans and their government. In November, 1886, Secretary Bayard dissented from the Mexican position that Americans residing in Mexico and having real estate there or having children born in Mexico were Mexican citizens unless their intention to retain their original nationality had been declared.[28]

Mexican prejudice against immigration which several times necessitated diplomatic intervention was reduced (and all relations were improved) by the more efficient policy which Diaz established. The decline of prejudice was indicated in the law of 1893 by which desirable settlers were permitted to purchase 6,250 acres and were exempt from military service and taxes (except municipal) for ten years.[29]

Apparently Americans became interested in Mexican mining territory as early as 1874. Possibly their activity was the only basis for certain rumors of pending negotiations for a Mexican cession of territory to the United States—rumors which were published in the *Commercial Herald* of San Francisco and other newspapers in the summer of 1874 and denied in the *Diario Oficiel* of August 16. As published in the *Journal* of St. Petersburg of August 12, the rumor was that Mexico had made overtures to the American government for cession of all territory north of a line drawn west from the mouth of the Rio Grande to the Pacific Ocean (by which the United States would obtain Nuevo Leon, Coahuila, Chihuahua, Sonora, Lower California, and a part of the states of Sinaloa and Durango) and that big capitalists and the boldest speculators of California had already begun the search for mines in the territory.[30]

In the early eighties, after the inception of the Mexican Central Railroad, several Americans became interested in mining development in Mexico. General Frisbie of California was interested at El Ora where he had been associated with some British interests. William Cornell Greene, who had obtained landed interests in California, purchased from the widow of Governor Pesquiera of Sonora the Cananea mines forty-five miles south of the Arizona line and organized the Greene Consolidated Copper Company. In September, 1884, the President of the Tecolote Silver Mining Company of Santa Barbara, Chihuahua, complained of the need of better protection. In the late eighties Senator Teller of Colorado sent agents to Chihuahua to obtain mining property. Many other Americans followed, usually beginning operations at abandoned Mexican mines of an earlier period, which were purchased direct from the Mexican owners and operated under general Mexican laws (without concessions). The new development in the old mining camps was of great economical benefit to the Mexican working classes, especially by the gradual increase in wages and the larger consideration of Americans for the interests of the Mexican workman. Americans with latest improved methods of mining contributed greatly to the mineral wealth of Mexico both by increasing the output of the older mines and by opening new mining districts. In 17 months from April, 1887, to September, 1888, 2,077 new mining claims and 33 stamp mills appeared; and under a law of June 6, 1887, the executive had signed 100 contracts for exploration and development of mineral zones. In 1888, the estimated capital engaged in the development of mining was $30,000,000.[31]

Following the development of mining interests came the establishment of smelting plants. Among the earliest Americans who became interested in this industry was Solomon R. Guggenheim who, after establishing smelting works in Pueblo, Colorado, in 1888, purchased silver mines in Mexico and in 1890, with his brother William, built at Monterey the first complete silver-lead smelting works in Mexico—works which had a capacity of 50,000 tons per month. In 1892-93 the Guggenheim firm built another large plant at Aguascalientes for lead and copper.

Early mining conditions were affected by disorderly acts of banditti, influenced in part by race prejudice, and necessitating intervention. In 1887 at Ventanas, Durango, six Americans, who were actively engaged in the development of Mexican resources and promoting Mexican property, were driven away—abandoning their property in order to save their lives—and three others, including Leon McLeod Baldwin, an American mining engineer, were murdered by a small band of outlaws (banditti). On the ground that the murders were due to race hatred and lack of government protection, Mrs. Janet Baldwin, through the American government, in 1888 asked reparation for the murder of her husband. In April, 1892, after almost five years of controversy, Secretary Blaine, refuting Mariscal's argument that the government was not responsible for the acts of the outlaws, through Mr. Ryan reiterated the justice of the claim based upon the legal responsibility of the Mexican government for its failure to observe its solemn pledges —a responsibility which he said was different from that of the United States in the recent cases of the lynching of Italians at New Orleans. "The Americans at Ventanas," said he, "like all other peaceable, industrious and law-abiding foreigners in Mexico, had entered the territory of the Republic in pursuance of invitations extended to foreigners, from the establishment of Mexican Independence to the present time, in the form of solemn decrees of the Mexican Government, holding out promises of protection and grants of rights and privileges as official inducements to immigration—offering the hospitality of the nation with the expressed expectation of benefits to be derived from the honest and intelligent labor, and the investment of capital in various departments of human industry, by the immigrants accepting the promised conditions." Finally in February, 1894, Romero, who had returned to Washington in March, 1893, offered to settle by payment of $20,000 in monthly installments without recognition of Mexico's liability. Secretary Gresham accepted with the understanding that payment would be in gold. Romero desired to pay in silver, but in August agreed to pay in gold by reducing the monthly installments—a proposition which Secretary Gresham accepted, resulting in the payment of the final monthly installment of $1,000 in August, 1895.[32]

In 1902, the American government, receiving complaints of grave irregularities by the local court of Sonora detrimental to the rights of the legitimate owners of copper mines in the Cananea near Nogales, instructed Clayton informally to ask the Mexican government to use its good offices to secure a speedy and impartial hearing and decision before the state court of Sonora. In January, 1903, presented with a claim of the Candelaria Gold and Silver Mining Company for diplomatic action on the ground of unjust and unlawful deprivation of valuable property by an administrative error, and of failure of repeated efforts to obtain a fair hearing, Secretary Hay suggested that the Mexican government might relieve the situation by indicating either the grounds of its refusal to take executive action or the remedy open to the claimant before the courts.[33]

In 1902, according to a consular report, the amount of American capital invested in Mexico was over $500,000,000, by 1,117 companies, firms and individuals. Practically all of this had been invested since 1877, and half of it after 1896. Apparently, investments were constantly growing in strength, and with the resulting impetus to Mexican industries appeared a large increase in trade. In 1902, Mexico bought from the United States 56% of her imports and sold to the United States 80% of her exports.

Of the total investments in Mexico in 1902 the larger amounts were invested in the following states: Federal District, $320,852,000 (of which $281,800,000 was credited to railways); Coahuila, $48,700,000; Sonora, $37,500,000; Chihuahua, $32,000,000; Oaxaca, $14,000,000; Nuevo Leon, $11,-000,000; Sinaloa, $7,000,000; Durango, $7,000,000; Vera Cruz, $4,455,000; Guanajuato, $3,000,000; Mexico State, $3,000,000; and Lower California Territory, $2,374,000.

Of the total American investments, 70% were in railways in which American capital still dominated and which had led the way to the large investments in various industries. Americans owned all the Mexican railroads except the Interoceanic and the Mexican between Mexico City and Vera Cruz (the first recently acquired by the Mexican government and the second controlled by English capital) and the National Tehuantepec (which had been reconstructed by S. Pearson and Son of London under contract with the Mexican government). Of the railways, the Mexican Central represented the largest single American interest in Mexico ($159,000,000) and the Mexican National (which about 1900 had changed from British to American control) was next ($107,350,000). The Mexican Central had the most enterprising record. Among its extensions within the twenty years since it began operations were the busy branch from Aguascalientes and San Luis Potosi to Tampico which was opened for traffic in 1890 (421 miles) and the Monterey division to Tampico (388 miles). A projected extension, a direct line from Tampico to Mexico City, furnishing a better route, was under construction with expectation of completion by the close of 1904. The Mexican National Railroad was in process of change from a narrow gauge to a broad gauge, the work of transition having been completed to Saltillo. Construction was in progress on the Kansas City, Mexico and Oriental Railroad, the proposed shortest line to the Pacific, with plans to enter Mexico at Presidio del Norte, Texas, and thence follow a route by way of Chihuahua to the Pacific coast at Topolobampo ("Port Stillwell"). From Chihuahua toward Port Stillwell $66,667 had already been expended for construction. At Port Stillwell, named for the enterprising president of the railway who had directed the work against almost insurmountable difficulties, provision had been made for connection with a line of ocean steamers owned by the railway and with an estimated capital of $100,000. At Ciudad Porfiro Diaz (formerly Piedras Negras) on the Rio Grande, one of the principal gateways to Mexico, opposite Eagle Pass, Texas, the Mexican International Railway connected with the Southern Pacific. It had a line into Durango. Its managers, the Harriman-Speyer combination of New York, had plans to extend the main line to Mazatlan on the Gulf of California, 130 miles from Durango.

Next to the railroads the chief Mexican industries in which American capital was invested in 1902 were: mining ($95,-000,000); haciendas, ranches and farms ($28,000,000); manufactories and foundries (nearly $10,000,000); banks and other financial institutions (over $7,000,000); assay offices and chemical laboratories, smelters and refineries (nearly $7,000,000); and public utilities—electricity, gas, telegraph, telephone and waterworks—(nearly $6,000,000).

Of the total estimated capital invested in mining in 1902 the largest amount was invested in Sonora ($27,829,000), Chihuahua ($21,277,000), Federal District ($8,430,000), Durango ($6,520,000), Coahuila ($6,000,000), Aguascalientes ($3,682,000), and Sinaloa ($3,183,000). In Sonora, Senator W. A. Clark of Montana had copper mines valued at $220,000, and near El Copete he had mines valued at $222,000. In Sonora, in Hermosillo District, the Creston-Colorado Gold Mining Company had mines valued at $2,222,000. At La Cananea, in Sonora, the Greene Consolidated Copper Company of New York owned copper works and two short railways with a total value of $7,500,000. At Nacosari the Moctezuma Copper Company and the Phelps Dodge Company controlled copper mining and production and even accompanying railways with a total valuation of $2,222,000. At Las Cruces the New York and Sonora Mining Company had lead-silver mines with an eighty ton smelter valued at $444,000. The Sinaloa and Sonora Mining and Smelting Company owned forty-two square miles of land at the junction of the states of Sinaloa, Sonora and Chihuahua, valued at $600,000. At Parral, Chihuahua, the Hidalgo Mining Company, of which John H. Wilson was president, owned eighteen mines and two lixiviation plants, with an estimated capital of $666,600. In Durango, at Santa Maria del Ora, the Lustre Mining Company of Pittsburgh had a gold mining and smelting plant with an estimated capital of $1,000,000 and at Topia the Gurney Mining and Milling Company of Franklin, Pennsylvania, with an estimated capital of $1,000,000 was engaged in mining silver and lead ores. In Guanajuato, the Consolidated Mining and Milling Company of New York, with an estimated capital of $266,000, was engaged in the mining and milling of gold and silver ores. In the state of Puebla the Teziutlan Copper Company of New York had mining and smelting properties valued at $1,000,000.

Closely allied to the mining interests were assay offices, chemical laboratories, smelters and refineries. All the large smelters were operated by American capital. The American Smelting and Refining Company (the Guggenheims), with its ore-buying agencies, had an estimated capital of $6,000,000. Its smelter at Monterey, Nuevo Leon, valued at $2,679,000, had an output of $5,818,000 in 1901, and its smelter at Aguascalientes, valued at $3,164,000, had an output of $8,298,000. In Coahuila its properties were valued at $750,000 and in Chihuahua at $600,000. The Guggenheims, who were reported in 1902 to have invested $12,000,000 in northern Mexico, planned larger investments. The two smelters at Monterey had nearly doubled their capacity.

Of the total estimated capital invested in haciendas, ranches and farms the largest amount was invested in Oaxaca ($10,-700,000), Sonora ($3,733,000), Vera Cruz ($3,513,000), Chihuahua ($1,822,000), Tabasco ($1,506,000), and Chiapas ($1,188,000). The largest haciendas were: the ranch and cattle properties of Mrs. Phoebe A. Hearst at Babicora, Chihuahua (with an estimated capital of $1,333,000); the cattle and horse property of Nelson and Weller Company at Musquiz, Coahuila ($436,000); the agricultural and dairy properties of General John B. Frisbie in Guerrero and elsewhere ($355,000); the extensive cattle-raising properties of the Greene Cattle Company (of Naco, Arizona) in Sonora; the cattle lands (500,000 acres) of M. M. Sherman (of Kansas City, Missouri) in Sonora; the Sonora Land and Cattle Company of Chicago (1,300,000 acres); the Sonora and Sinaloa Irrigation Company of New York (400,000 acres); the coffee and rubber plantations of the Mexican Coffee Trading and Planting Company of St. Louis in Vera Cruz ($200,000); the rubber, coffee and cattle plantation of United States Senator W. A. Clark in Vera Cruz ($113,800); the Mexican Gulf Agricultural Company of Vera Cruz ($500,000); the sugar and coffee plantation of the San Carlos Coffee and Sugar Company of Minatitlan, Vera Cruz ($300,000); the coffee and sugar plantation of the Vera Cruz Coffee Company of Omaha, Nebraska, in Vera Cruz ($102,000). In Lower California, at San Jorge, the McCormick Harvesting Machine Company controlled lands devoted to the exploiting of the maguey fiber, and along the west coast of Magdalena Bay Flores, Hale and Company owned and operated extensive tracts on which was produced orchilla (a moss used for dyeing purposes). The Pennsylvania Campeche Land and Lumber Company owned 522,000 acres in Campeche in which were the largest American investments in lumber and sawmills ($904,000). Several companies were organized to invest in haciendas for rubber cultivation which in Mexico was still in the experimental stage. In 1902 the Mexican lands near

Monterey, which were susceptible to irrigation, had attracted the attention of Americans following the success in the cultivation of rice on the Texas side of the river, and the American consul hoped that the Mexican government might be induced to remove the Mexican restriction prohibiting foreign ownership of property within the Free Zone, which had been an obstacle to development there.

In manufacturing, American capital was interested in several enterprises which were only in course of construction in 1902—such as the large iron and steel works at Monterey. Curiously the largest amount of capital invested in manufacturing enterprises in a single state was invested in Sinaloa (nearly $4,000,000), a state without a railroad. Most of this investment was in large sugar refineries. The largest single company was the Almada Sugar Refining Company ($3,111,000). Smaller companies were the Aguilla Sugar Refining Company ($350,000) and the Sinaloa Sugar Company ($222,000). Next to Sinaloa was Nuevo Leon in whose capital, Monterey, $2,500,000 of American capital was invested, the largest single plant being that of the Monterey Iron and Steel Company ($1,480,000) owned by the Edward Kelly estate of New York and others. In Aguascalientes, at Tepezala, the Guggenheim sons of New York had an investment of $2,500,000. At the city of Mexico the Waters-Pierce Oil Company of San Francisco had an estimated capital of $1,333,000 invested in the manufacture of oils and soap.

In 1902, American capital was beginning to assume some importance in banking interests in Mexico to which it contributed better business methods. It had recently acquired considerable interest in three of the leading banks and had taken a prominent part in starting two trust companies in Mexico. The largest American investments in public utilities (including also telegraphs and telephones) were in the Federal District ($4,000,000), Sonora ($666,000), Puebla ($350,000), Nuevo Leon ($222,000), and the State of Mexico ($222,000). The largest telephone enterprise was that of the Mexican Telephone Company ($2,000,000) which operated the telephones of

Mexico City, and the largest telegraph enterprise was that of the Mexican Telegraph Company ($2,000,000) which controlled a line from the capital to Vera Cruz and a cable from Vera Cruz to Galveston. Americans also built most of the lines for native and other foreign companies, and American material was largely used in the construction of electric street-car lines in the capital and other Mexican cities. Monterey had an Electric Light and Power Company with an estimated capital of over $220,000 and was planning an electric street car system to replace the two mule car lines and had granted concessions to Americans to construct gas and water works. At Tampico a water and sewer system was in contemplation. American manufacturers were advised to be ready to deliver bathtubs and water fixtures for which an early demand was expected. Outside the capital, telephones were in use in the State of Chihuahua at Chihuahua, Parral, Santa Barbara, Minas Nuevas; and Los Cuevos and Guaymas and Parral had waterworks. The Guaymas Water Company had an estimated investment of $444,000. Toluca, San Luis Potosi, Mazatlan and Aguascalientes had plants for electric lighting. Mazatlan, which reflected American influence in the improvement of business houses and dwellings, and which had expectations of large commercial advantages to result from the plans for the extension of the Kansas City, Mexico and Oriental Railway and the reported decision of the Harriman-Speyer combination to extend the International from Durango westward, had taken steps to install a system of street sewers which offered a good business opportunity to enterprising American contractors. Puebla had an Electric Light and Power Company with an estimated capital of $350,000. Jalapa, Parral and Minas Nuevas also had smaller plants for both light and power. At Ciudad Juárez electric cars had supplanted the mule cars across the international bridge to El Paso, Texas.

Considerable American capital was invested in churches in Mexico; especially the Methodist Episcopal (about $250,000), the M. E. South ($160,000) and the Presbyterian ($111,000).[34]

Within the decade after 1902 American investments rapidly increased. From 1884 to 1910 Mexican railway mileage increased from 3,682 to 15,360, of which 3,025 represented small local lines constructed under state concessions. American capital still dominated in railroad investments. Of an estimated total American investment of $1,057,770,000 in Mexico in 1912 the capital invested in railway shares was $235,464,000, and in railway bonds $408,926,000. By 1909 Americans probably controlled over three-fourths of the active mining in Mexico. By 1911 American mining properties, including the smelting industry, were valued at $250,000,000, chiefly owned by large interests— such as the Hearsts, the Guggenheims (American Smelting and Refining Company), the Batopilas Company of New York, the Anaconda group, the Greene-Cananea interests and the United States Steel Corporation. The increase of the acreage of American landed interests continued. A dozen or more large companies purchased large tracts of Mexican tropical lands, especially in Vera Cruz and Oaxaca, varying in size from ten thousand acres to a million acres. By 1912 over 15,000 Americans were residing in Mexico—some in almost every Mexican state—cultivating small holdings; and the value of all American holdings in farms, ranches and timber lands was over $50,000,000.[35]

Among the prominent new enterprises were the oil industry, the automobile business, insurance business and the manufacture and sale of soap.

The largest single new development was in the production of petroleum and its products. As early as 1864 small quantities of asphalt and crude oil were discovered and used in the Panuca River region—especially in central Tamaulipas and the northern part of the state of Vera Cruz. In 1886, in the zone of Maxuspana, Tabasco, were drilled several large wells from which commercial quantities of fine petroleum were obtained for a short time. Another small beginning in production of crude oil was made in 1888 by a company financed by Cecil Rhodes which drilled a few unproductive wells.

Although in May, 1887, Manning asked Mariscal to take steps to prevent the approval of the new oil refining concession to a Mexican company (the Martinez Company) which threatened injury and destruction to two earlier small American companies

—J. J. Findlay & Company and the Waters-Pierce Company—
the real beginning of Mexican oil development by Americans
was made after 1900 by E. L. Doheny and his associates whose
early adventures in the business were full of incidents more
interesting than romance. Doheny first visited the Mexican border in 1873, taking a bunch of pack mules from Fort Leavenworth for use in the survey of the boundary between Arizona
and New Mexico. Thereafter he prospected for gold and silver
until 1892 after which he began to prospect for oil. In the fall
of 1892 he discovered the Los Angeles oil field. In May, 1900,
with his associates, C. A. Canfield and A. P. McGinnis, and
partly at the suggestion of A. A. Robinson, president of the
Mexican Central Railroad, he made a prospecting trip to the San
Luis Potosi region west of Tampico. Encouraged by Robinson,
who planned to use oil for fuel on the Mexican Central, he and
several associates promptly purchased a hacienda of 280,000
acres for which he paid $325,000, securing a release from all
rights of the subsoil. To this he later added an adjoining
abandoned hacienda of 150,000 acres. Through Ambassador
Clayton, he met President Diaz who welcomed the proposed
efforts to develop a production of petroleum but exacted from
Doheny a promise not to sell to the Standard Oil Company
without first giving the Mexican government an opportunity to
buy the property. To obtain concessions from the government
with privileges of free importation of foreign materials needed
for starting the enterprise he submitted proofs that no oil industry was in operation in any of the states in which he proposed
to inaugurate the enterprise and agreed to spend a minimum
sum within five years on the property chosen for the first tests.
He arranged for protocolization of the company. In February, 1901, he established a camp ("Ebano") in the uncomfort-
able jungle on the Tampico branch of the Mexican Central
which penetrated a wild country of dense tropical jungle and
at great expense and in the face of dangers of disease, and difficulties of securing satisfactory labor, he equipped it with
homes, ice plant, water-distillation plant and electric plant (and
electric fans) to make life endurable there and also mills and

shops to facilitate the work incident to drilling and oil tanks to save any oil which he might discover. On May 1, he began to drill, and, on May 14, the first well, a shallow one (525 feet), began to produce (about 50 barrels a day). Unable to sell the oil to the railroad company, he organized a paving company which used it for asphaltum pavements in Mexico City, Guadalajara, Morelia, Tampico, Puebla, Chihuahua and other Mexican cities. Meantime, in October, 1902, he placed H. G. Wylie in charge of the oil development. After completing several shallow wells he sought, in 1904, a deeper producing formation and was successful in completing, at a depth of 1,450 feet, a well which began with a production of 1,000 barrels and soon increased to 1,700 barrels, greatly surprising the Mexican geologist (Aguilera) who soon thereafter made an unsuccessful effort to nationalize petroleum. In 1905, after equipping a railway engine to prove that the oil could be used as a locomotive fuel, he contracted with Henry Clay Pierce of the Mexican Central to supply it as a fuel for that road for fifteen years.

Meantime, still without competition in the business, Doheny (with Canfield) prospected north and south on horseback and foot or by aid of the railway, and up the rivers by a yacht, finding enormous oil "exudes" which to the natives were only ancient death traps for animals—and a source of danger to children—but to these American prospectors indicated the existence of profitable pools of undeveloped oil. With a confidence unshaken by earlier discouragements, he had increased his ownership of one-eighth to 40% of the earlier properties by purchases from stockholders who wished to sell. With the assurance that Diaz desired the prosperity of his business for its value as an example to Mexican workmen, he continued to extend his purchases of subsoil rights or of surface with subsoil rights, but was unable to secure leases on a royalty basis. In 1909, he began the development of Huasteca properties in the unfrequented region south of Tampico, near the scene of the abandoned efforts of Cecil Rhodes many years before. Before the end of 1909 he had proved the Juan Casiano field. Soon thereafter he organized subsidiary companies and built, at great cost, roadways, a pipe line and ten pumping stations for transportation to Tampico and facilities for storage of oil. The first Huasteca well soon filled all the storage tanks. The second started to flow in September, 1910, with a daily production of 70,000 barrels unrestrained. The oil production of the Doheny lands which in 1907 was one million barrels was increased to over sixty million fifteen years later.[36]

The Doheny oil interests in Mexico were followed by several competing interests after 1905. Among the most prominent of the many American competing groups were the Waters-Pierce Company, the Standard Oil Company, the Texas-Mexican Company, the Gulf Refining Company, the Texas-Mexican Fuel Company, the Penn-Mexican Fuel Company, the Sinclair Company and the Panuco-Boston Company. The Waters-Pierce Company and other large oil interests acquired land in the vicinity of Tampico in 1902 and soon planned to sink wells. Possibly the earliest competition was from a foreign group—the Pearson interests of Great Britain (Canada) which appeared by 1906, and discovered the San Cristobal in July, 1908, and was later followed by two other foreign competing companies (the Dutch Royal and the Spanish-Mexican).

The estimated value of American investments in Mexico increased from $500,000,000 (gold) in 1902 to near $1,500,000,000 by 1912—including ownership of 78% of the mines, 72% of the smelters, 58% of the oil and 68% of the rubber business, and exceeding the total investments of all other foreigners in Mexico.

The extension of American influence in Mexico was also expressed in the statistics of trade relations. Commerce, which had increased from $7,000,000 in 1860 to over $15,000,000 in 1880, grew to $36,000,000 by 1890 and to $63,000,000 in 1900. It reached $92,000,000 in 1905 and $117,000,000 in 1910.[37]

In the decade after 1900, usually associated with the increasing Mexican opposition to Diaz and his policies, appeared evidences of anti-American feeling based largely on economic conditions connected with the recent American railway and industrial invasion of Mexico. In 1900 and 1901 the Mexican arrest and imprisonment of American railway employees was a source of American diplomatic complaint. One case was that of Turner, a member of the Brotherhood of Locomotive Engineers in the United States, who had died after an imprisonment of over ten months, during five of which the American government had continuously and earnestly requested a prompt trial. After Turner's death, which was followed by considerable criticism of the American government for its failure to secure an adjudication of the case, Clayton, stating that a prompt trial could have been obtained by a few words from President Diaz to the officials, expressed plainly to Mariscal the opinion that the Mexican government, independent of its duty to accord to accused persons a prompt trial, should spare the American government such criticisms "by using every proper effort to avoid similar occurrences." In the spring of 1903 the Department of State was requested to present many complaints of arrest and imprisonment of railway employees. In March, 1906, Thompson found a new cause for complaint. In a dispatch to his government he reported that aliens were excluded from mining concessions in the districts of Sonora and Lower California.[38]

Meantime, after 1899, Limantour, Minister of Finance since 1893 (successor of Romero under whom he had served as subsecretary), fearing financial domination of Mexico by American capitalists, induced Diaz to adopt a more restrictive railroad policy, and between 1902 and 1909 put into operation a plan for national control of the larger part of the railway mileage, including the Mexican Central, National, Mexican International, Pan-American and Vera Cruz and Isthmus lines. The problem, resulting from the tendency to consolidate the lines controlled by rival American interests, was complicated by the fear that foreign interests would become predominant through the acquisition of the control of shares of railway stock. In 1903, Limantour, by the purchase of a new issue of its securities, got control of the Interoceanic which its rival, the Mexican National, desired to acquire in order to secure an outlet to the Gulf, and by this control he later effected an agreement which also gave the government control of the National. In 1906, he obtained a controlling interest in the Mexican Central which, by its financial needs, was threatened by a change of control. In the same year he had an interview with E. H. Harriman who, while on a visit to Mexico City, submitted to him a plan for merging into one great system several of the Mexican railways with a view to greater economy than could be obtained from the system of competition. To Harriman, after consultation with the President, he gave an unfavorable reply; but, utilizing Harriman's idea, he framed a plan for the nationalization of the principal railroads of Mexico, and, with the approval of Diaz, he obtained consent of Congress to his nationalization plan—using the bogy of a possible absorption of all Mexican railways by Americans to carry his point. To forestall the consolidating schemes of Harriman and H. Clay Pierce he proceeded to organize the National Railways of Mexico as an operating company in which the Mexican government held a majority interest, and which began operation in 1909, resulting in later discriminations against American railway employees whose discharge Mexican laborers sought to enforce in August, 1911, by a strike.[39]

The Southern Pacific interests, which had begun in 1898 by a lease of the Sonora railway from the Atchison, Topeka and Santa Fe to get access to Guaymas, remained under American control. In 1903, the Southern Pacific also acquired control of the Cananea, Yaqui River and Pacific from which a short line had been constructed from Naco on the boundary to the Cananea mines under a concession of 1900. In October, 1905, it got a concession for an extension line southward from Guaymas to Guadalajara by way of Mazatlan upon which construction was promptly begun and was completed to Mazatlan in 1909. Between 1903 and 1906 Sinaloa felt a subtle change of life resulting from a great wave of industrial development. The construction of a strategic west coast railroad (the Yaqui, Guadalajara and Pacific) through its fertile coastal plain by the Southern Pacific company, the activities of the well-financed American Sinaloa Land Company in acquiring rich agricultural and grazing lands by conveyance of a large grant from the astute lawyer Don Luis Martinez who had received a "survey concession" from the Mexican government, the arrival of many adventurers and investors, and the increase in the price of labor paid by railroads and at the Cananea mines had a disquieting influence on many of the residents who distrusted the impending commercial invasion and who, fearing the prospect of changes subversive of the old standards of living, were soon regarded by the newcomers as anti-American. The railway, already completed from Guaymas to Torin on the Yaqui by May, 1906, and advancing to meet construction northwestward from Mazatlan, was another evidence that Mexico was steadily growing more and more American by peaceful penetration or invasion of economic and social influences which stimulated new Mexican wants and new American markets, and also, unfortunately, was accompanied by some anti-American feeling.

In June, 1906, the American government became apprehensive of reports of anti-American activities in Mexico, evidently beginning with disturbances resulting from a strike of Mexican workmen at Cananea in which several persons were killed, resulting in a rumor that Arizona Rangers were en route to cross the border. Secretary Root, on June 2, following a telegram from the American consular agent at Cananea informing him of the murders and destruction of property and asking assistance, promptly (on June 3) wired Ambassador Thompson to request prompt and effective control and protection of American citizens and to invite suggestions as to any desired action of the American government to prevent violation of international obligations by American citizens. Thompson wired on the same day that the Mexican government assured him of its ability promptly to control the situation. Later, on the same day, Root, without wishing to make any offer which would not be agreeable and acceptable to the Mexican government, wired Thompson discreetly to ascertain "whether the Mexican Government would welcome or acquiesce in assistance of United States troops to preserve order in the special emergency, pending arrival of Mexican troops."

On June 3, Thompson, after a conference with President Diaz who seemed much agitated over the Cananea incident, wired to Secretary Root the following reply:

". . . In an interview today with President Diaz concerning Cananea matters, he said that the foundation of the whole thing is revolutionary and aimed at his Government. There were in Cananea about twenty revolutionists, he thinks all Mexicans, inspired from headquarters in St. Louis, Missouri. A reduction of wages in a Cananea mine from abnormally high to something like Mexican normal caused this outfit to put forth the claim that the Government was responsible. The result was that a large number, all Mexicans, followed the revolutionists, while on the other side were both Americans and Mexicans. The fight and attempted destruction of property, some buildings and lumber being destroyed, was the early result, immediately followed by twenty imprisoned and the scattering and fleeing of the attacking party. The Mexican Government is in perfect military control of Cananea and in pursuit of offenders. The President says he would be much pleased if the American side of the line could be patrolled by any authorized forces to prevent escape into American territory of fugitives, and that should further serious trouble develop, which he thinks not likely, he would, if bad, be glad to have Federal soldiers' assistance. No armed American force should cross line unless authorized." [40]

In July, 1906, coincident with the cooperation of President Roosevelt and President Diaz in efforts to adjust difficulties between Guatemala and Salvador, further American apprehensions arose from certain Associated Press dispatches. One, of July 12, from New Orleans published the sensational statement of F. A. Sturdevant, a dismissed employee of the Mexican Central Railway, that the recent troubles in Cananea were but the beginning of the anti-foreign activities of a secret society of Mexican laborers, with which the Mexican army would be unable to cope, that Americans had been warned to leave Mexico by September 4, and threatened with death thereafter, and that the American government would be compelled soon to send troops into Mexico to protect American interests there. Another of July 20, from El Paso, referred to a proposed demonstration against foreigners, planned for September 16, under the auspices of the League of Mexican Railroad Employees with a purpose of expulsion of all foreigners who held official positions with railroads, mines and smelters. It stated that President Diaz was calling a governors' conference to prepare measures to prevent the uprising. To prevent the harm which might result from the exaggerations and falsities of these dispatches the Mexican *Herald* of July 21 in contradicting them stated that discontent was only local and added the following explanation:

"It is understood that the authorities here are of the opinion that American and other foreign foremen in large industrial concerns often fail to display a proper degree of tact and judgment in their treatment of their Mexican labor. They are, it is averred, harsh and rough, at times, both in word and deed, and moreover do not give, it is said, their Mexican employes a fair show either as to pay or advancement, but under all circumstances give the preference to their own compatriots.

"It is furthermore understood to be the intention of the authorities, in so far as they properly may, within their legitimate sphere of action, to impress on large foreign employers of Mexican labor for their own benefit the expedience of treating their Mexican help well and with strict justice. In other words, the authorities intend to be properly solicitous for the growing working class in Mexico." [41]

In an official dispatch of July 25 Thompson reported to his government that for a month he had heard rumors of the suggested expulsion of Americans on September 16, and that recently an inflammatory circular calling Mexicans to prepare for a general uprising had been distributed at night, but that he had been assured by President Diaz that the inflammatory program was "the work of about three agitators whose efforts would end in nothing." On July 31 he cabled his government to notify the Associated Press that the reported statements relative to a Mexican anti-foreign uprising on September 16 were without foundation. The chief officers of the Mexican railway labor union stated that the members had "no grievances against either the Mexican Government or the foreigners, their whole object being to propagate peaceably a better condition for the railway employees." [42]

On the same date, following another talk with President Diaz, to whom he was privileged to have access at any hour, and feeling certain that local race troubles would arise in sections where Americans and Mexicans were employed together, and recognizing that "Mexico with all the Americans in it, and streaming into it, is essentially a land of emergencies," Thompson telegraphed directly to thirty-one of the principal American consular officers in Mexico to secure further information. Prompt replies practically agreed that rumors of a monster uprising were largely without foundation or justification and had been exaggerated. Several, however, mentioned a "deep seated hatred and dislike of Americans," especially along the border. The most pronounced evidence of this character came from Lewis A. Martin, the American consul at Ciudad Porfirio Diaz, who, on August 2, after referring to some disorderly incidents resulting from animosities endangered by labor troubles, and partly from inherited animosities arising from the Mexican War of 1846-48, stated that in many places Americans were unsafe. As a remedy for the situation he suggested that American business should be safeguarded and that it should treat with equal and exact justice the Mexican laborers who complained that they were paid less than Americans received for the same work. Thomas D. Edwards, consul at Ciudad Juárez whose laborers were chiefly employed at El Paso, admitted the existence of a feeling of enmity among the Mexican laboring class against the same class of Americans—a feeling which was deeper among skilled laborers. He suggested that the best way to remedy the situation was to impress upon the Mexicans that their antagonistic policy would probably cause a similar American movement which would result in a far larger exodus of Mexican laborers from the United States and a consequent reduction of wages in Mexico. From Aguascalientes, at which a large number of skilled laborers and miners were employed by the Mexican Central Railway and the American Smelting and Refining Company, Consul Wardman reported (on August 1) that the strike there was evidently directed against Hungarians recently employed, but that following so soon after the events of Cananea it had been construed as an anti-foreign uprising. From Chihuahua, where Americans were intimately associated with the Mexicans in business, and socially by marriages and friendships, Consul Mills (on August 1) reported that the railway strike, although based on complaints of favoritism to foreigners and dissatisfaction with the local government, was peaceful. He had no more apprehension of violence than at any other time during his residence of eight years there. From Coatzacoalcos Mr. Stubbs, although he admitted that a great wave of anti-foreign feeling had swept over that section within the past year and had been alarmingly increased since the affair of Cananea, reported that he did not share the opinion of Americans that an outbreak was bound to occur and that he had full confidence that the local authorities were capable of handling any situation which might arise.[43]

From Durango, Consul Le Roy on August 3 sent an extract from a bitterly anti-American periodical, *La Evolucion*, which, although condemning the recent publications in the American press which had disturbed the confidence of Americans in Mexico, admitted a well-defined Mexican anti-American feeling which did "not yet display itself in the form of antagonism actually hostile." Explaining the movement, the writer of the extract said:

"It is a case of natural reaction in the wills of the workingmen, which have been for long rendered as things null in the power of capital which exploited them to the full extent, till the day when the fabulous increase of speculative activity in the country made plain the miserable medium in which the laborer lived, compared with that enjoyed by the men who are factor of riches. Into a country like Mexico, day by day entered powerful trusts that in a short time multiplied the capital they invested; it was naturally right that the condition of the laborer should improve in proportion to the 'speculation' (meaning, increase of investments). This has not happened, and this is the reason why, under the pressure of the unjust (under whatever aspect) preference for foreign laborers, the movement has been provoked into being.

"But this movement, we repeat, is far from bearing the alarming character ascribed to it by the American press. It is a pacific demonstration of the rights of the laborer, who, abandoned to himself in what pertains to his labor, is protesting through the only means open to him, the strike. . . ."

From Guanajuato Mr. Furness, although stating that a small class of agitators recruited from skilled laborers had proposed to expel the better paid American laborers, after careful inquiry reported on August 5 that relations between the Americans and natives were cordial. In presenting the situation, he said: "The large investment of American Capital in this District is quite recent and the prosperity of the camp so largely due to Americans that there seems to be among all elements a feeling of gratitude toward the Americans. The existing relations between American managers and foremen and the Mexican laborers, except in isolated cases, are most cordial and satisfactory. Wages here have been practically doubled within the past two years and the demand for skilled, as well as common, labor is constantly on the increase."

Although Thompson's telegram (of August 3) to the Department of State was submitted to the press and although the Mexican journals published articles denying and disproving the rumored plans for an early uprising, the American newspaper reports of an imminent anti-foreign revolt persisted. Thompson, deeply surprised, attributed the action to love for the money speculators or to thoughtlessness of the New York journalists. On August 28, in a dispatch to Bacon, he complained of the harmful articles which had appeared in the New York *Herald* of August 19 and *Harper's Weekly* of August 25 which he said were breeding a decided spirit of unrest among foreigners in Mexico and exciting the common Mexican "to thoughts of what might be done along lines declared certain by the American press." He especially objected to the *Harper's* article which referred to "a bitter anti-American feeling cultivated by a powerful opposition to President Diaz." He suggested that President Diaz would feel a deep gratification if the American government could treat as anarchists the publishers of the radical St. Louis journal *Regeneracion* to which the origin of the troublous rumors and apprehensions had been traced.[44]

Influenced by an earlier undercurrent of feeling of discontent, Diaz had already contemplated retirement by resignation for which a way was prepared by a constitutional amendment of

1904, providing for a vice president, but he was doubtful whether the conditions were favorable for his retirement. He continued to watch the feeling of unrest which after 1905 led to several armed movements and became more pronounced in the next half decade. In 1908 he was subjected to increased criticism and opposition, following a newspaper interview in which he declared that Mexico was ready for democracy and that he would welcome the formation of an opposition party.[45] In November, 1910, he was further embarrassed by violent anti-American expressions of the press which he had sought to curb and which the American ambassador urged him further to restrict. Finally, in May, 1911, eight months after the centennial celebration of the beginning of the first struggle for Mexican independence, he checked a threatened revolution by an agreement to retire from the power which he had wielded so long. Although under his administration foreign investments were encouraged by the argument that railway extensions and accompanying telegraph lines greatly diminished the chances of revolution, he was finally overthrown by the middle class of Mexicans created chiefly by the employment furnished by the railroads and other foreign enterprises which this class regarded as instruments of exploitation.

Luis Cabrera, in an address at a Clark University Conference in 1913, attributed the revolution of 1911 to the maladministration of the previous thirty years—to the "porfirista" régime which placed power in the hands of the large landholders and was marked by the gradual disappearance of the small holdings through absorption into the large estates and by the maintenance of a condition of servitude of the rural peons, and the conditions of which were complicated by the establishment of large business enterprises and the formation of large corporations through the offer of special advantages.[46]

In 1915 Francisco Bulnes, a prominent Mexican statesman and financial expert, wrote a book in which he undertook to prove that the origin of the recent Mexican revolution of 1911 "had a markedly 'Boxer' character and was directed principally against the influences, prestige and interests of the United

States" which had been favored under Diaz. Among the chief causes of the increasing Mexican opposition to Diaz, according to contemporary criticisms (some false, some exaggerated or based on misinterpretations, and some true) published by General Bernardo Reyes and mentioned by Bulnes, were the following: the encouragement of the American immigration and economic and industrial invasion as illustrated in the sale of half of Lower California to Louis Haller for an American colonizing enterprise; the modification of the Mexican mining code to enrich grantees of unclaimed lands in Coahuila who had acquired them with plans to sell to (C. P.) Huntington, the American railway magnate; encouragement of the Guggenheims in monopolizing the "metallurgic industry" upon which depended the progress of mining; the grant of large concessions in Sonora copper lands to Colonel Greene, an American who "established the famous Cananea plant where four thousand employees were treated like slaves"; the sale of large tracts of land in Chihuahua to two favorites of the Mexican government who purchased for sale to the American millionaire, Mr. Hearst, who later sought American armed intervention; special official consideration to the recommendations of Ambassador Powell Clayton "for private American affairs" even when they involved "injustice to the rights of the Mexican people"; "personal concessions" to Ambassador Thompson, "by means of which he organized the United States Banking Company and the Pan-American Railroad"; special favors granted through Limantour to the Tlahualilo Company whose chief protector was the American ambassador, Henry Lane Wilson; "scandalous concessions in rubber lands . . . to John Rockefeller and Nelson Aldrich" in Durango; sale of large tracts of fertile lands to twenty-eight favorites for transfer to American and other foreign companies; expulsion of the Yaquis from their lands which thieving "bureaucrats" desired to sell to American investors; the granting of oil concessions and exemptions from export duties on oil; the purchase, at great advance, from piratical Mexican and American financial speculators, of stocks of various railroads, and the appointment of Americans to the important positions in the nationalized railway system; negotiation of foreign loans through the banking firm of J. Pierpont Morgan and other New York banks in 1899, 1904 and later; prostitution of Mexican courts to American litigants; the lending of Magdalena Bay to the United States and rejection of honorable Japanese propositions to establish colonies in Lower California and elsewhere (which might have displeased the United States); enactment of an immigration law against the Japanese and Chinese in 1908 at American dictation; and neglect (in the Chamizal question) to obtain possession of the territory upon which El Paso was built.[47]

Notwithstanding the falsity or unreasonableness of many of these criticisms and indictments, Diaz, who had adopted a policy of encouraging foreign enterprises and investments with the expectation of large benefits and improvements to his country and its people, recognized his inability to continue his liberal policies in defiance of popular prejudices which he could not dispel. Therefore, in 1911 (at the age of 80), he resigned the presidency, leaving to his critics and a group of youthful agitators the opportunity to experiment with the problems of government including the problems relating to foreign residents and foreign investments in industrial enterprise, and to encounter the difficulties of maintaining a government as orderly as that which he had administered for so many years with the aid of trained and well-matured officials, governors and congressmen, many of whom, like the President, had grown old in service—so old that unfriendly newspapers, referring to the officials as mummies, called the government offices "Pyramids of Egypt joined to the Pyramids of Teotihuacan."

REFERENCES

1. FRED W. POWELL, *The Railroads of Mexico*, Chap. XI.
2. *For. Rels.*, *1868-69*, Vol. 2, p. 390; *31 Mexico, Despatches*, (No. 47) Dec. 13, 1867; *32 Mexico, Despatches*, (No. 115) Apr. 21, 1868; *35 Mexico, Despatches*, (Unofficial) March 10, (No. 43) March 28, (No. 48) Apr. 10, (No. 58) May 10, 1869.
3. *38 Mexico, Despatches*, No. 165, Jan. 28, 1870.

4. *House Rp. 701*, 45-2, App. A, pp. 42-43.
5. *37 Mexico, Despatches*, (No. 115) Nov. 20, 1869; *39 Mexico, Despatches*, (No. 202) Mar. 24, 1870 (Enclosure).
6. *45 Mexico, Despatches*, (No. 563) May 1, 1872; *48 Mexico, Despatches*, (No. 746) June 12, (No. 6) June 28, 1873; *54 Mexico, Despatches* (No. 302) June 10, 1875; *47 Mexico, Despatches*, (No. 691) Dec. 7, 1872; *51 Mexico, Despatches*, (No. 171) Aug. 19, 1874; *53 Mexico, Despatches*, (No. 226) Dec. 23, 1874.
7. *48 Mexico Despatches*, (No. 6) June 28, 1873; *50 Mexico, Despatches*, (No. 74) Nov. 23, 1873, (No. 98) Jan. 24, 1874; *53 Mexico, Despatches*, (No. 226) Dec. 23, 1874; *54 Mexico, Despatches*, (No. 298) June 5, and (No. 302) June 10, 1875; *57 Mexico, Despatches*, (No. 472) Dec. 8, 1876; *For. Rels.*, *1873*, p. 673, 1874, pp. 718 and 723, 1875, pp. 853, 893, and 927-36, 1877, pp. 386-87 and 392-93, and 1879, pp. 774-81.
8. *59 Mexico, Despatches*, (Confidential and Unofficial) May 16, and July 9, 1877; *60 Mexico, Despatches*, (Unofficial) July 30, 1877.
9. *Ib.*, (No. 586) Aug. 3, 1877; *62 Mexico, Despatches*, (No. 702) May 6, (No. 712) May 29, 1878; *For. Rels. 1878*, pp. 549-52.
10. *64 Mexico, Despatches*, (No. 805) Oct. 9, 1878; *66 Mexico, Despatches*, (No. 874) Jan. 28, 1879; *68 Mexico, Despatches*, (No. 1014) Aug. 16, 1879; *For. Rels.*, *1878*, Vol. 1, p. 638, 1879, pp. 774, 826 and 834-40; *Cong. Globe*, May 8 and 15, 1878, pp. 3254 and 3476-81.
11. *For. Rels.*, *1878*, Vol. 1, pp. 636, 649-52, and 1880, p. 719; *64 Mexico, Despatches*, (No. 805) Oct. 9, 1878; *68 Mexico, Despatches*, (No. 1014) Aug. 16, 1879; *69 Mexico, Despatches*, (No. 1075) Dec. 24, 1879; *70 Mexico, Despatches*, (No. 26) June 7, 1880.
12. *72 Mexico, Despatches*, (No. 205) June 7, 1881; *73 Mexico, Despatches*, (No. 229) July 12, 1881.
13. *La Patria*, June 6, 1881; *Harper's Magazine*, Oct., 1882, pp. 745-47; *International Review*, XIII, 1882, pp. 477-506.
14. *Rp. A. T. and S. F. Ry.*, 1880; *U. S. For. Rels.*, 1879, p. 778; *Commercial Rels. of the U. S.*, 1882-83, p. 226; CY WARMAN, *Story of the Railroad*, pp. 213-21; POWELL, *Railroads of Mexico*, p. 196; M. ROMERO, *Mexico and the U. S.; Highways of Commerce* (Spl. Consular Rps., XII).
15. *98 Mexico, Despatches*, (X) Feb. 28, 1889, pp. 39-41.
16. *37 Mexico, Despatches*, (No. 99) Oct. 21, 1869; *38 Mexico, Despatches*, (No. 159) Jan. 22, 1870; *39 Mexico, Despatches*, (No. 218) Apr. 20, 1870; *102 Mexico, Despatches*, (No. 239)

Feb. 7, 1890; *103 Mexico, Despatches*, (No. 256) March 5, 1890; — *Mexico, Despatches*, (Tel.) Aug. 26, 1892; *160 Mexico, Despatches*, (No. 1634) Nov. 26, 1902; *18 Mexico, Instructions*, (No. 11) June 10, 1869, (No. 113) Oct. 22, 1870; *22 Mexico, Instructions*, (No. 354) Oct. 3, 1890.

17. *For. Rels., 1881; 20 Mexico, Instructions*, No. 133, June 1, 1881.

18. *Ib.*, No. 137, June 16, 1881.

19. *73 Mexico, Despatches*, (No. 254, Confidential) Aug. 13, (No. 229) July 12, 1881.

20. *20 Mexico, Instructions*, (No. 166) Aug. 31, (No. 199) Nov. 20, 1881.

21. *73 Mexico, Despatches*, (No. 254, Confidential) Aug. 13, (No. 273) Sept. 22, 1881.

22. *20 Mexico, Instructions*, (Tel.) Feb. 20, 1883; *Mexico, Despatches*, (No. X) Feb. 28, 1889.

23. *87 Mexico, Despatches*, No. 0, Aug. 31, 1885.

24. *18 Mexico, Instructions*, (No. 141) Feb. 25, 1871; *68 Mexico, Despatches*, (No. 1013) Aug. 15, 1879; *38 Mexico, Despatches*, (No. 118) Nov. 26, 1869; *44 Mexico, Despatches*, (No. 498) Jan. 9, 1872; *45 Mexico, Despatches*, (No. 515) Feb. 14, (No. 537) March 25, 1872; *69 Mexico, Despatches*, (No. 1074) Dec. 23, 1879, (No. 1089) Jan. 7, 1880; *Misc. Letters*, March, 1878, Part I; *122 Domestic Letters*, p. 196, March 18, 1878; JOHN W. FOSTER, *Memoirs*, I, p. 14.

25. *For. Rels., 1888*, II, p. 1189; *93 Mexico, Despatches*, (No. 157) June 16, 1887; *94 Mexico, Despatches*, (No. 288) Dec. 23, 1887.

26. *For. Rels., 1879; House Doc. 305, 57-2, I, p. 506; 20 Mexico, Instructions*, (No. 715) Jan. 27, 1880; *Mexico, Despatches*, (No. 718) July 28, 1891.

27. *79 Mexico, Despatches*, No. 606, Apr. 25, 1883.

28. *For. Rels., 1882*, p. 394, 1885 and 1886; *20 Mexico, Instructions*, (No. 288) July 24, 1882; *21 Mexico, Instructions*, (No. 905) Dec. 20, 1884, (No. 732) Feb. 17, 1885, and (No. 18) Nov. 20, 1886.

29. *28 Mexico, Despatches*, (No. X) Feb. 28, 1889; *House Doc. 305, 57-2, I, p. 522.

30. *For. Rels., 1874*, pp. 766 and 842; *51 Mexico, Despatches*, Aug. 12, 1874; *52 Mexico, Despatches*, Oct. 2, 1874.

31. *21 Mexico, Instructions*, (No. 656) Sept. 11, 1884; *Sen. Exec. Doc. 285, 66-2, I*, pp. 1462-63; *98 Mexico, Despatches*, (No. X) Feb. 28, 1889, pp. 44-46.

32. *For. Rels., 1888*, pp. 1087 and 1184, and 1894, pp. 418, 420 and 422-24; *23 Mexico, Instructions*, No. 716, Apr. 14, 1892.

33. *25 Mexico, Instructions*, (Tel.) Nov. 18, 1892, and (No. 834) Jan. 28, 1903.
34. *House Doc. 305, 57-2*, 1902; *Commercial Rels.* I, pp. 433-539 *passim*.
35. *Sen. Doc. 285*, 66-2, I, p. 1464.
36. *Sen. Doc. 285*, 66-2, I, pp. 208-18, 229-30.
37. *House Doc. 305, 57-2*, I, p. 507; *Sen. Exec. Doc. 285*, 66-2, II, pp. 3322 and 3313.
38. *25 Mexico, Instructions*, (Nos. 509 and 513) Apr., 1901; *145 Mexico, Despatches*, (No. 64) May 2, 1900; *For. Rels., 1906,* II, p. 1142.
39. *For. Rels., 1912*, p. 910; *Collier's Weekly*, July 1, 1916, pp. 22-23.
40. *183 Mexico, Despatches*, No. 79, June 5, 1906.
41. *184 Mexico, Despatches*, No. 131, July 25, 1906.
42. *Ib.*, also cablegram, July 31, 1906.
43. *184 Mexico, Despatches*, No. 144, Aug. 6, 1906 (Enclosures).
44. *22 Numerical File*, 1906-10, Case 97 to 100, (No. 160) Aug. 15, (No. 182) Aug. 28, 1906.
45. CREELMAN in *Pierson's Magazine*, March, 1908; *For. Rels., 1911,* p. 354.
46. *Journal of Race Development*, Jan., 1914, pp. 243-61.
47. BULNES, *The Whole Truth About Mexico: President Wilson's Responsibility*, pp. 103, 121-27.

CHAPTER XIV

WILSON'S POLICY TOWARD MEXICO IN REVOLUTION

AMERICAN relations with Mexico after the *coup d'état* of Huerta, in February, 1913, is naturally divided into two periods: that in which questions of the establishment of order was most prominent, until near the end of the American administration of President Wilson; and the period after 1920 in which adjustment of claims, and questions arising from certain land and subsoil provisions of the Mexican constitution of 1917 were most prominent.

In the Mexican situation of confusion and disorder and insecurity, resulting from the struggle of rival factions, the Wilson administration encountered a task far more difficult than it suspected. In the patient policy of watchful waiting which it adopted it was strongly opposed by certain American business interests which demanded intervention to protect suffering American interests in Mexico. Its policy was regarded with impatience by many leading men in both American parties and by European governments which, refraining from acts of intervention which would have aroused American hostility, deferred to the American government for diplomatic guidance. In the directing of his policies the President was aided by three successive secretaries of state. He first appointed William Jennings Bryan who, although he had served as a member of Congress (in 1891-95) and as a colonel in the Spanish American War, and had been three times the Democrat candidate for the presidency, and in the Baltimore Democrat convention of 1912 had determined the nomination of Wilson, had little knowledge of diplomatic practice and international law. He therefore was expected by Wilson to lean heavily upon Professor John Bassett Moore, the counselor of the Department (until March, 1914), who was well equipped by training and experience for diplomatic duties. In June, 1915, Bryan resigned and was succeeded by Robert Lansing, who had served as counselor of the Department since March, 1915, and was well trained for his duties by various diplomatic experiences—beginning as associate counsel in the Bering Sea arbitration in 1892 when his father-in-law, Hon. John W. Foster, experienced diplomat, was Secretary of State. In March, 1920, Lansing was succeeded by Bainbridge Colby, who had performed valuable business duties as commissioner of the United States Shipping Board and member of the mission to the Inter-Allied Conference at Paris in the period from 1917 to 1919. In Mexican relations the administration for several months issued instructions to Ambassador Henry Lane Wilson who had been appointed by President Taft, and in the early summer of 1913 the President appointed William Bayard Hale to report on the ambassador's actions in connection with the diplomatic corps; and, according to the ambassador, Secretary Bryan also sent a Mr. del Valle of California to watch Mr. Hale.[1] After the departure of Ambassador Wilson from Mexico in July, 1913, the administration for a time issued instructions to the American chargé, Nelson O'Shaughnessy, until he withdrew from Mexico City on April 23, 1914, and, in the same period, also sent ex-Governor Lind of Minnesota as a personal representative of the President to act as "adviser of the American embassy" (to give advice to General Huerta). On February 25, 1916, after the decision to recognize the government of General Carranza, the President appointed as ambassador to Mexico Henry P. Fletcher who, after service with the Rough Riders in the Spanish American War and later service in the Philippines, had been employed in the diplomatic service as secretary of the American legation in Cuba, China and Portugal and as minister to Chile after 1909 (and as ambassador to Chile since October, 1914).

On February 21, 1913, near the close of the Taft administration, Ambassador Wilson had wired that the diplomatic corps, which he had assembled to consider the invitation to meet Huerta, agreed that recognition of the new government was imperative in order to enable it to impose authority and re-establish order. Secretary Knox, on the same day, had wired a reply that the American government must carefully consider whether the Huerta provisional government of Mexico was able and disposed to comply with the rules of international law and amity, the obligations of treaties and the general duties to for-eigners and foreign governments. He especially desired assur-ances that it would satisfactorily arrange for the adjustment of outstanding questions, including the Tlahualilo controversy, the Chamizal dispute, a convention for the equitable distribution of the waters of the Colorado, the settlement of American claims resulting from recent political disturbances in Mexico and improvement of the administration of justice in Mexican courts. Three days later, following the news of the murder of Madero, Ambassador Wilson had wired that Huerta verbally agreed that all questions mentioned would have "immediate action over everything else" and that Minister De la Barra agreed that immediately after the reception of instructions from Huerta he would proceed to the solution of all difficulties except the Chamizal matter which would be referred to the new Mexi-can ambassador to Washington with instructions to arrange a satisfactory settlement; but Secretary Knox on February 25 wired the President's direction to accord no formal recognition to those *de facto* in control but to transact business in the in-formal manner usual in such an interval before formal recog-nition.[2]

The American government under Taft had reason for a re-served attitude while awaiting further information. On Febru-ary 26, Knox received from Wilson a telegram which reported that he was endeavoring in all possible ways to aid the new administration to establish itself firmly, stating that under it the anti-American sentiment which had characterized the Madero administration had almost entirely disappeared. On the same date, the President received another telegram from V. Car-ranza, governor of Coahuila, stating that the Mexican nation

condemned the "villainous *coup d'état* which deprived Mexico
of its constitutional rulers by cowardly assassination" and expressed confidence that the American government would not
accept the "spurious" government which Huerta was "attempting to establish upon crime and treason." "In order not to
hinder the efforts of the administration at Mexico City to come
to an understanding with the insurrectionary leaders in northern
Mexico," Knox on the following day wired permission for these
leaders to proceed to San Antonio, Texas, for a conference
which they had proposed to hold there. A day later, he wired
to Wilson a warning that his unofficial activities should be kept
within the limits of "cautious circumspection."[3]

The new American administration under President Wilson
continued a policy of "watchful waiting." On March 8, Secretary Bryan, wiring Ambassador Wilson of American interest in
the restoration of peace and order, said: "Without any interference on our part in the affairs of our sister Republic you will
exercise such influence as may properly be employed to bring
about cooperation between the various elements upon a basis of
justice to all at home and abroad."

In a long dispatch of March 12 to Secretary Bryan, chiefly devoted to the events of the *coup d'état* of Huerta and the legality
and prospects of the Huerta government, Ambassador Wilson,
in explaining the Carranza movement, mentioned his leadership
in a former movement of the border governors to form an independent republic and cautioned the Department not to
become involved in an evident movement in Sonora and Sinaloa
(whose people were a mixture of Texan origin) to combine
with Lower California to declare an independent republic—a
movement with which he had heard that certain American interests might have some connection. Ten days later, he evidently
expected early recognition, although he had no instructions indicating such intentions. On April 1, in reply to his telegram
concerning the need of an immediate meeting of the diplomatic
corps to consider recognition and claims, Secretary Bryan wired
him that there was no objection to his attendance at such a
meeting provided his attitude was noncommittal.[4]

On April 9, still without instructions as to the policy of his government concerning recognition which he thought should not await the result of proposals for an international claims commission, Ambassador Wilson wired Secretary Bryan urging the importance of American moral support of the Mexican government whose success he regarded as the only way to prevent absolute chaos involving the inevitable necessity of intervention. On April 11, pressed by De la Barra for an answer concerning the continuance of American vessels in Mexican waters of the Gulf—a continuance which he did not approve—he suggested to him the transfer of the discussion to the American embassy at Washington "by which results perhaps more satisfactory may be achieved." On May 8, he wired Bryan that Huerta, regarding as unwise and unfriendly the American policy of delay in official recognition, had decided that his embarrassed government did not feel justified in concluding the negotiations for settlement of pending questions—the Chamizal and Colorado River cases and special and general claims. Two days later he reported the public statement of Huerta that relations with the American ambassador would be confined to simple routine matters.

On May 15, in a long dispatch presenting the political situation as favorable to the administration of Huerta (who he said remained "calm, serene, active and vigilant"), Ambassador Wilson again referred to a general Mexican opinion propagated by the Mexican government that American policy in withholding formal recognition was influenced by "a more or less clearly defined interventionist organization in the United States" which was supposed to be contributing moral and material support to the revolutionary cause "with the primary object of forming (by secession) an independent republic from Mexican territory contiguous to the border and reaching as far south as the twenty-sixth parallel"—embracing Lower California, the states of Sonora, Chihuahua and Coahuila and parts of Nuevo Leon, Durango and Sinaloa—and with a view to later application for admission as states in the American Union. Again, in a telegram of June 9 to Secretary Bryan—expressing the disheartening impression resulting from injury to American interests, the increase of European advantages, the rapid growth of Mexican hostility and the difficulty and embarrassment in the business of the American embassy in relations with the Mexican government—he urged, "on highest grounds of policy," that the American government should without further delay accord official recognition as most of the other governments had done, and requested prompt instructions by telegraph concerning the views and policies of President Wilson. On July 9, again urging the pressing necessity of some drastic and convincing action to protect American interests and terminate the warfare in Mexico, he submitted two possible courses: (1) official recognition with demand for guaranties; (2) withdrawal of the ambassador as a protest against existing conditions. Incidentally he complained that the dignity of the embassy had been lowered by the recent presence of persons claiming to be representatives of the President. Two days later, in order to impress upon President Wilson the "grave responsibilities" which required "firm, formidable and impressive action," he wired Secretary Bryan that a practical boycott of the embassy by the Mexican government made practically impossible the transaction of business, and that the insolence of public officials to the embassy had become intolerable. Accompanying this situation was a rising tide of bitter resentment expressed by the press and by attempts at anti-American demonstrations against which he protested.[5]

On July 17, Ambassador Wilson departed for Washington, via Vera Cruz and Havana, leaving his secretary, Nelson O'Shaughnessy, in charge of the embassy as chargé d'affaires. On August 4, his resignation was accepted by Secretary Bryan with the explanation that "the part which he felt it his duty to take in the early stages of the revolution in Mexico would make it difficult for him to represent the views of the present administration in view of the situation which now exists."[6]

With this explanation Bryan announced the appointment of ex-Governor John Lind of Minnesota (a strong supporter of Bryan) as personal representative of the President to act as adviser of the American embassy in Mexico. On the following day O'Shaughnessy, learning through correspondents of American newspapers that Lind's mission was "to suggest peace terms and also to insist on the resignation of General Huerta as a *sine qua non*"—the publication of which he feared would thwart the mission and possibly incite the crowd to mob Mr. Lind at the station—he wired Secretary Bryan to authorize him to deny the latter part of the statement. On August 6, before the arrival of Bryan's reply stating that the mission was one of peace, he received from Garza Aldape, Acting Minister of Foreign Affairs, a notice from Huerta that if Lind did not establish his official character, or if he was not a bearer of recognition, his sojourn would not be pleasing.

Under President Wilson's new policy of using non-recognition as a means of discouraging the establishment of governments based on force and violence—a departure from the previous American recognition policy for *de facto* governments, and the latest extension of the Monroe Doctrine—the American government refused to recognize Huerta, unsuccessfully urged an early fair and free election in Mexico, warned Americans to leave that country and vigorously demanded both the *de facto* government of Huerta and insurrectionsts to respect lives and property of Americans.

Feeling a duty to volunteer good offices in effecting some arrangement to secure relief and peace for which the American government had long waited—a duty determined both by unselfish friendship and the expectations of the powers of the world—President Wilson, in his instructions to Lind to confer with "the persons who at the present time have authority or exercise influence in Mexico," stated that apparently no progress had been made toward the establishment of a central government which the country would obey and respect, and that the existing situation in Mexico was "incompatible." He suggested four things upon which a satisfactory statement seemed to be conditioned: (1) a definite armistice, scrupulously observed; (2) security for an early and free election in which all agree to participate; (3) consent of General Huerta to bind himself not to be a candidate for the presidency at this elec-

tion; and (4) agreement of all parties to accept the results of
the election and to cooperate in the organization and support
of the new administration. Lind, although treated with studied
courtesy, found that his advice fell on stony soil. After two
conferences he received from F. Gamboa, Secretary of Foreign
Affairs, a clever and dignified note of August 16, addressed to
"Mr. Confidential Agent," politely contradicting the "gross
imputation" that Mexico had made no progress in the establishment of a respected government, definitely declining the
friendly good offices and refusing to consider the four conditions which President Wilson had proposed—stating as reasons
that "bandits are not admitted to armistice," that Mexican laws
already provided the assurance of free elections, that the question
of the candidacy of General Huerta could be decided only by
Mexican public opinion expressed at the polls and that the
legality of the government of General Huerta (whom Ambassador Wilson had "congratulated upon his elevation to the Presidency") could not be disputed.[7]

Following Lind's report of the Mexican rejection of the
American proposals, President Wilson in a message of August
27 presented the situation to a joint session of both houses of
Congress, stating that the American government, while awaiting a Mexican awakening from misunderstanding to a realization of facts, must continue its duty to act with patient,
calm and disinterested deliberation, to maintain true neutrality,
to forbid the exportation of arms and munitions of war to
Mexico from any part of the United States, to urge Americans
to leave Mexico and vigilantly to watch and protect the lives and
interests of those who were unable to leave. In closing his message he expressed confident expectation that by the steady
pressure of moral force which would soon break the barriers of
pride and prejudice America would soon triumph as the friend
of Mexico.[8]

On August 25, Lind delivered to the Mexican government a
second note which Gamboa considered in essence the same as
the first, and which he answered by another note only because
"the President *ad interim* wishes to carry his forbearance to

the last point." It emphasized that in "seeking to counsel Mexico for her own good" the American government intended to pay the most scrupulous regard to the Mexican sovereignty and added that it would look with favor upon the extension of an immediate loan by American bankers in case President Huerta accepted the American suggestions. In a reply of August 25, Gamboa stated that Mexico could not compromise its sovereignty by an action which might encourage plans to submit future elections to the veto of the American executive, and, referring to the "disproportionate interest" which President Wilson had shown concerning Mexican "internal affairs," he said that no one in Mexico had ever yet proposed the candidacy of Huerta for the presidency.[9]

By October 11, the American government learned of new evidence which seemed to justify its policy. Huerta on that day ordered the arrest and imprisonment of one hundred and ten members of the Chamber of Deputies which was accompanied by the dissolution of the Chamber in which Huerta had been strongly opposed. Secretary Bryan in a telegram of protest, on October 13, stated that President Wilson would not feel justified in accepting the result of an election held at that time. Following demands for intervention, President Wilson, in a speech at Mobile, Alabama, on October 13, 1913, while expressing the hope that law and order would be maintained in neighboring republics, declared that the United States would never seek to add additional territory by conquest.[10]

On November 7, Secretary Bryan announced in a telegram to American diplomatic officers another step in President Wilson's policy—the employment of means necessary to secure the retirement of Huerta and the refusal to regard as binding on Mexico anything done by Huerta after his assumption of dictatorial powers. This policy he explained more fully in a report to various embassies and to John Lind on November 24.

"The purpose of the United States," said he, "is solely and singly to secure peace and order in Central America. . . . Usurpations like that of General Huerta menace the peace and development of America as nothing else could. They not only render the development of ordered self government impossible; they also tend to set law entirely aside, to put the lives and fortunes of citizens and foreigners alike in constant jeopardy, to invalidate contracts and concessions in any way the usurper may devise for his own profit and to impair both the national credit and all the foundations of business, domestic or foreign. It is the purpose of the United States therefore to discredit and defeat such usurpations whenever they occur. The present policy . . . is to isolate General Huerta entirely; to cut him off from foreign sympathy and aid and from domestic credit, whether moral or material, and to force him out. It hopes and believes that isolation will accomplish this end and shall await the results without irritation or impatience. If General Huerta does not retire by force of circumstances it will become the duty of the United States to use less peaceful means to put him out. . . . Each conspicuous instance in which usurpations of this kind are prevented will render their recurrence less frequent and in the end a state of affairs will be secured in Mexico and elsewhere upon this continent which will assure the peace of America and the untrammeled development of its economic and social relations with the rest of the world.

"Beyond this fixed purpose the Government of the United States will not go. It will not permit itself to seek any special or exclusive advantages in Mexico or elsewhere for its own citizens but will seek, here as elsewhere, to show itself the consistent champion of the open door." [11]

In his message, of December 2, President Wilson denied any intention of intervention. Meantime, at the White House, personally and through others, he had explained his policy to the private secretary of Sir Edward Grey, resulting in an early notification of Huerta that he could not rely upon British support and also the coincident representations of the British and other European diplomats in Mexico City advising him to yield to American demands. Recognizing that settlement by civil war was inevitable unless prevented by sweeping armed intervention which would result in more difficult problems, Secretary Bryan on January 29 instructed Ambassador W. H. Page to notify Sir Edward Grey, whose opinion had been sought, and to suggest: "If the European powers would jointly or severally inform General Huerta in plain terms that he could no longer expect countenance or moral support from them, the situation would be immensely simplified and the only possible settlement brought within sight. No one outside Mexico can now accommodate her affairs." Soon thereafter, without assuming responsibility, the American government acted as an intermediary for foreign powers in cases requiring protection of their citizens from acts of the revolutionary forces, but ignored all opportunities and temptations for territorial expansion or intervention—to establish a protectorate—although, in March, 1914, immediate intervention was urged by some who were apprehensive of contemplated action by Germany.[12]

Early in 1914 President Wilson decided to shift his position on neutrality. In August, 1913, recognizing no legitimate government in Mexico, he had sought to observe a strict impartiality between contending factions by forbidding exportation of arms and munitions of war from the United States to any part of Mexico as provided under the proclamation of March 14, 1912. He now found, however, that the Huerta faction, recognized as a legitimate government by several other governments, was in a position to obtain arms and ammunition elsewhere. On February 3, desiring to place the Mexican contending factions on an equality, he removed the inhibition on export of arms or munitions which had existed under the law of March 12, 1912, thereby favoring the Constitutionalist party whose operations had already caused the American government considerable concern. Coincidentally, the American government through its consuls submitted to the Constitutionalist leaders in Mexico many unofficial representations in behalf of non-American foreign persons and interests—especially in favor of Spanish subjects, against whom Carranza and Villa were prejudiced by the supposed pro-Spanish attitude of Huerta. When General Carranza, through his Secretary of Foreign Affairs, stated that representations and claims must be presented by the diplomatic representatives of the countries whose citizens were concerned, Secretary Bryan replied (on March 2) that the American unofficial consular representations and protestations for citizens of countries were in conformity with the usages and necessities incident to the grave situation, and in accord with international law, and were made in a friendly spirit and especially with a view to prevention of the adoption of coercive measures by foreign powers to secure redress of grievances. Through Special Agent Carothers he received a telegraphic reply (on April 14) that Carranza would receive through the American Secretary of State and American consuls representations requested by foreign diplomatic representatives at Washington.[13]

On February 12, following the violation of American jurisdiction by Mexican federal military officers at Nuevo Laredo, Acting Secretary J. B. Moore instructed O'Shaughnessy to request immediate action to stop such acts which showed disregard of international rights and obligations and had tended to create grave international complications.[14]

Meantime O'Shaughnessy, who remained in Mexico in charge of the American legation, was on very friendly terms with Huerta. He handled with tact and courtesy many complicated questions while expecting, sooner or later, a complete break of diplomatic relations. After the arrival of Wilson's ultimatum of November he remained at the Palace in discussion with Huerta until after midnight. He smoothed the difficulties connected with the visit of John Lind. He still remained *persona grata* with Huerta after Garza Aldape's "demission" on November 16 for presentation of the American note. In January, he received from Secretary Bryan a suggestion that he should not be too cordial with Huerta in public, but he could not fail to respond to the cordiality and affection with which Huerta continued to treat him until the day he left Mexico City. Early in March, he and his wife were "aghast at the resignation of John B. Moore" who, as counselor of the Department of State at Washington, had occasionally written him a letter of appreciation of his service in delicate transactions. At the same time he had little faith in the usefulness of the mission of John Lind, the "cloister agent," who was still watching and waiting at Vera Cruz and cabling his views to Washington—and who so continued until April 2.[15]

The Wilson policy in refusing to recognize the Huerta government and in demanding the elimination of Huerta from the list of candidates for the election was widely regarded as a mistake. It instigated Huerta to turn from a conciliatory policy to one of hostility—illustrated in the Mexican inexcusable arrest and imprisonment of American unoffending marines in American uniform at Tampico early in April, 1914, and (following their release) the refusal to comply with the American demand (of Admiral Mayo) for an apology by public salute of the American flag on shore. When the Huerta government, claiming that Tampico was under martial law at the time of the arrest, requested through O'Shaughnessy a withdrawal of the ultimatum requiring prompt salute of the American flag on shore, President Wilson promptly pressed the demand and O'Shaughnessy (on April 12) urged the necessity for quick action. The Mexican reply of April 12 through the young new Sub-Secretary Esteva Ruis insisted that the salute, regarded as humiliating by a stretch of "courtesy" which "would be equivalent to accepting the sovereignty of a foreign state," might result in serious anti-American outbreaks in Mexico. On April 14 Bryan, although expressing appreciation of the conciliatory attitude of General Huerta but doubting whether he realized the serious character of the situation, wired O'Shaughnessy firmly to impress upon him the grave consequences involved and the American expectation of his prompt compliance with the American naval demands. Huerta, although he agreed to investigate further, insisted that his position required him to uphold the dignity and sovereignty of Mexico; and he suggested that the whole question be submitted to the Hague or to settlement by arbitration under the treaty of 1848. On the following day (April 15) at noon, hesitating to salute first, he offered to compromise on a simultaneous salute to the two flags—to which Bryan objected (on April 16) on the ground that it would deprive Huerta's action of its significance. On April 18, Secretary Bryan wired O'Shaughnessy to say to Huerta that President Wilson, much disappointed, had determined that if the demand was not met by 6 o'clock P.M. April 19 he would present the matter to Congress and take steps to advise the withdrawal of all Americans from Mexico. When Huerta, warned by O'Shaughnessy that refusal to salute would probably result in armed intervention, agreed to accept the American terms if O'Shaughnessy would sign a formal protocol agreeing to a return salute, Bryan replied that the American authorities could be relied upon to observe the international custom and courtesy without the protocol—to which he objected (partly on the ground that it might be interpreted as a recognition of the Huerta government).[16]

President Wilson, disgusted with the series of international irritations and insults which had resulted from the year of Mexican disorder, was finally instigated to seek reparation by a naval and military force which, after its occupation of Vera Cruz, produced some apprehension of intervention on a larger scale involving the danger of a war with the possibility of conquest. In a message to a joint session of Congress, on April 20, he presented the Tampico incident as only one of a series which indicated a purpose to disregard the dignity and rights of the American government; and, without any purpose of aggression or intervention, he asked approval of his proposal to use American armed forces to enforce respect for the American government. He was supported in the House by a vote of 323 to 29 and in the Senate by 72 to 13. On April 21, he directed Admiral Fletcher at Vera Cruz to seize the customhouse to prevent delivery of arms and ammunition from Germany—an act which was promptly accomplished and was followed by an advance to occupy the entire city. The result was the severance of diplomatic relations by order of Huerta (through Minister Portillo y Rojas) and the immediate retirement of O'Shaughnessy from Mexico (April 24) accompanied by a large escort and by General Huerta's son as a guarantee of safety. O'Shaughnessy left the embassy in charge of the British embassy for which Bryan soon substituted the Brazilian minister.[17]

A few days later (April 28), Secretary Bryan wired Special Agent Carothers to endeavor to secure from the Constitutionalist authorities a written agreement to neutralize the great oil-producing region between Tampico and the Tuxpam River and at Ebano in which, since the Tampico incident, the wells in charge of inexperienced Mexican employees were running wild, threatening great destruction and danger. He received a prompt reply (of May 1) that Carranza, claiming that his forces now dominated the region, regarded neutralization as unnecessary and inexpedient but suggested that the experienced foreign oil operators should return to their work.[18]

From Carranza, who had been notified of the seizure of the port of Vera Cruz, Secretary Bryan was probably surprised to learn (on April 22) that this act was not regarded with favor by the "Constitutionalist Army," but as an unexpected "violation of the national sovereignty," an invasion which might result in war and a recognition of Huerta by a demand for reparation which he had no authority to grant. He was invited to suspend the hostile acts already begun and to evacuate Vera Cruz. From the American special agent (G. C. Carothers) at El Paso, however, he learned that Villa was friendly and that through him there was hope of establishing the neutrality of the Constitutionalists which was regarded essential in facilitating the elimination of Huerta. On April 25, he received assurance that Carranza would not fight American troops and would not join Huerta, whom Villa said must not be allowed to succeed in the use of his "satanic abilities" to start a war with the United States.

At the same time Bryan welcomed the generous offer of good offices from the diplomatic representatives of the A. B. C. powers (Brazil, Argentine and Chile) for a peaceful and friendly settlement of the difficult question, and he promptly accepted—followed by the acceptance of Huerta and the appointment of commissioners or delegates by each government by March 12. The American representatives were Associate Justice Lamar of the Supreme Court and Frederick Lehmann, former solicitor of the Department of Justice. The Mexican representatives were Emilio Rabasa, Agustin Rodriguez and Luis Elguero, all prominent men in their country. The conference convened at Niagara Falls, Canada (at the Clifton Hotel), on May 20. As the negotiations proceeded and the situation developed, questions of increasing difficulty and delicacy arose—especially concerning the personnel of the proposed provisional government to replace Huerta, the American proposal to renew the invitation to the Constitutionalists to send delegates to the conference and the proposed armistice between the Mexican armed factions. Bryan, on May 24, following new victories of the Constitutionalists which reënforced the expectations of the inevitable elimination of Huerta, wired the American special commissioners suggesting that a prompt agreement upon a clear program acceptable to the victorious Carrancistas was the only way to guard against further use of force or armed intervention. On May 27, satisfied that the success of the Constitutionalists was inevitable, he insisted that the provisional government, if it had any hope of success, must not be neutral as Huerta's representatives desired, but that it must be "actually, avowedly and sincerely in favor of the agrarian and political reforms" proposed by the Mexican revolution. Two days later he urged that it should be disconnected from the Huerta régime and the previous régime and that it should be explicitly pledged and bound to undertake the reforms. He still urged the representation of the advancing Constitutionalists at the conference, although the mediators insisted that Carranza's recent decision to enter the conference was the result of his want of ammunition and especially determined not to admit his representatives except upon conditions to which the other parties had agreed, including an armistice to which Carranza refused to agree. In reply to the demand of the Huerta representatives for the establishment of a neutral provisional government, and their criticism of the American plan which they said aimed at "absolute triumph for the revolution and the direction of Mexico's internal affairs" which would lead to "immediate intervention," Mr. Lehmann of the American delegation, reiterating the American policy to seek no advantage at the expense of Mexico and to make no claim for indemnity except what would be settled on principles of international law, insisted (on June 13) that any adjustment for pacification with hope of permanency must include the assurance of the agrarian and other reforms which had been promised by Diaz, Madero and Huerta, and a provisional government which would be acceptable to the majority of the Mexican people (i.e., the Constitutionalists) who could not be expected to yield everything gained by arduous struggles. Three days later (June 16), the American commissioners in a disappointing interview of four hours at Buffalo with the representatives of the Constitutionalists were told that "the mediators ought to stop attempting to settle internal affairs of Mexico" and that "under no consideration would Carranza accept the result of the mediation, no matter how much it might be in his favor"(!).[19]

On June 24 the Mediation Conference approved the provisions of the articles of a mediation protocol: (1) the constitution of a provisional government by agreement of the delegates representing the parties to the internal struggle in Mexico; (2) agreement of the American government to recognize the provisional government and to restore diplomatic relations through it, and to claim no war indemnity or other international satisfaction; (3) requirement that the provisional government proclaim absolute amnesty to all foreigners for all political offenses committed during the period of civil war in Mexico and negotiate for a commission for the settlement of indemnity claims of foreigners for damages resulting from military acts or acts of the national authorities in the period of the civil war; (4) agreement of the three mediating governments to recognize the provisional government.

The American delegates, who had signed all the minutes subject to a protest against recognizing the Huerta delegates as representatives of the United States of Mexico, on June 29 telegraphed Secretary Bryan concerning "the apparent incongruity of making an agreement as to international affairs when we ourselves claim that there is no representative of Mexico before the Mediators." On July 1, Bryan wired that the President directed the delegates to sign with a conditional stipulation that in doing so they expressly denied any American recognition of the government of Huerta.[20]

On July 3, Secretary Bryan still urged upon the American

special agent, Carothers, the importance of bringing the inharmonious Constitutionalist leaders into hearty cooperation, and the imperative necessity of conference of Carranza representatives with Huertista representatives, but he urged in vain. On July 9, he received a telegram from the American consul at Monterey stating that Carranza and his military chiefs agreed that a continuation of the fighting was "the only way to permanent peace," and, on the following day, another telegram from the American consul at Saltillo stating that Carranza, who planned no provisional government, would treat with the Huertistas only on the basis of unconditional surrender.[21]

On July 8, the Niagara protocol was read before the Congress at Mexico City. On July 10, a step toward the formation of the provisional government was taken by the appointment of Chief Justice Francisco Carbajal to the position of Minister of Foreign Affairs, through which he automatically became Provisional President in case of a vacancy. Huerta, weakened by his failure to secure prompt American recognition and worried by the inability to obtain arms and credit from abroad to suppress the opposition forces led by Carranza and Villa, resigned and fled from his country (July 15) leaving rival factions to solve the problem of administrative control. Secretary Bryan, keeping in touch through the Brazilian minister, Oliveira, at Mexico City, expected that Carbajal would immediately enter into negotiations with Carranza whom he sought to put in a receptive mood through Consul Silliman of Monterey. On July 20, he wired that Carranza would confer with representatives of President Carbajal at Saltillo and had agreed to temporary suspension of military operations during the conference. Three days later (July 23), seeking to stop the discord between the Constitutionalist leaders, by direction of the President he sent to Carranza by wire through Silliman a note of warning that the subsequent acts of the Constitutionalist leaders would determine the question of the recognition of the proposed new government by the American government, which "forced by circumstances must practically speak for the rest of the world."

On July 31, he sent a second warning indicating that excesses or extreme measures against political opponents might make morally impossible American recognition, without which the new government could obtain no loans and could have no hope of success.[22]

Meantime, on July 27, at Bryan's suggestion, Carranza issued a statement to allay anxiety and inspire public confidence, especially in Mexico City which was threatened with a dangerous situation as a result of threats attributed to Carranza. On July 29, he left for Saltillo to meet in person the representatives of Carbajal who three days later complained of the discourteous treatment of Constitutionalist officials at Tampico. On August 3, his representatives announced that the Carbajal propositions —including armistice and reinstatement of the dissolved Congress which was required to issue an amnesty, select Carbajal's successor and arrange the financial question—were in disagreement with the Constitutional Plan of Guadalupe. They also declined to treat on any plan which implied a recognition of the acts of Huerta or did not include the basis of unconditional surrender. Although Carbajal was willing to withdraw all conditions except amnesty and guaranties, and although Bryan tried to prevent the lack of consideration shown to the Carbajal delegates, Carranza terminated the negotiations—causing military threats to resist the entrance of the Constitutionalists into the capital. After further warnings from Bryan who also urged Carbajal to reach an agreement, Carranza finally agreed to a plan of the able Brazilian representative (in Mexico City) by which Carbajal on (August 12) dissolved his government and delivered the capital to the governor of the Federal District (Iturbide) who arranged the transfer of power, resulting in the peaceful but triumphal entry of General Carranza, on August 20, and the installation of a new government by September 8.[23]

Significant is the telegram of Bryan to the Brazilian minister, on August 22, requesting him to urge upon Carranza "the avoidance of any thing which could be construed as a lack of courtesy to the diplomatic representatives." Significant also was the later telegram of Acting Secretary Lansing announcing that the American government could not submit to losses of American citizens by application of the provisions of a decree of August 29 cancelling mining titles started under Huerta's administration and requiring prompt revalidation. More alarming than the latter decree was the earlier decree of the governor of Chihuahua (on July 27) requiring the prompt renewal (within one month) of local mining and industrial operations suspended by revolutionary conditions—a decree in which many Americans saw the beginning of a policy of the radical wing of the Constitutionalist party, represented by Villa, to drive foreigners from Mexico through discriminatory legislation and executive decrees.[24]

The American government still regarded with apprehension the unfriendly attitude of the rebel Zapata who demanded that Carranza must meet him in a conference at his remote military camp forty miles south of Cuernavaca, and refused to meet elsewhere. In attempts to arrange this conference at a suitable place, Bryan was unsuccessful, partly because Carranza obstinately insisted on arranging it by "his own efforts" which (by September 14) resulted in an open rupture. On September 15, he wired through the Brazilian minister, Oliveira, the information that President Wilson was arranging to withdraw American troops from Vera Cruz as soon as satisfactory plans could be made for transfer of authority; but, two days later, Acting Secretary Lansing requested discouragement of any immediate requests for recognition of the new government.[25]

Evacuation of Vera Cruz was delayed by the requirement of a clear understanding with Carranza concerning guaranties to avoid possible improper conduct following withdrawal, and, also, by a hopeless break of Carranza with Villa, who (on September 22) disowned Carranza and refused to participate in the proposed military convention of October 1, and who on September 26 proposed that Carranza should resign and deliver the provisional government to Señor Calderon—a demand which Carranza refused unless so determined by all the Constitutional chiefs in the convention. Attention was transferred to the military convention which at its meeting in Mexico City refused to accept Carranza's resignation, but which later, after adjournment to Aguascalientes, besought him to resign and finally (at midnight on November 1) declared the election of General Gutierrez as Provisional President for twenty days and on November 5 sent Carranza a telegraphic ultimatum to deliver his office to Gutierrez by November 10.

On November 13, Bryan wired a notification for "General Carranza" (who was still in office) stating that, as both Carranza and the Convention of Aguascalientes had given the assurances requested, American troops would be withdrawn on November 23. In the order (of November 20) for the evacuation, Acting Secretary of War Breckenridge instructed General Funston to leave in the best practical fashion without any arrangement or declaration which might be construed as a commitment to the recognition of Carranza or the authority of any individual or faction. The Americans departed as planned, without friction.[26]

On the following day Carranza, hard pressed by Zapata, left Mexico City; and, a few days later, he established the Constitutionalist government at Vera Cruz. On December 3, President Gutierrez accompanied by General Villa arrived at Mexico City. On December 12, Carranza issued a long declaration and decree stating that, as the military convention had acted under Villista threats and pressure, he was constrained to "accept the challenge to fight the reaction led by Villa"—to continue the revolution started in 1913, to organize a government, to provide for the election of a congress which would provide for the election of a chief executive and to enact and enforce the laws for required political and economic reforms. For the next six months a triangular contest continued.[27]

Bryan, distressed by news of executions at Mexico City, on December 13, wired Special Agent Silliman to use every possible influence in behalf of political prisoners, and especially to save Iturbide who had cooperated in the transfer of the city to the Constitutionalists and to protect from harm or insult the representatives of religious orders. In reply he received satisfactory assurances by Gutierrez who, however, was unable to control some of his most bloodthirsty generals and (after threatening to resign) practically became a prisoner (on December 28) by Villa's establishment of a military presidential guard and assumption of censorship of the federal telegraph. Later, after leaving the city, Gutierrez was deposed by the convention on January 16 but replaced by it under the presidency of General Gonzalez Garza. The American government could have seen little basis for hope in the convention plan of government which provided for an elective constitutional president whose ministers were chosen by the convention and were responsible directly to it for all their actions.[28]

Viewing the changes and unexpected situations which appeared with kaleidoscopic rapidity while the factions were contending for supreme power, President Wilson continued his policy of watchful waiting. On February 6, Acting Secretary Lansing, in response to Carranza's attempt to force the transfer of the diplomatic corps to Vera Cruz, wired instructions to the American consul to represent discreetly that his action was producing a harmful impression abroad, but authorized withdrawal whenever it was considered advisable by the majority of the corps. A month later, anxious concerning the food situation in Mexico City and deeply concerned as to the possible results of a threatening speech of General Obregon to merchants there tending to incite outrages in which innocent foreigners might become involved, Secretary Bryan wired a message, for delivery to Obregon and to Carranza, stating that the American government, which could no longer endure intolerable conditions for which they were responsible, was determined to hold them personally responsible if Americans should suffer by the conduct of the Constitutionalist forces in Mexico City or by failure to provide means of protection to life and property.[29]

President Wilson (on March 10) received by wire the personal reply of Carranza in which, although displeased with the reference to his personal responsibility which he said furnished cause for refusing to answer, he emphatically denied that Obregon had intended to incite the hungry populace or that he had

wilfully created the distressing conditions at Mexico City which
he said had been aggravated by the conduct of the merchants
in closing their stores as a protest against Obregon's "humani-
tarian relief tax," and gave assurance that at the time of the
planned evacuation of Mexico City every facility within his
power would be afforded all foreign residents. Bryan promptly
wired the personal reply of the President to Carranza explaining that as friends of Mexico "it is our duty to speak very
plainly about the grave dangers which threaten her from without whenever anything happens within her borders which is
calculated to arouse the hostile sentiment of the whole world."
At the same time, he was considering a telegram from Americans in Mexico City who explained why they could not leave
as the President and Carranza had advised and asked for effective guaranties of protection in their lawful occupations. On
March 20, in response to his telegram that Carranza had "renewed his promise to exert himself to protect lives and property," he received through Oliveira another telegram from the
American colony urging that the time had come "to accept the
Mexican situation for what it is and not for what it may be
hoped that it may become," and naming many arbitrary acts
which indicated that Mexico was "drifting toward total destruction from which a mistaken altruism is powerless to save
it." Four days later (March 24), he received a note from José
Vasconcelos expressing his "mission to the United States as the
envoy of President Gutierrez of Mexico," who with his cabinet,
after leaving Mexico City, disgusted with the new and smaller
military convention dominated by Villa and Zapata, had established his government in Nuevo Leon while awaiting an opportunity to reassemble the Convention of Aguascalientes before
which he planned to resign his power with a view to the establishment of "peace by peaceful means." On March 29, he
learned that the crisis in Mexico City had been reached by the
decision of President Garza to move to Chihuahua with the
Convention. At the suggestion of Oliveira, he promptly recommended to Carranza and Villa the establishment of the city as a
neutral zone, and also suggested the neutralization of the rail-

road to Vera Cruz, but without success. Later he learned that, although the capital with no railway communication with Vera Cruz was "suffering a lingering death," General Garza's Convention had remained. On May 24, following the news of a split in the convention, he saw some hope in General Garza's appeal for unification of all revolutionary parties to save the country by cessation of fighting in order to go to work.[30]

On June 2, Secretary Bryan wired to Oliveira for delivery to the Mexico City authorities for their information a public statement issued by President Wilson in which, after reference to the belligerent rivalry of the Mexican revolutionary leaders and the consequent lack of progress in reaching a solution of the tragic troubles, he announced that when Mexico was "starving and without a government," the American government must frankly state the policy which it must in duty adopt—that it "must presently . . . lend its active moral support to some man or group of men, if such may be found, who can rally the suffering people of Mexico to their support in an effort to ignore, if they can not unite, the warring factions . . . return to the constitution . . . and set up a government at Mexico City which the powers of the world can recognize," and that, if the Mexican leaders and factions could not promptly accommodate their differences and arrange within a very short time to act together, it must decide upon means to adopt "to help Mexico save herself." From General Garza, "President of the Sovereign Convention," he received a reply through the "Official Mayor of the Department of Foreign Relations," politely expressing cordial appreciation of American interest in the problem of unification which the Convention had under consideration, but noting with regret that Wilson's final remarks were "not in accord with the policy" previously followed by the government at Washington. He soon learned that Garza, who had submitted Wilson's frank statement to the Convention, was disposed to arrange at once for a general armistice and to deliver the executive power within twelve hours to the Provisional President who might be nominated by the united revolutionists, but that the Convention, wasting its time in useless discussions of factional dissensions, deposed Garza on June 9, replaced him with a Villista delegate from Chihuahua and promptly ordered the committees of public health to punish the enemies of the revolution. From Carranza he received no reply. From Villa, on June 11, he received a long reply by telegram of Special Agent Silliman—"a public and solemn" declaration refuting the general charges of President Wilson, denying that Mexico needed foreign assistance and intimating that Mexican motives in seeking concord were not based upon submission to foreign suggestions.[31]

Already, on June 8, Bryan, disagreeing with the President on American policy in the case of the British vessel *Lusitania* sunk by German torpedoes, had resigned from the office of Secretary of State and soon thereafter was succeeded by Robert Lansing, who was a son-in-law of the well-known diplomat, John Watson Foster, and who, as the tactful counselor of the Department, had been Secretary Bryan's chief assistant in handling questions requiring a knowledge of international law and diplomatic precedent.[32]

Within the next week after Secretary Bryan's resignation the American government was encouraged by the promises of Carranza's "Manifesto" (of June 11) to the nation, and the news of the advance of Carranza's forces under General Gonzales from Puebla toward Mexico City. On June 18, Acting Secretary Lansing wired Silliman, while emphasizing to Carranza the American determination to adopt measures to preserve Mexico for herself and the world, to intimate to him the possibility of American recognition if conciliatory conferences could effect union of the contending parties—an intimation which "did not in the least affect his impassive face." On June 19, he wired a warning that Carranza should order General Gonzales to use discretion in entering the capital (which, however, he did not occupy until July 11). On July 8 (after his appointment as Secretary of State), denying the assertion of the Conventionist government that the American government was openly in favor of Carranza and influenced by the reports of Carranza's discourteous treatment of peace commissioners sent to him by the

Convention, he wired Oliveira: "In view of this inflexible attitude of General Carranza a situation of the gravest nature is
forced upon this government." On July 16, considering the
situation at Mexico City, he was favorably impressed with the
attitude of General Gonzales, who evacuated the city two days
later but again occupied it (on August 3) after it had been
evacuated and reoccupied by the violent Zapatistas three times
in five days.[33]

Meantime, the American government was confronted with a
new problem relating to the suave General Huerta who had
sailed from Spain to New York in April, apparently with plans
to provoke further armed resistance in Mexico, and by cooperation of Lansing was later detained north of El Paso (on June
27) by an invitation to visit the Federal Building from which
he was soon removed to Fort Bliss. Secretary Lansing, within
a few days from June 30, received several requests for his
extradition as a fugitive criminal. One request, of July 1, came
from Arredonda, the confidential agent of Carranza's government, who also requested the detention of General Felix Diaz
and others supposed to be implicated with Huerta's plan. On
July 2, Lansing telephoned the War Department to prevent any
attempt of Huerta to cross the boundary into Mexico, resulting
in his second arrest and imprisonment in the county jail on
failure to furnish bond of $15,000 and his later return to Fort
Bliss without bond but under careful watch. All requests for
extradition were declined because of the absence of a recognized
government in Mexico.[34]

On July 10, following informal oral conferences of July 6
and 7, Secretary Lansing, by authority of the President, invited
the ambassadors of Brazil, Chile and Argentina and the ministers of Guatemala, Bolivia and Uruguay (at Washington) to
confer with him concerning an opportune time to recognize in
Mexico some party to establish order there. On August 11,
following several conferences, he and the diplomatic representatives of the six powers agreed upon a form of communication
which discreetly suggested that the political and military chiefs
directing the armed movements in Mexico should agree to meet

at a neutralized place, "far from the sound of cannon," to exchange ideas with a view to an agreement on the first steps toward constitutional reconstruction, and offered (if invited) to aid by arranging the time and place and other details. At a meeting of the Pan-American Conference, on September 18, Lansing announced to the conferees that an analysis of the replies from the various chieftains showed only two factions—the Carrancista and the Conventionist or Villista (including the Zapatistas). He announced that all the Conventionists had practically accepted the invitation and that Carranza (who sent the last and longest reply), while refusing to enter into a Mexican conference, had invited the seven Pan-American conferees to join in a conference with him to consider international affairs (Mexican affairs from an international standpoint with the sole object of determining whether Carranza exercised a *de facto* government). At this meeting, in reply to Suarez who doubted whether the revolutionary chiefs should be invited to appear before the conference to furnish information, he clearly indicated that the situation in Mexico was becoming intolerable and that if the conference could not agree to request the factions to present their cases with a view to the determination of what government should be recognized the United States would do it alone.[35]

By agreement of the conference, Lansing notified the Mexican chiefs that the representatives of the conference, contemplating an early recommendation of a Mexican government resulting from independent action of the Mexicans and "possessing the material and moral capacity to protect the lives and property of nationals and foreigners," invited the factions to furnish any statements which might aid a decision. On October 11, following a meeting of October 9, he announced that the conferees after a careful consideration of the facts had reported to their governments the decision that the Carrancista party was "the only party possessing the essentials of recognition as the *de facto* government of Mexico," and on October 19 he announced that President Wilson had "recognized the *de facto* government of which General Carranza is the Chief Executive," and that this recognition was promptly followed by the six Latin American governments represented in the recent conference. In his annual message of December, 1915, the President, expressing satisfaction with his unselfish Mexican policy and stating that whether it had benefited Mexico only time could determine, declared: "We shall aid and befriend Mexico, but we will not coerce her." Soon thereafter he appointed Henry P. Fletcher as ambassador to Mexico and received Elisey Arredondo as Mexican representative at Washington. Finding that General Carranza was ungrateful and suspicious, and that he was not in the saddle in all parts of his distracted country, he detained Fletcher while waiting and hoping for improved conditions.[36]

This recognition, interfering between the contending factions and followed by President Wilson's embargo on all shipments of arms to anti-government factions in Mexico, ignored the claims of the rival chief, Villa, whose revolutionary "bandits" still held part of the country, and who, on first reception of the news of the recognition, became very indignant and defiant and apparently was liable to seek further trouble. On December 27, General Obregon, at Juárez which he reached by way of American territory from Nogales (Arizona) to El Paso, mustered out former soldiers of Villa who was outlawed but had escaped capture and was still leading a band of about 800 men.[37]

In the early part of 1916, American attention in Mexico was directed chiefly to protection of American financial and economic interests—especially mining and oil interests—subjects which soon became complicated with other difficulties. In January, General Pershing from Fort Bliss reported rumors of an early attempt of revengeful Villa to incite Mexicans of the northern border to commit acts of violence against Americans in order to provoke intervention. At the same time he stated that practically all Americans returning from Mexico expressed little confidence in Carranza, regarding him as powerless to establish a stable government. The rumors of Villa's plans of revenge were soon followed (on January 10) at Santa Ysabel by the Villista murder of eighteen Americans who had entered

Mexico to reopen mines at Carranza's invitation. Instigated by this wanton atrocity the American Congress by resolutions demanded armed intervention. The American administration, however, accepted the promise of Carranza to punish the perpetrators of the massacre.[38]

A new adventure in American policy, resulting from the condition of the Mexican experimentation, soon followed. In March, when the American government found itself facing a new trouble which arose directly from a hostile attack of Villistas on the American town of Columbus, New Mexico,— President Wilson was instigated to send by motor trucks a punitive American force of 15,000 men under General Pershing into Mexico and across the Chihuahua desert in hot pursuit to hunt and disperse the bandits without formal notice to the Mexican government and practically without its consent. When Carranza protested and insisted upon American withdrawal, the American government refused to recede from a settled determination to maintain its national right and its duty to remove the peril which Americans on the frontier had borne too long, and it promptly called 150,000 militia to the border. The situation during a period of negotiations was complicated by a new raid of Mexican bandits into Texas.

The details of this adventure show the difficulties of the situation. They indicate that war with the stubborn Carranza was avoided only by the forbearance of President Wilson and leave one in doubt whether the recognition was wise. On March 9, Lansing wired Special Agents Silliman and Belt to convey to General Carranza the American expectation that the *de facto* government of Mexico would exert all its power to exterminate the lawless element. Receiving information that little confidence could be placed on Carranza's ability to protect with his inadequate forces, and impressed by General Funston's opinion that Villa's force should be relentlessly pursued, the President (on March 10) authorized the War Department to send an adequate armed force to capture Villa and disperse his band but to observe scrupulous regard for the sovereignty of Mexico. At six P.M. on the same day Lansing notified all American

consular officers in Mexico. On the following day, in reply to
a telegram of March 9, he received from Carranza a proposal
that "Mexican forces be permitted to cross into American territory in pursuit of the bandits led by Villa" and that recipro-
cally American forces be allowed to cross into Mexican territory
if a Mexican raid should unfortunately be repeated at any
other point on the border. Later, he received a rather discourteous message urging that the American crossing in pursuit of
Villa would be regarded as an unjustified and war-provoking
invasion if the American government failed to consider the
proposal for mutual permission to cross. On March 13, following
Carranza's press notice intimating that war was imminent, in
very courteous language he instructed Special Agent Silliman
by wire to accept the proposed arrangement for reciprocal
crossing "in pursuit of lawless bands who have committed outrages" and to state that the American government, understanding that the arrangement was in force without further exchange
of views, would exercise the privilege granted with the expectation that by mutual efforts border lawlessness would be
eradicated. At the same time, he sent Arredondo, the Carranza
representative at Washington, a copy of President Wilson's
statement that the military operations contemplated would not
be allowed to develop into intervention of any kind but were
"deliberately intended to preclude the possibility of intervention." On March 15, a force of 12,000 regulars commanded by
General John Pershing was sent to capture Villa. On March 17,
the punitive expedition was approved by Congress. On the following day, in response to a request for a permit to transport
supplies over the Northwestern Railway from Juárez to Casas
Grandes for the use of the American troops in pursuit, Acting
Secretary Polk received through Arredondo a message from the
Carranza government stating that the general consent for an
arrangement for mutual crossing of troops did not grant permission for the crossing of an expedition in pursuit of Villa
and that the Mexican government could not authorize any
right of crossing before the terms of the mutual agreement had
been definitely and concisely fixed. Regretting the misunder-

standing, Polk promptly explained (on March 19) that the orders for the expedition had been given under the impression that the Carranza government had understood and acquiesced in the arrangement, and with the realization "that no time was to be lost if the pursuit was to be effective." On the same day, he received from Arredondo a draft of the reciprocal agreement which was tentatively accepted; and on March 27 Secretary Lansing received a revised draft with certain restrictions as to the location of the crossing and distance of penetration from the border, but was still unable to get a satisfactory reply in regard to transportation—the consideration of which was evidently evaded and delayed because of political embarrassment resulting from publicity, and possibly with the hope of embarrassment to the punitive expedition.[39]

On March 31, while the question of the terms of the reciprocal arrangement was still pending, Lansing learned that Carranza and General Obregon, fearing the political effect of the expedition, contemplated the early necessity of a request for withdrawal in case of failure to capture Villa whose trail had grown cold. Two weeks later, following a clash between a small body of American soldiers and citizens of Parral, he received through Arredondo a telegram from Aguilar, Secretary of Foreign Relations in the Carranza government, stating that the pursuit of Villa was without previous agreement between the two governments and without warrant, urging that further pursuit was unnecessary and useless, suggesting the advisability of suspending all discussions or negotiations relating to the proposed arrangement for reciprocal crossing and expressing Carranza's wish to treat upon the subject of American withdrawal of military forces from Mexico. In reply of April 14, again disclaiming any intention of violating the sovereignty of Mexico, he declared that America's only purpose was "to endeavor to take the bandit Villa" whose capture was expected to prove more beneficial to the Mexican government than to the American government, and suggested that Mexican cooperation for speedy capture of the bandit was the best way to hasten the withdrawal of American troops. Three days later, after receiving fuller details of the Parral incident indicating that the attack was deliberately planned by Villista followers, he learned through the War Department that General Funston, in view of the state of anarchy and convinced that Carranza's policy was intentionally to obstruct the American military mission, had recommended immediate capture of the city and state of Chihuahua and the seizure of the railroads there as a necessary preliminary of the military expedition against Villa. War seemed imminent.[40]

On April 22, after further information of increasing antagonism to Americans in Mexico and the evident purpose of the superior Mexican authorities to force withdrawal, Lansing wired Special Agent James L. Rodgers to suggest to Carranza a conference near the border between General Scott and General Obregon or other high military officers to prevent misunderstanding—a suggestion which Carranza promptly accepted. Generals Scott and Funston received General Obregon at El Paso on April 30, and at his request agreed to hold the conference at Juárez. They presented the view of the American government: that with the desire to cooperate with the Mexican government and to avoid anything which had the appearance of intervention in Mexican domestic affairs, its pursuit of Villa was for the sole purpose of removing a menace to the common security and friendly relations—a menace which would be increased by American withdrawal and might threaten to irritate American public opinion to the point of demanding general intervention. They requested cooperation and the use of the railroad. Obregon, politely avoiding a discussion of cooperation, always contended for immediate withdrawal of American troops, stating that Villa was either dead or innocuous and that the continued presence of the troops made difficult his task of explanation to the Mexican people. With new telegraphic instructions, Scott and Funston suggested that, in order to avoid exposure of the border, withdrawal should be gradual, with an understanding that it would be complete as soon as the border was safe from further aggression. Encountering only polite rejections they suspected that the Mexican generals, certain of

American lack of military preparation, would arrogantly demand immediate withdrawal. Such a flat ultimatum they avoided by a diplomatic adjournment on May 1. War seemed imminent and was not easily averted.[41]

Finally, at a private and secret meeting, arranged with Scott at the request of Obregon through friends and beginning at midnight on May 2, an "agreement was reached after a struggle of twelve hours" which Scott said "was not equalled by any similar struggle with the wildest and most exasperated Indian heretofore encountered." Although the conference was usually amicable, arguments seemed interminable. Obregon's main object, to put a time limit upon the American stay in Mexico, was amicably thwarted with great difficulty. The agreement, after referring to the achievements of the American punitive expedition and the augmentation of the Constitutional forces to prevent disorders, explained that the American decision to continue gradually the withdrawal already begun "was inspired by the belief that the Mexican government is now in a position and will omit no effort to prevent the recurrences of invasion of American territory," and stated that "the completion of the withdrawal of American troops will only be prevented by occurrences arising in Mexico tending to prove that such belief was wrongly founded." The agreement was subject to the approval of the two governments. It was not satisfactory to Carranza, who especially wished to omit all introductory explanations of the withdrawal and to set a definite time for complete withdrawal. Scott and Funston no longer hoped for a peaceful solution. On May 10, the American government urged remaining American nationals to leave Mexico. The situation was complicated by the repetition of a border raid at Glen Springs and Boquillas, Texas, on May 5, by the consequent American dispatch of another force in pursuit one hundred and sixty miles into Mexican territory and by later reports of Mexican preparation for war. In the American Senate, where since the news of the Santa Ysabel massacre a considerable group led by Albert Fall had demanded armed intervention, efforts were made to force the administration into a more vigorous policy. In a long speech (of June 2) Senator Fall, who had demanded the complete occupation of Mexico by an American army of a half million soldiers, severely criticized the policy of President Wilson.[42]

On May 31, the Department of State received from Arredondo a very long note of Aguilar written on May 22 in an aggressive and recriminatory tone and style calculated to create irritation. In this note, Aguilar, after reviewing recent negotiations relating to the American expedition and making a sweeping charge that the American government had placed every obstacle to prevent pacification of Mexico, and especially protesting sharply against the latest American "invasion and violation of sovereignty" which, he said, created new complications and rendered more distant the possibility of a satisfactory solution, requested a categorical definition of the true political intentions of the American government in maintaining its troops "inactive and idle on Mexican territory"—intentions which he intimated were hostile, "in absolute contradiction to the continued declarations of friendship." On the following day, Lansing learned by wire that the note had just been published at Mexico City. Within the following week, he learned from reliable sources that Luis de la Rosa, planning border raids into Texas, was being aided and abetted by officials of the inefficient Carranza government. By June 18, through the War Department he learned of General Trevino's order to "prevent American forces from moving to the South, East or West" and of Pershing's reply that the American government had placed "no such restrictions on the movement of the American forces."[43]

On June 20, after three weeks' reflection, Lansing sent through Arredondo a long and complete reply to the Aguilar communication of May 22. In it, after expressing the surprise and regret caused the American government by the discourteous tone and temper of the communication, and the deep concern and disappointment resulting from the continuous bloodshed and disorders incidental to the revolution, he stated that in the face of continued depredations whose perpetrators were unpunished by the impotent Carranza the American government had been forced to accept a necessary but unsought duty to employ force to disperse the Mexican bands of outlaws. He clearly disproved the erroneous Mexican sweeping charges that the American government had placed obstacles in the way of Mexican pacification, and he declared unreasonable any expectations that American forces would be withdrawn while amidst conditions of anarchy American protection required safeguards which Carranza was manifestly unable or unwilling to give. "The United States government," said he, "can not and will not allow bands of lawless men to establish themselves upon its borders with liberty to invade and plunder American territory with impunity, and, when pursued, to seek safety across the Rio Grande, relying upon the plea of their government that the integrity of the soil of the Mexican republic must not be violated." Warning the Mexican government that the execution of its threat to appeal to arms to defend its territory against American forces, performing responsibilities and obligations which it had ignored, would lead to the gravest consequences, he said: "While this government would deeply regret such a result, it can not recede from its settled determination to maintain its national rights and to perform its full duty in removing the peril which Americans along the international boundary have borne so long with patience and forbearance." A résumé of this note he telegraphed on the following day to all missions in Central and South America with the statement that if the critical relations should eventuate into hostilities the American object would be defense of American territory and not intervention in Mexican affairs.[44]

Another crisis, threatened by an encounter of American with Mexican troops at Carrizal on June 22 resulting in casualties on both sides and the capture of seventeen Americans as prisoners, was averted only by Mexican acquiescence in the American demand for immediate release of the prisoners. Lansing, learning from Arredondo that the encounter was the result of the Mexican orders to General Trevino to prevent the American advance eastward, or any other direction except northward, in his telegraphic instructions of June 25 to Rodgers interpreted the Mexican act as a deliberately hostile one; and, after demanding immediate release, he expressed his expectation of an early statement of the Mexican plan of action—a statement which the Carranza government sought to avoid.

The strain of the situation continued until complications were solved in August by agreement upon a joint commission of six members—for which the American government selected Secretary Franklin K. Lane, George Gray and John R. Mott and the Carranza government selected Luis Cabrera, Ygnacio Bonillas and A. J. Pani. This commission, whose appointment relieved the tension of a grave situation, met at New London, Connecticut, on September 6; but after deliberations at New London and at Atlantic City, New Jersey, Philadelphia and New York, extending into January of the following year (during which time conditions in Mexico were growing worse), it failed to reach an acceptable plan of action—chiefly because Carranza would not agree to approve or allow the crossing of American troops in pursuit of raiders and refused to authorize negotiations on other questions of vital interest to the United States. On November 21, Secretary Lane, after returning to Atlantic City from a conference with President Wilson, informed the Mexican commissioners that the American government, in proposing to withdraw its troops and with no desire to dictate a policy to Mexico, expected the Mexican commissioners to submit frankly a larger constructive program which would offer some assurance of Mexican fulfilment of obligations to protect the lives and property of foreigners in Mexico and to cooperate in the establishment of a claims convention, and which would otherwise indicate Mexican desire to cooperate with the United States. At the same time, he said that a Mexican policy of isolation, by refusal to seek American cooperation could lead only to the downfall of the Carranza government. On the following day, the American commissioners submitted a proposed protocol of seven articles to which the full commission agreed, on November 24, subject to the approval of Carranza and the assurance that the Mexican commissioners were

authorized to proceed to the consideration of other questions of
vital importance to the American government. To this protocol
of November 24, signed at Atlantic City, providing for American withdrawal within forty days, a border patrol by each
government and American right to cross the border in hot
pursuit of bandits, Carranza obstinately withheld his approval
on the ground that he could not compromise the dignity of
Mexico.[45]

Although the Mexican commissioners (on December 19) at
Philadelphia, submitted proposed changes in the protocol, the
American commissioners regarded them as impractical and
unwise and announced that the rejection of the protocol would
terminate the function of the commission. On January 3, 1917,
convinced by the exhaustive discussions of three months that
the attitude of Carranza's *de facto* government would make
further discussion fruitless and delay the solution of questions
pending, the American commissioners reluctantly closed the
conferences by a polite suggestion of the advisability of conducting further negotiations under conditions which would
make impossible the embarrassment felt by the Mexican commissioners in negotiating so far from their seat of government.
At the same time, in a report to President Wilson, they stated
that the information submitted created in their minds the
"deepest misgivings with reference to the course of events in
Mexico" which seemed to present a grave menace. On January
15, at the last meeting preceding the adjournment of the conference, they proposed that the commission in adjourning
recommend the reestablishment of full diplomatic relations
under which direct negotiations might be conducted to secure
protection of life and property, to establish a claims commission
and to eliminate causes of further misunderstanding or friction
or clash. To this the Mexicans would not agree unless preceded
by a recommendation of the American commissioners for withdrawal of the American troops. To the latter the American
commissioners refused to concede, stating that since the Mexican refusal to agree to the protocol the matter of withdrawal
must be left entirely to the determination of the President.

After the adjournment, however, they recommended the re-establishment of full diplomatic relations. A week earlier (on January 8), Consul-General Hanna had wired from San Antonio his opinion that withdrawal of American troops, placing on the *de facto* government of Mexico the responsibility of restoring order there or of failing to restore it, would produce satisfactory results. To these suggestions President Wilson, with attention increasingly directed to the problems of the World War and to his proposals of bases of peace to terminate that war (two months before he asked Congress to declare war against Germany), listened with favor; and he prepared to act accordingly, with plans to hold the Carranza government responsible for American interests in the territory affected by American withdrawal but to maintain along the American border a patrol which would be ready to cross into Mexico if needed to protect American rights. Although Carranza gained some prestige for his success in baiting the American government, President Wilson achieved larger success by preventing a war with Mexico which would have interfered seriously with larger American duties in the termination of the World War. Unfortunately, American regular troops completely withdrawn by February 5, 1917, were replaced by Villa forces instead of Carranza forces.[46]

In February, 1917, the American government, after completing the withdrawal of American troops as already planned and with Arredondo's assurance of protection of American interests and indemnities for damages caused by the revolution, resumed regular diplomatic relations by sending Henry P. Fletcher as ambassador to the Mexican *de facto* government of Carranza under whose auspices preparations for better conditions were begun by the adoption of a new national constitution (published February 5 and effective May 1). On March 3, at Guadalajara, Fletcher, who had been detained because of unsatisfactory conditions in Mexico, presented his letters of credence to the "First Chief" Carranza who, eight days later, was elected President. Unfortunately, at Carranza's inauguration, Fletcher was greeted with hisses as he entered the Chamber of Deputies, in strange contrast to the applause which greeted the German ambassador, Von Eckhardt, the close friend and adviser of Carranza. On April 17, President Wilson accorded formal recognition to Señor Ygnacio Bonillas as Mexican ambassador at Washington, completing the establishment of official diplomatic intercourse which had been closed since the American refusal to recognize Huerta.[47]

Already, on January 22, Lansing, in touch with the discussions of the Mexican constitutional convention in regard to expropriation of private property and other provisions affecting the rights of American citizens in Mexico, had wired a warning that the American government could not concede the right of Mexico to limit the American right of intervention to protect the rights of American citizens in Mexico and could not acquiesce in any direct or indirect confiscation of foreign-owned property in Mexico. Later, as earlier, he found frequent occasions to insist upon the protection of Americans and American interests, especially in connection with land ownership and mining and oil properties and Mexican forced loans. On June 6, regarding with grave concern the evidences of Carranza's intention to apply retroactively certain provisions of the Constitution of 1917, he instructed Fletcher to request the views of the Mexican government and the suspension of enforcement of any confiscatory or discriminatory enactments. At the same time the American government continued to show a friendly spirit toward the Mexican *de facto* government. On June 19, upon the recommendation of Ambassador Fletcher in favor of the Carranza government, President Wilson ordered the release of 2,733,000 cartridges which had been detained at the border under the embargo of 1916 on export of arms and munitions into Mexico.[48]

Later relations with Mexico were affected by issues and conditions relating to the World War, which assumed primary importance. In February, 1917, when the American government was becoming more determined in its resistance to Germany's piratical acts against American rights upon the seas, the Carranza government, influenced by German propaganda, proposed

to the American and other neutral governments to invite the
belligerents to terminate the conflict, or, in case of failure, to
reduce the conflagration by placing an embargo on war imple-
ments and by suspending commercial relations. In reply, the
American government (in March), declining the proposal,
exposed a recently discovered plot (the infamous Zimmermann
note) of the German government to induce Mexico to negotiate
an alliance with Japan for war against the United States by
offering Mexico as the price of her cooperation with Germany
the recovery of territory ceded to the United States in 1848.
Although the Mexican government denied any participation in
the plot, Zimmermann acknowledged he had sent the note to
Carranza; and German influence in Mexico continued inimical
to the United States until the end of the World War in which
American forces turned the tide of battle against the military
masters of Germany. In Carranza's thinly veiled "neutrality"
the American government had reason to suspect a wish for the
success of Germany who might prove valuable as a friend to
check American hegemony on the American continent. In his
internal policy of "revindication" of the rights of the nation
to subsoil deposits, however, it found the source of a larger
controversy which grew more tense when attempts were made
to extend the policy retroactively to lands obtained by Americans from Diaz in full private ownership including subsoil
minerals.[49]

While diverting his chief attention to the World War, which
he had entered to secure guaranties for peace and respect for the
territorial integrity of weaker nations, President Wilson
through Lansing, who had repeatedly protested against any
proposed confiscation of property under the Constitution of
1917, continued to keep a watch on American interests in
Mexico with the purpose, under the right of diplomatic interposition, to hold Mexican authorities responsible for injuries
to Americans and American interests. In accord with American
policy and acting under Lansing's instructions of March 19,
Fletcher on April 2, after he had been notified that no modification of the Mexican petroleum decree of February 19 would

be made, submitted to the Mexican government a "formal and solemn protest" against violation or infringement of legitimately acquired American private property rights involved in the enforcement of the decree.

President Wilson also sought to remove Mexican suspicions and doubts of the sincerity of his Mexican policy and purposes. On June 8, 1918, in an address to a party of visiting Mexican editors, aiming especially to reduce the evil effects of German influences and to remove the suspicion which created misunderstanding and consequent trouble in Mexico, he stated that his policy had been based on the principle of non-interference with the internal affairs of the country and the desire to render moral assistance to constitutional order. Unfortunately, this address, although well received in other parts of Latin America, was not appreciated by the government of Carranza who proceeded to furnish the inspiration for a series of press articles comparing the address with Ambassador Fletcher's recent protest (of April 2) against the Mexican petroleum decree, advocating a vigorous Mexican policy of complete independence from the American influence which had resulted from the "complacency" of the Diaz régime, and explaining that the Monroe Doctrine had been cancelled and annulled by the practices of the New Carranza doctrine against American representation of European countries in regard to incidents affecting citizens of those countries. Feeling that German influences were seeking to discredit American friendly assurance and desiring to negative these adverse influences, Secretary Lansing (on June 24) proposed to show Mexico that the President was determined to translate his expressions into action by offering to settle at once all pending questions by a joint conference and to facilitate a loan to the Mexican government by private American interests. On June 29, in a telegram referring to the recent Mexican press comment, he replied that the President asked only justice and fair dealing, with no disposition to interfere in Mexico's internal affairs and that "seizure of property at the will of the sovereign without due legal process equitably administered and without just compensation has always been regarded as a denial of justice and a cause of diplomatic representation." Fletcher, meantime, had arranged a conference with Carranza who suggested that all resentment would quickly disappear if the American restrictions on exports could be reduced to a minimum, intimated that arbitration of difficulty concerning the decree would be possible and seemed agreeable to suggestion that the official reply to the note concerning the decree should be delayed or couched in terms which would not preclude further friendly negotiations, but regarded as unnecessary the proposed conference to facilitate a loan. Fletcher promptly wired to Lansing a recommendation of an immediate announcement of a more liberal export embargo policy and suggested the advisability of a visit to Washington for a conference with the Department on the President's plan to gain the good will of Mexico. This recommendation Lansing approved and (on July 6) wired a reply that the Department was arranging for a more liberal policy governing the granting of export licenses for shipment to Mexico, subject to restrictions imposed by the war act to prevent trade with the enemy powers of Europe and to satisfy the needs of the United States and allied powers, and on the assumption that Mexico would not permit reëxport of the commodities and food received by her from the United States.[50]

Meantime, on May 15, Fletcher had arranged with Carranza to give an audience to James R. Garfield and Nelson O. Rhodes who appeared at Mexico City as the representatives of all the American oil companies which had adopted plans to act as a unit in efforts for adjustment with the Mexican government. Although he did not participate in the negotiations, he was kept fully informed by Mr. Garfield; and later (July 31) he reported that although Secretary Pani was pleasant and might approve proposed modifications of the oil decree, Carranza would not yield and that the negotiations had not served in any way to remove the great obstacle to settlement of the question.[51]

On August 12, advised of the unsatisfactory results of the Garfield-Rhodes conferences, and learning of two new oil-land decrees which were announced to be effective on August 15, Lansing wired Fletcher to repeat the grave apprehensions of the American government concerning the effects of the decrees and the circumstances which might arise to impel it to protect the property of its citizens, and to request the postponement of the operation of the decrees. Fletcher promptly conferred with Carranza who declined to postpone the operation of the decrees (which he said were purely fiscal), explained that Congress alone had the power to decide the conflict in regard to subsoil ownership, and declared that in case of foreign interference with Mexican sovereign rights he was prepared to confront it with war if necessary, but stated his willingness to adopt peaceful means of settlement and especially advised appeal to the Mexican courts. On August 21, Fletcher, recognizing that an acute crisis had been avoided and expecting court decisions against the constitutionality of the decrees, was hopeful of peaceful adjustment. He even hoped that the government might propose to the next Congress an entirely new petroleum law.

Following the American warning of grave changes of policy which might follow, the editor of the *Nation* suggested that President Wilson had already tried every policy except real cooperation. Regarding the anti-American attitude of Carranza as entirely justified, he especially criticized the administration for refusing to Carranza the arms necessary to protect Americans in Mexico as required by the American government and recommended further patience in preference to a change of policy which threatened to lead to intervention.[52]

In the following December, Acting Secretary Polk, after referring to the pleasure resulting from the information of the improvement in the situation rendering unnecessary further immediate protest, took occasion to reply calmly to certain allusions and critical statements of the Mexican undersecretary, E. Garza Perez, in a note (of August 17) to Fletcher in reply to the latter's note of April 2. He especially defended the right of American diplomatic interposition, in cases of threatened spoliation of vested rights, to obtain protection due American citizens in Mexico under the generally accepted rules of international law, stated that it might be justified (as a distinctly friendly method of supporting legitimate national interests in order to avoid injustice) even when made before the exhaustion of legal remedies in the courts of Mexico, and asserted that the right had never been renounced by President Wilson who had sharply distinguished it from the policy of armed intervention. Although he had hoped that in legal proceedings already initiated the Mexican tribunals would protect the legitimately acquired rights of American citizens and thus hopefully end the controversy, he gave notice that if this hope should unfortunately be disappointed the American government "must reserve to itself the consideration of the questions of interesting itself further on behalf of American citizens in this important and serious matter." The hope was not entirely disappointed and found new basis in the later action of the Mexican Congress in breaking with Carranza—by refusing to enact the oil legislation which he recommended and by withdrawing the extraordinary war powers under which he had exercised dictatorial control.[53]

At the close of the World War, the American government viewed with great concern Carranza's waning power while confronting difficult problems in the continued struggle against revolts and in attempts to establish internal order. In 1919-20, when the Mexican issue again became prominent, it found difficulty in controlling certain American forces which, displeased with Mexico's friendliness with Germany during the war and demanding a radical change in Wilson's Mexican policy in order to suppress an international nuisance, again threatened aggression against Mexico as they had done in 1916, largely under the leadership of Senator Albert B. Fall. In the Senate, Ashurst proposed an attempt to purchase Lower California and part of Sonora. Before the Senate (Fall) sub-committee of the Committee on Foreign Relations, E. L. Doheny, the interesting pioneer oil operator in Mexico and a leader of the National Association for the Protection of American Rights in Mexico, appeared (on September 11, 1919) to urge action on the imperial theory of the American obligation to use force to compel Mexico to observe international obligations. "I say today," said he, "that the United States ought to hold for its industries and its people—the people who use the flivver, as well as the people who use the limousine—the oil lands that have been acquired by Americans anywhere in the world, and they should not be allowed to be confiscated by any government, whether it be British, Mexican or any other." A few days later this sub-committee began to publish an extensive and interesting report of its investigation of Mexican affairs upon which it based its recommendation for a more vigorous Mexican policy—a policy which was also favored by some members of the Wilson cabinet and by Ambassador Fletcher who returned to Washington to present his views. With this sub-committee Secretary Lansing cordially cooperated, especially after November 14 and especially through Ambassador Fletcher and Boaz Long (the American minister to Cuba) who were in Washington and in almost constant touch with the sub-committee. In the midst of this investigation and while Chairman Fall was on a brief trip to El Paso, William O. Jenkins, the American consular agent at Puebla, was captured and held for ransom. The American chargé at Mexico City demanded his immediate release. Fall returned at once to Washington and was driven directly to Secretary Lansing's home, on December 1, for consultation concerning the situation. Lansing, on the following day, notified Fall that he had designated Fletcher to represent the Department in consultation concerning certain proposed resolutions in regard to Mexico. Fletcher agreed on the proposed concurrent resolution which Fall promptly offered—approving the action of the State Department in the pending controversy and requesting the President to withdraw the recognition hitherto accorded to Carranza and "to sever all diplomatic relations with the pretended government of Carranza." Lansing, on December 4, appeared before the committee to request that the two parts of the resolution should be separated and that action on the later part should be deferred—possibly because of the President's illness. Learning from Lansing that the President since his illness had not been consulted on Mexican affairs, the committee designated Senators Hitchcock and Fall to call upon him to present the reasons for offering the resolution. On this visit, on December 5, Fall reported verbally on the Mexican situation, and, at the request of the President, submitted on the same day a written memorandum, especially referring to Carranza's propaganda with American radicals to prevent American intervention in Mexico, his attempts to influence American opinion favorable to the example set by Mexico in the nationalization of property and in refusing to yield to American demands, his assistance in the fantastic "Plan of San Diego" (of February, 1915) for the revolt and independence of Texas and other trans-Rocky American territory south of 42° (indicating his sympathy with the German proposition contained in the Zimmermann note of June 19, 1917), his purpose to exclude Americans from investments in Mexico and his failure to keep promises upon which the recognition of his government was based. To this written memorandum indicating the various subjects which, in connection with the Jenkins case, would justify withdrawal of recognition, President Wilson replied (on December 8) that he would "be gravely concerned to see any such resolution pass the Congress," that the initiative in directing foreign relations constitutionally belonged to the executive, and that the safest course was "to adhere to the present method of the Constitution." He was relieved from immediate pressure for war by the liberation of Jenkins, following the payment of the ransom by a peaceful-minded Mexican. Apparently he disapproved the recent action of Lansing in regard to Mexican policy. In the following February, he accepted the resignation of Lansing, and in March he appointed Bainbridge Colby as Lansing's successor.[54]

Before the Fall sub-committee completed its investigation and its final report on the question of withdrawal of recognition, the American government, by the success of a new revolution in Mexico, was relieved of further contention with the conditionally recognized Carranza and consequently from the increasing demand for a policy of armed coercion. Again it had an opportunity to ask for an understanding with a new government as a prerequisite to recognition—to demand assurances of protection of American citizens in Mexico and on the border and of future Mexican performance of national and international duties, and to offer aid in restoring peace. In April, 1920, it saw the beginning of this new revolution in Sonora led by General Obregon, Mexico's most popular military hero, who had lost an arm in defeating Villa and whose candidacy for the Mexican presidency was opposed by the inefficient Carranza—who, through his son-in-law, Candido Aguilar, had chosen Señor Ygnacio Bonillas (the Mexican minister at Washington) as the administration candidate. It observed with apprehension the serious aspects of this revolution which, beginning in Sonora with the incidents of a Southern Pacific railway strike, rapidly spread to other parts of Mexico and soon resulted in the independence of the seceded "republic of Sonora," an insurgent announcement of the formation of a Mexican government with Governor Adolfo de la Huerta of Sonora as "Supreme Commander," the subsequent flight of Carranza and his cabinet (and officials and employees) from the capital in twenty-one trains with expectation of establishing the government at Vera Cruz (early in May), and the later murder of Carranza in the mountains (late in May). After the assumption of authority by General Alvaro Obregon who, following a period of administration under Huerta as "Substitute President," was elected President in the following September under plans to continue the Constitution of 1917, it promptly recognized that it was confronted with another serious situation which might result in counter revolutions and demands for American intervention—a situation which was the subject of wide discussion. At a Clark University conference on Mexico and the Caribbean (on May 20) Henry Lane Wilson, who, at the time of his retirement from the American legation in Mexico in 1913, had recommended armed intervention as an alternative to recognition of Huerta, suggested that the crop of the larger Mexican revolutions might be reduced or prevented by a division of Mexico at the twenty-second parallel and the erection of Lower California and the northern border states (the "breeding ground" of the chief recent revolutions), by force if necessary, into an independent republic—a "buffer state." Possibly so. Certainly a shorter and more logical boundary could be found along the Sierra Madre range, and possibly a better boundary could be found along the general route proposed by Marcy in his instructions of October, 1853, for use of Gadsden; but the American government could hardly expect Mexico to agree to cede the rich mining area south of the present boundary.

The Fall committee in its recommendations of May 28, 1920, following its long report which indicated that Mexico under Carranza was not a safe place for an American citizen or American investments, stated that the American government should defer recognition until assured that the Mexican people had approved an administration of stability to endure and a disposition to comply with international obligations; that it should give a clear notice of its intention to insist upon responsibility for American lives and property; that recognition should be made with a plain understanding or agreement that certain provisions of certain articles (130, 3, 27 and 33) of the new Constitution of 1917 would not apply to American citizens; that it should require the appointment of commissioners at once to decide all claims and to settle disputes concerning the international boundary and waters of the Rio Grande and the Colorado (especially the Chamizal dispute and the Colorado River irrigation complication); that, after recognition upon these conditions, it should extend to the new government moral support and aid in securing financial support necessary for Mexican rehabilitation; and that, if the conditions were refused and if disorder continued, it should issue a warning of its purpose in the name of humanity (and without warring upon the Mexican people) to terminate conditions which parties to the conflict were unable or unwilling to stop.[55]

Before the election of Obregon, the provisional President (Governor Huerta) successfully prepared the way for internal peace by suppressing two revolts—one started by General Gonzales who was soon captured, and the other by the elusive Pancho Villa who was hired to stop by a grant of a large estate with privilege to keep fifty retainers at government expense and by additional grants of a tract of land to each of his eight hundred men. At the same time Obregon sought American favor by personal unofficial promises to restore order and protect property—and especially by his announcement that he would not enforce Article 27 of the new Constitution, an article which was based upon the theory that subsoil products were never legally alienated by the Diaz government and which Americans feared would endanger the holdings of foreigners (particularly in the oil fields).

Although agitation for immediate armed intervention was diverted, deflated and neutralized by the personal declarations and assurances of General Obregon, both before and after the date of his assumption of executive duties (on December 1), the Wilson administration, acting through Secretary Colby, after some consideration of the question of extending recognition to the new government (which was promptly recognized by Japan, Brazil, Holland and Germany), did not complete satisfactory arrangements for action in the matter and preferred to defer the question for decision of the incoming administration.

REFERENCES

1. *Sen. Doc. 285*, 66-2, Vol. 2, pp. 2290-91.
2. *For. Rels., 1913*, pp. 726-29 and 737-38.
3. *Ib.*, pp. 741-47.
4. *Ib.*, pp. 761, 774, 785-86.
5. *Ib.*, pp. 790, 792, 799-804, 807-10.
6. *Ib.*, pp. 812, 817.
7. *Ib.*, pp. 818-27.
8. *Ib.*, pp. 822-23.
9. *Ib.*, pp. 832-35.
10. *Ib.*, pp. 836, 838.
11. *Ib.*, p. 856; *For. Rels., 1914*, pp. 443-44.
12. *For. Rels., 1914*, p. 445.
13. *Ib.*, pp. 784—, 794-95, 806.
14. *Ib.*, p. 904.
15. EDITH O'SHAUGHNESSY, *A Diplomat's Wife in Mexico*.
16. *For. Rels., 1914*, pp. 448, 450, 454-55, 460-61, 466, and 468-71.
17. *Ib.*, pp. 474-77, 481, 484-85, 636-45.
18. *Ib.*, pp. 690-91 and 695.
19. *Ib.*, pp. 485-89, 503, 506, 510, 512-14, 518, 527-33.
20. *Ib.*, pp. 548-50.

21. *Ib.*, pp. 538, 556-57, 560, 562.
22. *Ib.*, pp. 561, 563-64, 568, 577.
23. *Ib.*, pp. 574, 579-81, 583, 585, 588, 595.
24. *Ib.*, pp. 589, 720-22, 724, 726.
25. *Ib.*, pp. 591-92, 596, 598-99.
26. *Ib.*, pp. 602-03, 605-06, 609, 612, 618, 621-22, 625.
27. *Ib.*, pp. 627-28 and 631-33.
28. *Ib.*, pp. 629, 635-36; *For. Rels.*, *1915*, pp. 644-45.
29. *For. Rels.*, *1915*, pp. 650-52, 660.
30. *Ib.*, pp. 666-68, 672-73, 676-78, 682-84, 691-92.
31. *Ib.*, pp. 694-99, 701-04.
32. *Am. Jr. Int. Law*, July, 1915, pp. 659-66.
33. *For. Rels.*, *1915*, pp. 705-07, 715-17, 721-22, 732.
34. *Ib.*, pp. 827, 829-35.
35. *Ib.*, pp. 723, 735-36, 746-48, 754-62 and 758.
36. *Ib.*, pp. 760, 767, 771.
37. *Ib.*, pp. 775, 778, 780.
38. *For. Rels.*, *1916*, pp. 662-63.
39. *Ib.*, pp. 480-96, 502-04, 508-12.
40. *Ib.*, pp. 505, 513-18, 521-22.
41. *Ib.*, pp. 525, 527-36.
42. *Ib.*, pp. 537-39, 541, 543-44, 547; *Cong. Record*, 64-1, Vol. 53, pp. 3884, 9150-67.
43. *For. Rels.*, *1916*, pp. 552-63, 566-73, 577.
44. *Ib.*, pp. 581-92.
45. *Ib.*, pp. 593, 595, 597, 599-608 and 625; *For. Rels.*, *1917*, pp. 916-38.
46. *Ib.*, pp. 905-08, 928-31, 935-38; *Am. Jr. Int. Law*, Apr., 1917, pp. 399-406.
47. *For. Rels.*, *1917*, pp. 910-12, 915, 951-81; *Sen. Doc. 285*, 66-2, Vol. 2, p. 2967.
48. *For. Rels.*, *1917*, pp. 947-49, 982, 1017-58, 1067-68, 1080-82, and 1085.
49. *Ib.*, p. 1021.
50. *Sen. Doc. 285*, 66-2, Vol. 2, pp. 3119—, 3156-58, and 3349; *For. Rels.*, *1918*, pp. 577-600, 631, 627-29, 702, 705-07, 712-14.
51. *Ib.*, pp. 720, 724-32, 745-46.
52. *Ib.*, pp. 754-55, 757-59, 766-70, 784; *The Nation*, Aug. 23, 1919, Vol. 109, p. 234.
53. *For. Rels.*, *1918*, pp. 767-70, 784-89.
54. *Cong. Record*, 64-1, Vol. 53 *passim*, and 65-3, p. 1088; *Sen. Doc. 324*, 64-1, Feb., 1916; *Sen. Doc. 285*, 66-2, Vol. 1, pp. 843 A-J, and Vol. 2, pp. 2966-67; *The Nation*, Nov. 29, 1919, Vol. 109, pp. 680-82.
55. *Sen. Doc. 285*, 66-2, pp. 3369-73.

CHAPTER XV

THE LATEST DECADE OF ADJUSTMENT

IN the decade after 1921 the most important subjects of American policy in diplomatic negotiations with Mexico were adjustments of claims and questions arising from the land and subsoil provisions of the Mexican Constitution of 1917—adjustments necessitated largely as a result of the Mexican economic and social policies of the preceding revolutionary decade. Incidental to these at the beginning of the period was the question of recognition of the Mexican government of General Obregon which seemed to be firmly established in Mexico but which, in accord with the recommendations of Senator Fall and other members of the Foreign Relations sub-committee of 1919, was asked to "agree in writing" to certain requirements as a price for recognition.[1] In the Mexican agrarian problem, the American government encountered a difficult situation arising from the possible clash of local laws and movements with foreign vested economic rights under international law. The whole controversy is an illustration of the almost inevitable collision between two antagonistic principles—the rising spirit of nationalism and the vested rights of foreigners. The American government was apprehensive that American vested interests and legal rights were threatened by the significant Mexican economic and social reform program which sought the welfare of the nation by the distribution of land to the landless, a noble experiment of statesmanship in the attempt to reverse the tendency toward monopoly. Although it offered no objection to the agrarian program, it recognized a duty to protect the rights of its nationals who had obtained large holdings of land and natural resources in Mexico in the period of Diaz.

584

American secretaries of state for the period were Charles
Evans Hughes of New York (to March, 1925), Frank Billings
Kellogg of Minnesota (1925-29) and Henry Lewis Stimson
of New York (from 1929). Secretary Hughes had won distinction in law (both as a professor and as a practitioner), as
governor of New York (1907-10), as associate justice of
the United States Supreme Court (1910-16), and as Republican candidate for President in 1916. Secretary Kellogg, after
experience as special counsel for the United States in several
anti-trust cases, had served as United States senator (1917-
23), as delegate to the Fifth International Conference of
American States (at Santiago, Chile, 1923) and as ambassador
to Great Britain (1924). Secretary Stimson, after valuable legal
experience (for several years with the firm of Root & Clarke),
had served successively as United States district attorney (1906-
09), Secretary of War (1911-13), special representative of the
President to Nicaragua (1927) and Governor-General of the
Philippines (1927-29).

From 1924, the American legation at Mexico City, which for
a time was managed by George T. Summerlin of Louisiana (acting as chargé *ad interim*, 1919-24), was successively directed
by Ambassadors Charles Beecher Warren of Michigan (1924),
James Rockwell Sheffield of New York (1924-27), Dwight
Whitney Morrow of New Jersey (1927-30) and Joshua
Reuben Clark of Utah (1930). Summerlin had served with
the army in Porto Rico and the Philippines, as clerk in the Department of State (1909-10) and as a secretary in the American legations at Tokyo (1910), Peking (1911-14) and Chile
(1914-15), and had been connected with the Mexican legation since February, 1917. Warren, who had earlier been counsel
for the United States before the commission to determine the
Bering Sea claims (in 1896) and before the Hague Tribunal in
the Atlantic Coast Fisheries arbitration (in 1910), had later
served as ambassador to Japan (1921-23) and was head of the
American high commission which in May-September, 1923,
negotiated the terms for resumption of diplomatic relations with
Mexico. Sheffield, after experience as secretary to Senator

W. B. Allison of Iowa (1883), had practiced law in New York City and had been somewhat prominent in New York politics (since 1893). Morrow had practiced law in New York City since 1899 and had been a member of the firm of J. P. Morgan & Co. since 1914. In 1918 he had served as adviser to the Allied Maritime Transport Council and since 1925 he had been chairman of the President's Aircraft Board. Although he had no experience in the diplomatic service before 1927, he had always had the instinct for diplomacy and he brought to his new task the valuable experience of financial negotiations with foreign governments and a recent self-training in concentrated study of Mexican history and international law. Clark, who had served at the Department of State as assistant solicitor (1906-10) and then as solicitor (1910-13), and had acted as counsel for the United States before the British claims commission in 1913 and as counsel and agent before the American-Mexican claims commission in 1926, had returned to the Department of State as Under Secretary in August, 1928.

That the administration of President Harding would delay Mexican recognition was indicated by Senator Fall who, a few days before his appointment as Secretary of the Interior by President Harding, wrote: "So long as I have anything to do with the Mexican question, no government of Mexico will be recognized, with my consent, which does not first enter into a written agreement promising to protect American citizens and their property rights in Mexico." President Obregon, however, ready to welcome American business men and American enterprise (in strange contrast to Carranza), believed that the new administration would be influenced by Henry P. Fletcher (as American Under Secretary of State) to pursue a course favorable to recognition; and, in the following July, he purchased at Washington on Sixteenth Street the McVeagh house for use as an embassy.[2]

Under the administration of President Harding, the American government, representing American public opinion, and setting the example for Great Britain and France, adopted a policy of conditional recognition of Obregon based upon a pre-recognition written understanding as to Mexico's international obligations and intentions concerning American claims and the protection of American citizens and American vested interests in Mexico. Like other foreign governments, it became concerned whether the provisions of the new constitution asserting ultimate ownership of the Mexican nation in all lands and waters (including subsoil minerals) would be interpreted as retroactive. Adopting the demands of American capitalists whose Mexican investments were large, it requested a treaty guaranty of property rights (by protection against confiscation) as a preliminary to recognition—a guaranty which Obregon refused to grant, on the grounds that such a pledge would give to foreigners greater security than Mexican citizens had and that it would threaten to impair Mexican sovereignty and his own prestige. By demanding Mexican concessions as a consideration for recognition, it postponed recognition for over two years—until the late summer of 1923.

On June 7, 1921, Secretary Hughes outlined the general American policy, urging that the fundamental and vital question was "the safeguarding of American property rights against confiscation" by retroactive application of the provision of the Mexican Constitution of 1917—a question to which the question of recognition was only subordinate. Therefore, he explained, as a preliminary to recognition he had proposed a treaty of amity and commerce, presented by Mr. Summerlin to General Obregon on May 27, in which the Mexican government was invited to make clear its assurances and purposes "by guarantees in proper form," binding itself to discharge primary international obligations. In this draft treaty, he provided for liberty of travel and residence, all rights incidental to the management of business or exercise of professions, protection and security for persons and property, proper restriction of expropriation, restoration of property rights or interests which had been destroyed and compensation for damages, freedom of religion and worship, freedom of commerce and navigation, exemption from transit duties, privileges of the most favored nation, protection of patents and trade marks, recognition of responsibility for damages from acts of representatives of the government or from acts of persons engaged in brigandage or insurrection or revolution against the Mexican government, and conventions for the settlement of claims and adjustment of pending differences.[3]

The editor of the *Nation,* (on June 22) following Hughes' demands for a treaty to safeguard American property rights, announced that "bumptious bullying" had succeeded "watchful waiting" in the American-Mexican policy and fearfully suggested that the new policy, under the influence of the "pliable and two-faced mentality" of President Harding and the hostile and aggressive Secretary Fall of the cabinet, and directed by oil interests who wished to continue private development and larger profits without government control or increase of taxes, would lead to a situation which would result in an invasion by a "protective force" or "temporary occupation" of territory on grounds of "necessity." Later he predicted that the continuation of the Harding-Hughes policy would "lead straight to intervention and bloodshed," for which the stage was being rapidly set by cessation of oil operations as a protest against the Mexican export tax and by the sudden appearance of American warships at Tampico; and he suggested that it would cause America to be regarded as a menace by the Latin American countries.[4]

Obregon, who had already rejected the proposition to sign a convention as a basis for recognition, in his message to Congress (on September 1), although he recognized protection of American interests in Mexico as one of the most urgent duties, stated that the Mexican government preferred the natural development of an administrative policy which would avoid the necessity for promises which might humiliate it—a policy which might later result in recognition without prejudice to national dignity and sovereignty and treaties, on equality of conditions. This expression of policy Señor Pani submitted to Summerlin (on November 19) with the statement that it represented "all that the Mexican government can do in this connection." At the same time he repeated a suggestion (which his government had previously made) that the first step toward the renewal of relations should be an agreement for the establishment of a special commission for the settlement of American claims for damages to American interests in the recent Mexican revolutions (since 1910), as planned in the Mexican political program; and he proposed that this agreement should be followed by recognition and then by the signing of another convention to establish a mixed commission to decide all claims and difficulties since 1868 except the American claims arising from the revolution.[5]

Summerlin in an informal reply (of February 6, 1922), following his telegraphic instructions from Secretary Hughes, invited the Mexican government to indicate specifically the objections to the proposed treaty clause safeguarding rights acquired by American citizens before May, 1917, and declared: "Unless General Obregon is willing to put the draft of the Treaty of Amity and Commerce into a form acceptable to both parties beforehand, it would be futile to engage in any discussion of the Claims Conventions."[6] From Señor Pani he received a prompt informal response (of February 9), stating that after the field of past and present obstacles was cleared by his proposed conventions providing for the claims commissions his government would be enabled to discuss the proposed treaty, and insisting that the American desire for assurances should already be satisfied by the practical effects of the policy adopted by President Obregon which rendered unnecessary the proposed formal stipulations—stipulations which the scrupulous Obregon said he could not sign without invading the exclusive sphere of legislative and judicial action.

The American government, although gratified that the Mexican government was disposed to sign at once the two proposed claims conventions, was still "concerned with the importance of suitable assurances for the adequate protection of American citizens and their property rights . . . some better assurance than any mere temporary abstention from the prosecution of the confiscatory policies which had been officially avowed." In this concern and in the policy of obtaining treaty assurances, it was justified by the absence of appropriate government action binding Mexico to afford the protection of valid titles and by previous unfortunate experience of eleven years—especially by the experience with Carranza who after recognition had ignored the "most explicit personal promises" upon which recognition was based. These views Summerlin expressed to Pani in a note of April 20. After emphasizing the importance, in the interest of friendly relations, "that there should be no misunderstanding" as to the future policy of Mexico, and suggesting that any Mexican impediment to the execution of an appropriate treaty (if such impediment existed) could be readily removed by the Mexican Congress, and at the same time urging that these questions should be settled at an early date, he significantly said: "Hence there would appear to be no reason . . . for delay in the signing of the treaty unless it is supposed that the Congress of Mexico will insist upon a confiscatory policy, and if this be the case, it is necessary to say that such an attitude would be a bar to the resumption of diplomatic relations." In a long reply (of May 4) Pani again urged the Mexican way as the least embarrassing and the most logical—the result of "efforts to reconcile moral obligations and conditions and political necessities with American demands." In stating his objections to the treaty proposed by the American government he said that it proposed as a *sine qua non* to the granting of recognition an imposition of obligations which were an affront to the dignity of a sovereign people, that it contained flagrant violations of the Constitution of Mexico and that it had no chance of ratification by the Mexican Senate.

On May 16, Summerlin sought information concerning any points of the Mexican political and administrative program which had a bearing on foreign interests in Mexico. In Pani's long reply (of May 24) he was furnished a statement of various evidences of Obregon's offer of hospitality to foreigners and foreign capital together with equitable reparations for damages suffered by revolution, an explanation of the origin and difficulty of the Mexican agrarian problem and indications of the purpose of the government as illustrated by several concrete cases. He was assured that the Mexican government, although founded on the principle that the nation owned the national resources and would demand an equitable participation in their development, had no wish to adopt a policy of isolation nor a policy of confiscation and would respect and protect all rights of private property acquired prior to May 1, 1917. He was also told of the expectation that the Mexican Congress at its next session (in Sepember) would enact an organic law regulating the application of Article 27 of the Constitution in accord with this established principle of irretroactivity.

Secretary Hughes, after some delay while awaiting Mexican action on its political and administrative program, on July 28 forwarded instructions for informal reply to Mr. Pani. He considered the situation very unsatisfactory. He had received new American complaints that under the retroactive application of Article 27 of the Mexican Constitution American subsoil rights acquired prior to May 1, 1917, were not respected—complaints emphasizing the necessity of adequate Mexican assurance in some appropriate form and of some adequate government action. He had no objection to any proper non-confiscatory legislation, but stated that the Mexican agrarian program should be made effective in accord with the fundamental conceptions of justice. After reading Pani's excuse concerning the limitation of the treaty-making power, he thought it "hardly necessary to discuss the inconclusive effect of General Obregon's personal statements," the inefficiency of which had been demonstrated. Still left to consider the Mexican expression of an expectation, he concluded: "It would thus appear that General Obregon's administrative and political program, which Mr. Pani invokes, has not yet progressed to such effective action as could be regarded as a satisfactory substitute for the binding engagements which I have desired in order to assure proper protection to the rights of American citizens in Mexico." He still expressed the hope that the Mexican authorities would see their way clear to give in an appropriate manner the reasonable assurances requested for the security of valid titles.[7]

In these instructions, submitted by Summerlin to the Mexican government on August 3, Pani saw the possibility of an American change of procedure in the conditions proposed precedent to recognition. He delayed his reply while awaiting definite acts of the Obregon government which might prove advantageous in determining the question of recognition.

Meantime, despairing of the success of further efforts to induce Obregon to sign a treaty of guaranties (which Obregon said would have changed the Mexican Constitution), President Harding on February 17, 1923, announced that he saw no early prospect of resumption of official relations. On February 15, he ordered troops on the border to be ready to protect American lives and property. By the end of February, however, he learned that the tax disputes with American oil companies were finally settled by a payment of $6,750,000, only 40% of the amount claimed.[8]

Finally, on March 3, 1923, in a long note to Summerlin, Minister Pani announced that three of the five obstacles to recognition had disappeared: (1) The questions relating to the public debt had been adjusted by the Lamont-Huerta agreement (of June 16, 1922) providing guarantees to the holders of the bonds and, also, the return of the National Railways of Mexico to the owning company; (2) the non-retroactive character of the petroleum clause of Article 27 of the Constitution had been clearly defined by decisions of the Supreme Court, based on the "rule of sane logic," in five cases of injunction (*amparo*); (3) the question of protection of the rights of petroleum companies would be satisfactorily defined by future organic law which had been debated in the Chamber of Deputies. At the same time, by presenting statistics of the "fabulous development" of the Mexican petroleum industries for the preceding six years (1917-22), he claimed to demonstrate that the new constitutional régime had placed no obstacle in the way of the increase of petroleum production. Explaining the conditions which had necessitated haste of official action in administration of the new land policy, resulting in the expropriations without indemnification, he stated that Obregon, having solved other difficulties, was now "able to proceed to the legal indemnification for the expropriations affected." [9] A few days later, Obregon in a decree confirmed a Mexican Supreme Court decision that the constitutional provision concerning rights to subsoil could not be construed as retroactive.

Influenced by this decree and by Pani's recent note, the American government was encouraged to test Obregon by direct negotiations with a view to recognition. The editor of the *Nation*, referring to the pre-recognition program of the Harding administration, later complained that even after the "well-oiled exit of Senator Fall into oblivion, Secretary Hughes persisted in seeking to impose on Mexico a legislative program conceived in petroleum and dedicated to the proposition that American property rights take precedence over Mexican national needs and aspirations." [10] On May 2, 1923, President Harding appointed two American commissioners, Charles Beecher Warren and John Barton Payne, who promptly met with Mexican commissioners at Mexico City (on May 15) to consider the questions in controversy which had delayed American recognition—chiefly the issues relating to Mexican nationalization of subsoil mineral deposits and the confiscation of agricultural lands. They heard the Mexican arguments concerning the rights under police power to enact legislation to protect natural resources as the United States had abolished slavery and prohibited the liquor traffic. These they did not deny, provided the legislation was not retroactive in destroying rights acquired by Americans before the operation of the new Constitution of 1917.[11] They found that the Mexican government was ready to disclaim a policy of retroactivity of the Mexican Constitution as to American acquired rights, but not ready to admit that American owners of Mexican land had acquired rights to subsoil without performance of some positive act indicating a purpose to use it. They were able to obtain an understanding (1) that American nationals who owned the surface before May 1, 1917, and had performed some "positive act" which was evidence of a purpose to utilize the subsoil deposits, were protected against nationalization, (2) that those who had performed no "positive act" had preferential rights against third parties, and (3) that claims to vested rights challenged by the Mexican government would be settled by arbitration. On the question of confiscation of agricultural lands, although they insisted upon a cash indemnity, they finally agreed to consider the proposed payment of indemnity in Mexican bonds for tracts not in excess of 4,335 acres, contingent upon the conclusion of a general claims convention to provide for consideration of claims for losses or damages by persons dispossessed.

In the records of the conference (signed on August 15) the Mexican commissioners interpreted the subsoil and agrarian legislation satisfactory to the American delegates and expressed the Mexican government's intention to follow these interpretations in good faith. Thus they finally reached a definite pre-recognition executive agreement that subsoil rights acquired by Americans (before May, 1917) should be respected, that Americans should receive fair compensation for lands lost by Mexican expropriation for the landless peons, and that commissioners should be appointed to adjust all claims. According to this agreement, American rights to titles in land acquired before the Constitution of 1917 were regarded as valid, under the laws then in force and under the Constitution of 1857; but lands acquired after May, 1917, were subject to the subsequent agrarian legislation concerning the division of estates in connection with agrarian reforms. One point of contention was apparently untouched in the official agreement: The question whether subsoil petroleum rights acquired prior to 1917 *but not exploited* were "acquired rights" under the Mexican law. On this point the Mexican government was unwilling to commit itself, but the American commissioners specifically reserved the rights of Americans who had acquired them.[12]

For the first time since 1913 America and Mexico were well on the way to resumption of regular diplomatic relationship. On August 31, the American government formally recognized the Obregon government, which was later recognized by France and England, and which promptly proceeded to inaugurate reforms based on the principles or pledges of the revolution, including the nationalization of subsoil mineral and oil deposits. Early in September, two conventions were signed. One, covering general claims since 1868, was signed at Washington on September 18 and ratified on February 23, 1924. The other, covering special claims originating during the recent revolutionary period- (from November 20, 1910, to May 31, 1920), was signed at Mexico City on September 10 and ratified on February 19, 1924. It included claims arising from acts of both federal and revolutionary forces and, also, from acts of mutinies, mobs or bandits which the proper authorities had not taken reasonable measures to suppress.[13] On February 29, 1924, President Coolidge appointed as ambassador to Mexico Mr. Warren who had succeeded in obtaining the understanding and who, after his resignation, was succeeded by James Rockwell Sheffield in the following September. Ambassador Sheffield in presenting his credentials to President Obregon said the American government sought no rights or privileges which it was not disposed to grant freely.

Meantime the American government had watched with some concern a new and menacing revolution, begun in December, 1923, by the followers of Huerta who had resigned from the Obregon cabinet (Secretary of the Treasury) with ambitions to defeat Plutarco Elias Calles in the race for the presidency in 1924. Regarding the early suppression of the revoluton as desirable, it aided the newly recognized government by sending to it a large consignment of surplus war equipment and by placing an embargo on all shipments of arms to the revolutionists—and, also, by allowing Mexico federal troops to cross Texas territory to El Paso. As Secretary Hughes later explained, it did not intervene nor invade the sovereignty of Mexico, but simply aided a neighboring constitutional government in preventing a revolutionary attempt to conduct a political campaign by force of arms, and thereby aided stability and peace in the American hemisphere. On October 31, 1924, Secretary Hughes gave, at the Pan-American Building at Washington, a dinner in honor of President-elect Calles who was welcomed as a distinguished visitor, and who three days earlier in a speech at a banquet given in his honor at the Waldorf-Astoria Hotel in New York City had explained his reform policy of reconstructive development —to secure the social and economic elevation of 12,000,000

submerged Mexicans, but at the same time to invite the cooperation of capitalists and industrialists of good will.[14]

Unfortunately, in 1925, after the retirement of Secretary
Hughes, the Coolidge administration became involved in a serious controversy with President Calles who, while planning to
continue and to expand the policy of Obregon for general improvement of economic and social conditions, unwisely decided
to favor a retroactive interpretation of Article 27 of the Constitution relating to nationalization of subsoil deposits and the
breaking up of large landed estates. For the latter decision the
American ambassador, James R. Sheffield, and the new American
Secretary of State, Frank B. Kellogg, were in part responsible—
the first by his unsympathetic interpretations of the Mexican
government in his communications to the Department, and the
latter by his indiscretion (in June, 1925) in furnishing to the
American press an undiplomatic and unjustifiable statement to
which Calles replied in language equally undiplomatic. In the
press statement, following a visit of Sheffield to Washington,
Kellogg announced that the American government was expecting the Mexican government to restore American properties
illegally taken and to agree to indemnity for losses, and, referring to a press report that another revolution was possibly
impending, he declared that the American government, although
its policy was to favor stable government and orderly constitutional procedure, would continue to support the government in
Mexico only so long as the latter complied with its international
engagements and obligations by protection of American lives
and rights in Mexico. "The government in Mexico," said he, "is
now on trial before the world."

President Calles, resenting the suggestion concerning a new
revolution, declared his government would "reject with energy
any imputation that Mexico was on trial in the guise of a de-
fendant . . . which in essence would only mean an insult."
The editor of the *Nation* characterized Kellogg's prepared press
statement as "a naked club, publicly brandished in the face of a
friendly government," as "lacking in the niceties of diplomatic
courtesy with which brutal international ultimatums are usually

disguised," and as sounding "like a sour-faced teacher reporting to a bad boy's father" with no hint of understanding of the problem.[15]

The new Mexican legislation of December, 1925—the petroleum law and the land law, which precipitated new and serious controversy—required owners of Mexican oil properties, in order to avoid confiscation, to transfer (before January 1, 1927) their concessions for a new concession terminating in fifty years; and later, as modified under a subsequent act, the law required foreign corporations which owned agricultural lands to sell to the Mexican government enough shares to enable the latter to control the vote in the organization. It also required compliance with the constitutional provision in regard to the waiving of nationality in order to prevent application for diplomatic protection and, also, enforcement of the prohibition of foreign ownership of lands or waters within thirty miles from the seacoast and sixty-two miles from the frontier. It also sought to prevent foreign control of any Mexican corporations. The first-mentioned law the larger American oil companies resisted and refused to obey—resulting in Mexican retaliatory cancellation of drilling permits and consequent reduction of oil production.

The American government, objecting to the retroactive and confiscatory features of the new legislation, began a correspondence which, although conducted with courtesy and probably useful in clarifying the points at issue, was finally closed without any visible basis of settlement and with apprehension of the danger of a break in relations. Following certain inquiries concerning the alien land bill while it was before the Mexican Congress, Secretary Kellogg, perceiving on the horizon of friendship clouds which he desired to remove, (on November 17, 1925) submitted through Ambassador Sheffield an *aide memoire* of friendly personal message to the Mexican Minister of Foreign Affairs. Influenced by the proposed legislation, which caused him some concern, but wishing to avoid any criticism of Mexican prospective legislation or any appearance of assuming the rôle of uninvited adviser, he suggested that the time was opportune for beginning the contemplated negotiations for the proposed new treaty of amity and commerce, and he ventured to hope that the Mexican government in its economic legislation intended to take no action in contravention of the understanding of the American-Mexican commission which convened at Mexico City in May, 1923.[16]

On November 27, Ambassador Sheffield received the reply of President Calles who, after stating that he saw no cause for perceiving clouds upon the horizon and that the Mexican government was disposed to fulfill all its obligations under international law and to negotiate the proposed treaty with fair stipulations for protection of mutual legitimate interests, explained his view that the conferences (of May-August, 1923) were confined to an exchange of views in order to find a way for resumption of diplomatic relations and that the policy of Obregon, which was made known at that conference, was the basis for the pending legislation which, while fully protecting acquired rights, aimed especially to dispel the vagueness of Article 27 of the Constitution. In concluding his reply, Calles said: "I should regret your being misinformed on this point and without any wish to take the part of an adviser I venture to call your attention to the very human fact that men and money are generally opposed to any innovation even though it does not mean any invasion of their rights."

On the same day, after the petroleum bill had passed the Mexican Chamber of Deputies, Secretary Kellogg instructed Sheffield to present to the Mexican government another *aide memoire* renewing the expression of apprehension which he regarded as justified by certain apparent retroactive and confiscatory features of the bill which seemed to affect American vested rights and to be in contravention to the understanding of the conference of 1923. He especially objected to the requirement that foreign holders of corporate stock must consider themselves Mexican nationals (as to such stock) and renounce the right to appeal to their government, or in the alternative forfeit their interests, and he also mentioned the requirement that the holdings of foreigners in Mexican agricultural companies must be less than 50% of the total stock. Concerning the proposed requirement of a waiver of nationality, he reminded the Mexican government that the American government had "always consistently declined to concede that such a waiver can annul the relation of a citizen to his government or that it can operate to extinguish the obligation of his government by diplomatic intervention to protect him in the event of a denial of justice within the recognized principle of international law." Sheffield, who promptly submitted the *aide memoire*, on December 7 received the reply (of December 5) which, after referring to the extraordinary American action in making representations (concerning pending legislation) which to suspicious minds might seem to involve pressure upon Mexican legislative bodies, suggested that the proposed land law pending in the Mexican Senate was similar to laws which were in force in states of the American Union and was not novel in Mexico (as illustrated by the railroad law of April, 1899, and various executive decrees of the last seven years), denied that it was retroactive and confiscatory or that it was in conflict with international law (even in its limitation upon the right of inheritance) or that it disregarded any of the rights of foreigners, and especially explained that the required agreement of foreigners acquiring real property "not to invoke diplomatic protection" (in matters relating thereto) was really not a renouncement of nationality.[17]

On January 8, 1926, following the enactment of the land law and the petroleum law, Ambassador Sheffield, under instructions from Secretary Kellogg, notified the Mexican Foreign Office that the objections previously advanced against certain retroactive and confiscatory features of the pending bills were considered as applicable to the enacted laws which, according to the American view, were in violation of the principles of international law and justice. He specifically objected to the failure of the petroleum law to recognize rights lawfully acquired before 1917 and to respect the recent decisions of the Mexican Supreme Court as to non-retroactivity and "positive acts," and also objected to its apparent contradiction to the statements solemnly made by the Mexican commissioners at the conference of 1923. Concerning the provision requiring a limited waiver of nationality, he repeated the American consistent refusal to concede that such a waiver could annul the relation between the American government and American citizens or that it could extinguish the obligation of the American government to protect American citizens in case of a denial of justice. He also gave notice that his government could not assent to any retroactive or confiscatory application of the laws to American-owned properties.[18]

In reply, Sheffield received from the Mexican minister a long note (of January 20) making a complete denial of any basis for the various objections. In this reply the minister (Aaron Saenz) stated that the later law might modify a status created by a previous law without being retroactive, that legislation should not be judged on the strength of a single legal precept, that the promise of the executive in 1923 to grant a preferential right was not intended to constitute an obligation for an unlimited time to grant preferential rights of subsoil to owners of the surface, that promises made by an executive could not exceed the limitations imposed upon his constitutional powers, that all governments had power to impose conditions or limitations upon aliens in regard to ownership of real property, and that the Supreme Court's judicial decisions before the enactment of a law did not restrict the power of Congress to enact laws under the Constitution. He said, however, that the executive with a view to satisfactory adjustment of difficulties resulting from the laws had extended a "spontaneous invitation to the petroleum companies to attend a conference for consultation." In conclusion he suggested that "a diplomatic representation is not considered appropriate in connection with the enactment of a law but is only justified when the enforcement of such a law involves an injury." [19]

The danger of the situation was seen in a Washington press dispatch to the New York *Times* which stated that "representations made by Ambassador Sheffield are believed to carry the implication that should the Mexican government be unwilling to abrogate or amend the sections deemed harmful to American interests, America may withdraw its official recognition which was granted in 1923 on the understanding that Mexico would protect American lives and American rights." [20]

Secretary Kellogg noted with satisfaction that the Mexican executive proposed to frame the executive regulations in the application and enforcement of the land and petroleum laws to prevent retroactivity against legally acquired rights. While awaiting further information, he reiterated (on June 28) the chief American contentions against retroactivity and individual waiver of diplomatic protection, and as to the threatened conflict between the terms of the recent legislation and the decisions of the supreme court and the agreements of 1923. In a long explanatory and courteous reply of February 12, Minister Saenz, after summarizing the points of agreement, announced that "the entire question is reduced to determining whether the laws under consideration are retroactive in their application." The American statement against individual waiver of diplomatic protection he regarded as apparently "due to some confusion" which he undertook to explain and dissipate by reference to the obligations of an individual in a private contract which did not infringe the rights of the state to which he belonged. In referring to modification of the right of ownership by legislation he ventured to suggest that the American government in enforcement of the prohibition law was not deterred by consideration of the destruction of lawfully acquired rights by paralyzing an established business. He closed by the assurance that in the regulation of the laws all points which had been the object of explanations would be defined. [21]

Meantime in a newspaper interview early in February, 1926, following rumors of a rupture in diplomatic relations with the United States, President Calles stated that the American government in assuming that the new Mexican laws in regulation of Article 27 of the Constitution were retroactive and confiscatory had based its position upon an incomplete legal comprehension of the situation, and he intimated that the existing diplomatic *status quo* in its origin had been influenced by interests which were liable to be affected by new Mexican laws in regulation of

Article 27 of the Constitution. Earlier, in January, 1926, in addressing a group of American "good will" visitors and agreeing with them that the American withdrawal of recognition from Mexico would strengthen the cause of rebels who were seeking to overthrow his government, he declared that in the existing crisis the source of the trouble was a small group of American capitalists, chiefly interested in Mexican oil, who, although amply protected by the Mexican legislation, were trying to induce the American Department of State to aid them by force.[22]

Pleased by the Mexican statement of February 12, that the two governments were in accord as to the principle which should be applied in the adjustment of the question of retroactivity, Secretary Kellogg (on March 1) submitted inquiries for specific information concerning the practical application of certain provisions of the alien land law and expressed the hope that in accord with the statements of Minister Saenz the Mexican government would be able to give the assurance that the rights of American citizens in respect to the products of the subsoil would be confirmed. He also explained that the liquor business in the United States had never been a property right but a licensed occupation subject to the police powers, and for the purpose of clarification again referred to the binding nature of the proceedings and understanding of the American-Mexican conference of 1923. From Minister Saenz he received a very satisfactory note (of March 27) indicating that the clauses in question were not retroactive and that an individual's waiver or renunciation of diplomatic protection did not extinguish the right of his government to extend it in case of a denial of justice, also acknowledging the declaration of the Mexican commissioners at the conference of 1923 as to the American express reservation of rights in subsoil deposits, and extending assurances that by executive regulations the subsoil rights of Americans (who had performed the enumerated "positive acts") would be affirmed.[23]

Secretary Kellogg at the end of the following July, after a review of the correspondence and a careful examination of the subsequent regulations of April 8 for enforcement of the petroleum law, "in the interest of a complete understanding" courteously submitted to Minister Saenz a brief summary of the American view of the situation indicating that, although there was general agreement on basic principles involved in the questions under consideration, there were still differences arising from practical interpretation and specific application of the general conceptions. He suggested that the Mexican attitude and declarations of intentions were calculated to defeat legitimate expectations justified by the accord on general principles. He especially stated that the American government was unable to acquiesce in the Mexican conception of a vested interest, or the theory under which the Mexican government by the simple device of a forced exchange of title proposed to convert unqualified exclusive ownerships into mere authorization to exercise rights for a limited period of time. Declaring that a vested interest is inviolable, he announced that his government could not accept the Mexican conception that a title was subject to curtailment or destruction by enforcement of laws enacted subsequent to the date of the acquisition of the title. He urged that, under the unequivocal understanding and express reservation of the American commissioners in the conference of 1923, the Mexican doctrine of "positive acts" did not apply to vested interests in subsoil deposits of petroleum which were acquired with the surface prior to May 1, 1917, in accord with the Mexican laws of 1884, 1892 and 1907—that such vested rights should not be construed as merely optional rights. Again referring to the nature of the conferences of 1923 which Calles had not regarded as a condition for recognition, he asserted that the paramount issue was that of recognition which would not have been extended without the assurances which were received in the course of negotiations and upon the fulfilment of which the American government still relied.[24]

Minister Saenz in his reply of October 7, although courteous, showed some impatience with the American insistence upon "purely academic discussion of abstract questions" with a view to a definite understanding in regard to the precise application of constitutional precepts in cases which had not yet arisen. Although he agreed to the principle that acquired rights may not be impaired by retroactive or confiscatory legislation, he remarked that the mere retroactive character of law could not properly be a subject of objection nor diplomatic representation until it had produced confiscatory or other harmful effects. Although he agreed to the right of a state to protect its nationals, he stated that diplomatic intervention was properly confined to concrete cases requiring protection of an alien and that an attempt of a state to insure beforehand in another state the trend of judicial decisions in the application of a law to future cases was equivalent to intervention or meddling in the administration of justice in the other state. Although his government on grounds of courtesy had answered unofficial American inquiries and diplomatic representations concerning the recent legislation, he reminded the American government that "*a priori* discussion" of the possible effects of a law upon the nationals of another country was unusual. Believing that the concrete points of difference between the American and Mexican positions offered only a remote possibility of injury to foreign interests, he suggested that the line of least resistance was to reserve protests while awaiting concrete specific cases of violation of American rights under international law by administrative application and judicial interpretation of the law. In reply to the American position that the recent Mexican Supreme Court decisions should determine future legislative and executive acts in regulation of the petroleum cases he explained that the influence of the decisions in injunction (*amparo*) cases upon legislation must be decided by Mexican constitutional principles which in such cases forbade judicial decisions of a general character concerning the laws. Concerning the Mexican proposal to transform the ownership right to subsoil into an administrative concession for fifty years with a lifetime limitation of certain alien rights, he asserted that such a permit to aliens who had interests incompatible with the new laws, to retain them until death, was the most that could properly be demanded as a protection of the rights acquired, although the Mexican government had allowed the natural beneficiaries of inheritance rights a reasonable period of five years for divestment of those rights, and to artificial persons a period of ten years.[25]

Secretary Kellogg, after careful consideration of the note of Minister Saenz and with full appreciation of the gravity of the situation which the American government had sought to avoid by efforts to secure a clear understanding, (on October 30) closed the correspondence with the reply that the American government would maintain its positions "with the utmost emphasis" (including the American reservation and the Mexican statements of August 2, 1923), and would expect the Mexican government, in accord with the "true intent and purpose of the negotiations of 1923" culminating in American recognition, to respect all acquired property rights of Americans under discussion and to take no action which would operate either directly or indirectly against such rights. In a reply of November 17, the Mexican minister reiterated the statement that the results of the conferences of 1923 did not have the force of a treaty and were not a condition for renewal of diplomatic relations, urged that the Mexican reservation of Mexican rights was as important as the American reservation, denied any justified motive for misunderstanding and declared that the Mexican government expected that the American government would indicate the concrete cases of violation of American legal rights so that Mexico could consider them with a disposition to repair them.[26]

In December, the American government apprehended further complication of the situation by the Mexican recognition and support of the Nicaraguan government of Sacasa which was in opposition to the Nicaraguan government (of Diaz) recognized by the United States. During the Nicaraguan revolution of 1926-27 it had unsuccessfully suggested to Mexico an agreement for a general arms embargo against Nicaragua. Later, Secretary Kellogg stated that the Washington government viewed with concern the export of arms from Mexico for the use of the revolutionary troops of Sacasa—which was regarded as an attempt to interfere in Nicaraguan politics.[27]

The situation was for a time complicated and aggravated by certain mysterious American documents, both stolen and forged, evidently intended to precipitate a crisis in American-Mexican relations and regarded by Calles as evidence of a plot to start a revolution or a war, but fortunately exposed as fraudulent by a New York newspaper man who visited Mexico City for that purpose early in 1927. Late in March, President Coolidge sought the identity of the person who had evidently taken copies of papers from the American embassy and who after changing them by addition of forged matter had placed them in possession of the Mexican government. By the disclosure of the pilfering and the forgery the hope of accord was advanced. In June, following inquiry of the thefts, an American lieutenant was relieved from his official duties as military attaché. Some of the forged documents were later published by the Hearst press with an intention to discredit certain American senators who, however, were exonerated by the Senate (in December, 1927) to the discredit of Hearst.[28]

On January 1, 1927, when the Mexican anti-alien land and petroleum laws became effective, a diplomatic *impasse* was apprehended. At the same time, influenced by rumors that Mexico was distributing radical propaganda in Central America, Secretary Kellogg submitted to the Foreign Relations Committee of the Senate a memorandum on "Bolshevik aims and policies in Mexico and Latin America" which tended to intensify the situation. On January 25, however, the Senate, in accord with the treaty of 1848, and doubtless influenced by public sentiment against any war which might result from the oil controversy and possibly by the lifting of the arms embargo, voted unanimously for the Robinson resolution in favor of arbitration of the controversy—in opposition to the views of President Coolidge who, apparently after some wavering, declared in favor of further attempts at adjustment through diplomatic negotiations. On February 16, in response to a Senate resolution of February 3, he reported certain information concerning American concessions and oil holdings in Mexico, and the American policy relating thereto, and stated his understanding that the corporations which had refused or failed to accept the provision of the new petroleum law controlled about 90% of the actively petroleum-producing lands of Mexico acquired before 1917 and were producing about 70% of the total oil production in Mexico—a statement which, however, was in conflict with that of Minister Morones, the Mexican Minister of Labor.[29]

Following the Mexican cancellation of drilling permits resulting from failure of applications of corporations to apply for confirmation of title, the Mexican Petroleum Company of California appealed to the courts for a restraining order (*amparo*) which was granted by the district judge, but the case was not decided until the following November. Senator Borah in a public address on March 20, 1927, while advocating American duty to insist that Mexico must not destroy vested rights in connection with the establishment of a new land system, expressed sympathy with the Mexican government in its task and recommended cooperation by refraining from false and unfair statements concerning dangerous communistic activities in Mexico.[30]

In the heat of the land and oil controversy with the Calles government, President Coolidge, through his action (of March 28, 1927) in terminating an anti-smuggling convention of 1926, apparently intended to make a veiled threat to lift the arms embargo with a view to the weakening of the Calles government by improving the chances of any possible Mexican revolutionists. Late in April, possibly without any intention to assert the extraterritoriality of American investments in Mexico, and expressing no desire for strife, he declared at a dinner of the United Press Association that "the person and property of a citizen are a part of the general domain of the nation even when abroad" and again asserted the duty of the American government to protect its citizens abroad. At the same time, he predicted a peaceful settlement which would prevent confiscation of American property in Mexico. A few days later, Senator Borah made a statement in opposition to force in the protection of American property rights.[31]

A few weeks later, early in July, and following recent indications of irritating diplomatic relations, the way for more satisfactory negotiations and a new period of improved relations was prepared by the resignation of Ambassador Sheffield who, after a conference with President Coolidge (at the summer executive home at Rapid City, South Dakota), sailed for Europe for a needed rest.[32] In Mexico the way was further prepared by the need of money to pay interest on the public debt and by the recognition of the value of external credit and confidence to the success of orderly government. Already in March, 1927, a writer in the *Atlantic Monthly* under the heading "Wanted, A Mexican Policy," undertaking to explain the reasons for the confusions and failures in Mexican relations, had suggested the wisdom of good-will diplomatic conferences for making friends with Mexico in connection with the presentation of problems for solution.[33] Evidently President Coolidge had reached a similar view of the situation. The American government, although it had used all the means of diplomacy in defense of American property rights in Mexico and under strong pressure of American oil interests in Mexico had been inclined to adopt drastic measures to coerce Mexican acquiescence to American views, had been unable to divert Calles from the determined pursuit of reform policies which he regarded as more important than the legal rights of prosperous individuals and companies favored by the policies of Diaz. Finally, after the demand of the American Senate for arbitration of the Mexican controversy, and possibly influenced by certain expressions of public opinion, it became somewhat reconciled to the Mexican policy of expropriating agricultural lands for restoration of the Indian community holdings provided the Mexican government would arrange satisfactory payment for lands taken from American citizens and saw a possible way for the adjustment of the application of the "positive act" doctrine of oil lands in which Americans had invested. Therefore, it decided to adopt a more conciliatory and sympathetic course of action in the negotiations for protection of American interests. Apparently, it finally withdrew any serious opposition to the Mexican claim to the legal right, under the alien law of December, 1925, to prevent inheritance by aliens—a claim based on the idea that an expectation of acquiring rights by inheritance was not yet an acquired right.[34]

President Calles, in his message to Congress on September 1, although he recognized that relations with the American government had unfortunately assumed an indeterminate character, was confident that the acerbities of controversy would be softened at the proper time by a cordial American comprehension of Mexican problems.[35]

Meantime President Coolidge, following the resignation of Sheffield and after his brief announcement from Rapid City that he did "not choose to run" for the presidency in 1928, decided to select as ambassador to untangle and tranquillize the Mexican situation his former classmate, Dwight W. Morrow, who had become well known as an able lawyer and financier of New York City, who in an article in *Foreign Affairs* in 1926 had expressed his view of the folly of using force to collect debts, and who fortunately was ready to retire from business with a wish for public service. After a conference, and the later consent of Morrow to serve, the President wired Secretary Kellogg, early in September, to inquire whether the appointment would be acceptable to Mexico City. Receiving a favorable reply (on September 21), he announced the appointment which was generally well received. Among senators, and in other quarters, he at first found some unimportant objection to the appointment on the ground that Morrow had been connected with the firm of J. P. Morgan & Co. which held a small part of the Mexican loan dating from the period before Morrow became a member of the firm. Borah guardedly stated that he wanted to know whether Morrow would favor friendly cooperation with Mexico and adjustment of controversy upon peaceful and just lines.[36]

Following the acceptance of the appointment, Morrow promptly applied himself to a study of the problems of his task, including in his work of preparation some study of Mexican history and of international law. He knew his task was not easy. Among the causes of misunderstanding or irritation, after the oil controversy which had resulted in a diplomatic *impasse*, he considered the Mexican failure to meet payments on the public debt, the Mexican zoning law, confiscations of land without adequate compensation, the Mexican requirement that individual contracts should surrender the right of diplomatic appeal, and the Mexican suspicion of plots based upon secret documents and propaganda. Before he arrived in Mexico, cynical Mexicans prematurely indicated their doubts by the expression "After Morrow come the marines"—an expression which they quickly revised after the first acquaintance with Morrow's manner and methods.

Morrow arrived at his post on October 23, and, on October 29, he formally presented his credentials to President Calles with a brief statement emphasizing respect for Mexican sovereignty. Within a week after his arrival he made a vigorous public speech at the Chamber of Commerce banquet urging American residents to have faith in the Mexican government and to comport themselves creditably in Mexico by their personal conduct and by showing proper respect to Mexican sovereignty. On November 1, he had his first informal breakfast of sausages and buckwheat cakes with President Calles whose firmness of decision he admired and with whom he immediately established a direct friendship based upon an attitude of honesty, fair play, justice and cooperation. In connection with the private negotiations between the Mexican government and the International Committee representing the holders of Mexican bonds he informally used his influence to advise and encourage the Mexican government to adopt a sound financial policy which would treat in a comprehensive manner the bonded debt and all classes of debt—a policy which he advised in the interest both of Mexico and of all classes of creditors. He elicited from Calles views of the future in which he was interested. Soon he was invited to informal breakfasts at the home of President Calles, at which the clouds of suspicion and misunderstanding were partly cleared away and replaced by an atmosphere of friendly confidence. He also made close contacts with other leading government officials, even at the risk of criticism from members of the American colony who cynically declared

"Calles will eat Morrow." In this way he and the Calles government reached a basis of agreement that Mexico could be independent and prosperous and at the same time protect the rights of aliens. While continuing to present to the Mexican government legitimate claims or grievances which could not be settled in the Mexican courts, he discouraged trivial or unreasonable claims. Incidentally, by his democratic habits and by his interest in Mexican life and activities, he won unusual popular favor. In dispelling suspicion, tenseness and indifference and in stimulating confidence, he was doubtless aided by the psychological effect of the visit of two popular Americans: (1) the irrepressible Will Rogers; and (2) Charles A. Lindbergh who, following the world enthusiasm resulting from his famous trans-Atlantic flight, arrived (on December 14) by a non-stop airplane flight from New York. He also contributed to the current of common interest and mutual understanding by encouraging the visits of professors and experts who were interested in improved relations.[37]

On November 8, at the first conference on the oil question, in the adjustment of which he was ably aided by J. Reuben Clark, Jr., Morrow began neighborly business negotiations which resulted in a steady improvement of relations—probably influenced in part by President Calles' recognition of the importance of the advice of a financial expert such as Morrow. Dropping for the time old legal controversies in which a deadlock had been reached, he tried to be helpful in regaining for Mexico a financial and economic standing in which its government was interested. In presenting the American view of international problems, he recognized the wisdom of perspective obtained by approaching the study of Mexican problems from the Mexican standpoint. He indicated that he respected Mexico's sovereign rights and appreciated its point of view, that he had faith in the Mexican desire and ability to play fair, that he believed Mexican laws should be upheld and asked no special privileges for Americans, and that he held to the recognized precepts of international law. Fortunately, he found no irreconcilable conflict of interest between Mexicans and the

American nationals. By December 4, according to a friend of Calles, he had won a victory for the United States [38] in the progress of negotiations for adjustments of difficulties.

In the settlement of the oil dispute Morrow was greatly aided by a Mexican supreme court decision of November 17 in the case of the Mexican Petroleum Company of California. This decision, unanimously confirming the judgment of the district judge, declared unconstitutional and void sections 14 and 15 of the petroleum regulations which had required application within one year for the substitution of a fifty-year concession for full titles held by those who had performed positive acts—regulations which had resulted in cancellation of permits to drill. At the same time, it declared that a requirement for a confirmation of acquired rights without any substantial alteration of them was no violation of constitutional guaranties. Its basic principles were in harmony with the declaration in the Texas case in 1921. Although the decision sustaining the American Oil Company (a subsidiary of the Standard Oil Company of Indiana) against the Mexican government, was not a blanket decision and could not operate as a precedent until followed by decisions in four other similar cases, it was generally regarded as an indication of the amicable ending of an old and ominous controversy. It proved that Americans could obtain justice in a Mexican court and that the Mexican government could not confiscate American oil interests through the device of an *ex post facto* law. It was a victory for both governments. It sustained the American contention, and therefore was an American victory—although the Louisville *Courier Journal* skeptically regarded the decision "not as a diplomatic victory except upon the cynical theory that the Mexican Supreme Court functioned to save the administration's face." Editorial opinion was usually very hopeful concerning the importance of the decision which, fortunately, was announced after the American government had changed its policy of pressure to one of more pacific methods of seeking adjustment.[39]

On December 26, President Calles, in view of this decision and after many informal conferences with Ambassador Morrow, submitted to the Mexican Congress proposed amendments to the laws which Congress promptly (December 27) enacted into a law providing for confirmatory concession, without cost and without limit to time, of certain rights derived from lands on which petroleum exploitation had begun prior to May 1, 1917, of rights derived from contracts closed before the same date with surface owners for the purpose of oil exploitation and of rights of operators of pipe lines and refineries under concessions or authorizations from the Department of Industry, Commerce and Labor. This new law, promulgated on January 10, 1928, indicated the determination of the legislative and executive departments of the Mexican government to recognize all rights held by foreigners in oil properties before May, 1917, and removed from discussion the most serious cause of American controversy with Mexico. It represented a compromise. Although it abolished the fifty-year concession on pre-1917 lands (those worked before 1917), it created a stricter interpretation of pre-1917 rights for which confirmation was required within one year by application for concession.[40]

In February, 1928, following the action of foreign oil companies in submitting a draft of proposed amendments to the petroleum regulations, Ambassador Morrow arranged informal conferences with Minister Morones of the Department of Industry with a view to framing amendments in harmony with the amended law. After several weeks of negotiations he felt satisfied that the substantial objections to the old regulations were eliminated. To the regulations Mexico attached a draft concession which, instead of the Calvo clause, contained a less harsh provision that any attempt to transfer the concession to an alien or to a foreign government would be null and of no effect. President Calles on March 27, 1928, signed regulations validating in perpetuity all oil titles obtained prior to May 1, 1917—regulations which were acceptable to the Washington government.[41]

Ambassador Morrow issued a statement announcing that these new petroleum regulations, completing the steps voluntarily taken by the different departments of the Mexican government to conclude the controversy of a decade, indicated clearly "that those who take confirmatory concessions under the amended law get a confirmation of their old rights rather than a new grant of rights." He added that there remained only the determination of what rights the oil companies held on May 1, 1917—a question of rights which he thought could be satisfactorily settled through the due operations of the Mexican governmental departments and the Mexican courts. This statement Secretary Kellogg approved and published. In the face of this official statement the American holders of oil rights yielded to the Mexican legislation.[42]

The new law, although it furnished proof of Morrow's capacity to secure better relations with Mexico, was regarded by some as "a symbol of the failure of our previous diplomacy of harassment." A critical writer in the *Nation* of January 25, in an article on "Dwight Morrow Agrees with Mexico," referred ironically to the new law as representing "the crowning failure of seventeen years of . . . inept and unsuccessful American diplomacy in Mexico," and the success of the astute, clever diplomacy of Calles in granting what the American government could have obtained long before by better diplomacy. Although it did not represent what many of the oil companies had demanded, nor all that the Department of State had asked in the earlier stages of the futile controversy, it came as the voluntary sovereign act of Mexico influenced by the agreeable tactics of Morrow, after the State Department offered less argument against the Mexican contention that diplomatic coercion should be deferred until after the actual violation of American rights and the exhaustion of Mexican legal recourse. It was a vindication of the direct, frank and friendly method of discussion inaugurated by Morrow.[43]

For the remaining period of his mission Ambassador Morrow devoted the larger part of his official attention to the adjustment of land questions and considerable unofficial attention to the church question. By March, 1928, he had mapped a program on the agrarian land dispute with a view to handling it gradually, case by case. He began his efforts with the expectation of the Coolidge administration that Mexico would either stop taking land or organize the agrarian procedure to take lands only under due forms of law, with compensation. At the same time he saw that future orderly government in Mexico was threatened by the seeds of civil conflict, which lay dormant in the Mexican church question with its constant tension and intrigue and, with the approval of the Mexican government and without mixing unduly into Mexican domestic affairs, he undertook certain friendly and impartial secret negotiations in an effort to effect a reconciliation between the government and the church.[44]

The church situation was the immediate result of the legislation of 1926, precipitated by previous verbal clashes between Church and State, and enacted on the recommendation of the Calles administration to make effective the anti-clerical provisions of the Constitution of 1917 which had been ignored by the Obregon administration. This legislation required prompt registration of all clergy, placed restrictions on foreigners engaged in the religious ministry and forbade the teaching of religion in the primary schools. It had resulted in a Catholic religious strike which began on August 1, 1926, and had continued since, although by government order the churches were kept open with services conducted by laymen. President Gil, who assumed the presidency temporarily in place of Obregon who had been assassinated after his reelection, indicated in a public statement (of May 1, 1929) his readiness to negotiate with the clergy for resumption of their functions on the basis of respect for the Mexican laws. Influenced by good advice, the Mexican archbishop agreed to negotiate. In June, 1929, the negotiations for adjustment resulted in a *modus vivendi* agreement under which the Catholic priests resumed their religious duties but which provided for state registration and prohibited parochial schools. The church resumed its services on the assurance of the President that the government in the enforcement of the law did not plan to destroy the identity of the Church or to interfere with its internal discipline. At the same time, although it made no concessions of its basic claims, it declared its desire and intention to abstain from participation in politics and its hope that in time and by the regular constitutional methods the laws might be somewhat modified.

Meantime Morrow, having acquired a fondness for Mexico, had become interested in every problem which had a relation to the future stability and order of the country. Early in August, 1928, following the assassination of President-elect Obregon, he made at Mexico City a sympathetic speech in which he expressed American confidence in the future of Mexico. By this simple expression of faith, indicating that his government had a sympathetic attitude, he stimulated the Mexican recognition of a call to responsibility to merit the faith. In the following month, when President Calles (three months before the end of his administration) astonished Mexico by his declaration that "Never, for any reason, shall I return to the presidency," he expressed faith in the ability of Mexico to select a successor by peaceful methods. Although he had never admitted that he had much influence in Mexican financial affairs, he had been in close and sympathetic touch, both officially and as a personal friend, with Señor Montes de Oca, the Mexican Minister of Finance, in connection with Mexican problems of financial recovery and rehabilitation.[45]

Early in 1929, in connection with the new Mexican revolution which was precipitated the day before the inauguration of President Hoover at Washington and which was strong in Mexican states with large American property interests—in Sonora, Chihuahua, Coahuila and Vera Cruz—the American government supported President Gil and ordered troops to the border to preserve neutrality. Later, Secretary Stimson announced that the American government would not recognize the revolutionary agent whom General Escobar had sent to Washington; and, in reply to Escobar's denouncement of Morrow for propaganda in favor of the established Mexican government, he asserted that Morrow's actions were in accord with diplomatic practice. In his steps to discourage the new revolutionists he apparently did not have full sympathy of the oil interests whose representative, Guy Stevens, clashed with Moises Saenz in a discussion at a luncheon before the Foreign Policy Association in New York City. Stevens, formerly director of the association of the oil producers in Mexico and evidently very friendly to the former American ambassador (Sheffield), writing pessimistically in March, 1929, stated that the facts furnished no justification for the general impression that the matters at issue between Mexico and the United States for two years had been settled, and indicated that the only possible cause for the outward change in Mexican relations was the change in American policy by ceasing to press outstanding matters to a solution. Economic conditions in Mexico, he said, had grown steadily worse instead of better. In Mexican politics he saw little hope, especially mentioning the fact that long before the presidential election of July, 1928, all the candidates except one had been eliminated by death and that the successful candidate at the polls had been overtaken seventeen days later by the same fate (by the act of a religious fanatic).[46]

Late in May, 1929, after the suppression of the threatened revolution under General Escobar, Ambassador Morrow, seeking a rest from official duties, went to the United States for a visit—a visit which was misinterpreted by certain press writers who erroneously reported that he was seeking aid for his task of adjustment in Mexico, especially concerning the question of land expropriation, and partly to encourage tolerance and patience of American creditors in regard to renewal of loans to Mexico and postponement of debt pourparlers in seeking a new agreement. Following the virtual settlement of Mexico's religious controversy, resulting in the restoration of spiritual nourishment to the country, in his relations with the new executive, President Gil, (according to press reports) he sought the further adjustment of the question of compensation for Mexican expropriations of lands of American citizens for communal grants. His chief problem was to satisfy Americans, who, instead of gold, had received for their lands securities of negligible value —a problem which involved the difficult process of handling each case separately, unless it could be facilitated by a lump-sum settlement before the American-Mexican claims commission. While seeking to adjust individual cases in which American citizens were interested he consistently advised the Mexicans to seek a stabilization and coordination of agrarian and financial policies. In all negotiations for the settlement of the land question he attempted to minimize friction in the application of the land laws, to restrict as much as possible the amount of land expropriated and to secure the assurance of prompt adjustment of the payments. Although he was in sympathy with the Mexican plan to stabilize the peon on the land, and recognized the Mexican right to expropriate land for that purpose, he suggested the importance of paying cash for the land as taken—in order to develop a more definite policy and to prevent a too rapid increase of the public debt. His ultimate purpose was to induce Mexico to balance its budget, to lay plans under which the Mexican government could meet its foreign obligations and have more money for constructive enterprises. José Vasconcelos, presidential candidate of the anti-reelectionist party, in the campaign before the election of November 17, 1929, in denying to the Associated Press that he was anti-American, expressed his belief that the agrarian problem could best be solved by opening to settlement and cultivation the jungle wastes of the Mexican tropics. A similar view was attributed to President-elect Rubio, who was received at Washington on a friendly visit following his election, and who on his return to Mexico entered office under the most favorable auspices—indicating that the era of *caudillos* would be succeeded by the era of institutions as announced by President Calles at the close of his administration in 1928.[47]

Meantime, Ambassador Morrow had exerted an influence in the arbitration of American claims. In March, 1928, he became interested in the question whether the claims commissions could be revived into active operation. The Special Claims Commission had been inactive since the decision of its first case, the Santa Ysabel case, adversely to the United States which entered a reservation. Resentment had resulted in abandonment of further efforts at meetings and a rehearing of the Santa Ysabel case was regarded as possible. The General Claims Commission which had been meeting in Washington had also struck snags by withdrawal of its neutral member whose place had not been filled. A year later, near the close of a second extended period of two years, the commissioners were far from the completion of their work. Under the authority of the Borah resolution, adopted by the Senate, Secretary Kellogg in June suggested to Mexico another two-year extension of time for the activities of the two American-Mexican claims commissions. At that time American citizens had filed before the General Claims Commission 2,780 claims aggregating $513,694,267, and before the Special Claims Commission 3,148 claims aggregating $420,435,256. Mexican citizens had filed before the General Claims Commission 836 claims amounting to $245,158,395. The total awards to that date including interest were $3,043,799 in favor of Americans and $39,000 in favor of Mexicans. Fred K. Nielson, who was appointed American commissioner on the General Claims Commission in July, 1926, was also appointed American commissioner on the Special Claims Commission in January, 1931. In December, 1930, Ambassador Clark reported that by an arrangement with the Mexican government the Special Claims Commission would meet in Mexico City from February 1 to May 1, 1931, and the General Claims Commission would meet at Washington from May 5 to July 15, 1931.[48]

In his mission to Mexico, with tasks complicated by the domestic uncertainties incident to three successive Mexican national elections, Morrow successfully shattered the century-old tradition of harassing diplomacy in Mexican relations and stimulated in Mexico a determination to solve its problems of prosperity and orderly government without injuring the rights of Americans who had contributed to the economic development of the country. On the eve of his departure from Mexico City in September, 1930, he delivered a radio address which the press fittingly described as a prescription for improved international relations.

The accord accomplished by Morrow with Mexico was possibly endangered in May, 1930, by a bill in the American Congress which proposed to place Mexico on a quota basis as to immigration—a proposed restriction which was not applied to any other American nation and which threatened to result in Mexican retaliatory immigration measures and tariff reprisals. The bill, which was reported without the advice of Ambassador Morrow and the Department of State, was finally abandoned, possibly because of threatened executive veto. The problem of new immigration to the United States from Mexico has been satisfactorily solved by the enforcement of the regular immigration laws by American consular officers in Mexico, reducing the number of *visas* from a monthly average of 4,848 in the fiscal year 1927-28 to a monthly average of 257 after July 1, 1930. In the year ending December 31, 1930, the departure of Mexicans from the United States exceeded the admissions by 45,086. In the first three months of 1931, over 30,000 Mexicans hastily returned to Mexico from southern California, chiefly influenced by lack of employment but, also, by apprehended local legislation for segregation of Mexican children in the public schools.[49]

Meantime delicate boundary questions have remained unsettled—especially the Chamizal dispute which has not changed since the attempted arbitration of 1913, and the Colorado problem which remains practically as it was in 1913. Associated with the latter are some unsettled problems of the Rio Grande. In 1919, a bill introduced into the lower house of Congress, through the influence of the irrigation district of the Imperial Valley of California, proposed American construction of an all-American canal to receive the waters of the Colorado north of the Mexican boundary and to convey it through American territory to the Imperial Valley. The interdepartmental committee (representing the Departments of State, War, Treasury and Commerce) to which the bill was submitted, suggested possible negotiations with Mexico and stated that the entire problem would be greatly simplified if the complications resulting from the international boundary line could be removed by an adequate convention with Mexico. In August, 1922, Secretary Hughes had occasion to consider the question with Herbert Hoover, who was then Secretary of Commerce. Although no final solution of the Colorado problem has been attained, much valuable information bearing upon it, and also upon the Rio

Grande and the Tia Juana problems, has been collected by the International Water Commission and published under order of April 21, 1930, as a House document.[50]

In considering the question of El Chamizal, possibly, some Mexicans still hope for a large indemnity. In March, 1931, Pedro Merla, former president of the Mexican House of Representatives, in an article criticizing Secretary Stimson's general statement of American policy, fancifully suggested that if the United States would accept the decision of the Canadian arbiter (La Fleur) in the Chamizal controversy, Mexico would receive enough indemnity to pay the greater part of its international debt.[51]

The American-Mexican International Boundary Commission has continued its work of elimination of *bancos* on the Rio Grande with a view to a straighter and more convenient boundary. On June 19, 1928, the press announced it had unanimously agreed on 42 decisions concerning changes of territory in adjustment of difficulties arising from capricious changes in the bed of the Rio Grande—an adjustment based on the principle of equal trading of the segregated areas resulting from the changes in the stream. At a meeting of the Commission at Mexico City in August, 1929, further consideration was given to the *banco* problem which had increased in importance in connection with difficulties encountered in the suppression of rum-runners and smugglers by the American border patrol. Late in July, 1930, at Mexico City, the Commission was planning further revision of the Rio Grande boundary for the purpose of straightening it, thereby shortening the distance from El Paso to Fort Quitman and to lower points on the river. It recommended that the cost of the straightening, estimated at $6,000,000, should be divided between the two governments— 88% to the American and 12% to the Mexican.[52]

The American-Mexican International Water Commission, in seeking an agreement on the problems of the Colorado and the Rio Grande, including especially the problem of an agreement on principles to control the division of the water for irrigation purposes, and also the problem of river improvement for protection from floods, is confronted by the fact that all the Colorado water used in Mexico is obtained from the United States and that about two-thirds of the Rio Grande water used in Texas (below Fort Quitman) is obtained from Mexico. At the conferences of the Commission at Mexico City in August, 1929, and at Washington in October, 1929, appeared considerable divergence of views concerning the use of waters of the Rio Grande and the Colorado for irrigation and other beneficial purposes. The American view was based on the theory that the navigability of these streams, ignored in practice and no longer regarded as of any use under changed conditions, should be abandoned; and the Mexican view was based on the idea that any modification of the treaties concerning navigability should be made only in case a more advantageous use of the waters could be obtained. At the August conference the American commissioners could not agree to the Mexican claim to equal participation in the distribution of the waters of the Colorado after the completion of the construction of Boulder Dam —a claim which Mexico based upon treaties, international law and precedent of prior use. The American section claimed freedom from any restriction on the complete American sovereignty over the Colorado within American territorial boundaries. It denied the Mexican contention that the Boulder Dam reservoir, planned for delivery of water for domestic use of distant cities, violated any provisions of the boundary treaties or that it would operate to the injury of Mexico. It proposed to settle the question of equitable division of the water by recognition of the right of Mexico to claim the largest amount of water ever applied to irrigation or other beneficial uses in a single year under the earlier Mexican contract of 1904 with the Mexican corporation which was authorized to divert waters from the river for consumptive use, and it emphasized the absolute necessity of cooperative efforts for further expensive regulation of the river by levees to prevent floods. To the American fundamental proposal as an act of comity to extend the doctrine of prior appropriation for the protection of exist-

ing uses of Colorado water in Mexico, and of existing uses of
Rio Grande water in both countries, the Mexican section could
not agree—on the ground that it was a restriction on the complete sovereignty of Mexico.[53]

Late in July, 1930, the American government denied a report
in congressional circles that the International Water Commission had suggested the purchase of Lower California. At the
same time President Hoover in a letter to Senator King of Utah
denied the report that the American government through Morrow had negotiated with the Mexican government concerning
Mexican claims to the Colorado. A few days later, the American
embassy in Mexico denied a report that Mexico had agreed to
sell its rights in the river in return for liquidation of American
claims against Mexico. In February, 1931, Senator Ashurst, renewing an earlier effort of January 7, 1919, proposed to the
American Senate a plan to request the Department of State to
purchase Lower California and all northern Sonora extending to
the parallel of 31.21° from Nogales to the Gulf of California, in
order to enable the United States to secure sole use of the waters
of the Colorado River. Although the proposal was regarded as
a joke by President Rubio of Mexico, it stimulated in the Mexican press a serious movement in favor of development of Lower
California by better communications, increased population and
self-government.

Under an appropriation act, approved March 4, 1931, Lawrence M. Lawson, the American member of the water commission, was authorized by the American government to proceed
with proposed investigations on the lower Colorado River, with
a view to the determination of the effect of the storage of water
at the proposed Hoover Dam, and the development of international plans for proper channel control and removal of the
menace of such discharges as may be expected from uncontrolled
drainage area sources. He was also authorized to proceed with
preliminary surveys and office studies of conditions on the lower
Rio Grande, including the development of engineering plans for
storage dams and flood control and such hydrographic and topo-

graphic investigations as will give a full understanding of the availability, conservation and use of the water supply in that region.

REFERENCES

1. *The Nation*, June 1, 1921, pp. 783-84.
2. *Current History*, Vol. 14, N. Y. *Times*, Apr., 1921, pp. 145-46, and Sept., 1921, pp. 1075-77.
3. N. Y. *Times*, June 8, 1921; *Dept. of State Confidential Release*, May 8, 1926; *U. S. Daily*, May 15, 1926.
4. *The Nation*, June 22, 1921, Vol. 112, p. 864, and July 20, 1921, Vol. 113, p. 60.
5. N. Y. *Times*, May 17 and 21, 1921.
6. *Department of State Confidential Release*, May 8, 1926; *U. S. Daily*, May 17, 1926.
7. *Dept. of State Confid. Release*, May 8, 1926; *U. S. Daily*, May 19, 1926.
8. *Current History*, Vol. 16, N. Y. *Times*, Apr., 1922, pp. 177-78.
9. *Dept. of State Confid. Release*, May 8, 1926; *U. S. Daily*, May 19, 1926.
10. *The Nation*, Feb. 10, 1926, Vol. 122, pp. 130-31.
11. *Proceedings of the Commission*, Washington, 1925.
12. N. Y. *Times*, Aug. 16, 1923; *Literary Digest*, Sept. 8, 1923, Vol. 78, pp. 14-15.
13. *Am. Jr. Int. Law*, July, 1924, pp. 143-51.
14. *Ib.*, Apr., 1924, pp. 235-36; Public Docs. and Addresses of Plutarco Elias Calles, *Mexico Before the World*, pp. 165-66.
15. N. Y. *Times*, June 13 and 15, 1925, and July 9, 1927; *The Nation*, June 24, 1925, Vol. 120, p. 706.
16. *Sen. Doc. 96*, 69-1, Apr. 12, 1926.
17. *Sen. Doc. 96*, 69-1, Apr. 12, 1926.
18. *Atlantic Mo.*, March, 1927, Vol. 139, pp. 381-91.
19. *Sen. Doc. 96*, 69-1, pp. 15-21.
20. *Literary Digest*, Jan. 23, 1926, Vol. 88, p. 13.
21. *Sen. Doc. 96*, 69-1, pp. 21-35; (Calles), *Mexico Before the World*, p. 80.
22. *Ib.*, pp. 150 and 152.
23. *Sen. Doc. 96*, 69-1, pp. 35-44.
24. *Am. Property Rights in Mexico* (Dept. of State, 1926), pp. 1-10.
25. *Ib.*, pp. 10-26.
26. *Ib.*, pp. 26-28; N. Y. *Times*, Apr. 26, 1927.

27. PRESIDENT COOLIDGE, *Message to Congress*, Jan. 10, 1927; *Cong. Record*, Vol. 68, p. 1324; N. Y. *Times*, Nov. 18, 1926, and March 10, 1927.
28. N. Y. *Times*, March 28 and 29, Apr. 10 and 16, June 21 and Dec. 20, 1927.
29. *Ib.*, Jan. 9 and Feb. 20, 1927; *Cong. Record*, Jan. 25, 1927, Vol. 68, p. 2200; *The Nation*, Feb. 2, 1927, p. 103; *Sen. Doc. 210*, 69-2, p. 4; *Current History*, N. Y. *Times*, Apr., 1927, p. 136.
30. *The Nation*, Apr. 13, 1927, Vol. 124, pp. 392-94.
31. B. H. WILLIAMS, *Economic Foreign Policy of the U. S.*, p. 149; *Dept. of State Press Release*, March 22, 1927; N. Y. *Times*, March 23 and 27, 1927.
32. For a defense of the work of Sheffield by W. F. SAUNDERS, see N. Y. *Times*, Nov. 11, 1927, III, p. 5.
33. *Atlantic Mo.*, Vol. 139, pp. 381-91 (article by Wallace Thompson).
34. *Am. Property Rights in Mexico.*
35. (Calles), *Mexico Before the World*, pp. 172-73.
36. N. Y. *Times*, Sept. 21 and 22, 1927.
37. *Collier's*, Aug. 4, 1928, Vol. 82, pp. 9 and 34.
38. N. Y. *Times*, Dec. 2 and 4, II, p. 1, 1927, and July 7, 1929; *Current History*, Vol. 30, N. Y. *Times*, Sept., 1930, pp. 1046-51.
39. *U. S. Daily*, Nov. 19, 1927; *Am. Jr. Int. Law*, Vol. 22, p. 421; *Literary Digest*, Dec. 10, 1927, Vol. 95, pp. 5-7.
40. *Dept. of State Press Releases*, Jan. 12 and March 28, 1928; *Current History*, N. Y. *Times*, March, 1928, p. 882.
41. *Foreign Affairs*, July, 1928, Vol. 6, pp. 600-14. (J. R. Clark, Jr., on "Oil Settlement with Mexico").
42. N. Y. *Times*, Mar. 28, 1928; *Dept. of State Releases*, March 27 and 28, 1928.
43. *The Nation*, Jan. 25, 1928, Vol. 126, pp. 91-93.
44. N. Y. *Times*, March 29, 1929.
45. *Ib.*, Aug. 5, 1928, and Jan. 25, 1929; *Literary Digest*, Sept. 29, 1928, p. 17.
46. N. Y. *Times*, March 6 and Apr. 7, 1929; *Current History*, March, 1929, Vol. 29, pp. 928-31.
47. N. Y. *Times*, May 27, pp. 1 and 10, and July 2, p. 12, 1929; *ib.*, Jan. 5, 1930, V, p. 18; N. Y. *Herald-Tribune*, Oct. 11, 1929; *Current History*, March, 1930, Vol. 31, pp. 1113-17.
48. N. Y. *Times*, March 29, 1928; *ib.*, June 22 and 23, 1929; *Dept. of State Press Release*, Jan. 7, 1931.
49. *Baltimore Sun*, May 25, 1930; *Dept. of State Press Release*, March 24, 1931; N. Y. *Times*, Apr. 12, 1931; *Current History*, Aug. 31, 1931, p. 756.

50. *House Doc. 359*, 71-2 (492 pp.).
51. N. Y. *Times*, March 22, 1931, III, p. 2.
52. *Ib.*, June 19, 1928; *ib.*, Aug. 4, 1929; *ib.*, July 18 and Aug. 7, 1930; *ib.*, Apr. 12, 1931.
53. *House Doc. 359*, 71-2, pp. 4-9 and 13-14; N. Y. *Times*, Aug. 4, 1929.
54. *Ib.*, July 27, Aug. 1 and Aug. 5, 1930; *Literary Digest*, Feb. 21, 1931, Vol. 108, pp. 13-14; *Dept. of State Press Release*, Apr. 3, 1931.

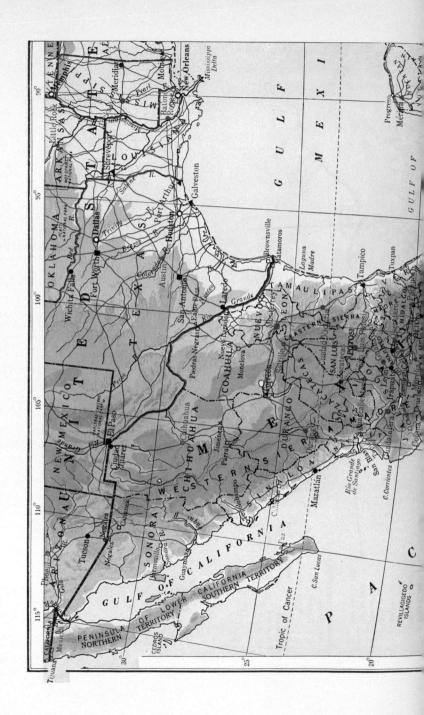

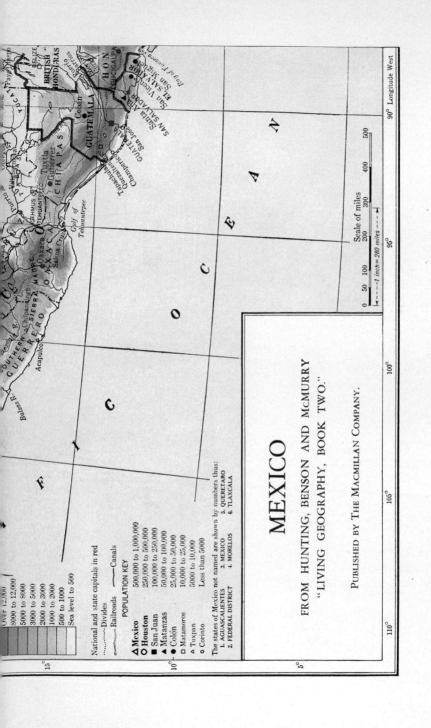

Over 12,000
8000 to 12,000
5000 to 8000
3000 to 5000
2000 to 3000
1000 to 2000
500 to 1000
Sea level to 500

National and state capitals in red
.... Divides   —— Canals
—— Railroads

POPULATION KEY

▲ **Mexico**   500,000 to 1,000,000
○ Houston   250,000 to 500,000
■ San Juan   100,000 to 250,000
▲ Matanzas   50,000 to 100,000
● Colón   25,000 to 50,000
□ Matamoros   10,000 to 25,000
△ Tuxpan   5000 to 10,000
○ Corinto   Less than 5000

The states of Mexico not named are shown by numbers thus:
1. AGUASCALIENTES   3. MEXICO   5. QUERETARO
2. FEDERAL DISTRICT 4. MORELOS   6. TLAXCALA

MEXICO

FROM HUNTING, BENSON AND McMURRY

"LIVING GEOGRAPHY, BOOK TWO."

PUBLISHED BY THE MACMILLAN COMPANY.

Scale of miles

0 50 100   200   300   400   500

‹----1 inch = 280 miles ----›

90° Longitude West

INDEX

A B C powers, 548-50, 559-61

Adams, J. Q., on question of recognition of Spanish American republics, 14; on Spanish claims (1818), 15; negotiations for settlement of the Louisiana-Texas boundary, 16; opposition to American Texan policy, 97, 110, 114, 130

Agrarian reforms (*see* Reforms)

Agents, special, executive or secret, 5, 9-10, 88, 96, 119, 146, 160, 166, 201, 259-60, 378-82, 426, 535, 539, 547, 554, 565

Agriculture (haciendas and farms), 513-14

Alamán, Lúcas Ignacio: confidential report on American policy, 65; his Texan policy and effect, 65-66, 67; unofficial adviser of Paredes, 162; death of, 215

Aldape, Manuel Garza, 540; ("demission") 545

Aldrich, Nelson, 529

Aliens, rights of, 425, 456

Alliance, American-Mexican (suggested or proposed), 240, 247, 263, 265-66, 270

Almonte, Juan N., 102; protest against American policy to annex Texas (without negotiation with Mexico), 114-15, 116; on pan-American policy, 115; terminates his mission, 131; later, Secretary of War in Mexico, 162; later, Mexican minister at Washington, 190, 215; influence on Gadsden's negotiations, 223

Amenities, international, 331, 332-33, 448, 450-51, 452, 595, 618

American investments in Mexico, protection of: Webster's views, 195 (*see* Diplomatic interposition)

Americanization of Mexico, 253, 331 (*see* Economic penetration)

American pacific economic penetration (*see* Economic)

American policy (*see* under subjects and under names of Secretaries of State)

American sympathy: with Texans, 81, 108

"American system" (republican): a factor in Poinsett's negotiations, 34-38, 55-56; Canning's views of the, 35; a factor in American recognition of Juárez, 260; basis of American opposition to French intervention in Mexico, 236, 292, 317, 323 (*see* Monroe doctrine)

Annexations: negotiations for (*see* Territory, Texas, California, etc.); views of Jefferson Davis concerning, 183; later suggestions concerning, 430-431

rumored plans of, 371, 507, 623; Mexican suspicions concerning, 332, 424, 430, 485

Anti-American feeling in Mexico, 399, 453, 519-27 (*also see* Mexican suspicions)

Arbitration, proposals for, 96, 97, 457, 458, 546, 606, 608

Ariola, raid of, 401

Armistice, in the Mexican War, 173-74, (terminated) 176; (effect of failure of, on American territorial plans, 177)

Armistice, proposed between Mexican factions, 549

Arredondo, Eliseo, 559, 561, 567

Arrests, 98, 103

Aspiroz, 446, 477, (death) 448. 462

Astor, John Jacob, encouraged in establishment of Astoria, 17

627